Ecclesiastes

BAKER COMMENTARY *on the* OLD TESTAMENT

WISDOM AND PSALMS

Tremper Longman III, EDITOR

Volumes now available

Psalms, vol. 1, *Psalms 1–41*, John Goldingay
Psalms, vol. 2, *Psalms 42–89*, John Goldingay
Psalms, vol. 3, *Psalms 90–150*, John Goldingay
Proverbs, Tremper Longman III
Ecclesiastes, Craig G. Bartholomew
Song of Songs, Richard S. Hess

Ecclesiastes

Craig G. Bartholomew

Baker Academic

a division of Baker Publishing Group
Grand Rapids, Michigan

Published by Baker Academic
a division of Baker Publishing Group
P.O. Box 6287, Grand Rapids, MI 49516–6287
www.bakeracademic.com

Paperback edition published 2014
ISBN 978-0-8010-9744-7

Printed in the United States of America

The Library of Congress has cataloged the hardcover edition as follows:
Bartholomew, Craig G., 1961–
    Ecclesiastes / Craig G. Bartholomew.
        p.   cm. — (Baker commentary on the Old Testament wisdom and Psalms)
    Includes bibliographical references and indexes.
    ISBN 978-0-8010-2691-1 (cloth)
    1. Bible. O.T. Ecclesiastes—Commentaries. I. Title.
BS1475.53.B378 2009
223′.8077—dc22   2008051064

In memory of my mother,
Laurel Dorothy Bartholomew (1923–2005),
and with gratitude to Carolyn Gird,
a friend at the right time

Contents

Series Preface

At the end of the book of Ecclesiastes, a wise father warns his son concerning the multiplication of books: "Furthermore, of these, my son, be warned. There is no end to the making of many books!" (12:12). The Targum to this biblical book characteristically expands the thought and takes it in a different, even contradictory, direction: "My son, take care to make many books of wisdom without end."

When applied to commentaries, both statements are true. The past twenty years have seen a significant increase in the number of commentaries available on each book of the Bible. However, for those interested in grappling seriously with the meaning of the text, such proliferation should be seen as a blessing rather than a curse. No single commentary can do it all. In the first place, commentaries reflect different theological and methodological perspectives. We can learn from others who have a different understanding of the origin and nature of the Bible, but we also want commentaries that share our fundamental beliefs about the biblical text. Second, commentaries are written with different audiences in mind. Some are addressed primarily to laypeople, others to clergy, and still others to fellow scholars. A third consideration, related to the previous two, is the subdisciplines the commentator chooses to draw from to shed light on the biblical text. The possibilities are numerous, including philology, textual criticism, genre/form criticism, redaction criticism, ancient Near Eastern background, literary conventions, and more. Finally, commentaries differ in how extensively they interact with secondary literature, that is, with what others have said about a given passage.

The Baker Commentary on the Old Testament Wisdom and Psalms has a definite audience in mind. We believe the primary users of commentaries are scholars, ministers, seminary students, and Bible study leaders. Of these groups, we have most in mind clergy and future clergy, namely, seminary students. We have tried to make the commentary accessible to nonscholars by putting most of the technical discussion and interaction with secondary literature in the footnotes. We do not mean to suggest that such information is unimportant. We simply concede that, given the present state of the church, it is the rare layperson who will read such technical material with interest and profit. We hope we are wrong in this assessment, and if we are not, that the future will see a reverse in this trend. A healthy church is a church that nourishes itself with constant attention to God's words in Scripture, in all their glorious detail.

Since not all commentaries are alike, what are the features that characterize this series? The message of the biblical book is the primary focus of each commentary, and the commentators have labored to expose God's message for his people in the book they discuss. This series also distinguishes itself by restricting its coverage to one major portion of the Hebrew Scriptures, namely, the Psalms and Wisdom books (Proverbs, Job, Ecclesiastes, and Song of Songs). These biblical books provide a distinctive contribution to the canon. Although we can no longer claim that they are neglected, their unique content makes them harder to fit into the development of redemptive history and requires more effort to hear their distinctive message.

The book of Psalms is the literary sanctuary. Like the physical sanctuary structures of the Old Testament, it offers a textual holy place where humans share their joys and struggles with brutal honesty in God's presence. The book of Proverbs describes wisdom, which on one level is skill for living, the ability to navigate life's actual and potential pitfalls; but on another level, this wisdom presents a pervasive and deeply theological message: "The fear of the LORD is the beginning of knowledge" (Prov. 1:7). Proverbs also raises a disturbing issue: the sages often motivate wise behavior by linking it to reward, but in reality, bad things happen to good people, the wise are not always rewarded as they expect. This raises the question of the justice of God. Both Job and Ecclesiastes struggle with the apparent disconnect between God's justice and our actual life experience. Finally, the Song of Songs is a passionate, sensuous love poem that reminds us that God is interested in more than just our brains and our spirits; he wants us to enjoy our bodies. It reminds us that we are not merely a soul encased in a body but whole persons made in God's image.

Limiting the series to the Psalms and Wisdom books has allowed us to tailor our work to the distinctive nature of this portion of the canon. With some few exceptions in Job and Ecclesiastes, for instance, the material in these biblical books is poetic and highly literary, and so the commentators have highlighted the significant poetic conventions employed in each book. After an introduction discussing important issues that affect the interpretation of the book (title, authorship, date, language, style, text, ancient Near Eastern background, genre, canonicity, theological message, connection to the New Testament, and structure), each commentary proceeds section by section through the biblical text. The authors provide their own translation, with explanatory notes when necessary, followed by a substantial interpretive section (titled "Interpretation") and concluding with a section titled "Theological Implications." In the interpretation section, the emphasis is on the meaning of the text in its original historical setting. In the theological implications section, connections with other parts of the canon, both Old and New Testament, are sketched out along with the continuing relevance of each passage for us today. The latter section is motivated by the recognition that, while it is important to understand the individual contribution and emphasis of each book, these books now find their place in a larger collection of writings, the canon as a whole, and it is within this broader context that the books must ultimately be interpreted.

No two commentators in this series see things in exactly the same way, though we all share similar convictions about the Bible as God's Word and the belief that it must be appreciated not only as ancient literature but also as God's Word for today. It is our hope and prayer that these volumes will inform readers and, more important, stimulate reflection on and passion for these valuable books.

The book of Ecclesiastes is one of the most intriguing and difficult books in the canon. Qohelet concludes time and again that life is enigmatic, and at times so is the interpretation of the book of Ecclesiastes. Craig Bartholomew is marvelously prepared to guide us in an exploration of this small, yet important book. He combines his expertise as a scholar of the Hebrew Bible with an understanding of the canon as a whole, the history of interpretation of the book, and philosophy. He calls on all these skills in his exposition of the book, and we, his readers, are the beneficiaries.

Tremper Longman III
Robert H. Gundry Professor of Biblical Studies
Westmont College

Author's Preface

Writing a lengthy commentary on Ecclesiastes is a privilege and a challenge. Undoubtedly myriads of my predecessors in this respect have felt as I have about this enigmatic book: as befits its content, it is like an octopus—just when you think you have all the tentacles pinned down, you notice one still waving around!

Many friends have helped in the writing of this book. My research assistant David Beldman has been of inestimable help in tracking down sources, assembling the bibliography, and in interacting with my work and getting it into final shape. After David left for the UK, Sean Purcell took on this role. I am most grateful to John Hultink and Redeemer University College for making it possible for me to have such resourceful assistants. Al Wolters, Ryan O'Dowd, and Tremper Longman III have helped improve the manuscript through their close reading of it. Brenda Stephenson, my colleague in psychology at Redeemer, was particularly helpful in developing the psychological reading of Ecclesiastes in the postscript to the commentary. Jim Kinney and Wells Turner of Baker Academic have been a joy to work with, and I am grateful both for their patience in waiting for the commentary to appear and for the work of Baker's editorial team.

Readers should note that because the Hebrew in this commentary is all transliterated, I have gone against common practice by putting Hebrew verse numbers in brackets after the English number where the numbers differ.

I am glad to dedicate this volume to my mother, who remains sorely missed, and to Carolyn Gird, a true friend. They are both women who fear the LORD and are worthy of praise.

A good commentary leads the reader to the text, and my hope and prayer is that this volume will encourage readers to wrestle themselves with the fecund text of Ecclesiastes.

Craig Bartholomew
Ancaster, Ontario, Canada
October 2007

Abbreviations

Bibliographic and General

ANET	*Ancient Near Eastern Texts Relating to the Old Testament*, ed. J. B. Pritchard, 3rd ed. (Princeton, NJ: Princeton University Press, 1969)
ANF	*The Ante-Nicene Fathers*, ed. A. Roberts and J. Donaldson, 10 vols. (repr., Grand Rapids: Eerdmans, 1978)
b.	Babylonian Talmud
BDB	Francis Brown, S. R. Driver, and Charles A. Briggs, *A Hebrew and English Lexicon of the Old Testament* (repr., London: Oxford University Press, 1962)
BHK	*Biblia Hebraica*, ed. R. Kittel, 3rd ed. (Stuttgart: Württembergische Bibelanstalt, 1937)
BHS	*Biblia Hebraica Stuttgartensia*, ed. K. Elliger and W. Rudolph (Stuttgart: Deutsche Bibelstiftung, 1977)
CD	Karl Barth, *Church Dogmatics*, ed. G. W. Bromiley and T. F. Torrance, trans. G. W. Bromiley et al., 4 vols. in 14 (repr., London: T&T Clark, 2004)
chap(s).	chapter(s)
d.	died
DJD	Discoveries in the Judaean Desert
GKC	*Gesenius' Hebrew Grammar*, ed. and enlarged by E. Kautzsch, trans. A. E. Cowley, 2nd ed. (Oxford: Clarendon, 1910; repr. with corrections, 1966)
GNB	Good News Bible
IBHS	B. K. Waltke and M. O'Connor, *Introduction to Biblical Hebrew Syntax* (Winona Lake, IN: Eisenbrauns, 1990)
KJV	King James (Authorized) Version
lit.	literally
LXX	Septuagint
MS(S)	manuscript(s)
MT	Masoretic text
NASB	New American Standard Bible

NCBC	New Century Bible Commentary
NIV	New International Version
NRSV	New Revised Standard Version
NT	New Testament
OT	Old Testament
RJW	Ronald J. Williams, *Hebrew Syntax: An Outline*, 2nd ed. (Toronto: University of Toronto Press, 1976)
RSV	Revised Standard Version
Symm	Symmachus
Syr	Syriac
TDNT	*Theological Dictionary of the New Testament*, ed. G. Kittel and G. Friedrich, trans. G. W. Bromiley, 10 vols. (Grand Rapids: Eerdmans, 1964–76)
TDOT	*Theological Dictionary of the Old Testament*, ed. G. J. Botterweck et al., trans. D. E. Green et al., 15 vols. (Grand Rapids: Eerdmans, 1974–)
Tg	Targum
v(v).	verse(s)
Vg	Vulgate

Old Testament

Gen.	Genesis	Song	Song of Songs
Exod.	Exodus	Isa.	Isaiah
Lev.	Leviticus	Jer.	Jeremiah
Num.	Numbers	Lam.	Lamentations
Deut.	Deuteronomy	Ezek.	Ezekiel
Josh.	Joshua	Dan.	Daniel
Judg.	Judges	Hosea	Hosea
Ruth	Ruth	Joel	Joel
1–2 Sam.	1–2 Samuel	Amos	Amos
1–2 Kings	1–2 Kings	Obad.	Obadiah
1–2 Chron.	1–2 Chronicles	Jon.	Jonah
Ezra	Ezra	Mic.	Micah
Neh.	Nehemiah	Nah.	Nahum
Esther	Esther	Hab.	Habakkuk
Job	Job	Zeph.	Zephaniah
Ps(s).	Psalms	Hag.	Haggai
Prov.	Proverbs	Zech.	Zechariah
Eccles.	Ecclesiastes	Mal.	Malachi

New Testament

Matt.	Matthew	1–2 Thess.	1–2 Thessalonians
Mark	Mark	1–2 Tim.	1–2 Timothy
Luke	Luke	Titus	Titus
John	John	Philem.	Philemon
Acts	Acts	Heb.	Hebrews
Rom.	Romans	James	James
1–2 Cor.	1–2 Corinthians	1–2 Pet.	1–2 Peter
Gal.	Galatians	1–3 John	1–3 John
Eph.	Ephesians	Jude	Jude
Phil.	Philippians	Rev.	Revelation
Col.	Colossians		

Introduction

As far back as we go in the history of the interpretation of Ecclesiastes, this book has provoked controversy. And it still does, with contemporary commentators polarized as to how to read it, whether as a positive book affirming life or as deeply pessimistic. Beyond biblical studies in the academy and in popular culture, Ecclesiastes attracts attention and resonates deeply with the existential struggles of people today. Indeed, sometimes it is easier to see how Ecclesiastes applies today than what it meant in its original context. Ecclesiastes takes the reader on a roller-coaster ride as its main character, Qohelet, sets out to explore the meaning of life. It is a sign of the richness and depth of Scripture that we have such a book in the canon, and of God's desire to meet us where we are and to lead us to full life in Christ amid the brokenness of the world.

This introduction provides the background for the interpretation of Ecclesiastes as Scripture. Any commentary must take account of the considerable work that has been and continues to be done on Ecclesiastes. The aim throughout is to assist readers in hearing Ecclesiastes as what it is: part of God's address to us. Ecclesiastes has powerful things to say to us today, and it invites us into a conversation in which much is at stake.

Title

In Hebrew Ecclesiastes is titled *qōhelet* (Qohelet), after its main character, who is introduced by a narrator in 1:1 and then addresses readers himself from 1:12 through 12:7.[1] It is therefore important to distinguish Qohelet and his

---

1. The narrator's voice returns once in the main body of Ecclesiastes in 7:27.

speeches from the book of Ecclesiastes as a whole, and in this commentary I will reserve "Qohelet" for the name of the main character and "Ecclesiastes" for the book as a whole. Qohelet is not a proper name like "Solomon" but probably more of a nickname.[2] The Hebrew word *qōhelet* is the Qal feminine singular participle of the verb *qāhal*, meaning "to call," "to assemble." Thus the nickname may allude to one who gathers an assembly to address it or to one who gathers words for instruction. The feminine participle is used elsewhere in the OT to refer to particular offices or occupations (Ezra 2:55; Neh. 7:57, 59).

The English title derives from the Septuagint (*ekklēsiastēs*) via the Latin Vulgate (*Liber Ecclesiastes*). The Septuagint translator(s) interpreted *qōhelet* to refer to a citizen of the assembly or *ekklēsia*. English translations have traditionally translated *qōhelet* as "Preacher" (KJV, RSV), which goes back to Luther's translation of *qōhelet* as "der Prediger."[3] This translation is somewhat anachronistic, with its overtones of the NT concept of the *ekklēsia* as the church. Qohelet's "office" is clearly identified in the epilogue (12:8–14) as that of a wise man, but "preacher" is helpful in that it alerts us to the fact that Qohelet was wise *and* taught the people knowledge (12:10).

Canonicity

The Council of Jamnia convened in AD 90, a session of the rabbinic academy at Jamnia to discuss whether certain books "make the hands unclean," a technical expression for divine inspiration. Central to this discussion was Ecclesiastes: did it make the hands unclean, or should it be "stored away."[4] The origin of this particular dispute is uncertain,[5] but it centered on Ecclesiastes' secular character, the great difficulty of harmonizing its contradictions,[6] and

2. Longman, *Ecclesiastes*, 1; N. Lohfink, *Qoheleth*, 10.

3. This interpretation of the word is already attested in Gregory Thaumaturgus in the third century AD.

4. The expression "defiling of the hands" derives from rabbinic literature. Broyde ("Defilement of the Hands," 66) asserts, "Defiling the hands is a status of ritual purity (or impurity) that is completely rabbinic in nature and was enacted by the Talmudic Sages not to promote ritual purity, but to protect holy works from destruction or desecration." This concept was initiated to ensure careful handling of holy scrolls and to prevent their defilement. Suffice it here to note that books that were deemed to defile the hands were regarded as holy and authoritative (i.e., canonical). For a more extensive discussion of the origin and meaning of this terminology, see Beckwith, *Old Testament Canon*, 278–83.

5. Beckwith, *Old Testament Canon*, 297–302.

6. The Talmud mentions the conflicts between Eccles. 7:3 and 2:2 and between 8:15 and 2:2 (*b. Šabbat* 30b). See Beckwith, *Old Testament Canon*, 284–87, where he points out that the rabbis were experts at scriptural harmonization, and thus their problems with Ecclesiastes meant that they found its contradictions especially difficult to harmonize.

the passages with supposed heretical tendencies, such as 1:3 and 11:9.[7] The Mishnah reports the dispute over Ecclesiastes between two Pharisaic schools, the disciples of the two great Pharisaic teachers who taught up to about AD 10. Beth Shammai maintained that Ecclesiastes does not make the hands unclean, but Beth Hillel claimed the reverse. The position of Hillel was confirmed during the session, but the decision was not authoritative and the dispute continued. Their disciples were active throughout the first century and into the second, although after the destruction of the temple in AD 70, the house of Hillel gained the upper hand.

This discussion at Jamnia has led many scholars to adopt the theory, first propounded by the Jewish historian Heinrich Graetz in 1871,[8] that the OT canon was closed at Jamnia but open prior to this time. However, this view has been thoroughly refuted by J. Lewis, Leiman, and Beckwith.[9] The council was not a "council" in the sense of the later church councils but a session of the elders. With regard to the disputed books, discussion was confined to Ecclesiastes and the Song of Songs, or possibly just to Ecclesiastes. Furthermore, the decision was not regarded as authoritative, and debate about Ecclesiastes continued throughout the second century. Indeed much of the rabbinical dispute about Ezekiel, Proverbs, Ecclesiastes, the Song of Songs, and Esther dates from well after the Council of Jamnia. "So either this evidence shows that the canon was still open long after AD 90 (incredibly long afterwards!), or it does not show that the canon was open at all."[10] Hillel's opinion that Ecclesiastes is inspired would appear to be the older view,[11] and it is better to regard Jamnia not as the process of canonization but as the result of a fresh wave of biblical exegesis and examination.[12]

The history of the development of the OT canon is complex. Childs, who supports the view of "a relatively closed Hebrew canon by the beginning of the Christian era," nevertheless asserts that "the Jewish canon was formed through a complex historical process which is largely inaccessible to critical reconstruction."[13] That Ecclesiastes was found among the texts at Qumran probably indicates, however, that is was regarded as authorita-

7. These verses are instanced in the Pesiqta de Rab Kahana 68b; Lev. Rabbah 28.1.

8. Graetz, *Kohelet*, 147–73. Aune, "On the Origins of the 'Council of Javneh' Myth," 492–93, notes the similarities between Spinoza and Graetz in this respect, upon whom Graetz may have been dependent for his view.

9. J. Lewis, "What Do We Mean by Jabneh?" 125–32; Leiman, *Canonization of Hebrew Scripture*, 120–24; Beckwith, *Old Testament Canon*, 276–77.

10. Beckwith, *Old Testament Canon*, 275.

11. Ibid., 298–302.

12. Ibid., 315.

13. Childs, *Introduction to the Old Testament*, 66, 67.

tive well before the time of Christ.[14] Indeed, Beckwith, who has done the most thorough work on the history of the OT canon in the latter part of the twentieth century, argues that the OT canon was closed by the second century BC.[15]

Ecclesiastes is quoted only once in the NT (Rom. 3:10), but it appears on the "Bryennios List" in the second century AD, the lists of Epiphanius (possibly second century), the list of Melito of Sardis (second century), the list of Origen (third century), and that of Jerome (fourth century). From the late third century we have a paraphrase of Ecclesiastes from Gregory Thaumaturgus, indicating its authoritative status among Christians.[16] Thus it would appear that the early Christian church accepted Ecclesiastes without question as part of the canon.[17]

Abraham asserts that "to have a canon of Scripture is to have a sophisticated means of grace which is related to formation in holy living in a host of ways. On this . . . reading, Scripture functions to bring one to faith, to make one wise unto salvation, to force one to wrestle with awkward questions about violence and the poor, to comfort those in sorrow, and to nourish hope for the redemption of the world."[18] This is helpful to remember in terms of the canonicity of Ecclesiastes. Thiselton notes, "Such texts as Job, Ecclesiastes, and the parables do not function *primarily* as raw-material for Christian doctrine. . . . Their primary function is to invite or to provoke the reader to wrestle actively with the issues, in ways that may involve adopting a series of comparative angles of vision."[19] Ecclesiastes is one of those books that force us to wrestle with very difficult questions that are pursued relentlessly. In the process it leads us back to the starting point of faith, but this time to know it more fully. Faith, we might remind ourselves, is a gift, but Ecclesiastes reminds us that it is not cheap.

14. Beckwith, *Old Testament Canon*, 321. Muilenburg ("Qoheleth Scroll," 27) suggests, "In any event we must reckon with the possibility that Qoh[elet] had attained canonical status, or something approaching it, in the Essene community by the middle of the second century B.C."

15. See Beckwith (*Old Testament Canon*, 164–66) for a summary of the results. The most recent examination of the development of the canon of the OT is that by Haran, *Biblical Collection* (Hebrew). Haran rejects the recent view of James Barr and John Barton and argues that the canon was well established before the rabbinic and Christian periods.

16. Gregory Thaumaturgus's (210–270) *Metaphrase of the Book of Ecclesiastes* is the earliest extant Christian work on Ecclesiastes.

17. Theodore of Mopsuestia, who lived in the late fourth century and early part of the fifth, is often regarded as having rejected Ecclesiastes as canonical. However, in the twentieth century a sizable part of his commentary was recovered, and in the light of this, Jarick ("Theodore of Mopsuestia and Interpretation") argues that Theodore did not deny the canonical status of Ecclesiastes but rejected its allegorical interpretation. For further details, see below under "History of Interpretation."

18. Abraham, *Canon and Criterion in Christian Theology*, 6–7.

19. Thiselton, *New Horizons*, 65–66.

The History of Interpretation

> Research into the book also shows that it reflects the interpreter's world view. That is why, I think, opinions vary so widely with regard to such basic matters as Qohelet's optimism or pessimism, his attitude toward women, . . . and his advocacy of immoral conduct.[20]

> It is always interesting to see where the "interpretative sweat" breaks out in dealing with such an iconoclastic book; moreover, the history of interpretation of Ecclesiastes sheds an important light on contemporary exegesis.[21]

Scholars are increasingly aware that the interpretation of a biblical book takes place in the context of the history of its reception.[22] Awareness of the reception history of approximately 2,300 years of readings of Ecclesiastes is vital for its interpretation today. Three main turns in the interpretation of Ecclesiastes can be identified. In the fifth century AD Jerome established the Neoplatonic allegorical and christological reading of Ecclesiastes that dominated interpretation of the book for over a thousand years. Luther, Melanchthon, and Brenz challenged this interpretation decisively in the sixteenth century and ushered in a literal and theological reading of Ecclesiastes quite contrary to that established by Jerome. The post-Enlightenment period represents the third watershed in the interpretation of Ecclesiastes, and its historical-critical fruit presses in upon the reader of Ecclesiastes as the immediate and weighty scholarly context in which to read the text. However, since the progressive relativizing and questioning of modernity[23] in the context of the literary and postmodern turns, there are welcome signs of a reappropriation of precritical readings of Ecclesiastes, albeit in a postcritical mode.[24] No commentator can ignore the contribution made by historical criticism, but in terms of the interpretation of Ecclesiastes today, the contribution of the evangelical Reformers should not be underestimated as a resource for a renewal of theological interpretation.

20. Crenshaw, *Ecclesiastes*, 47.
21. Newsom, "Job and Ecclesiastes," 191.
22. Important sources for the history of the interpretation of Ecclesiastes are Ginsburg, *Coheleth*; Kallas, "Ecclesiastes." More recently, see Bartholomew, *Reading Ecclesiastes*, 31–205; and Christianson, *Ecclesiastes through the Centuries*.
23. I use "modernity" to refer to the Enlightenment legacy in the West.
24. Childs (*Introduction to the Old Testament*, 580–89) and Dell ("Ecclesiastes as Wisdom") are good examples of this postcritical reassessment. For theological interpretation of Ecclesiastes, this relativizing of modernity is most important, for, as we will see, "precritical" interpretation was not uncritical but operated with very different presuppositions than most "critical" biblical scholars.

Intertestamental Interpretations

Ecclesiasticus (or Sirach, approximately 180 BC) and the Wisdom of Solomon[25] are both wisdom texts and chronologically fairly close to Ecclesiastes. Their relationship to Ecclesiastes has been much discussed,[26] but according to Murphy there is no serious sign of dependency between Ecclesiasticus and Ecclesiastes.[27] Although the Wisdom of Solomon is often seen as anti-Ecclesiastes, "the general run of claims and counter-claims has the appearance of being more impressionistic than substantive."[28] Holm-Nielsen seeks access to early interpretations of Ecclesiastes through analyzing the LXX and the Peshitta.[29] However, neither these versions nor the Qumran fragments yield much in terms of how Ecclesiastes was read at this early stage.[30] With regard to the Peshitta of Ecclesiastes, it should be noted that it is not strictly speaking intertestamental. The Peshitta translation of the Pentateuch was probably started by Jews in the first century AD, but the bulk of the translation extended over a long period of time and is probably the work of Christians.[31]

Premodern Readings

Murphy argues that because of common presuppositions of exegesis there is a real homogeneity in the history of interpretation of Ecclesiastes.[32] This is certainly true of the premodern era.[33] Murphy identifies three such common assumptions: Solomonic authorship, the interpretation of "utterly enigmatic"[34] against the perspective of immortality in the next life, and the recognition of tensions within the book. The assumption and foregrounding of the immortality of the soul is more dominant in Christian than in Jewish interpretation of Ecclesiastes, where the stress is rather on obedience to God and the blessings of the afterlife.[35] In both cases,

25. According to Perdue, *Wisdom and Creation*, 291, the author probably lived in Alexandria as early as the first century.

26. Cf. Murphy, *Ecclesiastes*, xlv–xlviii.

27. Ibid., xlvi.

28. Ibid., xlvii; cf. Crenshaw, "Ecclesiastes, Book of," 278.

29. Holm-Nielsen, "Book of Ecclesiastes."

30. See discussion under "Text" below. For a useful, brief discussion of these early texts and versions, see Murphy, *Ecclesiastes*, xxiv–xxv.

31. Beckwith, *Old Testament Canon*, 21. For a useful discussion of the Peshitta and the OT, see Weitzman, *Syriac Version of the Old Testament*.

32. Murphy, "Qohelet Interpreted."

33. I use "premodern" rather than "precritical" to dispel the notion that premodern interpretations were not critical.

34. My translation of the more traditional "vanity of vanities" (*hābēl hăbālîm*).

35. Cf. Murphy (*Ecclesiastes*, liv), who argues that the rabbis reinterpreted Ecclesiastes in the light of the Torah, whereas Christians reinterpreted it in the light of their beliefs. With its

however, this difference in nuance alerts us to a deeper assumption that they share: their recognition of Ecclesiastes as Scripture. This powerful assumption dominates the interpretation of Ecclesiastes up until the end of the nineteenth century. With regard to interpretive method, Jewish and Christian exegetes use both literal and allegorical interpretive approaches, and of course mixtures of both.

PREMODERN JEWISH READINGS

That the literal sense was not neglected by the rabbis is indicated by the well-known rabbinic debate about whether Ecclesiastes "makes the hands unclean."[36] The rabbinic debate about the inspiration of Ecclesiastes indicates a tendency to read it literally in the period of intense exegetical activity from the second century BC to the third century AD. However, Hirshman examines the interpretation of Ecclesiastes in the tannaitic[37] literature (AD 1–250) and concludes that because of the difficulties the rabbis experienced with reading it literally, its message could be appropriated only by radical methods of interpretation such as allegorization, contextualization, or standard midrash strategies.[38]

From Jerome's commentary it is evident that by the fourth century the Jews largely allegorized Ecclesiastes.[39] The allegorical and spiritual approach dominated Jewish reading of Ecclesiastes in the following centuries, as is evident from the Talmud and the Targum; the latter was the first entire commentary on this book. In it, for example, the *carpe diem* passage[40] in 2:24 is explained as the gathering of strength for the service of God.

---

strong emphasis on creation and the OT, the Jewish tradition was less amenable to the influence of Greek dualism, which strongly influenced Christianity at an early stage.

36. The premodern history of the interpretation of Ecclesiastes is thoroughly investigated by Ginsburg (*Coheleth*, 27ff.), on whom I depend for much that follows.

37. The Tannaim (*tannā'îm* = repeaters [of the law]) were the early rabbinic scholars who produced the Mishnah, Tosefta, Pirqe 'Abot, and other tractates found in the Babylonian and Palestinian Talmuds.

38. Hirshman, "Qohelet's Reception." See also idem, "Rabbinic Views of Qohelet"; idem, "Preacher and His Public"; Schiffer, *Kohelet*; and Hayman, "Qohelet, the Rabbis."

39. Ginsburg, *Coheleth*, 34. I use "allegorize" here in a broad sense. For more detailed analysis, see Hirshman, "Qohelet's Reception"; idem, "Greek Fathers and the Aggada"; idem, *Rivalry of Genius*, esp. 95–108.

40. With many other scholars, I call those passages in Ecclesiastes that refer positively to eating and drinking *carpe diem* passages. This Latin phrase originates in the poem *Odes* (1.11) by the great Latin poet Horace (65–8 BC). Horace's poetry advocates the enjoyment of good wine and pleasurable experiences but at the same time promotes moderation and the avoidance of extremes. The phrase appears repeatedly in Western literature and has two main senses: (1) casting off of moral restraint in the face of human mortality, and (2) making the most of current opportunities because of the transience of life. See the discussion of repetition on p. 79 of the introduction.

A breakthrough for literal interpretation came with Rashbam (1085–1155). He interprets according to the principle that the text has only one meaning.[41] Rashbam displays great sensitivity to the literary nature of Ecclesiastes and was the first to realize that Qohelet was set within a framework; 1:1–2 and the last seven verses were written by those who edited the book.[42] Rashbam locates the essence of the argument of Ecclesiastes in 1:2–11. Ecclesiastes here contrasts the transience of human life with the permanence of nature, thus showing the latter's advantage. None of the experiments in Ecclesiastes is successful in dispelling this melancholy; the only adequate response is to live in conformity to traditional values, to enjoy life calmly while resigned to providence. Present mysteries will be rectified in the future life.

In the following centuries, as literal interpretation progressed, the skeptical passages in Ecclesiastes attracted closer attention from Jewish exegetes. In the thirteenth century it is argued in the *Zohar* that in Ecclesiastes Solomon quotes ignorant unbelievers in order to expose their folly. However, this foregrounding of the skeptical passages in Ecclesiastes also drew forth an allegorical and spiritualizing response, particularly evident in the kabbalistic interpretation of E. Loanz (1631) and M. Landsberger (1724). Loanz defends the retention of Ecclesiastes in the canon by proposing a spiritualistic interpretation of it.

> Now, why the sages did not burn it, but intended to hide the book, is because Solomon was no infidel; on the contrary, if his words are properly examined, it will be seen that they are perfectly true, and becoming such a wise man as he was. That an empty-headed man may shelter himself under the literal meaning of the words, is no reason why the wise men should have burned a book of such sublime sentiments.[43]

Loanz argues, for example, that the reference to rejoicing in one's youth is to be understood as referring to the mind, which reaches its highest stage by studying the law.

In the tradition of Rashbam, L. Herzfeld (1838) strongly reasserted the literal interpretation of Ecclesiastes. He argued that Qohelet seeks to show the universal vanity of life and thereby to comfort the Israelites in their experience of life as vain. It is a sign of the developing ethos of biblical criticism that seventeen years later Herzfeld felt free to challenge Solomonic authorship for Ecclesiastes. He argued that Solomon could not be the author of Ecclesiastes and that it was written shortly before the era of Alexander the Great.[44]

41. See Japhet and Salters, *Commentary of R. Samuel Ben Meir.*
42. Ibid., 34ff. They point out that Gordis (*Koheleth*, 349) attributes the recognition of this framework to Döderlein, but that it is Rashbam who first reached this conclusion.
43. Quoted by Ginsburg, *Coheleth*, 76.
44. See ibid., 94–96, for Herzfeld's reasons.

By the end of the nineteenth century, those assumptions common to the precritical Jewish reading of Ecclesiastes were beginning to unravel. Nathan Rosenthal in his work on Ecclesiastes (1858) still maintains Solomonic authorship.[45] In his view, Solomon wrote the book to demonstrate that wisdom is only useful when combined with the fear of God and the keeping of his commands. By contrast, in 1860 Samuel Luzzatto developed a strikingly contemporary view of Ecclesiastes.[46] In his view, it denies the immortality of the soul and recommends carnal pleasure as all that is left. It was written in the postexilic period by one Qohelet who ascribed it to Solomon in order to give it authority. Contemporary sages recognized this forgery, deleted "Solomon," inserted "Qohelet," and left in "son of David, king in Jerusalem," knowing that such a juxtaposition would ensure recognition of the book for what it was. Later sages never knew this, and thinking it to be Solomonic, they added verses to make it more orthodox.

Premodern Christian Readings

Ecclesiastes was passed over in relative silence in the first, second, and early part of the third centuries AD by the early Christian writers.[47] The first significant study of Ecclesiastes was undertaken by Origen in the third century. He never wrote a commentary on the book, but his prefatory remarks to his *Commentary on the Song of Songs* are the earliest known discussion of Ecclesiastes within the church. Origen argues that Ecclesiastes and the Song of Songs, both written by Solomon, form a pair, with Ecclesiastes preparing the ground for the Song of Songs by teaching that all knowledge deserves contempt and that the physical realm merits little more than our disdain. The Song of Songs then recounts Solomon's positive progress toward Christ, with whom he seeks a marriagelike union.

---

45. Ibid., 96.
46. Ibid., 97.
47. Inter alia, see ibid., 99–243. For the references to Ecclesiastes in the literature of the church fathers, see Allenbach et al., eds., *Biblica Patristica*, vols. 1–7; and *Supplément: Philon d'Alexandrie*. Because of the relative silence on Ecclesiastes in the first two centuries, it is hard to determine whether, as with the interpretation of the Prov. 31 woman, there is first of all a literal interpretation, later replaced by an allegorical one. Commenting on the interpretation of Prov. 31, Wolters (*Song of the Valiant Woman*, 99) says, "It is remarkable how similar the patterns are in both the Jewish and Christian traditions. Both began with a literal understanding, both moved to a variety of allegorical interpretations, and both developed a standard allegorical reading in the Middle Ages which crowded out the others. For the Jews the Valiant Woman represented the Torah; for the Christians she symbolized the Church. For more than a thousand years, in both traditions, there was an overwhelming consensus that the Valiant Woman should be understood allegorically. It was this consensus which was challenged by the Reformation." Theodore of Mopsuestia read Ecclesiastes in a literal way even though he lived ca. 350–428, but his writings were later condemned. On Theodore, see Murphy, *Ecclesiastes*, xxiii, and see below.

Shortly after this preliminary exploration of Ecclesiastes by Origen, two of his disciples, Gregory Thaumaturgus (d. 270) and Dionysius the Great (d. 265), prepared more formal studies of Ecclesiastes. In attempts to expand on Origen's approach to Ecclesiastes, Dionysius prepared a verse-by-verse exegesis of the first three chapters and Gregory a metaphrase of the book. *A Metaphrase of the Book of Ecclesiastes* is thus the earliest extant Christian work on Ecclesiastes as a whole. In Gregory's view Solomon speaks to the whole church of God and shows them the vanity of servitude to transient human things in order to lead them to contemplation of heavenly things. In his comments Gregory recognizes the unorthodox sayings in Ecclesiastes but seeks to defuse them. In his comments on chap. 1, he presents Solomon as reflecting on a time when he thought that he was an expert on the nature of things but now realizing that such pursuits achieve no purpose. In chap. 2, on the discussion of pleasure, Gregory presents Solomon as coming to the orthodox conclusion that "the perfect good does not consist in eating and drinking, although it is true that it is from God that their sustenance cometh to men. . . . But the good man who gets wisdom from God, gets also heavenly enjoyment."[48]

The tendency to allegorize the reference to joy and eating is evident in this quotation. However, there is a tension in Gregory's understanding of the *carpe diem* passages in Ecclesiastes. On the one hand they are allegorized to refer to heavenly enjoyment, but on the other they are read as a manifestation of folly. At the same time Gregory recognizes that a Christian understanding of creation necessitates a positive approach to eating and drinking. In his paraphrase of chap. 5, he attempts to reduce this tension: "I am persuaded, therefore, that the greatest good for man is cheerfulness and well-doing, and that this short lived enjoyment, which alone is possible to us, comes from God only, *if righteousness direct our doings.*"[49] Not surprisingly, the epilogue is understood by Gregory as Solomon's apt conclusion to Ecclesiastes.

During the fourth century, Christians continued to take an interest in Ecclesiastes. Victorinus of Pettau (d. 304) wrote the first exposition of Ecclesiastes in Latin, and another important commentary on Ecclesiastes was that by Apollinarius of Laodicea (d. 390), but neither of these works is extant. These commentaries form the background and tradition from which Jerome (d. 420) wrote his commentary on the Hebrew text, which became the standard interpretation of Ecclesiastes until it was challenged by the Lutheran reformers.

Jerome's resort to the text in its original language is significant, as is his pastoral interpretation of Ecclesiastes.[50] It is written as a guidebook on spiritual devotion for one Blesilla, an aristocratic Roman, in order to "provoke her

48. Gregory Thaumaturgus, *Metaphrase of the Book of Ecclesiastes* 2 (*ANF*, 6:10).
49. Ibid., 11 (italics mine).
50. Note also Jerome's use of Jewish sources. See, for example, Kraus, "Christians, Jews, and Pagans."

to contempt of the world" and thus encourage her to adopt a monastic-like vocation.[51] Two principles govern Jerome's allegorical[52] reading of Ecclesiastes, namely *contemptus mundi*—the world is worthy of contempt—and that the entire earthly scene may be considered valueless, that is, *pro nihilo*. Jerome asserts the vanity of every enjoyment under the sun and the necessity of an ascetic life devoted to the service of God. He likens "the present world to a prison, jail and valley of tears."[53] "All told, Jerome develops a 'world view' for Ecclesiastes that is logically consistent and thoroughly consonant with his primary interpretive principle of the *contemptus mundi*. Indeed, Jerome concludes, the earthly scene that is investigated by the author in its entirety throughout Ecclesiastes is spurned *en bloc*."[54] The references to eating and drinking are allegorically interpreted as references to partaking of the sacrament, and inconvenient passages are put into the mouths of skeptics and opponents.

Drawing on Origen, Jerome finds a parallel between Ecclesiastes and the second component of the tripartite division of the classical sciences, the physical sciences. Like the physical sciences, Ecclesiastes reflects on the natural order, but rather than pursue the ontological implications of this, Jerome is more interested in the author's personal disposition toward nature, as evidenced by 1:2. Jerome resolves the potential contradiction with Genesis's positive view of creation by asserting that Qohelet sets out the comparative worth of union with God. "Jerome, however, never maintains that the author considers the created order *nihil boni*, that is, not good in an unconditional sense. . . . By means of this comparative relationship between the author's personal estimation of the created order and his exclusive devotion to God, Jerome justifies the negative attitude towards the natural realm that is apparent in 1:2."[55] Drawing on rabbinic tradition, Jerome reads Eccles. 3 as an outline of world history, demonstrating that history is in a constant state of change and uncertainty.[56] On the basis of verses like 1:3, Jerome takes Ecclesiastes to be passionately opposed to civic life. In line with the Alexandrian school of exegesis Jerome frequently resorts to a christological form of exegesis. Jerome notes that 1:1 asserts Solomonic authorship but that as "son of David" Jesus is *noster Ecclesiastes* (our Ecclesiastes). When Qohelet asserts in 4:9 that "two are better than one," this is not an affirmation of communal and civic life; the other "one" is Jesus. In 4:10 the one who lifts one up is likewise Jesus. At

---

51. On Jerome, Blesilla, and Ecclesiastes see Kallas, "Ecclesiastes," 58–66.
52. Although I think "allegorical" is the right description of his reading, this should not be taken to imply a complete neglect of the literal sense. See Hirshman, *Rivalry of Genius*, 95–108.
53. Kallas, "Ecclesiastes," 87.
54. Ibid., 88.
55. Ibid., 73.
56. See ibid., 73–79.

a literal level, 9:13–16 demonstrates the fragility of civic life, but if one reads this passage christologically, the powerful king is the devil, the besieged city the church, and the poor wise man Jesus.

Jerome's commentary was widely influential and became the standard interpretation of Ecclesiastes up until the time of the Reformers; for example, his equating of eating with the Eucharist is followed by Philastrius (380), Ambrose (ca. 339–397), and Augustine (354–430).[57] In effect Jerome standardized the interpretation of Ecclesiastes for over a thousand years. As Kallas observes,

> No expositor within the medieval exegetical tradition subjects the Ecclesiastes commentary of Jerome to direct criticism, or disputes its positive worth within the interpretative tradition of the church. In short, the Ecclesiastes commentary of Jerome may be likened to a plumb line from which medieval expositors may, on occasion, take a new orientation, but never without sight of this fundamental standard for an authentic interpretation of the text.[58]

The extent of Jerome's influence on the interpretation of Ecclesiastes can be gauged by the case of Theodore of Mopsuestia, who lived in the latter half of the fourth century and the first half of the fifth century. His insistence on the literal interpretation of the Bible combined with the opinions of his pupil Nestorius led to the condemnation of Theodore's works at the Second Council of Constantinople in the mid-sixth century. Part of the reason for the condemnation of his works is that he was said to deny the canonicity of Ecclesiastes.[59] Because of this condemnation Theodore's commentary on Ecclesiastes was lost until the twentieth-century discovery of a Syriac translation of the extensive introduction and commentary on the first seven chapters of his original Greek commentary. This discovery, combined with the medieval Syriac commentary of Dionysius, which is heavily dependent on Theodore, has enabled Theodore's view of Ecclesiastes to be reassessed.[60] Theodore, contrary to fifteen hundred years of tradition, did not deny the canonicity of Ecclesiastes but sought to rescue it from the dominant allegorical style of interpretation standardized by Jerome. He insisted on a literal reading of the text and rejected Jerome's allegorical and christological exegesis.[61]

Tradition dominated medieval interpretation of Scripture, and so it is not surprising that allegorical interpretation characterizes most medieval exegesis of Ecclesiastes.[62] However, just as the early Christians were influenced by

57. On these three see Ginsburg, *Coheleth*, 103–5.
58. Kallas, "Ecclesiastes," 93.
59. On Theodore's interpretation of the OT see Zaharopoulos, *Theodore of Mopsuestia*.
60. These documents are now available in published form in Strothmann, ed., *Das syrische Fragment*.
61. See Jarick, "Theodore of Mopsuestia and Interpretation."
62. On the interpretation of the Bible in the Middle Ages, see Lampe, ed., *Cambridge History of the Bible*, vol. 2: *The West from the Fathers to the Reformation*; and Smalley, *Study of the Bible*.

secular methods in their reading of Scripture, so too were theologians in the Middle Ages, and toward the end of the Middle Ages this led to a renewed interest in the literal sense. Smalley points out that for theologians in the medieval schools the rediscovery of Aristotle's *Politics* led to a renewed interest in politics and ethics and thus to a fresh examination of the sapiential OT literature that shared these interests.[63] The result was an increased output of commentaries on all the sapiential books in the thirteenth century. Amid the renewal of biblical studies in the thirteenth century, no less than thirteen commentaries on Ecclesiastes were written, the most significant of which is that by Bonaventura.

The Neoplatonic influence mediated by Augustine and Jerome privileged the spiritual reading, whereas the influence of the rediscovery of Aristotle favored the literal reading. Thus, in his postill on Ecclesiastes, Bonaventura (1221–1274) exploits the possibilities in the literal sense that Guerric had opened up as a result of the growing influence of Aristotle without, however, abandoning the tradition of interpretation established by Jerome.[64]

Bonaventura's renewed interest in the literal sense manifests itself in his argument that Ecclesiastes provides positive metaphysical truths about the natural order. Bonaventura appropriates from Hugh of St. Victor (d. 1141) the notion of a *triplex vanitas* (triple vanity), although he applies it systematically to Ecclesiastes, which he views as a logically structured whole: 1:3–3:15 deals with the *vanitas mutabilitatis*; 3:16–7:23 with the *vanitas iniquitatis*; and 7:24–12:7 with the *vanitas poenalitatis*. *Vanitas mutabilitatis* relates to the transience and mutability of the natural order that Qohelet is able to *observe*, an epistemology that Bonaventura finds paralleled in Aristotle, whose writings had recently been rediscovered. "In the realm of the senses, for example, Aristotle is given much authority by Bonaventura. Inasmuch as the author of Ecclesiastes apparently probes into the workings of the natural order and draws certain conclusions from his observations, the similar observations of Aristotle are also found to be of some assistance to Bonaventure for the interpretative task."[65] Bonaventura invokes Rom. 8:20 in support of his reading that the entire creation is subject to vanity, that is, mutability. He reads Eccles. 3 as teaching that time is an objective part of the natural order but connects it with the vanity of the natural order: "*Vanitas* is a general category that is attributable to the extended natural realm on account of its temporality just as temporality itself is that which defines, more specifically, the particular condition of *vanitas*."[66]

Vanitas iniquitatis and *vanitas poenalitatis* relate to the human condition, which is likewise subject to vanity. In the second section of Ecclesiastes the

63. Smalley, *Study of the Bible*, xxxi, 308–28.
64. Ibid., 292ff.
65. Kallas, "Ecclesiastes," 117.
66. Ibid., 138.

theme moves from the natural order to epistemology: "The *vanitas* manifest within the objective order of things, genuinely affects the powers of human perception and the field of knowledge within human beings."[67] In the third section the author deals with death and other aspects of the miserable human condition. Like Jerome, Bonaventura recognizes the potential conflict with his reading of Ecclesiastes and Genesis's positive view of creation. He resolves the contradiction by making a subtle distinction between the creation as good in a relative sense or *in ordine* while, at the same time, being subject to mutability and thus vanity.[68] In an effort to explain how the world can be regarded as vanity, Bonaventura compares the world to a wedding ring. The wife must regard the ring as nothing relative to her love for her husband, and our attitude to the world must be the same.

Bonaventura's more literal reading in relation to the natural order and the human condition in no way contradicts Jerome's reading. He continues to read Ecclesiastes christologically,[69] and his analysis of the metaphysics of Ecclesiastes is seen to support the mystical life through its negative view of present earthly life. "Ecclesiastes is treated accordingly by Bonaventure as though the author, too, proceeds as a 'wayfarer' through his investigations into the natural order of things unto more sublime eternal realities and finally the beatific life."[70]

Among fourteenth-century commentaries on Ecclesiastes, that by Nicholas of Lyra (d. 1345) deserves mention. Ginsburg singles him out as inaugurating a new era in the exegesis of Ecclesiastes with his knowledge of Hebrew and his emphasis on the literal meaning of the text. The contribution of the Reformers is regarded by Ginsburg as little more than a continuation of this recovery begun by Nicholas. When he deals with the Reformers, Ginsburg notes that Nicholas is "at last crowded by a host of Reformers."[71] As Kallas rightly argues, however, Nicholas manifests no major break with the Jerome-Bonaventura tradition of interpretation.[72]

The enduring influence of Jerome on the interpretation of Ecclesiastes is manifest in Thomas à Kempis's classic *The Imitation of Christ*.[73] Completed around 1427, the *Imitation* continues to be widely read to this day. Eugene Peterson notes, "This is the most widely published and read book on spirituality in our tradition. It is amazing how well its medieval monkishness carries over into

67. Ibid., 128.
68. See ibid., 147–54.
69. See ibid., 194–95.
70. Ibid., 161n97.
71. Ginsburg, *Coheleth*, 111.
72. See Kallas, "Ecclesiastes," 165–67.
73. The *Imitation* is probably a collation of the wisdom of the Brothers of the Common Life, a Dutch order that Thomas joined at the age of thirteen and remained with for the rest of his life.

the modern world. When Dag Hammarskjold was killed in an airplane crash in Africa, the books found in his briefcase were the Bible and *The Imitation*."[74] The opening section of *The Imitation* is entitled "Imitating Christ and Despising All Vanities on Earth."[75] Thomas emphasizes the importance of the grace and love of God and says, "Vanity of vanities and all is vanity, except to love God and serve him alone. This is the greatest wisdom—to seek the kingdom of heaven through *contempt of the world*."[76] Thomas advises the reader: "Often recall the proverb: 'The eye is not satisfied with seeing nor the ear filled with hearing' [Eccl. 1:8]. Try, moreover, to turn your heart from the love of things visible and bring yourself to things invisible."[77] The influence of Jerome's reading of Ecclesiastes on this devotional manual is obvious and frames Thomas's approach from the outset.

Jerome's reading of Ecclesiastes held sway for over a thousand years, and it was the enduring contribution of Luther, Melanchthon, and Brenz to break the stranglehold of this interpretation and to open up truly fresh ways of reading Ecclesiastes.[78] Calvin drew on Ecclesiastes some twenty-one times in his *Institutes* but never wrote a commentary on it. Zwingli paid little attention to Ecclesiastes; in his works seven glosses are compiled on selected verses.[79] "Though a seemingly insignificant event within the history of the Reformation and centered upon a text far removed from the mainstream of evangelical theology, this decisive break with Jerome that is initiated by the evangelical commentators on Ecclesiastes marks an important and still unrecognized event in Reformation history."[80]

Luther blazed the trail in the new interpretation of Ecclesiastes with his translation and exegesis of the Hebrew and was ably complemented in this task by Melanchthon and Brenz. Like Jerome, Luther noted the unique language of Ecclesiastes but completely rejected Jerome's notion that Ecclesiastes teaches contempt of the world. "That the household and politics are left forsaken, that persons flee to the desert, that society is abandoned for the solitary life, that human existence is merely lived in silence, are the manifold ramifications of the simple counsel Jerome offers to Blesilla

74. Peterson, *Take and Read*, 7.
75. Thomas à Kempis, *The Imitation of Christ*, Hendrickson Christian Classics (Peabody, MA: Hendrickson, 2004), 3.
76. Ibid. (italics mine).
77. Ibid.
78. See Kallas, "Ecclesiastes," in this respect. Kallas's work is a major contribution in terms of understanding the Reformers' achievement. In stark contrast to Kallas's positive reading of Luther on Ecclesiastes, G. White ("Luther on Ecclesiastes," 181) refers to "Luther's exegetical rape of Ecclesiastes." Additional important sources for the Lutheran reformers' interpretation of Ecclesiastes are Wölfel, *Luther und die Skepsis*; and Rosin, *Reformers*.
79. Kallas, "Ecclesiastes," 8.
80. Ibid., 172.

within his prefatory remarks."[81] Contra Jerome, Luther, Melanchthon, and Brenz insist that Ecclesiastes is fundamentally positive about civic life even as it wrestles with the difficulties of poor leadership, a problem with which the Reformers were only too familiar. Luther read Ecclesiastes as a book about politics and the family, about human existence in the context of creation order. He envisaged Solomon not as a solitary but as a political figure deeply concerned about social life. In contrast to Jerome's allegorical and christological exegesis of 4:4–12, Luther read this text as a strong affirmation of communal and civic life.

As we have seen, an issue in the Jerome–Bonaventura tradition of interpreting Ecclesiastes was how to reconcile contempt for the world with Genesis's affirmation of it as good. With their recovery of a rigorous doctrine of the goodness of creation, the Reformers demolished the doctrine of *contemptus mundi*. This is particularly evident in their reading of the *carpe diem* passages, particularly 5:18–20 [17–19]: "The ardent enjoyment of various things such as food, drink, labor, wealth and possessions are urged. Not only are such matters worthy of pleasure, but the very enjoyment of the manifold gifts is considered in the passage to be a gift of God. The great enthusiasm of Luther for this section leads him to maintain that this remark is an appropriate *conclusio* to the entire book, and especially the earlier chapters."[82] Similarly, in the first Protestant commentary on Ecclesiastes to be published,[83] Johannes Brenz (1527) comments,

> There is nothing better than to be cheerful, and enjoy one's life; to eat, drink, and delight in one's employment. . . . Some foolish persons, not understanding these things, have absurdly taught contempt for and flight from the world, and have committed many foolish things themselves; as we read in the lives of the Fathers that there were some who even shut themselves up from ever seeing the sun . . . living above the world is not living out of the world.[84]

In relation to Eccles. 3, time is now viewed positively as part of God's providential ordering of creation.

If one major contribution of the Reformers was to reassess Ecclesiastes' view of the world, then the other related contribution was to reassess the function of *hebel* (*vanitas*) in the book.[85] *Hebel* is taken to refer not to God's creation order but to the self, the human condition. "No longer is it assumed by Luther that the self and the very ontological structure of the created realm

---

81. Ibid., 178.
82. Ibid., 309.
83. Luther's commentary was written first, but publication was delayed until 1532. See ibid., 7–18.
84. Ginsburg, *Coheleth*, 112.
85. In Ecclesiastes, Hebrew *hebel* is traditionally translated "vanity," but I translate it as "enigma."

are positively linked through their mutual condition of *vanitas*. . . . What Solomon rather speaks about in Ecclesiastes and calls vain, Luther argues, is not the extended creation, but solely the human condition."[86] *Hebel* relates not to the created realm but to anthropology; more specifically, contra Origen, not to the body but to the heart, the volitional center of the human person that with its errant appetites "spawn *vanitas* within the self."[87] With regard to Rom. 8:19–20, Luther argues against Aquinas that the created order is good and that it is solely humans misusing the good creation that results in its being subjected to vanity.[88]

As we will see below, Luther's contribution is also significant in his view of the authorship of Ecclesiastes. In his commentary, he maintains that the material comes from Solomon but is assembled by his disciples. However, in his *Table Talk* he is the first to explicitly deny Solomonic authorship.

This fresh understanding of Ecclesiastes that emerged out of the Reformation results from a new emphasis on the text in its original language interpreted literally, *and* a strong theological recovery of the doctrine of creation with a corresponding stress on the vocation of all believers in all spheres of life.[89] Kallas is thus quite right in his assessment that "the evangelical reformers take upon themselves the responsibility for the inauguration of a break with the medieval exegetical tradition that effectively begins an altogether new stage for the interpretation of Ecclesiastes during the reformation in advance of the modern era."[90] Throughout the seventeenth century Ecclesiastes remained controversial as Catholic commentators strenuously defended Jerome's line of interpretation.[91]

In the eighteenth and nineteenth centuries, as the Enlightenment legacy gradually took hold in biblical studies, it became more common to deny Solomonic authorship of Ecclesiastes and to question the orthodoxy of the book (see discussion of authorship below).[92] The father of modern OT criticism, de Wette, published his mature views of Ecclesiastes in 1844 in the final edition of his introduction to the OT. De Wette maintains that Qohelet asserts the vanity of all things and the reality of enjoyment alone. Qohelet gives no hope of a future life, and his life view inclines toward fatalism, skepticism, and Epicureanism.

---

86. Kallas, "Ecclesiastes," 255.
87. Ibid., 277–78.
88. Aquinas specifically links Ecclesiastes to Rom. 8:19–20 (*Opera Omnia* [Rome: Commissio Leonina; Paris: Librairie philosophique J. Vrin, 1989–], 20:76ff.). See Kallas, "Ecclesiastes," 257.
89. See Wingren (*Luther on Vocation*, 2–3, 172–73, 226), who takes note of Luther's work on Ecclesiastes.
90. Kallas, "Ecclesiastes," 316.
91. Ibid., 317–27.
92. For a fuller discussion, see Bartholomew, *Reading Ecclesiastes*, 42–50.

Writing in 1881, Plumptre is a good indication of the state of Ecclesiastes scholarship at that time. He finds Ecclesiastes enigmatic but fascinating. He regards it as remarkably and providentially relevant to the needs of his day "to meet the special tendencies of modern philosophical thought, and that the problems of life which it discusses are those with which our own daily experience brings us into contact."[93] The hypocritical religion of Qohelet's wealthy parents and their friends was disillusioning for him. As he entered his adult years, Qohelet traveled to Alexandria, where he was exposed to the royal court. He lived an extravagant life and indulged in reckless sensuality. Qohelet experienced one great love but had been terribly disillusioned by this woman; she had proved to be "more bitter than death." Deeply affected by this broken relationship, he sought meaning in Greek philosophy, where for a time he found solace. The dark days returned, however, until a male friend, who was a great help to him at this and other times, finally reawakened him to the fear of God. Ecclesiastes is thus in Plumptre's view an intensely personal book whose main purpose is to warn those in quest of the chief good against the quicksands in which Qohelet nearly sank. Qohelet desires to deepen in his readers the fear of God, in which he at last found the anchor of his soul.

Although Plumptre denies Solomonic authorship[94] and in this sense agrees with the modern critical consensus, in most ways his work remains within the precritical framework. The type of speculative biographical analysis of Qohelet he develops is rare in twentieth-century works,[95] and his introduction addresses none of the source-, form-, and tradition-critical questions that are commonplace in twentieth-century commentaries. In line with the precritical tradition, Plumptre's reading is a theologically orthodox one in which the epilogue provides the key to the message of the book and resolves the tensions in the text. Plumptre comments on the epilogue (12:13–14):

> This is what the Teacher who, as it were, edits the book, presents to his disciples as its sum and substance, and he was not wrong in doing so. In this the Debater himself had rested after his many wanderings of thought. . . . From the standpoint of the writer of the epilogue it was shown that the teaching of Ecclesiastes was not inconsistent with the faith of Israel. . . . From our standpoint we may say that it was shown not less convincingly that the book, like all true records of the search after Truth, led men through the labyrinthine windings of doubt to the goal of duty, through the waves and winds of conflicting opinions to the unshaken rock of the Eternal Commandment.[96]

93. Plumptre, *Ecclesiastes*, 11.
94. Note, however, that he feels the need to devote fifteen pages to the issue in his relatively small commentary.
95. Zimmermann (*Inner World of Qohelet*) is a notable but eccentric exception.
96. Plumptre, *Ecclesiastes*, 229–30.

Modern Readings

In the second half of the nineteenth century the critical reading of Ecclesiastes gathered momentum, but it was only with the source-critical commentaries of Siegfried, Laue, McNeile, Podechard, and G. Barton that historical-critical reading of Ecclesiastes emerged in the way that it had done for the Pentateuch during the nineteenth century.[97] By the end of the nineteenth century pentateuchal criticism had already accrued the contributions of de Wette and Wellhausen. Driver published his *Introduction to the Literature of the Old Testament* in 1898. A comparison of his extensive treatment of the source criticism of the Pentateuch with his treatment of Ecclesiastes is instructive. The source criticism of Ecclesiastes was still in its infancy.[98]

There were reasons for this relative lack of interest in Ecclesiastes and Wisdom literature in general. Wellhausen paid almost no attention to Wisdom literature because he regarded it as late and secondary. He was especially concerned with the history of Israel's religious institutions, and there was no clear indication how wisdom was related to these. Duhm also affirmed the secondary status of wisdom; wise men were heirs of the prophets because they took the great moral principles of justice and applied them to everyday life.[99]

Two developments challenged the belief in the secondary and late emergence of wisdom. First, Gunkel applied form criticism to wisdom. The forms and character of wisdom teaching were discerned to be so distinctive that they could not be derived from prophecy or law. They must have emanated from a special class of wise men who were concerned with education and humanity's general progress and advancement in life.[100] Form criticism has been particularly important in identifying wisdom as a specific genre of literature within the OT. This is taken for granted nowadays, but it was really only in the late nineteenth century that wisdom was "discovered."[101] The second stimulus was the discovery in 1888 of the Teaching of Amenemope. Erman recognized the original of Prov. 22:17–23:11 in this text,[102] and this led to a heightening of

---

97. Siegfried, *Prediger und Hoheslied*; Laue, *Koheleth*; McNeile, *Introduction to Ecclesiastes*; Podechard, *L'Ecclésiaste*; G. Barton, *Ecclesiastes*. Cf., for example, the development of the historical-critical approach to Deuteronomy in the nineteenth century. See Bartholomew, "Composition of Deuteronomy," 13–19.

98. Driver, *Introduction*, 1–159 and 465–78.

99. Clements, *Century of Old Testament Study*, 100.

100. Ibid., 102.

101. Cf. Crenshaw, "Prolegomenon," in *Studies in Ancient Israelite Wisdom*, 3–5. The debate continued throughout the twentieth century as to what exactly constitutes a wisdom writing in the OT. See Whybray, *Intellectual Tradition*; Crenshaw, "Method in Determining Wisdom Influence."

102. See Reventlow, *Problems of Old Testament Theology*, 172–73, for bibliographic references.

interest in Wisdom literature against its background in the ancient Near East, especially during the years 1924–36.[103]

However, toward the end of the 1930s this interest waned. Old Testament Wisdom literature might have early and international roots, but it seemed to have little to contribute to the theology of the OT.[104] Zimmerli had argued that its central concerns were exclusively anthropocentric, and the notion that earlier wisdom had been secular and utilitarian was widely endorsed.[105] Recent decades, however, have seen a reawakening of interest in OT Wisdom literature. Zimmerli showed that creation was fundamental to OT wisdom,[106] and it became increasingly apparent that, like ancient Near Eastern wisdom, OT wisdom was deeply religious.[107] Von Rad himself came to argue that wisdom was a branch of Yahwism.[108] These developments have led to renewed interest in the theology of wisdom, its development within the OT, and its relationship to other strands of OT thought.[109] Scholars are divided over how to understand wisdom and its relationship to the rest of the OT, but by the end of the twentieth century wisdom was firmly on OT and theological agendas.[110]

The interpretation of Ecclesiastes in the twentieth century needs to be seen against this background. All the issues that have dominated wisdom study have had their impact on the interpretation of Ecclesiastes. Characteristic methods of historical criticism have been source, form, redaction, and tradition criticism. These were applied to Ecclesiastes at the end of the nineteenth century and the beginning of the twentieth, and their influence remains strong in the most recent commentaries on Ecclesiastes, albeit in modified form.[111]

103. Crenshaw, *Studies in Ancient Israelite Wisdom*, 5–6.

104. Or at least to the theological interests of contemporary OT scholars. Especially through von Rad's influence, the doctrine of creation, which is fundamental to Wisdom literature, was made subsidiary to redemption. Only in recent decades has there been a renaissance of interest in creation in the OT (cf. Reventlow, *Problems of Old Testament Theology*, 134–86).

105. Zimmerli, "Concerning Structure." Cf. G. Wright, *God Who Acts*, 102–5; and McKane, *Prophets and Wise Men*, 48ff.

106. Zimmerli, "Place and Limit of Wisdom."

107. Reventlow, *Problems of Old Testament Theology*, 174–78.

108. Von Rad, *Wisdom*, 106.

109. Reventlow (*Problems of Old Testament Theology*, 181) suggests, "It is at this point, i.e. over the question of the relationship between the various areas of Old Testament thought, that the discussion will have to be continued: in other words, between the conception of order which is characteristic of wisdom (and not just wisdom) and the areas governed by the tradition of salvation history."

110. A number of overview essays have been published that help one to get a feel for the development of wisdom study. Most recently see Day et al., eds., *Wisdom in Ancient Israel*. For a useful overview of the current issues on the "wisdom agenda," see Murphy, "Wisdom in the OT."

111. Very little redaction criticism has been done on Ecclesiastes. It has been suggested that Childs's canonical approach is really a redactional one, but see Murphy, "Old Testament as Scripture," 41, for a contrary view.

Siegfried pioneered the source-critical approach to Ecclesiastes,[112] identifying nine different sources in the book. Within English-speaking circles, McNeile and G. Barton developed more moderate source-critical approaches to Ecclesiastes.[113] As the twentieth century progressed, a radical source-critical approach to Ecclesiastes became rare, and the book came to be seen more and more as a unity,[114] with the exception of the epilogue, which is almost universally seen as a later addition. The prime legacy of source criticism in the interpretation of Ecclesiastes is this tendency to read the book without the epilogue. By comparison, in almost all precritical interpretation of Ecclesiastes the epilogue provides the interpretive key.

Gunkel initiated form-critical analysis of Wisdom literature, and assessment of the forms used in Ecclesiastes has continued to play a fundamental role in the interpretation of the book.[115] Crenshaw suggests that the dominant literary type in Ecclesiastes is reflection arising from personal observation.[116] He notes that scholars have also drawn attention to *mashal*, diatribe, and royal testament forms, and that Qohelet also uses autobiographical narrative, example story, anecdote, parable, antithesis, and proverb (as distinct from *mashal*).

Galling developed a form-critical interpretation in which he divided Ecclesiastes into a large number of originally independent sections.[117] Such an approach clearly militates against reading Ecclesiastes as a strongly unified text. However, on the macro level of the form of Ecclesiastes, no consensus has been reached regarding its genre and structure,[118] although A. Wright's New Critical analysis of the structure has convinced a number of scholars.[119] The problem of whether Ecclesiastes is prose or poetry remains, with the majority of scholars treating it as a mixture of both.[120]

The tradition history of Ecclesiastes was a matter of concern throughout the twentieth century.[121] Within the OT wisdom tradition most scholars have seen Ecclesiastes as a negative, skeptical reaction to mainline wisdom as rep-

---

112. Siegfried, *Prediger und Hoheslied*.

113. McNeile, *Introduction*; G. Barton, *Ecclesiastes*.

114. Gordis (*Koheleth*, 73) notes the growing recognition of the unity of Ecclesiastes.

115. Cf. Michel, *Qohelet*, 76–81; Crenshaw, "Wisdom Literature," 377–78; and Murphy, *Wisdom Literature*, 125–49.

116. Crenshaw, "Ecclesiastes, Book of," 275.

117. Galling, "Kohelet-Studien"; idem, *Prediger*.

118. A. Wright, "Riddle of the Sphinx"; and Schoors, "Structure littéraire de Qohéleth," contain useful overviews of the great variety of structures that have been proposed.

119. A. Wright's analysis is followed, for example, by Murphy, *Ecclesiastes*, xxxii–xli, and is drawn upon by Perdue, *Wisdom and Creation*, 203ff.; cf. Michel, *Qohelet*, 9–45.

120. Cf. Murphy, *Ecclesiastes*, xxvi–xxxii. As Towner ("Ecclesiastes," 270) notes, the NIV considers 60 percent of Ecclesiastes to be poetry, the NRSV thinks it is only 25 percent, and the Good News Bible/Today's English Version and the Revised English Bible regard 3:2–8 as the only poetic passage in the book.

121. Cf. Michel, *Qohelet*, 66–75.

resented by Proverbs.[122] Gese identified Ecclesiastes with a crisis of wisdom in Israel, but scholars remain divided over the existence and extent of this "crisis."[123] To what extent do we have a rigid doctrine of retribution in the OT and to what extent is Ecclesiastes a reaction to this?[124] By the end of the twentieth century there was no consensus about the development of the wisdom tradition and how Ecclesiastes fits into that development. Using sociological analysis, Brueggemann has suggested that "Ecclesiastes articulates a conservative ideology that reflects social control and a concern for stability. . . . The emancipatory side of wisdom is reflected in the embrace of creation in the Song of Solomon, the ideological dimension is articulated in Ecclesiastes."[125] This view is a development of Brueggemann's discernment of a royal (order) and a liberative trajectory in the OT.[126]

The relationship of OT wisdom to international wisdom was an issue throughout the twentieth century. Ranston, for example, published a monograph in 1925 in which he explored the relationship between Ecclesiastes and the early Greek wisdom literature. He concludes:

> The evidence strongly suggests that Ecclesiastes was not widely or deeply acquainted with the early Greek literature, i.e. he had not read much of it. . . . The conclusion reached is that Koheleth, in his search for suitable proverbs (ix.9f.), moved for a time in circles where the minds of the people were stored with the wisdom-utterances of the early sages mentioned by Isocrates as the outstanding teachers of practical morality, Theognis being the most important.[127]

Studies of Ecclesiastes continue to concern themselves with Ecclesiastes' relationship to Mesopotamia, Egypt, and Greece.[128] The Jewishness of Ecclesiastes has received greater recognition, but its relationship to Greek thought in particular continues to be debated.[129]

122. Cf., for example, Baumgartner, "Wisdom Literature," 221–27.

123. Gese, "Crisis of Wisdom in Koheleth." Cf. Crenshaw, "Wisdom Literature," 381–82; and Murphy, "Wisdom in the Old Testament."

124. Cf. Van Leeuwen, "Wealth and Poverty."

125. Brueggemann, "Social Significance," 129. On the sociological analysis of Ecclesiastes, cf. also Crüsemann, "Unchangeable World."

126. Brueggemann, "Trajectories in Old Testament Literature." Cf. Middleton's critique of Brueggemann's view of creation order, "Is Creation Theology Inherently Conservative?"; and Brueggemann's reply, "Response to J. Richard Middleton."

127. Ranston, Ecclesiastes and Early Greek Wisdom Literature, 149–50.

128. Cf. Michel, Qohelet, 52–65; Murphy, Ecclesiastes, xli–xlv.

129. Cf., for example, N. Lohfink (Qoheleth, 4–7), who tends to assume the Hellenistic character of Ecclesiastes, with Murphy (Ecclesiastes, xlv), who is far more cautious. Lohfink thinks that Ecclesiastes may have been written between 190 and 180 BC, just before the Maccabean revolt. In this context, Judea belonged to the Hellenistic world, and Hellenistic ideas were pervasive and competed with the Jewish tradition. Lohfink assumes a high degree of Hellenistic influence, whereas C. Harrison ("Qoheleth in Social-Historical Perspective") argues that

With regard to the message of Ecclesiastes, historical-critical scholarship differs notably from precritical readings in its general rejection of the need to harmonize Ecclesiastes with theological orthodoxy. This loss of theological constraint has not, however, produced agreement about the message of Ecclesiastes, as, for example, the huge variety of proposals about how to translate *hebel* (enigma) indicate.[130] Some, like Crenshaw, regard Qohelet as deeply pessimistic; others regard him as also positive but to differing extents.[131] Crenshaw asserts,

> Qoheleth taught by means of various literary types that earlier optimistic claims about wisdom's power to secure one's existence have no validity. No discernible principle of order governs the universe, rewarding virtue and punishing evil. The creator, distant and uninvolved, acts as judge only (if at all) in extreme cases of flagrant affront. . . . Death cancels all imagined gains, rendering life under the sun absurd. Therefore the best policy is to enjoy one's wife, together with good food and drink, during youth, for old age and death will soon put an end to this "relative" good. In short, Qoheleth examined all of life and discovered no absolute good that would survive death's effect. . . . Qoheleth bears witness to an intellectual crisis in ancient Israel.[132]

In a similar vein to Crenshaw, F. Watson describes Qohelet's vision as "rigorously hopeless." "Nowhere else in holy scripture is there so forthrightly set out an alternative vision to that of the gospel, a rival version of the truth. . . . In the light of the gospel, nothing could be more illusory than the consolation of Qoheleth's celebrated 'realism.'"[133] Loader likewise argues that Ecclesiastes is a negative witness to the gospel.[134] Whybray by contrast has argued that Qohelet was mainly a preacher of joy.[135] And Ogden asserts that Ecclesiastes' thesis "is that life under God must be taken and enjoyed in all its mystery."[136] Ellul sums up Ecclesiastes' message thus: "In reality, all is vanity. In truth, everything is a gift of God."[137]

Despite this polarization with respect to the message of Ecclesiastes, a certain consensus has emerged out of a historical-critical interpretation of Ecclesiastes. Very few scholars nowadays defend Solomonic authorship; most regard Ecclesiastes as written by an unknown Jew around the late third century

---

it was minimal in Judea, although he does argue that Ptolemaic economic policy was deeply affecting Judean society.

130. See commentary on 1:2.

131. Crenshaw, *Ecclesiastes*, e.g., 23–28. Cf., for example, Murphy, *Ecclesiastes*, lvi–lxix, with Ogden, *Qoheleth*, 9–10, 13–15.

132. Crenshaw, "Ecclesiastes, Book of," 277.

133. F. Watson, *Text, Church, and World*, 283–87.

134. Loader, *Polar Structures*; idem, *Ecclesiastes*. Cf. also Hertzberg, *Prediger*, 237–38.

135. Whybray, "Qoheleth, Preacher of Joy." Cf. also Maussion, *Mal, le bien*.

136. Ogden, *Qoheleth*, 14.

137. Ellul, *Reason for Being*, 31.

BC. Most scholars regard the book as a basic unity with the exception of the epilogue. With the possible exception of the discernment of different voices/strands in Ecclesiastes, all three assumptions that Murphy identified as common to precritical interpretation of Ecclesiastes have been undermined by historical criticism. However, as regards Ecclesiastes' structure, message, and relationship to OT traditions and to international wisdom, there is no consensus.

To a great extent, historical criticism has sought to exclude theological presuppositions from its methodology by insisting that the OT should be read in the same way as any other ancient Near Eastern text. In the latter half of the twentieth century, there was a growing reaction to that tendency.[138] Childs has sought to develop a hermeneutic that takes the OT seriously as canon.[139] The intriguing effect of his canonical approach upon his reading of Ecclesiastes is that in what we might call a postcritical move he reappropriates the epilogue as the key to the canonical function of Ecclesiastes, thereby undermining the one universal fruit of source criticism of Ecclesiastes. In Childs's view the epilogue alerts us to Ecclesiastes' nature as a corrective within the broader wisdom tradition.

J. Barton has suggested that the canonical approach of Childs stands or falls with New Criticism.[140] It is more likely that Childs's approach is part of a general reaction to positivism in the humanities, but it is important to note that the application of New Criticism to Ecclesiastes has resulted in new insights. A. Wright has sought to analyze the structure of Ecclesiastes by means of a close reading of the text along New Critical lines,[141] and N. Lohfink describes his creative approach to Ecclesiastes as that of *Werkinterpretation*, the German equivalent of New Criticism.[142] Although both Wright and Lohfink see the epilogue as an addition to Qohelet by another hand, their approaches indicate the developing tendency to read Ecclesiastes as carefully crafted literature. Loader also fits with this literary trend in his modified structuralist reading of Ecclesiastes whereby he discerns polar opposites as at the heart of its structure.[143] Fox proposes that we read Ecclesiastes as a narrative literary whole, with a focus on distinguishing between narrator, implied author, and Qohelet.[144] In terms of stimulating research into Ecclesiastes as a literary whole, Fox's work has been by far the most significant in recent decades.[145] Fox has

---

138. See, for example, Vanhoozer et al., eds., *Dictionary for Theological Interpretation*.
139. Childs, *Introduction to the Old Testament*.
140. J. Barton, *Reading the Old Testament*, 153–54.
141. A. Wright, "Riddle of the Sphinx."
142. N. Lohfink, "Freu Dich, Jüngling," 160.
143. Loader, *Polar Structures*.
144. Fox, "Frame-Narrative and Composition."
145. Followed, for example, by Longman, *Ecclesiastes*. See also Christianson, *Time to Tell*; and Bartholomew, *Reading Ecclesiastes*.

also made a major contribution in highlighting epistemology as a, if not the, major concern of the book.[146]

Perry too has argued for a literary reading of Ecclesiastes, but one in which Ecclesiastes is approached as the transcript of a debate between Kohelet (K) and the presenter (P). This dialogical approach, according to Perry, is the correct way to understand the "contradictions" that have plagued commentators for so long. Ecclesiastes is an essay, a collection, a debate, and the reader's task is to discern the alternating voices, which is what Perry attempts in his translation and commentary. He argues that Ecclesiastes elaborates on the paradigmatic contradiction in Hebrew Scripture that is introduced in the creation story of Genesis. It has to do with the way religious consciousness distinguishes itself from empirical or experiential modes of viewing life.

> What seems clear is that, as against the empirically based conclusions of K that all is vanity, P counters with a series of concepts that take on the density of myths of beginnings and ultimate ends, challenging the narrowness of experiential empiricism with notions that cannot possibly be verified by the same methods. P creates a tension by reinterpreting K's devalued image of total vanity with a reenergized version of the same: "less than All cannot satisfy man" (Blake).[147]

Since 2000, sustained attention has been given to the literary tropes of Ecclesiastes, following on from Fox's refocusing on Ecclesiastes as a literary whole.[148] Post-structuralism and postmodernism have inevitably started to impact the reading of Ecclesiastes,[149] as have queer[150] and postcolonial readings.[151] Regarding women's experience and Ecclesiastes, attention has tended to focus

146. This is anticipated in the tradition by Bonaventura (Kallas, "Ecclesiastes," 128), Nicholas of Lyra (ibid., 165–66), the evangelical Reformers (ibid., 245–316), and Nordheimer, "Philosophy of Ecclesiastes." More recently, see Bartholomew, *Reading Ecclesiastes*; Frydrych, *Living under the Sun*, 53–82; Schellenberg, *Erkenntnis als Problem*; Crenshaw, "Qoheleth's Understanding of Intellectual Inquiry."

147. Perry, *Dialogues*, 36.

148. See, e.g., D. Miller, *Symbol and Rhetoric in Ecclesiastes*; Ingram, *Ambiguity in Ecclesiastes*; Lee, *Vitality of Enjoyment*; Salyer, *Vain Rhetoric*.

149. Examples of postmodern readings are Koosed, *(Per)mutations of Qoheleth*; Beal, "C(ha)osmopolis"; Sherwood, "Not with a Bang"; Sneed, "(Dis)closure in Qohelet"; George, "Death as the Beginning of Life." The last is in a volume dealing with the Bible and the Holocaust, and in this respect Christianson, "Qoheleth and Existential Legacy," should also be noted.

150. Wernik, "Will the Real Homosexual"; Lyons, "'Outing' Qoheleth." The latter is a response to Wernik's argument that Qohelet is a homosexual. This queer reading of Ecclesiastes is anticipated by Zimmermann. See below.

151. Examples are Tamez, *When the Horizons Close*; idem, "Ecclesiastes 3:1–8"; Drewes, "Reading the Bible in Context"; Kabasele Lumbala and Grey, "Ecclesiastes 3:1–8"; Song, "Ecclesiastes 3:1–8"; Prior, "When All the Singing Has Stopped."

on 7:27–29 in particular, in an attempt to determine whether Qohelet was a misogynist.[152]

Psychoanalytic readings are in vogue, and Zimmermann has made a serious attempt to read Ecclesiastes along these lines, using insights from Freud, Rank, Jung, and Adler. Zimmermann maintains that Qohelet was a court official who had respect for the wealthy but was himself poor. He was married and had a son. Zimmermann analyzes his psychological condition as follows:

> He is a pathological doubter of everything, stemming from a drastic emotional experience, a psychic disturbance. He is doubtful about himself as a person of worth and character. He has no self-esteem or value of himself. His doubt has destroyed all values. He is an inferior, of no account, and he demeans himself constantly. His doubt comes from a parapathy, a disease of the mind which he shares with many neurotics.[153]

"A time to murder" in 3:1–8 indicates criminal elements in Qohelet's makeup. He represses these drives, but at the cost of the disintegration of his psyche. "To throw stones" indicates Qohelet's suspicion that his wife was adulterous. "To sow" hints at Qohelet's latent homosexuality. Indeed, Qohelet struggles with sexual impotence, as is evident from chap. 12. The picture is of an old man with declining physical powers. The symbols refer to the futility of using aphrodisiacs; "voice of the bird becomes faint" refers to lost sexual potency. Referring to 11:3, Zimmermann says, "When his gonads fill up, inevitably he experiences an emission. . . . And yet when the tree, a familiar symbol of erection . . . once falls it lies there prone and inert, and Qoheleth's potency is not aroused even by proximity to a woman."[154] Qohelet's hostility to women revealed in 7:26 could stem only from a hostile relationship with his mother. "The hatred which was directed against women (at first his mother, then his wife) enlarges, and then is levelled against all womankind."[155] "The first feminine relationship in his life with his mother/sister, on the other hand, fixated a love which he yearned to find again but could not under society's rule of morality and law."[156]

Crenshaw is surely justified to say of Zimmermann's analysis: "Such flights of fantasy possess more entertainment value than truth."[157] Zimmermann's reading presents us with an appropriate point to end our overview of readings

---

152. See, e.g., N. Lohfink, "War Kohelet ein Frauenfeind?"; Loretz, "'Frau' und griechisch-jüdische Philosophie."

153. Zimmermann, *Inner World of Qohelet*, 8.

154. Ibid., 27.

155. Ibid., 29.

156. Ibid., 36.

157. Crenshaw, "Wisdom Literature," 382; cf. also Michel's response to Zimmermann in *Qohelet*, 89–90. See the postscript at the end of this commentary for an alternative psychological reading of Ecclesiastes.

of Ecclesiastes.[158] It certainly alerts us to the diversity of readings of Ecclesiastes that have been proposed.

As with OT studies in general, research into Ecclesiastes thus finds itself in a condition of pluralism and fragmentation. Newsom's assessment is probably correct: "Scholarly work on Ecclesiastes has remained, with very few exceptions, the province of traditional historical criticism."[159] The implications of the literary turn in reading Ecclesiastes, inaugurated by Fox in particular, remain to be fully appropriated. However, the growing corpus within the literary paradigm and the minority recovery of theological interpretation in biblical studies make this a fertile time to write on Ecclesiastes.[160]

Authorship and Date

The description of Qohelet as "the son of David, king in Jerusalem," in Eccles. 1:1 clearly identifies him with King Solomon. In the precritical era scholars were more or less unanimous that Solomon was the author. Thus the Targum, for example, identifies Qohelet as Solomon and regards the book as Solomon's words of prophecy. The affirmation of Solomonic authorship of Ecclesiastes appears very early in Christian interpretation, at least as far back as Origen (185–254).[161] In the preface to his commentary on the Song of Songs, Origen notes that in Proverbs Solomon teaches moral science, in Ecclesiastes he teaches natural science—by distinguishing the vain from the profitable and essential, he counsels us to forsake vanity and cultivate things useful and upright—and in the Song of Songs Solomon teaches inspective science, in which he instills into the soul the love of heavenly things.[162] The

158. I have not considered the widespread cultural use of Ecclesiastes. Representative sources are Bozanich, "Donne and Ecclesiastes"; Christianson and McWilliams, "Voltaire's Précis of Ecclesiastes"; de Lacy, "Thematic and Structural Affinities"; Jacob, "Post-Traumatic Stress Disorder"; Schwartz, "Koheleth and Camus"; Middlemas, "Ecclesiastes Gone 'Sideways'"; Branick, "Wisdom, Pessimism, and 'Mirth'"; Harris, "Ecclesiastical Wisdom and *Nickel Mountain*"; Helsel, "Warren Zevon's *The Wind* and Ecclesiastes"; Turner and Chubin, "Another Appraisal of Ortega"; Harsanyi and Harter, "Ecclesiastes Effects." Kreitzer (*Old Testament in Fiction and Film*) explores the relationship between Hemingway's *Farewell to Arms* and Ecclesiastes; Bono, lead singer for the band U2, asserts that Ecclesiastes is the key to understanding U2's album *Achtung Baby* (Bill Flanagan, *U2 at the End of the World* [New York: Delta, 1995], 434); R. Johnston's *Useless Beauty* explores Ecclesiastes through the lens of contemporary film. The cultural use (and abuse) of Ecclesiastes is vast and has yet to be thoroughly investigated.

159. Newsom, "Job and Ecclesiastes," 184.

160. Bonhoeffer's use of Ecclesiastes is an example of the appropriation of the Lutheran reading in the twentieth century by an influential theologian. See Paulson, "Use of Qoheleth in Bonhoeffer's *Ethics*"; Limburg, *Encountering Ecclesiastes*, 47–52.

161. Origen, *Song of Songs*, 41.

162. Origen understood "inspective science" as a kind of perception of the mind that transcends the senses and grasps things divine. For Origen, this clearly surpasses natural science,

tradition of Solomonic authorship is affirmed by Jerome, whose interpretation dominated the patristic and medieval periods.

Luther is significant in his anticipation of the modern rejection of Solomonic authorship. In contrast to his commentary, in which he suggests that Ecclesiastes is Solomonic although assembled by his disciples,[163] in his *Table Talk* it is recorded:

> About Solomon's book the Preacher, called Ecclesiastes (which the Doctor [i.e., Luther] has read and seen through the press), he says, "This book should be more complete, it is too fragmentary, it has neither boots nor spurs, it only rides on stocking feet,[164] the way I did when I was still in the monastery." "I do not believe," he [Luther] said, "that Solomon was condemned, but this was written in order to frighten kings, princes, and rulers. Thus he did not himself write the book, but it was composed at the time of the Maccabees, by Sirach. However, it is a very good book, and useful, because it contains much excellent teaching about how a household should be run. Furthermore, it is like a Talmud, drawn together out of many books, perhaps from the library of King Ptolemy Euergetes in Egypt."[165]

Although it was only at the end of the nineteenth century that the historical-critical method was resolutely applied to Ecclesiastes, modern biblical criticism has much earlier roots, and these roots gradually become manifest in readings of Ecclesiastes. Hugo Grotius (1644) argues that we have in Ecclesiastes a collection of different opinions concerning happiness that the author mixes with his own arguments before giving his final opinion. Grotius was the first since Luther to argue against Solomonic authorship: "I believe that the book is not the production of Solomon, but was written in the name of this king, as being led by repentance to do it. For it contains many words which cannot be found except in Ezra, Daniel, and the Chaldee paraphrasts."[166] Grotius's view is significant for its focus on the language of Ecclesiastes as that of late Hebrew; this has become the major argument from contemporary scholars for a late date for Ecclesiastes.

---

which merely comprehends the things of this world: "The study called inspective is that by which we go beyond things seen and contemplate something of things divine and heavenly, beholding them with the mind alone, for they are beyond the range of bodily sight." See ibid., 21–44.

163. Luther, *An Exposition of Salomons Booke*, 9, where Luther affirms Solomonic authorship of Ecclesiastes.

164. According to the philological notes on this passage, *Tischreden*, in *Luthers Werke*, 1:630, "riding on stocking feet," i.e., without spurs, means being without power.

165. Ibid., 1:207, lines 12–22. Ginsburg (*Coheleth*, 113) is correct in his assessment of Luther's position, contra Christianson (*Ecclesiastes*, 95), who thinks Luther did not deny Solomonic authorship.

166. Ginsburg, *Coheleth*, 146. The reference is to H. Grotius, *Annotationes in Vetus Testamentum*, 1:434–35.

After Grotius the view that Solomon was not the author gradually gained ground. In 1751 J. D. Michaelis argued that Ecclesiastes was written by a postexilic prophet who wrote the book in Solomon's name so as to be able to philosophize more tellingly about the vanity of happiness. Similarly Bishop Lowth (1753) maintained that Solomon is "personated" in Ecclesiastes and that the language of the book is "low."[167] J. C. Döderlein (1784), J. Jahn (1793), J. E. C. Schmidt (1794), and H. Ewald (1826, 1837) also rejected Solomonic authorship of Ecclesiastes. Boehl (1860) and Vegni (1871), however, tried to show that linguistic arguments do not undermine Solomonic authorship.[168] Boehl attempted to show that the Aramaisms entered into Hebrew in the Solomonic age as did the two Persian words, *pitgām* (8:11) and *pardēsîm* (2:5). Vegni used poetic and historical reasons to account for Ecclesiastes' language.

Hengstenberg (1845) was the first to deny Solomonic authorship of Ecclesiastes in an orthodox English encyclopedia.[169] In his commentary Hengstenberg argues that the aim of Ecclesiastes is to encourage the fear of God in the difficult circumstances of its hearers, and he is adamant that the historical context is not that of Solomon.[170] Hengstenberg examines the issues Qohelet struggles with and concludes, "The picture thus drawn corresponds to no period but that when the Persians held dominion over the people of God,"[171] the period of Ezra and Nehemiah and about which Malachi prophesied. In the tradition inaugurated by Grotius, Hengstenberg argues that the language and style of Ecclesiastes is late. For example, he says of the phrase "a striving after the wind" in 1:14, "The usage of speech in Chaldee from which they are evidently borrowed, decides their meaning."[172] In addition to the historical context implied by Ecclesiastes, Hengstenberg argues that 1:1 does not introduce Solomon as a historical figure but as an ideal person—the ideal of wisdom; that the language and style of Ecclesiastes is of the late Hebrew of the postexilic period; and finally that the position it occupies in the canon—placed after Lamentations[173]—separates it from the literature of the Solomonic era. The reign of Xerxes was one of corruption and decay, and this, combined with the similarities between Ecclesiastes and Malachi (cf. Mal. 2:7 with Eccles. 5:5 and their agreement about the inner condition of the people), allow us to narrow down the period in which Ecclesiastes was produced, in the time of Ezra and Nehemiah.

---

167. Ginsburg, *Coheleth*, 178.
168. Boehl, *De aramaismis libri Koheleth*; Vegni, *L'Ecclesiaste secondo il testo ebraico*.
169. In an 1845 article in Kitto's *Cyclopaedia*; see Hengstenberg, "Ecclesiastes," 594–95.
170. Idem, *Commentary on Ecclesiastes*, 1–16.
171. Ibid., 6.
172. Ibid., 63.
173. It is not uncommon in the Jewish tradition for Ecclesiastes to follow Lamentations. See Beckwith, *Old Testament Canon*, 452–68.

Franz Delitzsch's 1875 commentary was influential in sweeping away attempts to continue to argue for Solomonic authorship of Ecclesiastes. He famously asserted, "If the book of Ecclesiastes were of old Solomonic origin, then there is no history of the Hebrew language."[174] Delitzsch developed a full list of the *hapax legomena* as well as idioms and forms in Ecclesiastes and asserted that these occurred mainly in mishnaic language. "Delitzsch's analysis shaped all the following studies about Qohelet's language. W. Nowack, C. Siegfried, G. Wildeboer, V. Zapletal, G. A. Barton closely quoted many of Delitzsch's linguistic arguments."[175] At the end of the nineteenth century Plumptre has an extensive discussion of Solomonic authorship in his commentary but concludes that the evidence is against it.[176] He takes "Qohelet" to mean "debater," and suggests that Qohelet was a debater in the Museum at Alexandria. He dates the book between 240 and 181 BC. Historical-critical commentary on Ecclesiastes got going at the end of the nineteenth century and the start of the twentieth century, and, following Delitzsch, it is unanimous in its rejection of Solomonic authorship. In the course of the twentieth century, scholars became divided as to whether Ecclesiastes affirmed joy or was deeply pessimistic, but on the denial of Solomonic authorship they agreed. Even conservative readers who were critical of historical criticism argued against Solomonic authorship.[177] Indeed, very few scholars nowadays defend Solomonic authorship, and most regard Ecclesiastes as written by an unknown Jew around the late third century BC. The evidence against Solomonic authorship is internal and external.

Internal Evidence

The description of Qohelet as "the son of David, king in Jerusalem" in 1:1 can only be a reference to Solomon. However, a number of aspects of the content of Ecclesiastes suggest that neither the author nor Qohelet is Solomon:

1. There is the use of the nickname "Qohelet" to describe the main character of Ecclesiastes. Unlike Proverbs (cf. 1:1), Solomon is not mentioned by name, and it is hard to see what is gained by not mentioning Solomon if his authorship is intended to be understood.

---

174. Delitzsch, *Ecclesiastes*, 190.

175. Bianchi, "Language of Qohelet," 212. Bianchi refers to authors who published their works on Ecclesiastes at the end of the nineteenth century and the beginning of the twentieth. The continuing influence of Delitzsch is witnessed, inter alia, in Seow, *Ecclesiastes*, 16–17.

176. Plumptre, *Ecclesiastes*, 19–34.

177. Examples are Hengstenberg, *Commentary on Ecclesiastes*, 7; Stuart, *Commentary on Ecclesiastes*, 67–79; C. H. Wright, *Book of Koheleth*, 79–106; Young, *Introduction to the Old Testament*, 347–49; Kidner, *Time to Mourn*, 21–22. An exception is Archer, "Linguistic Evidence."

2. Even if Qohelet is Solomon, it is important to note that this still does not solve the problem of authorship, because Qohelet's speeches are cast in a third-person framework (1:1, 2; 7:27; 12:8–14) and thus are introduced by a narrator, and we simply do not know who the narrator is.

3. Some verses in Ecclesiastes make it very difficult to see how Qohelet could be Solomon. In 1:12 Qohelet says that he "*was* king over Israel in Jerusalem." Implicit in this claim is that he is no longer king over Israel and looks back on such a time. However, the historical books of the OT know of no such period in Solomon's life. In 1:16 Qohelet comments, "I have demonstrated greatness and added to wisdom more than all who were over Jerusalem before me." This sounds like he is comparing himself to several kings who preceded him, but if he were Solomon, there would be only David who had been king *in Jerusalem*. Such verses count against Qohelet being Solomon.

4. As many have noted, the Solomonic fiction disappears after the first three chapters as Qohelet's journey develops. The Solomonic fiction fits with the first three chapters since in them Qohelet explores wisdom, wealth, women, and building projects as possible sources of meaning, and these all resonate well with what we know of Solomon. He was rich and wise, married many women, and engaged in many building projects, including that of the temple (see 1 Kings 4:29–34; 10:14–29; 11:3). However, after chap. 3 the Solomonic fiction fades, and in line with this is Qohelet's observation of oppression and his critique of the abuse of power (see 4:1–3; 5:8–9; 10:5–7, 16–20), whereas if he were Solomon, he would be in the perfect position to establish justice and rule appropriately.

The internal evidence thus makes it impossible to affirm Solomon as the author. Decisive in this respect is the third-person narrative frame that introduces Qohelet and concludes his speeches in 12:8–14. Even if Qohelet is Solomon, Solomon would not be the author. However, the internal evidence indicates that the clear, imaginative association of Qohelet with Solomon—only Solomon could be the son of David, king in Jerusalem—is a Solomonic fiction. Solomon was wealthy, wise, and great, and the reader is intended to think of Qohelet as such a person as he embarks on his journey of exploration, as someone who has all the resources necessary for an exploration of meaning "under the sun." By "fiction" we do not mean untrue. Ecclesiastes is literary artistry of a high order; in 12:9–10 the narrator tells us, "Besides being wise, Qohelet taught knowledge to the people, and he pondered and sought out and arranged many proverbs. Qohelet sought to find delightful words and he wrote truth plainly." The narrator here describes Qohelet as someone who carefully crafted his speeches, and the narrator's (1:1) and Qohelet's description of himself as "Qohelet . . . king over Israel in Jerusalem" (1:12), is a mark of this literary artistry. The narrator and Qohelet intentionally evoke in the reader's mind a figure like Solomon, and this lends considerable weight to the journey on which Qohelet embarks.[178]

If Qohelet is not Solomon, then who is he? The narrator describes him as a wise man who instructed the people and as an author (12:8–9). This would seem to argue in favor of Qohelet being a historical personage, but it is also possible that he is a literary construct. Fox and N. Lohfink suggest this as a possibility, and Fox draws an analogy with the Brer Rabbit stories, in which there is a comparable relationship between the main character Uncle Remus, who speaks, and the frame-narrator.[179] It is hard to be certain on this issue and there is nothing at stake theologically either way. The description of Qohelet by the narrator in 12:8–14 seems to favor him being a historical person whose teaching is presented by a narrator.[180]

External Evidence

As we will see under "Genre and Literary Style" below, there have been many attempts to establish the genre of Ecclesiastes by comparing it with other ancient Near Eastern texts. Such comparisons are inconclusive, however, and thus do not help in discerning the date of Ecclesiastes. It was Grotius who observed the unusual language and style of Ecclesiastes, and nowadays this is the main argument for a late, generally third-century BC, dating.

Everyone accepts that the Hebrew of Ecclesiastes is unusual compared to the rest of the Hebrew Bible. Words, grammatical peculiarities, and syntactical issues are puzzling. In the light of these characteristics scholars have advanced theories of Aramaic, Phoenician, Persian, and Greek influence, all of which are used to assert a late date.

One scholar arguing for Aramaic influence is Whitley. He examines the language of Ecclesiastes closely and comes to the following conclusions:

1. Ecclesiastes is familiar with the language and literature of the OT. Whitley gives numerous examples of this,[181] including the following: Eccles. 5:15, "As he came from his mother's womb, naked, so he will return to go," is based on Job 1:21; Eccles. 8:4, "and who will say to him, 'What are you doing?'" is reminiscent of Job 9:12; in Eccles. 5:1, "Approach to listen," "approach" is pointed as the infinitive absolute whereas we

---

178. Thus, Baldwin ("Is There Pseudonymity in the Old Testament?" 9) notes that "Qoheleth is no more pretending to be Solomon than Shakespeare is pretending to be Hamlet, but he is inviting his readers to see life through the eyes of that superbly endowed king."

179. Fox, "Frame-Narrative and Composition," 94–96; N. Lohfink, *Qoheleth*, 9–10.

180. So N. Lohfink, *Qoheleth*, 10.

181. Whitley, *Koheleth*, 119–21.

would expect the infinitive construct, although parallels for this usage
are found in Job 25:2[182] and Jer. 10:5.
2. Ecclesiastes also, however, contains many Aramaisms. Examples are
taqqîp (to contend with) in 6:10; *'al-dibrat še* (so that) in 7:14; *pēšer*
(interpretation) in 8:1; *'ăbādêhem* (their deeds) in 9:1; *gûmmāṣ* (pit) in
10:8; and *šiplût* (inactivity) in 10:18. Qohelet's tendency to use occasional
Aramaisms is paralleled in the Masada Scroll of Ben Sira and in the
marginal readings of the B text.[183] Furthermore, some words and usages
occur elsewhere only in Ben Sira, apart from in the Mishnah. For example,
šilṭôn (supreme) in 8:4 and 8 appears elsewhere only in Ben Sira.[184] In
Whitley's view, Ben Sira is earlier than Ecclesiastes, and Ecclesiastes is
dependent on it. He argues that we cannot find references to historical
figures in Ecclesiastes that would help us date it more precisely, but its
unique use of *Elohim* rather than *Yahweh* is helpful.[185] Whitley thinks
that Greek notions of God as remote and distant underlie Qohelet's
doctrine of God and that the more general *Elohim* is therefore more
attractive to Qohelet than is the personal *Yahweh*. Ecclesiastes seems to
be critically aware of the book of Daniel and its belief in resurrection (cf.
Dan. 12:2) and seems to lean on the Aramaic of Daniel; thus Ecclesiastes
must be dated later than Daniel, that is, later than 167–164 BC.

Whitley also argues that another characteristic of Ecclesiastes is a number
of phrases and words found only in the Mishnah and Talmud. He notes that
the mishnaic period probably extended from the start of the second century
BC to the close of the third century AD. The talmudic period began after this,
and the Talmud was probably in writing by AD 500. Examples of these words
and phrases are *bêt-'ôlām* (eternal home) in 12:5, which is found only here in
Biblical Hebrew but also occurs in the Mishnah; *ba'ălê 'ăsuppôt* (collected
sayings) is found only in 12:11 in the Hebrew Bible and occurs nowhere else
other than in the Talmud. Whitley notes as well that words are used with the
same secondary meaning in Ecclesiastes as in the Mishnah and Talmud; there
is a similarity of syntactical usage between Ecclesiastes and the Mishnah,
and Ecclesiastes corresponds with the Mishnah in its omission and use of the
definite article. However, Ecclesiastes contains too many elements of Biblical
Hebrew to have been written in a predominantly mishnaic era. Fragments of

182. Since the date of Job is disputed, the influence could be the other way around. Scholars
have tried to date the book of Job on the basis of theology, language, biblical and extrabiblical
literary dependence, and historical issues, but none of the evidence is conclusive. Nevertheless,
contemporary scholarship tends toward a date within the late biblical period (between the sixth
and fourth centuries BC). See Hoffman, *Blemished Perfection*, 19; Habel, *Job*, 40–42.
183. The B text is the Cairo Geniza Hebrew fragments of Ben Sira.
184. On Ecclesiastes and Ben Sira, see Whitley, *Koheleth*, 122–31.
185. Ibid., 135–36.

a manuscript of Ecclesiastes have been found at Qumran that the sectarians apparently took with them when they fled from there. Whitley suggests the time of Simon's decree (140 BC) as this time, and thus places the origin of Ecclesiastes between 152 and 145 BC.[186]

Some have regarded the influence of Aramaic on Ecclesiastes as so strong that they have proposed an Aramaic original of which Ecclesiastes is a translation. Zimmermann proposed this view and was supported by Torrey and Ginsberg, both experts in Semitic linguistics.[187] This was, however, robustly critiqued by Gordis, who scrutinized the passages Zimmermann used to argue his case and concluded that Ecclesiastes' Hebrew was too difficult to be a translation, noting that translations tend to smooth out difficulties and not exacerbate them. Gordis acknowledged Aramaic influence but argued that Ecclesiastes' Hebrew was closer to that of the Mishnah than to Aramaic. Consequently no recent commentary supports Zimmermann's view.[188]

A view as equally radical as Zimmermann's was put forward by Dahood in 1952, when he argued for strong Phoenician influence on Ecclesiastes, proposing that the author was a Jew who lived in a Phoenician city.[189] However, few supported Dahood's position, particularly because his evidence can be accounted for by a Palestinian origin without Phoenician influence.[190] The most that can be said is that some idioms in Ecclesiastes may be the result of Phoenician influence.[191]

It has become common to take the two Persian words found in Ecclesiastes, *pitgām* (8:11) and *pardēsîm* (2:5), as further evidence of a late date. However, Fredericks notes it is possible that Persian influenced Hebrew early on,

186. Ibid., 147–48.

187. Zimmermann, "Aramaic Provenance of Qohelet"; idem, "Question of Hebrew in Qohelet"; idem, *Inner World of Qoheleth*; idem, *Biblical Books Translated from the Aramaic*; Torrey, "Question of the Original Language"; Ginsberg, *Studies in Koheleth*, 17.

188. However, Fox (*Qohelet*, 155) expresses sympathy for the view that the Hebrew text of Ecclesiastes is a translation from Aramaic. In his 2004 commentary (*Ecclesiastes*, xxxiv), Fox notes that "the theory of an Aramaic original is plausible, given the discovery of certain books in Hebrew and Aramaic at Qumran (particularly Tobit), but the arguments Ginsberg brings are not adequate. This theory has been criticized (but not disproved) by Gordis . . . Whitley . . . and Schoors."

189. Dahood, "Language of Qoheleth"; idem, "Canaanite-Phoenician Influence"; idem, "Phoenician Background."

190. See Gordis, "Qoheleth and Qumran"; Whitley, *Koheleth*, 117–18; Schoors, "Use of Vowel Letters"; Fredericks, *Qoheleth's Language*, 18–24. Schoors (*Preacher*, 1:223) concludes, "Throughout this study I have been confronted with Dahood's 'Phoenician' theory. Being a former student of Dahood, who was an outstanding and inspiring teacher, I started my research with a favourable prejudice towards his approach. Nevertheless, out of some 30 linguistic phenomena which Dahood has involved in favour of his theory, barely one could more or less stand the test."

191. Seow, *Ecclesiastes*, 16.

without being mediated through Aramaic.[192] Fredericks compares Ecclesiastes' Persianisms with those in other books, noting how comparably sparse they are and that this sparseness is "especially relevant since at least a dozen of these Persianisms found in post-exilic books are related to governmental terminology, vocabulary that could well have been used in Qoh[elet] with its many political contexts."[193] Of the supposed Greek influence on Ecclesiastes' vocabulary, Fredericks maintains that such instances have adequate precedent in Biblical Hebrew or have natural Hebrew meanings.[194]

Controversy about the origins of Ecclesiastes continues. Fredericks concludes from his analysis of Ecclesiastes' language that the book should not be dated later than the exilic period and there is no strong linguistic evidence against a preexilic date.[195] By contrast, N. Lohfink, for example, notes that Ecclesiastes is indeed written in the traditional language of Hebrew, but "Greek syntax and stereotypes of speech in Greek mark the Hebrew just as today in central Europe elements of English are heard in the technical jargon of many intellectuals."[196] According to Seow, however, there is no trace of linguistic Graecisms in Ecclesiastes.[197] Around the same time that Fredericks published his work on the language of Ecclesiastes, two other major works appeared: Isaksson, *Studies in the Language of Qoheleth* (1987), and Schoors, *The Preacher Sought to Find Pleasing Words: A Study of the Language of Qoheleth* (1992). Schoors interacts seriously with Fredericks but concludes, "The language of Qoh[elet] is definitely late in the development of [Biblical Hebrew] and belongs to what scholars recently have called Late Biblical Hebrew."[198]

In his rigorous commentary on Ecclesiastes Seow reviews the debate and focuses on the following issues:[199]

1. The two Persian loanwords *are* significant for dating, and contra Fredericks, Seow notes that there is no substantial evidence for Persianisms prior to the Achaemenid period; all Persianisms in the Bible occur in postexilic literature; there are no Persianisms in Haggai, Zechariah, and Malachi, the literature associated with the first returnees from exile;[200] and Persian names are found only in Chronicles, Ezra, Nehemiah, Esther,

---

192. *Qoheleth's Language*, 242–45. For a detailed review of Fredericks, see Hurvitz, review of *Qoheleth's Language*.

193. Fredericks, *Qoheleth's Language*, 244.

194. Ibid., 246–49.

195. Ibid., 262.

196. N. Lohfink, *Qoheleth*, 7. See also Bühlman, "Difficulty."

197. Seow, *Ecclesiastes*, 16.

198. Schoors, *Preacher*, 1:221.

199. Seow, *Ecclesiastes*, 11–21.

200. Seow (*Ecclesiastes*, 12) incorrectly associates Malachi with the first returnees from exile.

and Daniel. Fox likewise is adamant that "contact with Persia did not precede the sixth century B.C.E."[201]

2. As regards Aramaisms, Seow affirms Fredericks's argument that some of these occur already in preexilic literature and that others are in Jewish Aramaic, which is too late for determining the date of Ecclesiastes. However, Seow points out that several terms in Ecclesiastes "are paralleled by their Aramaic equivalents specifically in Persian period texts."[202] Particularly significant is the occurrence of *šlṭ* in Ecclesiastes, meaning "to have right or power." This meaning is typical of the fifth and fourth centuries BC, but not of the third.[203]

3. There are important differences between preexilic and Late Biblical Hebrew. Schoors finds thirty-four aspects of Ecclesiastes' Hebrew that are typical of Late Biblical Hebrew.[204] However, not all the unusual linguistic features of Ecclesiastes can be explained as symptomatic of Late Biblical Hebrew. Moreover, the assumption that these differences indicate an even later date for Ecclesiastes is false. Fredericks is correct in his observation that there are more discontinuities than continuities between the language of Ecclesiastes and that of Mishnaic Hebrew.[205]

For Seow, on the basis of linguistic evidence, Ecclesiastes should be dated to the postexilic era and no earlier than the fifth century. The two Persian loanwords are decisive in this respect. Ecclesiastes must therefore be dated in the Persian period;[206] however, "The language of the book reflects not the standard literary Hebrew of the postexilic period. . . . Rather, it is the literary deposit of a vernacular, specifically the everyday language of the Persian period, with its large number of Aramaisms and whatever jargons and dialectal elements one may find in the marketplace."[207]

On all accounts the language of Ecclesiastes confirms that it is not Solomonic. But in terms of a precise date the arguments about language are not conclusive. The debate has continued since Longman published his commentary in 1998, but his conclusion remains valid: "We do not know the history of the Hebrew language or the foreign languages that influenced it well

---

201. Fox, *Ecclesiastes*, xxxiii.

202. Seow, *Ecclesiastes*, 13.

203. However, on this point, see Rudman, "Note on the Dating," who argues that Qohelet's use of *šlṭ* in its technical sense survived throughout the Hellenistic period and into the Christian era.

204. Schoors, *Preacher*, 1:221–24.

205. Contra N. Lohfink, *Qoheleth*, 4, who asserts that the Hebrew of Ecclesiastes is akin to that of the Mishnah.

206. Fox (*Ecclesiastes*, xxxiv) argues that the evidence for Seow's assigning of Ecclesiastes to the Persian period is inadequate. Ecclesiastes might also have originated in the early Hellenistic period (332 BC to mid-second century BC).

207. Seow, *Ecclesiastes*, 20–21.

enough to use Qoheleth's language as a barometer of the book's origin. Are certain features late, or do they reflect vernacular or dialectal peculiarities in Hebrew? We can never be certain. My conclusion is that the language of the book is not a certain barometer of date."[208] The state of the current debate favors a postexilic date for Ecclesiastes, but more precision will depend on one's interpretation of Ecclesiastes as a whole and of its social setting.

We can conclude that Ecclesiastes is not written by Solomon, nor should Qohelet be literally equated with Solomon. But if not Solomon, then who did write it? It might seem a waste of time even to pursue this, but Weinberg asserts that we should not quickly dispense with this issue.[209] He notes that in the Near East of the Axial Age (the end of the second millennium and start of the first millennium BC) consciousness of authorship became a real issue and the authority of a teaching was connected with its authorship.[210] This is evident, for example, in Egyptian wisdom literature in which the author is named at the beginning and/or end of the book as well as in the self-presentations. Weinberg discerns two ways in which authorship is attested: first by direct naming and second by an indirect concealing or hiding of the author's identity in the text. Job and Ecclesiastes are examples of the latter. Weinberg argues for Elihu as the author of Job and for Zerubbabel as the author of Ecclesiastes.[211]

Weinberg contends that 1:1 and 12:9 imply that Ecclesiastes is a "distinct author text and thus make the search for the author a legitimate one."[212] The main trend in linguistic analysis nowadays, according to Weinberg, is to date Ecclesiastes in the Persian period, so this limits one's search to the sixth to fourth centuries BC and within the Achaemenid empire, particularly Judea. The "author" of Ecclesiastes presents himself as Davidic, and in the history of Israel in the sixth century BC an outstanding Davidide was Zerubbabel. He was a founder and leader of the postexilic community and an organizer of the restoration of the temple. In the biblical texts of this time the temple is described as the "house of God," a description we also find in Ecclesiastes (4:17). Zerubbabel does not appear in the story of the consecration of the temple, an absence that according to Weinberg is best accounted for in terms of the Achaemenid tendency to remove high-ranking officials lest they become too powerful.[213] Such a fate resonates with Qohelet as one who looks back to a time when he was influential. In Jewish tradition, Zerubbabel was also a wise man and a skillful teller of parables. This connects with 12:10, in which Qohelet is described as skillful with words. A distinctive of Ecclesiastes is its

208. Longman, *Ecclesiastes*, 15.
209. Weinberg, "Authorship and Author," 157–69.
210. Cf. Baldwin, "Is There Pseudonymity in the Old Testament?"
211. Ibid., 160–66, 166–69. The same idea was launched independently by van der Waal in his series *Search the Scriptures*, 4:86–87.
212. Weinberg, "Authorship and Author," 166.
213. This is debatable. Zerubbabel could have died of old age.

abundance of economic and political vocabulary—such terms would have been well known to Zerubbabel, engaged as he was in the economic and political matters of his time. Zerubbabel's being born and brought up in Babylon could explain the presence of Persian words and Aramaisms.

Weinberg's is an intriguing revisitation of the authorship of Ecclesiastes. In my opinion the Greek influence on Ecclesiastes weighs against the view that Zerubbabel is the author, unless Greek influence was already being felt in Judah at this time, which is unlikely. We simply cannot be sure who wrote the book. In our interpretation of it the main concern must be to ascertain what the author has actually written, whoever he was.

Social Setting

The shifts in Ecclesiastes from third and first person to second-person exhortation indicate that the text is designed for instruction, as indeed 12:9–11 says of Qohelet's teaching. "My son" (12:12; cf. 11:9) implies a young male readership within Israel, although it is unclear whether this is within the family, school, or court.[214] Hā'ām ("the people," 12:9) alerts us that Qohelet's teaching as a whole was not confined to young males but was relevant to the whole people of God.[215] The implication is that Ecclesiastes is read within the community of God's people. This is confirmed by the orthodox ending.

However, one assumes that the readership would identify with the questions that Qohelet raises, the individualism that he embodies, and the tension that these create with his Israelite perspective on life. Thus it is more likely that Ecclesiastes is aimed at a particular group within Israel, namely, more learned members and perhaps advanced students, who were familiar with the sort of struggle Qohelet articulates. As Crenshaw notes,

> The books of Job and Ecclesiastes, moreover, seem ill-suited as parental instruction for young boys; like Sirach and Wisdom of Solomon, they raised theoretical questions more appropriate for a learned audience. Did such texts offer guidance to advanced students, or did they represent serious intellectual activity of ordinary adults who sought answers to existential questions? The striking use of *hakamim* in Ecclesiastes as a technical term and ben Sira's high regard for sages when compared with other professionals imply that something more than parental advice has found expression.[216]

Ecclesiastes presupposes an advanced level of cognition and a struggle with an alternative worldview(s) that is different from traditional wisdom as found

214. Whybray, *Proverbs*, 7–12.
215. See commentary on 12:9.
216. Crenshaw, "Unresolved Issues in Wisdom Literature," 218.

in Proverbs. As Crenshaw notes, Ecclesiastes assists in forming character and charting a worldview by making clear what things to avoid and what things to nurture.[217] As is so often the case in the history of the church, faith is sharpened and a worldview configured in opposition to outside challenges. But can we gain a clearer sense of the source of the individualism and autonomy with which Qohelet wrestles?

Ecclesiastes is the most philosophical book of the OT, and if one dates it in the third century BC, then its individualism and autonomy are best accounted for by the Greek influence to which Jews were being exposed at this time. However, it is difficult to be precise about such Greek influence.[218]

Fox suggests that Qohelet's affinities with Epicureanism are particularly significant, with its view that sensory experience is the ultimate source and arbiter of knowledge.[219] It is true that Qohelet's concern with pain and vexation in 1:18 and 2:23 and his exploration of pleasure focus on a problem that was a major concern to Epicurus. However, the positive enjoyment of life that Qohelet commends is quite different from the hedonism of Epicurus: "The good life for the Epicurean involves disciplining of the appetites, curtailment of desires and needs to the absolute minimum necessary for healthy living, detachment from most of the goals and values that are most highly regarded, and withdrawal from active participation in the life of the community, in the company of a few select friends—in a word, plain living and high thinking."[220] Epicurus valued spiritual over bodily satisfactions because these are more likely to bring the soul to rest, which is his ideal.[221] This is quite different from Qohelet's affirmation of eating and drinking and enjoying the wife of one's youth. Furthermore, we find nothing of Epicurus's atomism or his atheism in Ecclesiastes. Moreover, his epistemology is akin to but also different from that of Qohelet. For Epicurus the only criterion of the truth of concepts is their repeated confirmation by perception.[222] Observation is a major element in Qohelet's epistemology but so too are experience and reason.

Affinities with Stoic philosophy have also been noted by scholars. Fox notes the following affinities: determinism, strong restrictions on free will, the repetition of history in cycles, and the doctrine of the four elements in fire, air, water,

---

217. Ibid., 218–19.

218. I deal with the main Greek comparisons below, but the list is vast. For example, Müller ("Plausibilitätsverlust") finds parallels to Qohelet's skepticism in some tendencies of the pre-Socratics. Von Loewenclau ("Kohelet und Sokrates") discerns similarities between Qohelet and Socrates.

219. Fox, *Qohelet*, 16.

220. Strodach, *Philosophy of Epicurus*, 77.

221. Windelband, *History of Ancient Philosophy*, 324.

222. Ibid., 328. On Epicurus's epistemology, see also Everson, ed., *Epistemology*, chaps. 7 and 8. On Epicurean physics, see D. Sedley, "Hellenistic Physics and Metaphysics," in *The Cambridge History of Hellenistic Philosophy*, ed. K. Algra et al. (Cambridge: Cambridge University Press, 1999), 362–82.

and earth.[223] Gammie too notes that there are similarities between Qohelet and the Stoics: 1:6 is similar to Stoic assertions of the circular motion of air; 1:4, in which the author affirms that generations come and go but the earth stands forever, is akin to the Stoic view that "all things both fall back to the earth and arise from the earth"; Stoic determinism is similar to Qohelet's teaching in 3:11 and 7:13;[224] Qohelet's teaching that there is nothing new under the sun is echoed in Stoic teaching; Qohelet employs the Stoic diatribe, including rhetorical questions; as with Stoic ethics Qohelet sharply distinguishes between the wise and the foolish, the good and the bad; for Stoics and Qohelet wisdom involves knowing what is fitting in a situation or "timely behavior."[225]

However, Gammie also rightly notes important differences between Qohelet and Stoicism. For example, on the circular motion of air, Gammie notes that there is a sophistication in the Stoics not present in Ecclesiastes.[226] Regarding death, a major theme in Ecclesiastes, Gammie concludes that Qohelet ended up with a very different view from the Stoics—he agrees with them only in seeing death as part of a larger pattern. Moreover, Gammie argues that with regard to death Qohelet is deliberately *anti-Stoical*. He concludes that

> the Stoics, along with other Hellenistic philosophies, had an impact on the ancient Israelite sage, not only in specific teachings of divine causation, the cyclical nature of events, the relative value of education/wisdom, etc., but also in form of argumentation and, because of its advanced philosophy of language, possibly also in making Qoheleth more sensitive to the range of connotations in his use of terms such as *hebel*. In Qoheleth's reflections on death the influence of Stoicism is less traceable, yet even here his stance appears to be deliberately anti-Stoic as it also does with respect to the sage, sin, enduring fame, and the possibility of firmly grasping knowledge or impressions.[227]

Particularly significant is Gammie's last point; epistemologically Qohelet is very different from the Stoics. Although like the Stoics Qohelet relies heavily on observation and perception, for the Stoics it was precisely through perception that genuine knowledge could be obtained.[228] For Qohelet his autonomous epistemology leads him again and again to finding life ungraspable.

223. Fox, *Ecclesiastes*, xii. On Stoic physics and metaphysics, see Sedley, "Hellenistic Physics and Metaphysics," 382–411.

224. See commentary for my view of these verses. For the debate about the precise nature of Stoic determinism, see in particular S. Bobzien, *Determinism and Freedom in Stoic Philosophy* (Clarendon: Oxford, 1998). A helpful introduction is D. Frede, "Stoic Determinism," in *The Cambridge Companion to the Stoics*, ed. B. Inwood (Cambridge: Cambridge University Press, 2003), 179–205.

225. Gammie, "Stoicism and Anti-Stoicism in Qoheleth."

226. See ibid., 174–77, for details.

227. Ibid., 185.

228. See Windelband, *History of Ancient Philosophy*, 307–19. On Stoic epistemology, see J. Allen, "Probabilism and Stoic Epistemology," *Classical Quarterly*, n.s., 44.1 (1994): 85–113; R. J.

With his insistence that Ecclesiastes be dated in the Persian period, Seow pays little attention to possible Greek influence on the book. He argues that Ecclesiastes fits well with the economic and social realities of the second half of the fifth and the first half of the fourth centuries BC.[229] The Achaemenid government instituted a monetary economy that illuminates many sayings in Ecclesiastes, such as 5:10–12. Qohelet draws on traditional wisdom but addresses an audience facing a different economic world, using the economic vernacular of his day to make his points. An example is Qohelet's repeated use of *yitrôn* (benefit), which is found on an accounting document from the late fifth century BC, in which it means profit or net gain. Seow asserts that the Persian system of royal grants illuminates texts like 5:18–20 in which Qohelet presents life's opportunities in the language of royal grants. Seow also argues that the period was one of economic opportunities and arbitrariness, a time to make much wealth but also one vulnerable to oppression, and that this context fits well with Qohelet's observations and concerns.

It is notoriously difficult to pin down the specific influences affecting Qohelet. Seow is right in noting the strong economic elements affecting Qohelet,[230] but need this reflect only the Persian period? C. Harrison, for example, discerns the impact of Ptolemaic economic policy in the background rather than Persian influence.[231] And the Persian background may explain the monetary concerns and language, but how does one account for Qohelet's autonomous epistemology? No source in Persian philosophy would account for Qohelet's epistemology. Seow thinks that Qohelet's epistemology is the same as that of the wise in Proverbs, so this is not a problem for him. As Fox has shown, however, epistemology is central to Ecclesiastes; his quest is about how one can *know* whether work in its broadest sense is meaningful. Qohelet's epistemology is very different from that of Proverbs and traditional wisdom, and

---

Hankinson, "Stoic Epistemology," in *The Cambridge Companion to the Stoics*, ed. B. Inwood (Cambridge: Cambridge University Press, 2003), 59–178; and Rist, *Stoic Philosophy*, chap. 8. Rist (ibid., 149) concludes: "If we are right in thinking that Chrysippus at least was aware that our statements, whether true or false, are interpretations of reality, does that mean he despaired of reaching reality itself? This does not seem to be the case, because it is clear that he would allow presentations as well as propositions to be true or false."

229. Seow, *Ecclesiastes*, 21–36.

230. Kugel ("Qohelet and Money," 46), however, argues that commercial terms are largely absent from Ecclesiastes. Nevertheless, he sees Qohelet as belonging to "a world, . . . a class, of financial high-rollers." Kugel locates Ecclesiastes somewhere in the fifth century BC.

231. C. Harrison, "Qoheleth in Social-Historical Perspective." Harrison ("Qoheleth among the Sociologists," 164) notes that Judah's position under the Ptolemies was different from that under the Persians: "The Ptolemies required much more (in terms of direct tribute and taxes) from their Judean subjects than did any Achaemenid dynasty. More importantly, while the Persians were content largely to collect their conscription from Judea and leave undisturbed the basic economic processes and structures of antiquity, the Ptolemies instituted an affirmative policy aimed toward thoroughly incorporating Judea into the complicated international economic infrastructure of their empire."

thus it is vital to inquire of its source. Although Fox's description of Qohelet's epistemology as empirical is too restrictive,[232] I agree entirely with his comments that "Qoheleth's epistemology is . . . foreign to the ancient Near East, but it is paralleled in his Hellenistic environment. . . . He does . . . incorporate the fundamental tenet of Greek philosophy—the autonomy of individual reason, which is to say, the belief that individuals can and should proceed with their own observations and reasoning powers on a quest for knowledge and that this may lead to discovery of truths previously unknown."[233]

In terms of Greek philosophy, Qohelet's epistemology cannot be pinned down to any particular school of Greek thought. As the sort of studies referred to above show, Qohelet seems to be aware of general (and some specific) tendencies in Greek thought but represents no one school of such thought, though he may interact with several. He is best thought of as a believing Israelite who has become aware of and attracted by tenets of Greek thought that were in the air. Such thought stressed human autonomy in knowing, and the central role of experience, observation, and reason in arriving at truth, while being suspicious of tradition. In this respect, it is probably more important to note the major shifts inaugurated by Greek philosophy rather than to try to find one school that Qohelet embraced.

Greek philosophy has its origins in the sixth century BC, and soon after that the basic frameworks of naturalism and rationalism are evident in Greek thought.[234] In terms of the role of observation and reason, Aristotle is crucial; he brought Plato down to earth. For Aristotle, however, true knowledge could indeed be arrived at inter alia through reason and observation,[235] whereas for Qohelet observation and reason and experience lead him to confusion and enigma. Thus, whereas Qohelet may have an epistemological stress on autonomy and reason and observation in common with Aristotle, his regular conclusion that "all is enigmatic" is more akin to the Sophists, who thought that one simply could not know the true nature of reality. But, once again, Qohelet does not share the Sophists' atheism or their positive acceptance of such limits of knowledge.[236]

---

232. See Crenshaw ("Qoheleth's Understanding of Intellectual Inquiry," 212–13) for a legitimate critique of describing Qohelet's epistemology as empirical. "Autonomous" is a better description, and I agree with Fox against Crenshaw that this is very different from the epistemology of Proverbs.

233. Fox, "Wisdom in Qoheleth," 122–23.

234. See Tarnas, *Passion of the Western Mind*, 3–72, for a good overview.

235. On Aristotle's epistemology, see C. C. W. Taylor, "Aristotle's Epistemology."

236. The Sophists operated in the fifth century BC. In the fourth century BC, a parallel to Qohelet's skepticism might also be sought in the skeptics of the Middle Academy, namely, the later Platonists such as Arcesilaus (about 315–241 BC). Arcesilaus argued that although one cannot be certain of the truth of Ideas, in practice one must content oneself with a certain trust according to which some Ideas may be more probable and reasonable. Once again, however, the parallel with Qohelet is not precise.

The postexilic context of Israel, with what appeared to be the demise of the great Israelite experiment, must have led Qohelet and his educated contemporaries to question the reality of the Israelite vision of life into which they were born and nurtured. Qohelet thus sets out to explore the meaning of life with the tools of his autonomous "Greek" epistemology, while being unable to refute the genuine insights of his Israelite tradition. To such Jews the analysis that Qohelet models, put in the mouth initially of the wise man par excellence, Solomon, but still running up continually against the enigma of life, would speak with exceptional power. It is the tension between these two trajectories that lies at the heart of Ecclesiastes. It would be a bomb on the playing field of those seeking answers in Greek philosophy while being unable to shake off their nostalgia for the biblical tradition.

Text

This commentary is based on the *BHS* Hebrew text of Ecclesiastes, prepared for publication by F. Horst in 1975. This is an updated version of *BHK*, in which S. R. Driver edited Ecclesiastes (1905, 1913).[237] As with *BHK*, *BHS* is based on the Tiberian MT as preserved in the Leningrad Codex, MS B 19[A], which was completed in AD 1008.

The Hebrew text is without major problems, with few textual corruptions. The difficulties encountered in translation have more to do with the unusual language and subject matter than with the text itself. As Murphy notes, "It is only a small exaggeration to say that the book of Ecclesiastes defies translation more than other books in the Hebrew Bible. . . . In fact, the text of Qoheleth has been transmitted fairly exactly. The paradox is that although we have a relatively sound text, there is little consensus about the translation . . . of several passages."[238] Other significant witnesses to the text include Qumran fragments, the Septuagint translation, the Syriac Peshitta, the Aramaic Targum, and the Latin Vulgate.

Hebrew fragments of two MSS of Ecclesiastes were found in Cave IV at Qumran. The larger one, known as 4QQoh[a], was published by James Muilenburg in 1954.[239] This MS preserves portions of 5:14–18 [13–17]; 6:1?, 3–8, 12;

---

237. See K. Elliger and W. Rudolph, "Prolegomena," in *BHS*, xi–xiii, for the changes made to *BHK*.

238. Murphy, "On Translating Ecclesiastes," 571.

239. Muilenburg, "Qoheleth Scroll." Muilenburg (ibid., 23) notes that "the writing is a beautiful specimen of Essene scribal art. The letters are large and spacious, superbly wrought both in their prevailing uniformity and in the artistic flourishes of which the scribe appears to be especially fond."

7:1–10, 19–20.[240] The smaller MS, 4QQoh[b], was published by Ulrich in 1992.[241] It contains portions of 1:10–14. Apart from orthography, the Qumran portions agree with the MT and are of little text-critical value. They are significant, however, for the dating of Ecclesiastes; 4QQoh[a] is dated to 175–150 BC,[242] while Ulrich dates 4QQoh[b] to around the mid-first century BC, although he thinks it may be as late as the first century AD.[243] The Qumran portions are the earliest extant witnesses to Ecclesiastes and provide a *terminus ad quem* for its dating.

The LXX is the most important ancient translation of Ecclesiastes and is preserved in six uncial MSS. Codex Vaticanus (LXX[B]) is regarded as the most reliable MS.[244] The LXX translation is literal and adheres rigidly to the Hebrew word order and details. The translation style is unique among the books in the OT, and it would appear therefore that the translator of Ecclesiastes was different from those of the other books.[245] Similarities with the translations of Aquila of Pontus, a second-century BC convert to Judaism, have led many to take him as the LXX translator of Ecclesiastes.[246] However, this hypothesis has been refuted,[247] so that it appears that LXX Ecclesiastes is not Aquila's work but "a version that, like Aquila, is motivated by the desire to facilitate certain kinds of exegesis promoted by the rabbis. . . . Indeed, there is some indication in LXX of significant interpretive moves (e.g., 2:15; 11:9)."[248] In the commentary, I take note, where appropriate, of the differences between the LXX and the MT. Generally, I conclude that the LXX mistranslates the MT when they differ, although it is occasionally helpful in supporting a variant that makes better sense in context. The Latin, Syriac, and Coptic bear witness to the LXX from which they are translated and do not refer to a Hebrew original.

The Syriac version is known as the Peshitta ("the simple"), and its oldest MS is from the fifth century AD, although the Peshitta Pentateuch was probably begun in the first century AD. It is likely translated from the Hebrew, although it shows dependence on the LXX at points.[249] The Targum of Ecclesiastes is a

---

240. Ulrich, "Ezra and Qoheleth Manuscripts," 142.

241. Ibid.

242. Muilenburg ("Qoheleth Scroll," 24) suggests that "a temporal locus some time in the third or late fourth century seems likely." This refutes Whitley's (*Koheleth*, 147–48) dating.

243. Ulrich, "Ezra and Qoheleth Manuscripts," 148.

244. Seow, *Ecclesiastes*, 6.

245. Ibid., 7.

246. This was first argued for by Graetz, *Kohelet*, 173–79. This argument was furthered by Barthélemy, *Les devanciers d'Aquila*, 32ff.

247. By Hyvärinen, *Übersetzung von Aquila*, 88–99; and Jarick, "Aquila's Koheleth," 131–39.

248. Seow, *Ecclesiastes*, 8.

249. Ibid., 10. On the Peshitta of Qohelet, see Kamenetzky, "P'šita zu Koheleth"; Lane, "Lilies That Fester"; Salters, "The Word for 'God' in the Peshiṭta of Koheleth"; and Weitzman, *Syriac Version of the Old Testament*.

paraphrase and thus interpretive, although at times it translates the Hebrew directly, and remains therefore a valuable witness to the original text. As Jerome translated the OT in the late fourth century AD into Latin, first on the basis of the Greek text, he became more and more aware of the need to work with the Hebrew, and his new translation became the Vulgate. (On his own account, he completed Proverbs, Ecclesiastes, and Song of Songs in three days!)[250] His translation of Ecclesiastes is made from the Hebrew, but he also made use of Origen's Hexapla[251] and other Greek translations.

Genre and Literary Style

Part of the problem with interpreting Ecclesiastes is that there is no consensus about its genre. For example, scholars disagree about how unified Ecclesiastes is. Galling represents one extreme, N. Lohfink another. Galling argues that Ecclesiastes consists of twenty-seven *Sentenzen*, disparate sections dealing with different themes that were collected together after Qohelet's death by one of his disciples.[252] One must thus allow for the relative independence of the sentences and their free ordering. Lohfink, however, acknowledges, "I consciously go against current majority opinion that the Book of Qoheleth is no more than a very loose agglomeration of single proverbs, sentences, and 'mashals.' . . . In my opinion, the Book of Qoheleth is a very organized text."[253]

At a micro level a variety of different genres can be identified in Ecclesiastes:

1. *The proverb.*[254] Examples are 1:15, 18, and the multiple proverbs in 7:1–12. Their form, generally containing parallelisms, and their pithy content identify these sayings as proverbs. A special group of proverbs in Ecclesiastes are the "better-than" sayings (e.g., 2:13; 7:1, 2, 5, 8).[255]
2. *Autobiographical sections.* Several sections in Ecclesiastes are presented as reports from Qohelet as he reflects on his journey (1:12–2:26;

---

250. Jerome, "Preface to Proverbs, Ecclesiastes, and the Song of Songs," in *The Nicene and Post-Nicene Fathers*, ed. P. Schaff and H. Wace, 2nd series (repr., Grand Rapids: Eerdmans, 1983), 6:492.

251. On the four Greek versions of Ecclesiastes in Origen's Hexapla, see Beckwith, *Old Testament Canon*, 302–4, 472–77. See also Gentry, "Hexaplaric Materials."

252. Galling, *Prediger*, chap. 3.

253. N. Lohfink, "Qoheleth 5:17–19," 628n21.

254. Murphy (*Wisdom Literature*, 4–6) identifies the proverb as one of three types of "the saying." His other two types are the experiential saying and the didactic saying. I include all these under the type "proverb."

255. Ogden, "Qoheleth's Use."

3:10–4:16; 5:13–6:12). A major characteristic of these sections is the first-person narration.

3. *Reflection arising from personal observation and experience.* This is the dominant literary form in Ecclesiastes and is found throughout the book. It includes subgenres such as the proverb. The reflection is closely related to the autobiographical nature of Qohelet's journey and thus could be included under 2 above.

4. *Poems.*[256] Most agree that 1:4–11; 3:1–8; and 11:7–12:8 are poems. It is unclear whether 1:4–11 is to be attributed to the narrator or to Qohelet; in all probability it is part of the frame introducing Qohelet's thought that starts in 1:12.

5. *Rhetorical questions.* These are common throughout Ecclesiastes (1:3; 2:2, 15, 19, 25; 3:9, 21, 22; 4:8, 11; 5:6, 11, 16 [5, 10, 15]; 6:8, 11; 7:13, 16, 18; 8:1, 4, 7; 10:14).

6. *Quotations.* Gordis drew attention to Qohelet's use of quotations.[257] A proverb may, for example, be quoted to support Qohelet's argument or as a basis for deconstruction as in 7:1a. There can be no doubt that Qohelet does use quotations in his explorations, but the attempt to determine these with any precision is inconclusive. Although Gordis's attention to this issue helped move studies of Ecclesiastes toward a consideration of it as literature, the search for quotations is redolent of the source-critical attempt to get behind the text, a quest that is inevitably speculative and minimalist in terms of any probable conclusions.[258] For example, the poem on time in 3:1–8 may be a quotation, but it could also be a poem by Qohelet. We simply cannot be sure. The interpreter needs to be able to identify the different views Qohelet articulates and how he interacts with them. Excessive concern with whether he is quoting a source is speculative and detracts from the primary exegetical task.

7. *The example story.* Qohelet recounts anecdotes to support his argument (e.g., 4:13–16 and 9:13–16).

8. *The woe oracle* (e.g., 4:10 and 10:16).

9. *The blessing* (e.g., 10:17).

256. The extent to which Ecclesiastes is poetry and prose remains a matter of debate. Cf. Murphy, *Ecclesiastes*, xxviii–xxix.

257. *Koheleth*, 95–108. See also idem, "Quotations in Wisdom Literature"; and idem, "Quotations as a Literary Usage." Gordis himself notes the difficulty of identifying quotations in Ecclesiastes: "Whether Koheleth is quoting proverbs already extant or composing them himself is difficult to determine" (*Koheleth*, 100). Whybray, "Identification and Use of Quotations," is an attempt to answer this question. It took time for Gordis's inquiry to gain ground, but in the period 1961–1980 Kroeber, Zimmerli, R. B. Scott, Hertzberg, Lauha, and N. Lohfink took note of Gordis's proposal in their commentaries and endorsed it in various sections. See Beentjes, "Recente visies." More recently, see von Loewenclau, "Kohelet und Sokrates"; and Spangenberg, "Quotations in Ecclesiastes."

258. See Whybray's ("Identification and Use of Quotations") conclusions in this respect.

10. *Commands and prohibitions.*[259] With its numerous imperatives, 5:1–7 is a good example of this subgenre.

At the macro level, however, there is considerable difference of opinion about the genre of Ecclesiastes. Proposals seek a background in the ancient Near East or in Greek literature or in a combination of both. Regarding comparison with ancient Near Eastern texts there has been considerable disagreement, as we will see below. Von Rad considered Ecclesiastes a royal testament.[260] Braun argues that it has the genre of a Hellenistic diatribe.[261] N. Lohfink suggests that the genre is a combination of diatribe and palistrophe, a book from the world of education.[262] Uehlinger thinks that Ecclesiastes reflects the philosophical symposium that took place in the early Hellenistic Judah of the third and second centuries BC.[263] Longman maintains that Ecclesiastes is a fictional royal autobiography modeled on Akkadian literature.[264] Not surprisingly, Murphy maintains that there is no satisfactory solution to the problem of the literary form of Ecclesiastes.[265]

Regarding the comparison of Ecclesiastes with a Greek diatribe, one should note the extensive discussion of just what constituted the diatribe and whether there was a fixed genre of the diatribe in ancient Greece.[266] Bultmann's 1910 dissertation was important in highlighting that diatribe was not only a genre of ethical exhortation but dialogical, with statements by one and a response by another.[267] Giese identifies the following characteristics in common with Ecclesiastes and a diatribe:

1. In diatribes it is common for the narrator to address an imaginary interlocutor, often in the form of a command. Giese finds inter alia an example of this in the switch from discourse in 4:9–16 to exhortation in 5:1–7.
2. Diatribes, like Ecclesiastes, consist of short, simple sentences.
3. Diatribes repeat a theme or words, and repetition is a major characteristic of Ecclesiastes.
4. Diatribes use illustrations to make a point and so does Qohelet.

259. See Crenshaw, "Prohibitions," 120–21, where he identifies eight or nine varieties of prohibitions in Ecclesiastes.
260. Von Rad, *Wisdom*, 226.
261. Braun, *Kohelet*, 165; cf. Krüger, *Qoheleth*, 12–14.
262. N. Lohfink, *Qoheleth*, 7–8, 13–14. For an analysis of Ecclesiastes as a diatribe, particularly as represented by the LXX, see Giese, "Genre of Ecclesiastes."
263. Uehlinger, "Qohelet," 205–6.
264. Longman, *Fictional Akkadian Autobiography*, 120–23.
265. Murphy, *Ecclesiastes*, xxxi.
266. Giese, "Genre of Ecclesiastes," 22–43.
267. Bultmann, *Der Stil der paulinischen Predigt und die kynisch-stoische Diatribe*.

5. Diatribes use analogies to make points and so does Qohelet, especially in his proverbs.
6. An aspect of diatribes is the ironic command, and Giese reads the *carpe diem* passages as ironic commands.
7. Rhetorical questions are common in diatribes and in Ecclesiastes.
8. The importance of wisdom for a king is a common motif in diatribes, and this fits with the royal emphasis in Ecclesiastes.
9. Indictment of the arrogant and a critique of the pursuit of wealth are common to diatribes and Ecclesiastes.
10. The moralists were conservative about sex, and in 7:26 Qohelet manifests such a conservatism.[268]

Giese notes that many of these characteristics are not exclusive to diatribe, and this is certainly true of points 3, 4, 5, 7, 8, and 9. Furthermore, while the comparison with a diatribe is helpful in alerting us to the dialogical nature of Ecclesiastes, Qohelet does not address an imaginary interlocutor but struggles with himself.[269] Ecclesiastes does not consist only of short simple sentences, as any translator knows, and in 1:8 Qohelet manifests anything but a conservative approach to sex.

Another genre analysis in comparison with ancient Near Eastern texts was done by Perdue.[270] He points out that scholars usually place Ecclesiastes in one of two form-critical categories: it is either a sayings collection or a first-person narrative. Compared with Proverbs, Ben Sira, and Pirqe Abot, Ecclesiastes does look like a sayings collection, according to Perdue, with a loose rhetorical structure. However, first-person narration is Ecclesiastes' most distinguishing characteristic among the Israelite and Jewish wisdom corpus. Thus to determine the genre of Ecclesiastes, Perdue explores the following ancient Near Eastern forms, which are all characterized by first-person usage.

1. *Righteous sufferer poems.* These are modeled on the style of the individual lament in which a righteous sufferer narrates his trials and calamities, including his questioning of traditional wisdom and cultus. Finally he is redeemed by his personal god. The Sumerian "Man and His God" and the Akkadian "I Will Praise the Lord of Wisdom" fit into this category.[271] For Perdue these poems differ from Qohelet in that he experiences a radical gulf between God and the world, a gulf that they do not manifest.

268. Giese, "Genre of Ecclesiastes," 51–75.
269. Berger ("Qohelet and Exigencies," 157) notes that "although the objection may be raised that a dialogue requires a response or a partner, I would suggest that Qohelet is in dialogue with himself and his heart."
270. Perdue, *Wisdom and Creation*, 194–205.
271. *ANET*, 589–91 and 596–600, respectively.

2. *The Dialogue of Pessimism.*[272] Ecclesiastes has in common with the "Dialogue" the use of the first-person voice and structures that support opposite decisions. However, Qohelet never advocates suicide. In Perdue's opinion the smell of death surrounds Ecclesiastes, and he suggests that the following three categories of Egyptian literature, which are all set in situations involving death, provide the closest form-critical parallels to Ecclesiastes.

3. *Egyptian banquet songs.* These songs were sometimes used in funerary contexts. Although in a funerary context they tended not to question the afterlife and not to emphasize the present, as did their secular counterparts, "A Song of the Harper" represents an intriguing difference.[273] Composed at a time of social and political disintegration, this song is skeptical about the afterlife and encourages the reader, "Fulfill thy needs upon earth, after the command of thy heart, until there come for thee that day of mourning." In common with Ecclesiastes, according to Perdue, this song shares the context of death, first-person narration, and skepticism about the future life, as well as celebration of present life.[274]

4. *Grave biographies.* These were placed in the mouth of the deceased; they are first-person posthumous speeches addressed to tomb visitors, and contain an autobiographical narrative, ethical maxims, and instructions to visitors.[275] In the later inscriptions, the gods act without the constraint of retributive justice; according to Perdue, this pessimistic element reveals a remarkable parallel with Ecclesiastes, as do the fictional narrator's voice, the above literary features, and the pervasive autobiographical style.

5. *Royal instructions.*[276] The longer form of Egyptian royal instruction inserts an introductory narrative between the title and admonitions. In this way the biography provides the occasion for the instruction. Within the OT, royal instructions are found in 1 Kings 12:1–12 and Prov. 31:1–9. The longer form of royal instruction parallels Ecclesiastes in terms of the royal voice of the narrator, the list of royal achievements, and the giving of instruction.

Perdue concludes that "the book of Qoheleth is best seen as the fictional testament of Israel's most famous king, who is presented as speaking to his

272. *ANET*, 600–601.

273. *ANET*, 467.

274. In this respect, see also Fischer, "Qohelet and 'Heretic' Harpers' Songs," who argues that the *carpe diem* passages in Ecclesiastes are dependent on the Egyptian Harpers' Songs of the New Kingdom.

275. See Perdue, *Wisdom and Creation*, 365, for bibliographical details.

276. *ANET*, 412–14, 421–25.

audience either in his old age, shortly before death, or perhaps from the tomb."[277] "In Qoheleth we have the fiction of Israel's greatest and wisest king, presumably the one best able to master life and to know by wisdom the meaning of existence, undertaking the quest to determine the 'good' in human living."[278] In Perdue's view Ecclesiastes is thus imaginative Wisdom literature with a narrative structure in a form that is close to that of grave biographies and royal testaments—Qohelet is perhaps presented as a dead person who undertakes to instruct from the tomb.

Longman has also contended for the fictional autobiographical nature of Ecclesiastes, but by means of a comparison with Akkadian fictional autobiography.[279] He argues persuasively that fictional autobiography is a genre of Akkadian literature. He discerns three subgroups within this genre: fictional autobiography with a blessing and/or curse ending, fictional autobiography with a didactic ending, and fictional autobiography with a prophetic ending. As regards the comparison with Ecclesiastes, Longman maintains, "What has not been examined before, however, is the close similarity that exists between Qoheleth and the Akkadian genre of autobiography, particularly fictional autobiography with a didactic ending."[280]

For Longman, 1:1–11 and 12:9–14 are the frame of Ecclesiastes provided by a second wisdom figure who is using Qohelet's sayings to instruct his son. If one removes these, Ecclesiastes may be divided into three sections: (1) a first-person introduction (1:12–18), (2) an extended first-person narrative in which Qohelet describes his search for meaning in life (2:1–6:9), and (3) first-person instruction from Qohelet (6:10–12:8). Analyzed in this way, Ecclesiastes exhibits the same threefold structure as the Akkadian Cuthaean Legend, the best preserved Akkadian didactic autobiography. There is also a similarity at the level of form. Qohelet shares the forms of royal fiction and self-discourse with the Cuthaean Legend. Longman concludes that Ecclesiastes has an obvious Akkadian background in terms of genre. "Thus the literary structure and the use of royal fiction and self-discourse in the book of Qoheleth and in the Cuthaean Legend demonstrate a generic relationship between the two."[281]

Longman is well aware that this analysis does not provide a detailed explanation of the whole structure of Ecclesiastes. Without careful analysis of the

---

277. Perdue, *Wisdom and Creation*, 202.

278. Ibid., 205.

279. Longman, *Fictional Akkadian Autobiography*, 120–23. This book is a development of idem, "Comparative Methods in Old Testament Studies." Surprisingly, Perdue (*Wisdom and Creation*) does not mention Longman, and he does not consider the genre similarities between Ecclesiastes and Akkadian fictional autobiography. Longman (*Fictional Akkadian Autobiography*, 118ff.) notes the similarity between Akkadian fictional autobiography with a didactic ending and Egyptian instruction texts but does not suggest a comparison with the Songs of the Harper or with Egyptian grave biographies.

280. Longman, *Fictional Akkadian Autobiography*, 120.

281. Ibid., 122.

relationship between 1:12–12:8 and the frame, he argues that the frame is a crucial part of the book since it provides a hermeneutical guide by instructing the reader how to understand the text. Indeed, for Longman the frame warns the reader against Qohelet's skepticism. Longman also suggests that understanding Ecclesiastes as autobiography may help to explain its contradictions: "Perhaps . . . if there is a development within the structure of Qoheleth, it is that of a temporal thought progression. In other words, the book traces Qoheleth's thoughts on subjects at different periods in his life. The so-called 'contradictions' in the book may thus be explained as being different conclusions reached at different times in his life."[282]

Longman's and Perdue's analyses of the genre of Ecclesiastes are stimulating and helpful in confirming the autobiographical and didactic wisdom nature of Ecclesiastes. Some questions about the detailed comparisons remain. As is widely acknowledged, for example, the royal fiction in Ecclesiastes is soon dropped, and this militates to some extent against its being a royal instruction or the testament of Israel's most famous king.[283] The similarity to grave biographies also depends on Perdue's pessimistic reading of Ecclesiastes, a reading that is far from firmly established. As will become apparent, this is not my reading of Ecclesiastes. Furthermore, Ecclesiastes may be closer to righteous sufferer poems than Perdue suggests, depending on how one understands the total message of the book.[284] However, Qohelet describes not so much his own suffering as his experiences, observations, and conclusions, and this brings a more philosophical, perhaps Greek, diatribe-like element into his discussion that none of the proposed parallels accounts for. Longman points out that all the Akkadian fictional autobiographies are written in prose, and he regards this as an important element of their genre.[285] Most Akkadian literature was

---

282. Ibid., 121–22.

283. See Perdue (*Wisdom and Creation*, 201–2) for an attempt to defend the royal fiction of Ecclesiastes. Longman refers to all Akkadian autobiography as royal. He acknowledges that while the royal fiction is adopted throughout the Cuthaean Legend, some think it is present in only part of Ecclesiastes. According to Longman (*Fictional Akkadian Autobiography*, 122), "This question is not important to adjudicate; it is clear that royal fiction is employed in both Qoheleth and the Cuthaean Legend." However, if the author adopts the fiction and then drops it, this deviation from the form may be significant, since the norms of a genre provide a basis for conformity and divergence. As a heading to the entire book, however, 1:1 does confirm the royal fiction. For the continuing relevance of the analysis of 1:12–2:11 as a royal fiction, see Seow, "Qohelet's Autobiography."

284. Perdue's main reason for distinguishing Ecclesiastes from righteous sufferer poems is that in the latter the sufferer is rescued by his personal god, whereas Qohelet experiences a great gulf between God and the world. In my view, the difference is more at the level of the type of problem the sufferer is experiencing than the view of God. But see Fisch (*Poetry with a Purpose*, 158–59), who distinguishes the subjective, personal "I" of the Psalms from the autobiographical "I" in Qohelet.

285. Longman, *Fictional Akkadian Autobiography*, 199.

written in poetic form,[286] and fictional autobiography takes its form from non-fictional autobiography, which used prose rather than poetry as a way to stress its authenticity. What Longman does not comment on is that Ecclesiastes is highly poetic, although admittedly scholars are still not agreed as to whether its style is that of poetry or prose, as noted above.

Isaksson's *Studies in the Language of Qoheleth* confirms the autobiographical and reflective nature of Ecclesiastes. He argues that the autobiographical feature of Ecclesiastes is one of its central characteristics. Syntactically this trait is manifested through a chain of suffix conjugation forms in the first person singular, sometimes preceded by *waw*. *Waw* + prefix conjugation forms of the verb are very rare in Ecclesiastes.

> My conclusion is that the choice of conjunctive SC [suffix conjugation] and wSC [suffix conjugation used immediately after a *waw*] forms in the autobiographical thread is due to the special kind of narrative that constitutes this thread. The narrative of the thread is of the résumé type, in which, with the words of F. Rundgren, "the events are not given according to the historical process of the (usual) narrative, but are picked out as important single events and then juxtaposed." There are many examples of this kind of résumé narration from all genres of the Old Testament, which means that this special feature of the book is not a valid proof of lateness. . . . The infrequent usage of waPC [prefix conjugation used in syntagmatic connection with *wa-*] forms is noted. . . . My conclusion is that the low frequency of this verbal usage is a matter of literary genre: the philosophical approach of the book and the absence of straightforward historical narration.[287]

Thus the comparison of the form of Ecclesiastes with that of ancient Near Eastern texts[288] focuses its autobiographical and instructional nature, and the comparison with the diatribe highlights its dialogical nature, but do Perdue and Longman successfully explain how Ecclesiastes as a whole fits together? A crucial test in this respect is explaining how the epilogue relates to the rest of the book. For Longman the form of the material within the frame of Ecclesiastes is that of a fictional autobiography. Longman had earlier argued that the frame provides an orthodox warning against the skeptical pessimism of Qohelet.[289] Qohelet is pessimistic; the *carpe diem* passages represent resignation and not hope. Qohelet is a skeptic because he has not allowed God to enter into his

---

286. Ibid., 210.
287. Isaksson, *Studies*, 190.
288. I have not explored here in detail comparisons with Greek genres. N. Lohfink (*Qoheleth*, 7–8) argues that the form of this *Lehrbuch* results from the confluence of two forms: Greek philosophical diatribe and Hebrew chiasm. For a brief evaluation of Lohfink's view of a close relationship between Ecclesiastes and Hellenistic thought, see Murphy, *Ecclesiastes*, xliii–xlv.
289. Longman, "Comparative Methods."

thinking. Longman quotes Fox's translation of 12:10–12 with approval;[290] it fits with Longman's view that the narrator distances himself from the pessimistic Qohelet. "Qoheleth's speech (1:12–12:7) is a foil, a teaching device, used by the second wise man in order to instruct his son (vs. 12) concerning the dangers of speculative, doubting wisdom in Israel."[291]

Perdue recognizes the need to analyze the literary structure of Ecclesiastes in terms of narrator and so on, but he ends up with an uneven mixture of a source-critical and narrative analysis. Nowhere is this more evident than where he mentions in one paragraph that 12:9–14 consists of three parts attached by an editor, and then goes on in the next paragraph to say, "The narrator then turns to his or her own understanding."[292] This type of diachronic analysis cannot simply be juxtaposed with a narrative, synchronic reading in this way.

A weakness of both Longman's and Perdue's comparative approaches is thus that neither explains in any detailed or satisfactory way how the epilogue relates to the rest of the book.[293] Indeed, their comparative approaches rest on a diachronic analysis of Ecclesiastes, which identifies the first-person narration as the main element. Perdue, for example, argues that first-person narration is Ecclesiastes' most distinguishing characteristic, and he then looks for parallels to this among ancient Near Eastern literature. For Longman as well, self-discourse is utterly central to the parallel with Akkadian autobiography. Thus for both Longman and Perdue comparative genre analysis is done after diachronic analysis of Ecclesiastes in which the first-person narration is identified as the main characteristic of the book. Diachronic analysis can thus be said to shape their comparative analysis.

Diachronic analysis of Ecclesiastes often works on the historical assumption that "even though in the first part of the book he [Qohelet] uses the device of pretending to be King Solomon . . . there is no doubt that throughout the book this 'I' is a real and not a fictitious 'I.'"[294] In light of this assumption, many make every effort to locate the historical Qohelet and interpret the text on this basis. Old Testament scholars have become increasingly skeptical

290. See commentary on 12:8–14.

291. R. Dillard and Longman, *Introduction to the Old Testament*, 254.

292. Perdue, *Wisdom and Creation*, 237.

293. Longman (e.g., *Ecclesiastes*, 21) has followed Fox in his view that the frame narrator distances himself from Qohelet in the epilogue. Longman's frame, however, includes 1:1–11, and even if one accepted Fox's translation of the epilogue, Longman would need to explain how the opening poem is part of the orthodox hermeneutical guide that Longman takes it to be (ibid., viii). Longman's approach fails in terms of that circular intent at totality of New Criticism. The parallel to Akkadian autobiography is not strong enough to warrant taking 1:12–12:7 as an enclosed, unified section. The *carpe diem* sayings should not be read just as representative of resignation. And as I will argue in my comments on the epilogue, Fox's interpretation is not convincing. All this points toward the limits of the comparative approach; the nature of Ecclesiastes has to be argued primarily from the text itself.

294. Whybray, *Two Jewish Theologies*, 6.

about source-critical analyses of Qohelet, but the method of finding the real Qohelet and then reading the book on this basis remains in place and shapes comparative genre analysis.

I am not suggesting that Perdue or Longman would necessarily argue that the "I" of Ecclesiastes is historical in the sense that Whybray does. Indeed, the comparison of Ecclesiastes with *fictional* autobiography confirms what literary studies of autobiography alert us to: the "I" of autobiography can be very elusive.[295] Perdue's and Longman's analyses indicate that the "I" of Ecclesiastes is fictional. But they fail to pursue the implications of the "I" being fictional, for the presentation of a fictional Qohelet in the context of a frame narrative raises in an acute way the question of the relationship between the first-person narration and the frame narrator. As Fox has argued, 7:27 in particular indicates that the frame cannot be regarded as just a frame put on a complete first-person narration. The evidence points to deliberate shaping.

An important methodological issue is at stake here. Comparative genre analysis must be based on literary analyses that, initially at least, are performed independently of studies of comparative genre.[296] That Perdue and Longman are in danger of privileging diachronic at the expense of synchronic analysis will become apparent when I examine below Fox's proposals for ancient Near Eastern texts with a similar genre to Ecclesiastes. The hermeneutical spiral operates here as well, but the effort has to be made to compare Ecclesiastes with other genres without reading comparative genres into Ecclesiastes at the outset, as part of that continual move between source and discourse that Sternberg describes so well.[297] Furthermore, we must avoid working with a static understanding of genre. Wellek and Warren refer to genre helpfully as an "institution": "One can work through, express oneself through, existing institutions, create new ones, or get on, so far as possible, without sharing in polities or rituals; one can also join, but then reshape, institutions. Theory of genres is a principle of order. . . . Any critical and evaluative—as distinct from historical—study involves, in some form, the appeal to such structures."[298] Comparative genre can be helpful in a general way, but priority has to be given to the individuality of the text in the form we receive it.

Fox, by contrast, begins with a literary analysis of Ecclesiastes as "frame-narrative" and then looks for ancient Near Eastern texts comparable to "the use of an anonymous third-person retrospective frame-narrative encompassing

295. For contemporary studies of autobiography, see Marcus, *Auto/biographical Discourses*.

296. A similar example of the importance of correct methodology is that of the comparison between Deuteronomy and ancient Near Eastern treaties. See Bartholomew, "Composition of Deuteronomy," 203–20.

297. Sternberg, *Poetics of Biblical Narrative*, 7–23. See also Bartholomew, *Reading Ecclesiastes*, 215–18.

298. Wellek and Warren, *Theory of Literature*, 226.

a first-person narrative or monologue."[299] Fox finds examples of this style in various genres, including wisdom literature, particularly in Egypt but also in Israel:[300]

1. *The Instruction for Kagemeni*. Only the final portion of this text is preserved, but the overall design is clear. In the body of the text the old vizier who is the father of Kagemeni instructs his children and records his instruction. The epilogue speaks about the vizier in retrospect and explains how his son benefited from his instruction and became vizier himself. The narrative frame that surrounds and presents the instruction of the old vizier looks back on the life of the old vizier and evaluates his work.

2. *The Prophecy of Neferti*. Although written in the reign of Amenemhet I in the Twelfth Dynasty, this text begins with a frame narrative presenting itself in the reign of Snefru in the Fourth Dynasty looking back on the life of the ancient sage Neferti, whose words are respectfully introduced. The work is fictional, presenting a prophecy *ex eventu* of the triumph of Amenemhet I.

3. *The Complaint of Ipuwer*. The introduction has been lost but, according to Fox, it must have explained the setting that is implied in the ending of the work, that is, how Ipuwer was called to address the king. The body of the work consists of Ipuwer's lament about the breakdown of the social order. His "I" occurs only occasionally. Thus the speech of Ipuwer, which forms the body of the text, is presented within a framework by an anonymous narrator who looks back on the sage, quoting and evaluating him.

4. *'Onchsheshonqy*. The Instructions of 'Onchsheshonqy consists of an anonymous frame narrator relating the story of 'Onchsheshonqy. It opens by explaining how he came to write his instruction on ostraca while in prison. The body of the book consists of a long quotation of his words. It is uncertain whether he ever existed; according to Fox, the introductory story is probably fictional and the instruction contains references to the introduction and is probably contemporaneous with it.

5. *Deuteronomy*. Fox argues that in its present state, but excluding the additions in 4:41–43; 32:48–52; 34:1–12, Deuteronomy is a first-person monologue by Moses set in a third-person framework. Thus we have a narrator telling about Moses, looking back on him, while remaining in the background. Fox acknowledges that Haran suggested the parallel be-

---

299. Fox, "Frame-Narrative and Composition," 83–92.

300. Ibid., 92–96; and idem, *Qohelet*, 312–15. The latter list is longer than the former one, which adds Duachety, Shuruppak, and Ahiqar. These additions do not add much to the overall argument, and I have omitted them from my consideration of Fox's examples.

tween Ecclesiastes and Deuteronomy to him, arguing that the "narrative form may be another sign of wisdom influence on *Deuteronomy*."[301]

6. *Tobit*. According to Fox the title and brief identification are not part of the frame narrative. Immediately after this, Tobit begins speaking in a reflective manner similar to Qohelet. The book as a whole is a third-person narrative, as, for example, 3:7ff. indicate, in which the author speaks about Tobit. The essential narrative design is the same as Ecclesiastes. Fox notes with interest that the first-person speaker in Tobit can appear immediately after the title without an introduction by the frame narrator, contrary to the expectations of modern readers, who would anticipate that the frame narrator would be more prominent at the outset. Fox finds this a helpful parallel to Ecclesiastes: "The frame-narrator's voice in *Qohelet* as in *Tobit* is scarcely heard at the beginning of the work—only 'Qohelet said' in 1:2. The author allows the first-person speaker to introduce himself in order to establish him immediately as the focal point."[302]

7. *Uncle Remus*.[303] Fox also employs an analogy from modern literature to help elucidate the function of the narrative framework. He notes the difference between Qohelet and "Uncle Remus" and explains that he is concerned only to compare the rhetorical function of the narrative framework as a literary technique. Fox does note, however, that models from far afield can help to draw our attention to phenomena we might be unaware of and help us to break out of unjustified assumptions that arise from working with a restricted body of texts.

Like Qohelet, Uncle Remus's words are surrounded by a frame narrative. The words "said Uncle Remus," interrupting a first-person sentence, are equivalent to "says Qohelet" in Eccles. 7:27. As with Ecclesiastes, the frame narrator presents himself not as the creator of the story but merely as the transmitter, "a relatively passive agent between their creator (Uncle Remus) and the reader."[304] The narrator stays well in the background, and indeed the author Harris once referred to this narrator as a "dull reporter." Fox notes that the narrator is not to be identified with the author himself: "Harris was far more than simply a collector and transmitter of Negro folklore. He utilized old slave tales but altered and polished and sharpened them until the products were far from pure folk tales. He once showed a friend sixteen introductions

---

301. Fox, "Frame-Narrative and Composition," 93n24. Weinfeld (*Deuteronomy and the Deuteronomic School*, 244ff.) discusses at length the relationship between Deuteronomic literature and Wisdom literature.

302. Fox, "Frame-Narrative and Composition," 94.

303. A series of novels by Joel Chandler Harris. Fox ("Frame-Narrative and Composition," 94) holds that "the various volumes really form a single work."

304. Ibid., 95.

he had written for a single story."[305] Why does Harris employ a frame narrator? According to Fox, this was done to cause the reader to treat Uncle Remus seriously—without the frame it would be too easy to laugh him off—and to create some distance from Uncle Remus. The frame narrator embodies an attitude of respect at a distance from Uncle Remus. The frame narrative also attests to the reality of Uncle Remus, thus calling for a suspension of disbelief in the reader since he is a fictional character. "In other words, a bizarre character, one whose voice we are not used to encountering in literature, needs a plausible, normal voice to mediate him to us and to show us how to relate to him. Qohelet too receives this type of mediation from his frame-narrator."[306]

Remarkably there is no overlap between the ancient Near Eastern texts that Fox invokes and those that Perdue and Longman call upon. This indicates the extent to which one's initial decisions about Ecclesiastes shape comparative investigations of the genre as well as the limitations of comparative genre at least with regard to Ecclesiastes. What are we to make of these different approaches? If one were forced to choose between them, then Fox's approach would be preferable because it seeks to do justice to the genre of Ecclesiastes as a whole. However, I suggest that in accordance with their starting points Fox, Perdue, Longman, and the comparison with the Greek diatribe recognize real but partial aspects of Ecclesiastes, aspects that in my view need not be antithetical. The diatribe approach foregrounds the dialogical nature of Ecclesiastes. Perdue and Longman are alert to the royal fiction, the dominant first-person narrative, and Perdue is sensitive to the pessimism and ethos of death that surrounds Qohelet. Indeed, the fictional testament or royal autobiography closely parallels these. Fox is above all concerned with the frame-narrative aspect of Ecclesiastes, and he correctly finds that this is a style that extends across particular genres. Fox's comparisons do not, however, account for the royal fiction and the skepticism in Ecclesiastes. For example, not one of the main characters in his examples is the king.

In my view the diatribe approach, as well as Fox's, Longman's, and Perdue's approaches, pick up correctly on different aspects of Ecclesiastes:

- first-person narration is a dominant characteristic
- there is a royal fiction and 1:1 relates that to the entire book
- there is a pessimistic element in Ecclesiastes
- death is a dominant feature of Ecclesiastes
- there is a dialogical dimension

305. Ibid., 95n30.
306. Ibid., 96.

- frame narrative is integral to the book and cannot simply be read as a late addition to a complete text

Any understanding of the genre of Ecclesiastes must do justice to all these features. My suggestion, therefore, is that we have in Ecclesiastes a developed wisdom form of the royal testament or fictional autobiography cast in a frame narrative. The explosive material in Qohelet requires careful presentation, and the frame-narrative technique that was common in the ancient Near East lends itself to such caution and is developed accordingly in Ecclesiastes. Contra Longman and Perdue, however, the fictional autobiographical aspect of Ecclesiastes undermines diachronic analysis that quickly isolates the first-person narrative as the "real Qohelet." The recognition of this possible fictionality should have led Longman and Perdue to see that the way in which Qohelet is presented and the relevance of the framework to this are integral parts of interpreting Ecclesiastes. Fox is thus right that it is the literary implications of the third-person sections, that is, of the "editing" in Ecclesiastes, that we should focus on in our interpretation of the book.

Further development of our understanding of Ecclesiastes requires that we move beyond comparative genre analysis, but certainly not without the insights it has brought, to the sort of narrative literary analysis pursued by Fox.[307] Comparative genre analysis helpfully alerts us to many of the characteristics of Ecclesiastes, but these must lead us to deepened close analysis of the text itself. This enables us to take the whole text of Ecclesiastes seriously.

By 1977 Fox had begun to focus on the literary shape of Ecclesiastes. He maintains that Ecclesiastes is Wisdom literature and narration.

> It tells something that happened to someone. I would like to take some first steps in the investigation of the literary characteristics of *Qohelet* as narrative: Who is speaking (the question of *voice*), how do the voices speak, and how do they relate to each other? I will argue that the *Book of Qohelet* is to be taken as a whole, as a single, well-integrated composition, the product not of editorship but of authorship, which uses interplay of voice as a deliberate literary device for rhetorical and artistic purposes.[308]

Fox argues that while modern scholarship correctly recognizes more than one voice in Ecclesiastes, its presuppositions prevent the voice other than Qohelet's from being listened to carefully. This other voice is the one we hear speaking in

---

307. While I am using narrative theory to develop a methodology for discerning the message of Ecclesiastes, I am aware that Ecclesiastes' genre is composite in the sense that it is not pure narrative. The autobiographical and wisdom elements are also important parts of the total genre. Autobiography has a strong narrative element to it, however, and it does seem to me that a narrative structure constitutes Ecclesiastes, so that a narrative approach provides a useful way into the text.

308. Fox, "Frame-Narrative and Composition," 83.

1:2; 7:27; and 12:8, for example. This third-person voice is not that of Qohelet, as is made particularly clear by the way the voices interact in 7:27. It is unlikely, according to Fox, that Qohelet would speak of himself in the third person in the midst of a first-person sentence,[309] while a writer quoting someone else can put a *verbum dicendi* within the quotation wherever he wishes.

But if it is not Qohelet, who is this other voice? Generally scholars speak of the editor(s). But, Fox says, what signs are there of editing in Ecclesiastes? Fox suggests that the notion of editorship needs closer examination. The other voice could be that of a passive editor who receives a finished book and only adds glosses. G. Barton, for example, holds this view.[310] However, 1:2 (the addition of a title), 7:27, and the epilogue make this impossible; whoever is responsible for these "insertions" is far more active than a mere phrase inserter.

Nor could the other voice be that of an editor-rearranger, as Loretz suggests.[311] The way the voice appears in 1:2; 12:8; and especially 7:27 betrays activity at the level of sentence formation. Fox wonders by what criteria one could distinguish editorial rearrangement of a previously completed book. Loretz uses the criterion of logical order, but, as Fox demonstrates, illogical order is not evidence for editorship, and in the absence of a strong structure it is difficult to say what violates original structure. Ellermeier alone has investigated precisely what this editor did and concludes that Ecclesiastes was compiled by a redactor (QohR1) who wrote 1:1a, 2–3; 12:8, 9–12. QohR1 had before him fifty-six small independent *meshalim* that he joined on the basis of "thematische Begriffe" and "Stichwörter." A second editor (QohR2) was responsible for 12:13–14 and some glossing.[312] Fox finds Ellermeier's view wanting on four accounts.[313] First, it is not at all clear whether we can distinguish originally independent units. Second, it is often not clear whether Ellermeier's "Begriffe" and "Stichwörter" join or are internal to units. Third, to the extent that there are connections, how does one know that these are editorial rather than from the author? "While I agree with Ellermeier that in 1:2 and elsewhere we can hear another voice speaking besides Qohelet's, I see no evidence that that voice belongs to an editor who arranged numerous units he received from Qohelet."[314] Fourth, Qohelet's words are presented to us as the search by one man. The language of search and observation are found throughout the book and "provide a matrix that unites the disparate observations that Qohelet reports."[315]

309. Ibid., 84.
310. G. Barton, *Ecclesiastes*, 43–46.
311. Loretz, *Qohelet*, 136–44.
312. Ellermeier, *Qohelet*, 1/1:122–24, 131–41.
313. Fox, "Frame-Narrative and Composition," 88–90.
314. Ibid., 89.
315. Ibid., 90.

How then should we understand this other voice speaking in the third person about Qohelet in 1:2; 7:27; 12:8; and the epilogue?

> Here we should not ask what Qohelet or an editor could have written, but rather—what are the literary implications of the words? What are we meant to hear in the third-person sections? . . . I believe the questions raised can best be answered by the following understanding of that voice and its relation to Qohelet. That certain words are in a different voice does not mean that they are by a different hand. . . . I suggest that all of 1:2–12:14 is by the same hand[316]— not that the epilogue is by Qohelet, but that Qohelet is "by" the epilogist. In other words, the speaker we hear from time to time in the background saying "Qohelet said" . . . is the teller of the tale, the external narrator of the story of Qohelet. That is to say, the epic situation of the third-person voice in the epilogue and elsewhere is that of a man looking back and telling his son the story of the ancient wise-man Qohelet, passing on to him words he knew Qohelet to have said, appreciatively but cautiously evaluating his work in retrospect. Virtually all the "story" he tells is a quotation of the words of the wise-man he is telling about. The speaker, whom I will call the *frame-narrator*, keeps himself well in the background, but he does not make himself disappear. He presents himself not as the creator of Qohelet's words but as their transmitter.[317]

Fox thus understands Ecclesiastes as operating on three levels: the first (1) is that of the frame-narrator who tells about the second (2a), Qohelet-the-reporter, the narrating "I," who looks back from old age and speaks about the third level (2b), Qohelet-the-seeker, the younger Qohelet who made the investigation in 1:12ff. Level 1 is a different person from levels 2a and 2b; levels 2a and 2b are different perspectives of the same person.[318]

Fox's approach leads him to explore in detail the meaning of the epilogue in terms of its relationship to the main body of Ecclesiastes.[319] The didactic tone of the father-son instruction situation would have been easily recognized by the early readers of Ecclesiastes. In this way the epilogist identifies himself as a wisdom teacher. The frame narrator's first function in the epilogue is to testify to the reality of Qohelet so that we react to him as having lived.

> The reader's acceptance of the reality of literary figures is important to certain authors even when writing the most outlandish tales. . . . What the author seeks is not necessarily genuine belief in the character's existence (though that may be the intention in the case of *Qohelet*) but *suspension of disbelief* for the purposes of the fiction. . . . The epilogist of *Qohelet* succeeded in convincing

316. To an extent, Fox had already recognized this in his doctoral thesis. In "Book of Qohelet," xii, Fox argues that the editor and Qohelet are the same person.
317. Fox, "Frame-Narrative and Composition," 90–91.
318. Ibid., 91–92.
319. Ibid., 96–106.

many readers that he had an intimate familiarity with *Qohelet*, and it is clear that this is one of the epilogue's purposes.[320]

The second function of the frame narrator in the epilogue is to convey a certain stance toward Qohelet and his teaching. Qohelet is acknowledged as a wise man and his goals are praised, but according to Fox, the frame narrator is subtly noncommittal about the truth of Qohelet's words. In 12:10, Qohelet is said to have sought fine words and truth, but it is not said that he succeeded. This caution becomes more pronounced in v. 12 with the warning against excessive writing and speaking, the very activities Qohelet is engaged in. Fox takes the comparison of the words of the wise with goads/nails to indicate not positive stability but their dangerous nature—they both prick and hurt. The dogmatic certitude with which the overall duty of humans is stated contrasts with Qohelet's insistence on the uncertainty of everything. In a sense the epilogue can be seen as a call to allow expression of unorthodox opinion as long as the right conclusion is arrived at. But

> it is not only in offering a proper conclusion that the frame-narrative makes the book more easily tolerated. The use of a frame-narrative in itself puts a certain protective distance between the author and the views expressed in his work. This distance may be important even when the author is anonymous, because it may prevent the book as a whole from being violently rejected. The author blunts objections to the book as a whole by implying through use of a frame-narrator that he is just reporting what Qohelet said, without actually rejecting the latter's ideas.[321]

Finally, Fox considers the relationship between the frame narrator and the implied author, "the voice behind the voices."[322] Fox refers to the work of Wayne Booth, who has argued that every work of literature has an implied author, our sense of whom "includes, in short, the intuitive apprehension of a completed artistic whole; the chief value to which *this* implied author is committed, regardless of what party his creator belongs to in real life, is that which is expressed by the total form."[323] This is important because the view of the frame narrator may not be the same as that of the implied author, particularly in a book like Ecclesiastes where the conventional view of the frame narrator does not cancel out Qohelet's skepticism unless the reader allows it to. Indeed, by ending such an unorthodox book with an orthodox epilogue, the author creates an ambiguity that gives the reader freedom to choose which position to align with.

320. Ibid., 100.
321. Ibid.
322. Ibid., 104.
323. Ibid., 104n43, quoting Booth, *Rhetoric of Fiction*, 74–75.

Fox's understanding of the relationship between the frame narrator and the implied author is questionable, as we will see below and in the commentary on 12:8–14. However, he has certainly demonstrated the value of a literary approach to Ecclesiastes and raised one of the most important questions in the interpretation of Ecclesiastes, namely how, in a final-form approach, one understands the epilogue to relate to the main body of the text. Fox is the only recent commentator on Ecclesiastes who has focused intensively on this problem.

The way to discover the message/theology of Ecclesiastes, then, is decidedly not by reconstructing original versions of the text for which there is no text-critical evidence, but by inquiring after the implied author of Ecclesiastes. In other words, the way to arrive at the message of Ecclesiastes is by exploring the following diagrammatically expressed relationships in Ecclesiastes (E = Ecclesiastes).

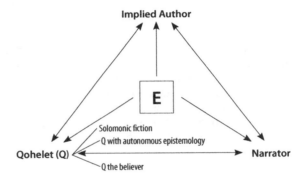

According to this approach the way to discover the message of Ecclesiastes is to inquire after the Implied Author (IA). One inquires after the IA by first exploring the characters in the text, namely, the narrator and Qohelet, and their interrelationship. Qohelet is represented in a number of ways: as king in Jerusalem (the Solomonic fiction), as an explorer in the grip of an autonomous epistemology (Greek), and as a believing Israelite who affirms the meaning of life in the *carpe diem* passages and other sections such as 5:1–7. We ought to distinguish more closely between the "Greek" Qohelet and the "orthodox" Qohelet rather than between the younger and older Qohelet, as does Fox. The tension between these two Qohelets is central to the book and accounts for its dialogical nature. To discern the message of the text, it is important also to ask how the implied author relates to the narrator and to Qohelet. Sternberg maintains that in biblical narrative the implied author and the narrator are the same.[324] Fox and N. Lohfink suggest that in Ecclesiastes they are not.[325]

324. Sternberg, *Poetics of Biblical Narrative*, 74–75.
325. I learned this in a discussion with N. Lohfink.

My conclusion in the commentary is that the voices of the narrator and the implied author are one and the same.

Such an analysis of Ecclesiastes as carefully crafted literature foregrounds three further literary characteristics:

1. *Irony*.[326] The common definition of irony is saying one thing and meaning the opposite. Irony may be taken literally, "yet a nagging doubt hints at a meaning hidden behind the mask."[327] Irony is criticism that perceives an incongruity in things as they are, but it is distinguished from other perceptions of incongruity by two characteristics. First, it is stated by means of understatement or a method of suggestion rather than of plain statement. Second, the perception comes from a supposed stance in truth.

   An ironic mode of speech dominates much of Ecclesiastes,[328] and throughout Qohelet's journey, until the epilogue, the irony is only suggested, albeit ever more strongly, rather than plainly stated. Central to Qohelet's irony is his repeated description of his epistemology as "wisdom." With Proverbs as the immediate context this suggests that Qohelet will pursue his explorations with the fear of the LORD as the foundation and beginning of wisdom. As we will see in the commentary, however, as his journey progresses the reader is indeed left with a nagging doubt as to whether this epistemology is "wisdom" at all. In 7:23–29 the irony of Qohelet's "wisdom" comes clearly into view when he finds that it has brought him into the hands of Dame Folly. But it is not until 11:7–12:14 that the irony is finally resolved.

2. *Repetition in Ecclesiastes*. Repetition is common in Proverbs and Ecclesiastes, and yet it has rarely received sustained attention. Snell asserts, "Clearly, no commentary ever written on Proverbs takes repetitions, clichés, and the shapes of the collections seriously."[329] Ecclesiastes is full of repetition, as Murphy, for example, recognizes: "While judgment

---

326. Good (*Irony in the Old Testament*, 168–95) was the first to write on irony in Ecclesiastes. The first edition of his book appeared in 1965. Since then, see Polk, "Wisdom of Irony"; Fisch, "Qohelet: A Hebrew Ironist," chap. 9 in his *Poetry with a Purpose*; W. Anderson, "Ironic Correlations and Scepticism"; Spangenberg, "Irony in the Book of Qohelet," who concludes (ibid., 69) that "the book is not only one of the dominant ironic writings in the Old Testament, but further that its author was an ironist *par excellence*"; and Sharp, "Ironic Representation." Studies have also been made of irony in Job (see Clines, *Job 1–20*, xcvii) and, to a lesser extent, in Proverbs, e.g., Alonso-Schökel, *Manual of Hebrew Poetics*, 165. Vílchez Líndez (*Eclesiastés o Qohélet*) deals with irony at certain points in his exegesis of Ecclesiastes (see esp. 201, 274, and 317). Irony has a significant background in Greek thought, of course; see Vlastos, "Socratic Irony."

327. Good, *Irony in the Old Testament*, 22.

328. Fisch (*Poetry with a Purpose*, 158–78) argues that Ecclesiastes as a whole has an ironic tone.

329. Snell, *Twice-Told Proverbs*, 84.

about the peculiar grammatical characteristics of the language is still out . . . there can be no doubt about the distinctiveness of Qoheleth's literary style. The poem on the repetition of events in 1:4–11 is as it were a symbol of this style; repetition is its trademark. This repetition is manifest in vocabulary and also in a phraseology that is almost formulaic." Murphy then lists twenty-eight favorite words of Qohelet.[330] Qohelet also repeats the following set phrases: "who knows," "under the sun," "all the work that is done," "labor," "eat" and "drink," and of course "everything/all is enigmatic."

What Snell says of commentaries on Proverbs remains true of commentaries on Ecclesiastes; the way in which this literary device of repetition manifests itself in *the whole book* is not generally explored. As part of his analysis of repetition in Ugaritic and Hebrew poetry, Zurro refers to numerous types of repetition in individual verses in Ecclesiastes.[331] Useful as this analysis is, it remains at the level of the individual verse and does not examine the structure of repetition within a book as a whole, like Ecclesiastes. In terms of this larger analysis Sternberg has done the most thorough work on repetition in biblical texts, although he limits himself to OT narrative,[332] and clearly there are some important differences between the structures of repetition in narrative as opposed to poetic texts.[333] Most relevant to Ecclesiastes is Sternberg's point that in literary texts the dismissal of redundancies as "noise" must be the last resort. There is a prima facie case in Ecclesiastes, as in biblical narrative, for a functional approach.[334] This is certainly true of repetition in Ecclesiastes.

Particularly significant is one major type of repetition in Ecclesiastes, that of the *carpe diem* passages,[335] 2:24–26; 3:10–15, 16–22; 5:18–20 [17–19]; 8:10–15; 9:7–10; 11:7–12:7. A variety of ways are proposed for reading these passages, which I will note in the commentary section.

330. Murphy, *Ecclesiastes*, xxix–xxx.

331. Zurro, *Procedimientos iterativos*.

332. Sternberg, *Poetics of Biblical Narrative*, 365–440. For Sternberg's earlier work on repetition, see his *Expositional Modes and Temporal Ordering in Fiction* (Baltimore: Johns Hopkins University Press, 1978). Sternberg's more recent work on the legal literature of the OT includes discussion of repetition. See his *Hebrews between Cultures: Group Portraits and National Literature* (Bloomington and Indianapolis: Indiana University Press, 1998), 426–638.

333. See Sternberg, *Poetics of Biblical Narrative*, 386; and Alter, *Art of Biblical Poetry*, for a consideration of repetition in Hebrew poetic texts.

334. Contra Whybray, *Ecclesiastes* (OT Guides), 44–45, who maintains that "the theory that the material originated as separate, individual pieces . . . also accounts for the frequent repetitions and duplications which are so characteristic of the book. This feature, regarded in this way, points rather to the literary disunity of the book than to its unity."

335. As Robert Alter commented to me, this may not be the most appropriate term for these passages, because it implies a hedonistic attitude that they do not teach.

Suffice it here to say that I do not read these passages as representing a hedonistic response to Qohelet's despair, but as a confessional evocation of a holistic, positive approach to life that we find in so much of the OT. These passages present the voice of Qohelet the Israelite believer who affirms life as God's good creation. They stand in strong tension with the *hebel* conclusions that Qohelet keeps coming to, and they increase in intensity as the book progresses. The tension between them and the *hebel* conclusions also increases and comes close to deconstruction in 9:7–10.

3. *Juxtaposition and gaps.* How to relate the *carpe diem* passages to the *hebel* conclusions has perplexed commentators for centuries, and there is always the temptation to flatten the book out in one direction or the other. We should resist both of these temptations. The opposing perspectives are *deliberately* juxtaposed so that gaps[336] are opened up in the reading, and the book is precisely about how to resolve the tension between these contradictory juxtapositions. The juxtaposing of contradictory perspectives producing gaps is part of the very fabric of Ecclesiastes. This has never been consciously studied by commentators,[337] although of course they work with the phenomenon all the time. Those who see Qohelet as ultimately positive tend to smooth over the gaps, whereas those who recognize the gaps tend to see Qohelet as a pessimist with the *carpe diem* passages as hedonistic resignation or as additions. Good is one of the few to recognize the role of gaps in Ecclesiastes, but even he writes, "The book is not a systematic or complete presentation of theology, a philosophy, an ethic, a way of life. The large gaps that remain, Qoheleth's sardonic wit might have filled delightfully, but we must leave them blank."[338]

Why is it that the gaps in Ecclesiastes have not been attended to? The answer lies in the failure of commentators to take the literary nature of Ecclesiastes seriously. As Sternberg points out, a literary work is a system of gaps that need to be filled.[339] Gaps are not the same as blanks; gaps are relevancies that demand closure. Gaps are created by opposition in juxtaposition: "The narrative juxtaposes two pieces of reality that

---

336. I am using "gaps" in the sense that Sternberg (*Poetics of Biblical Narrative*, 186–263) does. See below.

337. In his examination of the composition of Ecclesiastes, Eaton (*Ecclesiastes*, 41) says of the contradictions, "It is surely more likely that juxtaposed contradictions (e.g., 8:12f.) are calculated to draw our attention to the viewpoint of faith in contrast to that of observation." However, Eaton does not pursue the presence of such juxtapositions in Ecclesiastes as a whole. Gladson ("Retributive Paradoxes in Prov. 10–29," 146) notes that literary juxtaposition is one way the OT handles retributive paradox, and he refers to the final chapter of Ecclesiastes as an example.

338. Good, *Irony in the Old Testament*, 195.

339. Sternberg, *Poetics of Biblical Narrative*, 186.

bear on the same context but fail to harmonize either as variants of a situation or as phases in an action."[340] According to Sternberg, filling gaps is not arbitrary but should be controlled by the text's norms and directives. Although they arise from a lack in the telling, gaps move the reader between the truth and the whole truth and thereby give rise to a fullness in the reading.[341]

Structure

There has been considerable debate about the structure of Ecclesiastes. Is it just a loosely assembled collection or is it carefully crafted literature? A. Wright discerns two major sections to the book: Qohelet's investigation of life in 1:12–6:9 and Qohelet's conclusions in 6:10–11:6. Wright drew on New Critical insights in analyzing Ecclesiastes according to its form, whereas form *and* content are indispensable in tracing the development of Qohelet's thought. Wright's approach does not fit with the back-and-forth but progressive nature of Qohelet's journey that continues throughout the main body of the text.[342] Loader applied the insights of structuralism to Ecclesiastes and discerned polar structures in virtually every literary unit of the book.[343] In his commentary on Ecclesiastes, however, he simply divides the book into thirty-two sections.[344] In his rigorous analysis of the structure of Ecclesiastes, Backhaus argues that the body of Ecclesiastes divides into two halves of approximately equal length, with two compositions in each half: 1:3–3:22; 4:1–6:9; 6:10–8:17; and 9:1–12:8.[345] The first section in each part deals with a situation that people encounter, whereas the second section deals with advice on how to cope in such a situation. The first section of the first half deals with the problem of everything being ephemeral and uncertain, and the first section of the second half deals with the elusiveness of wisdom. With some adjustments, this is the structure Seow follows.[346]

Ecclesiastes is indeed carefully crafted, but this does not mean that the sort of logical objective structure that Wright and Backhaus seek can be discerned. It is the nature of Qohelet's journey that in his quest to answer the programmatic question of 1:3 he moves from subject to subject and that he often

340. Ibid., 243.
341. See ibid., 186–263, for a detailed discussion of gaps and the reading process in biblical narrative.
342. A. Wright, "Riddle of the Sphinx." See Bartholomew, *Reading Ecclesiastes*, 107–22. See also Seow (*Ecclesiastes*, 44–46) for a critique of Wright.
343. Loader, *Polar Structures*. See Bartholomew, *Reading Ecclesiastes*, 131–34.
344. Loader, *Ecclesiastes*.
345. Backhaus, *Denn Zeit und Zufall*, 1–332.
346. Seow, *Ecclesiastes*, 46–47.

doubles back on himself, picking up earlier themes. This fits the excruciating nature of his experience as he seeks to put the pieces of his world together, a world that has disintegrated in his hands.[347] The journey into and through despair is anything but linear, and as is typical in such experiences, moments of great insight are often followed by lapses back into the old struggles so that the journey is far more of a spiral than a straight line. The *carpe diem* passages (5:1–7 [4:17–5:6]; 7:23–29; 11:7) stand out as moments of poignant insight. The first, 5:1–7, which N. Lohfink understandably sees as the center of the book[348] and which resonates strongly with 12:13–14, is immediately followed, however, by Qohelet's further struggles with injustice and the problem of wealth. The second, 7:23–29, in which Qohelet recognizes that his exploration has led him into the arms of Dame Folly, is followed by a relentlessly dark chapter. Moreover, 11:7, which marks a true turning point in his journey, still does not yet provide final resolution. Thus the structure of Ecclesiastes is *literary and organic*, as befits Qohelet's experience, rather than logical in a scientific sense.[349] His journey is carried forward by the *hebel* conclusions and their contradictory juxtaposition with *carpe diem* passages, the developing tension between the juxtapositions, as well as the growing sense of the irony of the autonomous epistemology driving his journey.

Approaching Ecclesiastes as frame narrative divides the book into three main parts: the introduction by the third-person narrator, the main body of the work with Qohelet speaking apart from the brief voice of the narrator in 7:27, and the epilogue by the narrator in 12:7–14.

I. **Frame Narrative (1:1–11)**
   A. Title (1:1)
   B. Statement of the Theme of the Book (1:2)
   C. The Programmatic Question (1:3)
   D. A Poem about the Enigma of Life (1:4–11)
II. **Qohelet's Exploration of the Meaning of Life (1:12–12:7)**
   A. Qohelet's Description of His Journey of Exploration (1:12–18)
   B. Testing Pleasure and the Good Life (2:1–11)
   C. The Problem of Death and One's Legacy (2:12–23)
   D. Eating, Drinking, and Enjoying One's Labor (2:24–26)

347. See the psychological analysis of Ecclesiastes in the postscript. Nowadays, scholars pay little attention to the experience underlying Ecclesiastes, but some sense of its trauma is essential to grasping its structure.

348. N. Lohfink, *Qoheleth*, 8.

349. In this respect, see Ellul's perceptive comments about the presuppositions that dominate study of Ecclesiastes (*Reason for Being*, 6–16). The first presupposition he identifies is "the necessity of formal, logical coherence in a text" (ibid., 7). As he notes, "Such a criterion proves utterly inadequate if we want to *understand* the text" (ibid., 9). In a similar vein, see Carasik, "Qohelet's Twists and Turns."

Reading Ecclesiastes within the Context of Proverbs and Job and Its Connection to the Torah

Since Ecclesiastes is an OT wisdom text, Proverbs and Job provide the immediate intertextual context for reading it. Qohelet's relationship to traditional wisdom has featured large in twentieth-century interpretation of Ecclesiastes, with Qohelet regularly seen as reacting strongly against traditional wisdom. Hengel, for example, argues that Qohelet's empiricism results in his denying the traditional Jewish doctrine of retribution.[350] Perdue goes so far as to suggest that Qohelet develops an alternative worldview to that of the sages: "In his writings the foreground is not occupied by the manifold traditional motives; rather, he transforms them in his extremely individualist criticism by shattering the traditional worldview of earlier wisdom, denying a fixed connection between action and result, and proclaiming the absolute inexplicability of the divine action in nature and history."[351]

Crüsemann maintains that "this difference between Koheleth and his predecessors must be taken as the starting point for understanding Koheleth"[352]

350. Hengel, *Judaism and Hellenism*, 1:126.
351. Perdue, *Wisdom and Creation*, 116.
352. Crüsemann, "Unchangeable World," 61.

and suggests that Ecclesiastes brings Job to its logical conclusion.[353] This type of approach to the relationship between Ecclesiastes and the wisdom corpus/movement rests on a developmental reconstruction of wisdom in the OT in which Qohelet becomes associated with a crisis in wisdom.[354] Preuss is an extreme example of such a position.[355] In his view,

1. Wisdom is marginal to Israel's faith.
2. The God of wisdom is not Yahweh.
3. Wisdom concentrates on the orders in reality.
4. Retribution is one of these orders. The sages sought to discover this mechanical correspondence between action and consequence, as reflected in Proverbs.
5. A deed-consequence viewpoint is the basic dogma of early wisdom.

Clearly, if one understands early wisdom in this way, then Qohelet will be seen as reacting against this mechanical understanding of retribution and thereby participating with Job in a crisis of wisdom. The critical question is whether early wisdom was of this sort and whether wisdom in Proverbs is of this sort. Murphy points out that although this notion of a wisdom crisis looms almost as large in scholarly discussion as the exile of 587 BC, the earliest tradition clearly interpreted Qohelet as working within the wisdom tradition. As he tersely puts it, "There is no record that the book of Ecclesiastes was received with consternation."[356]

The subject of the origin and development of Wisdom literature in Israel is complex and cannot be pursued in detail here. As far as intertextuality goes, however, there are good reasons for rejecting the sort of understanding of the Ecclesiastes-Proverbs relationship that Preuss advocates. Gladson persuasively argues that "retributive paradox" occurs in all strands of OT literature including Proverbs,[357] so that taken as a whole Proverbs by no means presents a mechanical act-consequence understanding of retribution. This has been clearly demonstrated in an excellent article on wealth and poverty in Proverbs by Van Leeuwen.[358] He points out that there are large groups of sayings in Proverbs that assert a simple cause-and-effect relationship whereby righteousness leads to wealth and wickedness to poverty. These are examples of the "character-consequence nexus." However, they do not concern concrete, individual acts

353. Ibid., 61; idem, "Hiob und Kohelet," 381.
354. See Gese, "Crisis of Wisdom in Koheleth"; and Schmid, *Wesen und Geschichte der Weisheit*, on the crisis of wisdom.
355. Preuss, *Einführung*, 114–36.
356. Murphy, *Ecclesiastes*, lxi. For Murphy's understanding of Qohelet's relationship to traditional wisdom, see pp. lxii–lxiv.
357. Gladson, "Retributive Paradoxes in Prov. 10–29."
358. Van Leeuwen, "Wealth and Poverty."

and their consequences: "It is the long-term character and direction of a person or group (as 'righteous' or 'wicked') which determines life consequences and 'destiny.'"[359] It is a failure to recognize this long-term character that leads scholars to the mechanical view of retribution in Ecclesiastes.

> These proverbs, when taken by themselves, are the basis for the view of some scholars that the tidy dogmatism of Proverbs does not correspond to reality and is doomed to collapse under the weight of reality, as happened in Job and Qoheleth. Since the foregoing sayings are not always exemplified in human experience, their falsification presumably led to a crisis of faith in Yahweh's maintenance of a just world order.[360]

However, by their very nature proverbs are partial utterances, and this type of mechanical approach does not do justice to the many sayings in Proverbs that manifest a more complex understanding of the way God works in creation. Particularly noteworthy in this respect are the "better-than" sayings in Proverbs (cf. 15:16–17; 16:16, 19; etc.). The overall picture is a far more complex one, which Van Leeuwen sums up as follows:

> *In general*, the sages clearly believed that wise and righteous behavior did make life better and richer, though virtue did not *guarantee* those consequences. Conversely, injustice, sloth, and the like generally have bad consequences. The editor-sages who structured Proverbs sought first to teach these basic "rules of life," thus the heavy emphasis on character-consequence patterns in both Proverbs 1–9 and 10–15. We must first learn the basic rules; the exceptions can come later. Though very aware of exceptions to the character-consequence rule, the sages insisted that righteousness is better than wickedness. The most fundamental and profound reason for this is that they believed that God loves the one and hates the other. . . . For Israel's sages that sometimes seems the only answer. . . . The sages knew that there are limits to human wisdom. General patterns may be discerned, but many particular events may be unjust, irrational, and ultimately inscrutable.[361]

Van Leeuwen also notes that there is a future-oriented retribution perspective in Proverbs; it lacks a doctrine of resurrection and yet insists on the triumph of God's justice. He regards this as a hallmark of Yahwistic faith. "The sages' stance is to maintain faith in God's justice, even when they personally cannot see it or touch it, even when the recorded past does not verify it. Here religion provides no escape from the pain or absurdities of existence. The book of

359. Ibid., 27; cf. Fox, *Qohelet*, 132–33.
360. Van Leeuwen, "Wealth and Poverty," 28–29.
361. Ibid., 32–33.

Job was inevitable, not because Proverbs was too simplistic, but because life's inequities, as reflected in Proverbs, drive faith to argue with the Deity."[362]

Once one recognizes that Proverbs' understanding of retribution is more complex than a mechanical deed-consequence notion, then one has to re-evaluate Ecclesiastes' relationship to Proverbs and traditional wisdom. Admittedly, Van Leeuwen's understanding of this greater complexity is only one possibility among many. Gladson, for example, makes retributive paradox a function of pluralism and dissent already present in early wisdom traditions.[363] For Van Leeuwen, by comparison, "whatever their historical origin, within Proverbs they have come to express one broad worldview which acknowledges the conflict of dogma and experience, yet maintains both."[364] Either way, it is clear that Qohelet's autonomous methodology demands a certainty that traditional wisdom was aware that it could not provide. Consequently, rather than representing a crisis in wisdom, Qohelet should be seen as focusing on the retributive paradox that Proverbs is aware of and subsumes under its more general, long-term, character-consequence understanding. Because Qohelet's epistemology is based on observation, experience, and reason alone, he moves in the direction of deconstructing the tradition by always focusing on the individual exceptions.

One should also note that Ecclesiastes does not as a whole recommend Qohelet's autonomous epistemology, but ironically deconstructs it and arrives at a "remembering your Creator" position that is similar to the "fear of God" that Proverbs declares to be foundational to its wisdom. In this way, the focus of Ecclesiastes is far more specific than that of Proverbs, but their views of wisdom and retribution are not necessarily that far apart.

As regards the relationship between Job and Ecclesiastes, it seems quite unhelpful to regard Ecclesiastes as bringing Job to its logical, pessimistic conclusion. Rather, these two books should be seen as parallel representations of the struggle with the paradoxes of life in which the character-consequence structure appears not to apply. Job focuses on the devastating experience of an individual, whereas Ecclesiastes is more of an intellectual quest with the question of epistemology at its heart. Both books find resolution to the problems they wrestle with through a painful and hard-won recovery of the doctrine of creation.[365]

Another intertextual issue that has featured centrally in the interpretation of Ecclesiastes is the relationship between wisdom and law, especially as this is focused in 12:13b: "Fear God and keep his commandments." For many

362. Ibid., 34.
363. Gladson, "Retributive Paradoxes in Prov. 10–29."
364. Ibid., 26.
365. See in this respect C. Gunton, "Trinity and Trustworthiness," in *The Trustworthiness of God: Perspectives on the Nature of Scripture*, ed. P. Helm and C. R. Trueman (Grand Rapids: Eerdmans, 2002), 275–84.

scholars the introduction of law is alien to the wisdom tradition in which Ecclesiastes is situated, thus indicating that the epilogue, or at least this part of it, is a later attempt to make Qohelet appear orthodox or to thematize a relationship between wisdom and the commandments in the Law.[366]

However, there is no text-critical evidence—and there are good reasons for resisting attempts—to conclude that the epilogue is a later addition.[367] The genre of Ecclesiastes and the circular intent at totality drive us to explore other avenues before concluding that the reference to law must make the epilogue a later addition. There are clear indications that the reference to law may not be as alien to Ecclesiastes as some suggest. For example, as N. Lohfink points out, law is not alien to the fear of God in Ecclesiastes.[368] He makes the point that 5:7 [6] concludes the section 5:1–7 [4:17–5:6]. Indeed, 5:1–7 contains in vv. 3–4 a restatement of the law of Deut. 23:22–24, and the background to 5:6 is Num. 15:22–31. Moreover, this section with its allusions to the Torah concludes with the exhortation to "fear God."[369] Finally, 5:1–7 makes clear too that Qohelet is well acquainted with the cultus of the temple, as does the reference to "clean" and "unclean" in 9:2.[370]

This evidence of awareness of pentateuchal cultic legislation needs to be combined with the vocabulary in Ecclesiastes that also appears to relate to the domain of torah, namely "judgment" (3:17; 11:9), "sinner," "sin" (2:26; 5:5 [4]; 8:12), "wicked" and "righteous" (3:17), "wickedness [is folly]" (7:25), "one who pleases God" versus "the sinner" (7:26), and so on. Many try to minimize the religious and ethical nuance of this vocabulary in Ecclesiastes. Even so evenhanded a commentator as Murphy, for example, says of the one who is good versus the sinner in 2:26 that these terms should be understood "not as moral qualifications, but as designations of human beings in terms of the inscrutable divine will."[371] Similarly, regarding "the sinner" in 7:26 Fox argues, "As many interpreters recognize, the *ḥoṭe'* here [2:26 and 7:26] is not a transgressor against the law or moral norms, but rather one who has somehow incurred God's disfavor."[372] This person "may be no more or less virtuous than

---

366. See Sheppard, *Wisdom as a Hermeneutical Construct*, 121–29.

367. The introduction of law does strike the reader initially as strange, but strangeness is not alien to endings. In the twentieth century, considerable work was done on the theory of endings, and this may provide helpful insights with respect to the epilogue. See Kermode, *Sense of an Ending*; Rogers, "Parthian Dart"; and for a fascinating application of this type of theory to Jonah, see Crouch, "To Question an End."

368. N. Lohfink, "Qoheleth 5:17–19," 633.

369. There is considerable disagreement, however, as to how to understand Qohelet's view of the cult. Cf. Perdue, *Wisdom and Cult*, 178–88; and Ogden, *Qoheleth*, 75ff., for two different views. Ogden's view is more satisfactory. See commentary on 5:1–7.

370. On the similarities between Deuteronomy and Ecclesiastes, see note 45 of the chapter on 12:8–14.

371. Murphy, *Ecclesiastes*, 76.

372. Fox, *Time*, 189.

others. Qohelet calls a man pleasing or offensive to God in accordance with his fate rather than his deeds."[373]

It is not only the language in Qohelet that overlaps with that of Torah that is denied moral significance. Schoors, for example, argues that nowhere does "folly" have a moral connotation in Ecclesiastes.[374] Fox says of wisdom in Ecclesiastes, "In sharp contrast to Proverbs, but not to most of the Bible, Qoheleth does not regard wisdom as an ethical or religious virtue. . . . He does pair righteousness and wisdom in 7:16 and 9:1, but he is bracketing the categories as positive values, and not pairing them."[375]

The reasons modern scholarship fails to recognize the moral and religious significance of these terms are multiple. First, the developmental notion of wisdom as originally secular and only later connected with Israel's faith lingers and continues to influence studies of wisdom. In the OT and the ancient Near East, however, wisdom is inherently religious and thus moral; the OT knows nothing of the sacred-secular dualism common to modernity. As Hubbard notes, "*We should fight shy of any theory of simple, straightline evolutionary development in Israel's wisdom movement*. . . . Solomon's enterprising ways spurred on a movement which had existed in the popular life of Israel from her earliest days and which had taken on semi-official status under David."[376]

Second, "wisdom" (*ḥokmâ*) and its associated vocabulary[377] covers a range of meaning including technical skill and intelligence, abilities that can be misdirected, so that *ḥākām* can have, for example, the negative meaning of "crafty" as in 2 Sam. 13:3.[378] By focusing on the religious base of wisdom, Proverbs does not abandon the notion of wisdom as expertise but grounds it in the doctrine of creation.

373. Ibid., 269.

374. Schoors, *Preacher*, 2:169; he asserts, "It seems that in Qoh[elet], folly as such has no moral connotation, nor does wisdom."

375. Fox, "Wisdom in Qoheleth," 128.

376. Hubbard, "Wisdom Movement and Israel's Covenant Faith," 17–18. The view that Israel's wisdom evolved from secular to religious has implications for one's view of wisdom's epistemology. McKane (*Prophets and Wise Men*, 61) argues that the older secular wisdom was "primarily a disciplined *empiricism* engaged with the problems of government and administration" (italics mine). In his discussion of whether early wisdom was secular, Weeks (*Early Israelite Wisdom*, 73) concludes, "The theory that early Israelite wisdom was a secular tradition has been examined in some depth, and found wanting in almost every respect. The internal evidence of Proverbs cited by McKane and others is, I have argued, largely illusory, while the Egyptian and other non-Israelite evidence suggests that Wisdom literature conventionally incorporated religious elements long before it reached Israel, if, indeed, it ever lacked them."

377. See Fox, *Proverbs 1–9*, 29–38, for a discussion of the main vocabulary of wisdom.

378. In arguing that Qohelet is in line with the rest of the OT, Fox (*Time*, 72) refers also to Isa. 29:14; 47:10; Ezek. 28:5. These verses, however, have a strong religious overtone contrasting the wisdom followed by the Israelites and Tyre in Ezekiel with the LORD's wisdom. See Van Leeuwen, "Wisdom Literature," 848, on wisdom as a totality concept.

Third, there is the tendency to see torah, prophecy, and wisdom as distinct and separate categories, whereas, as Ecclesiastes demonstrates, they were far more organically interwoven than is generally recognized. In OT theology the relationship between law and wisdom remains a controversial and difficult issue.[379] Murphy has helpfully suggested that "the problem of the relationship between Wisdom literature and other portions of the Old Testament needs to be reformulated in terms of a shared approach to reality."[380] Similarly, Reventlow seems on the right track in his recovery of Schmid's comprehensive notion of righteousness as order of the world.[381] "The starting point for his deliberations is the remarkable breadth of the term 'justice': it comprises, beyond the juridical scope and wisdom, also nature/fertility, war/victory, cult/offering and kingdom. Behind these special fields a comprehensive world-order becomes visible, which as a whole can be characterized by the term 'righteousness.'"[382]

We need to remember that the strong distinction between law and wisdom is a modern construct and that by the third century BC, wisdom and law would certainly not be considered separate paths to successful living in the minds of teachers and populace, since both relate to ordering life in all its dimensions. This becomes particularly clear when one notes that "a distinction between religious and secular is not applicable to Old Testament wisdom teaching."[383] Neither is it applicable to torah, which also orders all areas of life. How then might these two approaches have been understood to relate to each other?

This is an extremely complex issue, and here I want to make a suggestion along the lines of Murphy's proposal of a shared reality. The wisdom and legal traditions in the OT are clearly distinct, and yet they manifest some awareness of each other, as we have seen with Ecclesiastes.[384] Both have in common the ordering of the life of God's people.[385] Van Leeuwen has analyzed the root metaphors of Prov. 1–9 and argues persuasively that

379. For useful discussions of the relationship of these two traditions, which both seek to order the lives of God's people, see Hubbard, "Wisdom Movement and Israel's Covenant Faith"; and Blenkinsopp, *Wisdom and Law in the Old Testament*.

380. Murphy, "Wisdom—Theses and Hypotheses," 38.

381. Schmid, *Gerechtigkeit als Weltordnung*.

382. Reventlow, "Righteousness as Order of the World," 165. Crenshaw ("In Search of Divine Presence," 365) notes that for biblical wisdom, "order derives from divine presence." In the same article (497), he refers positively to J. Lévêque's point that the Israelite called into covenant relationship with God was at the same time an "everyday man."

383. Murphy, "Wisdom—Theses and Hypotheses," 40.

384. See Van Leeuwen, "Liminality," 122, for some of the links between Proverbs (and Job) and the Pentateuch. Van Leeuwen argues that certain texts in Proverbs and Job presuppose the historical tradition of the gift of the land.

385. Murphy ("Wisdom—Theses and Hypotheses") is critical of the close association of wisdom with the search for order, arguing that this question is a modern one that focuses on a presupposition of Israel's wisdom approach. However, see Van Leeuwen, "Liminality," for a powerful defense of taking the tacit presupposition of cosmic order seriously in Wisdom literature.

underlying the bipolar metaphorical system of positive and negative youths, invitations/calls, "ways," "women," and "houses" in Prov. 1–9, is a yet more fundamental reality which these images together portray. These chapters depict the world as the arena of human existence. This world possesses two fundamental characteristics. First is its structure of boundaries or limits. Second is the bipolar human eros for the beauty of Wisdom, who prescribes life within limits, or for the seeming beauty of Folly, who offers bogus delights in defiance of created limits.[386]

Van Leeuwen argues that the worldview Proverbs exhibits is a "carved" one in that "cultural and personal exhortation is grounded in the reality of the created world with its inbuilt normativity."[387] Justice and righteousness are built into the world.

This link of wisdom with creation has long been recognized. What is often not noted, though, is that the order that Proverbs finds in the "carved" creation is not and cannot be simply read out of the creation. This is the point that Fox makes about Israelite wisdom; it is not empirical[388] in the way that Ecclesiastes is, but assumes ethical principles that it uses observation to support. This is the sort of position exemplified in Gen. 1–3. The ordering of creation is not antithetical to instruction from Elohim/Yahweh Elohim. Order and instruction/torah go hand in hand, and obedience requires both a good creation and instruction. The point is that Wisdom literature assumes certain ethical principles that are not just read off creation but are often very similar to the principles found in the Law. Van Leeuwen, for example, argues that Prov. 1–9 indicates that it is in "the liquid abandonment of married love" that healthy *communitas* takes place, and he notes, "This reality has its parallel at Sinai."[389]

Thus one can argue that while wisdom is most closely related to creation, it presupposes instruction. Similarly, when the narrative frame, within which law always occurs in the final form of the OT, is foregrounded, it becomes apparent that the law of Yahweh the redeemer God is also the law of the creator God. This link between Yahweh as creator and redeemer is central to covenant in the OT,[390] and alerts us to the link between law and creation.

My suggestion therefore is that law and wisdom share an underlying and often tacit presupposition of a "carved" creation order. This is their shared reality. Instruction from Yahweh would therefore not be seen to conflict with the way he ordered his creation, but would provide the ethical principles for discovery of that order. If this is even close to the situation that prevailed in Israel,

386. Van Leeuwen, "Liminality," 116.
387. Ibid., 118.
388. Fox refers to Qohelet's epistemology as empirical, but I prefer the term "autonomous." Classically, empiricism is the view that true knowledge derives exclusively from sense perception, whereas Qohelet depends on reason, experience, and observation.
389. Van Leeuwen, "Liminality," 132.
390. See Bartholomew, "Covenant and Creation."

then it would confirm the argument for caution about insisting that the epilogue must be an addition because it mentions keeping God's commandments.

Both torah (covenant)[391] and wisdom have their roots in creation theology, so that in general the torah vocabulary in Ecclesiastes needs to be read with its full religious and ethical connotations. Furthermore, the indications that Ecclesiastes has a strong link with Genesis and several strong links with Deuteronomy make it more and more difficult to insist that the reference to law means that the epilogue must be a later addition or that the torah vocabulary of Ecclesiastes must be voided of religious significance.[392] Certainly if Qohelet had Gen. 1–4 in mind, then the use of *Elohim* and the reference to "your Creator" should not be set in opposition to the lawgiver, Yahweh, as Gen. 2 makes particularly clear with its description of God as *Yahweh Elohim*, thereby stressing that the creator Elohim is the Yahweh of Israel.[393]

The fourth reason modern scholarship fails to recognize the moral and religious significance of these terms is the complex nature of Ecclesiastes, and much depends on how one reads it as a whole. Qohelet's method, which he describes as "wisdom" (1:13), is very different from wisdom in Proverbs. Fox notes that "Qoheleth's epistemology is . . . foreign to the ancient Near East, but it is paralleled in his Hellenistic environment. . . . He does . . . incorporate the fundamental tenet of Greek philosophy—the autonomy of individual reason, which is to say, the belief that individuals can and should proceed with their own observations and reasoning powers on a quest for knowledge and that this may lead to discovery of truths previously unknown."[394] What Fox does not recognize is that this usage of "wisdom" is ironized in Ecclesiastes itself, and the irony points clearly toward the Proverbs-type understanding of wisdom rooted in the fear of the LORD. Furthermore, the struggle and tension in Ecclesiastes is between the autonomous, "Greek" Qohelet and the believing, Israelite Qohelet, who is fully aware of the religious connotations of sin, wickedness, righteousness, and so on.

Many other aspects of biblical intertextuality in relation to Ecclesiastes could be considered. A strong connection between Ecclesiastes and the early chapters of Genesis has rightly been noted.[395] Alter notes a connection with

---

391. See ibid.

392. See my discussion of the epilogue, 12:8–14. It is possible to argue that Qohelet knows the Torah but is very negative toward it. This will depend on one's understanding of the passages in which this vocabulary occurs.

393. See L'Hour, "Yahweh Elohim"; and Bartholomew, "Covenant and Creation."

394. Fox, "Wisdom in Qoheleth," 122–23.

395. Forman, "Koheleth's Use of Genesis"; Clemens, "Law of Sin and Death"; Hertzberg, *Prediger*, 227–30; W. Anderson, "Curse of Work." Hertzberg (*Prediger*, 230) asserts that there can be no doubt: the author of Ecclesiastes wrote the book with Gen. 1–4 in front of him. Similarities with as well as differences from Genesis are important. For example, as Robert Alter pointed out to me in conversation, much of Qohelet has a very different understanding of time compared with Gen. 1:1–2:4.

Ps. 39,[396] and I have noted earlier the similarities between Ecclesiastes and psalms like Ps. 73.

Message

Ecclesiastes is not first a kerygmatic book, but rather one that calls the reader to engage with Qohelet's journey and to enter into the dialogue he evokes. Thus any attempt to summarize his message is in real danger of the "heresy of paraphrase."[397] His message unfolds, and needs to unfold, as the journey develops. Thus the readers of this commentary are encouraged to work closely with the text of Ecclesiastes, to feel the agony of Qohelet's journey, and to return to this section again at the end of their journey with Qohelet.

Qohelet articulates his quest in terms of the meaningfulness of work or labor (1:3), so that in one sense Ecclesiastes is a book about work. However, this question backs him into the deeper question of the meaning of life "under the sun." As his journey unfolds, the still deeper question surfaces of *how* to explore such a question wisely—the central issue of epistemology.

Commentators remain polarized as to whether Ecclesiastes is fundamentally positive, affirming joy, or basically pessimistic. The majority incline to the latter view. In my view scholars continually fall into the trap of leveling Qohelet toward his *hebel* pole, or toward his *carpe diem*–affirmation-of-joy pole. This is to ignore the literary juxtaposition of contradictory views that is central to the book and the life-death tension it embodies. Qohelet's autonomous epistemology, depending on observation, experience, and reason alone,[398] leads him continually to the *hebel* conclusion, which is juxtaposed again and again with his *carpe diem* confessions of the goodness of life. The book is about the struggle to live with and resolve the agonized tension between these two poles.

As we will see in the commentary, there have been many proposals for how to translate *hebel*, ranging from "absurd" (Fox), "meaningless" (Longman), "useless" (GNB), to "vanity" (KJV), and "a puff of breath" (N. Lohfink). In my opinion "enigmatic" is the best translation because, in line with the parallel expression "a striving after wind," *hebel* does not indicate that there is *no* meaning but that it appears ungraspable or incomprehensible.[399] There is thus an important difference in nuance between "enigmatic" and "meaningless, useless, absurd," and so on because "enigmatic" leaves open the possibility

---

396. Alter, *Art of Biblical Poetry*, 68–70.

397. See Cleanth Brooks, "The Heresy of Paraphrase," in *The Well Wrought Urn: Studies in the Structure of Poetry* (New York: Harcourt Brace, 1947), 192–214.

398. See the discussion of the theological implications of 7:23–29 for a full discussion of Qohelet's autonomous epistemology and its comparison to that of Proverbs.

399. See Gammie's ("Stoicism," 178–79) helpful comments in this respect.

of meaning—it is just that Qohelet with his autonomous epistemology cannot find it. McKenna, therefore, is quite correct in seeing in Ecclesiastes' use of *hebel* a reflection on the contingency of creation, its total dependency on its creator God.[400] *Hebel* does indeed have a distinctly negative connotation in Ecclesiastes, but it does not finally close the door on meaning. As Berry perceptively notes, "A person who marks his trail into despair remembers hope—and thus has hope, even if only a little. But if he speaks of despair, he must know it, and he must speak as one who knows it."[401] *Hebel* repeatedly marks Qohelet's trail through autonomy toward despair, but his very marking of that despair and his refusal to give up "remembers hope."

Most significant for the message of Ecclesiastes is that Qohelet's epistemology and his trail into *hebel* is ironized in the book itself. This is most clear in 7:23–29, in which Qohelet finds that his epistemology had led him right into the arms of Dame Folly, and it is stated most plainly in 11:7–12:7, in which remembering one's Creator resolves the acute tension in Qohelet's experience. McKenna thus notes regarding Ecclesiastes and its use of *hebel*, "We must recognize here the fact that this concept of the contingent rationality of created reality denies validity to the Graeco-Roman foundations for knowledge. Mother Wisdom in Israel is an attack upon the very heart of the effort in the ancient world to relate God and the world by some necessary means discovered in the laws of the cosmos, usually a cosmos whose eternity reflected in this way the eternity of God himself."[402] Or, as Ricoeur puts it, "Nothing is further from the spirit of the sages than the idea of an autonomy of thinking, a humanism of the good life; in short of a wisdom in the Stoic or Epicurean mode founded on the self-sufficiency of thought. This is why wisdom is held to be a gift of God in distinction to the 'knowledge of good and evil' promised by the Serpent."[403]

Ecclesiastes seems to have been written for third-century Israelites who lived in a period when Yahweh's promises seemed to have come to nothing and there was little empirical evidence of his purposes and promises. The Israelites were exposed to pervasive Greek thought and culture at this time, and a common temptation especially among the more educated was to apply a sort of autonomous Greek epistemology to their experience of desolation, leading many of their young people to conclude that God's purposes in the world are inscrutable and utterly enigmatic.[404]

Ecclesiastes is crafted in this context by a wisdom teacher as an ironical exposure of such an autonomous epistemology that seeks wisdom through

400. McKenna, "*Hebel* in Ecclesiastes."
401. Berry, *What Are People For?* 79.
402. McKenna, "*Hebel* in Ecclesiastes," 24.
403. Ricoeur, "Toward a Hermeneutic," 88.
404. As Muilenburg ("Qoheleth Scroll," 20) notes, "ultimately Qoheleth must be read as a product of the Hebrew mind in the Greek period."

personal experience and analysis without the glasses of the fear of God. As such Ecclesiastes is an example of contextualization of biblical faith or what N. Lohfink calls "a model of enculturation."[405] Qohelet puts himself into the shoes, as it were, of the autonomous Greek worldview and applies it to the world he observes and experiences, but only in order to show that it leads again and again to enigma rather than truth. His autonomous epistemology keeps running up against the enigma of life when pursued from this direction, and it appears impossible to find a bridge between this enigma and the good that he experiences and that the biblical tradition alerts one to. The resolution of this paradox is found in the fear of God (rejoicing and remembrance), which enables one to rejoice and apply oneself positively to life in the midst of all that one does not understand, including especially death.

Ecclesiastes thus exhorts Israelites struggling with the nature of life's meaning and God's purposes to pursue genuine wisdom by allowing their thinking to be shaped integrally by a recognition of God as Creator so that they can enjoy God's good gifts and obey his laws amid the enigma of his purposes. As Langdon Gilkey notes, one of the religious affirmations implied by the Christian doctrine of creation is that "because of God's creative and ruling power our finite life and the events in which we live have, despite their bewildering mystery and their frequently tragic character, a meaning, a purpose, and a destiny beyond any immediate and apparent futility."[406] In this way Ecclesiastes is an exhortation to be truly wise in difficult and perplexing situations. This is where the implied author wants readers to stand in relation to the enigmas of life.

Ultimately, therefore, Qohelet affirms joy, but not of course cheap joy, much as Bonhoeffer affirmed grace, but costly grace, not cheap grace.[407] The section 12:1–7 remains as a testament to the vale of tears in which and through which one is to remember one's Creator with joy and lovingly obey his commandments, which, as the Psalms remind us (e.g., Pss. 19; 34; 119), are our food and drink. As Ford asks, "But what about joy-destroying evil? The saints offer no conceptual solution to this, but they wrestle with reality at its darkest points and still testify to the joy of God."[408] The great metaphor arising from Ecclesiastes for this is "feasting":

> To envisage the ultimate feasting is to imagine an endless overflow of communication between those who love and enjoy each other. It embraces body language, facial expressions, the ways we eat, drink, toast, dance and sing; and

405. N. Lohfink, *Qoheleth*, 6. However, I am less optimistic than Lohfink about Qohelet's attempt to draw as much as possible from the Greek worldview without abandoning Israel's wisdom.

406. Gilkey, *Maker of Heaven and Earth*, 30–31.

407. D. Bonhoeffer, *The Cost of Discipleship* (New York: Macmillan, 1948; 2nd ed., 1959).

408. Ford, *Self and Salvation*, 266.

accompanying every course, encounter and artistic performance are conversations taken up into celebration. We can imagine a "great feast of languages" (Shakespeare), with cultures and traditions in conversation. There can be a pluralism without divisiveness—there is only a limited number of exchanges any guest can take part in, and nobody needs to know what is going on in every conversation. Aesthetics, ethics and metaphysics converge in this performance that is "infinitely communicative" (Traherne).[409]

This brings us close to the great feast of the kingdom that Jesus proclaimed and embodied.

Ecclesiastes and the New Testament

The Nestle-Aland edition of the Greek NT indicates one literal quotation from Ecclesiastes, in Rom. 3:10, where Paul is thought to refer to Eccles. 7:20 as part of his argument that all have sinned and fallen short of the glory of God.[410] Scholars also discern a link with Ecclesiastes in Rom. 8:20, in which "futility" (*mataiotēs*) is the same word the LXX uses to translate *hebel* in Ecclesiastes.[411] In Rom. 8 Paul speaks of the creation as having been subjected to futility or frustration, but in hope that it will be set free. This is a reference to the effect of the fall on the whole creation and likewise to the cosmic implications of there being "no condemnation in Christ."

Ecclesiastes is certainly in touch with the frustration and sense of futility that can grip one in our fallen world, and Qohelet emphasizes in his explorations how this futility touches every aspect of our lives. This is what the Reformed tradition means by *total depravity*: precisely *not* that everything is as bad as it can be, but that the fall affects every aspect of created life. The catholic tradition also teaches that every aspect of life has been, is being, and will be redeemed in Christ.[412] However, we do need to be careful how we see Ecclesiastes as articulating the futility of life. According to Longman, "he [Qohelet] presents a true assessment of the world apart from the light of God's redeeming love. His perspective on the world and life is restricted; he describes it as life 'under the sun,' that is, apart from heavenly realities,

409. Ibid., 271.
410. Aland et al., eds., *Novum Testamentum Graece*, 789.
411. In the entry on *mataiotēs*, O. Bauernfeind notes that "R[om]. 8:20 is a valid commentary on Qoh[elet]. The passage does not solve the metaphysical and logical problems raised by *vanitas*. In detail it allows of different possibilities of understanding. . . . But it tells us plainly that the state of ματαιότης ('vanity') exists, and also that this has a beginning and end. Before its beginning and beyond its end is God" (*TDNT* 4:523).
412. On the Reformed side, see Wolters, *Creation Regained*; from the Roman Catholic side, see *Catechism of the Catholic Church*, part 1, section 6; and on the Eastern Orthodox side, see Schmemann, *For the Life of the World*.

apart from God. In other words, his hopelessness is the result of the curse of the fall without recourse to God's redemption."[413] Ecclesiastes is more nuanced than this. Qohelet demonstrates the futility of trying to find meaning in a fallen world apart from remembering one's Creator and starting with the fear of the LORD, but he also affirms life, and he resolves this tension at the conclusion of his journey precisely through his exhortation to remember one's Creator. Thus the futility Ecclesiastes exposes is that of trying to find meaning while embracing human autonomy in a world that depends at every point on its Creator.

As the NT story unfolds, it becomes apparent that Jesus redeems us from this futility and our sinful autonomy and suppression of the truth about this world (Rom. 1:18–23).[414] He does this by ushering in the kingdom of God, the main theme of Jesus's teaching. As Spykman perceptively notes, "Nothing matters but the kingdom, but because of the kingdom *everything matters*—especially the ministries of the church and the Church's daily living."[415] Just as *hebel* casts its shadow across all areas of life, so too does Christ claim all areas of life as rightly his and thus to be redeemed and brought to their fulfillment under his rule. Christ does not just teach about the kingdom; through his incarnation he enters the very history that is subject to futility and embodies the kingdom in his acts and ultimately in his death and resurrection and ascension. In his death he takes upon himself the full weight of the futility of separation from God and thereby opens the gate to entrance into the kingdom, in which full meaning is found in Christ.

The NT therefore provides a more comprehensive perspective on the problems that Qohelet struggles with. The problem of death, for example, overshadows his journey of exploration, but in the light of the Christ event we know that history is indeed headed toward the final judgment and resurrection, something no OT believer saw with comparable clarity. Death is not the end but a stepping stone into the presence of the living and true God. In terms of history too, from an NT perspective we now have the contours—if not the details—of the full story, something that Qohelet lacked. In terms of the ongoing relevance of Ecclesiastes, we should note that the era of mission inaugurated at Pentecost is the age that falls between the coming of the kingdom and its consummation. In this era the whole creation still groans, and thus Ecclesiastes

413. Longman, *Ecclesiastes*, 39.

414. See Bruns, "Some Reflections," for comparable points. Bruns notes that similarities to Sadducean teaching have been discerned in both the Gospel of John and Ecclesiastes. Steinmann (*Ainsi parlait Qohèlet*, 125) refers to Ecclesiastes as "the Sadducean breviary." Bruns ("Some Reflections," 415) asserts that "surely it is apparent that the Jesus of John's Gospel is the anodyne to this melancholic philosophy of life. Almost all of the 'I AM' sayings of Jesus parallel the negative attitudes of Coheleth."

415. Spykman, *Reformational Theology*, 478 (italics mine).

remains a book of great pastoral and evangelistic significance as believers and unbelievers struggle with the meaning of life amid its many enigmas.

It is important, however, that we not limit the relationship of Ecclesiastes to the NT to the places where it is quoted or alluded to.[416] Ecclesiastes has much to say about a range of ethical issues such as politics, wealth, community, and hedonism, and these need to be taken into account in biblical theology and theological ethics.[417] Furthermore, Jesus fulfills the whole of the OT, including the wisdom tradition, and as Witherington rightly argues, the wisdom traditions of the OT form an important background to the Jesus tradition in the Gospels.[418] What is rarely explored is Ecclesiastes' role in this respect, and yet its celebration of life and its affirmation of feasting resonate deeply with Jesus's ministry, especially as it is described in Luke's Gospel, in which Jesus seems to go from party to party: "Jesus literally ate his way through the Gospels."[419]

> Jesus went to meals, weddings and parties and had a feast-centred ethic. The images are vivid: water turned into wine; guests jockeying for places at table and being told to aim for the lower places . . . a woman sinner shocking the company by anointing Jesus and being forgiven by him; the reversal of expectations as the poor, handicapped and outsiders of all sorts are welcomed at the feast of the Kingdom of God while those who thought themselves sure of a place are left out; advice about not inviting to your banquet those who will invite you back; a master sitting a servant down and serving him; the Prodigal Son welcomed back unconditionally with the best robe, a ring, shoes, the fatted calf and a celebration; Jesus's last supper, which was probably also a celebration of Passover; Jesus washing his disciples' feet; and the mysterious meals of the risen Jesus.[420]

H. Anderson and Foley describe Jesus as "a Storyteller with Bread." They remind us

> how much of his ministry is remembered through the food and dining metaphors that provide the vernacular for narrating the Jesus event. His food was the will of the one he called Father, and this divine will, in turn, became the enduring banquet for any who dared to follow him. Jesus' ministry, his evangelizing, his

416. There are other echoes of Ecclesiastes in the NT, and I will refer to these in the commentary. See Krüger, *Qoheleth*, 32–34.

417. O'Donovan, whose writings I draw on repeatedly in this commentary, has done exceptional work on a theological ethics that is rooted in exegesis. However, he has not paid much attention to OT wisdom, and this remains to be excavated as a source, not least for political theology.

418. Witherington, *Jesus the Sage*. Hubbard ("Wisdom Movement and Israel's Covenant Faith," 28) notes that "Christ was not only master of the wise man's techniques. He was steeped in the wise man's message. He not only personifies wisdom, after the manner of Prov. 8, but He virtually identifies Himself with it. Surely it is *His* wisdom that will be justified by her deeds (Mt. 11:19)."

419. H. Anderson and Foley, *Mighty Stories, Dangerous Rituals*, 155.

420. Ford, *Self and Salvation*, 268.

legacy were so intimately linked to the ritual metaphors of dining and food that, in his fascinating book *Six Thousand Years of Bread* (1944), H. E. Jacob could title his chapter on Jesus as "Jesus Christ: The Bread God." . . . And as remembered over and over in the Gospels, they killed him because of the way he ate; that is, because he ate and drank with sinners.[421]

Ecclesiastes, with its particular emphasis on celebration and feasting, offers itself as a major source from which Jesus would have taken this understanding of the kingdom. In Matt. 11:16–19 Jesus specifically relates his eating and drinking to wisdom. The book of Revelation looks forward to the marriage feast of the Lamb, and John in his final exhortations encourages all those who thirst—and this side of the consummation of the kingdom we do indeed thirst—to come and drink of the water of life. Commenting on the Mary-Martha story in Luke's Gospel, in which Martha is busy while Mary sits at Jesus's feet, Augustine asks, "What was she doing? I know," he says, "She was eating Christ!"[422] That is ultimately the place to which Ecclesiastes must lead us. Only thus will we be able to love God with our whole hearts as "a kind of *cantus firmus* to which the other melodies of life provide the counterpoint. . . . Where the *cantus firmus* is clear and plain, the counterpoint can be developed to its limits."[423] Or as Simone Weil states in terms that resonate strongly with Ecclesiastes, "Man's great affliction, which begins with infancy and accompanies him till death, is that looking and eating are two different operations. Eternal beatitude is a state where to look is to eat."[424] Thereby we will interweave a theology of the cross with full involvement in the life of the world.[425]

One emerges from a study of Ecclesiastes with a strong sense that this book does indeed "make the hands unclean." For a sense of its contemporary relevance, as well as a psychological reading and its relationship to spiritual formation and preaching, see the postscript at the end of the book.

---

421. H. Anderson and Foley, *Mighty Stories, Dangerous Rituals*, 154–55.

422. Augustine, *Sermon* 179.5. Cf. *Ancient Christian Commentary on Scripture*, vol. 3: *Luke*, ed. A. A. Just Jr. (Downers Grove, IL: InterVarsity, 2003), 182.

423. Ford, *Self and Salvation*, 254.

424. Weil, *Gravity and Grace*, 90.

425. See Ford, *Self and Salvation*, 255.

I.
Frame Narrative:
Prologue
(1:1–11)

Translation

[1]The words of Qohelet, the son of David, king in Jerusalem.

[2]"Utterly enigmatic,"[1] says Qohelet, "utterly enigmatic, everything is enigmatic."

[3]"What is the benefit for humankind[2] in all one's labor at which[3] one labors under the sun?"

[4]A generation goes and a generation comes,
   but the earth stands forever.

[5]And the sun rises[4] and the sun sets,
   and it hurries to its place where it rises again.

---

1. The vocalization of the construct *hăbēl hăbālîm*, which occurs twice in this verse, is unusual. Many take it as an indication of Aramaic influence and thus as supporting a late date for Ecclesiastes. Fredericks (*Qoheleth's Language*, 222) disputes this. Cf. Schoors, *Preacher*, 1:75.

2. Literally "for the man." Qohelet has humankind in mind. See interpretation.

3. This is the first occurrence of the relative *še* in Ecclesiastes. Qohelet's extensive use of *še* (68 times) is used by scholars to argue for a late date for Ecclesiastes because *še* becomes dominant in late Hebrew. Fredericks (*Qoheleth's Language*, 102–4) disputes this. Schoors (*Preacher*, 1:56), however, asserts that "the distribution is such that Qoh[elet]'s use of ש betrays either a northern origin or a late date. Which of the two explanations must be preferred cannot be decided on the sole basis of the relative pronoun."

4. Because of the participles that follow in vv. 5–6, some commentators transpose the *waw* and *zayin* in *wĕzāraḥ* so as to read it also as a participle. However, the Hebrew MSS as a whole strongly attest to *wĕzāraḥ*, and I retain this form here. See Seow, *Ecclesiastes*, 106.

⁶Blowing northward and turning southward,
    round and round goes the wind,
    and the wind returns to its circuits.
⁷All the streams flow into the sea,
    but the sea is not full;
to the place to which the streams flow,
    there they continue⁵ to flow.
⁸Everything is wearisome;⁶
    humankind is unable to articulate it.
The eye is not satiated by seeing,⁷
    nor is the ear filled by hearing.⁸
⁹Whatever⁹ was¹⁰ is what will be,
and whatever has been done is what will be done,
    so there is nothing new under the sun.
¹⁰If there exists¹¹ a thing about which one can say,
    "See, this is new,"
it already existed in the ages
    that were before us.
¹¹There is no remembrance of those who came before;
    nor will those who are still to come
    be remembered by those who come after them.

Interpretation

---

¹The words of Qohelet, the son of David, king in Jerusalem.

1:1. *Title.* This verse is the title for the book. The expression "the words of" occurs frequently in the OT to introduce collections of sayings (cf. Jer. 1:1; Amos 1:1; Prov. 30:1; 31:1). Thus in the title the narrator introduces what follows as a collection assembled by one "Qohelet." "Words of" thus gives an

5. There is some debate about how to translate *šābîm*, as "return" or in the sense of "again," as here. Either way, the point of the text is the continuous, circular motion of the waters.

6. Whybray ("Qoheleth as a Theologian," 248–49) argues that *yĕgēʿîm* (wearisome) is more likely related to the noun *yĕgîaʿ* (effort or the result of effort) so that "wearisome" should rather be translated as "in constant activity." However, Whybray does acknowledge that in the two other places in the OT in which *yĕgēʿîm* occurs (Deut. 25:18; 2 Sam. 17:2), it does seem to mean "weary."

7. The use of *lĕ* here indicates the agent. See RJW §280.

8. *Min* is here used to indicate means (RJW §320).

9. Indefinite use of *mah*. See RJW §125.

10. There is some discussion of this verb's tense. See Isaksson, *Studies*, 75–76. There is nothing important at stake in the decision taken.

11. The Hebrew syntax here is difficult. I follow Gordis (*Koheleth*, 207) and Seow (*Ecclesiastes*, 110) in taking *yēš dābār* as having the force of a conditional sentence. Cf. RJW §479.

indication of the genre of the book. In 12:9–10 the narrator elaborates on the activity involved in bringing together this collection: Qohelet taught knowledge to the people, and he pondered and sought out and arranged many proverbs; he sought to find delightful words, and he wrote truth plainly. As we will see there, "words of" should therefore not just be thought of as sayings randomly assembled[12] but as a careful, reflective gathering and crafting of written material into a literary whole.

The nature of Ecclesiastes as collected and arranged sayings is probably further implied by the name *qōhelet*. Numerous suggestions have been made about the meaning of this name, which occurs seven times in the book (1:1, 2, 12; 7:27; 12:8, 9, 10), once with the definite article (12:8). The most likely derivation of the word is from the verb *qhl*, "gather" or "assemble." The feminine participial form here is not unusual in the OT in reference to particular offices in Israel.[13] Thus Qohelet could be thought of as the one who gathers Israel or who addresses the gathering[14]—hence the translation by some as "the preacher"—or, in my view, as one who gathers material for education of the public.[15] Indeed, there is no reason why *qōhelet* may not refer to both the one who teaches the public and the one who carefully gathers material for public education. The idea of *qōhelet* as the one who gathers the assembly seems less likely—the emphasis in 12:9–14 is on *qōhelet* as one who gathers material and teaches. Fox suggests that *qōhelet* means "teacher to the public," and he rightly discerns parallels with the personification of wisdom as a woman in Prov. 1–9 in which she preaches in the public areas of the city.[16] The title associates Qohelet with Solomon, as we will see below, and in 1 Kings the verb *qhl* is used of Solomon gathering the elders of Israel (1 Kings 8:1: *yaqhēl*),[17] and in 1 Kings 8:22 he addresses the

---

12. Galling (*Prediger*, 276–99) approximates this view. See Bartholomew, *Reading Ecclesiastes*, 73–74.

13. See Ezra 2:55, 57, and Neh. 7:59. On the feminine ending having a masculine referent, see *IBHS* §6.6b. Kamenetzky ("Rätselname Koheleth," 227) finds the comparison with Ezra 2:55, 57, and Neh. 7:59 unconvincing because the feminine forms there are family names. He argues that *qōhelet* is in the feminine form because it best expresses the individuality of the designated object. With regard to the feminine form, Hengstenberg ("Ecclesiastes," 594) notes, "The only correct explanation of this is, that Solomon was called Koheleth because he was personified Wisdom, *hḥkmh*, and that Wisdom spoke through him."

14. Joüon ("Sur le nom de Qoheleth") argues that Qohelet is an orator of the people, not just of an elite. See my discussion of 12:9.

15. Ullendorff ("Meaning of *qhlt*") follows Ginsberg's suggestion that *qōhelet* can only be a translation of an Aramaic form, and he goes on to note that in Aramaic-Syriac *qhl* means not only "to summon an assembly" but also "litigiosus, pertinax." Thus he suggests that *qōhelet* may mean "the arguer." However, as discussed in the introduction, it is unlikely that Ecclesiastes is a translation from Aramaic.

16. Fox, *Ecclesiastes*, 3.

17. Hiphil imperfect third-person masculine singular jussive of *qhl*. In the Hiphil, *qhl* means to summon an assembly.

assembly (*qěhal*).[18] Of particular relevance to Qohelet as the one who gathers the material set before us in this book is all the wisdom that Solomon gathered (cf. 1 Kings 4:29–34).

That we are to think of Qohelet as Solomon is made clear by the phrase "the son of David, king in Jerusalem." "King in Jerusalem" could refer to David or Qohelet, but in the light of 1:12 it is best to take it to refer to Qohelet. Only David and Solomon were kings over Israel in Jerusalem. "The son of David" must refer to Solomon. As established in the introduction, Qohelet is not really Solomon; what we have here is a royal fiction. In the interests of the journey in quest of wisdom that is to unfold in this book around the figure of Qohelet, we are to think of him as a Solomonic figure: wealthy, particularly wise, and with great authority.

As king *in Jerusalem* we should also note that this is the leader of God's people and someone familiar with the Israelite traditions as they have been embodied in the Sinai covenant and the Davidic covenant. We would not therefore expect Qohelet to be an unbeliever but someone who knows the ways of the LORD and whose responsibility it is to promote those ways among God's people.

"Qohelet" is thus a kind of nickname[19] for the central character of the book whose journey of gathering wisdom for the people the narrator presents to us. It is hard to know whether we are to think of Qohelet as a historical person. The literary nature of Ecclesiastes means that Qohelet may be a fictional construct by means of which the narrator presents his teaching. However, the narrator's comments about Qohelet in 12:9–14 incline me toward the view that Qohelet is most probably a historical person.

> [2]"Utterly enigmatic," says Qohelet, "utterly enigmatic, everything is enigmatic."

1:2. *Statement of the theme of the book.* Verse 2 and its virtual repetition in 12:8 are an inclusion that states the theme of Ecclesiastes. It is common in biblical literature to find a theme stated at the beginning and end of a section as a way of indicating what the section is all about. The word for "enigmatic" is *hebel*, which occurs here twice in a superlative construction and once in

---

18. Kamenetzky ("Rätselname Koheleth") argues that the background to the name Qohelet is found particularly in Chronicles, in which forms of the root *qhl* are regularly associated first with David (1 Chron. 28:1, 8; 29:1, 10, 20), then with Solomon (2 Chron. 1:3, 5; 5:2–3; 6:3). Kamenetzky argues, therefore, that the author of Ecclesiastes had access to the books of Chronicles and that Ecclesiastes must be dated later than Chronicles (ibid., 228). Chronicles was most likely written in the Persian period (539–333 BC), though some argue for a dating as late as the mid- to early third century. See discussion on dating in R. K. Duke, "Chronicles, Book of," in *Dictionary of the Old Testament: Historical Books*, ed. W. T. Arnold and H. G. M. Williamson (Downers Grove, IL: InterVarsity, 2005), 164–71.

19. So Longman, *Ecclesiastes*, 1; and N. Lohfink, *Qoheleth*, 10.

relation to "everything." In Hebrew, the way to express a superlative is to say "enigma of enigmas," which means "utterly enigmatic." Similar expressions in the OT are "holy of holies" (that is, most holy) and "song of songs" (that is, the best song).[20] This thematic statement by Qohelet is thus strong and emphatic. This is further enhanced (as if it needed it) by the repetition of the superlative, the further statement that everything is enigmatic, and the repetitive alliteration in the Hebrew of the letter *h*.[21] Qohelet here is represented as making as strongly as possible his point that he sees everything as utterly enigmatic. This shocking statement of the theme by the ruler of God's people in Jerusalem anticipates the journey he will embark on and the conclusions he will come to.

Hebel is a key word in Ecclesiastes, occurring thirty-eight times. Traditionally translated as "vanity," in recent decades an astonishing variety of translations of *hebel* have been proposed, such as "meaningless,"[22] "useless" (GNB), "absurd,"[23] "futility,"[24] "bubble,"[25] "trace,"[26] "transience,"[27] and "breath."[28] The literal meaning of *hebel* would appear to be breath or vapor. Isaiah 57:13 is an example of this usage, in which *hebel* parallels *rûaḥ* (wind): "When you cry out, let your assemblage of idols deliver you! But the wind will carry them off; a breath [*hebel*] will take them away. But the one who takes refuge in me shall inherit the land and possess my holy mountain."[29] However, in the majority of places in the OT where *hebel* is used—and in Ecclesiastes in particular—it is used metaphorically, and the challenge is to work out in *this* context the connotations of *hebel*.

Seow, with others, maintains that Ecclesiastes uses *hebel* in a variety of ways, so that no one translation covers all uses. He retains "vanity" as the translation "for want of an adequate alternative."[30] He notes the clear negative connotation of *hebel* in Ecclesiastes and points out that *hebel* is used of human life and experience, not of God or the universe in general. "The view that 'everything' is *hebel*, then, reflects not so much Qohelet's cosmology as

---

20. *IBHS* §14.5b.

21. See Jarick, "Hebrew Book of Changes," for insightful comments about the poetic implications of the orthographic similarities between "everything" (*hakkōl*) and "enigmatic" (*hebel*).

22. Longman, *Ecclesiastes*, e.g., 59.

23. Barucq, *Ecclésiaste*, 27–28; and Fox, *Ecclesiastes*, xix, although he translates *hebel* as "futility" in his translation.

24. See Crenshaw, *Ecclesiastes*, 57, but note that he changes his translation of *hebel* as he finds appropriate throughout the book. Krüger (*Qoheleth*, 42) translates v. 2 as "Futile and fleeting, said Qoheleth, futile and fleeting! All (that) is futile."

25. Burkitt, "Is Ecclesiastes a Translation?" 27–28.

26. Levy, *Qoheleth*, 12; and Braun, *Kohelet*, 45.

27. Fredericks, *Coping with Transience*, 11–32.

28. N. Lohfink, *Qoheleth*, 19.

29. Cf. also Job 7:16; 9:29.

30. Seow, *Ecclesiastes*, 102.

it does his anthropology. What is *hebel* cannot be grasped—neither physically nor intellectually. It cannot be controlled."[31]

Seow's approach alerts us that how we translate *hebel* will depend to a significant extent on how we read the book as a whole; thus the hermeneutical spiral of interpretation is unavoidable. Rather than his anthropology, what is at stake in Qohelet's quest is his *epistemology*, how we come to know such that we can trust the results of our explorations. Qohelet embarks on a quest for knowledge, and it is this exploration of the meaning of life that continually runs down into the conclusion: utterly *hebel*. In this respect Qohelet's quest does indeed include his view of God—Qohelet is after all king in Jerusalem—and of the cosmos.

Douglas Miller rightly notes that in order to understand *hebel* in Ecclesiastes we need to take seriously its metaphoric and symbolic nature.[32] He argues that *hebel*, whose basic meaning is vapor, is a tensive symbol: it holds together a set of meanings but cannot be exhausted by any one of them. Miller discerns three referents of *hebel* in Ecclesiastes: insubstantiality, transience, and foulness. He notes the significance of *hebel* being both motto (1:2 and 12:8) and refrain in the book. In the motto, according to Miller, *hebel* functions multivalently to refer to the totality of human experience, whereas in the refrains the referents are focused by the contexts.

Ecclesiastes does use *hebel* with a variety of nuances, and as here in 1:2, it always carries a negative connotation, but an important question is whether the symbol has a core meaning or referent. The common element in relation to Qohelet's epistemological quest is that if there is meaning and value, it cannot be grasped and is thus *enigmatic* or *incomprehensible*. As Miller notes, a live metaphor like *hebel* guards its meaning by the descriptive phrases associated with it. The proximity of *hebel* to "wind" is instructive in this respect, for Qohelet will repeatedly associate his *hebel* refrain with the phrase "striving after wind." The wind is real enough, but it cannot be grasped. This does not mean that there is no meaning, but that if there is it cannot be grasped. I thus suggest that the core meaning of *hebel* is "enigmatic." Seow notes, "Something that is *hebel* cannot be grasped or controlled. It may refer to something that one experiences or encounters for only a moment, but it cannot be grasped—neither physically nor intellectually."[33] Such an approach finds support in

31. Ibid.

32. D. Miller, "Qohelet's Symbolic Use of *hbl*"; idem, *Symbol and Rhetoric in Ecclesiastes*.

33. Seow, *Ecclesiastes*, 47. Murphy ("On Translating Ecclesiastes," 573) similarly argues with respect to *hebel* that "the nuance is incomprehensible rather than irrational." See also Gammie, "Stoicism," 178–80. Gammie (ibid., 179) notes, "It is apparent that the author of Qoheleth intends to stress in the passages where *hebel* is linked with *rĕ'ût/ra'yôn rûaḥ* the 'incomprehensible, ungraspable' nature of his quest for meaning." Ogden (*Qoheleth*, 22) similarly asserts that "the term *hebel* in Qoheleth has a distinctive function and meaning: it conveys the notion that life is enigmatic, and mysterious." For an older but similar argument see Staples, " 'Vanity'

light of the repetition of *hebel* in Ecclesiastes (and this almost always in the manner of a conclusion) and the central role of *hebel* in the motto embracing Qohelet's teaching, and it also alerts one to the value in translating *hebel* with one word, although we must be attentive to nuances as we proceed with Qohelet's journey. Even where *hebel* does not appear in a conclusion, its occurrence invariably connects with the *hebel* refrain throughout the book, and it is a vital clue for picking up on Qohelet's thought and irony. A good example of this is 5:7 [6], where Qohelet offers a clue as to the source of *hebel*. See the commentary on 5:1–7.

"Says Qohelet" reminds us that we are here busy with the narrator's introduction of Qohelet, who will not come onto the stage until v. 12. Verse 2 is thus the narrator's provocative summary of Qohelet's quest for meaning.

> [3]"What is the benefit for humankind in all one's labor at which one labors under the sun?"

1:3. *The programmatic question.* This verse expresses the programmatic rhetorical question that informs the whole of Ecclesiastes, not just the immediate context.[34] Qohelet's quest described in vv. 12–18 and continued throughout the book is an attempt to answer this question. This also means that although the question is laden with a sense of the agony of life "under the sun," it is a real question, and thus it is unhelpful to transform it into "a thesis statement of the preface: human beings have no advantage in all their toil 'under the sun.'"[35] Qohelet's autonomous epistemology *will* lead him to this conclusion, but to close the question down before his journey even gets going ignores the literary character of Ecclesiastes. The rhetorical question is common in Ecclesiastes; the thirty-two questions account for about 12 percent of the book.[36] The function of the rhetorical questions is to engage the reader by creating a gap in the reading: "These gaps 'beg to be filled, and as a result hook the audience, the pure psychology of interrogation guarantees the capturing of the reader's attention.' The intellectual 'vacuum' created by the rhetorical question pulls its victim into its circle of influence and drives the reader to solve its intellectual challenge."[37] Thus, although Qohelet will regularly conclude that he cannot find any benefit in labor, the openness to the rhetorical question of v. 3 is important to maintain—this openness invites the reader to participate in Qohelet's struggle about the meaning of life.

---

of Ecclesiastes." Ravasi (*Qohelet*) makes much of Ecclesiastes as enigmatic but translates *hebel* with the Italian *vuoto* (space, gap, void).

34. See Ogden, *Qoheleth*, 28–30.

35. Seow, *Ecclesiastes*, 111.

36. Christianson, *Time to Tell*, 219.

37. Salyer, *Vain Rhetoric*, 258. For a full discussion of the rhetorical questions in Ecclesiastes, see R. E. Johnson, "Rhetorical Question."

The noun "benefit" (*yitrôn*) occurs ten times throughout Ecclesiastes and only here in the OT.[38] It is one of several words that are repeated again and again and contribute to the repetitive literary style of the book. *Yitrôn* comes from the root *ytr* and means advantage, profit, or benefit. It may have a background in business with the meaning of profit.[39] Seow finds it important to translate *yitrôn* as "advantage" rather than "benefit" because he believes that *yitrôn* here is not just benefit but a surplus, something additional. He argues that for Qohelet it is not that labor has no meaning but that it gives one no additional "edge."[40] However, Qohelet's scrutiny of labor and the meaning of life will bring them into question at the deepest level so that it makes no sense to read *yitrôn* as an additional edge—the question becomes whether labor and life are of any *benefit* at all.[41]

"Humankind" (*'ādām*, lit. "man") occurs forty-nine times in Ecclesiastes and always refers to humankind in general, apart from in 2:8.[42] This alerts us to the universal nature of Qohelet's quest—he is asking fundamental questions about human existence. "Under the sun," another expression that occurs repeatedly (twenty-nine times), confirms this universality—Qohelet is concerned with the whole range of human experience.[43] "Under the sun" occurs only in Ecclesiastes in the OT.[44] Occasionally Qohelet uses the alternative expression "under the heavens" (1:13; 2:3; 3:1), but the meaning is the same as "under the sun."[45]

The noun "labor" occurs twenty-two times in Ecclesiastes, the verb "to labor" thirteen times.[46] Seow argues that labor has a distinctly negative

---

38. In addition to 1:3 it is found in 2:11, 13 (twice); 3:9; 5:9, 15 [8, 14]; 7:12; 10:10, 11.

39. Seow, *Ecclesiastes*, 103.

40. Ibid., 103–4. "Edge" is Seow's word.

41. Ogden ("Qoheleth's Use," 343) notes of *yitrôn* that "its usage is distinctive in being quite generalized in this context."

42. Most scholars regard 7:28 as an exception to this, but see the commentary on 7:23–29.

43. Longman (*Ecclesiastes*, 66) takes this expression to indicate the restricted scope of Qohelet's inquiry; it excludes the possibility of a transcendent yet immanent God. While Qohelet's focus *is* on human life, as "Solomon" he is clearly portrayed as one in the tradition of Yahwism, and in v. 13 he is clear that the task of work is one given to humankind by God. Thus his viewpoint certainly includes God and how belief in God bears on life "under the sun." Kline ("Is Qoheleth Unorthodox?") argues that in the OT "under the heavens" is primarily associated with God's curse and judgment and that "under the sun" and "on the earth" by association have similar connotations in Ecclesiastes. However, Qohelet's preference is for "under the sun" rather than "under the heavens," and his quest is about the meaning of life "under the sun"; to assume a negative meaning is to close down the quest before it has begun. Furthermore, in 5:18 "under the sun" is a positive expression, as is "sun" in 11:7.

44. See Seow, *Ecclesiastes*, 104–5, for nonbiblical, ancient Near Eastern uses of the phrase.

45. Seow (ibid., 105) discerns a different nuance between the two expressions. "Under the heavens" is a spatial distinction referring to the cosmos, whereas "under the sun" is a term for this world in contrast to the netherworld. As Seow notes (ibid., 104), however, both terms refer to the universality of human experience.

46. The verb *'āśâ* (to make) is also used to refer to work. See de Jong, "Book on Labour," 112.

connotation in Ecclesiastes and translates it as "toil" to indicate its implications of struggle and pain.[47] There is no doubt that Qohelet wrestles with the struggle and meaninglessness associated with much of human endeavor, but "labor," with its broad connotations of human endeavor in Ecclesiastes, is not always negative. Examples of a positive use of "labor" are 3:13 and 5:18 [17]. Indeed, Qohelet is out to explore the meaning(lessness) of all that humans engage in, and to interpret labor as negative here prejudges the very question Qohelet will explore. De Jong thus appropriately describes Ecclesiastes as "a Book on Labour" and rightly notes the centrality of the theme of labor in Ecclesiastes: "All sorts of aspects of human labour are investigated: for example, striving after wisdom, seeking pleasure, doing justice and the fruits of labour."[48]

> [4]A generation goes and a generation comes,
>   but the earth stands forever.
> [5]And the sun rises and the sun sets,
>   and it hurries to its place where it rises again.
> [6]Blowing northward and turning southward,
>   round and round goes the wind,
>   and the wind returns to its circuits.
> [7]All the streams flow into the sea,
>   but the sea is not full;
> to the place to which the streams flow,
>   there they continue to flow.
> [8]Everything is wearisome;
>   humankind is unable to articulate it.
> The eye is not satiated by seeing,
>   nor is the ear filled by hearing.
> [9]Whatever was is what will be,
> and whatever has been done is what will be done,
>   so there is nothing new under the sun.
> [10]If there exists a thing about which one can say,
>   "See, this is new,"
> it already existed in the ages
>   that were before us.
> [11]There is no remembrance of those who came before;
>   nor will those who are still to come
>   be remembered by those who come after them.

1:4–11. *A poem about the enigma of life.* Verses 4–11 are a poem that is deliberately placed between the programmatic question and Qohelet's first-person introduction of himself in 1:12. The distinction between poetry and

---

47. Seow, *Ecclesiastes*, 104. So too Longman, *Ecclesiastes*, 65.

48. De Jong, "Book on Labour," 112. For a stimulating discussion on work in the OT and Ecclesiastes, see W. Brown, "Whatever Your Hand Finds to Do."

prose is complex in Biblical Hebrew, and commentators debate as to whether vv. 4–11 are poetry.[49] However, the parallelism throughout these verses,[50] their chiastic structure,[51] and the abundance of participles in the early part of the poem argue in favor of this being poetic.[52]

It is unclear whether this poem is from Qohelet himself or the narrator, and if from Qohelet whether he wrote it or is quoting it. Whatever the case, it sets the context for 1:12–18 and what follows by giving us some idea why the programmatic question in 1:3 is such a tough one. Chiasmus in longer passages such as this one is not easy to determine, and one must be clear as to why one thinks it is chiastic.[53] It is mainly a careful examination of the *content* of these verses accompanied by the repetition of a key word in the center of the chiasm that inclines me toward the view that the poem has a chiastic structure:

A generations come and go, but the earth remains fixed (v. 4)

  B the repetitive circularity of nature (vv. 5–6)

    C as the sea is never full, so neither the eye nor ear are ever satisfied, so that everything is wearisome (vv. 7–8)

  B' there is nothing new under the sun (vv. 9–10)

A' there is no remembrance of people (v. 11)

The repetition of the root *ml'* in vv. 7–8 indicates their interrelatedness. The sea is never filled and neither is seeing or hearing, both of which are governed by the verb *ml'*. The "conclusion" to the poem that anticipates Qohelet's repetitive conclusions is also found in this center, at the start of v. 8: "Everything is wearisome."[54] Thus the chiasmus functions to indicate the midpoint of the poem,[55] its climax, and thereby to alert us to the sort of conclusion that Qohelet will come to again and again. The way in which the different parts of the poem parallel one another will become clear as we work through the poem.

49. The majority of commentators read these verses as a poem, but Longman (*Ecclesiastes*, 59) argues that they are prose since they lack the heightened presence of traits that define Hebrew poetry, namely, parallelism, terseness, and wordplay.

50. As indicated in the translation.

51. W. Watson (*Traditional Techniques*, 386–87) notes that "chiasmus does seem to indicate (in combination with other factors) that a particular passage is poetic in character."

52. For two very different poetic analyses of this text, see Backhaus, *Zeit und Zufall*, 8–11; and Good, "Unfilled Sea." Backhaus's analysis is part of a comprehensive "scientific" analysis of the text whereas Good's has the flavor of a literary reading. Backhaus (*Zeit und Zufall*, 8–9) concludes that 1:4–6 and 8–9 are poetry and that 1:7 and 10–11 are prose.

53. W. Watson, *Traditional Techniques*, 354–68.

54. Contra Krüger, *Qoheleth*, 49, who sees v. 9 as the summary or conclusion.

55. W. Watson, *Traditional Techniques*, 370.

The immediate context of the poem is the programmatic question of v. 3, and the following issues are raised in it as indications of why the benefit of labor is such a problem:

1:4	The earth exhibits permanence, but not so humankind. Generations come and go, and as we will see later in Ecclesiastes, this transience raises major questions for Qohelet of the value of labor (see, e.g., 2:18–23).[56] There is some debate as to whether *dôr* means generation or cycles of nature. Ogden has argued for the latter meaning, but semantically it is hard to be sure which meaning is intended.[57] However, if these verses do have a chiastic structure, then v. 11 supports reading *dôr* as "generation"—it is the coming and going of *human* generations that results in there being no remembrance of individuals. The text of 1:3, with its focus on "humankind," may also support reading *dôr* as "generation."[58]
1:5–6	In contrast to the earth, which *stands* forever, there is a lot of activity in nature, as indicated by the large number of participles in vv. 5–7,[59] evoking continuous action.[60] The sun and the wind are very active, but their activity is circular and repetitive and seems to go nowhere.
1:7–8	Amid this circularity nothing final seems to be achieved. Although the streams flow into the sea, it is never full, and the process is endless.[61] So too it is with human experience; as much as the eye can observe and the ear take in, there seem to be no final answers from these sources of seeing and listening to the programmatic question. Hence Qohelet's conclusion at the outset of v. 8: "Everything is wearisome."
1:9–10	There is nothing new in history. These verses connect with the repetitiveness in nature portrayed in vv. 5–6. Human action in history seems to be as circular as nature—it repeats itself without ever reaching closure.
1:11	This connects with v. 4. As generations come and go, people are forgotten, and so it will continue to be. One may labor very hard and achieve many things, but what is their value if all is lost in time?

56. Transience is part of *hebel*, but in the context of 1:2 it is clear that the permanence of the earth indicates that *hebel* is about more than transience. As Good ("Unfilled Sea," 64) muses, "Perhaps the point of the metaphor in *hebel* is not impermanence."

57. Ogden, "Interpretation of *dwr*." Building on this, Fox ("Qohelet 1.4") argues that "the earth" (*hā'āreṣ*) refers not to the physical earth but to humanity as a whole. For the same view as that of Ogden, see Whybray, "Ecclesiastes 1:5–7." Whybray argues that nothing is said about the futility of the phenomena described in 1:5–7 but that implicitly the reader is invited to contemplate their activity with wonder.

58. Good ("Unfilled Sea," 64) notes, "*Dôr* seems in some way to continue *'ādām*, since the word has to do with human generations."

59. In v. 5 "sets," "hurries," and "rises again" are participles. In v. 6 "blowing," "turning," "round and round goes," and "returns" are participles. In v. 7 "flow" (twice) and "continue to flow" are participles.

60. GKC §116a notes, "The *participle active* indicates a person or thing conceived as being in the continual uninterrupted *exercise* of an activity."

61. Ogden (*Qoheleth*, 31) suggests that the author may have the Dead Sea in mind, which, although it has no outlet, has many streams feeding into it but is never full.

Clearly, discerning the poetic, chiastic nature of this section is important and helpful for its interpretation. The continual passing of generations (v. 4) results in individuals not being remembered (v. 11). The way in which individuals are forgotten is a problem to which Qohelet will return again and again. If we are forgotten, then what is the value of all our labor? The circularity of nature (vv. 6–7) is paralleled by the repetitiveness of history (vv. 9–10). This too is a topic to which Qohelet will return. If history simply repeats itself and has no telos, then of what value is labor? Identification of the chiastic structure of this section is helpful in focusing our attention particularly on its center, vv. 7–8. Verse 8 expresses a conclusion that will recur in Qohelet's journey—here observation of the repetitiveness of nature and its parallel in human history leads to the conclusion that everything is wearisome, and neither *observation* (a major theme of Qohelet) nor *instruction* (what wisdom offers) resolves the question of what benefit there is to humankind's labor under the sun. The adjective "wearisome" occurs only here in Ecclesiastes but is akin to *hebel*, expressing the struggle and depression involved in trying to discern the meaning of work and thus life amid what one sees and hears.

The poem thus powerfully evokes the issues that Qohelet will struggle with as he seeks to explore the meaning of labor and life itself, and serves as an excellent lead into Qohelet's journey. As part of the frame, the statement in v. 8 that the eye is not satiated by seeing nor the ear filled by hearing is particularly significant. Observation is central to Qohelet's epistemology. As Crenshaw notes, "If asked, 'How do you know?' Qoheleth readily offers the answer, 'I saw it.'"[62] But already here we learn that observation by itself will not satisfy. Nor, it appears, will instruction, the domain of traditional wisdom teaching. In this way the poem evokes the horns of the dilemma on which Qohelet will find himself painfully perched; he problematizes the instruction of wisdom but cannot find resolution through observation.

Theological Implications

The primary background to reading Ecclesiastes is Proverbs. Like Proverbs, Ecclesiastes is associated with Solomon. As argued in the introduction, however, the association with Solomon is deliberately employed as a royal fiction, whereas in Proverbs, despite the complexity of authorship, the historical association with Solomon is stronger.[63] The title of Ecclesiastes thus creates an expectation for wisdom along the lines of that in Proverbs so that

62. Crenshaw, *Ecclesiastes*, 28.
63. See Waltke, *Proverbs 1–15*, 31–36. Of Ecclesiastes, Waltke notes (ibid., 35) that "although many allege that *The Sayings of Qoheleth* claims Solomonic authorship, in truth the late editor of that work credits *Qoheleth's* words to a Solomon-like figure, not to Solomon himself, in what appears to be a studied attempt to avoid the morally questionable practice of pseudonymity."

nothing prepares us in the opening verse for the shock both of the statement that everything is enigmatic and of the poem centered in the assertion that everything is wearisome.

That the central character in this book is called Qohelet—that is, the gatherer—is significant. To gather is to pull together into a unity, and wisdom involves seeing how things fit together in God's complex world. Ecclesiastes is full of irony, and it is likely that the name Qohelet is ironic or a parody. The figure introduced here is the great gatherer of wisdom and its literary articulation, but the question that will quickly emerge is whether even someone like Solomon is up to the challenge of holding together the riddles of human existence in this world.

Intriguingly, the notion of gathering plays an important role in Heidegger's understanding of human "Being" in his *Being and Time*. Heidegger calls the Being of humankind in the world *Dasein*, and Krell argues that "Dasein is the kind of Being that has *logos*—not to be understood derivatively as reason or speech but to be thought as the power to gather and preserve things that are manifest in their Being."[64] Heidegger asserts that logos has the "structural form of συνθεσις. Here 'synthesis' does not mean a binding and linking together of representations. . . . Here the συν has a purely apophantical signification and means letting something be seen in its togetherness."[65] Thus for Heidegger, gathering has to do with the intricate contexts of meaning in human life. Such contexts become visible particularly when things go wrong.[66] This bears directly on Qohelet and his quest and exposes the irony in Qohelet's name. For Qohelet things are badly wrong in the world, and he cannot see how things fit together—the intricate contexts of meaning have been shattered for him, and he does not know how to put things back together again. Irony is a central feature in the literary character of Ecclesiastes, and here already we see it in play. Qohelet is a Solomonic figure who gathers wisdom for the people, but ironically the gatherer's great problem will be how to hold the disparities in life together.

After 1:1 with its Solomonic associations, v. 2 comes as a tremendous shock. Traditional wisdom presupposes the meaning of life as God's good creation and seeks to trace the intricate contexts of meaning within that order. Qohelet appears to throw a grenade into the heart of that approach, affirming emphatically that everything is enigmatic, utterly incomprehensible! At the outset of Ecclesiastes, v. 2 alerts us not only to the conclusion that Qohelet will come to again and again but also to the content of the journey on which he will embark. His struggle is whether life is meaningful, and v. 2 alerts us to his struggle to

---

For the more common view that Proverbs has little if any connection historically with Solomon, see Fox, *Proverbs 1–9*, 56–58.

64. Krell, "General Introduction," 19.
65. Heidegger, *Being and Time*, 56.
66. Krell, "General Introduction," 19.

come to grips with where his research appears to lead him again and again: all is enigmatic. But it is important to note that this summary statement does not close the debate but rather opens it—the shock of the statement engages the reader in Qohelet's own struggle as we begin to wrestle with how a wise person akin to Solomon could make this sort of statement.

In terms of the interpretation of Ecclesiastes and of the theology of the book, there is much at stake in how we translate *hebel*. McKenna is exceptional and insightful in his theological reflections on *hebel*.[67] He argues for a concept of *hebel* that permeates the whole of Ecclesiastes as well as the particular contexts that Qohelet explores. McKenna asserts the importance of reading *hebel* against the background of the wisdom *and* covenantal traditions of the OT, and theologically he discerns as central the distinction between God as Creator and creation as contingent reality, whose meaning derives always from God and in relation to him. He finds Karl Barth's doctrine of the "nothingness" of creation helpful in explicating *hebel*. The nothingness of creation is not nothingness in the existentialist or nihilist sense but creation as nothing *in itself*; its existence and knowability depend entirely on God. Thus *hebel* positively means something like "contingency": "What doctrine is this? I would suggest it is the concept of the contingent rationality of the created reality of the world developed out of the belief that God created out of nothing and by his Word all that has been made to be outside of himself."[68] McKenna notes that such a doctrine of contingency polemically sets itself against the Greco-Roman approach to knowledge, which seeks to find truth starting from a point *within* the creation.[69]

McKenna discerns that the canonical and theological context within which we read Ecclesiastes will shape how we interpret *hebel*. Contrary to the aspirations of much historical criticism, objective, neutral interpretation is a myth.[70] As Gadamer has noted, it is our very prejudices—prejudgments—that make interpretation possible. This does not mean that we simply impose them on Ecclesiastes, but we allow them to illuminate the text as we wrestle with it. McKenna's theological interpretation of *hebel* indicates just how fruitful such an approach can be.

A close reading of *hebel* in Ecclesiastes would, however, nuance McKenna's approach as follows. *Hebel* has more of a negative connotation in Ecclesiastes

67. McKenna, "*Hebel* in Ecclesiastes."
68. Ibid., 22.
69. According to Gilson, *Spirit of Mediaeval Philosophy*, 64–83, whereas Greek philosophy could understand contingency in the order of intelligence, it could not extend that to the order of existence because the Demiurge or the Unmoved Mover does not grant existence. It is the identification of God with Being and all its post-Parmenedian predicates that led Christian philosophers to explore the existential contingency of the creation and its creatures. The notion of contingency is not found in the Greek world at all.
70. See Clouser, *Myth of Religious Neutrality*.

than McKenna allows for. *Hebel* does indeed relate to the contingency of creation, but in the context of Qohelet's autonomous epistemology, which he articulates in 1:12–18, contingency means that the order of creation is enigmatic and incomprehensible, and this is decidedly not good for Qohelet.

As philosophers of science have come to recognize, all data are interpreted within a framework, so that actual data are always *underdetermined* by a particular theory and the same data can be read differently in the context of a different paradigm or framework.[71] Popper expresses this evocatively in his images of the bucket and the searchlight.[72] According to the bucket theory of knowledge our minds are like containers in which knowledge accumulates. Popper rejects this approach to epistemology and argues instead for the searchlight theory, according to which a hypothesis or theory precedes and informs observation. In the framework of Qohelet's epistemology, *his searchlight*, the paradoxes of creation and life "under the sun" lead him again and again to the *hebel* conclusion. The very real data he discerns will need to be recontextualized in a very different framework for the positive side of creation as contingent to emerge. But this is to anticipate the later stages of Qohelet's journey. At this stage it is sufficient to note that Qohelet's intense struggle with the *hebel* of creation holds out hope for a resolution to the problem he wrestles with.

In the OT *hebel* is also the name for Adam and Eve's second son, Abel (Gen. 4:2). "Abel's name thus alludes unwittingly to the fate that is in store for him, for his life will be cut short."[73] The name of Abel's brother, Cain, is connected in Gen. 4:1 with Hebrew *qānâ*, meaning "to get, acquire," or, more rarely, "to create." The precise nuance is unclear, but "there is an ambiguity about her [Eve's] expression which may suggest that she covertly compares her achievement with Yahweh's greater works and hoped that he would be her own son."[74] There is good evidence that Ecclesiastes reflects at many points on Genesis, and it is possible that Qohelet's use of *hebel* has Abel and Cain in mind. Abel's unjust and meaningless murder is just the kind of datum that Qohelet wrestles with. The ambiguity in Eve's naming of Cain may also be helpful in our overall interpretation of Ecclesiastes. As in Gen. 2–3, what sets the world adrift is the human desire for autonomy and to play God, rather than embracing one's creatureliness.

71. In philosophy of science, the underdetermination theory was first articulated by Poincaré, *Science and Hypothesis*, in 1905. It was further developed by Reichenbach, *Philosophy of Space and Time*, in 1953. Glymour ("Epistemology of Geometry," 485) states the theory as follows: "There is a philosophical tradition going back to at least Poincaré, which argues that the geometrical features of the universe are underdetermined by all possible evidence, by all of the actual or possible coincidences and trajectories of material things, whatever they may be. Many different geometrical and physical theories can encompass the phenomena, can account for the motion of things."

72. Popper, *Objective Knowledge*, 341–61.

73. Wenham, *Genesis 1–15*, 102.

74. Ibid.

The programmatic question about labor in v. 3 frames the whole of Ecclesiastes, which is a response to this question. Labor/work is notoriously difficult to define. As Meilander notes, "In the history of the West work has no single meaning or significance. St. Augustine once said that he knew what we meant by time until asked to explain it; then he found that he did not really know what it is. Something similar is likely to be true of work."[75] It includes leisure and pleasure, architecture and landscape design, law courts and justice, work in general—indeed the gamut of human endeavor under the sun. In Ecclesiastes the range of human endeavors explored in Qohelet's quest to answer this programmatic question indicates the breadth of meaning in mind in the reference to labor in 1:3.

Qohelet is perplexed about the meaningfulness or benefit of labor as he observes the world around him. In *Shantung Compound* Langdon Gilkey describes in a similar way how he and others experienced work in an internment camp: "Work and life have a strange reciprocal relationship: only if man works can he live, but only if the work he does seems productive and meaningful can he bear the life that his work makes possible."[76] Through focusing on work in a comprehensive sense, Qohelet's quest thus becomes an interrogation of the very meaning of human life, thus exemplifying Gilkey's comment about the reciprocal relationship between life and work. The goodness of creation is in question: "The Rabbis . . . pointed out that the seven 'vanities' of 1:2 (vanity [1] of vanities [2] + vanity [1] of vanities [2] + all is vanity [1] = 7) refers to the seven days of creation and that K[ohelet]'s complaint is therefore directed against the entire creation and, by extension, the goodness theology that the Genesis narrative supports."[77]

The contemporary and pastoral significance of Qohelet's quest should not be underestimated. As with all biblical religion, Qohelet's concern is with *all* of human life as God has made it. The refrain "under the sun" evokes this comprehensive range as does the variety of areas of life on which he will focus. We find here no sacred/secular dualism that has contaminated much Christian thought historically. Qohelet is concerned with all of life under the sun, and he will cast his eye across all aspects of human life. One of the most significant missiologists of our time, David Bosch, poses the question, "What is it that we have to communicate to the Western 'post-Christian' public? It seems to me that we must demonstrate the role that plausibility structures, or rather, worldviews, play in people's lives."[78] To do this Christians would first need to recover the comprehensive range of biblical faith, that it deals with all of life as God has made it. Qohelet can help us with this in his albeit negative insistence that the question of meaning and thus faith, which of course he

75. Meilander, *Working*, 1.
76. Gilkey, *Shantung Compound*, 52.
77. Perry, *Dialogues*, 24.
78. Bosch, *Believing in the Future*, 48.

puts into question, relates to all of life and not just to a part of life that some call the sacred dimension.

The poem alerts us to two key issues that Qohelet will struggle with as he explores the benefit of labor and thus the meaning of life: the repetitiveness of history and the fact that people are not remembered. These issues are dealt with in more detail by Qohelet in the following chapters, and we will deal with their theological implications in detail there. Suffice it here to note that this poem expresses, on the basis of observation, a cyclical view of history, in contrast to the OT's cyclical *and linear* view. In the poem *observation* of the repetitiveness of nature leads to finding an analogical repetitiveness in history. As we will see in the next section, observation (v. 8) is central to Qohelet's epistemology, and if on the basis of observation one concludes that history is endlessly repetitive, then it is indeed hard to see the value of labor and of life.[79] One might find meaning in the fact that one's hard work and achievements will be remembered, but as the poem notes, no matter what one's achievements, people are quickly forgotten, so that meaning cannot be grounded in remembrance.

Theologically, the poem therefore raises the issue of how we view history and of where we locate our identity or meaning in life. Scripture and the Christian tradition rightly recognize, with this poem, that a cyclical view of history is hope-less, and also alert us to the fact that we cannot root our identity in others and their remembrance of us.

79. Tamez ("When the Horizons Close upon Themselves," 54) suggests that in the assertion that there is nothing new under the sun, Qohelet is reacting to a context in which all was new. Innovations in all areas of life took place in the period after the death of Alexander the Great and during the Ptolemaic period. She suggests that Qohelet rejected novelty because "he was sharp and daring in his ability to discern the negative consequences that the new Hellenistic economic order would bring to the non-Greek population." However, this poem and Qohelet make the less contextual and more ontological point that as far as one can see, history repeats itself again and again.

II.

Qohelet's Exploration
of the Meaning of Life

(1:12–12:7)

In this main body of Ecclesiastes, Qohelet himself comes onto the stage, introduces himself and his quest for meaning, and then proceeds to scrutinize different aspects of life and experience to see if meaning is to be found. In the light of his autonomous epistemology, he keeps coming to the conclusion that all is enigmatic. Regularly this conclusion is juxtaposed with the *carpe diem* passages, which evoke the joyful appreciation of life that he has learned from the Israelite tradition. The contradictory juxtaposition that results opens up gaps in the reading, gaps that indicate the excruciating tension emerging from Qohelet's journey of exploration. Breakthroughs occur in 5:1–7 and 7:23–29, but in both cases the breakthroughs, which illuminate the autonomous nature of Qohelet's epistemology, are followed by passages full of despair and struggle. Resolution comes in 12:1–7 through "remembering" and "rejoicing" but not apart from the struggles of life.

A.
Qohelet's Description
of His Journey of Exploration
(1:12–18)

Translation

¹²I, Qohelet, was[1] king over Israel in Jerusalem.

¹³I set my heart to seek and to explore by[2] wisdom all that is done under the heavens. It is an evil task that God has given to human beings with which to be afflicted.

¹⁴I have seen all the works that are done under the sun, and see,[3] everything is enigmatic and a striving after wind.

¹⁵What is crooked cannot be made straight, and what is lacking cannot be counted.

¹⁶I dialogued with my heart, saying, "I have demonstrated greatness and added to wisdom more than all who were over Jerusalem before me." And my heart observed much wisdom and knowledge.

¹⁷And I set my heart to know wisdom, and to know madness and folly. I know that this also is a striving after wind,

¹⁸for in much wisdom is much vexation, and the one who increases knowledge increases pain.

1. Longman (*Ecclesiastes*, 76) translates *hāyîtî* as "have been" in order to imply "was and still is." It seems to me that Qohelet is describing a past exploration of the meaning of life, and at that stage he was king over Jerusalem.

2. *Bĕ* here expresses means or instrument (RJW §243). "By wisdom" is a preferable translation to Longman's (*Ecclesiastes*, 77) adverbial translation "to explore wisely" because Qohelet here sets out not only his program but his methodology.

3. *Wĕhinnēh* often focuses attention on what follows.

Interpretation

Here for the first time we hear Qohelet's own voice, and until we come to the end of Ecclesiastes the book will be dominated by the first person "I" as Qohelet narrates his explorations and conclusions along the way. This first-person characteristic of Ecclesiastes alerts us to its autobiographical nature. For Whybray, "Even though in the first part of the book he [Qohelet] uses the device of pretending to be King Solomon . . . there is no doubt that throughout the book this 'I' is a real and not a fictitious 'I.'"[4] Such an assumption has been used by historical-critical scholars to locate the historical Qohelet and thereby discern later additions and sources. However, the comparison of Ecclesiastes with *fictional* autobiography confirms what we know from contemporary studies of literary autobiography: the "I" can be very elusive.[5] Much will depend here on whether we think Qohelet to be a fictional construct of the author or a historical person whose teachings are presented by the narrator. In the light of 12:9–14, I incline toward the view that Qohelet was a historical person. Nevertheless, his teachings are presented by the narrator, and his personal reflections must therefore be read in the light of the literary whole of Ecclesiastes. Qohelet's own voice is framed by the words of a third-person narrator, whose voice is evident in vv. 1–2; 7:27; and 12:8–14. Thus what we have in Ecclesiastes is the presentation of Qohelet and his quest by a narrator, and we cannot simply assume that the narrator and Qohelet agree. Indeed, a key element in the theological interpretation of Ecclesiastes is to be aware of the different voices and to inquire about their interrelationship (see pp. 77–79 of the introduction).

> **12**I, Qohelet, was king over Israel in Jerusalem.

1:12. In 1:12–18 Qohelet introduces himself and explains his project while also giving vent to the struggle and frustrations this journey evokes in him. Verse 12 repeats the royal fiction of v. 1. The royal dimension is important because we are to imagine Qohelet as the leader of God's people, that is, as a believer in the LORD, with wisdom akin to that of Solomon and with all the power and resources to embark on his project. Thus, when Qohelet asserts that he has seen all the works done under the sun (v. 14) and that he demonstrated greatness and added to wisdom more than those over Jerusalem before him (v. 16),[6] we are to take his resources for such an endeavor and achievements

4. Whybray, *Two Jewish Theologies*, 6.
5. See Bartholomew, *Reading Ecclesiastes*, 153–54.
6. It is unclear whether to interpret "before me" (*lĕpānay*) temporally or spatially. Solomon was only the second king of Israel to reign in Jerusalem, whereas a temporal interpretation implies many predecessors. Plumptre (*Ecclesiastes*, 111) thinks that Melchizedek and the Jebusite kings who reigned in Jerusalem before its capture by the Israelites are in view. Whybray (*Ecclesiastes*

seriously. As Seow notes, this section has the form of the ancient Near Eastern royal testament in which the king bequeaths his wisdom to his readers, but ironically this royal testament leads only to enigma and pain.[7]

> **13**I set my heart to seek and to explore by wisdom all that is done under the heavens. It is an evil task that God has given to human beings with which to be afflicted.

1:13. In the OT the heart is the center of the human person. This is no casual investigation that Qohelet is engaged in or a purely mental one; it is one that involves his whole person, and much is at stake in his quest. Qohelet describes his quest as to explore by wisdom "all that is done under the heavens." "All that is done" is a synonym for "labor" in the programmatic question of v. 3 and indicates once again the range of Qohelet's exploration. It is nothing less than a universal quest for the meaning of life, a struggle to discern what the human condition is all about.

It is vital to note Qohelet's description of his method of investigation: it is *by wisdom* (v. 13). Ecclesiastes is one of the three OT wisdom books (Proverbs and Job), and with Proverbs in particular as the background the reader initially assumes that "wisdom" here has the same meaning as it does in Proverbs, where *ḥokmâ* is the approach to knowledge that begins with and makes its foundation the fear of the LORD. As we will see, Qohelet's use of "wisdom" here is ironic, because Qohelet's epistemology—the method he uses to find answers to his questions that he can trust as true—turns out to be very different from the wisdom of Proverbs. Indeed, the difference from Proverbs is already evident in the dominance of the "I" we encounter from this point on. The center of Qohelet's quest will be his own consciousness, as manifest in observation, reason, and experience. Having drawn attention to the dominance of first-person verbs in Ecclesiastes, Whybray notes that "Qoheleth's claim to have made a *personal* investigation is also unique— and in this respect the book probably owes a great deal to the Hellenistic spirit."[8]

[NCBC], 51) thinks Qohelet made a slip and refers to the many Judean kings. Rudman ("Qohelet's Use of *lpny*," 146–47) argues for a spatial interpretation whereby the phrase refers to all those around Qohelet. Perhaps we should understand "before me" both temporally and spatially. Certainly a comparison with David would be significant and indicative of Qohelet's hubris as well as hinting at the irony in his claim.

7. Seow ("Qohelet's Autobiography") relates the royal fiction to 1:12–2:11. See ibid., 284: "Against that background, Qohelet's imitation of the genre is poignant in its irony. . . . The mention of the king's deeds, and especially the superiority of his deeds to those of his predecessors, leads to a surprising conclusion, one that is quite contrary to the purpose of royal texts. The legendary acts, wealth, and wisdom of Solomon turned out not to have abiding significance after all."

8. Whybray, "Qoheleth as Theologian," 240.

This summary also gives us a clear insight into the frustration Qohelet encounters in his quest and of the conclusions he repeatedly reaches. He sees the quest for meaning as unavoidable—it is given by God (v. 13)—but evil! There are many parallels to Gen. 1–3 in Ecclesiastes,[9] and here there is a shocking reversal of what we find in Gen. 1 and 2. There the task given to humankind is good, but here, in almost blasphemous terms, it is described as evil.

> [14]I have seen all the works that are done under the sun, and see, everything is enigmatic and a striving after wind.
> [15]What is crooked cannot be made straight, and what is lacking cannot be counted.
> [16]I dialogued with my heart, saying, "I have demonstrated greatness and added to wisdom more than all who were over Jerusalem before me." And my heart observed much wisdom and knowledge.
> [17]And I set my heart to know wisdom, and to know madness and folly. I know that this also is a striving after wind,
> [18]for in much wisdom is much vexation, and the one who increases knowledge increases pain.

1:14–18. Verses 14–18 explain why Qohelet views this task as evil: he finds enigmas in life that he cannot resolve so that the quest for meaning is like trying to get hold of the wind (vv. 14, 17). In v. 14, the key word *hebel* occurs, expressing the frustration and pain Qohelet experiences in his journey of exploration. This is followed by "and a striving after wind," a phrase repeated in v. 17. *Rĕ'ût* (striving) can mean to shepherd or to feed, to associate with, to strive, and to desire.[10] "To shepherd" and "to strive" fit the context best. Either way the meaning is clear—just as one cannot shepherd the wind, so one cannot grasp the meaning of life under the sun. Meaning may be there but it cannot be grasped—it is like trying to shepherd the wind—and the enigmas cannot be reconciled. As v. 15 expresses it, there is something crooked in the world and something lacking, but the world cannot be made straight, nor can what is lacking be counted. It is important to note that Qohelet does not deny that there is meaning, but he finds it impossible to lay hold of. "Enigmatic" expresses this more clearly than proposed translations such as "meaningless" or "absurd," which close down the very struggle that the reader is being called to engage in. By "wisdom" Qohelet seeks to know wisdom and madness and folly, but this too he finds to be like striving after wind (v. 17). His experience of "wisdom" is that it leads to vexation and pain.

In stark contrast, Prov. 1:1–6 heaps item upon item as it evokes for the reader the value of wisdom. Here Qohelet finds the search for wisdom evil

---

9. See "Reading Ecclesiastes within the Context of Proverbs and Job and Its Connection to the Torah" in the introduction to this commentary.
10. BDB 944–46.

and painful. How can that be? A gap is thereby opened in the reading as the reader is invited to accompany Qohelet on his journey of exploration in which much is at stake.

Theological Implications

In the summary of his journey in vv. 12–18, Qohelet establishes his resources for his exploration of the meaning of life and explains his methodology. The word used for his epistemology is *ḥokmâ*, the dominant word for "wisdom" in Proverbs. Thus we are led to expect an approach that makes its foundation the fear of the LORD. However, we are perplexed by the radically different direction this takes Qohelet compared with Proverbs. In stark contrast to Proverbs, "wisdom" here leads to enigma and vexation and pain. This arouses suspicion in the reader about the true nature of "wisdom."

Qohelet's epistemology is centered in his self-consciousness, his "I," and in this respect probably owes much to the Hellenistic spirit. Although Ecclesiastes is not philosophical in any systematic sense, Qohelet's methodology is redolent of the quest for certainty in modernity. Descartes, the French philosopher whose *Discourse on Method* was hugely influential in getting the Enlightenment going, similarly sought solid ground for certain knowledge about life. Legend has it that Descartes spent a day in an oven wrestling with this issue and coming to the conclusion that the only solid ground was his *Cogito*—hence his famous saying, *Cogito ergo sum* (I think, therefore I am). Everything else could and must be doubted according to Descartes, but once one found the solid ground in one's consciousness one could build rational, trustworthy propositions from there. William Temple describes Descartes' day in the oven as the most disastrous day in Western history,[11] and postmodernism has rightly developed a hermeneutic of suspicion of such attempts to ground knowledge in self-consciousness. Nietzsche, Freud, Heidegger, and their postmodern successors such as Lyotard and Foucault have played a vital role in unmasking the self. Thus for Freud, for example, the self is not innocent but "brings illusion and self-deception to the epistemological task."[12]

Modernity presented its grand narrative of human autonomy, reason, science, and progress as "wise" par excellence. However, after two world wars, the Holocaust, the nuclear threat, and the ecological crisis, postmodernism has helped us to see that much of that wisdom was folly. Theologically, therefore, Qohelet's journey is important, as will become apparent as his journey progresses, in pointing to the legitimate role of a hermeneutic of suspicion—not everything that calls itself wise *is* wise. The extremes of

11. C. Brown, *Philosophy and the Christian Faith*, 52.
12. Thiselton, *Concise Encyclopedia*, 234.

postmodernism have taken suspicion too far so that nothing can be trusted, least of all the living and true God, but this should not obscure the legitimate role of suspicion.[13]

In terms of his quest for meaning we should note the resonance of Qohelet's quest with the twentieth and twenty-first centuries, in which the question of what life is about has become acute. The twentieth century began with great confidence in reason and progress to lead us forward to a utopia, but this hope has been thoroughly undermined, so that Qohelet's question is one that our age constantly wrestles with. Having been interned himself, the psychiatrist Viktor Frankl noted from his experiences that one could survive almost anything if one found meaning in life.[14] So too did the psychiatrist Carl Jung, who in the process stressed the importance of recovering living religion as a basis for such meaning.[15] But the poignant question remains of whether life *really* is meaningful. As Marxism demonstrated, modern styles of work made the lives of millions a kind of hell. Ellul comparably notes how the evolution of work in the West since the nineteenth century makes a vocational approach to work impossible.[16] Graham Ward and others note that work fares little better in our postmodern context.[17] Thus by articulating the question of labor and its inevitable relationship to life, Qohelet connects with the struggles of our age in a major way.

Finally, it is important to note that Ecclesiastes is not just a book for unbelievers, as though it were an evangelistic tract. Qohelet clearly presents himself as a Solomonic figure, and thus one who has been immersed in the biblical traditions.[18] His crisis and journey of exploration is one of a believer, not of one unfamiliar with the ways of the LORD. Believers are not exempt from this sort of profound crisis of faith, hence the pastoral relevance of Qohelet. What does one do when precisely as a believer everything one observes and experiences seems to lead to the conclusion that all is enigmatic and that the enigmas cannot be resolved? This is Qohelet's struggle, and it resonates with

13. See in this respect Westphal, *Suspicion and Faith*.

14. V. E. Frankl, *Man's Search for Meaning: An Introduction to Logotherapy*, 4th ed. (Boston: Beacon, 1992). On Frankl's logotherapy, see R. F. Hurding, *Roots and Shoots: A Guide to Counselling and Psychotherapy* (London: Hodder & Stoughton, 1986), 126–37.

15. In his description of a personal conversation with Jung, M. Kelsey (*Encounter with God* [London: Hodder & Stoughton, 1972], 160) notes, "In talking with him I learned that he did not get into the area of meaning and religious direction because he wanted to, but because he could find no clergy who knew this realm to whom he could refer patients who needed help along these lines, and therefore he had to enter this area himself."

16. Ellul, *Ethics of Freedom*, 495–506.

17. S. Sassen (quoted by G. Ward, *Cities of God*, 242) notes that "place no longer matters and . . . the only type of worker that matters is the highly educated professional."

18. Davidson (*Courage to Doubt*, 195) notes that "we cannot come to grips with Qoheleth unless we see him as one brought up within, and thoroughly familiar with, the wisdom tradition in Israel."

that of any believer in a crisis of faith. In this respect we should observe that in comparison with Job, Qohelet's struggle has more of an intellectual nature than an experiential one resulting from the sort of suffering Job experienced. In our age, which still values reason despite the attacks it has suffered under postmodernism, Qohelet's quest speaks poignantly.

B.
Testing Pleasure
and the Good Life
(2:1–11)

Translation

> [1]I dialogued with my heart: "Come now, I will test you with pleasure and taste the good life."[1] But this also was enigmatic.
> [2]Of[2] laughter I said, "Madness!" and of pleasure, "What can it[3] do?"
> [3]I explored in my heart how to sustain my body with wine—my heart still guided by wisdom—and how to grasp folly, until I could see what[4] was good for humans to do under heaven in the few days of their life.
> [4]I did great works. I built residences for myself and planted vineyards for myself.
> [5]I made gardens and parks[5] for myself, and I planted in them all kinds of fruit trees.

1. Literally "see good." But *r'h* often means "to experience" as in 9:9. Cf. also Pss. 27:13; 34:12 [13]; 128:5. Hence my translation "taste." See Schoors, "Word *ṭôb*," 694; idem, "Verb *r'h*."

2. The preposition *lĕ*, which precedes "laughter" and "pleasure," is the *lamed* of specification. See *IBHS* §11.2.10d.

3. *Zōh* is a feminine singular demonstrative pronoun; here and elsewhere in Ecclesiastes *zōh* stands for *z'ōt*, and this leads some to see this as an example of late Hebrew style. But see Fredericks, *Qoheleth's Language*, 100.

4. *'Ê-zeh* functions here interrogatively. Cf. 1 Kings 13:12. See *IBHS* 327n25.

5. The word for "parks" is *pardēs*, one of two loanwords from Persian in Ecclesiastes. The presence of such loanwords is commonly regarded as evidence of a late date for Ecclesiastes (e.g., Ginsburg, *Coheleth*, 349). Seow (*Ecclesiastes*, 128) notes that *pardēs* comes from the Old Persian *paridaiḏa, which is first attested in an Elamite text dated to around 500 BC. Akkadian has the cognate *pardēsu*, and Seow (*Ecclesiastes*, 128) suggests that it "is probably by way of Akkadian that the Persian word came into Hebrew in the fifth century." However, Fredericks

[6]I made myself pools to irrigate the forest of growing trees.

[7]I acquired male and female slaves, and I had house-born slaves[6] as well. I also had many herds of cattle and flocks,[7] more than anyone who preceded me in Jerusalem.[8]

[8]I also gathered for myself silver and gold and the treasure of kings and of the provinces. I assembled male and female singers,[9] and the delights of men[10]—many concubines.[11]

[9]So I became great and I surpassed all who were before me[12] in Jerusalem. Moreover, my wisdom stood by me.[13]

[10]I did not withhold from my eyes anything they desired. I did not withhold any pleasure from my heart that brought joy in all my labor. This was my reward from all my labor.

[11]But then I reflected on all the deeds that my hands did and on all the labor at which I labored to do, and see, everything is enigmatic and a striving after wind. And there was no benefit under the sun.

Interpretation

[1]I dialogued with my heart: "Come now, I will test you with pleasure and taste the good life." But this also was enigmatic.

[2]Of laughter I said, "Madness!" and of pleasure, "What can it do?"

(*Qoheleth's Language*, 242–45) notes that it is possible that Persian influenced Hebrew early on, without being mediated through Aramaic.

6. Literally "sons of the house," i.e., children of slaves who were born while their parents or mother belonged to the household.

7. *Ṣō'n* (flocks) may refer to a flock of sheep or to one of sheep and goats.

8. It is hard to be sure whether the expression "who preceded me" (*šehāyû lĕpānay*) is to be interpreted temporally or spatially. Cf. note on "before me" in my comments on 1:12. Rudman ("Qohelet's Use of *lpny*," 146) argues that the phrase is here used spatially to refer to the wealthiest people around him, or literally "before" him. Either way the point is clear: Qohelet amassed great wealth.

9. It is possible to read this phrase as "I made for myself chains and necklaces." See Seow, *Ecclesiastes*, 130.

10. Here it is clearly more appropriate to translate *bĕnê hā'ādām* as "men."

11. Seow (*Ecclesiastes*, 118) translates *šiddâ wĕšiddôt* as "(humanity's treasures) in chests." This reading depends on the postbiblical meaning of *šiddâ* as chest or box. The word occurs only here in the Hebrew Bible, and it is hard to be sure of its meaning. Crenshaw (*Ecclesiastes*, 81) notes that comparison with Song 7:7 confirms the suspicion that *šiddâ* refers to women. Longman (*Ecclesiastes*, 92) thinks the most likely etymology is from *šad*, meaning "breast," so that we have here a crude reference to the use of women for sexual pleasure.

12. See note 8 above.

13. "Stood by me" is the literal translation. However, the idiom *'āmad lĕ* means "to serve, to help, to attend." See 1 Sam. 16:22; 1 Kings 1:2; Ezek. 44:11; Neh. 7:65; etc. I retain the translation "stood by me" because it connotes continuity.

2:1–2. The first area that Qohelet observes and experiences in his quest for what benefit humankind has in all their labor under the sun is that of pleasure and the good life. The word for "pleasure" in vv. 1 and 2, *śimḥâ*, can also be translated as "delight" or "joy" and need not have negative hedonistic connotations, but here in 2:1–11 there is undoubtedly an abandonment to sensuality in Qohelet's experiment. Indeed, Seow suggests that we should translate "I will test you" as "let me make you experience."[14] Certainly the test is one of full immersion. At the end of v. 1 and in v. 2, Qohelet already tells us his conclusion, as he will again in v. 11. In v. 2 he exclaims that laughter is madness and that pleasure cannot fulfill his quest. In 1:17 he explains that part of his quest is to know "madness" (*hôlēlôt*); here he finds the laughter accompanying his immersion in pleasure as "madness" (*měhôlāl*), but it is unfulfilling. In 1:18 he observed that "wisdom" brings only vexation and pain. Perhaps then the answer is to pursue pleasure directly. But the result is enigmatic. Observation and experience of pleasure will not finally satisfy or answer his quest.

> [3]I explored in my heart how to sustain my body with wine—my heart still guided by wisdom—and how to grasp folly, until I could see what was good for humans to do under heaven in the few days of their life.

2:3. The verb for "explored" is *twr*, which occurs here and in 7:25. Seow argues that "explore" makes no sense here and translates the start of v. 3 as "I went about in my heart."[15] However, in OT wisdom the heart is the center of the person, and "explore" makes perfect sense in that Qohelet's person is fully engaged in his exploration of wine as a means to pleasure and fulfillment. The precise meaning of "to sustain" (*limšôk*) in v. 3 is not clear. Literally the word means to drag or pull, but commentators debate its nuance here.[16] "Sustain" fits well with the sense of drag or pull because Qohelet is looking for that which will hold him through his struggle as to whether life is meaningful and provide an answer. In the face of this struggle many have turned to alcohol for comfort, and Qohelet considers this option. We are told not that he gave himself over to drunkenness but merely that he explored this option in his heart. Because he immediately notes that his heart was still guided by *wisdom*, conservative commentators have been quick to defend Qohelet against such

---

14. Seow, *Ecclesiastes*, 125–26. He argues that when the verb *nsh* is accompanied as here by verbs of seeing, hearing, knowing, and learning, it means "to experience." See Greenberg, "*Nsh* in Exodus 20:20," 273–76.

15. Seow, *Ecclesiastes*, 126–27.

16. See Longman, *Ecclesiastes*, 89.

debauchery.[17] However, the reference to wisdom here is ironic, and there is no reason to doubt that Qohelet's test included giving himself over to wine. This is confirmed by the expression "and how to grasp folly." In Proverbs "folly" is the opposite of wisdom, and in Eccles. 7:25 it parallels "wickedness." Thus in Qohelet's test he is going to explore pleasure as the world defines it and to drink its cup to the bottom to see if it does indeed provide meaning in life. As he notes in v. 3, human life is short, and perhaps the answer to life is to seize the day and squeeze as much pleasure out of it as one can.

What then do we make of his aside: "my heart still guided by wisdom [ḥokmâ]"? Qohelet's approach is so contrary to wisdom in Proverbs, where the abuse of wine[18] and taking hold of folly are warned against, that suspicion is aroused as to what sort of "wisdom" this is. In Prov. 23:19–21 the reader is warned not to be inebriated with wine, for drunkenness and gluttony will lead only to poverty. In Prov. 23:29–35 lingering over wine and continually trying mixed wines is said to lead to woe and sorrow and strife. Wine looks great when it gleams in the wine glass (v. 31) but it bites like a snake and poisons like an adder. Particularly relevant for our purposes is Prov. 31:1–9, in which King Lemuel's mother advises that it is not for kings to drink wine or to desire or crave strong drink, because it undermines wise judgment and thus the provision of justice for citizens. Here in Eccles. 2 the royal fiction is clearly in operation and yet "Solomon" is trying to find meaning in wine and pleasure. A gap is thereby opened in the reading, and one is forced to reflect hard on what "wisdom" could possibly mean here. We start to realize that what Qohelet calls "wisdom" is something quite different from what Proverbs calls "wisdom," and as we will explore in the theological implications below, it starts to become apparent that his use of "wisdom" is ironic. It is the same word as used repeatedly in Proverbs for "wisdom" (ḥokmâ) but points in a very different direction.

> [4]I did great works. I built residences for myself and planted vineyards for myself.
> [5]I made gardens and parks for myself, and I planted in them all kinds of fruit trees.
> [6]I made myself pools to irrigate the forest of growing trees.
> [7]I acquired male and female slaves, and I had house-born slaves as well. I also had many herds of cattle and flocks, more than anyone who preceded me in Jerusalem.
> [8]I also gathered for myself silver and gold and the treasure of kings and of the provinces. I assembled male and female singers, and the delights of men—many concubines.

17. See, e.g., Leupold, *Exposition of Ecclesiastes*, 60; and Hengstenberg, *Ecclesiastes*, 75–77.

18. On alcohol in Proverbs, see Longman, *Proverbs*, 550.

> [9]So I became great and I surpassed all who were before me in Jeru-
> salem. Moreover, my wisdom stood by me.
> [10]I did not withhold from my eyes anything they desired. I did not with-
> hold any pleasure from my heart that brought joy in all my labor.
> This was my reward from all my labor.
> [11]But then I reflected on all the deeds that my hands did and on all
> the labor at which I labored to do, and see, everything is enigmatic
> and a striving after wind. And there was no benefit under the sun.

2:4–11. Qohelet's embrace of debauchery could lead us to think of him as a lowlife, a bum, but vv. 4–10 make clear that his experiment with pleasure was sophisticated and wide ranging. The royal fiction is strongly in evidence here since the projects Qohelet embarks on and the possessions he accumulates fit with what we know of Solomon[19] and kings in the ancient Near East. The word *ʿśh*, "to do" or "to make," occurs seven times in vv. 4–11 and is part of Qohelet's vocabulary of work. Qohelet's list of accomplishments is paralleled by comparable lists in royal inscriptions found in the ancient Near East.[20] The Tell Siran Bottle, for example, speaks of the works of Amminadab, which include a vineyard, a garden, an enclosed park, and a pool.[21] Qohelet built multiple residences for himself and planted vineyards from which would come the exquisite wines with which he would try to sustain himself. These residences would include gardens and parks. Gardens were an important part of the irrigation economies of Mesopotamia and Egypt, and in the case of wealthy and influential persons the garden could be expansive and generally adjoined the residence. The ancient Egyptians also cultivated gardens, orchards, and parks, and wealthy families often maintained country estates where the owners could relax amid flowers, fruit trees, and ponds.[22] The parks might also contain animals for the pleasure of hunting. Qohelet notes that he also planted all kinds of fruit trees, the produce of which would bring pleasure to his palate.

Qohelet made pools to irrigate his forest of growing trees. Several pools are mentioned in the OT, including some in the area of Jerusalem (2 Kings 18:17; 20:20). In terms of the royal fiction it is worth noting that Josephus was aware of "Solomon's Pool," situated between the Pool of Siloam and Ophlas.[23] These pools were used to irrigate the fruit trees. A useful later example is that of the Siloam canal, an aqueduct carrying water from the Spring of Gihon

19. Cf. 1 Kings 7:1–12; 9:15; and 2 Chron. 8–16.
20. Seow, *Ecclesiastes*, 128.
21. Thompson and Zayadine, "Tell Siran Inscription"; and E. Smit, "Tell Siran Inscription."
22. See R. Harrison, "Garden."
23. Josephus, *Jewish War* 5.145.

along the Kidron Valley into a large pool. The canal has several openings that water the orchards and gardens situated along the Kidron.[24]

Qohelet's residences required many slaves, and these he acquired as well as their offspring, which would belong to him.[25] Slaves would also be needed to care for his herds and flocks, of which he had many. In v. 8 he refers to his royal treasure, much of it acquired from foreign tribute—"the treasures of kings"—and through taxation of the provinces.[26] His residences were full of valuable and aesthetically pleasing objects, and his singers (v. 8) provided the best music of the day. Royal inscriptions from the ancient Near East often note the presence of singers as one of the king's achievements.[27] Furthermore, these residences provided the context for the full enjoyment of sex—Qohelet had many concubines (v. 8). Qohelet is thus not exaggerating when in v. 9 he asserts that he became great. In the ancient Near East of his time he bears all the marks of royalty and greatness. As in v. 3 he again notes that his "wisdom" stood by him in all these activities.

Verheij perceptively notes the remarkable occurrence of a cluster of words in vv. 4–6 that also occur in Gen. 1 and 2.[28] "To plant" (root *nṭʿ*) in v. 4 also occurs in Gen. 2:8. "Garden" (*gan*, v. 5) also occurs in Gen. 2:8, 9, 10, 15, 16. "All kinds of fruit trees" (*ʿēṣ kol-perî*) in v. 5 also occurs in Gen. 1:11, 12, 29; 2:9, 16, 17. "To irrigate" (*lĕhašqôt*) in v. 6 also occurs in Gen. 2:5, 9. The Hebrew root *ṣmḥ*, meaning "to sprout," is found in v. 6 (growing) and also in Gen. 1:7, 16, 25, 26. Finally, the verb *ʿāśâ* (to make or do) is found in vv. 5 and 6 and in Gen. 1:7, 16, 25, 26, 31; 2:2, 3, 4, 18. Verheij notes, "Taken separately, these words are not remarkable . . . [but] their combined occurrence here and in Genesis . . . establishes a firm link between the texts."[29] The point of this link is that Qohelet "not only poses as a king, but even—for a moment—as God."[30] He attempts, as it were, to re-create Eden.

With Proverbs and Gen. 1–2 as background it is thoroughly perplexing how Qohelet could think that this approach to life is "wise" (vv. 3, 9). By drawing his method to our attention in this way Qohelet alerts us to its ironic nature—

---

24. Seow, *Ecclesiastes*, 129.

25. Cf. Exod. 21:2–11.

26. *Hammĕdînôt* probably refers to the new districts that Solomon created to sustain the state. See 1 Kings 4:7–19 and Longman, *Ecclesiastes*, 92.

27. See Seow, "Qohelet's Autobiography," 282–83.

28. Verheij, "Paradise Retried."

29. Ibid., 114. With Hertzberg, *Prediger*, 227–31, Verheij thinks that several parts of Ecclesiastes reflect the influence of Gen. 1–4.

30. Verheij, "Paradise Retried," 113. Cf. Bolin's ("Rivalry and Resignation") intriguing analysis of Ecclesiastes using René Girard's concept of mimetic desire, which, Bolin argues (ibid., 258), clarifies Qohelet's "advice that humankind give up its illusory desire to be like God." Barth (*CD* 3.2:151) asserts, "Perhaps the fundamental mistake in all erroneous thinking of man about himself is that he tries to equate himself with God and therefore to proceed on the assumption that he can regard himself as the presupposition of his own being."

it is not what it seems. In Gen. 1, God continually reflects on his creation and declares it good. In Gen. 1:31 he declares it "very good." Qohelet's response to his "creation" is radically different. In v. 10 Qohelet sums up his experience of this test of pleasure—he did not withhold from himself anything that might bring pleasure and resolve the question of the meaning of life for him. But did it work? The answer is a strong no (v. 11). Once he reflected on all his projects and his experiment with pleasure, he finds no resolution—all remains enigmatic and a striving after wind. He does not explain here why this was so, but the following section gives us some reasons for his disillusionment with his projects.

Theological Implications

In this first test we get a good look at *Qohelet's epistemology* in action, the means by which he will try to answer the question of the benefit of labor under the sun. Experience and observation are core elements. Pleasure presents itself as an answer to his question, and he abandons himself to it relentlessly, using all the resources at his disposal. He explores the pleasure of wine, extensive building projects, gardens and parks, the accumulation of wealth and treasures, music, sex, and so on, but all to no avail. Once he stops and reflects on this test, he concludes that it too leaves his quest unanswered.

Qohelet is at pains to name his epistemology "wisdom" (*ḥokmâ*, vv. 3 and 9), but clearly this is something very different from *ḥokmâ* in Proverbs, in which abandonment to wine, women, and pleasure as a way to find meaning is folly, not wisdom. In Proverbs the fear of the LORD is the beginning of knowledge/wisdom.[31] With this motto Proverbs enunciates a fundamental principle in biblical wisdom, as von Rad observes:

> The thesis that all human knowledge comes back to the question about commitment to God is a statement of penetrating perspicacity. . . . It contains in a nutshell the whole Israelite theory of knowledge. . . . There lies behind the statement an awareness of the fact that the search for knowledge can go wrong . . . because of one single mistake at the beginning. To this extent, Israel attributes to the fear of God, to belief in God, a highly important function in respect of human knowledge. She was, in all seriousness, of the opinion that effective knowledge about God *is the only thing that puts a man into a right relationship with the objects of his perception.*[32]

The result is that wisdom in Proverbs, as Fox has noted, is not empirical but observes the world from the vantage point of the fear of the LORD.

---

31. See Prov. 1:7; 9:10.
32. Von Rad, *Wisdom*, 67–68 (italics mine).

Qohelet depends on experience and reason alone, and in this sense manifests an autonomous epistemology that is quite different from that of Proverbs. His consciousness, his "I," rather than the fear of the LORD, is the center from which he operates, hence the constant repetition of the first person "I" throughout the book. That this is very different from real wisdom is made even clearer if Verheij is right about the intertextual links with Gen. 1 and 2, which alert us that Qohelet is trying to play God by reenacting Eden. What Qohelet calls "wisdom" may be quite the opposite. This is not to detract from the existential pain of his exploration but to attend to his *means* of exploration. His repetition of *ḥokmâ* in vv. 3 and 9 is intentional and foregrounds his method in a context in which it is something very different from *ḥokmâ* in Proverbs. Indeed, his use of "wisdom" here is ironic.

Philosophically the test that Qohelet here embraces is that of *hedonism*, the pursuit of pleasure as the key to meaning in life. This is a perennial temptation,[33] and there are many possible sources for Qohelet's exposure to this option. In Greek philosophy hedonism has its origins in the philosophy of Aristippus, who lived in the fifth and fourth centuries BC,[34] and his followers, known as the Cyrenaics. "The question concerning the content of the concept of the Good, which was not really answered by Socrates, was answered by these Hedonists, in that they declared pleasure to be this content, and indeed all pleasures, whatever their occasion, to be indistinguishable. . . . The highest, the only good, for these Hedonists was the enjoyment of the moment."[35] Later in the fourth century BC hedonism was further developed by Epicurus in Athens. In his philosophy everything is made subservient to the attainment of pleasure—science and virtue are valuable only insofar as they result in pleasure. Pleasure involves painlessness, a state of rest, and the fulfillment of wants. Epicurus prized spiritual above bodily satisfactions and particularly valued aesthetic enjoyment.[36]

The revival of hedonism in modernity can be traced to a number of English philosophers: Hobbes, Hartley, Bentham, James Mill, John Stuart Mill, the two Austins, and, more recently, Alexander Bain. This stream of philosophy is known as *utilitarianism*. Contemporary hedonists are usefully classified as either egoistic or altruistic. The former make the happiness of the individual the goal, whereas the latter make the happiness of the greatest number the goal. Qohelet would certainly fit with the former category—his concern in chap. 2 is with himself and personal fulfillment.

---

33. For a contemporary defense of attitudinal hedonism, see F. Feldman, "The Good Life: A Defense of Attitudinal Hedonism," *Philosophy and Phenomenological Research* 65.3 (November 2002): 604–28.

34. Probably 435–360 BC. See Windelband, *History of Ancient Philosophy*, 146.

35. Ibid., 148.

36. Ibid., 319–29. See also Strodach, *Philosophy of Epicurus*; and Rist, *Epicurus*, esp. chap. 6.

The occurrence of hedonism in fifth- and fourth-century Greek thought raises the question of Qohelet's relationship to it. As discussed in the introduction, it is hard to show direct dependence, and the spirit of Qohelet's quest in chap. 2 has little in common with the hedonism of Aristippus and Epicurus. For Aristippus, "Right enjoyment is only possible through reasonable self-control";[37] spiritual joy is prized above the abandonment to bodily satisfactions. Similarly for the Epicureans, the good life "involves disciplining of the appetites, curtailment of desires and needs to the absolute minimum necessary for healthy living, detachment from most of the goals and values that are most highly regarded, and withdrawal from active participation in the life of the community, in the company of a few select friends—in a word, plain living and high thinking."[38] Although Qohelet's hedonism includes aesthetic enjoyment, his abandonment to bodily pleasures is therefore significantly different from the hedonism of Aristippus and Epicurus. If one assumes a postexilic date for Ecclesiastes, the experience of exile and the disappointment of the postexilic recovery of Israel[39] would make fertile ground for the attraction of hedonism, but, in Ecclesiastes at least, of a different sort from that of the Cyrenaic and Epicurean traditions.

However we resolve the issue of Qohelet's relationship to Greek thought, the contemporary relevance of his quest is clear. Consumerism, one can argue, is the dominant ideology of our age, and central to consumerism is the quest for pleasure through possessions and experience.[40] The heroes of Western culture have multiple houses, accumulate phenomenal wealth, and are able to buy all the pleasures of life they desire. The undermining of modernity and the shattering of socialism have created an ideological vacuum in the West, and it has been filled by the grand narrative of consumerism that is driven by market fundamentalism.[41] Thus pleasure attained through alcohol, sex, multiple residences on different continents, music, and art have become the Good of our day. Yet the quest for fulfillment and meaning remains as elusive as ever. Depression has become so common that some are calling our age the "age of melancholy," in contrast to the "age of anxiety" that followed World War II.[42] To this context Qohelet's test of pleasure and his decisive no to its effectiveness speaks powerfully. Central to the problem with hedonism is its idolatry—pleasure is a creational good but hedonism seeks in pleasure what can be found only in the Creator. The allusion to Gen. 1 and 2 and thus the

37. Windelband, *History of Ancient Philosophy*, 149.

38. Strodach, *Philosophy of Epicurus*, 77.

39. Intriguingly, the Tg, identifying Qohelet as Solomon, sees Solomon as prophesying in Ecclesiastes about the future division of the kingdom and destruction of the temple.

40. See Bartholomew and Moritz, eds., *Christ and Consumerism*, 1–12.

41. See Goheen and Bartholomew, *Living at the Crossroads*, 114–19.

42. G. Collins, *Christian Counseling*, 84.

depiction of Qohelet as playing God alert us to this danger—Qohelet is attempting to recover meaning and even paradise by playing God.

While looking at chap. 1 of Ecclesiastes, I noted that Qohelet's concern with life "under the sun" serves as a powerful reminder that faith relates to the whole of life. In a negative way that concern is given content in chap. 2. The extent of his explorations is remarkable and includes cuisine, architecture, farming, gardening, relationships, and gathering antique and other treasures. Life "under the sun" is comprehensive for Qohelet, and although in this section he despairs of finding it meaningful, positively it reminds us that the question of faith and meaning relates to the whole of life as God has made it.

C.
The Problem of Death
and One's Legacy
(2:12–23)

Translation

> [12]And I turned to observe wisdom and madness and folly, for what will the man do who comes after the king? Only that which has already been done.[1]
>
> [13]I observed that wisdom is more beneficial than folly just as light is more beneficial than darkness.
>
> [14]The wise person has eyes in his head, but the fools are walking in darkness. But[2] I also know that the same fate awaits all of them.
>
> [15]And I dialogued with my heart: I also will meet the same fate as the fool, why then have I become so wise?[3] And I reflected in my heart that this also is enigmatic.

1. The Hebrew of this phrase is difficult, lit. "for what the man who comes after the king that which already they have done." The ancient versions struggled with it, and many suggestions and emendations have been proposed. See Schoors, *Preacher*, 1:156–57; Lys, *L'Ecclésiaste*, 230–37; Backhaus, *Zeit und Zufall*, 101–5; Smelik, "Re-interpretation of Ecclesiastes 2,12b." With Longman (*Ecclesiastes*, 96), Murphy (*Ecclesiastes*, 20), Krüger (*Qoheleth*, 58), and others, I follow the proposal that the verb "will do" be inserted or understood to be implied after the interrogative *mâ* (what). As Hertzberg (*Prediger*, 80) asserts, this is an example of aposiopesis (cf. GKC §167a), a rhetorical trope that suppresses the verb.

2. The *waw* here is adversative.

3. Commentators differ over the force of "then" (*'āz*) and "so" (*yôtēr*). The latter can be a noun or adverb, and those who take it to be a noun generally emend *'āz* to an interrogative (usually *'êy*). Thus Whitley (*Koheleth*, 24–25) translates: "And why am I wise, where is the advantage?" However, if *ḥākamtî* is understood as "become wise" (as is often the case), if *yôtēr* is taken as an adverb (so), and if *'āz* is understood in the temporal sense of "then," then the

¹⁶For the remembrance of neither the wise person nor the fool endures forever because already in the coming days[4] everything will have been forgotten. O how[5] the wise person dies just like the fool!

¹⁷And so I hated life, for the work that is done under the sun is evil to[6] me. For everything is enigmatic and a striving after wind.

¹⁸And so I hated all my labor at which I labor under the sun, for[7] I have to leave it to the person who comes after me.

¹⁹And who knows whether that person will be a wise person or a fool? Yet he will lord[8] it over all the labor at which I labored so wisely under the sun. This too is enigmatic.

²⁰And so I gave up my heart to despair concerning all the labor at which I labored under the sun.

²¹For[9] there was a person who labored with[10] wisdom and knowledge and success,[11] but he had to leave his legacy to[12] a person who did not labor for it. This also is an enigma and a great evil.

²²For what does a person get for all one's labor and anxiety of one's heart with which one labors under the sun?

²³For all one's days one's task is painful and grievous; even at night one's heart does not rest. This also is an enigma.

Interpretation

¹²And I turned to observe wisdom and madness and folly, for what will the man do who comes after the king? Only that which has already been done.

MT makes sense as it stands. According to *IBHS* §39.3.1i, *yōtēr* occurs as an adverb only in Ecclesiastes and Esther.

4. The juxtaposition of "already" with "in the coming days" causes some difficulty. As Seow (*Ecclesiastes*, 136) notes, the tension is probably deliberate, the point being that only too soon both fool and wise person will be forgotten.

5. The particle *'ēk* introduces an exclamatory question indicating Qohelet's lament that the wise person dies just like the fool. For comparable uses of *'ēk*, see 2 Sam. 1:19, 25, 27; Hos. 11:8; Isa. 14:12; etc.

6. The use of *'al* in the dative sense of "to" is characteristic of Late Biblical Hebrew (see Joüon-Muraoka §133.f).

7. The function of *še* here is causal.

8. In the OT the verb *šlṭ* occurs only in late texts. In the Persian period, it is used as a legal expression referring to the right to dispose of property. See Seow, *Ecclesiastes*, 136–37.

9. *Kî* here is causal (RJW §444).

10. *Bĕ* has the sense of means or instrument here (RJW §243).

11. *Kišrôn* occurs only in Ecclesiastes in the OT, here and in 4:4 and 5:11 [10]. It refers to achievement or success.

12. I take the third-person masculine suffix on *yittĕnennû* as datival, i.e., give *to* him. See GKC §117x.

2:12. "And I turned" indicates a change in focus and thus the start of a new section. In this section Qohelet turns to observe wisdom and madness and folly. "Madness" and "folly" mean the same thing, referring to behavior that is senseless and irrational. Fox reads the pair as a hendiadys meaning "inane folly."[13]

> [13]I observed that wisdom is more beneficial than folly just as light is more beneficial than darkness.
> [14a]The wise person has eyes in his head, but the fools are walking in darkness.

2:13–14a. In evocative images Qohelet articulates the traditional view that wisdom is better than folly, an example of the character-consequence structure that is clearly taught in Prov. 1–9. In v. 13 he makes the contrast in the strongest possible way: wisdom is like light and folly like darkness. They are polar opposites. Verse 14a is a proverb that elaborates on why wisdom is like light and folly like darkness. The wise person has eyes in his head, but fools walk in darkness. In Prov. 2:13 "walking in darkness" is the opposite of walking in the paths of uprightness. Without the light of wisdom the fool stumbles around in the darkness. Darkness evokes both evil in the sense of disobedience to God (cf. Prov. 2:12–15) and a lack of knowing how to live successfully. The wise, by comparison, "are able to see their way around in life, while fools grope about in the darkness of ignorance."[14] The image of the wise having "eyes in their heads" points to the heart of what biblical wisdom is about: knowing how to negotiate life with all its challenges. Fools, by contrast, are like the blind—they have no idea how to live and hence make a mess of their lives. Wisdom thus has a double advantage: it pleases God and enables one to negotiate life successfully.

> [14b]But I also know that the same fate awaits all of them.
> [15]And I dialogued with my heart: I also will meet the same fate as the fool, why then have I become so wise? And I reflected in my heart that this also is enigmatic.
> [16]For the remembrance of neither the wise person nor the fool endures forever, because already in the coming days everything will have been forgotten. O how the wise person dies just like the fool!
> [17]And so I hated life, for the work that is done under the sun is evil to me. For everything is enigmatic and a striving after wind.

2:14b–17. In this section Qohelet elaborates on two reasons why all his projects do not bring closure to his quest for meaning. There is first of all

---

13. Fox, *Qohelet*, 183.
14. Seow, *Ecclesiastes*, 153.

the problem of death. In v. 14b and v. 15 Qohelet immediately deconstructs the traditional view. He can see that wisdom is better than folly, but what difference does this make if both fool and wise person end with the same fate, death? If death is the end and both wise and fool end up there, what difference does it make how one lives? What then was the point of Qohelet becoming so "wise"? Thus he declares such traditional wisdom to be *hebel* (v. 15)—it does not make sense and is enigmatic, a mystery.

As we will see, death is a problem to which Qohelet will return again and again, not least in 12:1–7. Von Rad notes of death in the OT, "The fact of ultimate death first finds expression as a real intellectual problem in the teachings at the point where faith in Yahweh's support of life begins to disappear. This new situation, with all its disturbing consequences, is depicted in very impressive terms in the book of Ecclesiastes."[15] To understand Qohelet's struggle with death, we need some sense of how death was viewed in Israel.

Burkes discerns three categories of texts or themes about death in the OT.[16] First are texts such as Pss. 39 and 90, which express human ephemerality. In the OT the common expression for the place to which one goes at death is Sheol, and the second category of texts are those that describe what Sheol is like, texts such as Ps. 30:9 [10]; Job 7:9–10; and 10:20–22. Sheol is described as a place of darkness and gloom. To what extent this represents a continuation of existence is unclear. This picture of death has parallels in Babylonian and Sumerian writings. Third are texts that speak of God saving his people from death/Sheol. Examples are Ps. 16:9–11; Prov. 15:24; and 21:16. Proverbs 15:24 is particularly interesting: "The path of life leads upward for the wise, so as to avoid Sheol below." Burkes sees such texts as not literally referring to life after death but as a reference to quality of life. Waltke, however, says of Prov. 15:24, "This synthetic proverb escalates the rewards of righteousness from present joy to everlasting life in relationship with the LORD."[17]

Burkes herself notes that some passages in the OT seem to intimate the possibility of life after death, such as Pss. 49:15 [16]; 73:26; Job 19:26; Hos. 6:1–2; 13:14; Isa. 25:7; 26:19; 53:10; Ezek. 37:12–14; and Dan. 12:2–3. Apart from the passage in Daniel, Burkes argues that these passages are ambiguous as to whether they refer to a literal life after death or national restoration.[18]

In his thorough examination of death and afterlife in the OT, P. Johnston comes to some rather different conclusions from Burkes, especially as regards Sheol. "Sheol" is indeed the most common term in the OT for the underworld, to which one descends, but it occurs only infrequently in the OT and thus would not seem to be an important concept for OT writers. "Sheol" occurs entirely in

15. Von Rad, *Wisdom*, 305.
16. See Burkes, *Death in Qoheleth*, 10–33.
17. Waltke, *Proverbs 1–15*, 634.
18. Burkes, *Death in Qoheleth*, 9–33. See P. Johnston, *Shades of Sheol*, 218–39, for a more positive reading of the OT evidence for a belief in the resurrection of the dead.

contexts of personal engagement, or what Johnston calls "first-person contexts," and never in contexts of narrative or prescription. In most cases Sheol refers to human fate, as a destiny the righteous are anxious to avoid or as descriptive of difficult situations that they see as God's judgment on them. Mostly it is a judgment wished on the ungodly. Johnston demonstrates that in the OT Sheol is almost exclusively reserved for those under God's judgment, and that it seldom refers to the destiny of all humanity and then only in contexts relating to human sinfulness and the absurdity of life, an example of which is Eccles. 9:7–10. He is adamant that "Sheol is not used indiscriminately to describe human destiny at death,"[19] and asserts, "The underworld truly was a place of little interest to the Hebrew writers. They praised and feared Yahweh in this life and this world alone, and had little interest in the world below."[20]

On the whole, the OT undoubtedly has no clear doctrine of life after death such as we find in the NT. However, there is a strong intimation in this direction. Qohelet appears to be aware of and interacting with the early chapters of Genesis, and there we do indeed find a sophisticated reflection on death. Death in Gen. 2 and 3 is primarily about the severing of life with God, and physical death is merely a symptom of this thicker dimension of death. Disobedience leads to expulsion from Eden, the place of blessing and of God's presence. But through Abraham (see Gen. 12:1–3) God sets about recovering his purposes of blessing for all nations. This is no less than a recovery of his purposes in creation of blessing, and thus by implication of the overcoming of the sting of death. The result is that although the OT never explores in detail how death will be overcome, the impetus in that direction is clear. Burkes asserts, "The Israelites had practically no notion of an afterlife for the individual because of their finely honed sense of the people's survival in general under God's guidance; community continuity provided comfort in the face of death."[21] This is, however, to raise the question: what did they understand God's purpose to be with them as his people? If Gen. 12:1–3 gives us an important clue in this respect, then being part of God's people meant being part of his purpose to recover blessing for the nations, and that includes a recovery of life with God forever. Johnston notes, "Yahweh's proclaimed power to renew life, its occasional experience in life and vision, his authority over the underworld, and the desire for unending communion with him all contributed to the development of Israelite belief in resurrection."[22]

According to Van Leeuwen, Proverbs, like Yahwism, holds out hope for the triumph of justice without articulating how this will happen. He notes that there is a future-oriented retribution perspective in Proverbs, which lacks a doctrine of resurrection and yet insists on the triumph of God's justice. Van

---

19. Johnston, *Shades of Sheol*, 83.
20. Ibid., 124.
21. Burkes, *Death in Qoheleth*, 31.
22. Johnston, *Shades of Sheol*, 238.

Leeuwen regards this as a hallmark of Yahwistic faith. "The sages' stance is to maintain faith in God's justice, even when they personally cannot see it or touch it, even when the recorded past does not verify it. Here religion provides no escape from the pain or absurdities of existence. The book of Job was inevitable, not because Proverbs was too simplistic, but because life's inequities, as reflected in Proverbs, drive faith to argue with the Deity."[23] We should also note that God's redemptive purposes in the OT consistently center on Israel, so that it is not surprising that it is sometimes hard to know whether visions of the future refer to life after death or national restoration—indeed, one would not expect the OT to distinguish closely between these because of God's intention to fulfill his purposes for creation through the line of Abraham.

For Qohelet, however, death is the end, and it is the destination of both wise and fool. It is important here to bear in mind Qohelet's epistemology, his torchlight that he brings to the data of death. In this respect von Rad's comment (referred to above) about death as an intellectual problem taking hold where Yahwism starts to disappear is most perceptive. Qohelet is living at a time in which Yahwism appears to have run into the ground—God's promises to Abraham and Israel appear to have come to nothing. In this context Greek philosophy with its emphasis on observation and reason and experience is a powerful attraction. Empirically it is true that both wise and foolish die, and from what we can *observe* this indeed is the end for both. If this is the truth about death, then it certainly raises the most acute questions about life. Why bother spending time becoming "so wise" (v. 15)? Qohelet's "wisdom" has led him to turn traditional wisdom on its head. The emphasis on his becoming "so wise" again arouses suspicion in the reader as to whether this is really the case. As so often in Ecclesiastes, irony is again at work here—has he really become wise through his test of pleasure and the good life?

Second, flowing out of the universality of death is the problem of one's legacy. All Qohelet's projects were hard work and involved much labor and anxiety (v. 22), but what is the long-term benefit? As we saw in the poem in chap. 1, and as he asserts in 2:16, generations to come will forget him. In v. 16 he generalizes the notion of memory: neither the wise nor the foolish will be remembered forever—soon everything will have been forgotten. Proverbs 10:7 asserts, "The memory of a wise person is a blessing, but the name of the wicked will rot." But Qohelet notes that both will soon be forgotten. According to Silberman, in the OT "death, though no less the dissolution of [the] individual, lost its ultimacy, for the corporate person, family or clan or all Israel, endured."[24] It may be this sort of view that Qohelet has in mind. However, he is adamant that meaning cannot be located in remembrance because sooner or later both wise and foolish are forgotten.

---

23. Van Leeuwen, "Wealth and Poverty," 34.
24. Silberman, "Death in the Hebrew Bible," 26. See Burkes, *Death in Qoheleth*, 28–33.

> ¹⁸And so I hated all my labor at which I labor under the sun, for I have
> to leave it to the person who comes after me.
> ¹⁹And who knows whether that person will be a wise person or a fool?
> Yet he will lord it over all the labor at which I labored so wisely
> under the sun. This too is enigmatic.
> ²⁰And so I gave up my heart to despair concerning all the labor at
> which I labored under the sun.
> ²¹For there was a person who labored with wisdom and knowledge and
> success, but he had to leave his legacy to a person who did not
> labor for it. This also is an enigma and a great evil.

2:18–21. One has no control over what is done with one's legacy (vv. 18, 19,²⁵ 21). In v. 12 Qohelet asks what the man will do who succeeds the king. His somewhat enigmatic answer, which presupposes his cyclical view of history, is "only that which has already been done." Verses 18–21 explain what this will involve. One has to leave one's labor to the person who comes after, and one has no control over that person—they could be wise or foolish (vv. 18–19). In v. 21 Qohelet narrates an anecdote:²⁶ he has observed a person who worked hard and was very successful, but at death he had to leave it to one who did not work for it. The implication is that since this person has not worked for what he receives, he may be thoroughly foolish in how he handles his inheritance. Experience and observation are key elements in Qohelet's epistemology, and we see them at work here in his anecdote (cf. 6:2).

> ²²For what does a person get for all one's labor and anxiety of one's
> heart with which one labors under the sun?
> ²³For all one's days one's task is painful and grievous; even at night
> one's heart does not rest. This also is an enigma.

25. Verse 19 is the first of four places in which the question "who knows" (*mî yôdēaʿ*) occurs (cf. 3:21; 6:12; 8:1). See Crenshaw, "Expression *mî yôdēaʿ*," for a discussion of the ten places in which this expression occurs in the Hebrew Bible. Crenshaw distinguishes between occurrences that leave open the possibility of redeeming action (open door) and those that do not (closed door). According to Crenshaw, the occurrences in Ecclesiastes fall in the latter category. He asserts (ibid., 285) that in these verses in Ecclesiastes the expression signifies that "the door of hope has been firmly shut." *Mî yôdēaʿ* does indeed occur in passages in Ecclesiastes in which Qohelet is in the grip of his struggle with the enigma of life, but this very struggle indicates that the door of hope remains ajar, however marginally.

26. Seow (*Ecclesiastes*, 137) argues that "for there was a person" does not refer to a specific historical situation that Qohelet observed but introduces a general reflection on the human condition. Seow bases this on a parallel expression, *wn p3 nty*, in Late Egyptian texts. However, observation is a key element in Qohelet's epistemology, and it is typical of him to generalize from specific situations, as here.

2:22–23. The result is that Qohelet cannot find meaning in work or in his experiment with pleasure and the good life. Verse 22 repeats the programmatic question of 1:3 with a strong sense of nothing but pain and grief and despair (v. 23) as the answer. His existential experience of the tension and frustration this generates is excruciating: in v. 18 he speaks in the strongest terms of hating his labor and in v. 20 of succumbing to despair. In v. 23 he articulates the agony this question causes him—even at night he cannot find rest. Sleeplessness is a sign of the extent of just how disturbed his inner being is. His experiment with pleasure and the good life, which has included much labor, has not succeeded—all remains enigmatic.

Theological Implications

For Qohelet the repetitiveness of history, the end of life for all in death, and one's lack of control over one's legacy lead him to his conclusion that all is enigmatic. Living prior to the Christ event, Qohelet would not have had access to a clear doctrine of the afterlife and the renewal of all things through Christ at the end of history. However, contrary to much of the OT he espouses a view of history as cyclical, rather than cyclical *and* linear. Ricoeur explores the complexity of the ways in which time is viewed in the OT and concludes his synchronic reading of the different genres of the OT by noting that "the model of biblical time rests on the polarity between narrative and hymn and on the mediation brought about between telling and praising by the law and its temporal anteriority, prophecy and its eschatological time, and by wisdom and its immemorial time."[27] It is the cyclical repetitiveness of history, however, that seems to be central to Qohelet's thought (vv. 12b, 16), and because Qohelet lacks a NT perspective on the coming and consummation of the kingdom, one needs to have some sympathy for his struggle with history and the problem of death. On this side of the Christ event there is less room for sympathy as regards such a struggle. In chap. 3 we will examine more closely Qohelet's view of time and contemporary approaches.

Suffice it here to note that among some postmodernists (e.g., Jacques Derrida) Nietzsche's doctrine of repetitiveness in history has again become popular. One of Nietzsche's cosmological propositions is that all events recur eternally.[28] Schacht notes that "once Nietzsche became convinced of its truth it is only reasonable that he should have become all the more concerned with the problem of our responses to the idea of eternal recurrence, and that he should have continued to regard one's reaction to the idea as a decisive test of one's attitude to life; for he knew, from personal experience, that the idea

27. Ricoeur, "Biblical Time," 180.
28. Schacht, *Making Sense of Nietzsche*, 43.

could appear terrible indeed. In moments of pessimism and weakness he found the idea unendurable; while in moments of exuberance and strength, he embraced it enthusiastically."[29] Qohelet (v. 12) rightly finds the idea of eternal recurrence unendurable and would warn against finding hope in a renewal of such a view of history.

As regards death in our age, Ellul discerns two tendencies: first, to be obsessed with suicide and nihilism; and second, to naturalize death.[30] Of obsession Ellul writes, "In the music and films of the 1980s death is always bombastic and glorified. Every so often another astounding vindication of Mishima appears, whereas we would react more appropriately with compassion or horror. . . . Such praise is misplaced, since Mishima represents the equivalent of World War II's kamikaze pilots and the best of the Nazis. They scorned death to the point where they gave it and sought for it with the same amount of pride."[31] Yukio Mishima (1925–70) was a Japanese author and playwright, famous for both his nihilistic postwar writings and the circumstances of his ritual suicide by *seppuku* (a form of ritual death by disemboweling). The obsession with suicide is also found in more recent philosophers such as Foucault, who celebrated suicide. No conduct, he asserted, "is more beautiful or, consequently, more worthy of thought than suicide. One should work on one's suicide throughout one's life."[32] The tendency to naturalize death also remains very strong in our culture. This involves viewing death as a mere biological phenomenon that is entirely natural—it should neither scare nor outrage us.

Qohelet will have neither of these approaches—he rails against death and refuses to go gently into the dying of the light.[33] He confronts us with the abnormality of death and rightly denaturalizes it. As Ellul notes, Qohelet thus, in a negative and ironic way, shows us the way to wisdom because he confronts us with our finitude, of which death is the ultimate symbol. "Our aim is to keep our actions and words from being a chasing after wind, or mist that evaporates from a mirror. The only way to achieve this is to begin by crashing into a reality that is anything but wind!"[34]

Any wisdom worth its weight has to come to grips with death, the great enigma of life. Qohelet confronts us with its reality but at this stage provides no answer to the enigma. From a theological perspective death remains "the last enemy" but is contextualized in the story of God's purposes with the world.

29. Ibid., 44.

30. Ellul, *Reason for Being*, 173, 174.

31. Ibid., 173. That death continues to be an obsession in Western culture is evident from Dollimore's book *Death, Desire and Loss in Western Culture*, published in 1998. The book describes the influence of the death obsession in Western culture.

32. Dollimore, *Death*, 305. Dollimore discusses the centrality of death in modern and postmodern philosophy, as well as its growing entanglement with desire.

33. Allusion to Dylan Thomas's poem, "The Dying of the Light." See idem, *Collected Poems* (New York: New Directions, 1957), 128.

34. Ellul, *Reason for Being*, 172.

Bringing God into the picture makes all the difference. Biblically, death is a consequence of sin and the divinely imposed penalty on it. Death is a thick concept that should not be reduced to physical death: "But no matter how we slice the pie of human existence, nothing in us or around us escapes the death-dealing power of sin. It affects the whole person and every life relationship, dragging us down to defeat. We hear echoes of our own death knell in the monotonous funeral march of earlier generations: 'And he died, . . . and he died . . .' (Genesis 5:3–31). . . . The grim reaper wields a host of strangely formed sickles by which to claim his victims."[35] Pornography can be more devastating than an automobile accident. Education can be murderous:

> Poor teaching, pedagogic routine, a style of instruction which is, consciously or not, cynical in its mere utilitarian aims, are ruinous. They tear up hope by its roots. Bad teaching is, almost literally, murderous and metaphorically, a sin. It diminishes the student, it reduces to gray inanity the subject being presented. It drips into the child's or the adult's sensibility that most corrosive of acids, boredom, the marsh gas of ennui. Millions have had mathematics, poetry, logical thinking, killed for them by dead teaching, by the perhaps subconsciously vengeful mediocrity of frustrated pedagogues. . . . The majority of those to whom we entrust our children in secondary education, . . . are amiable gravediggers. They labour to diminish their students to their own level of indifferent fatigue.[36]

The effect of sin is that God's image bearers forfeit their right to exist and their reason for existence—Qohelet's great struggle. But God does not give up on his good creation. "He grants his creatures a stay of execution. He holds the full force of the death penalty in abeyance. Thus he makes room for the renewal of life, for his unfolding plan of salvation, for Israel, for planting a cross on a hill outside Jerusalem, for the empty tomb, for the church, for the coming of the kingdom, and ultimately for a Paradise regained, where death will be forever banished and life in its fullness restored."[37] As Spykman notes regarding the biblical story, "Nothing matters but the kingdom, but because of the kingdom everything matters."[38] For the present, however, death remains as "a living enigma," "the riddle of our existence—the relentless grip of death in the midst of a divinely preserved life,"[39] but for the wise its sting is neutralized. Death becomes in Christ the gateway into God's presence. Death for the fool becomes the gateway to judgment and ultimate death. As the Catholic Prayer of Commendation puts it, "May you return to your Creator who formed you from the dust of the earth. . . . May you see your Redeemer face to face."[40] As

---

35. Spykman, *Reformational Theology*, 335.
36. Steiner, *Lessons of the Masters*, 18.
37. Spykman, *Reformational Theology*, 335.
38. Ibid., 478.
39. Ibid., 335.
40. *Catechism of the Catholic Church*, 288.

Paul notes in 1 Cor. 15:54, the effect of Christ's resurrection is that "death has been swallowed up in victory."

The biblical story also casts a different light on one's legacy. In a fallen, broken world, this is, as Qohelet asserts, an enigma. A friend of mine spent years of his life building up a fine biblical studies department with a growing international reputation. Then, for no apparent reason, the department was virtually destroyed overnight. What does one make of this kind of experience? Many colleges of education have been founded on Christian principles, only to have these abandoned by later generations.[41] The country of Lebanon had made considerable progress in developing its infrastructure and improving the country as a whole, only to have immense damage wrought by an Israeli invasion in 2006.[42] Is nothing permanent? Does nothing last? Once again the biblical story with its eschatology of a new heavens and new earth contextualizes this enigma in a way that creates hope amid the struggle. Paul in 1 Cor. 3:10–15 evokes the image of our lives as houses built on the foundation of Christ. One can build on the foundation in different ways: gold, silver, precious stones, wood, hay, or straw. "The Day" will disclose what has been built because it will be disclosed with fire, and for that which remains after the fire one will receive a reward. Revelation 21:24 speaks evocatively of the treasures of the nations being brought into the new Jerusalem—such glimpses intimate that that which is done wisely will survive somehow into the new creation and receive its just reward. From this perspective how we live and how we shape culture is enormously important and of lasting, indeed eternal, significance.

41. See Burtchaell, *Dying of the Light*.
42. See Mearsheimer and Walt, *Israeli Lobby and U.S. Foreign Policy*, 306–34.

D.
Eating, Drinking,
and Enjoying One's Labor
(2:24–26)

Translation

24There is nothing better for a person than[1] to eat and to drink and to find his soul well in his labor. This too I have observed, that it is from the hand of God.

25For who can eat and who can experience joy[2] apart from him?[3]

26For to a person who is good in his sight he gives wisdom and knowledge and joy, and to the sinner he has given the task of gathering and amassing only to give to the person who is pleasing to God. This too is an enigma and a striving after wind.

1. The comparative is not marked in the MT. Seow (*Ecclesiastes*, 139) notes that the phrase in Hebrew is probably elliptical for the comparative. The sense is clear.

2. The translation of *yāḥûš* is much debated. Should it be translated positively (experience joy) or negatively (to worry; Longman, *Ecclesiastes*, 109)? The usual meaning in Biblical Hebrew is "to hasten," but that is inappropriate here. It is hard to be certain, but I take *yāḥûš* as a synonym for *yō'kal*. See de Waard, "Translator and Textual Criticism," 521–27. Seow (*Ecclesiastes*, 140) argues for "gather" as the appropriate meaning, which is antithetical to "eat" and refers to the sinner who gathers in the following verse. The effect on the meaning of this pericope is minimal.

3. The first-person ending on the preposition in the MT poses a problem if Qohelet is speaking. With the LXX, Syr, and some Hebrew MSS, I emend this to "him." For a full discussion, see de Waard, "Translator and Textual Criticism." An alternative (cf. ibid., 520) is to take this verse as a quote from God, in which case "me" would refer to God. However, the first person in Ecclesiastes normally refers to Qohelet himself.

Interpretation

This is the first of five *carpe diem* passages that occur in Ecclesiastes (see the introduction, "Genre and Literary Style"). Scholars have been perplexed as to what to make of this text following on from 2:1–23—does it advocate hedonism, and if not, how does it relate to what precedes?

> ²⁴There is nothing better for a person than to eat and to drink and to find his soul well in his labor. This too I have observed, that it is from the hand of God.
> ²⁵For who can eat and who can experience joy apart from him?
> ²⁶For to a person who is good in his sight he gives wisdom and knowledge and joy, and to the sinner he has given the task of gathering and amassing only to give to the person who is pleasing to God. This too is an enigma and a striving after wind.

2:24–26. Verse 24 starts with the *'ên-ṭôb* (better-than) form. This form occurs four times in Ecclesiastes, here and in 3:12, 22; 8:15; on each occasion it occurs in the context of one of the *carpe diem* passages. A number of the elements of this form also occur in 5:18 [17]. Ogden's analysis of the form reveals that it has two basic modes of expression. As in v. 24 the introductory *'ên-ṭôb* is followed by a preposition plus *'ādām* and either the relative *'ăšer/še* with Qal imperfect verb forms or *kî 'im* with infinitive constructs.[4] The *'ên-ṭôb* form is unique to Ecclesiastes but is probably a development of the "better-than" form in Proverbs, of which Prov. 16:8 and 27:10 are good examples.[5] Ogden suggests that Qohelet created this form and notes, "It is his means of setting forth his advice on how best to cope with a life which is God-given but fraught with enigmas such that man's limited knowledge and ability to comprehend it leave him without the final and absolute answers for which he craves."[6]

For Ogden, as for Whybray,[7] these *carpe diem* passages function as the answer to Qohelet's struggle and programmatic question. In my opinion, rather than functioning as an answer they are *juxtaposed* with the *hebel* conclusions as an alternative response to the programmatic question. To see this we need to examine the content of this section in more detail.

God is the central character in this section, whereas he is not referred to once in 2:1–23. This in itself signals that vv. 24–26 move in a different direction from vv. 1–23. Eating and drinking and enjoying one's toil are interpreted by

4. Ogden, "Qoheleth's Use," 350.
5. Ibid. On the "better-than" proverbs, see Bryce, "'Better'-Proverbs." There are some twenty of these in Proverbs.
6. Ogden, "Qoheleth's Use," 342.
7. Whybray, "Qoheleth, Preacher of Joy."

different commentators in very different ways. Loader, for example, argues that Qohelet's exhortation here to joy in life "can only be a sort of intermezzo in a meaningless life." "The Preacher's conclusion of joy is strongly reminiscent of Paul's words when he writes to the Corinthians: 'If the dead are not raised, "Let us eat and drink, for tomorrow we die."' . . . If there is no prospect beyond the grave, then all that remains for man is to enjoy himself as long as he can."[8] This approach sees the *carpe diem* passages as a despairing hedonism in the context of the meaninglessness of life.

However, 2:24–26 should not be seen just as a response to Qohelet's experience of the enigma of the world. In 2:26 Qohelet affirms the character-consequence structure that is central to Prov. 1–9. To a person who is good in his sight God gives wisdom and knowledge and joy, and to the sinner he gives the task of gathering and amassing only to give to the person who is pleasing to God. Seow insists that the sinner (*ḥôṭe'*) is not a religious category in OT Wisdom literature.[9] The pair *ṭôb*/*ḥôṭe'* occurs twice elsewhere in Ecclesiastes, in 7:20 and 7:26. As we will see below, 7:23–29 is a crucial passage in the interpretation of Ecclesiastes. Suffice it to note that I think Seow is quite wrong to suggest that *ḥôṭe'* is not a religious category. Proverbs as a whole strongly militates against such a view, rooting wisdom as it does in the fear of the LORD. Wisdom is different from *torah* (law) in its quest for God's order in creation, but the two are inseparable and both have their origin in God; thus one may sin by breaking God's law and by being unwise. Rather than sinners prospering and enjoying life (cf. Ps. 73), they suffer God's judgment, and what they amass is given to the righteous. In technical wisdom terms the character-consequence structure is in operation.[10] Thus Qohelet here affirms what he has subverted in the preceding section. In v. 23 labor yields vexation and pain, whereas here it is a source of joy and fulfillment.

Eating, drinking, and enjoying one's labor are furthermore here positively evoked as the gift of God and resonate with the goodness of creation as it is articulated in Gen. 1 and 2 (cf. Gen. 1:29; 2:9), Deuteronomy (7:13), and multiple other passages.[11] As Barth notes,

> The creation story in Gen. 1 right up to the creation of man is one long account of how God ensured and fashioned this space for man to live on earth. The story of the covenant . . . is also the history of Israel's conquest of the land by the will of God and its settling in the land by the same faithfulness and goodness—each "under his vine and under his fig-tree." . . . Indeed the Old and

8. Loader, *Ecclesiastes*, 41–42.

9. Seow, *Ecclesiastes*, 141.

10. See Bartholomew, *Reading Proverbs with Integrity*, 11–13.

11. As is apparent in Eccles. 12:1–7, Qohelet is familiar with the eschatological language of the prophets, and thus it is possible that the vision of the messianic banquet in Isa. 62:8–9 is a further source for his vision of life.

151

New Testaments generally have an extraordinary amount to say about such things as man's dwelling, food, drink and sleep, labour and rest, health and sickness . . . nor are these statements incidental only, nor overshadowed by the greater and more decisive matters at issue.[12]

In this respect the evangelical Reformers with their robust doctrine of creation were right in their approach to the *carpe diem* passages (see introduction, "The History of Interpretation"). The *carpe diem* passages celebrate creaturely human life as God has made it. The attitude recommended will certainly include eating and drinking and working, those fundamental, embodied human activities, but these activities are also metaphors for an approach to life, and one that differs fundamentally from that of *hebel*. Von Rad is thus quite correct to assert:

> It has been rightly stressed that this exhortation to be aware of happiness and of anything that enhances life is not to be confused with that zest for life which so often settles in the shadow of despair.[13] The situation is rather the reverse. Here for the first time, Koheleth is aware that he is in accord with a divine purpose; here he sees himself face to face with a beneficent God. . . . How excitedly this unyielding theologian speaks about God when he comes to speak on this subject.[14]

Eating and drinking and enjoying one's work are an expression of the shalom that God intended for his creation and humankind in particular.[15] It is the vision evoked with Eden in Gen. 2 and in the promises to the Israelites about the good land of Israel (see, e.g., Deut. 6:10, 11; 30:9). Thus Eccles. 2:24–26 is neither a despairing response to *hebel* nor an answer to what has preceded, as Whybray and Ogden suggest. It is rather an alternative vision set in contradictory juxtaposition to the conclusion of *hebel* that Qohelet's epistemology leads him to.

One might well ask, where does Qohelet get this vision from? The answer is found in remembering that Qohelet is clearly portrayed as a believer, a Solomonic figure who knows the OT tradition. Thus this shalom perspective articulates what Qohelet knows from tradition and experience, but what he does *not* know is how to reconcile it with his epistemology and observations that lead him in the contrary direction. Hence his statement in v. 26 that this too is an enigma. The contradictory juxtaposition opens up a gap in the

---

12. Barth, *CD* 3.4:338.
13. Contrary to Crenshaw (*Ecclesiastes*, 89), who asserts that Qohelet here "offers practical advice for living under the shadow."
14. Von Rad, *Wisdom*, 231.
15. Tamez ("When the Horizons Close upon Themselves," 62) evocatively refers to this vision as that of the "utopia of the quotidian feast."

reading as Qohelet, and thus the reader, wrestles with how to relate these contradictory answers to the programmatic question.

Verses 24–26 are a wonderful and refreshing vision of life after the hedonism and despair of 2:1–23, but the challenge is how to relate these verses to what precedes. Interpreters are constantly tempted to reduce the obvious contradictions in visions toward the despair pole or toward the joy pole. As explained in the introduction, we must avoid both approaches and must allow the contradictory perspectives to stand side by side. What we have here is an example of deliberate contradictory juxtaposition. Verses 24–26 articulate the orthodox wisdom perspective on life, and Qohelet would have imbibed this vision of life as a believer and as an Israelite. However, his observation and experience of life seem to contradict this vision, hence his quest for where real meaning in life is to be found. He cannot deny the power of the shalom perspective but finds it deeply in tension with his reason, observation, and experience. Central to his journey is the resolution of the tension between these two perspectives that threatens to tear him apart inside. Contradictory juxtapositions open a gap in the reading; they ask to be filled in some way, and this mirrors the gap in Qohelet's experience. How does he reconcile the tensions between what he observes and what he knows as a believer? In a nutshell, Ecclesiastes is about the resolution of that tension.

Theological Implications

Verses 24–26 articulate a glorious vision of our creaturely, embodied humanity, and they do this through two groups of three: "eating, drinking, working" and "wisdom, knowledge, joy." Theologically this passage is an expression of the biblical doctrine of creation. Barth explores this aspect of creation as it relates to the embodied nature of human existence under the heading "Respect for Life,"[16] noting that if justice is not done to the particularity and embodiedness of human existence, humankind's "freedom for God and in fellowship would be singularly majestic but also singularly problematic and docetic, hovering over the dark abyss of his multi-coloured vital being rather as the strange, purposeless and inactive spirit of Elohim did over the waters of chaos in Gen. 1:2."[17] As Barth notes, "It is a matter of the whole man."[18] He refers in this respect to Col. 3:17 and most explicitly to 1 Cor. 10:31: "Whether therefore you eat or you drink, whatever you do, do everything to the glory of God." In a way that is relevant to the resolution of Qohelet's struggle, Barth stresses that respect for life is possible only when we recognize that "man's

16. Barth, *CD* 3.4 §55.
17. Ibid., 325.
18. Ibid., 326.

creaturely existence as such is not his property; it is a loan. As such it must be held in trust."[19]

Theologically, a useful way to enter this rich vision is through "eating."[20] Wendell Berry asserts,

> Eating with the fullest pleasure—pleasure, that is, that does not depend on ignorance—is perhaps the profoundest enactment of our connection with the world. In this pleasure we experience and celebrate our dependence and our gratitude, for we are living from mystery, from creatures we did not make and powers we cannot comprehend. When I think of the meaning of food, I always remember these lines by the poet William Carlos Williams, which seem to me merely honest:
>
> > There is nothing to eat,
> > > Seek it where you will,
> > > > But the body of the Lord.
> > The blessed plants
> > > And the sea, yield it
> > > > To the imagination
> > Intact.[21]

Berry here rightly makes the connection with eating and God—as Qohelet says, this is from the hand of God, it is a gift. As Berry notes, however, our approach to food nowadays is miles away from this perspective. We live in an age of fast food and mass production for the market, but "like industrial sex, industrial eating has become a degraded, poor and paltry thing."[22] Consumerism has enveloped the food chain, and our kitchens have become like filling stations, our homes like motels.[23] How do we escape this and recover Qohelet's vision for eating as a gift of God? "By restoring one's consciousness of what is involved in eating; by reclaiming responsibility for one's own part in the food economy."[24] Berry suggests seven ways to recover this responsibility:

1. Participate in food production by growing what one can.
2. Prepare one's own food.

19. Ibid., 327.
20. For a fascinating discussion of the relationship between eating and human nature, see L. R. Kass, *The Hungry Soul: Eating and the Perfecting of Our Nature* (New York: Free Press, 1994). See also M. Pollan, *The Botany of Desire: A Plant's-Eye View of the World* (New York: Random House, 2001); idem, *The Omnivore's Dilemma: A Natural History of Four Meals* (New York: Penguin, 2006); and idem, *In Defense of Food: An Eater's Manifesto* (New York: Penguin, 2008).
21. Berry, "Pleasures of Eating," in *What Are People For?* 152.
22. Ibid., 147.
23. Ibid.
24. Ibid., 149.

3. Know the origins of the food you eat, and eat locally produced food.
4. Where possible, deal directly with a local farmer or gardener.
5. Learn, for self-defense, whatever you can about the technology of industrial food production.
6. Learn what constitutes the best farming and gardening.
7. Learn what you can about the life histories of food species.[25]

Similar comments could be made about drinking and work. As noted in the discussion of 1:3, our consumer culture denatures work for billions of people, all in service of the economy and production. In contrast to such an economy of competition, Berry invokes the notion of an economy of pleasure. He refers to Rev. 4:11, according to which God created all things *for his pleasure*, and Berry suggests that our motivation for work should be similar: "Our truest and profoundest religious experience may be the simple, unmasking pleasure in the existence of other creatures that *is* possible to humans."[26] "Our responsibility, then, as stewards, the responsibility that inescapably goes with our dominion over the other creatures, according to Revelation 4:11, is to safeguard God's pleasure in His work. And we can do that, I think . . . by safeguarding *our* pleasure in His work, and our pleasure in our own work."[27]

One might think with all our pleasure industries that ours is an age of pleasure par excellence, just as was Qohelet's experiment with pleasure in 2:1–11. However, the very existence of pleasure industries "can only mean that our economy is divorced from pleasure and that pleasure is gone from our workplaces and our dwelling places."[28] Rightly understood, and as evoked here in 2:24–26, work perfects pleasure:[29] there is nothing better! After describing his experience of the tobacco-cutting season, Berry articulates the satisfaction that should come from work: "It is possible, as I have learned again and again, to be in one's place, in such company, wild or domestic, and with such pleasure, that one cannot think of another place that one would prefer to be—or of another place at all. . . . Being there is simply all, and is enough. Such times give one the chief standard and the chief reason for one's work."[30]

As noted in the interpretation section, Qohelet evokes a general attitude toward life with his activities of eating, drinking, and working. As with Berry's approach, Qohelet's attitude is God centered. It is also a vision of *justice* in which sin is punished and good rewarded (v. 26). A good OT word for this vision is that of shalom (peace), which is intertwined in the OT, as in 2:24–26, with justice. Nicholas Wolterstorff takes the title of his book *Until Justice and*

25. Ibid., 149–50.
26. Berry, "Economy and Pleasure," in *What Are People For?* 139.
27. Berry, "God and Country," in *What Are People For?* 100.
28. Berry, "Economy and Pleasure," 139.
29. Ibid., 140.
30. Ibid., 143.

Peace Embrace from that wonderful phrase in Ps. 85:10 [11]. As Wolterstorff notes, shalom is more than an absence of hostility; "At its highest it is *enjoyment* in one's relationships. . . . To dwell in shalom is to *enjoy* living before God, to *enjoy* living in one's physical surroundings, to *enjoy* living with one's fellows, to *enjoy* life with oneself."[31] Wolterstorff discerns three characteristics of such shalom:

1. It involves a right, harmonious relationship with God and delights in his service.
2. It involves right relationships with others and delights in community.
3. It involves a right relationship to nature and delights in the creation.[32]

Wolterstorff concludes that shalom is God's cause in the world and that it ought also to be that of the followers of Jesus. "Shalom is . . . our human calling. . . . We are workers in God's cause, his peace-workers. The *missio Dei* is *our* mission."[33]

With Qohelet we are not yet at the point of the church's mission, of course. But proclamation of the gospel must be in word *and* deed, and Qohelet's *carpe diem* passage gives us an important clue as to the contours of such embodiment of the gospel. In the introduction (see "Ecclesiastes and the New Testament"), I explored the connections between passages like 2:24–26 and Jesus's eating and drinking and the kingdom of God. Suffice it here to note that the goal of salvation in Christ is the restoration of our full humanity, and that as Irenaeus notes, "the glory of God is the human person fully alive."[34] Full humanity *will* involve eating and drinking and enjoying one's work.

Indeed, vv. 25–26 stress *joy* as part of this approach to life. In his discussion under the heading "Respect for Life," Barth argues that joy is a divine imperative for humankind.[35] Barth defines joy as a form in which life's movement in time is temporarily subjectively arrested so that one experiences a sense of fulfillment. Life at these moments presents itself as a gift, as Qohelet points out. Barth notes how common the theme of joy and celebration is in Scripture and asserts that in the light of the Christ event

> it is now genuine, earthly, human joy; the joy of the harvest, wedding, festival and victory; the joy not only of the inner but also the outer man; the joy in which one may and must drink wine as well as eat bread, sing and play as well as speak, dance as well as pray. . . . We must also remember that the man who

31. Wolterstorff, *Until Justice and Peace Embrace*, 69.
32. Ibid., 70.
33. Ibid., 72.
34. Irenaeus, *Against Heresies* 4.20.7 (cf. ANF, 1:490).
35. See Barth, *CD* 3.4:374–85.

hears and takes to heart the biblical message is not only permitted but plainly forbidden to be anything but merry and cheerful.[36]

It is, of course, this very vision of joyful eating and drinking that highlights the brokenness and contradictions and enigmas we experience in life. The tension between shalom and life as we often experience it is at the heart of Ecclesiastes. Qohelet confronts us with how we live the tension between what God intends for life and our often painful experience of it.

36. Ibid., 376. Barth notes, "Joy is really the simplest form of gratitude."

E.
The Mystery of Time
(3:1–15)

Translation

> [1]For everything[1] there is a season,
>   and for every matter[2] a time under the heavens.
> [2]A time to[3] give birth[4] and a time to die,
>   a time to plant and a time to uproot what has been planted.
> [3]A time to kill and a time to heal,
>   a time to break down and a time to build.
> [4]A time to weep and a time to laugh,
>   a time to mourn and a time to dance.[5]

1. *Lakkōl* (for everything) could be translated as "for everyone," i.e., for every person (so Kugel, *Great Poems*, 310–11). However, the generalized and comprehensive list of activities makes "everything" the better translation.

2. *Ḥēpeṣ* occurs seven times in Ecclesiastes (3:1, 17; 5:4, 8 [3, 7]; 8:6; 12:1, 10). In 5:4 [3]; 12:1, 10 it means pleasure, but here in 3:1 and in 3:17; 5:8; 8:6 it appears to mean matter or activity, as the parallel to "every deed" in 3:17 suggests.

3. Kugel (*Great Poems*, 311–12) translates the recurring *lě* (to) as "of," thus "a time of giving birth and a time of dying," etc. He does this because he understands Qohelet to mean that like it or not, we will do these activities at certain fixed times. However, this is to read into the poem a determinism that is not present. See the interpretation. The *lě* is rather that of purpose (RJW §277).

4. *Lāledet* means "to give birth" and cannot be taken as "to be born," contrary to many commentators. The passive form is attested in 7:2, and the opposites in Qohelet's poem are not all strict antonyms.

5. In vv. 4b, 5a, and 8b the *lě* is omitted before the infinitive constructs. This breaks the poem's rhythm, and there is no apparent reason for it.

158

⁵A time to throw stones and a time to gather stones,
   a time to embrace and a time to refrain from embracing.
⁶A time to seek and a time to do away with,
   a time to keep and a time to throw out.
⁷A time to tear and a time to repair,
   a time to be silent and a time to speak.
⁸A time to love and a time to hate,
   a time for war and a time for peace.
⁹What profit is there for the worker in all that in which he labors?
¹⁰I have seen the task that God has given humankind to be preoccupied with.
¹¹He has made everything fitting⁶ in its time. Furthermore,⁷ he has placed eternity⁸ in their heart, but still⁹ one is unable to discern what God has done from the beginning to the end.¹⁰
¹²I know that there is nothing better for them¹¹ than to rejoice and to do good¹² in one's days.
¹³And also everyone who eats and drinks and enjoys the fruits of his labor—it is God's gift.
¹⁴I know that everything that God does will last forever; nothing can be added to it and nothing can be taken from it. God has done this so that they should fear him.¹³
¹⁵What is, has already been. What will be, has already been. And God will seek out what has been pursued.¹⁴

Interpretation

That 3:1–15 is a new section in Ecclesiastes is indicated by the *hebel* conclusion at the end of 2:26 and the change in topic from death and one's legacy to that of time. The theme of death recurs in this section but only in a minor

6. *Yāpeh* can mean "beautiful," but Qohelet is concerned here not with an aesthetic judgment but with the right, the appropriate, time. A similar usage is found in 5:18 [17].

7. *Gam* is used here in the sense of addition (RJW §378).

8. The translation of *hāʿōlām* is much debated; see the interpretation.

9. The phrase *mibbēlî ʾăšer lōʾ* is without parallel in the OT, and its translation is contested; see the interpretation.

10. *Sôp* (end) is typical of Late Biblical Hebrew.

11. Seow (*Ecclesiastes*, 158) translates *bām* more literally as "among them." In English, "for them" more accurately captures the meaning. Some commentators find it problematic that the suffix on *bām* is plural whereas that on "day" is singular. But as my translation indicates, the image may move from the group to the individual.

12. Schoors ("Word *ṭôb*," 694–95) argues that the expression "to do good" means "to enjoy the good things" rather than having an ethical content, but this is a false dualism. For Qohelet, the way to do good is to rejoice, eat and drink, and enjoy the fruits of one's labor.

13. There is some debate as to how to translate *šeyyirʾû*. See the interpretation.

14. Scholars disagree as to how to translate *yěbaqqēš ʾet-nirdāp*. See the interpretation.

way, although it will loom large again in 3:16–22. In terms of the organic logic of Qohelet's quest it is more important to notice the recurrence of the programmatic question in v. 9. This question is now addressed in relation to the mystery of time.

The structure of this section is as follows:

STRUCTURE

1. A poem on time (vv. 1–8)
2. A rhetorical question about the benefit of toil in such a timed world (v. 9)
3. Observational response to the question (vv. 10–11)
4. First confessional (I know) response to the question (vv. 12–13)
5. Second confessional (I know) response to the question (vv. 14–15)

3:1–8. *A poem on time.* This new section begins with a poem about time in vv. 1–8. Verse 1, which is more general in content, is the heading of the poem and summarizes its content. It also has a chiastic form (*a b b′ a′*): everything—a season : a time—every matter, which is not clear in the English translation. This internal parallelism is used here to open the segment of poetry.[15] The poetic style is clear from the repetition of the infinitive construct form,[16] a consequent recurrence of the long ō sound, the repetition of the word "time" (*ʿēt*), the intricate chiasmus, and the way in which the verses set out twenty-eight contrasting activities. This poem has the longest set of lines—fifteen in a row—with internal (half-line) parallelism in the OT.[17] Also significant is the antithetic nature of the internal parallelism, since the preferred type of internal parallelism is synonymous.[18] Loader notes that in 3:2–8 "we have the most intricate chiastic composition in the Old Testament."[19]

Loader has analyzed the poem in detail.[20] He notes that each of the verses in vv. 2–8 consists of two poetic lines, and each of these lines consists of two halves, the one half stating the opposite of the other (e.g., birth vs. death, plant vs. uproot). The two lines in each verse run parallel to each other. Each statement, according to Loader, refers to a favorable and an unfavorable matter, and in each verse these are parallel to each other. For example, v. 2 can be depicted as follows (F = Favorable; U = Unfavorable):

(F) birth   (U) die

(F) plant   (U) uproot

---

15. W. Watson, *Traditional Techniques*, 162.
16. Except in v. 8b.
17. On internal parallelism see W. Watson, *Traditional Techniques*, 104–91.
18. Ibid., 157.
19. Loader, *Polar Structures*, 11.
20. For Loader's detailed analysis, see idem, "Qohelet 3:2–8."

However, in v. 3 the order is reversed:

(U) kill	(F) heal
(U) break down	(F) build

One should note that "favorable versus unfavorable" is not appropriate for all the opposites that are described in the poem. Some fit this pattern but not all. Mourning (v. 4) is certainly less favorable than dancing, and making war (v. 8) less favorable than peace. But in most of the other antonyms, such a judgment is not clear. Giving birth (v. 2) may be a tough experience, as dying may be. Planting (v. 2) may be just as hard work as clearing a field. Thus although Qohelet describes opposites, he is not necessarily describing favorable and unfavorable activities. His concern is that for all these different activities and events there would appear to be a right time. In depicting the structure of the poem it is preferable to use + and − to indicate the opposite activities, as does W. Watson.[21]

Thus one finds the following chiastic pattern in the poem:

A	+	−	(v. 2)
	+	−	
B	−	+	(v. 3)
	−	+	
	−	+	(v. 4)
	−	+	
B′	+	−	(v. 5)
	+	−	
	+	−	(v. 6)
	+	−	
A′	−	+	(v. 7)
	−	+	
C	+	−	(v. 8)
	−	+	

Loader discerns four strophes in the poem—vv. 2–3, 4–5, 6–7, and 8—and notes that the pattern resembles that of a modern sonnet. A. Wright has sought to refine this structure by arguing that vv. 4 and 7 both refer to mourning and are the endings of two stanzas, each one expressing separate ideas: vv. 2 and 3 express constructive/destructive actions, and vv. 5 and 6 express union/

21. W. Watson, *Traditional Techniques*, 366.

separation.[22] Clearly chiasm dominates the structure of the poem; however, much will depend on how we read the individual verses.

> ¹For everything there is a season,
>   and for every matter a time under the heavens.

We do not know whether the poem is a composition by Qohelet or a poem he quotes. Either way it expresses his thought at this point and is marshaled as part of his argument. The poem deals with a major concern of biblical wisdom, namely, what is fitting or appropriate at a particular time.[23] Proverbs 26:1–12 is an excellent example of this—there is an appropriate time to answer a fool and a time not to answer a fool. Wisdom involves knowing the fitting time. Verse 1 states the general principle, which is then fleshed out in the rest of the poem: there is an appropriate season and time for every activity in the creation.[24] This principle rests, as OT wisdom does, on the belief in creation and its orderliness.

Loader, however, argues that Qohelet here only describes but does not prescribe. He is not saying what people *should* do but is merely describing situations and events people find themselves in. "When the occasion arrives, the event that fits it occurs. This is a deterministic view according to which fate has fixed all things in advance and there is nothing anyone can do about it."[25] Similarly, Murphy says of the poem that "its purpose is to underscore that all events are determined by God and are beyond human control."[26] From this perspective, the poem teaches a strong doctrine of determinism.[27] This view seems clearly wrong. Two activities in vv. 2–8 are out of human control, namely, giving birth and dying. However, every other activity is one in which humans can respond at the right time or choose not to. The second line in v. 2, for example, has agriculture in mind. It has its own order—there is a time to plant and a time to uproot, with a view to replanting. A good farmer knows the right time but has the freedom to ignore the rhythms of nature and plant in the wrong season and uproot in the wrong season, to his own detriment. The background to Qohelet's thought at this point is to be found in traditional wisdom and OT teaching according to which God has ordered his creation in a fixed way but humans

---

22. A. Wright, "For Everything," 321–28.

23. As von Rad (*Wisdom*, 138–43) notes.

24. Wilch (*Time and Event*, 120) emphasizes the number of pairs; there are seven double pairs, which "represent all the possibilities that may take place within the range of human activity and experience."

25. Loader, *Ecclesiastes*, 35.

26. Murphy, *Ecclesiastes*, 33.

27. This view is argued for most extensively in Rudman, *Determinism in the Book of Ecclesiastes*, e.g., 177: "Qoheleth's statement in 3:1 . . . and the catalogue of items in 3:2–8 outline a deterministic worldview in which all human actions and emotions are controlled by the deity."

are free to respond to that order as they choose.[28] The creation order that holds for agriculture is fixed but the human response is not. The same is true of the other activities described in the poem. Thus the poem does not articulate the sort of determinism Loader and Murphy refer to but, like Proverbs, speaks of the propitious time that correlates with how God has made the world.

Two words are used for "time" in v. 1, but it is difficult to discern much difference in meaning between them. Both refer to specific times rather than to duration, and the first word, zĕmān (a season), is used of appointed or predetermined time.[29] The second word, 'ēt, is the one that recurs throughout the poem and some eleven times in Ecclesiastes after 3:1–8. Qohelet's point is that the order in creation extends across the whole of it and hence he enumerates the gamut of human life and activities. Verses 2–8 list fourteen pairs of opposites and thereby evoke completeness. Qohelet is concerned with life "under the sun."

> **2**A time to give birth and a time to die,
>   a time to plant and a time to uproot what has been planted.
> **3**A time to kill and a time to heal,
>   a time to break down and a time to build.

As often with poetry, the references are open ended, and we cannot always be sure precisely what activities Qohelet is referring to or even if he intends a single meaning. Verses 2 and 3, the first strophe, deal with beginnings and endings. Verse 2 refers to human life and its limits—a time to give birth and thus a time of new life, and a time to die, whereas v. 2b refers to plant life—in agriculture there is a time to plant and a time to pull up what was planted. Planting and uprooting may also have a wider metaphorical reference, as the intertextual parallels to Jer. 1:10 indicate: "See, I have appointed you this day over the nations and over the kingdoms, to pluck up and to pull down, to destroy and to overthrow, to build and to plant."[30]

Blenkinsopp translates lāmût (to die) as "to take one's life," and thus as a reference to suicide. This is an important part of his argument that the poem

28. Passages like Ps. 1:3; Gen. 8:22; and the emphasis on creation order in Prov. 1–9 are obvious examples.

29. Seow, Ecclesiastes, 159. For discussions of Qohelet's vocabulary of time and of time in 3:1–11, see Barr, Biblical Words for Time, 99–100; Brin, Concept of Time; Wilch, Time and Event, 117–28; Schultz, "Sense of Timing"; Ratschow, "Anmerkungen"; and Fox, "Time in Qohelet's 'Catalogue of Times.'" As Schultz ("Sense of Timing," 267) notes, 3:1 introduces a theme that is taken up in various places in Ecclesiastes, such as 7:17; 8:1–9; 9:7–10; 10:16–20. Of Qohelet's use of 'ēt, he says (ibid., 262) that "nearly every passage in Ecclesiastes that employs the word . . . can be understood as harking back to and further developing or illustrating the 'doctrine of the times' as set forth in chap. 3." Brin's is the most thorough analysis of time in the Bible, but he pays little attention to the Wisdom literature.

30. W. Watson (Traditional Techniques, 156) notes that Jer. 1:10 "evokes Qoh. 3:2–8."

is from a "stoicizing Jewish sage," because of the positive attitude of the Stoics to suicide.[31] Blenkinsopp thinks that Qohelet quotes this Stoic poem and then refutes it in the verses that follow. He rightly does not think that the poem teaches determinism. As Rist points out, however, there was no single Stoic approach to suicide, and it was not central to Stoic thought.[32] Their acceptance of suicide in certain circumstances fits with the whole of classical antiquity in which suicide was common and justified in certain circumstances. The more natural sense of *lāmût* is "to die."

Verse 3 starts with the endings and is thus in a chiastic relationship to v. 2. There is a time to kill and a time to heal. "Killing" could refer to legitimate capital punishment or holy war and "healing" to the cultic restoration of a person or medical treatment. "Breaking down" could refer to destruction of buildings in war and "building" to the consequent reconstruction or to the normal processes of knowing when to tear down a building and when to rebuild.

> [4]A time to weep and a time to laugh,
>   a time to mourn and a time to dance.
> [5]A time to throw stones and a time to gather stones,
>   a time to embrace and a time to refrain from embracing.

Verse 4 deals with emotions—there is a time for grief and a time to celebrate. This is given a more concrete expression in v. 4b: grief manifest as mourning and celebration manifest as dancing. It is unclear precisely what v. 5 refers to, and Murphy asserts that "the peculiar nature of the metaphor remains unexplained."[33] Qohelet Rabbah interprets the gathering of stones as a reference to sexual intercourse and the throwing out of stones as sexual restraint.[34] This would fit well as a parallel to the second line in v. 5; however, the biblical support for this reading of "stones" is weak. Whybray takes the gathering of stones to refer to clearing a field for construction and the throwing of stones to refer to ruining a neighbor's field by throwing stones into it.[35] The problem with this view is that it makes this the only activity that is clearly sinful in the list of twenty-eight, and from a wisdom perspective there would not be a right time for such an activity. It is better to take this verse to refer to clearing a field of stones (to throw stones) and to gathering stones for building. In parallel to the second line in v. 5, this could mean that the land is cleared for the building of a house, a home, in the context of which embracing and refraining from

31. Blenkinsopp, "Ecclesiastes 3:1–15," 64. See Rist, *Stoic Philosophy*, 233–55, on the Stoics' approach to suicide.
32. Rist, *Stoic Philosophy*, 233–55.
33. Murphy, *Ecclesiastes*, 33.
34. Gordis (*Koheleth*, 230) follows this reading.
35. Whybray, *Ecclesiastes* (NCBC), 71.

embracing take place.[36] Embracing can refer to sexual intercourse or the more general showing of affection.

> [6]A time to seek and a time to do away with,
>   a time to keep and a time to throw out.
> [7]A time to tear and a time to repair,
>   a time to be silent and a time to speak.

Verse 6 probably has to do with possessions. There is a time to seek new ones and a time to let them go, a time to hold onto possessions and a time to get rid of them. The context of v. 7 may be that of mourning—a time to tear could refer to the tearing of a garment that signified grief (cf. Gen. 37:29 and 2 Sam. 13:31). A time to repair would then refer to the repairing of the garments at the end of the mourning period. Similarly, being silent and speaking might also refer to fitting responses to those in mourning—the book of Job provides a good example of how hard it is to know when to keep silent and when to speak.

> [8]A time to love and a time to hate,
>   a time for war and a time for peace.

Verse 8 deals with personal emotions (love and hate) and with public correlates to those emotions (war and peace). Hate need not imply something wrong and sinful; in Deut. 12:31, for example, God is referred to as "hating" the ways in which the Canaanites worshiped their gods, and the example is given of child sacrifice.

> [9]What profit is there for the worker in all that in which he labors?

3:9. *A rhetorical question about the benefit of toil in such a timed world.* Verse 9 poses again the programmatic question (cf. 1:3; 2:22) that Qohelet is seeking to answer. Now it is asked in relation to time and discerning what is fitting or appropriate in a particular situation. He recognizes that there is an order to creation (v. 11a), but does this help with his quest? Clearly not, as Qohelet says in v. 11. "I have seen" in v. 10 is a constituent part of Qohelet's

---

36. W. Watson (*Traditional Techniques*, 158) suggests that 3:5 may be translated "a time to expose sons and a time to accumulate sons." This involves taking *'bn* as a form of *bn* (son) with a prothetic *aleph* and *haślik* in the sense of "to expose." Cogan ("Technical Term for Exposure") argues that *haślik* is also a technical term employed when referring to an item one wishes to abandon. See also Redford, "Literary Motif of the Exposed Child." Loretz ("Poetry and Prose," 176) notes that for reasons of colometry, this proposal is unlikely. It also involves unnecessarily reading the *aleph* in *'bn* as prothetic and introducing an alien thought into the poem, namely, the idea that there would be a right time to expose sons, i.e., abandon them. Such an idea is abhorrent to traditional wisdom and Yahwism.

response to the apparent order in time. It evokes his epistemology or search-light that he brings to the data of life. Empirically one cannot discern the order in creation and thus cannot determine the right time for an activity. The reason for this, according to Qohelet, is that God has put eternity in humans' hearts, but one cannot discern what God has done from the beginning to the end (3:11).

> ¹⁰I have seen the task that God has given humankind to be preoccu-pied with.
> ¹¹He has made everything fitting in its time. Furthermore, he has placed eternity in their heart, but still one is unable to discern what God has done from the beginning to the end.

3:10–11. *Observational response to the question.* There are a number of dif-ficult issues in 3:10–15. First, how is "eternity" (*hāʿōlām*) to be understood?[37] Is it "world" (LXX), "a sense of past and future" (NRSV), "a sense of duration,"[38] "ignorance,"[39] "distant time,"[40] or "a consciousness of the eternal"?[41]

Second, should *mibbĕlî ʾăšer lōʾ* (but still one is unable) in v. 11b be under-stood as introducing a purpose clause, thus indicating that the presence of *hāʿōlām* ensures that humans will not understand what God is up to, or should it be understood in the sense of "but still," that is, as introducing a result clause and thereby referring to the limitations of human knowledge?

Third, how should the last part of v. 14, "they should fear him," be under-stood? Is *šeyyirʾû* to be understood to refer to fearing/standing in awe (Murphy) or seeing (Ogden)? Ogden translates v. 14b, "God has done (this) so that they might see (what proceeds) from him."[42]

Finally, how should *yĕbaqqēš ʾet-nirdāp* (he will seek out what has been pursued) in v. 15b be translated? Murphy translates, "And God seeks out what has been pursued,"[43] suggesting that the reference is to the past or events of the past. On the basis of parallels between vv. 14b and 15b, Ogden suggests "God requests that it be pursued," with "it" referring to the enjoyment of vv. 12–13.[44]

---

37. Although the versions all support the MT, emendations have been proposed. Thus Mac-Donald ("Old Testament Notes," 212) proposes to emend *hāʿōlām* to *hāʿāmal* and translate v. 11 as "also toil he has appointed for their heart (or mind), so that man cannot find out from beginning to end the work which God has done." However, the support of the versions for the MT should make emendation a last resort.

38. Murphy, *Ecclesiastes*, 34.

39. Whybray, *Ecclesiastes* (NCBC), 73–74.

40. Krüger, *Qoheleth*, 87.

41. Ogden, *Qoheleth*, 55.

42. Ibid., 57.

43. Murphy, *Ecclesiastes*, 29, 36.

44. Ogden, *Qoheleth*, 58.

In vv. 1–8 time signifies the right occasion for things to take place in a creation ordered by God. Scholars are disagreed as to how positively the author regards this order, but there is agreement that, as Murphy puts it, "these are God's times, not our times."[45] This provides the background for the rhetorical question in v. 9: In such a timed world what is the value and purpose of human labor and toil?

The first response in vv. 10–11 is a negative one. Everything may have its divine time, but the human cannot discover that time. Two contextual clues help in deciding how to translate hāʿōlām. First, as Murphy notes, the contrast between "time" and hāʿōlām suggests a temporal meaning, something along the lines of "duration."[46] Similarly, Krüger takes hāʿōlām to refer to a distant time "that extends far beyond the life of an individual human being in the direction of either the past or future or both."[47] Second, we should not ignore the recurrence of ʿōlām in v. 14, where it characterizes God's activity. These clues suggest that we should think of hāʿōlām as something to do with the way God has made humans and the world. In a timed world, humans recognize that "there is a time and a place" and that in order to discern this they need a sense of the larger picture, what philosophers might call origin and telos. However, Qohelet's problem is that they cannot get access to this larger sense of "duration."[48]

If this understanding of hāʿōlām is correct, then "but still" is probably the better understanding of mibbĕlî ʾăšer lōʾ. To translate this clause as "so that" portrays God as deliberately setting up this tension in human experience, an unlikely view in an Israelite context, especially if the author has Gen. 1 in mind. It is rather the limitation of human knowledge that Qohelet sees as making humans' toil enigmatic in vv. 10–11. The "gift" of "eternity" is a terrible burden from this angle.

> [12]I know that there is nothing better for them than to rejoice and to do good in one's days.
> [13]And also everyone who eats and drinks and enjoys the fruits of his labor—it is God's gift.

3:12–13. *First confessional (I know) response to the question.* The second and third responses to the question of v. 9 are introduced by "I know" (yādaʿtî), whereas Qohelet's observation that humans cannot discern God's works is

45. Murphy, *Ecclesiastes*, 39.
46. Ibid., 30.
47. Krüger, *Qoheleth*, 87.
48. Davidson (*Courage to Doubt*, 198–99) intriguingly suggests concerning hāʿōlām: "It may well be that Qoheleth is deliberately playing upon different meanings of this word, particularly the time, past, present and future theme and the idea of hiddenness." One suggestion is that hāʿōlām comes from a root ʿlm, meaning "to hide." Scott (*Ecclesiastes*, 220–21) thus translates hāʿōlām as "enigma."

introduced by "I have seen." These two "I know" responses are very different in content from the first "I have seen" response. Here the opportunity that God's order of creation presents for eating, drinking, and working is seen as a positive gift, in line with 2:24–26. Murphy recognizes the contrast but then goes on to suggest that the gift of eating and drinking appears to be a compensation for *hā ʿōlām*.[49] However, a number of factors suggest that what we have here is a juxtaposition of different responses rather than vv. 12–15 being a compensation for the negative conclusion of vv. 10–11.

Apart from the contradictory content, there is the fact that the knowledge in vv. 12–15 is not arrived at by observation, especially that in v. 14. It is much more of a confessional or traditional nature. The tension between vv. 9–11 and vv. 12–15 is made even stronger if one follows Ogden in translating the last part of v. 14 as "God has done (this) so that they might see[50] (what proceeds) from him,"[51] since this stands in stark contrast to "yet they cannot find out" in v. 11. The juxtaposition of being unable to find out and yet knowing would strengthen the contrast in this section. However, even if one translates v. 14b along the lines of "stand in awe before him,"[52] this still forms a strong contrast with the frustrated enigmatic response of vv. 10–11. The recurrence of the opening rhetorical question in v. 9 (cf. 1:3), with its implied negative answer, plus the reference to the harsh task that God has given humans in v. 10, strengthen the enigmatic focus of vv. 9–11.[53]

> **14**I know that everything that God does will last forever; nothing can be added to it and nothing can be taken from it. God has done this so that they should fear him.
> **15**What is, has already been. What will be, has already been. And God will seek out what has been pursued.

3:14–15. *Second confessional (I know) response to the question.* Verse 15, especially v. 15b, is not easy to interpret. On all accounts, it expresses God's sovereignty but should not be interpreted negatively, contra Whybray.[54] The language of v. 15a is akin to that where Qohelet reflects negatively on the repetitiveness of history. As Krüger perceptively notes, however, v. 15a "takes up the concept of a constant repetition of similar things from 1:4–11 and

---

49. Murphy, *Ecclesiastes*, 39.

50. *Šeyyirʾû* could be the Qal imperfect of "to see" or "to fear."

51. Ogden, *Qoheleth*, 57.

52. I understand this sense of fearing God in a far more positive, mainstream OT way than Murphy ("Qohelet's 'Quarrel' with the Fathers," 241), who agrees with Zimmerli that such fear involves living under a closed heaven. Contra Crenshaw ("Eternal Gospel," 48) as well, I do not think that Qohelet here articulates a pessimistic determinism.

53. I agree with Murphy (*Ecclesiastes*, 34), contra Ogden (*Qoheleth*, 54–55), that *hā ʿinyān* ("the task," 3:10) here, as generally in Ecclesiastes, has a negative connotation.

54. Whybray, *Ecclesiastes* (NCBC), 75.

interprets it theologically (cf. Gen. 8:22)."[55] God's seeking out what has been pursued then refers to God's making sure that what happened once happens again, so that v. 15 "summarizes and combines the statements about God's work in both v. 11a and v. 14a."[56] In other words, the order that God puts into creation is sustained by him, so that there is always a fitting time and a place for things and activities. Whether or not Ogden is right in reading the last part of v. 15 as a reference to God calling humans to joy, v. 15 is a development of v. 14, and both should thus be seen as a positive expression of God's sovereignty. Verses 12–15 are therefore an answer to v. 9, but an answer that is juxtaposed to a very different and negative answer in vv. 10–11.

This section thus presents us with two contradictory approaches to the mystery of time. The one despairs of being able to discern the time and the place, whereas the other celebrates time as the context in which to rejoice, do good, eat and drink, and enjoy one's labor. The contrast is stark and opens up a gap in the reading—how is the tension between these two approaches to be resolved?

Theological Implications

Once again we see in this chapter the comprehensive reach of Qohelet's exploration: time, the limits of human life, namely birth and death, and the range of activities that make up human culture, including agriculture, war, reconciliation, medicine, grief, celebration, and so on.[57] Qohelet's quest is torn between two responses to the order in time that he observes—on the one hand, it leads him to despair over life being meaningful; on the other hand, he knows that time is the God-given context for enjoying one's work, doing good, and rejoicing. As already noted in chaps. 1 and 2, meaning for Qohelet and thus faith relate to the whole of life; "all of life is religion," as the late Evan Runner never tired of saying.[58]

In this section *time* and *creation order in time* come under scrutiny. Qohelet acknowledges the apparent existence of this order: "When we look at life, says Qohelet, it seems like a rich tapestry of contrasting colours; with every thread in place and everything seeming to fit."[59] This is a presupposition that is fundamental to biblical wisdom, but Qohelet despairs of humans being

55. Krüger, *Qoheleth*, 90.
56. Ibid.
57. There is an interesting reception history of 3:11 in Dutch philosophy and theology. See Botha, *Sosio-Kulturele Metavrae*, 81–87.
58. Runner was a neo-Calvinist Christian philosopher. The chair I occupy is named after him.
59. Davidson, *Courage to Doubt*, 198.

169

able *to know* this order. Epistemology is at stake once again.[60] To know this order, humans would require a sense of the origin and telos of creation, but from Qohelet's autonomous perspective it is precisely this they lack. God has constituted them with this need, but they lack such a sense of duration of time. The result is that they cannot discern his order, and everything is rendered enigmatic.

How to think about time *is* complex. As Augustine says in his *Confessions*, he knows what time is until he is asked to explain it.[61] As Ricoeur notes in his three-volume classic *Time and Narrative*, however, "A constant thesis of this book will be that speculation on time is an inconclusive rumination to which *narrative activity* alone can respond."[62] This brings us close to Qohelet's problem—in the context of his epistemology of reason, experience, and observation, he cannot access the larger *story* that will make sense of the order he observes in time. Humans need a grand story or metanarrative from which to make sense of life, but they are limited and thus live in the terrible epistemological tension between what they need and the realities of life.

In the OT era, in which the future of God's purposes is hazy and what happens after death is unclear, one would have some sympathy with Qohelet's struggle. Even bearing this in mind, however, I have noted his tendency toward a cyclical view of history as opposed to the general OT view of history as cyclical and linear. Even within his limited context he ignores the linear view of history that the OT opens up, and depends on his autonomous epistemology. However, it is precisely the narrative structure of Scripture that provides potential resolution to Qohelet's struggle with time. In an essay titled "Biblical Time," Ricoeur alerts us to the way in which the different genres of the OT interact with one another in generating a biblical view of time (if there is such a thing). But he concludes from this that "the project of a merely narrative theology is a chimera."[63] However, it is precisely a narrative theology of the Bible that helps develop a biblical view of time and history. The genres in the OT are all connected canonically into the grand story it tells, so that narrative holds the key to a biblical perspective on time. As Herrera notes,

---

60. Kugel (*Great Poems*, 315–16) perceptively notes that Qohelet "is out to speak the truth; but he is limited to what he happens to be able to see, and say, at any one time. Koheleth's position might be compared to that of a man in a room walking around some object in the center—say, a globe—at a distance of five or ten feet. At any given moment he is able to describe *part* of the globe in great detail. . . . But as he moves around everything changes. Where once in the middle of the picture there was water there is now dry land. So in order to describe the globe he ends up presenting a series of snapshots, each one slightly different from the one before it and the one after it; in fact, from opposite points of the room they have absolutely nothing in common."

61. On Augustine and time, see Ricoeur, *Time and Narrative*, vol. 1, chap. 1.

62. Ibid., 6 (italics mine).

63. Ricoeur, "Biblical Time," 179.

The foundational charter of the philosophy of history is found in one biblical verse: "God, at the beginning of time, created heaven and earth." . . . This
text, as traditionally interpreted, shattered the pagan conception of an eternal
universe parceled out in an infinity of cycles. That view was voiced by Berossus,
the Babylonian astrologer, who maintained that the universe passes through
a number of Great Years with each cosmic cycle reproducing that which had
preceded it. The doctrine of creation entailing linear time opened a vast horizon
of novel events that took history beyond the limits of the ancient chroniclers.
Even Herodotus . . . was imprisoned in a circle.[64]

Similarly M. Smit stresses the importance of creation in his articulation of a
Christian philosophy of history:

> When I maintain that *God is the meaning of history* I mean to say that history
> has meaning in that it is totally, in all its elements and phenomena, in all its
> subjects and objects, *related to, oriented to* God. He has created the world in
> relation to himself. . . . That means for history not only fullness of meaning but
> also freedom, since for its meaning it is not dependent on the historical process,
> nor on the autonomous person.[65]

This implication of the opening salvo of the biblical story is even clearer
when the whole canon of Scripture is taken into account, and while Cullmann's
discussion of Greek thought about history as cyclical may be questionable at
points,[66] his articulation of the significance of the Christ event for a biblical
view of time and history remains deeply insightful. He rightly asserts that
"the New Testament writings for the first time give to all revelation an essential anchorage in time; here for the first time the line is consistently carried
through in its central significance for salvation and faith. Thus it is not as if
we had to do with a Jewish survival; rather, that which is intimated in Judaism
is here completely carried out."[67] Qohelet had only the intimations, although
these are ignored in his discussion of time. But we have the full revelation in
Christ, and this provides the grand story within which it is possible to live
and to discern what is fitting and wise.[68] As Wolters notes, "An implication of
the revelation of God in creation is that the creation order is *knowable*. That
is also the significance of the *call* of Wisdom to all—she appeals to everyone
to pay attention and learn from her, for insight and understanding are genuinely available to them if they heed her. This fundamental knowability of the

---

64. Herrera, *Reasons for Our Rhymes*, 13.
65. M. Smit, *Toward a Christian Conception of History*, 325.
66. Ricoeur, "Biblical Time," 167–69. But cf. Herrera, *Reasons for Our Rhymes*, chap. 1.
67. Cullmann, *Christ and Time*, 38.
68. See Bartholomew and Goheen, *Drama of Scripture*.

creation order is the basis of all human understanding, both in science and everyday life."[69]

One of the major theological reflections on time is by Barth.[70] He notes that time "is the form of our existence. To be man is to live in time."[71] In terms strongly reminiscent of Qohelet, Barth acknowledges how time can confront us as a monstrous enigma: "Infinite, also, is the impossibility of escaping its enigma as the enigma of man himself, man who is, and who would like to be in time and have time, who is in point of fact temporal, and whose being in time is of this nature."[72] Time is a "given"; it is part of our *creaturely* condition, and for Barth it becomes a monstrous enigma because of our alienation from God and thus from ourselves. Time confronts us with the boundaries and limits of human existence. For Barth, we can come to terms with time only when we recognize God as Creator: "What emerges . . . is that man is not God, but a needy creature of God. . . . To say 'man' or 'time' is first and basically, even if unwillingly and unwittingly, to say 'God.' For God is for man as He has time for him. It is God who gives him his time. . . . Time as the form of human existence is always in itself and as such a silent but persistent song of praise to God."[73] The secret of time is, for Barth, "the will and act of God."[74]

Barth discusses time as present, past, and future. The loss entailed in "the past," a theme to which Qohelet returns again and again, can be profoundly disturbing, and two unhelpful ways of responding to this are by seeking to re-create it in memory[75] or by relegating it to oblivion. Again, for Barth, the problem of the past is resolved only in relation to God. Of the past he notes, "Because God was then, its reality and fullness cannot be taken away by the fact that it has gone. What he willed and created cannot disintegrate into nothing. It has merely lost its character as our present, which it once had. But it has not perished as one of the terms of our time."[76] And so it is with the future: "we can count on the fact that the will and act of God are the

69. Wolters, *Creation Regained*, 29. See the whole of chap. 2.
70. Barth, *CD* 3.2 §47. Titled "Man in His Time," this section is over two hundred pages long. I cannot discuss it in any detail here, but it is a deeply insightful examination of the theology of time. Particularly relevant for Ecclesiastes is subsection 2: "Given Time."
71. Ibid., 521.
72. Ibid., 511–17, quotation 515.
73. Ibid., 525.
74. Ibid., 527. The indispensability of relating time to God as Creator is underscored in Barth's emphatic statement (ibid., 551): "We understood time and our being in time as real by considering it as the form of human existence willed and created by God. We thus purged the concept of time from all the abstractions by which it is inevitably confused and darkened when the divine will and action are left out of account and time is not understood as His creation."
75. Barth defines memory (ibid., 534) in this context as "an attempt to restore to the past the duration and extension which it obviously does not have any longer."
76. Ibid., 537.

meaning and ground not only of our being in time generally but also of our being in the future."[77]

This resolution of the problem of time and the importance of understanding history as the move from creation through fall to re-creation has major implications for our response to postmodernism. It opposes and helps us to see the terror of the sort of recovery of the doctrine of eternal recurrence that I spoke of earlier as well as providing an alternative to the historicism that is endemic in postmodern thought.

Nietzsche posed the option between eternal recurrence and Christianity evocatively: "Have I been understood?—Dionysus versus the Crucified."[78] But the Dionysian vision is hardly a comfortable one to live with, as Qohelet discerns: "The Eternal Recurrence is hardly a panacea. It is a 'terrifying vision' which moves in the opposite direction and serves only to consolidate the power of time."[79] Furthermore, as Ingraffia shows, Nietzsche's critique rests on an incorrect understanding of Christianity's view of time and history.[80] The scriptural narrative operates with a now-and-not-yet vision of the accomplishment of God's purposes in history, not with a Greek spatial distinction between this world and that above.

Nietzsche's doctrine of eternal recurrence is closely related to *historicism*—the view that all is afloat in time and change without any all-embracing creation order. As Herrera notes, eternal recurrence, Nietzsche's "mightiest thought,"[81] attempts to deny Being and to deify Becoming:

> The Eternal Recurrence is a serious attempt to authenticate, and perhaps even deify, Becoming. Following in the steps of Heraclitus, Nietzsche proposed that Being, presumed to exist behind the mask of Becoming, is merely an illusion. If all is becoming, it follows that, "the complex of causes will recur . . . it will create man again. . . . I shall return . . . not to a new life or a similar life . . . [but] to this identical self-same life to teach once more the eternal recurrence of all things."[82]

Historicism means that everything is adrift and that there are no sure guides to how to live or how to know what is fitting at any particular time. As O'Donovan notes in relation to marriage,

---

77. Ibid., 545.

78. F. W. Nietzsche, *Ecce Homo*, in *On the Genealogy of Morals and Ecce Homo*, trans. and ed. W. A. Kaufmann (New York: Vintage Books, 1967), 335.

79. Herrera, *Reasons for Our Rhymes*, 172. On Nietzsche's philosophy of history, see ibid., chap. 11.

80. Ingraffia, *Postmodern Theory and Biblical Theology*, part 1.

81. Jaspers, *Nietzsche*, 357–58.

82. Herrera, *Reasons for Our Rhymes*, 145.

> A historicist account . . . must argue that this "natural good" is not given trans-historically in nature at all, but is the product of cultural development peculiar to a certain time and place. . . . By making marriage an item of cultural history in this way, historicism necessarily raises a question about it. . . . Historicism makes all created goods appear putatively outmoded. So that if there are currents of dissatisfaction evident in a society's practice of marriage, such as might be indicated by a high divorce rate or a prominent homosexual culture, they will be treated with great seriousness as signs of the evolution for which the institution is destined.[83]

Historicism has no transcendent norm; the best one can do is to support one element of culture against another. "To criticise the culture as a whole is unthinkable; one can only speak for the culture against the culture, as the representative of a new strand in the culture which will fashion its future."[84]

Qohelet's analysis of time leads him in a historicist direction—there may be an order to life under the sun, but we cannot know it! At the same time, as he confesses in the "I know" passages, he knows from his immersion in the Israelite tradition and from experience that finding the right time to eat, to drink, to marry, and to rejoice is wonderfully meaningful. "In theism, God may be said to give the gift of time as opportunity; as an interval for promise, hope and faithfulness; as a resource for which humankind is accountable; or as sheer gift for enjoyment."[85] But how is one to reconcile this with Qohelet's assertion that one cannot discern what God has done from the beginning to the end (v. 11)? Empirically, of course, one cannot, and one is left to flounder in the sinking sand of historicism. Reason and experience and observation lead Qohelet toward a terrifying view of time and history as complete mysteries. Simultaneously he confesses an alternative, positive vision of time as the stage for shalom. These perspectives, with their enormous consequences, sit side by side in an awful tension, crying out for resolution.

---

83. O'Donovan, *Resurrection and Moral Order*, 69–70.

84. Ibid., 73. Braaten and Jenson ("Preface," 4) find contemporary Western culture to be pervaded with gnosticism: "The hall mark of this Gnosticism is experiential religiosity divorced from dogma—and indeed from all concern for truth." In this respect, see also Lundin's excellent *Culture of Interpretation*, esp. chap. 4: "Postmodern Gnostics."

85. Thiselton, *Concise Encyclopedia*, 309.

F.
The Problem of Injustice and Death
(3:16–22)

Translation

[16]But[1] still I have seen under the sun: in the place of justice, there was injustice! And in the place of righteousness, there was injustice!

[17]I dialogued with my heart: God will judge the righteous and the unjust, for there is a time for every activity and for every deed as well.[2]

[18]I dialogued with myself concerning the manner of human beings. God has selected them in order to show that they are but animals.

[19]For the fate of humankind and the fate of animals is the same fate. As one dies so does the other. All have the same spirit. Humankind has no advantage at all compared with animals.[3] Truly[4] everything is enigmatic.

[20]All go to the same place. All came from dust and all will return to dust.

1. Adversative use of *wāw*.
2. It is hard to know how to translate *šām* (lit. "there") at the end of this verse. See Whitley, *Koheleth*, 34–36; and Seow, *Ecclesiastes*, 166–67. I follow Whitley here in treating *šām* as an asseverative, meaning "too" or "as well." Isaksson (*Studies*, 176) and Longman (*Ecclesiastes*, 125) agree.
3. The word order of this phrase, ending with "no/none," makes the meaning emphatic.
4. Asseverative use of *kî* (RJW §449).

²¹Who knows whether the spirit of humankind ascends upward and the
spirit of animals descends downward to the earth?
²²But I saw that there is nothing better than that one should enjoy
one's work, for that is their portion. Though⁵ who can bring one to
see what will be after one?

Interpretation

This section deals with injustice in the world and not knowing whether
or when it will be punished, and also revisits the problem of death. The
"But still" of v. 16 connects this section with the preceding confessions. As
a believer, Qohelet knows that life is good and to be affirmed, but . . . , and
here he picks up on another of his struggles that contradict the affirmation
of life, namely that of terrible injustice in the world. The idea of God having
a "time" (ʿēt) for judgment (v. 17) further links this section back into 3:1–15
and indicates why Qohelet finds God's order for creation so problematic. The
juxtaposition of different responses continues in this section, which can be
outlined as follows:

1. Statement of the problem (v. 16)
2. Confessional response—God has a time for judgment (v. 17)
3. Enigmatic response to the problem (vv. 18–19)
4. Ignorance of what happens to humans after death (vv. 20–21)
5. "There is nothing better than" saying (v. 22a)
6. Rhetorical question (v. 22b)

In vv. 18–19 the injustice of life again foregrounds the question of the meaning
of life as in v. 16. The injustice that Qohelet observes is for him God's means
of showing humans that they are but animals. From this perspective, humans
have no advantage over animals; they come from dust and return to dust, and
no one knows what happens to them after that.

¹⁶But still I have seen under the sun: in the place of justice, there was
injustice! And in the place of righteousness, there was injustice!

3:16. *Statement of the problem.* In v. 16, Qohelet evocatively introduces a
problem he has observed that makes nonsense of God's order for creation. The
synonymous internal parallelism evokes the horror of what he has observed,
as does the repetition of "injustice" (*hārešaʿ*):

5. Concessive use of *ki* (RJW §448).

> The place of justice—there injustice/evil!
> The place of righteousness—there injustice/evil!

In Israel, the place of judgment was the administration of justice practiced by the elders in the city gates. The parallel term to "justice," namely "righteousness," intensifies Qohelet's observation by reminding the reader what justice is all about: it is to punish evil and reward good and so maintain righteousness among God's people. But Qohelet observes terrible corruption; instead of righteousness he finds injustice.[6]

> **17**I dialogued with my heart: God will judge the righteous and the unjust, for there is a time for every activity and for every deed as well.

3:17. *Confessional response—God has a time for judgment.* Verse 17 picks up on the theme of time in 3:1–8 in a positive way and confesses that there will be a time for judgment that will resolve the problem of injustice. Verses 18–19 are juxtaposed to v. 17 in a contradictory way. Both of these responses to injustice are what Qohelet meditated on in his heart, but they represent radically opposed responses to the problem.

> **18**I dialogued with myself concerning the manner of human beings. God has selected them in order to show that they are but animals.
> **19**For the fate of humankind and the fate of animals is the same fate. As one dies so does the other. All have the same spirit. Humankind has no advantage at all compared with animals. Truly everything is enigmatic.

3:18–19. *Enigmatic response to the problem.* Verses 18–19 conclude from the observation of life that all is enigmatic and God is a cruel examiner whose purpose in the injustice is to remind humans that they are only animals. Genesis 1 and 2 clearly teach that humans are different from animals in that they are made in the *imago Dei*. But the common observable fate of both animals and humans raises for Qohelet the question as to whether there is any difference between them: they all have the same spirit (*rûaḥ*), and its destination is the same. The reality of death is brought into Qohelet's reflection on injustice: humans die just like animals. All—animals and the righteous and the wicked—go to the same place, and no one knows what happens after death, whether the spirits of humans ascend upward to God or not (v. 21).

6. Qohelet's vocabulary here (justice, injustice, righteousness) clearly has the same moral connotations as in the Torah (see "Reading Ecclesiastes within the Context of Proverbs and Job and Its Connection to the Torah" in the introduction).

> **20**All go to the same place. All came from dust and all will return to dust.
> **21**Who knows whether the spirit of humankind ascends upward and the spirit of animals descends downward to the earth?

3:20–21. *Ignorance of what happens to humans after death.* In v. 20 Qohelet asserts that animals and humans go to the same place, but then in v. 21 he raises the possibility of a different destination for their spirits. In 12:7 he indeed speaks of the spirit (*rûaḥ*) returning to God. This view is found also in Job and the Psalms (Job 34:14–15; Ps. 104:29–30). When humans die, the spirit returns to God, but the body returns to dust. The problem is, on the basis of observation (i.e., in the light of Qohelet's autonomous epistemology) it is impossible to know what happens after death.

Verses 20–21 mediate between the enigmatic conclusion of v. 19 and the positive saying in v. 22. Verses 20–21 deal with the limitations of human knowledge and could lead in one of two directions.[7] They could provide further support for the enigmatic conclusion. In the light of the animal analogy the rhetorical question in v. 21 could imply a negative answer. But the awareness of human limitations could also lead on to the positive approach of v. 22. Moreover, with its close proximity to 3:12–15 and its "better-than" form, v. 22a should not just be read as a statement of positive resignation in the light of human enigmas. The enjoyment here is a positive, "shalomic" appropriation of the human task in creation, a recognition of the task that God has assigned humans.

> **22a**But I saw that there is nothing better than that one should enjoy one's work, for that is their portion.

3:22a. *"There is nothing better than" saying.* Like v. 17, the saying in v. 22a is juxtaposed to vv. 18–19 in a contradictory way. Against the idea that v. 22 is the answer to the problem of injustice is the radical tension between "enjoying their work" and the injustice portrayed in v. 16. Verse 22a does not resolve this tension; how is the worker to enjoy life as his portion while being dragged unjustly into the corrupt law courts? Similarly the tensions between v. 17 and vv. 18–19 are not resolved. The reader is uncertain how the observations leading to the conclusion that "God has selected/is testing them in order to show that they are but animals" relate to the confession that there is a time appointed for judgment. Both are said in Qohelet's heart/mind, but do the observations deconstruct the former confession? One might think so, but what then of the positive saying in v. 22a? This fits closely with v. 17 and seems to be the conclusion of this brief

---

7. Compare the previous *carpe diem* passage, where the limitation of human knowledge in 3:11–15 can lead one to a joyful trust in God, but it can also be the basis of concluding that all is enigmatic.

discussion of injustice. The fact is that the juxtapositions of contradictory views set up gaps, and the gaps are not filled at this point.[8]

> [22b]Though who can bring one to see what will be after one?

3:22b. *Rhetorical question.* The uncertainty with which the reader is left is enhanced by the rhetorical question at the end of v. 22. As with most of the rhetorical questions in Ecclesiastes, this one can be answered in two ways. Like vv. 20–21 it could enhance the sense of meaninglessness and enigma. Alternatively, and especially in the light of v. 17, it could imply that even this enigma is under God's control.[9]

Theological Implications

In this section we see why Qohelet finds the apparent order of creation such a problem. Time and place are the two great coordinates of created life, and in v. 16 the focus moves from time to place. One would expect the law courts to be the *place* where justice finds its appropriate *time*, but Qohelet observes the opposite. And if there is no time for judgment, then the apparent order of creation is deconstructed. This problem is intensified by the issue of death, already discussed by Qohelet in 2:12–17. If death is just the end, then humans are no better than animals, and there never will be a time for judgment.

In terms of the biblical metanarrative there will indeed be a time for judgment. From the fuller revelation of the NT we know that at the consummation of history with the return of Christ there will be judgment and restoration, and this revelation answers Qohelet's probing questions about death and justice. "After the resurrection comes the judgment, an event pictured in the Old Testament as a victory of the Messiah over all Israel's enemies but described in the New Testament more spiritually as a judicial work of Christ in which he judges and sentences all people in accordance with the law God gave them."[10] In its vision of the future, Rev. 20 and especially vv. 11–15 are packed with imagery of judgment. In vv. 11–15 the picture is of a great white throne before which *all* the dead are brought for judgment: "And the dead were judged according to their works, as recorded in the books" (20:12).

---

8. For a good example of how commentators feel the need to fill the gaps that juxtapositions set up, see Fox's (*Qohelet*, 336–37) paraphrase of this section.

9. Commentators reflect these two options. Murphy (*Ecclesiastes*, 37) understands v. 22b to refer to humans being unable to see any real future for themselves, whereas Ogden (*Qoheleth*, 62–63) sees v. 22b as another reason for Qohelet's positive advice (i.e., it is no use inquiring into the future, because there is no tangible evidence; nevertheless there is something "after one," and this is part of our "benefit"). My translation of *kî* as "though" suggests the former option.

10. Bavinck, *Reformed Dogmatics*, 4:698.

Judgment will be followed by the renewal of all creation, a reality wonderfully evoked by Bavinck, summarized here by his editor:

> The renewal of creation follows the final judgment. According to Scripture the present world will neither continue forever nor will it be destroyed and replaced by a totally new one. Instead it will be cleansed of sin and re-created, reborn, renewed, made whole. . . . Biblical hope, rooted in incarnation and resurrection, is creational, this-worldly, visible, physical, bodily hope. The rebirth of human beings is completed in the glorious rebirth of all creation, the new Jerusalem, whose architect and builder is God himself. . . . The final rest of God's children is not to be conceived as inaction; his children remain his servants, who joyfully and in diverse ways serve him night and day.[11]

How this will all take place we do not know, but the biblical story assures us that there will be a time for judgment, in which justice will be settled once and for all, and mercy will extend as far as it possibly can.

This does not mean, however, that believers are exempt from Qohelet's struggle with injustice. In its terse style v. 16 conjures up a terrifying spectacle: in the place of justice, injustice! In our Western democracies with the relative justice they provide, it is too easy to underestimate the pain and horror of this vision. One needs to know something of the Nazi Holocaust, of the Rwandan genocide, or the day-to-day realities in Baghdad since its "liberation" in order to feel the problem that Qohelet here invokes.[12] Brennan Manning describes the allied problem of pain and suffering as "the enormous difficulty" in relation to faith:

> When pain and suffering are conjoined with the monstrous mystery of evil, we come to a crossroads from which there is no turning back. The tsunami of high school killings in Kentucky, Oregon, and Colorado, the rampage of serial killer Rafel Resendez-Ramirez, the sexual torture spree of thirty-eight-year-old Charles Ng, which led to the murder of six men, three women, and two baby boys, the horror of the seventy-eight-year-old mother who belatedly confessed to suffocating all of her eight children before they had reached the age of two, the mass graves of slaughtered ethnic Albanians in Kosovo—the list of evil incidents goes on and on, impressing believers and unbelievers alike more powerfully than the presence of God.[13]

Even within the fuller picture of the scriptural story, injustice remains a mystery. *The* story reveals that there will be a time of judgment, and believers trust that

11. Ibid., 4:715.
12. See Wiesel, *Night*, for an evocation of the horror of living through the Holocaust. See Ilibagiza and Erwin, *Left to Tell*, for an extraordinary story of one woman's discovery of God through the experience of the Rwandan genocide.
13. Manning, *Ruthless Trust*, 39–40.

justice will finally prevail. In the context of racist apartheid, Archbishop Tutu used to exhort his fellow South Africans to join the winning side, by which he meant that justice will ultimately triumph. Similarly Julian of Norwich confesses, "All shall be well, and all manner of thing shall be well."[14] But this remains a confession, and one that this side of the consummation of history is made from a position of ruthless trust, as Manning describes it. Faith here provides a place to stand and from which to hope in a way that an empirical epistemology, limited to what is observable, can never provide.

In his discussion of time as given, Barth explores the challenge of time as *future* for humans. Like Qohelet, Barth recognizes that the certainty of death complicates our understanding of time.[15] Theologically, time is part of the created order, but how does this square with death, which theologically is part of God's judgment?[16] For Qohelet, in terms of his autonomous epistemology, death is here portrayed as annihilation, the end. As Barth notes, this is a terrifying scenario:

> Our beginning is indeed behind us and constantly recedes. It does not attract our attention or arouse our concern. Yet it points to the same fact and confronts us with the same problem as our end: that our being is bordered by our non-being; that our non-being behind and before is a most terrible threat to our being; that we are menaced by approaching annihilation; and that our being thus seems to be a mere illusion and our life irretrievably forfeit.[17]

Barth observes that there are two ways for humans to face the future toward which all our human activity hastens. There is first the unreflective way. This is to

> stand firmly on the pretence and to assume that it affords solid support, never giving a thought to the fact that our future being in time is enclosed by a great bracket; that one day—we do not know when—we shall step and fall into the abyss, having a present without a future, encountering the further side not only of our present moment, but of our whole being in time; and that with every step we take our being is a being of unending terror under the threat of this catastrophe.[18]

Second, there is the reflective way, which faces up squarely to the fact that all that lies ahead is death. This is the path that Qohelet chooses, and Barth's description of this approach resonates with Qohelet's experience: "The way

14. *Revelations of Divine Love*, revelation 13, chap. 27.
15. In this respect, see Barth's (*CD* 3.2:587–640) discussion of "Ending Time."
16. Barth (ibid., 596) notes that "death, as it actually encounters us men, is a sign of God's judgment on us."
17. Ibid., 572.
18. Ibid., 543.

in which we look and step from the present into the future is determined by the fact that we see the whole of the path before us in this shadow."[19]

The problem for Qohelet is that the shadow his reflective approach to death casts sets up an unbearable tension with his affirmation of time as the context for humans to live positively in the present. With the OT's limited eschatology Qohelet's struggle is understandable; resolution comes from the larger metanarrative of the canon of Scripture as a whole, according to which death is not the end but the stepping stone into God's presence:

> Though it [death] is our last enemy, it cannot do what it likes with us. God has appointed it to its office, but He can also disarm it. . . . For with death the Lord of death is also present. To be sure, He will be present as the Judge and Avenger, as the One who causes us in death to reap what we have sown, as the One whom we must fear even now, and then still more. But He is also the Lord of death. If death has such terrors for us, it is because in death we shall finally fall into the hands of the living God.[20]

19. Ibid., 544.
20. Ibid., 608–9.

G.
Four Problems
(4:1–16)

Translation

[1]So I turned again[1] and I observed all the acts of oppression that
are done[2] under the sun, and oh, the tears[3] of the oppressed! But
there was no one to comfort them. In[4] the hand of their oppressors
was power, but there was no one to comfort them.
[2]So I praised[5] the dead who are already dead more than the living
who remain alive.
[3]But better than both of them is the one who does not yet exist,[6] who
has not seen the evil activity that is done under the sun.

1. The use of *šûb* here indicates the start of a new section and topic (cf. 4:7; 9:11).
2. For the tense of this verb here and in v. 3, see Isaksson, *Studies*, 69–74.
3. The singular noun is collective here, as in Isa. 25:8; Pss. 39:12 [13]; 42:3 [4].
4. *Min* indicates here the source of the power and could also be translated as "from."
5. The Piel infinitive absolute followed by the subject "I" is used here in place of a finite verb. *IBHS* (596n60) refers to this as a "systematic exception," which is called the *qatāli anāku* construction. Further examples of this are found in Exod. 36:7; 1 Chron. 5:20; Esther 2:3; 3:13; 9:1.
6. The phrase "the one who" (*'ēt 'ăšer*) normally indicates the object of a sentence. Thus Whybray (*Ecclesiastes* [NCBC], 83) suggests that we take this phrase either as the object of "I praised" in v. 2 or as the object of an implied verb that is not stated. However, the LXX and Syr take *'ēt 'ăšer* as nominative, and a similar usage is found in Jer. 38:16. Such usage is more frequent in Late Hebrew.

⁴Then I observed all the labor and the skill⁷ involved in work—it results from one person's jealousy of his neighbor.⁸ This too is enigmatic and a striving after wind.

⁵The fool folds his hands and consumes his flesh.⁹

⁶One handful of rest is better than two handfuls of labor¹⁰ and a striving after wind.

⁷And I turned again¹¹ and I observed enigma under the sun.

⁸There was one person without another.¹² He also¹³ had neither a son nor a brother; yet there was no end to all his labor, and his eyes¹⁴ were never satiated with his riches. "And for whom do I labor, depriving myself of good?" This also is enigmatic and an evil task.

⁹Two are better than one¹⁵ because¹⁶ they have a good reward in their labor.

¹⁰For if either of them falls,¹⁷ one will pick up the other, but woe¹⁸ to the person who falls, and there is no one to pick him up.

¹¹Also, if two people sleep together,¹⁹ they keep warm, but how can one person keep warm?

¹²And if one person can overpower²⁰ him who is alone, two can resist his opponent.

The three-stranded²¹ cord is not quickly severed.

7. *Kišrôn* can mean "skill, success, achievement." It also occurs in 5:10 [11], where it is more appropriately translated as "benefit." Here, however, "skill" fits the context better; the Ugaritic cognate *ktr* has this meaning.

8. The word for "neighbor" (*rēaʿ*) can have the stronger meaning of "friend." If so, it is used ironically (D. Miller, "Power in Wisdom," 155).

9. Ginsburg (*Coheleth*, 324–25) and N. Lohfink (*Kohelet*, 36–37) translate *bĕśārô* as "his meat," meaning that the fool still has food to eat. However, the four other times *bāśār* occurs in Ecclesiastes, it always refers to the human body (2:3; 5:6 [5]; 11:10; 12:12). Furthermore, *bāśār* with the pronominal suffix always refers to the human body or parts of it in the OT (see Seow, *Ecclesiastes*, 179). In the English version of Lohfink's commentary (*Qoheleth*, 69), *bāśār* is translated as "flesh."

10. My translation takes *kap nāḥat* and *ḥopnayim ʿāmāl* as construct chains, with the final *mem* on *ḥopnayim* being enclitic (see Whitley, *Koheleth*, 42). The alternative is to take "rest" and "labor" as adverbial accusatives (see Whybray, *Ecclesiastes* [NCBC], 85).

11. See the first translation note on v. 1.

12. The Hebrew reads lit., "There was one and not a second." The "and" (*wāw*) is explicative (RJW §434).

13. *Gam* is here emphatic.

14. Following the Ketib, rather than the singular Qere.

15. Literally "the two" and "the one." The definite articles may indicate that the reference is to those who are not solitary and those who are (Seow, *Ecclesiastes*, 181).

16. The particle *ʾăšer* is causal here.

17. The verb is plural, and with Gordis (*Koheleth*, 242) I take it as partitive.

18. The unusual form of *ʾilô* is generally taken as a sign of Late Hebrew.

19. Literally "lie down."

20. *Tāqēp* is attested only in Late Hebrew.

21. This is a Pual participle. According to *IBHS* §25.4c (p. 423), it means "to do three times," and the authors propose the translation "three-fold."

> [13]Better is a poor[22] but wise youth than an old but foolish king who no longer knows how to receive instruction.
> [14]One can indeed come out of prison[23] to reign, even though being born poor in one's kingdom.
> [15]I observed all the living, who walked under the sun, with the youth who replaced him.
> [16]There was no end to all the people, to all those he led. Yet those who came later did not like him. This too is enigmatic and a striving after wind.

Interpretation

In this chapter, Qohelet deals with four areas of life he observes that reinforce his view that all is enigmatic: oppression (vv. 1–3), rivalry as the motivation for work (vv. 4–6), isolation in work and life (vv. 7–12), and the problem of government (vv. 13–16). These may seem unrelated, but as will become clear there are unifying links between these sections.[24] A model of work based on rivalry can lead to oppression and undermine community, and a community without wisdom problematizes good government.

> [1]So I turned again and I observed all the acts of oppression that are done under the sun, and oh, the tears of the oppressed! But there was no one to comfort them. In the hand of their oppressors was power, but there was no one to comfort them.
> [2]So I praised the dead who are already dead more than the living who remain alive.
> [3]But better than both of them is the one who does not yet exist, who has not seen the evil activity that is done under the sun.

4:1–3. *Oppression.* Qohelet turns to another aspect of life that he observes, namely oppression. His observation of oppression extends his social critique of injustice in 3:16–22.

Oppression is a theme found throughout the OT, from the oppression of the Israelites under the Egyptians, to the prophetic voices critiquing oppression, to Israel's experience of oppression in the exile. The same root (*ʿšq*) from which "the acts of oppression" and "the oppressed" come in v. 1 also occurs

---

22. *Miskēn* occurs only here and in 9:15–16 in the OT. However, it is well attested in Post-biblical Hebrew.

23. *Hāsûrîm* is from *hāʾăsûrîm*, with the *aleph* elided (cf. 2 Kings 8:28; 2 Chron. 22:5; GKC §160b).

24. See D. Miller, "Power in Wisdom," for the different views of the interrelationship of the sections in chap. 4 and an argument for reading 4:1–16 as a unity with a chiastic structure. Cf. also Rudman, "Contextual Reading."

in Prov. 14:31: "The one who oppresses the poor reproaches his Maker, but the one who is gracious to the needy honors him"; Prov. 22:16: "Oppressing the poor to enrich oneself, and giving to the rich, will lead only to poverty"; and Prov. 28:3: "A poor man who oppresses the needy is like a beating rain that leaves no food." Qohelet merely describes the horror of what he has seen and moves to his conclusion.

N. Lohfink dates Ecclesiastes in the third century BC. During this period Judea was part of the province of Syria and Phoenicia in the Ptolemaic kingdom. A Greek elite permeated the kingdom, and the leading families in Jerusalem were becoming integrated with the Greek elite. In this context the wealthier classes oppressed the underclass, especially through the institution of debt slavery. Whole families could end up being sold into foreign slavery when they were unable to pay their debts. While we cannot be sure of the date of Ecclesiastes (see "Authorship and Date" in the introduction), it is doubtless this sort of phenomenon that Qohelet is referring to—the abuse of economic and political power leading to terrible oppression of the underclass.[25] His reference to "all the acts of oppression" (v. 1) indicates that oppression was pervasive in the society of his time.

The horror and pain of such oppression and its relentlessness is evoked in Qohelet's response, "Oh, the tears of the oppressed!" Power is in the hand of the oppressor, and there is no one to comfort the oppressed. The repetition of this latter phrase, "there was no one to comfort them," which evokes the repetition of "no one to comfort" in Lam. 1:2, 7, 9, 16, 21, reinforces the pathos of their situation.

Longman and others note here that Qohelet neither personally engages the subject nor exhorts others to resist the oppression.[26] But this is to miss the point of Qohelet's journey—it is a personal quest for meaning, and from this perspective his whole person is indeed engaged. His observation of oppression evokes horror in his mind, so much so that he goes on in vv. 2 and 3 to praise the dead and to declare that it is better to be dead than to be alive and to have to witness or be subject to such abuse by human beings. Verse 3 is the first of many "better-than" sayings in Ecclesiastes and is the first of four in this chapter.[27] This type of saying is common in Proverbs and in Egyptian instructional literature. Here it functions to intensify his feelings of horror by asserting it is better not even to be born than to have to witness such oppression. "The *ṭôb*-saying thus points to the irony of human existence: what is really 'better' in this regard is not within the grasp of mortals."[28] The extent of Qohelet's anguish is confirmed by the parallels to v. 3 that we find in Job 3:3–5 and Jer.

25. See N. Lohfink, *Qoheleth*, 68–69.
26. Longman, *Ecclesiastes*, 133.
27. "Better-than" sayings are found in 4:3, 6, 9, 13; 5:3 [4]; 6:3, 9; 7:1, 2, 3, 5, 8; 9:4, 16, 18. On this literary form in Ecclesiastes, see Schoors, "Word *ṭôb*," 687–94.
28. Seow, *Ecclesiastes*, 187.

20:18. Qohelet's quest is more intellectual than that of Job and Jeremiah, who suffer deep, existential pain, but the resulting anguish is comparable.

Longman's comment above is helpful in that it alerts us to the limited function of the royal fiction in Ecclesiastes. One might expect Qohelet as king to reflect on the king's role in reforming oppression, but the fiction is mainly about Qohelet's wisdom and has faded by this point.

> ⁴Then I observed all the labor and the skill involved in work—it results from one person's jealousy of his neighbor. This too is enigmatic and a striving after wind.
> ⁵The fool folds his hands and consumes his flesh.
> ⁶One handful of rest is better than two handfuls of labor and a striving after wind.

4:4–6. *Rivalry in Work.* "Then I observed" indicates that Qohelet turns here to a new topic, namely what motivates all the hard work that humans engage in. Work involves considerable energy and hard-won skills that often take years to acquire. But what is it that motivates all this labor? Qohelet observes that much of it—his simple assertion is an example of hyperbole—stems from rivalry and the desire to keep ahead of one's neighbors. There is some debate about how to understand "rivalry" (*qin'at*, v. 4). Rivalry can have positive connotations in the OT, and Ogden asserts, "There is nothing in the context . . . which suggests that the challenge to excel is unhealthy."[29] However, it is only in the divine-human relationship and the marriage relationship in the OT that jealousy/rivalry is normative.[30] As Prov. 14:30 asserts: "A tranquil heart gives life to the body, but rivalry [*qin'â*] makes the bones rot."[31] It is this type of negative rivalry that Qohelet has in mind. This connects back into his programmatic question of Eccles. 1:3; if *this* is what motivates all that labor under the sun, then work is an enigma and a striving after wind.

If rivalry motivates so much labor, then is it perhaps better not to work? In v. 5 Qohelet quotes a proverb very much in the spirit of Proverbs that addresses the importance of work.[32] The fool folds his hands, that is, he refrains from working, but then ends up consuming his flesh! The idiom of folding one's hands is found elsewhere in OT Wisdom literature as a synonym for rest or sleep and can refer, as here, to idleness. For example, Prov. 6:10–11 warns, "A little sleep, a little slumber, and a little folding of the hands to rest, and your poverty will come upon you like a robber and your need like an armed man." Verse 5 here evokes the result of inactivity and sloth in highly evocative

---

29. Ogden, *Qoheleth*, 67. Cf. Crenshaw, *Ecclesiastes*, 108.
30. See Longman, *Ecclesiastes*, 137.
31. Cf. also Prov. 27:4.
32. In content, this proverb has many parallels in Proverbs. See Prov. 6:6–11; 10:4–5; 12:24; 13:4; 19:15, 24; 20:13; 24:30–34.

imagery, that of self-cannibalism. The result of such laziness and inactivity: "They in essence become cannibals of themselves. The implication is that they will kill themselves by starvation."[33] As is so often the case in Ecclesiastes, however, this traditional proverb is given an ironic twist in v. 6. If work is of the sort observed in v. 4, then a little bit of rest is better than working and striving after wind. Perhaps the fool is right after all? This ironic twist leaves vv. 5 and 6 in tension with each other[34] and thus the question of the value of work unresolved. Work remains enigmatic for Qohelet.

> [7]And I turned again and I observed enigma under the sun.
> [8]There was one person without another. He also had neither a son nor a brother; yet there was no end to all his labor, and his eyes were never satiated with his riches. "And for whom do I labor, depriving myself of good?" This also is enigmatic and an evil task.
> [9]Two are better than one because they have a good reward in their labor.
> [10]For if either of them falls, one will pick up the other, but woe to the person who falls, and there is no one to pick him up.
> [11]Also, if two people sleep together, they keep warm, but how can one person keep warm?
> [12]And if one person can overpower him who is alone, two can resist his opponent.
> The three-stranded cord is not quickly severed.

4:7–12. *Isolation and a Lack of Community.* This section continues Qohelet's observations about labor, but the opening "And I turned again" indicates a shift in focus. As Qohelet tells us at the outset in v. 7, this new topic also leaves him with the view that labor is an enigma.

Observation is central to Qohelet's epistemology, and here he relates the anecdote of a person who is quite alone. He has neither a spouse nor a son nor a sibling. Nevertheless, he works exceptionally hard but is never satisfied with the wealth resulting from his labor (v. 8). In Semitic thought the eye is the seat of desire, and Qohelet evocatively notes that this loner's desire for more was never satisfied. Like Qohelet this person ends up finding labor deeply enigmatic. Qohelet allows the reader to hear the exasperated question of the loner:[35] "And for whom do I labor, depriving myself of good [*ṭôbâ*]?" *Ṭôbâ* can refer to pleasure or general well-being; in context the latter is more

---

33. Longman, *Ecclesiastes*, 138.

34. Contra Longman, *Ecclesiastes*, 138; and Seow, *Ecclesiastes*, 188, who sees v. 6 as the resolution of the dilemma.

35. Alternatively, the first person could indicate that Qohelet himself poses the question, but in context it is more likely that he dramatically allows us to hear the question of the loner himself.

likely,[36] but whatever its precise nuance the point is clear: pursuit of wealth by oneself does not fulfill.

Empirically one might suspect that wealth and riches would bring meaning to life, but Qohelet's conclusion is that they do not. Some commentators suggest that we have here a depiction of a lonely miser[37] or a sarcastic reflection on family life.[38] But these interpretations have to be read into the text, and it is important to take into account that Qohelet is merely reporting what he has observed. There are various reasons a person like this ends up alone. We can speculate as to why, and his workaholism may provide a clue. It is more likely that for circumstantial reasons this person has found himself alone, and in this tough situation, he has sought meaning in work and wealth. But they fail to provide the meaning he seeks. His question alludes to a possible reason for this: "for whom" does he labor? Far from being sarcastic about family life, the suggestion is that his lack of community may be a, or the, cause for his experience of life—with Qohelet—as enigmatic and evil.

In response to this anecdote Qohelet shifts to reflect on the value of community: "Two are better than one." Ogden suggests that this adaptation of a numerical saying to start with the larger number is a way to emphasize the value of community.[39] Qohelet is possibly deliberately alluding to Gen. 2:18 here, in which God asserts, "It is not good that the man should be alone. I will make him a helper as his partner." Like Gen. 2, Qohelet focuses strongly on the practical advantages of companionship. It is not clear what Qohelet has in mind by "a good reward" in v. 9.[40] It could refer to increased business profits, but as Hengstenberg notes, "Wherein the reward consists is detailed in ver. 10 ff. They afford each other protection and help, and mutually render life agreeable."[41] Verse 10 refers to a literal fall but undoubtedly also evokes any difficulty encountered. In ancient Near Eastern culture, falling could be perilous, putting one's very life at stake. In such a situation a companion could literally be a life-saver.

A companion will also provide warmth against the cold night (v. 11). Rashi understands sleeping together as a euphemism for sexual intercourse, but

36. Contra Schoors ("Word *ṭôb*," 697), who takes "good" here to mean "pleasure." But more is at stake here than pleasure; the quest is rather about finding out what makes life meaningful.

37. Longman, *Ecclesiastes*, 138–40.

38. Gordis, *Koheleth*, 242.

39. Ogden, "'Better'-Proverb," 499; idem, "Mathematics of Wisdom," 452–53. Seow (*Ecclesiastes*, 181) notes that this reversal has an ancient Near Eastern context earlier than Ecclesiastes. Indeed, 4:9–12 is one of several places in Ecclesiastes that manifest a close similarity to the Gilgamesh Epic (Seow, *Ecclesiastes*, 64–65).

40. Schoors ("Word *ṭôb*," 685) argues that *ṭôb* here means "better"; "it is a really good reward in contrast with what the solitary worker will obtain." I have retained the translation "good" because of its resonance with "good" in v. 8. This resonance suggests that the reward may be more than just really good but be a key to "the good" of life.

41. Hengstenberg, *Ecclesiastes*, 130.

the dominant view that the two are just companions goes back as early as 'Abot de Rabbi Nathan in the second century AD.[42] There is no reason why it could not include a marriage partner, but it need not be limited in this way. In Western society, the idea of adults sharing a bed evokes sexual connotations that it would not in the ancient Near East and many other non-Western societies today.

Verse 12 reflects on the security a companion provides. Isolated, one is more vulnerable to violent attack than in community. Longman suggests that the most natural setting here is that of a journey.[43] Roads outside cities and towns were often hazardous, and the isolated traveler would be particularly vulnerable to attack. A companion would lessen the danger.

Qohelet's reflection on the advantages of companionship climaxes in the well-known proverb that a three-stranded cord is not easily severed. The move from two (companions) to three is a typical example of numerical parallelism in Hebrew.[44] If two are better, then how good will three be! As Shaffer has shown, this proverb also has close parallels in the Sumerian text *Gilgamesh and Huwawa*, so that Qohelet is here probably quoting a well-known proverb about the benefits of friendship.[45]

This positive proverb concludes this short section on the benefit of community. Far from Qohelet being sarcastic about family and communal life, he recognizes its practical value in the provision of companionship, warmth, and security.[46] However, it is important to note that it does not resolve Qohelet's dilemma. His conclusion has already been stated in v. 7. Community is certainly better than isolation, but it is isolation that Qohelet has observed, so that his reflections on community intensify the problem of what he has seen rather than resolving it.

> [13]Better is a poor but wise youth than an old but foolish king who no longer knows how to receive instruction.
> [14]One can indeed come out of prison to reign, even though being born poor in one's kingdom.

42. Ibn Ezra also takes the verse literally. See Ibn Ezra, *El Comentario de Abraham Ezra al Libro del Ecclesiastes: Introducion, Traduccion y Edicion Critica*, ed. M. Gomez Aranda, Textos y estudios "Cardenal Cisneros" 56 (Madrid: Instituto de Filologia del CSIC, 1919).

43. Longman, *Ecclesiastes*, 142.

44. See Amos 1 for repeated examples of numerical parallelism. Cf. also W. Watson, *Classical Hebrew Poetry*, 282.

45. Shaffer, "Mesopotamian Background"; and idem, "New Light on the 'Three-Ply Cord.'" See also Landsberger, "Zur vierten und siebenten Tafel."

46. D. Miller ("Power in Wisdom," 170) links this section with the preceding one by noting that "for wisdom's power to be activated, Qohelet's audience will need to embrace the alternative community lifestyle he proposes." He argues (ibid., 146) that 4:1–16 is a unit in which individualism and materialism are identified as central elements in the persistence of oppression.

> ¹⁵I observed all the living, who walked under the sun, with the youth who replaced him.
> ¹⁶There was no end to all the people, to all those he led. Yet those who came later did not like him. This too is enigmatic and a striving after wind.

4:13–16. *Government.* As Qohelet has done in the previous two sections, he again starts with a proverb expressing traditional wisdom. Verse 13 is the fourth better-than proverb in this chapter. A poor but wise youth is of more value than a king who is no longer open to advice. Proverbs stresses the importance of listening: "An essential ingredient in the wisdom experience is the ability to listen. Solomon asked for a 'listening heart' as the gift by which he might govern the people of God (1 Kings 3:9). . . . The fool is precisely the one who will not listen, who lacks a sense of docility."[47]

Proverbs makes the point several times that a wise leader takes advice. For example, Prov. 20:18 asserts: "Plans are established by counsel; make war by taking instruction."[48] The king would decide to go to war, and this proverb highlights the importance of the king taking advice in making such a decision. A king no longer open to advice could be catastrophic for his people, hence Qohelet's comparison between a poor but wise youth and an old king.

In v. 14 we learn more about this youth. He is not only poor but has been imprisoned.[49] Seow notes that in the ancient Near East prisons were not penitentiaries; people were usually thrown into prison for economic or political reasons.[50] Out of prison he ascends to the throne and replaces the old king. Some commentators suspect that we have here an allusion to Joseph, who did indeed emerge from prison to become a leader, but crucially for our purposes not to be king (Gen. 37:41–57).[51]

The Hebrew in this section has its challenges; indeed, Irwin describes it as "Hebrew usage at its worst"![52] It is hard, for example, to know whether two or three people are involved in the action. Does v. 15 introduce a third character in "the youth who replaced him"? Debate centers on the meaning of *haššēnî*, which qualifies the youth and literally means "the second." Some commentators suggest excising the word as a gloss, but all the MSS attest the

---

47. Murphy, "Proverbs and Theological Exegesis," 89.

48. Cf. also Prov. 11:14; 15:22; 24:6.

49. Syntactically we cannot be sure whether it is the king or the youth who comes out of prison to reign, but in context it is clearly the youth.

50. Seow, *Ecclesiastes*, 184.

51. Crenshaw (*Ecclesiastes*, 112) notes that this anecdote "echoes the story about Joseph." Others who see in this narrative an allusion to Joseph are D. Miller, "Power in Wisdom," 164, 165; Ogden, "Historical Allusion," who argues for allusions to Joseph and David in this section; and Rudman, "Contextual Reading," who reads 4:13–16 in the light of the court story genre, examples of which are the Joseph narrative, Esther, and Daniel.

52. Irwin, "Ecclesiastes 4:13–16," 255. See also A. Wright, "The Poor but Wise Youth."

word. Others, and this is the majority view nowadays, understand it to introduce a third character, namely the youth who replaces the first youth on the throne.[53] Gordis, however, suggests reading *haššēnî* in apposition to *hayyeled* (the youth). He finds an exact parallel to this usage in Hos. 2:7 [9], in which "first husband" does not imply other husbands.[54] Thus "second" would simply mean "next," so that the youth here in v. 15 can be taken to be the same youth referred to in vv. 13–14. The context seems to favor this direction, for the point of the anecdote is not that even the wise youth is replaced, but rather that the people come to dislike their wise leader.

Qohelet observes that his following is immense (vv. 15–16). But, and here we have Qohelet's ironic twist to the tale, those who come later dislike him. A wise king may be better than an old king who refuses advice, but what if the wise king loses all popularity? Qohelet's observation of the exercise of political power thus leads him once again to conclude that this too is enigmatic and a striving after wind.

Theological Implications

In this chapter, Qohelet examines four problem areas that make life enigmatic for him: oppression, distorted motivations in work, isolation in work, and political leadership. The range of his exploration is once again evident—he really is concerned with life under the sun. Each area is examined through the grid of his epistemology of reason, observation, and experience, and in each case he comes to see life as enigmatic. In each section we are clearly told "I observed," and his conclusions follow from this. Characteristic of the last three sections is his starting with traditional wisdom and then deconstructing it through his experience and reason and observation.

The OT, and Proverbs in particular, addresses the issue of oppression. Qohelet shares their aversion to it but makes no attempt to advise against it or to propose any solutions. His empirical approach confines him to describing what he has observed and declaring that in such a context it is better never to have been born.

The problem of oppression that Qohelet wrestles with remains as relevant as ever in the twenty-first century. *Oppression* takes many forms today, and suffice it to mention one major example, the oppression of children. According to Wendell Berry, "In the course of our unprecedented inhumanity toward other creatures and the world, we have become unprecedently inhumane toward humans—and especially, I think, toward human children."[55] UNICEF reports

53. So Murphy, Fox, Whybray, Longman, N. Lohfink, Seow, etc.
54. Gordis, *Koheleth*, 245.
55. Berry, *Another Turn of the Crank*, 78.

that approximately 218 million children ages 5 to 17 work, with about 126 million working in hazardous situations, such as in mines, with chemicals and pesticides in agriculture, or with dangerous machinery.[56] They are everywhere, but invisible, toiling as domestic servants in homes, laboring behind the walls of workshops, hidden from view in plantations. Millions of girls work as domestic servants and unpaid household help and are especially vulnerable to exploitation and abuse. Children may be trafficked (1.2 million), forced into debt bondage or other forms of slavery (5.7 million), into prostitution and pornography (2 million), into participating in armed conflict (300,000) or other illicit activities (600,000). However, the vast majority of child laborers—70 percent or more—work in agriculture.

This is just one major example of contemporary oppression. One can add to it the oppression of women that we became more aware of in the twentieth century, oppression of one people by another such as the Palestinians by the Israelis, the oppression of the blacks in apartheid South Africa revealed in its horror through the Truth and Reconciliation Commission, Mugabe's brutal oppression of his opponents in Zimbabwe, the first genocide of the twenty-first century in Darfur, the practice of torture, and so on. Global economic inequality is another form of oppression. As Stiglitz notes, "Free trade has not worked because we have not tried it; trade agreements of the past have been neither free nor fair. . . . This asymmetric globalization has put developing countries at a disadvantage. It has left them worse off than they would be with a truly free and fair trade regime."[57] Similarly John Paul II observed that

> it is still possible today, as in the days of *Rerum novarum*, to speak of inhuman exploitation. In spite of the great changes which have taken place in the more advanced societies, the human inadequacies of capitalism and the resulting domination of things over people are far from disappearing. In fact, for the poor, to the lack of material goods has been added a lack of knowledge and training which prevents them from escaping their state of humiliating subjection.[58]

There is much today to evoke the anguish Qohelet felt as he observed oppression: "Oh, the tears of the oppressed!" Even with the fuller light of the whole canon of Scripture, the experience of oppression remains a mystery. Christians believe that with the consummation of history in Christ there will be justice, but this remains a confession of faith amid the enigma of oppression.

Certainly Christ gives us wisdom in terms of knowing how to respond to oppression. It has been well stated that the Beatitudes in Matt. 5 are a picture

---

56. What follows is taken almost verbatim from the UNICEF Web site: http://www.unicef .org/protection/index_bigpicture.html (accessed November 6, 2008).
57. Stiglitz, *Making Globalization Work*, 62. See also idem, *Globalization and Its Discontents*.
58. John Paul II, *Centesimus Annus*, 94.

of Christ, the king of the kingdom. He cultivates his character in his followers so that we too become those who hunger and thirst after righteousness—personal and social and global. William Barclay speaks evocatively in this respect of the "bliss of the starving spirit."[59] We are to manifest a deep hunger for justice. Luminous examples for Christian social and political activism include Mother Teresa; the social reformers of past days such as Shaftsbury, who labored in nineteenth-century Britain to reform the conditions of children and women workers amid the Industrial Revolution; and Wilberforce, who fought successfully for the abolition of the slave trade. In the twentieth century, particularly through the Lausanne Congress and the resulting Covenant of 1974, evangelicals recovered the imperative to serve Christ in word *and* deed. Even as we tell forth the good news of Christ, we need to give expression to it by doing what we can to undermine oppression.

The NT epistles also recognize that prior to the return of Christ oppression and persecution will often have to be endured. For example, in Rom. 12:14 Paul exhorts his readers to bless those who persecute them, before going on in Rom. 13:1–8 to outline a vision of a just state in which good is rewarded and evil punished. But the NT is strongly in touch with the fact that there will be oppression and that believers will have to endure many trials. Thus, even within the context of the metanarrative of the Bible, intellectually at least, we, like Qohelet, will have to continue to live with the mystery of oppression.

From a theological perspective rivalry is a complex topic to unravel. Rivalry and jealousy (v. 4) are certainly expressions of self-interest, but is all self-interest wrong? Skillen notes that in contemporary debate sometimes market and economic enterprises, interest-group politics, and even government itself are judged as selfish and self-serving, whereas "civil-society" projects are valued as constructive and selfless.[60] However, he asserts that self-interest has a legitimate place. Parents are not being selfish when they look out for the interests of their children and family. It is not selfish for a business to seek to increase its sales and to secure legal protection and the best tax policies. It is not wrong for states to protect their own national interests. The problem comes when these legitimate self-interests are skewed. Parents' concern for their family becomes skewed when they aim only at the benefit of their children and lose sight of the well-being of all families. With regard to business: "If the only thing business people do is to seek the interest of their own businesses and lobby for benefits to help their businesses regardless of all else, then they turn proper self-care into unjust and unstewardly selfishness."[61] National self-interest becomes skewed if a nation fails to take seriously its responsibility with other states to do justice internationally.

59. Barclay, *Gospel of Matthew*, 114–17.
60. Skillen, *In Pursuit of Justice*, 36–39.
61. Ibid., 37.

Another area where rivalry or competition has an important place is in sports. Zuidema expresses the views of some in the Christian community about competition this way: "Competition is morally wrong because it pits one player or team against another in rivalry which often results in hate."[62] Yet surely Zuidema is correct when he counters that competition is a "basic ingredient" of sports and athletics and that "no one can play responsibly to lose."[63] Yet competition in sport can be twisted by sin and turn ugly. The great Green Bay Packers football coach Vince Lombardi's comments express this distortion of competition: "Winning isn't everything; it's the only thing"; "To play this game you must have fire in you, and there is nothing that stokes fire like hate."

Theologically, therefore, it is important to discern the context in which competition is taking place and to distinguish between a distorted desire to be better than one's neighbor and the God-given desire to excel.[64] As Forsyth asserts:

> Christ is certainly no less concerned than Nietzsche that the personality should receive the fullest development of which it is capable, and be more and more of a power. The difference between them lies in the moral method by which the personality is put into possession of itself and its resources—in the one case, by asserting self, in the other by losing it. . . . We complete our personality only as we fall into place and service in the vital movement of the society in which we live. . . . The aggressive egotist is working his own moral destruction by stunting and shrinking his true personality. Social life, duty and sympathy are the only conditions under which a true personality can be shaped.[65]

What Qohelet fingers is the dominance of the "aggressive egoist" in labor, who is only out for his own gain and to be one-upping everyone else. In the context of the West today it may be hard to understand why rivalry as a motivation for work should be such a problem for Qohelet, because nowadays it is everywhere. Capitalism operates to such an extent on competition and rivalry that we struggle to see rivalry as the perversion of work that it is. In an essay titled "Economy and Pleasure," Wendell Berry analyzes the extent to which competition has come to dominate our lifestyles and the problems with it. Berry acknowledges that competition is a useful and important part of life but only within limits. He argues that in the world of work and economics, competition has gotten out of control: "It seems that we have been reduced almost to a state of absolute economics, in which people and all other creatures and things may be considered purely as economic 'units,' or integers of

62. Zuidema, "Athletics from a Christian Perspective," 185.
63. Ibid., 184–85.
64. On legitimate excellence see Peterson, *Run with the Horses.*
65. Forsyth, *Positive Preaching and the Modern Mind*, 178–79.

production, and in which a human being may be dealt with, as John Ruskin put it, 'merely as a covetous machine.'"[66]

Berry argues that the economic ideal of competition is false and silly; it requires that there be winners and losers, and a society dominated by winners never knows what to do with the losers. Unlimited competition leads to concentrations of economic power and the class of losers becomes ever larger. Such competition destroys life: "It is a fact that the destruction of life is a part of the daily business of economic competition as now practiced. If one person is willing to take another's property or to accept another's ruin as a normal part of economic enterprise, then he is willing to destroy that other person's life as it is and as it desires to be."[67] The problem with an economy of competition is that it is reductive: "Rats and roaches live by competition under the law of supply and demand; it is the privilege of human beings to live under the laws of justice and mercy."[68] An economy of competition undermines community and destroys nature. So Berry appeals for an economy of affection and pleasure, noting God's pleasure in his creation (Rev. 4:11).

Berry's articulation of an economy of pleasure is redolent of Goudzwaard and de Lange's *Beyond Poverty and Affluence: Toward a Canadian Economy of Care*. In both cases competition is decentered as the ruling motivation for work. It should therefore be clear that Qohelet's concern with rivalry as the motivation for work is an acute insight into the misdirection of labor and connected with his analysis of oppression. Rivalry as the motivation for work will lead to a class of winners and losers and is fertile ground for oppression. Work is a God-given task by which we serve God, our neighbors, and the creation and develop its potentials to the glory of God. Rivalry as the motivation for work violates the tenth commandment and denatures work and destroys community. Not surprisingly, therefore, Qohelet's next section in this chapter deals with community and its lack.

Qohelet outlines the advantages of community but observes an isolated individual. Qohelet's affirmation of community is theologically orthodox and insightful. Humans are made not for isolation but for community, as Gen. 2 makes clear. Indeed, we are constituted in relationship, first with God and then with one another.[69] It is the latter dimension that Qohelet focuses on in these verses; the importance of relationship to God comes to focus in 5:1–7. Gaede thus asserts, "The first biblical insight we must come to grips with if we are to pursue an alternative social science is this: God created the human as a social being. God designed the human being to be a relational creature. Note this point well. Humankind was created to relate to other beings. It was not an accident. It was not the result of sin. It was an intentional, creational

---

66. Berry, *What Are People For?* 130.
67. Ibid., 131–32.
68. Ibid., 135.
69. On Jesus and community, see G. Lohfink, *Jesus and Community*.

given."[70] The trinitarian God is a relational being at core, and his image bearers are likewise relational beings. Relationship with God is primary, but Gen. 2 is remarkable in its insistence that even with his relationship with God Adam was "alone." We are made to love others and to be loved by others. As Barth asserts, "Every supposed humanity which is not radically and from the very first fellow-humanity is inhumanity."[71]

As with the other issues Qohelet raises in chap. 4, the theme of community is of great importance today. It is widely recognized that modernity fractured community and that our well-being depends on its recovery. Western individualism and postmodern pluralism have left many in the West isolated and desperate for meaningful relationships. Colin Gunton argues that in the secularization of modernity, God was displaced into humankind with disastrous consequences for community. The other person becomes the one we must escape from or rule over. As a solution Gunton invokes the trinitarian concept of sociality: "Persons do not simply enter into relations with one another, but are constituted by one another in the relations."[72]

Individualism continues to characterize Western culture. Its attraction is that "to the degree one can successfully internalize the philosophy of individualism, one can reduce relational pain and maximize personal power."[73] Qohelet's loner is a graphic picture of this lifestyle, but as he discerns, it fails to fulfill. The opposite pole of individualism, namely communalism, also emerged as a major temptation in the twentieth century, with Marxism as the obvious example. In this approach the individual is suppressed for the sake of the larger whole. As Gaede notes, this is simply the other side of the coin of individualism and can be equally oppressive.[74]

Gunton's analysis is acute, but the question remains how we are to go about recovering life-giving community today. Much Western Christianity is privatized religion, and too often the church has succumbed to this privatization, so that the church often fails to be a community. Recovery of community will require a penetrating analysis of where Western culture is at present and the shape of a missional response to it. At the end of *After Virtue*, Alasdair MacIntyre argues:

> What matters at this stage is the construction of local forms of community within which civility and the intellectual and moral life can be sustained through the new dark ages which are already upon us. And if the tradition of the virtues was able to survive the horrors of the last dark ages, we are not entirely without grounds for hope. This time however the barbarians are not waiting beyond

70. Gaede, *Where Gods May Dwell*, 98.
71. Barth, CD 3.2:228.
72. Gunton, *The One, the Three, and the Many*, 214.
73. Gaede, *Where Gods May Dwell*, 136.
74. Ibid., 138.

the frontiers; they have already been governing us for quite some time. And it is our lack of consciousness of this that constitutes part of our predicament. We are waiting not for a Godot, but for another—doubtless very different—St. Benedict.[75]

Some have suggested that we need a "new monasticism" in order to recover the community we so urgently need, and this is an important way forward. In the Roman Catholic, Anglican, and Orthodox traditions, monasticism continues to thrive and offers to the catholic church a great resource for community.[76] Since the Reformation, Protestants have never fully recovered the opportunities that geographical community presents, but there are encouraging signs of a renewed interest in this and certainly plenty of models that Protestants could copy without in any way relinquishing their Protestantism. On several occasions I have visited the Mother of God Community north of Washington, DC. Single working persons live in apartments in the community with one or more priests also present. A school is part of the community. Catholic families in the area may also join the community and attend Mass each day in the chapel and participate in a variety of other ways. On Sundays community members attend and participate in local churches. This is an example of the sort of community that could go a long way to help the church recover community. Apart from this but certainly not in opposition to it, the challenge to local churches is clear—churches need to become bearers of the comprehensive Christian tradition so that they enable Christians to live out all of life in Christ *together*. This is no small challenge, and it will certainly entail a recovery of Christianity as a worldview or plausibility structure that relates to all of life under the sun, as well as to the communal nature of faith.

But, of course, the institutional church is not our only source of community. Indeed, Qohelet does not focus on the cultic community in this section. Nor does he restrict his vision to family life, but it is clearly part of what he reflects upon. As we know from Gen. 2, marriage and family life is the major source for companionship. In the West this too is in crisis, and a major need of our day is the recovery and nurturance of healthy families. The companionship that Qohelet describes would also include friendship, and since 1980 there has been a renewed interest in the theology of friendship.[77] Qohelet alerts us to the practical value of companionship, and Stearns similarly asserts: "Good friends are as basic to life and health as knowing how to cup your hands when there's

75. MacIntyre, *After Virtue*, 263. Benedict was responsible for forming monasticism such that it transformed Europe. See Bosch, *Transforming Mission*, 230–36.

76. See, e.g., Jean Vanier's classic, *Community and Growth*.

77. Theological reflection on friendship has a long tradition; see, e.g., Konstan, *Friendship in the Classical World*, 149–73; C. White, *Christian Friendship in the Fourth Century*; Southern, *Saint Anselm*, 138–65; Aelred of Rievaulx, *Spiritual Friendship*; etc. Recent discussions of the subject are Meilander, *Friendship*; Wadell, *Friendship and the Moral Life*; Burrell, *Friendship and Ways to Truth*; Soskice, *Kindness of God*, 157–80.

nothing else to drink from. The most self-loving action any of us can perform in a lifetime is learning how to develop and sustain close friendships."[78]

One of the best recent theologies of friendship is that by O'Callaghan, *The Feast of Friendship*. He describes the surprising blessing that friendships have been in his own life and notes Jesus's capacity for forming close friendships, not least with John, the beloved disciple. He concludes: "The full intensity of love, commitment, devotion, and inner unity that typify the best of friends is an initiation into the communion that all will experience in Christ in the everlasting kingdom. Therefore, to pursue friendships in the beauty of holiness is to drink deeply of the mystery of God's kingdom."[79]

A word should also be said here about solitude. Clearly the solitude depicted in Eccles. 4:8 is unhealthy. But a healthy solitude is an indispensable part of genuine community. Nouwen addresses this and the related issue of celibacy in his *Clowning in Rome*: "Solitude is the very ground from which community grows. Whenever we pray alone, study, read, write, or simply spend quiet time away from the places where we interact with each other directly, we are potentially opened for a deeper intimacy with each other."[80] Solitude is crucial because the center of Christian community is not the community itself but God. Solitude counters any tendency to absolutize the community and creates room for the individual to recenter in God and thus to rediscover one's unity in community. Thomas Merton's well-known experience of coming into Louisville after years of being in a monastery is exemplary in this respect:

> In Louisville, at the corner of Fourth and Walnut, in the center of the shopping district, I was suddenly overwhelmed with the realization that I loved all those people, that they were mine and I theirs, that we could not be alien to one another even though we were total strangers. . . . I have the immense joy of being *man*, a member of a race in which God Himself became incarnate.[81]

At times Qohelet's analysis is so contemporary that it is easier to apply it today than to grasp its ancient significance. This is true of his final section on leadership. In the autocracies in which Qohelet lived it is hard to see why a wise king losing popularity would be a major problem, whereas in our democracies it is only too easy to see the problem with a wise leader losing popularity. Qohelet is presumably getting at the fact that even when the good is provided, people cannot be relied on to embrace it. This is truly the nature of a fallen world—it is not that there are not solutions and salvation but so often humans do not want the good, do not want salvation.

78. Stearns, *Living through Personal Crisis*, 69.
79. O'Callaghan, *Feast of Friendship*, 136.
80. Nouwen, *Clowning in Rome*, 13.
81. Merton, *Conjectures of a Guilty Bystander*, 156–57.

Qohelet's analysis of the dangers of wielding power is acute and in line with the rest of the OT. Absolute power is always in danger of corrupting absolutely, and this is evoked in the image of the old king who no longer takes advice. This could be devastating for the people under such a king's rule. OT Torah and narrative emphasize repeatedly that God's law is over the king and not vice versa (cf. Deut. 17:14–20). The battle with monarchy and its ultimate demise as a model of government is all related to whether the king will facilitate Yahweh's rule over his people (cf. 2 Kings 17). Proverbs insists that the wise ruler listens to advice.[82]

Contemporary democracy does not exempt us from these problems. Wise governance remains a challenge. One thinks, for example, of the decision by U.S. President George W. Bush and British Prime Minister Tony Blair to invade Iraq. Which voices did they listen to, and did they fail to receive adequate instruction before acting so decisively? At the very least, it would appear that in many aspects they were ill-advised or chose to ignore certain voices that they did not wish to hear. The implications have been considerable.

In our times, in which democracy is the dominant political model, it is easier to see why a wise leader being unpopular is such a problem. The Bush administration claimed to seek to spread the gospel of political and economic freedom across the globe but often failed to note that successful democracy depends on much more than elections and a "free" market. Majority votes by themselves can easily simply reinforce evil and injustice. A wise populace is required to develop wise government. As Skillen notes: "'Civil society' cannot save a people from oppressive, unjust governments, but neither can such governments be changed without the emergence of a sense of civic purpose and the ability of citizens to mobilize in order to reform or replace oppressive governments. For the latter to occur, people need to become literate, publicly engaged, and willing to act in the public interest."[83] People get the leaders they deserve, and in our consumer culture, this bodes ill for the fate of wise leaders.

82. On OT wisdom and politics, see Bartholomew, "Time for War."
83. Skillen, *In Pursuit of Justice*, 34–35.

H.
Worship
(5:1–7 [4:17–5:6])

Translation

5:1 [4:17]Watch your step[1] as you go to the house of God. Approach[2] to listen[3] rather than[4] to offer the sacrifice of the fools, for they do not know that they are doing evil.[5]

1. Literally "steps," but the English idiom is singular and the Qere is singular.

2. Taking the infinite absolute *qārôb* as an imperative (GKC §113aa, bb). It is also possible to take *qārôb* as an adjective meaning "presentable" or "acceptable," or in the nominal sense of the infinitive absolute as "the approach." See Seow, *Ecclesiastes*, 194; and Murphy, *Ecclesiastes*, 44–45.

3. *Lišmōa'* is often taken to mean "obey," particularly in relation to 1 Sam. 15:22. However, in context Qohelet is concerned with speech and understanding, so that "listen" is the more appropriate translation.

4. This is an example of the "pregnant use of the *min*" in which the attributive idea is supplied by the context (GKC §133e).

5. Literally "they do not know to do evil." In context, this cannot mean that they do not know how to do evil. Various emendations have been proposed, for which see Seow, *Ecclesiastes*, 194–95. The solution is to recognize that the idiom *yāda' lĕ* means "to recognize, acknowledge, to know of" (cf. Ps. 69:5 [6]; 2 Sam. 7:20; Isa. 59:12; BDB 394.4.a). However, Spangenberg ("Century of Wrestling," 85) translates "for they do not know how to do evil" and argues that this is an ironic comment about fools.

²[1]Do not be hasty⁶ with your mouth nor let your heart be quick to bring forth a word⁷ before God, for God is in heaven and you are on earth. Therefore let your words be few.

³[2]For the dream⁸ comes with⁹ much work, and the voice of the fool with many words.

⁴[3]When you make a vow to God, do not delay in fulfilling it, for there is no pleasure in fools. Fulfill what you vow![10]

⁵[4]It is better that[11] you do not vow than that you make a vow and not fulfill it.

⁶[5]Do not let[12] your mouth cause your flesh to sin.[13] And do not say to the messenger that it was an error. Why[14] should God be angry on account of your voice and destroy the work of your hands?

⁷[6]For with many dreams come enigmas and many words.[15] Instead,[16] fear God.

Interpretation

This section follows on from Qohelet's exploration of the enigma of oppression, rivalry in work, lack of community, and the problem of good government.[17]

6. The Piel form of *bāhal* can mean "to dismay, terrify" or "to act quickly." The latter meaning, which is most appropriate here, is characteristic of Late Biblical Hebrew.

7. *Dābār* could mean "word" or "event" or "matter." Because of the focus on speech, "word" is more likely.

8. If one takes the definite article of "the dream" as generic, then "dreams" would be an appropriate translation. However, "the dream" (singular) parallels "the voice of the fool" (singular), and so I have retained "the dream" in the translation.

9. *Bě* here has the sense of accompaniment (RJW §248).

10. On the function of *'ăšer* in this exhortation, see Schwarzschild, "Syntax," 19.

11. As is often the case in Ecclesiastes, *'ăšer* here means "that," as does *še* in the parallel line in this verse. This usage of *'ăšer* is common in Late Biblical Hebrew.

12. See Whitley, *Koheleth*, 47, for this meaning of *ntn*.

13. The prefixed *h* that characterizes the Hiphil infinitive construct is elided in *lahăţî'* (see Whitley, *Koheleth*, 48).

14. *IBHS* §18.3c suggests that the use here of *lāmmâ* is quasi-rhetorical and could be translated as "otherwise." Whitley (*Koheleth*, 49) and Seow (*Ecclesiastes*, 196) suggest the meaning "lest."

15. The MT reads lit., "For in many dreams and enigmas and words very many." Various emendations have been proposed, but none is satisfactory (see Whitley, *Koheleth*, 49–50). Seow (*Ecclesiastes*, 197) takes *hălōmôt wahăbālîm* as a hendiadys meaning "vacuous dreams." Longman (*Ecclesiastes*, 150) takes *wahăbālîm* to be qualifying "words" and translates "meaningless words." With Murphy (*Ecclesiastes*, 44), I read the conjunction *wě* in *wahabālîm* adjunctively, meaning "also" (RJW §441). "Also" here has the sense of what accompanies, hence my translation.

16. Adversative use of *kî* (RJW §447).

17. On the reception history of Eccles. 5:1–7 [4:17–5:6] in the twentieth century, see Spangenberg, "Century of Wrestling." Astonishingly, the history of interpretation moves from seeing

A new section is indicated by the *hebel* conclusion in 4:16 and the change in tone from reflection to that of instruction,[18] as well as the change in subject matter. Qohelet now turns to the theme of speech and worship.[19]

> **5:1 [4:17]**Watch your step as you go to the house of God. Approach to listen rather than to offer the sacrifice of the fools, for they do not know that they are doing evil.

5:1 [4:17]. In v. 1 Qohelet exhorts to watch one's step when going to the house of God. In Prov. 1:15–16 and 4:27 feet are used as a graphic symbol for human conduct.[20] Proverbs 1:15–16 exhorts readers to keep "your foot from their [sinners] paths, for their feet run to do evil." "One's feet could lead one astray . . . or lead one aright. . . . People must be careful, therefore, to hold back their feet from the wrong way. . . . It appears that going to the temple is, for Qohelet, not synonymous with being on the right track."[21] Jeremiah was notoriously instructed to stand in the gate of the temple and to exhort the Israelites going in and out to amend their ways and not to trust in deceptive words: "This is the temple of the LORD, the temple of the LORD, the temple of the LORD" (Jer. 7:1–4). Similarly Qohelet exhorts his readers to "watch their step" as they go into the temple—it is the place where God dwells, and a casual approach to the temple is dangerous.

The reference to sacrifice and the quotation from Deuteronomy in vv. 4–5 make it likely that Qohelet has the temple rather than the synagogue in mind, so that the image evoked here is of the Israelite striding toward and through the temple. Qohelet urges that this not be done thoughtlessly—one should approach to listen rather than to offer "the sacrifice of the fools." The sacrifice of the fools should be thought of not as a denial of the value of sacrifice per se but as a critique of superficial religion that goes through the

---

5:1–7 in part or its entirety as an addition to Ecclesiastes to N. Lohfink's (*Qoheleth*, 8) view that 5:1–7 is integral to the book and a poem that stands at the center of Ecclesiastes.

18. There is some discussion as to whether 5:1–7 is prose or poetry. With Spangenberg ("Century of Wrestling," 85), I read this section as an instruction and thus prose, not poetry.

19. Scholars differ about the structure of this section. Spangenberg ("Century of Wrestling," 85) discerns four admonitions (5:1, 2, 4–5, and 6 and 7b) and two proverbs (5:3, 7a). Each admonition has three elements: a prohibition, a motivation, and a conclusion. There is a repetition of vocabulary in both admonitions and proverbs. The first proverb (5:3) follows the first two admonitions, whereas the second proverb (5:7a) comes between the motivation and the conclusion/advice of the fourth admonition. Spangenberg (ibid., 90) argues that the position of the second proverb is rhetorically significant: "The first proverb functions as a short break in the instruction. The second one . . . creates tension. Then the final injunction comes unexpectedly: 'Fear God!' Looking back at the other admonitions one may say that Qohelet was preparing for this injunction all along, but it still comes as a surprise to the implied reader and this reader cannot but endorse Qohelet's view and advice."

20. On the "foot" in Proverbs, see Pippert, *Words from the Wise*, 112–14.

21. Seow, *Ecclesiastes*, 198.

rituals with many words but no awareness of God. As N. Lohfink perceptively notes, "What alone matters is that the fear of God, which transcends any particular ritual act, must not be damaged."[22] "Not of 'sacrifices' in general does Koheleth here speak, but of the sacrifices of *fools*, which were not an outward form expressing the worship which is in spirit and truth, but the contrary thereof, namely an invitation whose purpose was to appease God and to silence the conscience."[23] Thus v. 1 is in the same spirit as 1 Sam. 15:22–23 and Ps. 40:6 [7]. For Qohelet such superficial cultic activity is evil and dangerous.

Indeed, the similarities between Eccles. 5:1 and Ps. 40:6 [7] are remarkable. Not only is there a warning against superficial sacrifice but also an exhortation to listen. Translated literally, Ps. 40:6b reads "ears you have dug for me." This evocative metaphor alerts us to how hard it is to be truly receptive to God's instruction. Peterson says of this verse: "God is speaking and must be listened to. But what good is a speaking God without listening ears? So God gets a pick and shovel and digs through the cranial granite, opening a passage that will give access to the interior depths, into the mind and heart. . . . The result is a restoration of Scripture: eyes turn into ears."[24]

This type of listening is precisely what Qohelet exhorts his reader to do in public worship: to be open to being taught wisdom by God. This is very much in the spirit of Proverbs, which has repeated exhortations to listen and to be open to being taught.[25] "The fool is precisely the one who will not listen, who lacks a sense of docility. The *tōkaḥat*, or 'reproof,' occurs about a dozen times in Proverbs; it is something to be heard and loved, for it leads to correction and improvement."[26] Proverbs 28:9 is particularly interesting in this context: "The one who turns his ear away from listening to the law, even his prayer is an abomination." Old Testament wisdom is sometimes thought to be unaware of OT law, but Proverbs and Qohelet stress that the wise person is open to being instructed from the law. By "listening to God" Qohelet presumably had in mind the instruction one would receive in the temple through the reading and teaching of the law by the priests. N. Lohfink rightly notes, therefore, that the fear of God in this section does "not at all exclude listening to the Torah of Moses."[27]

Indeed, in v. 1 Qohelet captures the twofold function of the temple: as the place where the torah was present and by means of which the priests in-

22. N. Lohfink, *Qoheleth*, 75.
23. Hengstenberg, *Ecclesiastes*, 136.
24. Peterson, *Working the Angles*, 71.
25. See Prov. 2:2; 4:20; 5:1; 15:31; 18:15; 21:13; 22:17; 23:12; 25:12; 28:9.
26. Murphy, "Proverbs and Theological Exegesis," 89.
27. N. Lohfink, "Qoheleth 5:17–19," 633. Spangenberg ("Century of Wrestling," 88) thus wrongly relegates "to listen" to being "probably only a typical wisdom topos."

structed the people, and the place of mediation between God and his people via sacrifices.[28] Vriezen notes that "the temple serves wholly to advance the communion between God and man, and is the meeting-place."[29] "When Yahweh manifests Himself in a certain place, this is in fact always done in order to proclaim His Word. . . . In a temple, a place sanctified forever by His presence, one may expect to receive His Word again and again."[30]

Such an attitude that is focused on God would mean that one's words should be few and carefully chosen. Once again this reflects the same spirit as Proverbs, which has much to say about the tongue and speech.[31] Proverbs 17:27–28 observes, "The one who withholds his words has knowledge. . . . Even a fool who keeps silent is deemed wise, when he closes his lips he is deemed intelligent." How much more so, Qohelet would say, when it comes to approaching God's house. One is dealing with God, and he is in heaven while you are on earth. Qohelet's caution with respect to many words is akin to Jesus's advice in Matt. 6:7–8: "And when you pray, do not heap up empty phrases as the Gentiles do."

> 2 [1]Do not be hasty with your mouth nor let your heart be quick to bring forth a word before God, for God is in heaven and you are on earth. Therefore let your words be few.

5:2 [1]. The theological basis for Qohelet's exhortation is God's transcendence: "God is in heaven and you are on earth." Some think that Qohelet here expounds a view of God as distant and inaccessible and uninterested in human affairs. Similarly critical scholars thought that Deuteronomy with its Name theology had moved from thinking that God was actually present in the temple to being only symbolically present there.[32] However, Qohelet's stress on God's transcendence, like Deuteronomy's (cf. Deut. 3:24), should not be taken to deny God's immanence in the temple. Such a view makes nonsense of Qohelet's exhortation to "listen," an imperative that implies that the temple is the place where one can hear God's address, and hence it is the place where he is present. Furthermore, his reference to God acting in judgment (v. 6) is clearly not a reference to a distant God uninvolved in human affairs. Here, as in Proverbs, the character-consequence structure of human life is in place; sin has consequences. Qohelet's point is that the God approached in the temple is the transcendent holy one, who must therefore be approached with reverence and fear.[33]

28. Vriezen, *Outline of Old Testament Theology*, 248.
29. Ibid., 249.
30. Ibid., 247.
31. See Prov. 13:3; 15:23; 17:27–28; 18:13; 21:23.
32. See Bartholomew, "Composition of Deuteronomy," 167–71.
33. See Ellul, *Reason for Being*, 271–78.

> ³ [2]For the dream comes with much work, and the voice of the fool
> with many words.

5:3 [2]. In v. 3 Qohelet quotes a proverb in support of his view of worship. It is hard to be sure exactly what the first half of the verse means—probably that overwork leads to many dreams. This was not an uncommon view in ancient cultures.[34] Seow notes that in the ancient Near East dreams were often a synonym for the ephemeral, the unreal, and he takes the first part of v. 3 to mean that much work amounts to an illusion.[35] However we interpret it, the comparison is clear: the voice of the fool similarly yields many words, which Qohelet regards as dangerous.

> ⁴ [3]When you make a vow to God, do not delay in fulfilling it, for there
> is no pleasure in fools. Fulfill what you vow!
> ⁵ [4]It is better that you do not vow than that you make a vow and not
> fulfill it.

5:4–5 [3–4]. Qohelet moves on to an example of using words before God, namely the case of making a vow before God. He quotes almost verbatim from Deut. 23:21 [22], indicating that he knows the Torah. A vow before God—Qohelet uses *Elohim* instead of Deuteronomy's *Yahweh*—should be speedily fulfilled; indeed, it is better not to make one than to make one and not fulfill it. In place of Deuteronomy's motive clause—"the LORD your God will surely require it of you, and you will incur guilt"—Qohelet notes that God has no pleasure in a foolish approach that says much but does little. Seow argues that Qohelet is here "typical of the wisdom's tradition to avoid any language of divine causality."[36] However, v. 6 clearly speaks of God becoming angry and destroying the work of one's hands. For Qohelet as for Deuteronomy, failure to fulfill a vow will evoke God's wrath.

Deuteronomy 23:22 [23] states that one will not incur guilt if one refrains from making a vow. Qohelet presents this in v. 5 as a better-than saying; by recasting the teaching in this form, he emphasizes the danger of a casual approach to God. One should err on the side of caution when it comes to approaching God.

> ⁶ [5]Do not let your mouth cause your flesh to sin. And do not say to
> the messenger that it was an error. Why should God be angry on
> account of your voice and destroy the work of your hands?

34. Seow, *Ecclesiastes*, 199.
35. Ibid., 200.
36. Ibid.

5:6 [5]. The reference to "the messenger" in v. 6 is perplexing. Longman suggests that it refers to people in Qohelet's time whose duty it was to follow up on those who had not fulfilled their public vows.[37] N. Lohfink takes the messenger to refer to the priest whose duty it was to oversee the declaration of unintentional sins.[38] Lohfink and Hengstenberg read v. 6 in terms of the fool claiming that his failure to fulfill his vow was an unintentional omission.[39] The law makes room for unintentional sins. Numbers 15:27–31 refers to the individual who sins unintentionally (cf. Lev. 4). However, such unintentional sin is carefully distinguished from acting "high-handedly," the punishment for which is to be cut off from among the people. Whatever the precise case in view, Qohelet here warns against taking such grace for granted and being duplicitous in worship. One is dealing with God, and he will recognize a foolish utterance, even if the messenger does not, and punish the fool accordingly.

> 7 [6]For with many dreams come enigmas and many words. Instead, fear God.

5:7 [6]. Qohelet quotes another proverb in support of his view: with many dreams come enigmas and many words. "Enigmas" (*hăbālîm*) here are clearly undesirable and connected unequivocally with folly. This attitude to *hebel* contrasts with Qohelet's repeated enigmatic conclusion elsewhere in Ecclesiastes. Instead, one should "fear God." This conclusion summarizes the entire passage. Here again Qohelet is one with Proverbs in his approach to wisdom. Proverbs makes the fear of God the beginning of wisdom and repeatedly exhorts its reader in this direction.[40] Fear of God describes an attitude of holy reverence toward God and a creaturely openness to being instructed by him.[41] As Whybray notes, "There is no reason to suppose that for him the fear of God . . . differed from that which is found in such texts as Deuteronomy: obedience, love, service, worship . . . conformity to God's

---

37. Longman, *Ecclesiastes*, 154.
38. N. Lohfink, *Qoheleth*, 77.
39. Ibid.; Hengstenberg, *Ecclesiastes*, 138–39.
40. See Prov. 1:7, 29; 2:1, 5; 3:7; 8:13; 9:10; etc.
41. Scholars regularly distinguish Qohelet's "Fear God" from that of Proverbs and the Torah, arguing that for Qohelet, God is the distant creator "in heaven" (5:2 [1]). For examples of this view, see Pfeiffer, "Gottesfurcht im Buche Kohelet"; and Becker, *Gottesfurcht im Alten Testament*, 249–55. Much is made of the fact that Ecclesiastes never uses *Yahweh* but only *Elohim*. However, in this section *Elohim* is present in the temple where he addresses his people, one can make vows to him, and he acts in judgment—all characteristics of Yahweh. Thus it is better to think of Qohelet's distinctive use of *Elohim* as part of his contextualizing his message rather than as a means of distinguishing *Elohim* from *Yahweh*.

moral commands . . . avoidance of sin . . . honest conduct . . .—in short, the reverence for, and the worship of God, characteristic of sincere Yahwists."[42]

Scholars are divided about the attitude Qohelet adopts toward the temple and temple worship in this section.[43] Crenshaw asserts, "Qoheleth advises caution lest one's action incur divine wrath. This advice neither recommends nor discounts traditional piety, although Qoheleth suspects the motives and conduct of some who approach the sacred place."[44] Longman notes that it is hard to be sure of Qohelet's tone in this section—he neither abandons the cultus nor affirms it wholeheartedly.[45] Gordis comments on v. 2b, "That God was distant from the affairs of men and hence unconcerned with their fate was the characteristic form of unbelief in Israel . . . as it was in the doctrine of Epicurus."[46] Hengstenberg reads this passage positively as a warning against superficial worship—and an exhortation to fear God, a real temptation to the Israelites "groaning under the yoke of the Persians."[47] Similarly, N. Lohfink acknowledges that the religious critique is present but sees this section as the center of Ecclesiastes and as an instruction to behave fittingly within religious worship. Lohfink also notes the similarity between this section and 9:7–12:7.[48]

As my interpretation has shown, one should read this section positively, as do Hengstenberg and Lohfink, and in the same spirit as the *carpe diem* passages. That this section differs from what precedes is clear from the absence of the first person singular and Qohelet's language of observation, the repeated reference to God, the series of imperatives, the reference to Deut. 23, and the negative reference to "enigmas" in v. 7. Lohfink is right to note the connection with 9:7–12:7, but we should also note the connection with 12:13 in which the reader is likewise exhorted to fear God.

N. Lohfink's proposal that this section is the center of Ecclesiastes bears further scrutiny. He argues that Ecclesiastes is formulated along the lines of a Greek diatribe while retaining Semitic palistrophe. "The organization of the text, as most convincingly perceived in its logic and rhetoric, satisfies a Greek sensibility. Yet the 'religious critique,' when judged by that premise, is located out of proper order. Indeed, it functions, for Semitic sensibility, as the center

42. Whybray, "Qoheleth as a Theologian," 264–65. On Qohelet's view of God, see also the helpful article by de Jong, "God in the Book of Qohelet."

43. For a useful discussion of wisdom and cult in the ancient Near East, see Perdue, *Wisdom and Cult*. As Perdue shows, ancient Near Eastern wisdom is largely positive, although not uncritical, toward the cult. He (ibid., 178–88) argues that Qohelet says one should engage in the cult with great caution and foreboding. In my view, Qohelet's approach to the cult is far more positive and more akin to that of the wise generally in the ancient Near East.

44. Crenshaw, *Ecclesiastes*, 116.

45. Longman, *Ecclesiastes*, 148.

46. Gordis, *Koheleth*, 248.

47. Hengstenberg, *Ecclesiastes*, 133ff.

48. See N. Lohfink, *Qoheleth*, 75.

of a palistrophic structure that also informs the text as a whole."[49] The overall structure of Ecclesiastes remains a matter of contention; the structure is more organic than clearly demarcated. As noted in the introduction, the comparison with a Greek diatribe is not compelling. Nevertheless, N. Lohfink's approach is helpful in alerting us to the central role of this section. It resonates with the *carpe diem* passages, with 9:7–12:7, and particularly with the epilogue and its conclusion of "Fear God." Delitzsch goes so far as to suggest that we call Ecclesiastes "The Song of the Fear of God."[50] This section, 5:1–7, is certainly in tune with that song. Even more interesting is that "enigmas" are here seen as folly and the product of many dreams and many words. There are many enigmas in Ecclesiastes, and they are here identified as folly and originating ultimately from not listening to God. The result is that at this point in his journey Qohelet approximates the teaching of Ps. 73, in which the psalmist finds the injustices of life an enigma, or in his words "a wearisome task" (v. 16). It is only when the psalmist goes into the temple that this enigma is existentially resolved for him (v. 17). Such resolution is not clearly stated in this section, but it represents a breakthrough of luminous insight in Qohelet's journey and provides important hints at possible resolution of Qohelet's struggle, as does the connection between enigma and dreams and overwork.

Theological Implications

Qohelet here manifests knowledge of the cultus (the house of God, i.e., the temple) and of OT law. In terms of OT theology this indicates a far more organic relationship between OT law and wisdom than is often recognized (see "Reading Ecclesiastes within the Context of Proverbs and Job and Its Connection to the Torah" in the introduction).

This section on public *worship* has much to teach us. Worship has to do with God, but we have a constant tendency to shift the focus elsewhere, for example, entertainment, one another, or growing the church. In his critique of being quick to speak and his example of making a vow but not fulfilling it, Qohelet is in line with much prophetic critique of Israelite religion. Word and deed must go together in worship, otherwise it becomes empty. The great ritual of the church is the Eucharist, and Paul's warning to the Corinthians in 1 Cor. 11:27–32 is reminiscent of Qohelet's warnings in this section. According to Paul, one will be held accountable for participating in the Eucharist in an unworthy manner. One should examine oneself before participating, lest one eat and drink judgment against oneself. Commenting on v. 27, Thiselton asserts: "The syntax therefore implies *not a sacrilege against the elements*

49. Ibid., 8.
50. Delitzsch, *Ecclesiastes*, 183.

of the Lord's Supper but answerability or being **held accountable** for the sin against Christ of *claiming identification with him* while using the celebration of the meal *as an occasion for social enjoyment or status enhancement without regard to what sharing in the Lord's Supper proclaims."*[51] Qohelet similarly wants to hold his readers accountable for their worship, to ensure that they understand what they are involved in, and to act accordingly.

The particular temptation Qohelet addresses is a careless approach to God and the use of many words, somehow thinking that this will satisfy God without accompanying deeds. Since the coming of Jesus, worship is no longer centered in the temple, but similar dangers remain. In mainline liturgical denominations the danger of empty ritual remains real. And nonliturgical churches have their own temptations, such as emotionalism and entertainment. As N. Lohfink says, "What alone matters is that the fear of God, which transcends any particular ritual act, must not be damaged."[52] Once holy reverence for God is subverted, then other things move into center spot and the danger of idolatry is never far away.

A particular danger in terms of decentering God nowadays, accompanied by many words but not always fitting deeds, is civil religion, in which the state is so closely identified with God that they become inseparable. Jim Skillen addresses this problem in America:

> The early sacralizing of America as the civil-religious community chosen to lead the world to its true destiny explains why Americans tend to believe that all people on earth really are destined (and should desire) to become like us: free, self-governing, and prosperous. Yet, according to the American self-understanding, the future cannot come to pass except through American leadership. . . . The city on a hill must be defended at all costs and by every means. Consequently, every grave threat seems to call for war.
>
> If it is necessary to recognize the religious depths of the Islamist ideology in order to understand Al Qaeda's actions, even if the religion of Osama bin Laden is not that of traditional Islam, so, too, it is necessary to recognize the religious depths of the American exceptionalist ideology, even if that civil religion is now two or three times removed from original Puritanism.[53]

Civil religion was a real danger in Israel—as part of the covenant nation, just being an Israelite seemed to bring assurance that God was on one's side and all was well. The danger with all civil religion is that God is co-opted to our cause and not taken seriously as God. Qohelet's comments are salutary in this respect—in worship we have to deal with God—we need to be instructed

51. Thiselton, *First Corinthians*, 890.
52. N. Lohfink, *Qoheleth*, 75.
53. Skillen, *With or against the World?* 130.

by him and to obey him. Faith without works, as James (2:17) says, is empty and useless.

Taking God seriously as God will mean that we engage with him personally—that, after all, is what worship is about. As Qohelet says, however, we will focus on *listening* to God and be slow to utter many words, especially vows. James 1:19–20 could well be a reflection on this section in Ecclesiastes. James exhorts his readers to be quick to listen, slow to speak, and slow to anger, for one's anger does not produce God's righteousness. As Peterson has noted, the art of listening to God is much neglected nowadays so that we do need to pray for ears to be dug into our heads, as it were. For Christians living between the coming of the kingdom in Jesus and its consummation, it is particularly in the Scriptures that we hear God's address. In a day of proliferation of words it is important to note, "Reading Scripture is not the same as listening to God."[54] As Peterson points out, "The intent in reading Scripture, among people of faith, is to extend the range of our listening to the God who reveals himself in word, to become acquainted with the ways in which he has spoken in various times and places, along with the ways in which people respond when he speaks."[55] A considerable effort is required nowadays to approach Scripture to listen. It will involve recovering such disciplines as sacred reading (*lectio divina*), in which time is taken with Scripture to listen for God's address.[56]

Just as Qohelet needed a priest to read and expound the law to him, so we need preachers and teachers who are themselves listening to Scripture in order to open up the Scriptures for us. As Barth notes, "The fact of the canon tells us simply that the church has regarded the Scriptures as the place where we can expect to hear the voice of God."[57] However, biblical preaching has fallen on bad days in recent decades. As Ellen Davis notes, "It is now widely regarded as axiomatic that one should not do exegesis in the pulpit. Conversely 'homiletical treatments' of Scripture are dismissed by biblical scholars as inherently lacking in substance."[58] A recovery of preaching that facilitates our listening to God is urgently needed today; as Qohelet reminds us, it is our primary reason for gathering around Christ in the Christian community.

Qohelet and Jesus encourage us to be sparing in the words we use with God. In the context of taking oaths Jesus tells us, "Let your word be 'Yes, Yes,' or 'No, No'; anything more than this comes from the evil one."[59] It is intriguing

---

54. Peterson, *Working the Angles*, 61.
55. Ibid., 62.
56. See Peterson, *Eat This Book*.
57. Barth, *Homiletics*, 78.
58. E. Davis, *Wondrous Depths*, xii.
59. Matt. 5:37 NRSV. Historically Matt. 5:33–37 has raised the question of whether Christians are permitted to swear oaths at all. In the light of other verses in the NT, such as Matt. 26:63–68; 2 Cor. 1:23; Gal. 1:20; and Heb. 6:13–18, it is generally argued that in Matt. 5 Jesus does not prohibit all taking of oaths. Thus the thirty-ninth of the Anglican Articles of Religion states: "As we confess that vain and rash Swearing is forbidden Christian men by our Lord Jesus

that with regard to prayer the desert fathers also advise that we nurture our communion with the Father with short prayers: "Abba Macarius was asked 'How should one pray?' The old man said, 'There is no need at all to make long discourses; it is enough to stretch out one's hand and say, "Lord, as you will and as you know, have mercy." And if the conflict grows fiercer say: "Lord, help." He knows very well what we need and he shows us his mercy.'"[60]

Then there is the marvelous Tolstoy story about three Russian monks on a faraway island. The bishop visits them, and he is disturbed to discover that they do not know the Lord's Prayer. He devotes all his time to instructing them in the "Our Father." When he is leaving in his boat he sees the monks running across the water toward the boat. "Father," they say, "we can't remember the 'Our Father.'" Amazed he asks, "Well, how do you normally pray?" "Well," they say, "'Dear God, there are three of you, and there are three of us, have mercy on us!'" The bishop is struck by their simplicity and holiness and tells them to return and be at peace.[61]

Anne Lamott, in her delightful *Traveling Mercies*, says that she and her friends, as busy, stressed-out moms, find that there are two prayers they pray continually: "Help me, help me, help me," and "Thank you, thank you, thank you"![62] The point is that communion facilitated by prayer from the heart requires fewer, not more, words. Words facilitate communion—that is their glory—but in a cerebral culture we use words to do too much. Vanier says:

> To abide or dwell in Jesus is to make our home in him
> And to let Jesus make his home in us.
> We feel at home with him and in him.
> It is a place of rest for one another and presence to one another.
> It is a place of mutual indwelling and friendship.
> This rest is also a source of life and creativity.
> Abiding in him, we bear fruit, we give life to others.
> We live a mutual indwelling.
> This indwelling is friendship.[63]

Rest, indwelling, friendship—words have their place in such intimacy, but so too do silence and resting, waiting, soaking, and basking. The essence of worship is that we deal with *God*, and Qohelet's short section is helpful in reorienting us in this respect.

Christ, and James his apostle, so we judge, that Christian Religion doth not prohibit, but that a man may swear when the Magistrate requireth, so it be done according to the Prophet's teaching, in justice, judgment and truth."

60. Nouwen, *Way*, 80.

61. Told in Nouwen, *Road to Daybreak*, 50.

62. Anne Lamott, *Traveling Mercies: Some Thoughts on Faith* (New York: Pantheon Books, 1999), 82.

63. Vanier, *Drawn*, 272.

We should note as well that this section is illuminating in terms of Qohelet's journey. With its focus on God, worship decenters the ego, the "I." Therefore, it is not surprising that this section gives us some clues as to the origin of Qohelet's struggle. In v. 3 [2] dreams are related to overwork, and in v. 7 [6] they are the source of "enigmas." N. Lohfink has noted the centrality of this section to Ecclesiastes, and we should also note here the clue as to the source of Qohelet's enigmas. They are related to overwork and dreams. As I discuss in the postscript, a psychological reading of Ecclesiastes should focus on the relationship between the ego and the self, and thus God. From a Jungian perspective, overwork and disturbing dreams are a signal that the ego and the self are misaligned. The role of worship is to keep the ego and the self properly aligned, and here in the context of worship we get some hints as to the source of Qohelet's struggles and hence their possible resolution.

I.
Oppression and Profit
(5:8–17 [7–16])

Translation

⁸ ⁽⁷⁾If you see oppression of the poor and robbery of justice and righteousness[1] in the province,[2] do not be astounded at the matter,[3] for one official watches out for another, and there are officials over them.[4]

⁹ ⁽⁸⁾But the profit of a land is for all: a king for a plowed field.[5]

1. The expression *gēzel mišpāṭ wāṣedeq* (robbery of justice and righteousness) is not found anywhere else in the OT, but the meaning is the same as *ligzōl mišpāṭ* in Isa. 10:2 (to rob of justice). Literally *gēzel* means "robbery" or "plunder," and I have retained this translation here because it evokes the injustice involved. Seow (*Ecclesiastes*, 202) translates *gēzel* as "violation," and Longman (*Ecclesiastes*, 157) as "deprivation."

2. See 2:8. The singular may mean that Qohelet is specifically referring to the province of Judah during the Persian period. So Longman, *Ecclesiastes*, 157.

3. On *ḥēpeṣ* (matter) see 3:1 and cf. 3:17; 8:6.

4. The last two clauses are difficult. Translation hinges on how we interpret *gābōaḥ* (official), which is normally an adjective meaning "high" and is generally taken here as a substantive meaning "high official." Kugel ("Qohelet and Money," 35–38), however, argues that *gābōaḥ* never has this meaning in the OT. Rather, when used as a substantive as here, it means "an arrogant one" or "a haughty one" (cf. Job 41:34; Ps. 138:6; Isa. 10:33; Ezek. 21:26). However, Kugel has to emend the text to fit with his reading, and Seow (*Ecclesiastes*, 203), who follows his translation, redivides the consonants to facilitate this translation. In terms of interpretation, there is not much at stake in the decision we make in this respect. See the interpretation.

5. The entire verse is difficult. The referent of the demonstrative pronoun *hî'* is unclear. The Qere has the masculine form *hû'*. Various solutions are proposed (see Seow, *Ecclesiastes*, 204–5). Reading the Qere of the demonstrative pronoun, and thus taking it as referring back to the "profit," and reading *bakkōl* as "for all (people)" rather than "in all respects," I arrive at my translation of this verse. Much depends on how one interprets Qohelet's logic at this point. See the interpretation.

[10] [9]He who loves money will not be satisfied with money, nor he who loves abundance[6] with gain. This also is enigmatic.

[11] [10]When goods increase, those who consume them increase. But what benefit is there to their owner except what his eyes see?[7]

[12] [11]Sweet is the sleep of the laborer whether one eats little or much, but the satiety of the rich person does not allow[8] him to sleep.

[13] [12]There is a sickening evil I observed under the sun; riches were kept by[9] their owner to the harm of the owner.

[14] [13]And those riches were lost in an evil situation. Though a son was born, he has nothing in his hands.[10]

[15] [14]As he came from his mother's womb, naked, so he will return to go, and he will take nothing from his labor that he can carry in his hand.

[16] [15]This also[11] is a sickening evil; just as[12] he came so also shall he go, and what benefit is there for him from toiling for the wind?

[17] [16]Indeed,[13] all his days he eats in darkness, with great vexation, sickness, and anger.

Interpretation

[8] [7]If you see oppression of the poor and robbery of justice and righteousness in the province, do not be astounded at the matter, for

6. Since *'āhab* (loves) never takes the preposition *bĕ* elsewhere, some think the *bĕ* may be the result of dittography. But see Seow, *Ecclesiastes*, 204–5.

7. The Ketib (probably *rĕ'iyat*) and the Qere (*rĕ'ût*) are nominal forms and *hapax legomena*. Whybray (*Ecclesiastes* [NCBC], 99) emends to the infinitive construct, *rĕ'ōt*, a reading supported by a small number of Hebrew MSS. The Ketib *rĕ'iyat* is well attested, however, in Postbiblical Hebrew meaning "seeing, sight." See Jastrow, *Dictionary*, 1436.

8. *Mannîah* is the Hiphil participle of *nwh*. For the Hiphil form meaning "allow," see Ps. 105:14; 1 Chron. 16:21; and Judg. 16:26. The meaning "allow" is also known in Postbiblical Hebrew; see Jastrow, *Dictionary*, 885–86.

9. The preposition *lĕ* indicates agent (RJW §280).

10. N. Lohfink (*Qoheleth*, 82) translates *bĕyādô* (lit. "in his hand") as "in his accounts." He argues that while *bĕyādô* normally means "in his hands," we have a Hebrew text from the historical period of Ecclesiastes that uses the expression in a business context with the meaning "on his account." See N. Lohfink, "Kohelet und die Banken."

11. 4QQoh[a] does not have a *waw* before the *gam*. Seow (*Ecclesiastes*, 207) and Longman (*Ecclesiastes*, 161) take this variant as genuine. However, the MT makes sense as it stands.

12. There is much discussion among scholars about the unique phrase *kol-'ummat še*. Ginsburg (*Coheleth*, 195) and du Plessis ("Aspects," 170) take it as an Aramaism. Isaksson (*Studies*, 195) reads it as a sign of vernacular speech. However, Ibn-Giat, known from Kimchi and referred to by Delitzsch (*Ecclesiastes*, 300), noted that the original form should have been *kil'ummat*, made up of the comparative *kĕ* plus the compound preposition *lĕ'ummat*. This yields the translation "just as" or in Delitzsch's (ibid., 299) terms "altogether exactly as."

13. *Gam* is emphatic.

> one official watches out for another, and there are officials over
> them.
> ⁹ [8]But the profit of a land is for all: a king for a plowed field.

5:8–9 [7–8]. A new section starts in v. 8, as indicated by the return to reflection and the change of subject matter.[14] Some scholars take vv. 8–9 as a separate section.[15] However, oppression, the subject of vv. 8–9, naturally leads on to the theme of pursuing wealth, which is often the cause of oppression. Comparable development of the theme of injustice is found in 3:16–22 and 4:1–3.

Verses 8 and 9 deal once again with *oppression*, a theme already examined in 4:1–3. There Qohelet observed with astonishment and horror that there was no one to comfort the oppressed, whereas here he exhorts the reader not to be surprised at oppression. "Robbery" evokes the injustice of such oppression—the legitimate rights of the oppressed are being snatched away from them. In v. 8b there are two difficulties: first how we translate *gābōah* (official), and second how we understand *šōmēr* (watches out for).

Gābōah literally means "high (one)" and could refer, as most commentators take it, to an official. In this case Qohelet is describing government corruption resulting in oppression. Alternatively, *gābōah*, used here as a substantive, could refer to "arrogant one," without a precise reference to government.[16] From this perspective *gābōah* "probably refers to anyone who is of higher socioeconomic or political status than the ordinary person, but not necessarily a bureaucrat."[17] One cannot be sure of the translation here, but the context in v. 8 of justice and righteousness, above all the domain of government, inclines me to the view that *gābōah* is best translated as "official."

---

14. Fredericks ("Chiasm and Parallel Structure") discerns an extended chiasm and parallel in 5:10 [9]–6:9, which is adopted with some modifications by Seow, *Ecclesiastes*, 216–17. A detailed evaluation is not possible here, but some aspects are not convincing. There are certainly important parallels between 5:8–17 and 6:3–9. However, Fredericks ("Chiasm and Parallel Structure," 26–27), for example, says of 5:18–20 [17–19] (his C) and 6:1–2 (his C′) that "the conceptual unity of these two scenarios is obvious as the rhetorical sequence from observation to conclusion is charted." This fails to recognize the contradictory juxtaposition at work. Seow (*Ecclesiastes*, 217) sees 5:20 as the center of the chiasm and the answer to Qohelet's discussion of insatiability and lack of contentment. However, 5:20 seems to be an integral part of 5:18–20 and as such is set in juxtaposition to what precedes and follows it. Contra Fredericks, 6:9 does not parallel 5:18–20 in relation to the theme of contentment, and this means that Frederick's ("Chiasm and Parallel Structure," 32–33) discernment of the overall movement in these verses is incorrect. Thus the debatable discernment of a chiasm gets in the way of discerning the developing argument rather than illuminating it.

15. Lauha, *Kohelet*, 103–5; Longman, *Ecclesiastes*, 156; Whybray, *Ecclesiastes* (NCBC), 97; Zimmerli, *Buch des Predigers Salomo*, 190–91.

16. So Kugel, "Qohelet and Money"; and Seow, *Ecclesiastes*, 203.

17. Seow, *Ecclesiastes*, 203–4.

The decision as to how to translate *gābōah* is connected with what one makes of *šōmēr*. Again it is hard to be sure, but in the context of government *šōmēr* is probably best translated as "watches out for,"[18] the implication being that the officials have an intricate network of corruption. Ellul comments, "So the problem is not with some rascal who gains power and does evil by accident. No: he obeys those who are above him, and they are worse. They in turn are under a still worse, higher person, and the higher we climb on the ladder of power, the worse the people we have to deal with (how naïve of us to think a court of appeals will hand down a better decision than a lower court!)."[19] The point of one official "watching over" another is that they protect each other's backs in the maintenance of oppression.[20]

Verse 9 is similarly read in a variety of ways. Gordis describes this verse as an "insuperable crux."[21] *Bakkōl* can be translated in a variety of ways: "for all," "by all" (Longman),[22] "in all" (RSV), "on the whole" (G. Barton, Leupold),[23] "over everything" (Gordis),[24] "after all" (NASB), or "always" (Delitzsch).[25] Verse 9b is also open to a variety of translations. Seow regards the reference to a king as sudden, odd, and meaningless, and omits it.[26] Then there are the questions of how to interpret the preposition *lĕ* in *lĕśādeh* (for a field) and whether the final Niphal verb, *neʿĕbād*, refers to the king or the field. Gordis, who takes *neʿĕbād* to refer to the king, proposes that the best rendering is: "Agriculture has an advantage over everything else, for even a king is subject to the land."[27] However, the Niphal of *ʿbd* is found only in Deut. 21:4 and Ezek. 36:9, 34, and has to do with cultivated land.

My decision is not to emend the text (emendation should generally be a last resort), to take *bakkōl* as "for all," to read the *lĕ* in *lĕśādeh* as the *lĕ* of interest or purpose,[28] and to take *neʿĕbād* as referring to the field. This pithy statement would then sum up what a just order should be. The profit of the land is not just for a select few, but is intended for the benefit of all. This principle is encapsulated in a proverb: "A king for a plowed field." This is confirmed by

18. Contra Ogden (*Qoheleth*, 80–81), who reads *šōmēr* as indicating that a system of checks and balances is in place.

19. Ellul, *Reason for Being*, 80–81.

20. With his interpretation of *gābōah* as "arrogant one," Seow (*Ecclesiastes*, 218) takes v. 8b to be a description of arrogant individuals everywhere trying at all costs to move up the socioeconomic ladder without any regard for the poor.

21. Gordis, *Koheleth*, 250.

22. Longman, *Ecclesiastes*, 157.

23. G. Barton, *Ecclesiastes*, 127; Leupold, *Ecclesiastes*, 123.

24. Gordis, *Koheleth*, 250.

25. Delitzsch, *Ecclesiastes*, 294. Seow (*Ecclesiastes*, 204) emends *bakkōl* to *bĕkīlāh* (in its yield).

26. Seow, *Ecclesiastes*, 204.

27. Gordis, *Koheleth*, 250. See Eaton (*Ecclesiastes*, 101) for a variety of possible translations. He proposes, "But an advantage to a land for everyone is: a king over cultivated land."

28. RJW §§271, 277.

the importance of the inalienable holding of land by kin-groups in OT law. As C. J. Wright explains, "That the land should be held in the form of patrimonies which should not pass out of the family was a cherished ideal in Israel that was protected by legislation and theologically justified and sanctioned."[29] Leviticus 25:23 asserts that the land belongs to Yahweh, and Mettinger notes, "The proper concept of this divine ownership appears to be that every Israelite was to regard his holding as deriving from God himself. . . . There existed the consciousness of an intrinsic equality among the Hebrews before God . . . which was expressed . . . by each head of a family holding his land as from God."[30] One's land was a symbol of one's share in the inheritance of Israel and the means of economic survival for one's family. The sort of oppression of the poor that Qohelet describes in v. 8 resulted very often from theft of land, which is why this is so frowned upon in the OT. Proverbs 23:10–11 warns precisely against this: "Do not move an ancient boundary stone or go into the fields of the fatherless, for their redeemer is strong, he will plead their cause against you!" The king was appointed to prevent this sort of thing from happening and to ensure justice for all, which included making sure that property rights were respected. Hence, "a king for a plowed field."

The image evoked is that just rule would facilitate plowed fields throughout the land so that all can benefit from the fruit of the earth. The land should be for all and the king should facilitate justice, but the tone is ironic. The corrupt power relations have spread to the top of the tree and offer no hope of justice for the oppressed. Land and its just distribution are central to OT law, and in an agricultural context one's survival depends on having one's own land to cultivate. This principle of equitable land distribution is powerfully portrayed in the unlawful "robbing" of Naboth's vineyard by King Ahab in 1 Kings 21. This sort of robbery was presumably rampant in Qohelet's day.

> **10 [9]**He who loves money will not be satisfied with money, nor he who loves abundance with gain. This also is enigmatic.
> **11 [10]**When goods increase, those who consume them increase. But what benefit is there to their owner except what his eyes see?
> **12 [11]**Sweet is the sleep of the laborer whether one eats little or much, but the satiety of the rich person does not allow him to sleep.
> **13 [12]**There is a sickening evil I observed under the sun; riches were kept by their owner to the harm of the owner.
> **14 [13]**And those riches were lost in an evil situation. Though a son was born, he has nothing in his hands.
> **15 [14]**As he came from his mother's womb, naked, so he will return to go, and he will take nothing from his labor that he can carry in his hand.

29. C. J. Wright, *God's People*, 55–56.
30. Mettinger, *Solomonic State Officials*, 109.

16 [15]This also is a sickening evil; just as he came so also shall he go, and what benefit is there for him from toiling for the wind?
17 [16]Indeed, all his days he eats in darkness, with great vexation, sickness, and anger.

5:10–17 [9–16]. Qohelet's reflection on oppression and unjust gain leads him to reflect on the problems that the love of wealth brings. He shifts his attention from the economic effect of unjust gain to look more closely at those who pursue wealth at all costs. In vv. 10–17 he discusses several reasons why the love of wealth is not the answer to the quest for meaning. First, he notes in v. 10 that the love of money does not bring fulfillment; one never has enough. In light of the oppression of the poor one might think that the pursuit of wealth would bring fulfillment, but empirically Qohelet discovers that this is not so. As so often, Qohelet does not wait to tell us his conclusion about wealth; already in v. 10 he informs us that this quest too is enigmatic.

Second, Qohelet notes in v. 11 that increased wealth increases costs so that all the owner can really do is observe rather than enjoy his increased wealth. "Increase" certainly includes cost, but it may also refer to increase in other ways: socially, in responsibilities, and perhaps even physically. The point is that the thing pursued, namely wealth, takes on a life of its own and starts to control the person pursuing it. All the owner can do is stand and watch as the problems gather momentum.

Third, wealth involves increased worries and cares so that the rich person does not enjoy the good sleep of the poor laborer (v. 12). "Qohelet here pits the working class against the rich."[31]

Fourth, Qohelet describes a sickening evil he observed: a rich man loses all his wealth in an unspecified evil situation, and even though he has a son, he cannot provide for him or pass on his legacy to him. Wealth can be here today and gone tomorrow.

Fifth, there is the problem of death (vv. 15–17). Even if one had a son, one comes naked into the world and cannot take one's labor along at death (cf. Job 1:21). Verses 16 and 17 most likely refer to the father. The father can carry nothing with him when he dies, and having lost his wealth he spends his remaining days in darkness and anger. In v. 16 Qohelet poses again the programmatic question (cf. 1:3) with the implied answer, "Nothing." "Toiling for the wind" is a graphic expression, a virtual synonym for everything being enigmatic and a striving after wind. The "sickening evil" of his situation is summed up in v. 17 in "eats in darkness," "great vexation, sickness, and anger." Ehrlich and Kugel propose reading *baḥōšek* as "in want" instead of "in darkness."[32] This does not much alter the meaning, but in 2:14 the fool walks in darkness, and

31. Seow, *Ecclesiastes*, 206.
32. Kugel, "Qohelet and Money," 38–40, esp. 39n17.

the birth and death analogies in these verses make darkness more appropriate. It is as though while living the man is already dead.

Theological Implications

With regard to oppression, see the discussion of 4:1–3, "Theological Implications." Qohelet's additional insight here is how power can become corrupt and how this corruption can spread like a cancer through the entire structure of authority and devastate the poor. Apart from 4:14 this is the only other place in which the poor (*rāš*) specifically come into view. Government, as Qohelet notes in 5:9 [8], is a good institution designed to facilitate justice for all. By design government wields power, and ideally this is to be for the benefit of all citizens (cf. Rom. 13:1–7). But from his observations, Qohelet knows that corruption can set in so that rather than promoting justice, government becomes the source of oppression and exploitation of the poor.

The struggle for government that will facilitate justice is found throughout the OT. Monarchy was always vulnerable to corruption and the abuse of power. Amos's powerful sermon in Amos 1–2 pronounces judgment on the nations surrounding Judah before directing God's word of judgment against Judah itself. The reasons for this judgment are religious but also social: "They sell the righteous for silver and the needy for a pair of sandals; they trample the heads of the poor into the dust" (Amos 2:6–7).

There have been many examples of government corruption and resulting oppression in our time, some of which I discussed in the comments on 4:1–3. It is notable that, as with Qohelet's observations, in countries emerging from or in the midst of oppression, land distribution is often a major cause of frustration. In apartheid South Africa 15 percent of the people owned 70 percent of the land. Similarly in Zimbabwe, amid the mismanagement of the Mugabe regime, land distribution has been a festering sore. In terms of Qohelet's specific focus on how corrupt government oppresses the poor, the struggles of the poor for justice in Central America deserve mention. It is in this context that liberation theology and the notion of the preferential option for the poor arose.[33] Archbishop Oscar Romero faced this kind of corruption head-on in El Salvador in the 1970s and asserted that "we know beforehand the destiny of the poor: to disappear, to be captured, to be tortured, to reappear as corpses."[34] As with Qohelet's description of the network of evil associations in 5:8 [7], the oligarchy, security forces, and death squads worked together to destroy any popular movement that challenged their control of the nation.

33. The latter phrase was coined by the Third General Conference of Latin American bishops at Puebla, Mexico, in 1979. See Bosch, *Transforming Mission*, 432–47.
34. Romero, *Martyr's Message*, 91.

"An entire generation of peasant leaders, union organizers, reform-minded teachers, base community workers, and catechists were being swept away in a massive wave of reprisals."[35]

Romero paid with his life for standing up to this oppression. Qohelet does not advise his readers how to respond to such oppression, but his statement of the divine intent of government in v. 9 [8] provides us with an important clue in this respect: government should facilitate public justice for all. In response to their investigation of the situation in Central America, Spykman and his colleagues propose that a justified faith evokes a threefold commitment: to life, to truth, and to the poor.[36] Intriguingly, Elsa Tamez, an evangelical from Mexico, uses Proverbs to support her call for a preferential option for the poor.[37] She invokes Prov. 14:31, "The one who oppresses the poor insults his maker, but he who is gracious to the needy honors him," and 29:13, "The poor person and the oppressor meet together; the LORD gives light to the eyes of both." Proverbs 29:14 goes on to note that a king's throne will be established forever if he judges the poor with equity.

The poor is a major biblical theme and also one central to Jesus's preaching. Luke manifests a particular concern with the poor as is evident in the Nazareth manifesto of Luke 4:18–19:

> The Spirit of the Lord is upon me,
> Because he has anointed me
> To preach good news to the poor.
> He has sent me to proclaim release to the captives
> And recovery of sight to the blind;
> To let the oppressed go free,
> To proclaim the acceptable year of the Lord.

Most of this statement is a quotation from Isa. 61:1 and 2a, but intriguingly Luke has inserted the phrase "to let the oppressed go free" from Isa. 58:6 between Isa. 61:1 and 61:2. As Bosch notes, this insertion has a "distinctly social profile"[38] in Isa. 58.

"The poor" in the Gospels should not be reduced to those who are materially poor.[39] They are also the disadvantaged, the devout, the humble, and those who live in radical dependence on God.[40] But "the poor" certainly includes those in poverty, and as the phrase "the oppressed" makes clear, those in poverty resulting from oppression. So there is a real sense in which Jesus manifests a

---

35. Cook et al., *Let My People Live*, 4.
36. Ibid.
37. Tamez, "La teología del éxito."
38. Bosch, *Transforming Mission*, 100.
39. Matt. 5:3 makes this clear.
40. Bosch, *Transforming Mission*, 99.

preferential option for the poor, and his followers ought to do likewise. This does not necessarily mean that one should appropriate liberation theology carte blanche. Apart from the diversity of liberation theologies, one should be wary of making a sociological analysis of "the poor" the grid through which to theologize, as do some liberation theologians.[41] Furthermore, as O'Donovan notes, the political issues that liberation theologies address—what he calls the Southern school—differ from the sort of political issues faced in the North.[42] He asserts, "It is proper to say to theologians of the Southern school that, just as poverty was their issue first, but also ours, so authority is our issue first, but also theirs."[43] As I noted in the comments on 4:1–3, Christian faith is comprehensive, and believers ought to pray and work for the ending of oppression, corruption, injustice, and poverty. The work of Mother Teresa's Sisters of Charity is exemplary in this respect, as they seek to serve the poorest of the poor. As with Romero the cost may be high. O'Donovan perceptively notes:

> The church's identification with the poor, then, has to be the goal, not the presupposition, of social reflection in the North. Modern society has hidden the poor by distributing wealth and distributing power, and not distributing them together; so that even fairly poor people assume the attitudes that belong to power. When a clerical student, one of the materially poor of the earth, boasts that the internet has redefined our relation to space so that we can buy things without going out, he commits the same error as an eighteenth-century slave-owner: he overlooks the fact that someone somewhere is running errands for him. To tyrannize over one's neighbour like a Roman emperor, one needs only the use of a computer and a phone-jack.[44]

In 5:10–17 [9–16] Qohelet reflects on the *love of wealth and its dangers*. Love of money and consequent work for it will not bring fulfillment. It is important to emphasize here that Qohelet is referring not simply to wealth per se but to love of it. As Paul says in 1 Tim. 6:10, "For the love of money is a root of all kinds of evil. Some people, eager for money, have wandered from the faith and pierced themselves with many griefs" (NIV). Qohelet elaborates on the type of grief that love of money can lead to. It never satisfies, because one always wants more; increasing wealth brings more stress into one's life so that one is unable to really enjoy it; and if one's identity is formed around wealth, then when it is taken away (v. 14), one's life becomes empty and meaningless. Furthermore, one cannot take one's wealth along at death.

41. For a useful and practical analysis, see Cook et al., *Let My People Live*.
42. O'Donovan, *Desire of the Nations*, 18. O'Donovan here enumerates thirteen typical questions about Northern societies on which Southern theology sheds little light.
43. O'Donovan, "Political Theology," 241.
44. O'Donovan, "Response to Peter Scott," 376.

This love of money contrasts with the gift of wealth by God in v. 19 and the proper enjoyment of it. Wealth by itself is not the problem, but where it fits in one's approach to life. Contemporary studies show that after a certain level of wealth, there is no relationship between increased wealth and happiness.[45] Qohelet perceptively analyzes just how destructive the love of wealth can be in a person's life. In our culture of relentless consumerism love of wealth is a constant temptation. As Susan White notes,

> If there is an overarching metanarrative that purports to explain reality in the late 20th century, it is surely the metanarrative of the free-market economy. In the beginning of this narrative is the self-made, self-sufficient human being. At the end of this narrative is the big house, the big car, and the expensive clothes. In the middle is the struggle for success, the greed, the getting-and-spending in a world in which there is no such thing as a free lunch. Most of us have made this so thoroughly "our story" that we are hardly aware of its influence.[46]

With the demise of socialism and the "triumph" of free-market capitalism, the love of money is commonly regarded as *the* goal to be pursued. But, as Qohelet rightly observes, it is not the answer to life and can bring its own share of grief.

45. Myers, "Money & Misery."
46. S. White, "New Story to Live By?" 4.

J.
The Gift of God
(5:18–20 [17–19])

Translation

> **18 [17]**This is what I have observed to be good and fitting:[1] to eat and to drink and to enjoy[2] all one's labor at which one labors under the sun during the few days of one's life that God gives to one, for this is his gift.
>
> **19 [18]**Furthermore, to every person to whom God has given riches and wealth,[3] he empowers[4] one to eat of it and to receive one's portion and to rejoice in one's labor. This is the gift of God.

1. The phrase *ṭōb 'ăšer yāpeh* (to be good and fitting) is challenging to translate. Fox (*Qohelet*, 218) argues that the relative pronoun *'ăšer* functions as a colon. N. Lohfink (*Qoheleth*, 84) translates the phrase as "perfect happiness." He argues that Greek phrases underlie this expression, but Fredericks (*Qoheleth's Language*, 246) and Lauha (*Kohelet*, 112) dispute such a background. Lauha notes that Qohelet's *'ăšer* construction is totally different from the cognate construction of the Greek idiom. The Greek expression is used to provide an aesthetic-ethical characterization of people, whereas Qohelet uses it to speak of concrete things. The masoretic accentuation is unhelpful, and scholars differ over whether *'ăšer yāpeh* is part of the first line or the second. With Lohfink, I take *'ăšer yāpeh* as part of the first line and take *'ăšer* to mean "that is," which can legitimately be rendered "and" in this context.

2. Literally "to see good." Cf. 2:1.

3. *Nĕkāsîm* is a loanword that came into Hebrew from Akkadian or Aramaic (Seow, *Ecclesiastes*, 209). However, it occurs in Josh. 22:8, and this indicates that it is not a late Aramaism.

4. *Hišlîṭô*, the Hiphil form of the verb, also occurs in 6:2. Seow (*Ecclesiastes*, 209) translates this verb as "he has authorized them" and argues that this is legal terminology. However, this makes less sense in 6:2, and thus the translation "empowers."

²⁰ ⁽¹⁹⁾For one will hardly brood over the days of one's life, because God will keep one occupied⁵ with the joy of one's heart.

Interpretation

There is a remarkable shift in tone here from the dark pessimism of vv. 8–17 [7–16] to these verses. It is the change in tone plus the repeated references to God,⁶ which are lacking in vv. 8–17, that indicate that this is a separate section. This *carpe diem* passage lacks the "better-than" element present in the others that we have looked at so far. Ogden notes, however, that all the other elements of the form are present and suggests that the nonuse of "better than" may be deliberate, relating to the fact that 5:18 is in a mediate position between 5:13–17 and 6:1–6. "In the context of life which may issue in these two 'evils' stands the one 'good' which Qoheleth can see."⁷ The context of this *carpe diem* section is that the love of wealth does not satisfy or last and may be lost more quickly than it is gained.

> ¹⁸ ⁽¹⁷⁾This is what I have observed to be good and fitting: to eat and to drink and to enjoy all one's labor at which one labors under the sun during the few days of one's life that God gives to one, for this is his gift.

5:18 [17]. According to Whybray and Ogden, v. 18 provides the answer to v. 16.⁸ However, a strong tension remains between the response to the problem of toil that leads to darkness, vexation, sickness, and anger, and the "response" of eating and drinking that Qohelet here observes to be fitting and good and

---

5. *Ma'āneh* is difficult on two accounts. It lacks the pronominal suffix, and I follow the LXX, Peshitta, and Tg in emending it to *ma'ānēhû* (he [God] will keep one). Second, the precise meaning is unclear. The root has several meanings: "to occupy," "to answer," "to reveal," and "to sing." Scholars focus mainly on the first two as possible meanings in this verse. N. Lohfink (*Qoheleth*, 84) translates *ma'āneh* as "continuously answers," but see G. Barton, "Text and Interpretation." There is not much at stake in which meaning one selects (see interpretation).

6. N. Lohfink ("Qoheleth 5:17–19," 631) notes that this section "contains one of the most dense concentrations of the word *'ĕlōhîm* in the whole book. This word occurs in Qoheleth 38 times. There are six cases in 3:10–15 which is *the* theological text of the book, and five cases in 4:17–5:6 MT which is Qoheleth's treatment of religious behavior. The rest of the passages are nearly evenly distributed throughout the book. The only exception is our text, 5:17–19 MT. In its three verses we find the word *'ĕlōhîm* four times, and we should even add the two occurrences in 6:2, because this verse is linked to our passage. Simply by reason of these statistical facts, we should consider 5:17–19 as the third 'theological' passage of the Book of Qoheleth." Lohfink does not count the two occurrences of *'ĕlōhîm* in the epilogue.

7. Ogden, "Qoheleth's Use," 341–42.

8. Whybray, "Qoheleth, Preacher of Joy," 89; Ogden, *Qoheleth*, 87.

the gift of God. Seow and Gordis recognize this tension.[9] Seow notes the consensus that *yizkōr* ("brood," v. 20) is indicative, but argues that in context it should be translated as an injunctive (they should not call to mind), because "Qoheleth's problem is precisely that people do brood about their days—too often and too much—although he thinks that they will not discover anything in all their brooding (3:11)."[10]

> 19 [18]Furthermore, to every person to whom God has given riches and wealth, he empowers one to eat of it and to receive one's portion and to rejoice in one's labor. This is the gift of God.

5:19 [18]. However, the tension is not resolved by seeing vv. 18–20 as an answer to vv. 8–17 or by changing these verses to fit the context. Verses 8–17 and vv. 18–20 represent radically different ways of approaching life "under the sun" in which wealth does not last, and the reader is left with a question mark about their relationship, as a comparison of v. 17 with v. 19 makes clear. In both v. 17 and v. 19 there is a reference to "eating," but this common activity serves only to contrast the different circumstances of that eating. In v. 17 one eats with darkness, vexation, sickness, and anger, whereas in v. 18 one eats and drinks with joy *coram Deo*, before the face of God. Furthermore, we might well ask, how is one to enjoy one's labor as the gift of God if one is deprived of justice and righteousness as in v. 8? Does not the oppression of v. 8 contradict the very possibility of v. 19? And in v. 12 and vv. 13–17 the person is unable to enjoy riches, whereas in v. 19 God empowers the person to enjoy the wealth he has given.

Verses 18–20 conjure up a marvelous vision of what life could be and should be: eating and drinking and enjoying one's labor. "God" occurs four times, and all the goodness is twice declared to be his gift. Verse 19 notes that everyone to whom God gives riches and wealth he empowers to "eat of it" and to rejoice in one's labor. Longman raises the question as to whether God grants his gift of wealth to many and suggests that the implied answer is no.[11] For Longman "the few days of one's life" in v. 18 sets a depressing tone, and the gift of wealth is a reference to wealth as an "anesthetizing pleasure" that only a few, and certainly not Qohelet, can enjoy.[12] In my opinion, however, this interpretation misreads this *carpe diem* passage. Qohelet acknowledges the brevity of life in v. 18, but his attitude toward it is positive rather than negative. The gift of wealth is referred to in different language in the *carpe diem* passage in 2:26, and it is a basic element of the character-consequence theme

---

9. Seow, *Ecclesiastes*, 209; Gordis, *Koheleth*, 255. Gordis simply asserts that the translation "keep one occupied" "is not appropriate to the context."

10. Seow, *Ecclesiastes*, 209.

11. Longman, *Ecclesiastes*, 168.

12. Ibid.

in Proverbs that wisdom leads to prosperity. Proverbs 3:9–10 is exemplary in this respect. "Honor the LORD from your wealth and from the first of all your produce, then your barns will be filled with plenty and your wine vats will be bursting with wine." Thus Qohelet is not referring to a minority group; the focus in this *carpe diem* section is rather on what he as a believer understands to be good and fitting—it represents a different perspective on life that he also knows to be true.

> **20 [19]**For one will hardly brood over the days of one's life, because God will keep one occupied with the joy of one's heart.

5:20 [19]. This *carpe diem* section contains a stronger emphasis on joy than the earlier sections. Joy occurs in 2:24–25 and in 3:22, but 5:20 evokes a sense of contentment and peace unparalleled in the earlier *carpe diem* passages. As noted in the translation, there is some debate about how to translate "keep one occupied" in v. 20. However, the root *'nh* can also mean "to answer, to reveal." N. Lohfink notes the connections between the *carpe diem* passage in 3:12–15 and this section. He points out that why joy is a gift from God and what it means are not developed in 3:12–15. He suggests that this question is answered in this *carpe diem* section. He proposes to translate 5:20 as "He will not brood much over the days of his life; on the contrary, God reveals himself (to him) by the joy of his heart."[13] Verse 20 implies that "the ecstasy of the good is given within the psychic phenomenon of 'joy' itself—insofar as this is also a divine 'answer,' something like 'revelation.' . . . In joy, then, the conclusion of right thinking—namely the perfection and the eternity of divine action within all events—is directly communicated as revelation."[14]

It is hard to be sure about the meaning of *'nh* in v. 20. In 1:13 and 3:10 it clearly means "to keep busy with, to keep occupied with." In both those contexts, however, *'nh* has negative connotations, whereas here in 5:20 the context is positive. It is therefore possible that there is a play on meaning, as Lohfink suggests, so that in contrast to the earlier references *'nh* here speaks of an answer, a revelation of God through joy. It may not be that important to decide between these translations. Even if we retain the meaning "to keep one occupied," in this section there is clearly an existential resolution of the problem of wealth, and this is God's gift through joy. This experience enables one "to know that there is a sense even if we cannot grasp it. The joy of the heart must be something like divine revelation. When we experience joy at least in one small moment, we come in touch with that sense of things which normally God alone sees."[15]

13. N. Lohfink, "Qoheleth 5:17–19," 634n45.
14. N. Lohfink, *Qoheleth*, 85.
15. N. Lohfink, "Qoheleth 5:17–19," 634.

Rather than this *carpe diem* section being the answer to the problem, we have two contradictory responses to the problem juxtaposed and the resulting gap left unresolved, as in the other *carpe diem* passages that we have looked at. Qohelet's use of "This is what I have observed" rather than "there is nothing better than" in v. 18 reinforces the contradictory juxtaposition, for he refers to seeing oppression in v. 8, and he observes "the sickening evil" of v. 13 as well as this *carpe diem* perspective in vv. 18–20. As we will see, 6:1–6 strengthens the tension between 5:12–17 and 5:18–20, because although it may be our portion to enjoy life as God enables us to, many are unable to enjoy life. Qohelet's struggle is how to resolve the tension between these perspectives.

Theological Implications

In vv. 8–17 [7–16] Qohelet describes the oppression of the poor and explores the problems encountered in the love of money and wealth. By contrast, in vv. 18–20 [17–19] Qohelet presents a vision of eating and drinking, of enjoying one's work and one's wealth, and of sustaining joy. I have already discussed the theological implications of much of this material in 2:24–26, and the reader is referred to my comments there. This section emphasizes joy, and I will focus on the theological implications of Qohelet's emphasis on sustaining joy.

Joy and the exhortation to rejoice is a theme found throughout Scripture. While the word "joy" does not occur in Gen. 1–11, it is implied by the theology of blessing and embodied in the human response to the good creation that is made as a home for humans. Not surprisingly, therefore, the theme of salvation as it develops in the OT and is fulfilled in Christ is constantly associated with joy. In the Pentateuch rejoicing is associated with the yearly festivals, enacted in God's presence. Deuteronomy in particular emphasizes joy in God's presence.[16] Deuteronomy 12:7 asserts, "You shall eat there before the Lord your God; and you shall rejoice in everything to which you put your hand, together with your households, because the Lord your God has blessed you." McConville notes of this verse, "The feasting is in itself a participation in the blessings given. Israel at worship, in obedience, togetherness, prosperity and joyful feasting, is a cameo picture of the covenant people in active and harmonious relationship with God."[17] The reference to feasting and joy in work resonates closely with Qohelet's emphases in 5:18–20.[18] Rejoicing is also a major theme in the Psalms and Isaiah. Jeremiah 31:12 evokes redemption in terms of the goodness of the Lord and speaks of grain, wine, and oil so

---

16. See Deut. 12:7, 12, 18; 14:26; 16:11; 26:11; 32:43; 33:18.

17. McConville, *Deuteronomy*, 223.

18. As I note in the introduction (see "Reading Ecclesiastes within the Context of Proverbs and Job and Its Connection to the Torah"), there are many similarities between Deuteronomy and Ecclesiastes.

that the life of the redeemed will be like a watered garden. The latter phrase evokes Eden, the original watered garden, and indicates that redemption will recover God's creation purpose of blessing and the human response of rejoicing that follows in Jer. 31:13.

Not surprisingly, therefore, the fulfillment of salvation in Jesus is encompassed with joy. Luke in particular emphasizes this theme, and it is embodied early on in his Gospel in the Magnificat, in which Mary rejoices in God (Luke 1:46–55). The theme of the messianic banquet, drawing on Deuteronomy, Ecclesiastes, and Isaiah, overflows with abundance and joy. An evocative image of this is the feasting and joy when the prodigal son returns home (Luke 15:11–32). In continuity with the Gospels, the Epistles exhort disciples to follow Jesus with joy. This is a major theme in Philippians, in which Paul exhorts his readers to "rejoice, . . . and again I say, rejoice!" (4:4; cf. 1:18–19; 2:17–18; 3:1). Similarly in 1 Peter, Peter exhorts his readers to rejoice amid their trials—though they have not seen Christ, they "rejoice with an indescribable and glorious joy" (1 Pet. 1:8).[19] And Rev. 19:7 brings the theme full circle with its exhortation to rejoice because the marriage supper of the Lamb has come. These biblical theological links help us to see that what Qohelet has in mind in the *carpe diem* passages is life as God intended it to be.

Joy is thus a major biblical theme, but one that receives scant theological attention. David Ford's work is exceptional in this respect.[20] He follows Levinas in seeing joy as constitutive of the human person. For Levinas the particularity of the person is *bonheur de la jouissance* (the happiness of enjoyment).[21] "Life is love of life, a relation with contents that are not my being but more dear than my being: thinking, eating, sleeping, reading, working, warming oneself in the sun."[22] "Only in enjoyment does the I crystallize."[23] Ford says of Levinas's philosophy of joy,

> In the formation of selfhood through enjoyment . . . hunger satisfied by eating is the paradigmatic case of immediacy—taste in contact with food—but none of our other activities and passivities have to do with a neutral "reality" either. All are encompassed by enjoyment. . . . The continuity of time is ruptured by the gathering of life into knots of enjoyment. . . . The pervasiveness of enjoyment in constituting the separated self and its interiority acts as a resistance to attempts to conceive the self primarily in other terms, while yet allowing for those terms to be taken into account.[24]

---

19. On 1 Pet. 1:3–9 and joy, see Ford, *Self and Salvation*, 174.
20. Ford, *Self and Salvation*. Barth is another theologian who addresses the topic of joy. See my comments on the theological implications of 2:24–26. For a brief treatment of the relationship between happiness and joy in Aquinas, see Pieper, *Happiness and Contemplation*, 43–49.
21. Levinas, *Totality and Infinity*, 115.
22. Ibid., 112.
23. Ibid., 144.
24. Ford, *Self and Salvation*, 35–36.

Ford develops his theology of the joyful self in dialogue not only with Levinas but also with Paul (Ephesians), Thérèse of Lisieux, and Dietrich Bonhoeffer. Bonhoeffer affirms joy in Christ but interrogates his Lutheran tradition not least in how it relates to natural life:

> It is in the joys of the body that it becomes apparent that the body is an end in itself within the natural life. If the body were only a means to an end man would have no right to bodily joys. It would then not be permissible to exceed an expedient minimum of bodily enjoyment. This would have very far-reaching consequences for the Christian appraisal of all the problems that have to do with the life of the body, housing, food, clothing, recreation, play and sex. But if the body is rightly to be regarded as an end in itself, then there is a right to bodily joys, even though these are not necessarily subordinated to some higher purpose. It is inherent in the nature of joy itself that it is spoilt by any thought or purpose.[25]

Where the love of God is firm, full enjoyment of the creation is possible and desirable: one is "completely in the arms of God and completely in the world."[26]

Ford notes that in the Christian tradition the saints do not affirm joy by ignoring joy-destroying evil. Rather, they affirm joy in the context of the worst forms of evil. An extraordinary example of this is Etty Hillesum, as reflected in her diary and letters. In the darkest days of Nazi occupation in Holland, Etty found a capacity for joy and celebration. Writing on 18 August 1943 while in Westerbork camp before being sent to death at Auschwitz, she addresses God:

> You have made me so rich, oh God, please let me share out Your beauty with open hands. My life has become an uninterrupted dialogue with You, oh God, one great dialogue. Sometimes when I stand in some corner of the camp, my feet planted on Your earth, my eyes raised toward Your heaven, tears sometimes run down my face, tears of deep emotion and gratitude. At night, too, when I lie in my bed and rest in You, oh God, tears of gratitude run down my face, and that is my prayer.
>
> I have been terribly tired for several days, but that too will pass. Things come and go in a deeper rhythm, and people must be taught to listen; it is the most important thing we have to learn in this life.
>
> . . . I always end up with just one single word: God. . . . The beat of my heart has grown deeper, more active, and yet more peaceful, and it is as if I were all the time storing up inner riches.[27]

Etty died in Auschwitz on 30 November 1943.

25. Bonhoeffer, *Ethics*, 113. This quote occurs in Bonhoeffer's discussion "The Rights to Bodily Life" (ibid., 112–22), which includes several references to Ecclesiastes.
26. Ford, *Self and Salvation*, 260.
27. Hillesum, *Interrupted Life*, 332.

This capacity for joy amid pain points toward a solution for Qohelet's struggle, but he is not yet there in his journey. His affirmation of joy and celebration of life and its goods as a gift of God does, however, resonate with the OT wisdom tradition and the Scriptures as a whole. "God loves to be enjoyed, so let us do so!"[28]

28. Ford, *Self and Salvation*, 278.

K.
Riches and Wealth Continued
(6:1–12)

Translation

[1]There is an evil[1] that I have observed under the sun, and it is common among humankind:
[2]There is a person to whom God gives riches, wealth, and honor,[2] and he lacks nothing that he desires. But God does not allow[3] him to eat of it, for a stranger[4] eats of it. This is enigmatic and a sickening evil.
[3]If a person produces a hundred children and lives many years, however[5] many are the days of his years, but his soul is not satisfied

1. Several Hebrew MSS add "sickening" (ḥôlâ), but this is probably a result of the influence of 5:13 [12] or 6:2.
2. The same three words, "riches, wealth, and honor," occur in 2 Chron. 1:11 in the same order with respect to Solomon. The precise nuance of kābôd (abundance, honor, glory) is unclear here. Salters ("Notes on the Interpretation of Qoh 6:2") argues that "honor" is incompatible with "to eat," even if the latter is taken as "to enjoy." But "to eat" is clearly a metaphor here, and one can certainly take delight in and enjoy honor.
3. Seow (*Ecclesiastes*, 210) translates yaślîṭennû as "authorize." See 5:19 [18].
4. *Nokrî* can also mean "foreigner," but here the point is simply that someone else enjoys this person's wealth.
5. The syntax is difficult here. I follow Gordis (*Koheleth*, 258) in reading wĕrab šeyyihyû as a concessive, hence "however."

with the good things, and he[6] does not even get a burial site,[7] then better I say is the stillborn baby than he.

[4]For it comes[8] in enigma, and in darkness it goes, and in darkness its name is obscured.

[5]Moreover,[9] it does not observe the sun, nor does it know anything, yet there is rest[10] for this one rather than for him.

[6]Even if[11] he lives a thousand years twice over but does not see the good—are not all[12] going to one place?

[7]All a person's labor is for his mouth, and yet his soul[13] is not satisfied.

[8]For what advantage does a wise person have over the fool? What do the poor have by knowing[14] how to live in the presence of the living?[15]

[9]Better is the sight[16] of the eyes than the passing of life.[17] This also is enigmatic and a striving after wind.

6. Crenshaw (*Ecclesiastes*, 126–27) takes *lô* (to him) as anticipatory and reads this phrase as referring to the stillborn, but the more natural reading is as referring to the rich man.

7. *Qĕbûrâ* probably refers to a burial site, not the act of burial (Seow, *Ecclesiastes*, 211).

8. The tense of *bā'* is unclear here. Isaksson (*Studies*, 131) argues that *bā'* is the perfect of the verb and that the other two verbs of the verse are imperfects. He argues that the coming is considered an established fact, whereas the departing is in the process of being fulfilled. 4QQoh[a], however, has *hlk* (probably perfect rather than a participle; Seow, *Ecclesiastes*, 212) rather than *ylk* (imperfect). Translating as "comes" or "came" makes no difference to the meaning.

9. Taking *gam* in an additional sense (RJW §378).

10. Gordis (*Koheleth*, 259), with many others, takes *naḥat* (rest) to be related to Postbiblical Hebrew *nwḥ* (satisfaction). In all the examples referred to, however, the form is *nwḥ*, not *nḥt*. Furthermore, elsewhere in Ecclesiastes (4:6; 9:17) *naḥat* means "rest," as it does elsewhere in the OT. See Muilenburg, "Qoheleth Scroll," 25.

11. *'Illû* occurs only here and in Esther 7:4 in the Hebrew Bible. However, the form is well attested in Jewish Aramaic, Syriac, and Mishnaic Hebrew. The form is most likely an Aramaism, the equivalent of Hebrew *'im . . . lû* (Seow, *Ecclesiastes*, 213).

12. Taking *hakkōl* as referring to all people rather than to the rich man and the stillborn.

13. This is the only place in which *hannepeš* occurs in Ecclesiastes, although *nepeš* without the article occurs in v. 9. Most commentators translate it as "appetite," but it has a variety of possible meanings, and I have used "soul" because even if "appetite" is used, it means more than just his hunger—the point is that his life is unfulfilled.

14. This line has caused difficulties to commentators because the function of *yôdēaʿ* (lit. "knowing") is unclear. Various emendations have been proposed (Whitley, *Koheleth*, 59). It is best to take this as an ellipsis with "by" implied (RJW §587).

15. *Lahălōk neged haḥayyîm* (to live in the presence of the living) is ambiguous (see Murphy, *Ecclesiastes*, 48). I take *hlk* to mean "to live" in the sense of "conduct oneself."

16. *Mar'ēh* can refer to the object of seeing or the act of seeing. As in 11:9, I take it to refer to the action of seeing.

17. I follow Seow (*Ecclesiastes*, 215) in translating *mēhălāk-nāpeš* as "than the passing of life." Most commentators prefer "wandering desire" or some such phrase, but as in v. 7 *nepeš* is best understood to refer to the life of the person as a whole.

10Whatever happens[18] has already been named. Also it is known what[19] a person is, for he is unable to contend with one who is stronger[20] than he.
11For there are many words that increase enigma. What advantage is there for the person?
12For who knows what is good for the person during the few days of one's enigmatic life? He makes them like a shadow,[21] so that[22] who can tell the person what will happen after one under the sun?

Interpretation

This section continues the theme of 5:10–17 [9–16], the problem of wealth. Thus 5:10–17 and 6:1–12 sandwich the *carpe diem* passage in 5:18–20.

1There is an evil that I have observed under the sun, and it is common among humankind:
2There is a person to whom God gives riches, wealth, and honor, and he lacks nothing that he desires. But God does not allow him to eat of it, for a stranger eats of it. This is enigmatic and a sickening evil.

6:1–2. Here Qohelet returns to the theme of the person who acquires riches but is unable to enjoy them, and his despair at this enigma intensifies.[23] Qohelet's observation in 5:18–20 [17–19] contrasts starkly with the evil he observes that is common among humankind (v. 1). As in 5:18, riches and wealth (and honor) are given by God to a particular person. The same three nouns appear in 2 Chron. 1:12, referring to God's gifts to Solomon. Thus we are to imagine an exceptionally wealthy person who also has honor, that is, who is well respected in his society. In v. 2, Qohelet also notes, as in 5:19, that this wealth is a gift of God, but unlike in 5:19 here God does not empower the

18. See Isaksson (*Studies*, 85–88) for an extended discussion of translation of the verbs in Ecclesiastes. The Qal form here would normally be translated with a past, but the context makes this unlikely. "Happens" is more appropriate than "exists." The phrase is essentially a synonym for all that is done under the sun.

19. Following the masoretic accents, Krüger (*Qoheleth*, 132) translates this phrase as I do. Seow (*Ecclesiastes*, 231) points out that it is unusual to translate 'ăšer as "what." One would expect *mah*. However, one could translate 'ăšer as a relative pronoun, "that which," a meaning that fits with my translation, since we are dealing here not with an explicit or implicit question but with a statement of what is known.

20. Reading the Qere šettaqqîp. Cf. Schoors, *Preacher*, 1:35–36.

21. Literally "the shadow," but Ecclesiastes' use of the article varies, and "a shadow" fits better in English.

22. The precise function of 'ăšer is unclear here. I take it to indicate a result (RJW §465).

23. This theme is also discussed in 2:18–23 and 4:7–8.

person to enjoy his wealth. The syntactical and vocabulary parallels between 5:18–19 and 6:1–2 highlight the contrast between the two situations:

| 5:18 | This is what I have observed to be good and fitting | 6:1 | There is an evil that I have observed |
| 5:19 | to every person to whom God has given riches and wealth | 6:2 | a person to whom God gives riches, wealth, and honor |

Instead of this person being able to enjoy his wealth and honor, however, a stranger "eats of it." The word for "stranger" often means a foreigner in the OT, but it need not mean that here. The point is simply that this person's entire wealth is enjoyed by a nonfamily member, an unknown person. "Eats" here is a metaphor and refers to enjoyment—the point is that this person works hard to acquire wealth, but the wealth is enjoyed by a stranger. We are not told why God does not empower this person to enjoy the wealth or under what circumstances it is passed on to a stranger, but that is beside the point; for Qohelet it is enigmatic, mysterious, that one works so hard and then is unable to enjoy the fruits of one's labor. Qohelet is here describing a common situation he has observed. He finds himself repulsed by what he observes—he describes this enigma in strong language as a "sickening evil" (v. 2).

> [3]If a person produces a hundred children and lives many years, however many are the days of his years, but his soul is not satisfied with the good things, and he does not even get a burial site, then better I say is the stillborn baby than he.

6:3. One might imagine, as Qohelet has argued before (4:7–8), that the enigma stems from not having children to pass the wealth on to, but v. 3 informs us that that is not the reason. Even if one has a hundred children and lives forever, as it were, all is enigmatic if one's soul cannot find rest and satisfaction in one's labor. Many translate napšô (his soul) as "appetite." However, nepeš often refers to the whole person in the OT (cf. Gen. 2:7), and the point here is not just that his appetite is unfulfilled but that his life is empty. Proverbs 17:6 tells us, "Grandchildren are the crown of the aged, and the glory of children is their parents."[24] Similarly, longevity is seen as a fruit of wisdom (Prov. 3:2).[25] But here Qohelet asserts that one may have all this and still not be at rest and fulfilled. Among the wealthy it was common to secure a site to ensure a proper burial (cf. Gen. 23:3–9; Isa. 22:16). This person's resultant

24. A similar emphasis is found throughout the OT; cf. Gen. 15:5; 22:17; 26:4; Ruth 4:11–12; Pss. 127:4; 128:3; etc.

25. In Isa. 65:20, 22–23; Zech. 8:4–5, longevity and children are signs of the age of salvation.

lack of a decent burial[26] indicates what was true of his life as a whole—it was unfulfilled despite his wealth and extended family, and lacking a burial site he will not be remembered.

> ⁴For it comes in enigma, and in darkness it goes, and in darkness its name is obscured.
> ⁵Moreover, it does not observe the sun, nor does it know anything, yet there is rest for this one rather than for him.

6:4–5. Qohelet's comparison of such a person with a stillborn child evokes the strength of his feeling at this point. In Ps. 58:8 [9], to be stillborn and never see the sun is one of the worst forms of judgment one can imagine. *Nēpel* (stillborn) is also found in Job 3:16, in which from out of his agony Job asks why he was not rather buried like a stillborn child, like an infant who has never seen the light. Such is the depth of Qohelet's struggle at this point that he regards the stillborn child as better off than this rich man, because even though it comes in enigma and goes in darkness and thus never observes the sun, at least it is at rest. The "birth" of the stillborn is enigmatic and mysterious; it departs in darkness without ever having lived, and its memory is erased (v. 4). The horror of such an experience is elaborated on in v. 5. To see the sun is to be alive (cf. 7:3). Not to "know anything" means that the stillborn lacks conscious awareness. As Longman comments, "The stillborn never reaches consciousness, with the implication that the stillborn never experiences the hardships and misery of the present life."[27] The stillborn is neither alive nor conscious, and yet according to Qohelet, it is better off than the rich person, because it has rest.

The value of rest (*naḥat*) has already been highlighted by Qohelet in 4:6 (cf. also 5:12 [11]). This also focuses the problem with the experience of the rich man in Qohelet's eyes: he lacks rest, and no matter how much wealth or how many children he accumulates, they are unable to deliver this sense of rest to his life. If Qohelet has Genesis in mind, and he appears to refer to it regularly, then his references to *rest* clearly evoke Gen. 5:28–29. Lamech names his son Noah (*nōaḥ*, lit. "rest") in the hope that from the ground that God has cursed Noah will bring relief from work and toil. In Genesis this hope for rest also harks back to Gen. 2:1–3, in which God rests after his work of creation. Qohelet's observation resonates with that of Lamech—so often work and rest do not go together. This is also the sense of v. 7, in which the mouth being the

26. Krüger (*Qoheleth*, 126) suggests that v. 3aα may be understood to refer to 364 years and thus be an allusion to Enoch (Gen. 5:23; 365 years). Like Elijah, Enoch had no burial, for he was taken directly to God. The lack of a burial site would mean therefore that even if one moves directly into a new life with God, this is of no value if one lacks fulfillment in this life.
27. Longman, *Ecclesiastes*, 171.

organ by which we eat is a metaphor for enjoyment and rest—all a person's labor is aimed in this direction, but by itself it cannot achieve its goal.

> [6]Even if he lives a thousand years twice over but does not see the good—are not all going to one place?
> [7]All a person's labor is for his mouth, and yet his soul is not satisfied.

6:6–7. In v. 6 Qohelet's struggle with what he observes is again compounded by the shadow of death—all go to one place, namely the grave. One expects the "even if" at the start of v. 6 to be followed by "then," indicating some kind of result. Commentators thus assume an ellipsis.[28] This is not necessary, however, as this is an example of Qohelet's organic logic. The shadow of death clouds his mind once again and deconstructs his argument—whatever the case about fulfillment, all end up in the grave. Murphy evocatively suggests that "mouth" in v. 7 is a reference to Sheol, clearly in view in v. 6.[29] Thus all human labor is for Sheol's mouth, which is never satisfied. However, Sheol is not explicitly mentioned in v. 6, and *nepeš* refers to people in this context (cf. 6:2, 3, 9).

> [8]For what advantage does a wise person have over the fool? What do the poor have by knowing how to live in the presence of the living?

6:8. Wealth cannot provide meaning (rest), and both the wise person and the fool have the same destination; what then if any is the advantage of "wisdom," asks Qohelet (v. 8). Verse 8 refers back to 5:8–9 [7–8]. Wisdom is all about skill in living, but what value is it to the poor if their lot is to be oppressed and exploited? How can wisdom help the poor if rising out of poverty, that is, becoming wealthy—one of the things wisdom is meant to produce (cf. Prov. 3:9–10)—merely compounds the problem of the meaning of life? Qohelet's use of "wisdom" here is surely ironic, for the context assumes that the person seeking wealth is wise, whereas the book as a whole will time and again show that this sort of wisdom is folly.

> [9]Better is the sight of the eyes than the passing of life. This also is enigmatic and a striving after wind.

6:9. In vv. 9–12 we have Qohelet's conclusions to this section. All that Qohelet can conclude in v. 9 is expressed with a "better-than" proverb. "Sight of the eyes" is a metaphor for being alive. Thus the proverb affirms life over death, contrary to Qohelet's argument in vv. 3–5 about the stillborn. Most commentators translate *mēhălāk-nāpeš* (than the passing of life) as "wandering desire,"

---

28. So Seow, *Ecclesiastes*, 213.

29. Murphy, "On Translating Ecclesiastes," 577–78. So also Ackroyd, "Two Hebrew Notes," 84–85.

in which case the proverb would affirm that observation of these enigmas is better than the "wandering of desire," that is, the restlessness that seeking meaning in wealth results in. *Nāpeš*, however, is the same word I translated as "soul" in v. 7 and evokes here life as a whole, so that "the passing of life" is a better translation. This affirmation of life is thoroughly in line with traditional wisdom, but after his exploration of the advantage of the stillborn all of this leaves Qohelet perplexed, and he unsurprisingly concludes once again that all is enigmatic and a striving after wind.

> ¹⁰Whatever happens has already been named. Also it is known what a person is, for he is unable to contend with one who is stronger than he.

6:10. Qohelet invokes once again his cyclical view of history, in which nothing new occurs (cf. 1:4–11). "Whatever happens" is equivalent in Qohelet's language to "all that is done under the sun." Literally in the Hebrew "has already been named" is "its name has already been called." In Ps. 147:4 and Isa. 40:26 this language is used of God assigning the luminaries their place in the cosmos. Qohelet may well, therefore, have Gen. 1 in mind in which God calls things into existence and names them. Just as the place of the luminaries is fixed, so too for Qohelet is "whatever happens." This allusion to an order in creation is extended to humankind—it is known what a person is, possibly referring to Gen. 1:26–28. As we saw with the poem in chap. 3, however, Qohelet's problem is how humankind fits in this order, and it is the same here. "One who is stronger than he" is thus an indirect reference to God and the limitations of the human before God. Qohelet finds God's creation order thoroughly oppressive.

> ¹¹For there are many words that increase enigma. What advantage is there for the person?
> ¹²For who knows what is good for the person during the few days of one's enigmatic life? He makes them like a shadow, so that who can tell the person what will happen after one under the sun?

6:11–12. In such a context many words simply increase the enigma of life (v. 11). This is not to say that *all* words increase the enigma of life, but this line raises in an acute fashion which words do not! Qohelet certainly seems unable to find them. Who then can say what the path to life and joy is in the few days of a person's enigmatic life? Verse 11b repeats the programmatic question of "what benefit" there is for the person (cf. 1:3). Verse 12a repeats the question with an emphasis on the brevity of life and its enigmatic nature. Seow insists that "enigmatic" must mean "fleeting" here but gives no reason for this,[30] presumably because it extends the idea of the brevity of one's days. As a conclusion to vv. 1–12, however, there is no reason why Qohelet should not refer to the brevity of life *and* its enigmatic nature. Transience is indeed a major theme in this section, but it contributes to the enigmatic nature of life. God, according to Qohelet, has made people like a shadow. This metaphor, which occurs elsewhere in the Hebrew Bible,[31] emphasizes the insubstantiality of the human person—shadows come and go, and this is just like humans, who have no idea what will happen after them under the sun.

Theological Implications

In 5:10–17 [9–16] and 6:1–12 Qohelet applies his epistemology outlined in chap. 1 to the problem of wealth. In chap. 5 he observes that the love of money does not answer the question of what life is about. In 6:1–12 his central concern is that acquisition of wealth does not by itself satisfy and bring the rest that meaningful life requires. Juxtaposed between these two sections on wealth is the *carpe diem* passage of 5:18–20. It is in strong tension with both 5:10–17 and 6:1–12.

Scholars continually try to flatten out the tension between these approaches to life. Longman, for example, argues that in 5:18–20 [17–19] "in the light of the absence of a meaningful life, Qohelet advocates a life pursuing the small pleasures afforded by food, drink, and work."[32] As we saw, however, the exhortation in 5:18–20 is much stronger than this and is at points in direct contradiction with what precedes and follows it. For example, in 5:19 God empowers a person to enjoy his wealth, whereas in 6:2 God does not allow a person to "eat of it." What we have, then, is not an answer to the problem of wealth in 5:18–20 but a contradictory vision of life set in juxtaposition to Qohelet's struggles with wealth in 5:10–17 and 6:1–12. This contradiction is stark and is not resolved by Qohelet at this point—indeed, having moved from 5:10–17 to his positive confession in 5:18–20, his despair at finding meaning through wealth intensifies in 6:1–12, which is a very bleak passage.

Are there any clues in the text as to how this tension might be resolved? Final resolution, insofar as it exists, will have to wait, but there are some clues in chaps. 5 and 6 that help us to see why wealth does not provide meaning in life by itself. In chap. 5, the *love of* money is explored, which gives us an important clue as to the problem there. In chap. 6, an important clue is that the person pursuing wealth is unable to find *rest*, which Qohelet clearly regards as essential to meaning in life. Indeed, this is at the heart of the powerful comparison with

30. Seow, *Ecclesiastes*, 233.
31. 1 Chron. 29:15; Job 8:9; 14:12; Ps. 144:4.
32. Longman, *Ecclesiastes*, 168.

the stillborn: for all the horror of not being born, at least the stillborn has rest, which the person pursuing wealth to find meaning lacks. Qohelet does not explore why the person pursuing wealth is unable to find rest, other than his provocative comment that God does not empower him to do so.

It is important to note that in 5:10–17 [9–16] and 6:1–12 Qohelet argues on the basis of his experience and reason alone and that the focus is on wealth as providing the meaning for life. The description by implication of the person seeking meaning in wealth as "a wise person" in v. 8 is thus ironic. Qohelet's autonomous epistemology leads him again and again to the despairing conclusion that all is enigmatic. The character of 5:18–20 is very different from these sections. In 5:18–20 Qohelet also reports something he observes, but it has more of a confessional character, one that starts with God rather than ends by bumping up against God as in 6:10.

Theologically what are we to make of Qohelet's exploration of wealth and possessions? This is a large topic, and one would ultimately need to examine the whole of Scripture, which we cannot do here. Qohelet does, however, offer some very important insights on this topic. We need to remember, first, that this exploration, as with all the others, operates under the rubric of 1:3. Qohelet wants to know what work and thus life is all about, and wealth is one of the areas he examines in this respect.

Second, we in the West should note the contemporary relevance of Qohelet's exploration of wealth. The accumulation of wealth is one of the great idols of our day, and huge amounts of energy are spent seeking meaning through greater and greater accumulation of wealth and possessions. Miles notes, "Consumerism appears to have become part and parcel of the very fabric of modern life. . . . And the parallel with religion is not an accidental one. Consumerism is ubiquitous and ephemeral. It is arguably *the* religion of the late twentieth century."[33] As Wuthnow asserts, "We cannot fully appreciate the depths of materialism unless we understand how economic behavior supplies us with meaning, purpose, and a sense of sacred order."[34]

It is precisely Qohelet's question as to whether wealth can ultimately provide us with meaning and purpose. His answer is a decisive no. In terms of his epistemology this still leaves him perplexed about wealth, but his reasons for replying in the negative are insightful. There is first the problem of motivation: the *love of* money will not lead to satisfaction in life. Qohelet, in other words, probes the inner attitude toward wealth and possessions. It has long been recognized that this is a central element in a Christian ethic of wealth. Clement of Alexandria (third century AD), commenting on the rich man who is told by Jesus to sell everything and come follow him, asserts that what is

33. Miles, *Consumerism—as a Way of Life*, 1.
34. Wuthnow, "Introduction," in *Rethinking Materialism*, 19. All the essays in this book are germane to our discussion. See also Bartholomew and Moritz, *Christ and Consumerism*.

at stake is not a call to poverty but "the inner spirit of passionate desire for goods."[35] Humans easily become attached to goods in a way that replaces the Creator with his gifts—such idolatry will never lead to fulfillment in life, for we are made first for God, and the creation can be properly enjoyed only as his gift.

Second, there is the effect that possessions can have on a person. As Meilander notes, "We have not exhausted all there is to be said about the Christian life when we have discussed motives and noted that a good tree will bring forth good fruit, for it is also true that a heart will be shaped by the location of our treasure."[36] In chap. 6 Qohelet gets at the effect of the love of money on a person: one is unable to find the rest and meaning one so desires. Qohelet never explicitly explains why God does not empower this person to enjoy his wealth, but the reference to "rest" as the missing element, with its allusions to Noah and the problem of work since the fall, provides an important clue. Since the fall, work is not easily integrated into life so that one works and then rests as does Elohim in Gen. 1:1–2:3. Work is a struggle and easily becomes an idol. Pursuit of wealth and honor above all things boomerangs back on the person and leaves one restless and unfulfilled. As the Genesis narrative makes clear, the lack of rest in work is integrally connected to a broken relationship with God.

Third, we should note that there is no glorification of poverty in Qohelet. The *carpe diem* passage of 5:18–20 [17–19] makes this clear. The freedom to eat, drink, work, and accumulate wealth are gifts of God and are to be enjoyed before him. As Meilander notes:

> In the Old Testament there is condemnation of those who oppress and show no concern for the poor, but there is little condemnation of wealth itself. After we have finished calling attention to prophetic woes uttered upon the rich who trample the poor, and after we have taken note of the legal provisions connected with the year of jubilee, we will still have to grant that the legitimacy of possessions is both presupposed and protected by the Decalogue's commandments. Radical poverty is not an ideal.[37]

What then is a Christian approach to possessions and wealth? This is a complex question, and Meilander discerns three main attitudes in the Christian tradition.[38]

1. Possessions are good but also dangerous. To avoid the dangers we need to pursue *simplicity and generosity*.

35. Meilander, *Things That Count*, 188–89.
36. Ibid., 186.
37. Ibid., 183. See also McConville, "The Old Testament and the Enjoyment of Wealth."
38. Meilander, *Things That Count*, 191–93.

2. Generosity may imply more than moderation; it may involve *renunciation*. Meilander asserts that not all Christians are called to this route but notes that the parable of the rich young ruler (Luke 18:22–27) surely teaches that some Christians are called to renounce wealth and possessions. Christian religious orders who take a vow of poverty are an important example in this respect. In *Vita Consecrata* John Paul II notes, "*Poverty* proclaims that God is man's only real treasure. When poverty is lived according to the example of Christ . . . it becomes an expression of that *total gift of self* which the three Divine Persons make to one another. This gift overflows into creation and is fully revealed in the Incarnation of the Word and in his redemptive death."[39] This encyclical speaks of the *prophetic witness of the consecrated life* and notes, "*Another challenge* today is that of a *materialism which craves possessions*, heedless of the needs and sufferings of the weakest. . . . The *reply* of the consecrated life is found in the possession of *evangelical poverty*, which can be lived in different ways and is often expressed in an active involvement in the promotion of solidarity and charity. . . . Its [evangelical poverty's] primary meaning . . . is to attest that God is the true wealth of the human heart."[40]

3. Attempting to practice simplicity and generosity may create a tension in the Christian life that will lead to a certain austerity.

Meilander notes that room must be left for Christians to make different choices in response to God's call. He himself argues for *enjoyment and renunciation*. At the heart of this problem he discerns the question of trust:

> But at the heart of our attachment to things is the need for security. In what or whom do we place our confidence? To say that our life consists not in what we possess but in our relation to God, not in the goods we have compared with what others have but in the affirming verdict of God upon our lives, is not to say that the things of this world are of no importance. But it does make the issue of trust central.[41]

That creation is fallen will always make trust in the created goods rather than the Creator a temptation. This is at the heart of what makes those pursuing wealth above all unable to find rest. Hence Christians should be ready to renounce the gifts, bearing in mind that the problem is not the gifts but "that greedy, grasping, fallen self."[42] This is particularly true in our materialistic age.

39. John Paul II, *Consecrated Life*, 33.
40. Ibid., 162, 163.
41. Meilander, *Things That Count*, 194.
42. Ibid., 198.

In the light of redemption and the full range of the biblical story, however, *enjoyment* remains the final goal:

> When they [Christians] attempt to understand their lives within the world of biblical narrative, they are caught up in the double movement of enjoyment and renunciation. Neither half of the movement, taken by itself, is the Christian way of life. In order to trust, renunciation is necessary, lest we immerse ourselves entirely in the things we possess, trying to grasp and keep what we need to be secure. In order to trust, enjoyment is necessary. . . . Indeed, affirmation must . . . have the final word . . . because created goods are channels through which the divine glory strikes us . . . to renounce all enjoyment of created things—to delight in nothing . . . must be hell.[43]

In developing a positive norm for possessions, Meilander notes, "Since such beneficence must ultimately flow from 'fear and love' of God, the problem of possessions is, finally, a problem of trust."[44] With this, no doubt, Qohelet would concur. As he concludes 5:1–7 [4:17–5:6]: "Instead, fear God."

43. Ibid., 200.
44. Ibid., 193.

L.
Knowing What Is Good for One
(7:1–13)

Translation

> ¹A good name is better than good[1] ointment, and the day of death better than the day of one's birth.
>
> ²It is better to go to a house of mourning[2] than it is to go to a house of feasting, for it is the destination of every person, and the living should take it to heart.[3]
>
> ³Vexation[4] is better than laughter, for through a sad face the heart is made well.
>
> ⁴The heart of the wise is in the house of mourning, but the heart of fools is in the house of joy.
>
> ⁵It is better to listen to the rebuke of a wise person than for a person to listen to the song[5] of fools.

1. *Ṭôb* (good) means "fine" or "precious" here, as Schoors ("Word *ṭôb*," 685) points out, but since there is a wordplay in the Hebrew (see the interpretation), I retain the translation "good."

2. *Bêt-'ēbel* (house of mourning) occurs only here in the OT, but it occurs often in the Mishnah and Talmud with this meaning.

3. Cf. 9:1 for the same idiom.

4. In order to harmonize this verse with 5:17 [16], in which vexation is clearly negative, some commentators follow Luther in translating *ka'as* as "sorrow." There is no philological justification for this, however, and it stems from a desire to reduce the contradictions, which are a vital part of Ecclesiastes. See the interpretation.

5. Zimmermann ("Aramaic Provenance," 24) and Gordis (*Koheleth*, 269) argue that *šîr* means "praise" and not "song" here. They believe that "praise" is a better parallel to "rebuke," and they also note that this meaning is supported by an Aramaic cognate. Seow (*Ecclesiastes*,

6For[6] like the crackling of thorns under the pot,[7] so is the laughter of a fool. This also is enigmatic.

7For oppression makes a wise person foolish,[8] and a bribe[9] destroys the heart.[10]

8The end of a matter is better than its beginning. Patience of spirit is better than haughtiness of spirit.

9Do not be quick to be angry in your spirit, for vexation lodges[11] in the bosom of fools.

10Do not say, "Why is[12] it that the earlier days were better than these?" For it is not from wisdom that you ask this.

11Wisdom is good with[13] an inheritance, a benefit to those who see the sun.

12For to be in the shadow of wisdom is to be in the shadow of money, and the benefit of knowledge is that wisdom maintains the life of the one[14] who possesses it.

13Observe the work of God, for who can straighten what he has made crooked?

Interpretation

The literary style changes at the start of chap. 7: the first twelve verses are proverbs, many of which have the "better-than" form. Scholars differ about section divisions in this chapter. Some take 6:10–12 as leading into chap. 7 and beyond. Most recent commentators take 7:1–14 as a unit. It is hard to be

---

236) suggests that *šîr* here refers to a song of praise or adoration. *Šîr* means "song" everywhere else, and this meaning fits well in the context.

6. The *kî* here and at the start of v. 7 is causal (RJW §444).

7. There is a wordplay between *hassîrîm* (thorns) and *hassîr* (the pot) and also between *hassîr* and *šîr* (song) in v. 5. The repetition of sibilants and palatals in this line is also probably onomatopoeic.

8. There is some difficulty in translating *yĕhôlēl* (make foolish), as the dictionaries list three different roots for *hll*. The NASB translates "makes . . . mad." I agree with Longman (*Ecclesiastes*, 186) that the context suggests that the root in the Polel, which we appear to have here, meaning "make foolish," is the right choice.

9. *Mattānâ* refers to a bribe and not just any gift. Cf. Prov. 28:16.

10. Verse 7b is difficult in that the subject (bribe) is feminine, whereas the verb (destroys) is masculine. Furthermore, the accusative marker *'et* is used without the article. Various emendations have been proposed, but they are not necessary. The use of feminine subjects with masculine verbs is not unknown in Biblical Hebrew (GKC §145o), and in Ecclesiastes the accusative marker is sometimes used with nouns lacking the definite article (3:15; 4:4; 7:7).

11. *Yānûaḥ* (lodges) may be deliberately chosen as a wordplay on the several uses of *rûaḥ* (spirit) in vv. 8–9.

12. For the tense of *hāyâ*, see Isaksson, *Studies*, 88–89.

13. *'Im* here has its common meaning of accompaniment, hence "with" (RJW §328), contra Schoors ("Word *ṭôb*," 686), who interprets *'im* as "like"; hence "Wisdom is as good as riches."

14. The plural noun here is an honorific. See *IBHS* §7.4.3c.

sure of precise parameters, but 6:10–12 is better taken as the conclusion to 5:8 [7]–6:12, and 7:14 is best taken as the introduction to Qohelet's discussion of moderation. The list of proverbs in 7:1–13 indicates a change in literary style and thus a new section. As is typical of Qohelet's organic logic, however, this section attempts to answer the question raised in the conclusion in 6:12: "Who knows what is good for the person during the few days of one's enigmatic life?" Unity is also provided by word repetition: *ṭôb* (better/good) occurs eleven times, *ḥākām/ḥokmâ* (wise/wisdom) six times, *lēb* (heart) five times, *kĕsîl* (fool) four times, and *kaʿas* (vexation) twice.[15] These proverbs are full of irony, and Qohelet often starts off sounding very much like Proverbs but then gives the proverb an ironic twist.

> ¹A good name is better than good ointment, and the day of death better than the day of one's birth.

7:1. According to Prov. 22:1, "A good name is to be chosen rather than great riches, and grace is better than silver or gold." Verse 1a sounds just like Proverbs—a good reputation[16] is better than good ointment, an expensive and highly desirable item. The Hebrew of v. 1a contains a wordplay that is arranged chiastically: *ṭôb šēm miššemen ṭôb* (lit. "good name—than ointment good"). Fine ointment is listed among the treasures of King Hezekiah (2 Kings 20:13) and was a highly desirable luxury item. However, this proverb affirms that one's reputation is more important than wealth, and thus should not be sacrificed in the pursuit of wealth. The ironic twist comes in the comparison in v. 1b—the day of death is better than the day of one's birth. The twist relates back to Qohelet's reflections on death in passages like 3:18–21; 4:2–4; and 6:1–6. If death is all that awaits us, then of what value is life and thus a good reputation? In this way, v. 1b deconstructs v. 1a. If all is enigmatic, then the day of one's death is better than being born.

> ²It is better to go to a house of mourning than it is to go to a house of feasting, for it is the destination of every person, and the living should take it to heart.

7:2. Verse 2 explains v. 1 in case we are in any doubt—it is better to go to the funeral parlor than to a feast. A house of mourning would be the mourner's home, where family and friends would gather to mourn the death of a person. However, in Jer. 16:5 the NRSV translates a different phrase

---

15. Whybray, *Ecclesiastes* (NCBC), 112.

16. Seow (*Ecclesiastes*, 234–35) argues that *šēm* (name) may here mean more than just reputation, but fame that outlasts life. However, Qohelet's ironic twist in v. 1b contrasts life with death, and thus it is better to think of *šēm* as something enjoyed during one's life, namely, a good reputation.

as "the house of mourning," which might refer to a building set aside for funerary purposes.[17] Either way, as Jer. 16:5–8 makes clear, mourning also involved eating and drinking, and this is confirmed by ancient Near Eastern texts.[18] The "house of feasting" may refer to a banquet hall or simply to a home in which a celebration is taking place. For Qohelet, it is better to go to the house of mourning, because that is our ultimate destination anyway. Presumably the corpse would be present in the house of mourning, so that this is the literal destination of every person.[19] As is often the case, this section contradicts the *carpe diem* passages, which encourage feasting and celebration. Typically, commentators try to reduce the element of contradiction. Thus C. H. Wright argues that the eating and drinking referred to in the *carpe diem* passages is only in the context of the fear of God, whereas verses like v. 2 discourage frivolous pleasure.[20] But there is nothing to indicate this in v. 2, and the contradiction with the *carpe diem* passages is deliberate and symptomatic of Qohelet's struggle.

> [3]Vexation is better than laughter, for through a sad face the heart is made well.

7:3. Verse 3 is a further example of this: in 5:17 [16] vexation is a bad thing, but here it is better than laughter. Ogden distinguishes healthy from empty laughter[21] and argues that we have here a reference to empty laughter, but as with v. 2 this laughter is that of the feast, something the *carpe diem* passages celebrate. The second half of v. 3 is difficult to understand. It echoes Prov. 14:13, "Even in laughter the heart suffers, and the end of joy is grief." In the context of Prov. 14:13 a person is pursuing a way that seems right, but its end is death, and thus the laughter and joy referred to there is empty. Qohelet appears to caricature this saying by turning it on its head to take its logic to the opposite extreme: if the end of laughter and joy is suffering and grief, then vexation and sadness are preferable because they should lead to laughter and joy![22] As Seow notes,

> Here in vv 3–4 he caricatures the teachings of the traditional sages, and exaggerates their general advice in extreme terms: vexation is better than merriment, sadness of the face equals happiness of the heart, the heart of the wise is in the house of mourning. The sayings are perhaps deliberately ludicrous. By their

---

17. See P. Johnston (*Shades of Sheol*, 184–85) for a discussion of Jer. 16:5–9.
18. Seow, *Ecclesiastes*, 235–36.
19. Our knowledge of Israelite funerary customs is limited. For a review of the evidence and the main sources of research, see Johnston, *Shades of Sheol*, 49–65.
20. C. H. Wright, *Book of Koheleth*, 381.
21. Ogden, *Qoheleth*, 103.
22. Longman (*Ecclesiastes*, 184) argues that for Qohelet a sad face is preferable because it reflects reality. However, this fails to account for how it would heal the heart.

sheer absurdity, Qohelet challenges the audacity of anyone to tell others what is good and how to have an advantage in life. . . . The realities of life are simply too contradictory for one to be governed by axioms.[23]

> ⁴The heart of the wise is in the house of mourning, but the heart of fools is in the house of joy.

7:4. Verse 4 confirms this view. The heart of the "wise" is in the house of mourning. This does not just refer to a healthy awareness of one's finitude but to an obsession with death. The heart is the center of the person, and for Qohelet the "wise" person's center dwells in the house of mourning. Qohelet's logic leads him to the view that the wise person is consumed with death and the fool with celebration and joy. Once again this thoroughly contradicts the *carpe diem* passages in which joy is recommended and alerts us to the ironic use of "wise."

> ⁵It is better to listen to the rebuke of a wise person than for a person to listen to the song of fools.
> ⁶For like the crackling of thorns under the pot, so is the laughter of a fool. This also is enigmatic.

7:5–6. Verse 5 finds the rebuke of one wise person to be better than the song of (many) fools. Again this is a common theme in Proverbs. For example, Prov. 17:10 asserts, "A rebuke strikes deeper into one who has understanding than a hundred blows into a fool." The laughter of fools here in v. 6 is compared to the irritating crackling of thorns set alight under a pot. The wordplay between "thorns" (*sîrîm*) and "pot" (*sîr*) is hard to reproduce in translation. This sounds very much like the traditional wisdom of Proverbs, but lest we think Qohelet has changed course, he immediately adds: "This also is enigmatic." It is hard to be sure of Qohelet's logic at this point; why exactly are the proverbs of v. 5 and v. 6 enigmatic? Possibly this relates back to v. 4. If the heart of the "wise" is in the house of mourning, then why should his rebuke be better than the songs of fools?

> ⁷For oppression makes a wise person foolish, and a bribe destroys the heart.

7:7. The "for" of v. 7 links its proverb back to the enigma of v. 6 and gives us a clue as to how to read this proverb. Commentators struggle with the link between v. 7 and v. 6 and have often concluded that there is something wrong with the text at this point.[24] But this is to ignore the organic, floundering logic

---

23. Seow, *Ecclesiastes*, 246.
24. Longman, *Ecclesiastes*, 186.

of Qohelet in his struggle with what is good for a human. Even the wise person buckles under oppression and is susceptible to a bribe, and bribery and corruption destroy the heart. Thus, "Even if the wise are relatively superior to fools, they are still susceptible to corruption."[25] This links back to v. 5—if even a wise person can be made foolish by oppression, then it is *not* always better to listen to the rebuke of such a person. It is important to see Qohelet's autonomous epistemology at work here once again. He has observed what oppression can do even to the wise, and observation of even one such case subverts the traditional wisdom of v. 5.

> [8]The end of a matter is better than its beginning. Patience of spirit is better than haughtiness of spirit.
> [9]Do not be quick to be angry in your spirit, for vexation lodges in the bosom of fools.

7:8–9. The context of trying to determine what is good for humans is important as we come to vv. 8–9. Verse 5 gives us a clue as to how the end of a matter may be better than its beginning: the rebuke of a wise person may be unpleasant, but its end or result may be good. Thus patience and waiting are better than haughtiness. But this is complicated by v. 9. In v. 4 vexation is recommended above laughter, but here it lodges unpleasantly in the bosom of fools, so that patience is no help when it comes to vexation. Thus the truth of v. 8 is subtly undermined.

> [10]Do not say, "Why is it that the earlier days were better than these?" For it is not from wisdom that you ask this.

7:10. In v. 10 we hear a question from Qohelet's audience: "Why are the former days better than the present?" But Qohelet responds that it is "not from wisdom" to ask such a question. He does not explain why this is a worthless question, but in the light of his view that history keeps repeating itself, such a question would be senseless. As so often in Ecclesiastes, the question is about the true nature of "wisdom." According to traditional wisdom and OT narrative and law this would be a sensible question to ask so that we could discern where we are going wrong in the present. It is the sort of question that 2 Kings 17:7–41 answers at length. But for Qohelet, with his view of history and his epistemology, such a question is folly, not wisdom.

> [11]Wisdom is good with an inheritance, a benefit to those who see the sun.

25. Seow, *Ecclesiastes*, 247.

> ¹²For to be in the shadow of wisdom is to be in the shadow of money, and the benefit of knowledge is that wisdom maintains the life of the one who possesses it.
> ¹³Observe the work of God, for who can straighten what he has made crooked?

7:11–13. Verses 11–12 initially seem to recommend traditional wisdom, but all is not what it seems. Some commentators take '*im* (with) in v. 11 to mean "as" and thus take wisdom to be compared positively to an inheritance. This meaning is attested in 2:14, but the common function of '*im* is to refer to accompaniment, and all the major versions apart from the Peshitta interpret it in this way. It is even possible that we have a play on the two meanings here, but "with" fits the ironic logic and context better. Verse 11 starts off in a traditional fashion declaring wisdom to be good, but the twist comes in that something extra is needed: an inheritance. Wisdom is closely tied here with wealth, described in terms of an inheritance and money, but both wisdom and money are likened to being in a shadow. A shadow can imply protection,[26] but we know from 6:12 that a shadow also speaks of insubstantiality. Thus the latter part of v. 12 is highly ironic. Wisdom may keep a person alive, but it will not bring meaning or rest. Qohelet has already demonstrated in previous chapters that wealth cannot provide meaning for life, and by equating wisdom and wealth so inseparably in vv. 11–12, he lets us know that they will not maintain but destroy one's life. This reading of v. 12 is confirmed by the comment in v. 13. God has made life crooked, and no one can straighten what he has made crooked. This harks back to and is in the same spirit as 1:15, although here Qohelet explicitly states that God has made things crooked. As in chap. 1, this assertion that God has made things crooked and one cannot straighten them is equivalent to saying that all is enigmatic.

Qohelet's exhortation to "*observe* the work of God" alerts us to the fact that his autonomous epistemology has led him to this conclusion; one is unable to determine from traditional wisdom what is good for humans. Neither achieving a good reputation, nor vexation, nor listening to the advice of a wise person, nor trying to discern why the present is worse than the past, nor money provides an adequate answer to the question of what is good for humans. All is enigmatic.

Theological Implications

In this section Qohelet attempts to answer the question as to *the nature of the good life* by looking again at traditional wisdom. Not surprisingly,

26. Longman (*Ecclesiastes*, 190) takes this as the meaning of "shadow" here.

therefore, the dominant form is that of the proverb. He starts with traditional wisdom and then problematizes this each time, so that we are left with no clear answer as to what constitutes the good life. The sort of wisdom that Proverbs offers would appear to be deeply problematic and to offer no secure place to stand. The cold shadow of death is felt throughout this section, and it regularly contradicts Qohelet's positive affirmation of life in the *carpe diem* passages. Empirical observation is central to Qohelet's deconstruction of traditional wisdom. The universality of death is observable; it is the destination of every person. Oppression can make a wise person foolish, and thus one cannot always trust the rebuke of a wise person. God is not excluded from these reflections, but the move is from them toward God: if this is the broken nature of reality demonstrated by his analysis, Qohelet asserts, then God must be the source of its enigma, and there is nothing we can do to straighten what he has made crooked.

Theologically this section demonstrates that an autonomous, empirical approach such as that of Qohelet is unable to discern what is good for humans. As Wendell Berry notes,

> Religion, as empiricists must finally grant, deals with a reality beyond the reach of empiricism. This larger reality does not manifest itself in the manner of laboratory results or in the manner of a newspaper front page. Christ does not come down from the cross and confound his tormentors, as good a movie as that would make. God does not speak loudly from Heaven in the most popular modern language for all to hear. The walls of the rational, empirical world are famously porous. What comes through are dreams, imaginings, inspirations, visions, revelations. There is no use in stooping over these with a magnifying lens. Beyond any earthly reason we experience beauty in excess of justice, love in excess of deserving or fulfillment. We have known evil beyond imagining and seemingly beyond intention. We have known compassion and forgiveness beyond measure.[27]

Qohelet's conclusion in v. 13 provides us with an important theological clue as to the problem with empiricism. His empiricism enables him to see that the world is bent and broken, but it cannot take him any further than that. It is as though his world is confined to that ushered in by Gen. 3, the fall. It is true, as Qohelet finds again and again, that an empirical approach to our present fallen world makes life appear utterly enigmatic. But the larger context of Gen. 3, of creation and redemption through the line of Abraham, alerts us that God *is* at work making straight what has been bent and broken. Shalom is a good biblical word for God's intention with creation:

27. Berry, *Life Is a Miracle*, 99–100.

The webbing together of God, humans, and all creation in justice, fulfillment, and delight is what the Hebrew prophets call *shalom*. We call it peace, but it means far more than mere peace of mind or a cease-fire between enemies. In the Bible, shalom means universal flourishing, wholeness, and delight—a rich state of affairs in which natural needs are satisfied and natural gifts are fruitfully employed, a state of affairs that inspires joyful wonder as its Creator and Savior opens doors and welcomes the creatures in whom he delights. Shalom, in other words, is the way in which things ought to be.[28]

This is what God made the world for and this is his goal in redemption, which is the medicine to heal the sickening evils of creation. True understanding of the gospel requires a "full disclosure on sin"[29] and brokenness, and Qohelet relentlessly confronts us with this. But such disclosure must also be contextualized in the intention and ultimate triumph of shalom; otherwise enigma will indeed become nihilism and despair.

28. C. Plantinga, *Not the Way It's Supposed to Be*, 10.
29. Ibid., 199.

M.
Moderation in Wisdom and Folly
(7:14–22)

Translation

> [14]On a good[1] day, enjoy yourself, but on an evil day, observe: God has made this one as well as that one, so that[2] no one will discover what comes after one.
> [15]I have observed everything[3] in my enigmatic life: there is a righteous person perishing in[4] his righteousness, and there is a wicked person who prolongs his life in his wickedness.
> [16]Do not be very righteous and do not be excessively wise. Why destroy yourself?
> [17]Do not be excessively wicked and do not be a fool. Why die before[5] your time?

1. Schoors ("Word *ṭôb*," 697) argues that "good" here means "well-being, prosperity."
2. *'Al-dibrat še* occurs only here. It is equivalent to Aramaic *'al dibrat dî* (Dan. 2:30; conjectured in 4:17 [14]). So Seow, *Ecclesiastes*, 240.
3. Alternatively, *kōl* could be translated here as "both."
4. The preposition *bě* before "righteousness" and "wickedness" here has been interpreted in three ways: concessively as "despite" (Podechard), instrumentally as "through" (Hertzberg; Bickell; Carlebach; Lamparter; Dahood, "Qoheleth and Northwest Semitic Philology"), and normatively (RJW §252) as "in" (G. Barton, *Ecclesiastes*; Power; Zimmerli, *Buch des Predigers Salomo*; Galling, *Prediger*; A. Williams; Loretz, *Qohelet*). "Through" would imply that there is something in the righteous man's righteousness that causes him to perish and something in the wicked person's wickedness that causes him to survive, and this interpretation is the most unlikely of the three. The first and third amount to the same thing. See the interpretation section.
5. Temporal use of *bě* (RJW §241).

> ¹⁸It is good that you grasp this one, and do not let go of that one from your hand, for the person who fears God will emerge⁶ with both of them.
> ¹⁹Wisdom strengthens⁷ a wise person more than ten officials⁸ who are in a city.
> ²⁰For there is not a righteous person on the earth who does good and does not sin.
> ²¹Also do not take to heart all the words that people speak, lest⁹ you hear your servant cursing you.
> ²²For, furthermore, your heart knows that you also have cursed others many times.

Interpretation

Verse 13, with its exhortation to observe the work of God, who has made the world crooked, is a link verse between these two sections. In vv. 14–22 Qohelet reflects on how to approach wisdom and folly if this is the state of the world. His advice boils down to this: be moderate in both and excessive in neither.

> ¹⁴On a good day, enjoy yourself, but on an evil day, observe: God has made this one as well as that one, so that no one will discover what comes after one.
> ¹⁵I have observed everything in my enigmatic life: there is a righteous person perishing in his righteousness, and there is a wicked person who prolongs his life in his wickedness.

7:14–15. In continuity with v. 13, v. 14 notes that both good and bad days are made by God, so one should enjoy the good days but be aware that God also makes bad ones and know that one can know nothing about one's future. "After one" most likely refers to one's earthly life rather than life after death. Qohelet's point is that God's ways with the world are so confusing that one should enjoy the good days but be aware that one has no idea what is to come. This leads on in v. 15 to another anecdote from Qohelet—he has observed a righteous person perishing despite his righteousness and a wicked person living

6. Grammatically, the verb here can be translated as "to escape from," but the context of holding onto militates against this.

7. Seow (*Ecclesiastes*, 256) translates *tā'ōz* as "is dearer." This is a possible meaning that Seow prefers because "be strong" does not seem to fit. As I argue in the interpretation, however, "strengthen" fits perfectly well.

8. The singular form is found in 8:8 and 10:5. Against the background of Aramaic documents of the fifth and fourth centuries BC, Seow (*Ecclesiastes*, 257) argues that a *šallîṭ* is a proprietor, one who has power over property.

9. *'Ăšer lō'* here expresses purpose, i.e., "so that not" or "lest" (RJW §466).

a long life despite his wickedness. In other words, Qohelet has found living examples that clearly contradict Proverbs' character-consequence teaching that righteousness will lead to blessing and folly to destruction.

> ¹⁶Do not be very righteous and do not be excessively wise. Why destroy yourself?
> ¹⁷Do not be excessively wicked and do not be a fool. Why die before your time?
> ¹⁸It is good that you grasp this one, and do not let go from your hand of that one, for the person who fears God will emerge with both of them.

7:16–18. Qohelet's exhortations that follow in vv. 16–18 build on this observation—one should not be very wise or very righteous, and at the same time one should not be very wicked or a fool. Verses 16 and 17 form a well-constructed literary unit. "Do not be very righteous" is paralleled by "do not be excessively wicked," and "do not be excessively wise" is paralleled by "do not be a fool." Both verses also end with a question. Strange identifies four interpretations of v. 16: it is a warning against scrupulosity in religious and moral matters (Podechard), against the dangers of intellectual and moral greatness (G. Barton), against legalism (van der Ploeg), or against the danger involved in the affectation of justice and wisdom (Castellino, Whybray, Murphy).[10] Strange argues that the fourth interpretation fits best in this context. Much in his interpretation hinges on the possibility of reading *tiṭḥakkam* (v. 16, "do not be wise") in its Hithpael form as "show yourself wise," thus implying affectation or playing a role. Strange thus reads vv. 15–18 as follows: Because of v. 15 one should not pose as a just person or make a display of wisdom; one should not be greatly wicked or a fool, as this can lead to an early death. The God-fearing person heeds both parts of this advice and thus escapes the dangers threatened. However, the only other use of the Hithpael of *ḥkm* in the OT is in Exod. 1:10, and there, contrary to Strange, it does not have the clear meaning "show yourself shrewd/wise." Furthermore, Strange's arguments for reading "do not be very righteous" as a warning against affecting righteousness are not compelling.[11] Moreover, pretense is clearly not involved in v. 17, which closely parallels v. 16.[12]

---

10. Strange, "Question of Moderation," 68. See Podechard, *L'Ecclésiaste*, 374–79; G. Barton, *Ecclesiastes*, 144; van der Ploeg, *Prediker*, 46–47; Castellino, "Qoheleth and His Wisdom"; Whybray, "Qoheleth the Immoralist?"; Murphy, *Seven Books of Wisdom*, 100. Murphy (*Ecclesiastes*, 70) says rather differently that "he is attempting to show that there are no privileged claims on life on the side of either wisdom or folly, of either justice or wickedness."

11. Strange, "Question of Moderation," 83–87. Longman (*Ecclesiastes*, 195) notes the significance of the lack of the Hithpael in the first part of v. 16.

12. On the internal arrangement of vv. 16–17, see Whybray, "Qoheleth the Immoralist?" 192.

The obvious reading, but by far the most shocking, is that in the light of v. 15 Qohelet logically argues from what he has observed that neither strenuous righteousness/wisdom nor wickedness/folly is to be recommended.[13] The person devoted to righteousness perishes, and so does the wicked. Both extremes, from Qohelet's observations, may destroy one. The only logical way forward would appear to be moderation in both. Seow, following Loader, argues that the terms used here should not be thought of as moralistic, but that depends on a false distinction between wisdom and law (see the introduction, "Reading Ecclesiastes within the Context of Proverbs and Job and Its Connection to the Torah").[14] Both righteousness (living according to God's torah) and wisdom (living according to God's order in creation) are aspects of obedience to God and therefore morally and religiously charged.

Typically, it is hard to know just what such moderation would involve; not being very wicked allows for moderate wickedness, a position contrary to the OT narrative, legal, and Wisdom literature and in stark contrast to the exhortations in the *carpe diem* passages in Ecclesiastes to "fear God." "The person who fears God" in v. 18 is an ironic reference to the fear of God and relates back to v. 13. If God has made the world crooked, then this is what fear of God should involve! Logically, this position flows from Qohelet's observation of v. 15; if this example is allowed to undermine the character-consequence structure taught by Proverbs, then the exhortation to moderation has a certain logic about it. Indeed, for Qohelet, on the basis of what he has observed, this is simply reality: God has made the world crooked so that, as he says in v. 18, one must hold onto righteousness-wisdom and wickedness-folly, for the person who reveres the God who has made the world crooked will emerge with both. As Seow points out, on the basis of his logic at this point, "Qohelet is simply stating a reality: the 'fearer of God' will venture forth in life *with* both righteousness-wisdom and wickedness-folly."[15]

Qohelet's affirmation of moderation raises the question again of a possible Greek background. In 1925 Ranston argued that Qohelet's recommendation of moderation finds an apt parallel in the thought of Theognis (d. ca. 525 BC). However, the similarities are more apparent than real.[16] Plumptre says of v. 16, "Even in that which is in itself good, virtue lies, as Aristotle taught, in a mean between opposite extremes."[17] Although Aristotle does indeed have a doctrine of means regarding moral virtues,[18] he is quite clear that this doctrine must not be applied to cases in which there is no mean: "But not every action

---

13. Proverbs is strongly opposed to such a view, e.g., Prov. 3:7; 4:27; 8:13.
14. Seow, *Ecclesiastes*, 253; Loader, *Polar Structures*, 47–48.
15. Seow, *Ecclesiastes*, 255.
16. See Strange, "Question of Moderation," 115–20.
17. Plumptre, *Ecclesiastes*, 167.
18. See his *Nichomachean Ethics* and *Eudemian Ethics*.

or feeling admits of the mean. For the names of some automatically include baseness, e.g., spite, shamelessness, envy, and adultery, theft, murder, among actions. . . . Hence in doing these things we can never be correct, but must invariably be in error."[19] Thus Qohelet's shocking affirmation of moderation is best understood as a result of his struggle with traditional wisdom under the general influence of Greek philosophy.

> [19]Wisdom strengthens a wise person more than ten officials who are in a city.
> [20]For there is not a righteous person on the earth who does good and does not sin.
> [21]Also do not take to heart all the words that people speak, lest you hear your servant cursing you.
> [22]For, furthermore, your heart knows that you also have cursed others many times.

7:19–22. Verse 19 is a proverb affirming the value of wisdom in the spirit of Proverbs. Scholars struggle to see the logic of introducing this proverb at this point.[20] However, the mention of "wisdom" connects back into the previous verses, and the orthodox proverb provides a basis for further deconstruction of traditional wisdom. Verse 19 is immediately partially subverted by v. 20, asserting as it does that no person is wholly righteous, not even the wise. In terms of Qohelet's epistemology this undermines the proverb. As in vv. 16–17, wisdom and righteousness/sin are held together. This reflection on the universality of sin and folly is extended in vv. 21–22 to speech. According to v. 21, we should not listen too closely to what others say, for we may hear our servant cursing or slandering us. Verse 22 provides the motive clause for v. 21: we know that we err in this way ourselves.

There is, of course, some irony in Qohelet ending his discussion of moderation in this way. If no one's words can be fully trusted, then why should we listen to him? He is, as it were, hoist upon his own petard. There is some discussion as to whether the word "cursing" and "curse" in vv. 20–21 may in this context have the less severe sense of "declare contemptible" or "revile."[21] However, the normal meaning of the root in the Piel stem is "to curse," and it is better to retain this sense here. Qohelet refers to cursing others, but one cannot help reflecting on how close he has come to calling evil good and good evil (cf. Isa. 5:20). In Isa. 5 such people are described as wise in their own eyes and ripe for God's judgment, his curse. In Job 2:9 Job's wife advises him to curse God and die, an indirect exhortation to suicide because it would bring

19. Aristotle, *Nichomachean Ethics*, 45.
20. Longman, *Ecclesiastes*, 197–98.
21. Gordis, *Koheleth*, 279–80.

God's judgment on him.[22] Qohelet has not reached that stage, but from an OT perspective, he has "sinned with his lips" (Job 2:10).

Theological Implications

If traditional wisdom does not work, then perhaps *moderation* is the answer. Qohelet explores this idea in this section. But his reflection is done in the shadow of his observation of a righteous person perishing despite his righteousness and the wicked living a long, good life, and his conclusions hardly provide a way forward. What could it possibly mean to be moderately righteous and moderately wicked? Qohelet's shocking advocacy of moderation is more a despairing protest than a viable way forward.

Qohelet's promotion of moderation stems from his struggle with *theodicy*—seeing the righteous perish while the wicked enjoy good, long lives. It is precisely the sort of problem the psalmist describes in Ps. 73. The wicked are prosperous and happy while the psalmist is plagued and punished and wearisome. Theologically and philosophically, much has been written about theodicy. The term "theodicy" was coined by the German philosopher Leibniz in 1710.[23] His aim was to show that the evil in the world is not in conflict with the goodness of God; indeed, this is the best of all possible worlds. As Christians have wrestled, like Qohelet, with the very real problem of evil, various theories have been formulated.

Christian theism believes that

1. There is one God (monotheism).
2. God is the creator of the world.
3. God is all-powerful.
4. God is personal.
5. God is wholly good.

Evil, both natural and moral,[24] problematizes these beliefs, because if God is all-powerful he is able to prevent evil, and if God is wholly good he must be willing to prevent evil.[25] "There is little doubt that the problem of evil is *the* most serious intellectual difficulty for theism."[26] David Hume put his finger

---

22. Violation of the second commandment merited the death penalty in the OT. The Hebrew word for "curse" in Job 2:9 is *brk*, which is usually translated as "bless." In the prologue, it appears to be used euphemistically, but, oddly, it is used in the normal sense as well. So there is some debate over whether Job's wife is advising Job to bless or curse God and die.

23. Leibniz, *Essais de théodicée*.

24. The latter refers to evil brought about by human and demonic agents.

25. S. Davis, "Introduction," 3.

26. Ibid., 2.

on the problem: "Is he [God] willing to prevent evil, but not able? Then he is impotent. Is he able, but not willing? Then he is malevolent. Is he both able and willing? Whence then is evil?"[27] In wrestling with this issue Christian philosophers and theologians have come up with the following proposals.

1. *Deny the omnipotence of God.* The tension between an omnipotent and wholly good God and the evil in the world has led to a recurring temptation either to drop the omnipotence of God or to face up to God not being wholly good. The latter is intolerable—C. S. Lewis's great fear was to discover that God is there but not wholly good. Thus the easier option has been to relinquish the omnipotence of God by coming to the view that he is not all-powerful and cannot therefore control evil and consequently cannot be held responsible for it. An example of this approach is Griffin's process theodicy. Griffin denies the doctrine of *creatio ex nihilo* and asserts, "My solution dissolves the problem of evil by denying the doctrine of omnipotence fundamental to it. . . . There has always been a plurality of actualities having some power of their own."[28] Qohelet, however, never moves in this direction; he holds on to a view of God as God and therefore omnipotent.

2. *Question the goodness of God.* Frederick Sontag's theodicy, which he calls anthropodicy, is a good example of this position.[29] For Sontag we need to start with the problem of evil and then slowly work toward an adequate view of God, rather than assuming that we know God is good and omnipotent; for too long apologies have been made for God. "It is the status of evil in God's nature which forces us to reconceive divinity. Some faults in our world can be explained by claiming that they are not seen as evil in God's sight but only in ours. However, such an event as a holocaust surely does not appear 'good' to God in any sense of the word."[30] Sontag thus loosens theism's hold on the perfect goodness of God and invokes mystery at these points. Aspects of Qohelet's struggle resonate with Sontag's theodicy. His struggle does lead him to question God's goodness. A development of his thought in 7:13, compared with 1:15, is his assertion that God has made the world crooked and that we are therefore powerless to make it straight. His logic runs something like this:

A. The world is observably crooked.
B. God made the world.
C. God made the world crooked.
D. By implication God is not wholly good.

27. Hume, *Dialogues concerning Natural Religion*, 198.
28. Griffin, "Creation out of Nothing," 105.
29. Sontag, "Anthropodicy and the Return of God."
30. Ibid., 148.

But this is not an easy position to live with, and it is what Qohelet would call "utterly enigmatic." Thus, as we will see below, Qohelet's theodicy perhaps best fits that of the protest sort.

3. *The Irenaean theodicy.* This is particularly associated with John Hick,[31] who finds in the thought of Irenaeus the framework for developing a theodicy. According to Hick, God's intention with humankind is to create perfect personal creatures in relationship with him. However, it is logically impossible for God to create humans already in this state, because spiritually such a state involves moving freely toward God and freely choosing good over evil. Thus humankind was initially created by means of the evolutionary process as a morally and spiritually immature creature and as part of an ambiguous and ethically demanding world. Thus moral and natural evil are necessary parts of the process by which God is making perfect finite creatures. Qohelet does not explore such an approach, but he would undoubtedly find the evil he observes difficult to square with some larger process whereby God is making perfect creatures.

4. *The free-will defense.* From this perspective, evil is a consequence of God giving humans free will. Without the potential to choose evil, humans would be like robots. The free-will defense has an ancient pedigree in Augustine: "At bottom, he says, it's that God can create a more perfect universe by permitting evil. A really top-notch universe requires the existence of free, rational, and moral agents; and some of the free creatures He created went wrong. But the universe with the free creatures it contains and the evil they commit is better than it would have been had it contained neither the free creatures nor this evil."[32] This approach was reformulated and critiqued by J. L. Mackie.[33] Mackie questions the claim that evil is a result of human free will. If the will is free, according to Mackie, then logically it is possible for a person always to choose the good. If such a virtuous world is possible, then it is within the power of a good, omnipotent God to create such a world. Thus the claim that God had to choose between a world of robots or one of free agents is a false dilemma.

In response to Mackie, the neo-Calvinist philosopher Alvin Plantinga has presented a robust defense of a free-will theodicy. He argues that evil is consistent with God's existence because there are some things that even an omnipotent God cannot realize, such as making $2 + 2 = 7$. For Plantinga there are logical truths, what he calls "counterfactuals of freedom," about our choices in various situations. The truths about these choices are necessarily and timelessly true. If, for example, in situation Y in which Mike is free either to cheat or not to cheat in an exam, it is either true that "If Mike were to be free in Y,

31. Hick, "Irenaean Theodicy," 39–52.
32. A. Plantinga, "Free Will Defense," 25.
33. Mackie, "Evil and Omnipotence."

he would cheat in the exam," or "If Mike were truly free in Y, he would not cheat in the exam." If the first proposition is true—Mike would cheat in the exam—then God cannot bring about the possible world in which Mike does not cheat in the exam.

Furthermore, Plantinga argues for the possibility that a person will sin at least once, no matter what context God puts them in. Such a person suffers from what Plantinga calls "transworld depravity." Though it is possible that one could choose to do good in every situation, it remains true that one will choose to sin. God can do nothing to bring about sinless possible worlds because they are up to the sinner, who will choose otherwise. God may be omnipotent, but he cannot alter free decisions. Perhaps all persons suffer from "transworld depravity" so that the actual world, though not the best possible world, is the best one God could create if he is to respect the free will of the human creature. This may account for moral evil but what of natural evil? Plantinga appeals to the idea of Satan as the cause of natural evil, which S. Davis calls Plantinga's "luciferous defense."[34] Furthermore, natural evil may also be the result of powerful, evil moral agents such as demons.

Richard Swinburne similarly argues for a free-will defense of evil: "A generous God . . . will seek to give us great responsibility for ourselves, each other, and the world, and thus a share in his own creative activity of determining what sort of world it is to be."[35] A realistic theodicy must be based on a "free-will defense [that] claims that it is a great good that humans have a certain sort of free will which I shall call free and responsible choice. . . . Necessarily there will be the natural [not predetermined] possibility of moral evil."[36] The life of humans is more valuable when they have "*genuine* responsibility for other humans, and that involves the opportunity to benefit *or* harm them."[37]

5. *A theodicy of protest, or against theodicy*. This approach has developed particularly since the Holocaust. Christian theology teaches that God cares about history, but J. Roth, who advocates a protest theodicy, agrees with Hegel that history is "the slaughter-bench at which the happiness of peoples, the wisdom of states, and the virtue of individuals have been sacrificed."[38] Roth wants evil acknowledged for what it is and God held accountable. The danger in this approach is that one relinquishes the notion that God is wholly good.

The Mennonite theologian John Howard Yoder discussed his approach to theodicy in an unfinished essay, "Trinity versus Theodicy: Hebraic Realism and the Temptation to Judge God" (1966). Yoder is opposed not to theodicy per se but to the approach often taken to the problem, which he regards as idolatrous. He asks:

34. Davis, "Free Will and Evil," 75.
35. Swinburne, *Is There a God?* 96.
36. Ibid., 98.
37. Ibid., 99.
38. Roth, "Theodicy of Protest," 10.

- Where does one get the criteria by which to judge God?
- Why do we consider ourselves qualified to judge God?
- If we think we are qualified, how does this adjudication proceed?

Yoder thus opposes the narrow sense of theodicy, as articulated by Leibniz, which aims to justify God.[39] In this vein, Braiterman, writing in the context of post-Holocaust theology, coined the term "antitheodicy," which means "refusing to justify, explain, or accept" the relationship "between God (or some other form of ultimate reality), evil, and suffering."[40] Two other Jewish post-Holocaust thinkers, Joseph Soloveitchik and Mordecai Kaplan, to whom Braiterman refers, are also cited by Yoder. Yoder describes their approach as the Jewish case against God, creatively updated since Auschwitz. The faithful continue with their prayers, after denouncing the LORD for what he has allowed to happen. Yoder sees this as a valid form of theology in the *mode* of theodicy, but it is the opposite of theodicy.[41]

Job fits well within Yoder's type of antitheodicy. In Job the problem of suffering is never resolved intellectually but only existentially in relation to God, and particularly God as creator. And his journey toward resolution contains much protest. Contra Yoder, Ecclesiastes provides ample *Hebraic* defense for an intellectual analysis of the problem of evil. However, the analysis often culminates in a protest, as it does in his conclusion that God made the world crooked and in the logical but shocking recommendation of moderation. It is thus another question altogether whether Qohelet thinks rational analysis of the problem of evil will get us anywhere. In terms of Qohelet's journey, we need to wait and see how his struggle is resolved.

Theologically we should also note that Eccles. 7:20 is the single example of a verse from Ecclesiastes quoted in the NT. In Rom. 3:10 Paul, at the start of a series of quotations from the OT, quotes v. 20 in the lead up to his assertion in Rom. 3:23 that "all have sinned and fall short of the glory of God." Paul immediately follows this with the glorious truth that just as all have sinned, now they are justified by his grace as a gift, through the redemption in Christ Jesus. This, indeed, is God's means for making straight what has become crooked.

---

39. An important discussion of theodicy in the Yoder tradition is that of Hauerwas, *Naming the Silences*. Hauerwas argues that theodicy generally takes place in the context of enlightenment presuppositions that are unacceptable from a Christian perspective. Historically speaking, he argues (ibid., 53), "Christians have not had a 'solution' to the problem of evil. Rather, they have had a community of care that has made it possible for them to absorb the destructive terror of evil that constantly threatens to destroy all human relations."

40. Braiterman, *(God) After Auschwitz*, 4.

41. Yoder, "Trinity versus Theodicy."

N.
Qohelet's Reflection on His Journey and the Inaccessibility of Wisdom
(7:23–29)

Translation

> [23]All this I tested by wisdom. I said, "I will be wise," but it was far from me.
> [24]That which is,[1] is far off, and extraordinarily[2] deep. Who can find it?
> [25]I turned my heart[3] to know and to explore and to seek wisdom and an explanation, and to know wickedness, stupidity, folly, and madness.[4]

1. Isaksson (*Studies*, 90–91) notes that this is an occurrence of *hāyâ* where the context requires that the verbs be translated by a present tense. Cf. 1:9; 3:15; 6:10.

2. So Crenshaw, *Ecclesiastes*, 144. For intensification by repetition—the adjective "deep" occurs twice—see *IBHS* §12.5a.

3. Literally "I turned, I and my heart." Although emendations of this somewhat awkward phrase are proposed (Longman, *Ecclesiastes*, 201–2), they are not necessary. The *waw* (and) prefixed to "heart" is explicative (GKC 484n1).

4. The sequence of four nouns is problematic. They may be an enumeration, as translated here, or two double accusatives dependent on "to know." If the latter, then one would translate v. 25b "and to know that wickedness is stupidity and folly is madness." Either translation fits well in the context. The use of the definite article only with "folly" is also unusual.

²⁶And I am finding⁵ more bitter than death the woman who⁶ is a snare, and whose heart is a trap,⁷ and whose hands are chains. The one who pleases God escapes her, but the sinner is seized by her.

²⁷Observe: "This is what I have found," says Qohelet, "adding one thing to another to find an explanation,⁸

²⁸which my soul still seeks but I have not found. One person⁹ among a thousand I have found, but a woman among all these I have not found."

²⁹Only¹⁰ observe this: I have found that God made the human being straight, but they have sought out many schemes.

Interpretation

²³All this I tested by wisdom. I said, "I will be wise," but it was far from me.

²⁴That which is, is far off, and extraordinarily deep. Who can find it?

7:23–24. "All this" (v. 23) refers immediately to vv. 1–22, but the similarities in this section to 1:12–18 extend Qohelet's reflections to his whole journey thus far.¹¹ "All this" also indicates the start of a new section as Qohelet pauses to reflect. Qohelet notes again his methodology or epistemology in v. 23, namely "by wisdom" (*baḥokmâ*). "By wisdom" occurs three times prior to 7:23 (1:13; 2:2, 21). As noted in chap. 1, it is important there as an indicator of Qohelet's epistemology. Its recurrence here is thus significant, encouraging the reader to reflect again carefully on Qohelet's epistemology. By now, however, it is far clearer than it was in 1:12–18 that this wisdom is autonomous and something very different from wisdom in Proverbs, for ironically his search "by wisdom" fails to yield wisdom! Thus Seow is quite wrong to assert, "The author claims to have the ability to test by wisdom, yet he admits that wisdom is beyond him.

5. The verb is the Qal active participle (*môṣeʾ*).

6. *ʾĂšer* could be relative (who) or causal (because, for). Both are true: the woman is a snare, and she is bitter because she is a snare.

7. *Ḥĕrāmîm* (trap) is the plural of complexity (Seow, *Ecclesiastes*, 263). The Hebrew accents indicate that the trap is related to the woman, but *BHS*, following the versions, separates the two, which is reflected in my translation.

8. Literally "one to one to find an explanation."

9. Seow (*Ecclesiastes*, 274) notes that the use of *ʾādām* here is unusual because elsewhere in Ecclesiastes it never refers to a specific person. He therefore concludes that v. 28b is a marginal gloss inadvertently included. But see the interpretation.

10. *Lĕbad* (only) is taken by many to relate to "this" and thus translated as "only this." However, *lĕbad* begins the verse and is separated from "this" by the verb "observe."

11. See Spears, "Theological Hermeneutics," 132–33, on "all this" as anaphoric; chapter 5 is a valuable close reading of 7:23–29.

There is no real contradiction, however. . . . He applied reason (as traditional wisdom does), but found that it did not make him as wise as he had wished."[12] This is to miss the irony that surfaces here strongly and to fail to note the difference between Qohelet's epistemology and that of traditional wisdom.

Wisdom is far from Qohelet, it is far off and deeply hidden (vv. 23–24). This evokes Job 28, in which wisdom is poetically described as "hidden." Even Abaddon[13] and Death have heard only rumors of it (Job 28:22)! Like the woman in Prov. 31, wisdom is hard to find. This inaccessibility of wisdom when pursued "by wisdom" raises acutely for the reader the question of whether Qohelet's methodology is "wise."

> [25]I turned my heart to know and to explore and to seek wisdom and an explanation, and to know wickedness, stupidity, folly, and madness.
> [26]And I am finding more bitter than death the woman who is a snare, and whose heart is a trap, and whose hands are chains. The one who pleases God escapes her, but the sinner is seized by her.
> [27]Observe: "This is what I have found," says Qohelet, "adding one thing to another to find an explanation,
> [28a]which my soul still seeks but I have not found.

7:25–28a. The rest of this section expands on Qohelet's failure to find the wisdom he sought. Verse 25 reminds us of the energy involved in his search (to know, to explore, to seek), the extent of his search (wisdom, an explanation, wickedness, stupidity, folly, madness), and its intensely personal nature: he turned his "heart" to know and explore. Qohelet has been fully invested in his journey of exploration, but the result is that wisdom is far from him (v. 23) and so deep that if it exists he cannot find it; indeed, who can (v. 24)? The metaphors of distance (far off) and depth (extraordinarily deep) evoke both the extent of Qohelet's quest and its dismal failure.

Verse 27 is unusual in that it is the only place apart from 1:1–2 and 12:8–14 in which we hear the voice of the narrator in the words "says Qohelet." This reminds us that the words of Qohelet are cast in a third-person framework, and also that this is a highly significant point of reflection in Qohelet's journey, thus reinforcing the opening imperative of v. 27. In v. 27 he refers to the rigorous logic of his analysis, "adding one thing to another," and says that his search is ongoing (v. 28), but still wisdom eludes his grasp.

In the process of articulating his anguish at the lack of resolution to his journey, Qohelet invokes in v. 26 the woman who is "more bitter than death" and notes in v. 28 that one person among a thousand he found, but not a single woman. Clearly these images are intended to evoke the inaccessibility

---

12. Seow, *Ecclesiastes*, 270.
13. The word means "destruction."

of wisdom, but the details of their interpretation have caused considerable debate. Longman thinks that Qohelet is speaking in v. 26 of women in general, whereas others argue that he has a specific type of woman in mind, namely the seductive type,[14] or a specific woman, his wife, for example.[15] Longman has no problem in seeing Qohelet here as a misogynist. N. Lohfink, however, translates *mar* as "strong" rather than "bitter"[16] and so translates v. 26: "Again and again I find the claim that womankind is stronger than death." According to Lohfink, Qohelet takes this literally, so that when he says he could not find a woman, he means that he could not find one who did not die.[17]

The context is crucial for deciding whether *mar* means strong or bitter. We have noted repeatedly the importance of reading Ecclesiastes against the background of Proverbs, and this is imperative for this passage. In Prov. 5:1–6 Dame Folly, portrayed as a dangerous seductress, is described as in the end "bitter [*mārâ*] as wormwood" (5:4). Van Leeuwen notes with regard to this woman that in the first instance she is a woman other than one's wife, but that, secondly, she is a metaphorical instance of folly.[18] It is surely this metaphorical Dame Folly that Qohelet has in mind in v. 26.

The latter part of v. 26 confirms that Qohelet has more than adultery or sexual deviance in mind—the one who escapes her (cf. Prov. 9:13–18) pleases God, but the sinner is seized by her. There is a tendency to interpret *ṭôb* (good)[19] and *ḥōṭē'* (sinner) as nonreligious or nonethical categories. Murphy asserts that these terms "are best understood as in 2:26, not as moral qualifications, but as designations of human beings in terms of the inscrutable divine will. Some will fall victim to this type of woman but others will not, as God pleases."[20] If this is correct then Qohelet's bitterness results from God's action, which is outside his control. In the vast majority of cases in the OT, however, *ḥōṭē'* refers to the sinner. Murphy's type of view rests on an understanding of the development of OT literature that fails to take account of the organic interrelation of the different genres. I have noted previously Qohelet's awareness of OT torah and the cultus. Furthermore, both law and wisdom theologically are grounded in creation—law gives specific expression to directives for living in God's ordered creation. As Qohelet and OT wisdom thus recognize, wisdom and

14. Longman, *Ecclesiastes*, 204.
15. See Spears, "Theological Hermeneutics," 159, for full bibliographical references.
16. This suggestion comes from Dahood, "Qoheleth and Recent Discoveries," 308–10; and idem, "Phoenician Background," 275–76. There is solid evidence that *mar* can mean "strong" as well as "bitter" in Hebrew. See Kutler, "'Strong' Case for Hebrew *mar*"; and W. Ward, "Egypto-Semitic *mr*."
17. N. Lohfink, *Qoheleth*, 101–3.
18. Van Leeuwen, "Proverbs," 71.
19. The Hebrew of v. 26b reads lit. "the good one before God."
20. Murphy, *Ecclesiastes*, 76. Schoors ("Word *ṭôb*," 700) argues that in 7:26 neither "good" nor "sinner" has the usual moral content but both "denote an element of divine favor without an ethical connection."

righteousness and folly and wickedness are correlates, albeit with their own nuances. We should therefore allow *ṭôb* (good) and *ḥōṭē'* (sinner) their full ethical and religious force at this point. Qohelet is speaking not of a kind of determinism in v. 26b but in very traditional wisdom language of the two ways of wisdom: if one pleases God, one escapes Dame Folly, but the sinner is seized by her.

Seow thus concludes, "The *femme fatale* is not, therefore, an individual woman. She is not necessarily a specific type of woman or women in general. Rather, she is a composite image of Folly herself (Prov 9:13–18). Folly is out on a hunt, as it were, trying to lure and trap people and lead them down the deadly path."[21] *Mar* is thus to be understood as "bitter" rather than "strong." Verse 26 therefore amounts to a statement that summarizes the message of Prov. 1–9: "Flee folly!" Ironically, however, Dame Folly is the very woman that Qohelet has found and *is finding* more bitter than death[22] (v. 26a). Qohelet himself is the sinner who has been seized by her (v. 26c). His epistemology has ironically led him right into her bitter embrace.

> [28b]One person among a thousand I have found, but a woman among all these I have not found."

7:28b. Verse 28 expands on Qohelet's inability to find wisdom. He can find one wise person among a thousand but cannot find one woman. The word for "person" in v. 28 is *'ādām*, which is always used in Ecclesiastes to refer to people in general rather than to a specific man. In my opinion it retains that meaning here, the point being that Qohelet has the ability to find one person among a thousand, that is, he is able to find a needle in a haystack, but one woman he cannot find. Much has been made of the comparison with one man versus one woman and whether Qohelet is a misogynist. There is nothing at stake theologically if he is expressing a misogynistic perspective—he expresses many unorthodox views, but this is to miss the point. *'Ādām* refers to a person rather than specifically to a man, and the emphasis here is on *finding* and *not finding* rather than on gender.[23]

With Proverbs in the background the most likely interpretation of this woman is as Lady Wisdom. As in Prov. 31:10 so here: she is hard to find and more precious than jewels.[24] However, the more important background may be Lady Wisdom's role in Prov. 1–9 in which she calls out in all the public

---

21. Seow, *Ecclesiastes*, 272. Perry (*Dialogues*, 132), Farmer (*Who Knows*, 179), and Spears ("Theological Hermeneutics," 156–71) make similar points.

22. The rhetorical combination of "seek" (v. 25) and "find" (v. 26) may deliberately evoke Qohelet's surprise. On this combination, see Fox and Porten, "Unsought Discoveries," 35–37.

23. Spears, "Theological Hermeneutics," 178.

24. Hugo of St. Cher already made this connection between this woman and the Prov. 31 woman. See Wolters, *Song*, 93.

spaces, offering wisdom to any who respond to her call. Ironically, for all his seeking Qohelet is unable to find her. Thus the reader is led again to reflect on what is wrong with Qohelet's search—he claims it is by "wisdom," but if Lady Wisdom offers herself freely, why is it that Qohelet's quest has led him into the arms of Dame Folly? Where has he gone wrong? What sin (v. 26) is Qohelet guilty of that has resulted in his being seized by her?

> [29]Only observe this: I have found that God made the human being straight, but they have sought out many schemes.

7:29. Verse 29 gives us an important clue. The unusual use of *lĕbad* (only)—this is the only place in the OT in which *lĕbad* introduces a main clause—alerts us to the importance of what is to follow. The exhortation to "observe" is intriguingly ironic here, because observation has been at the heart of Qohelet's methodology, but here he calls on the reader to observe the origin, as it were, of his faulty methodology. There is something wrong, says Qohelet, with humans and, by implication, not with God. In v. 13 Qohelet asserts that God made the world crooked. But here he presents a very different perspective. God made humankind "straight" and not crooked, but humans have sought out many schemes. In most cases in the OT when "straight" (*yāšār*) is used of humans it carries ethical and religious connotations, as it does here. Thus Qohelet's assertion is redolent of God seeing that everything was very good after his creation of humankind in Gen. 1. The human was created good, but something has gone terribly wrong.

What went wrong? The wordplays in this section point us in the right direction. "Seek" occurs in v. 29 for the third time in this section (vv. 25, 28, 29). In v. 25 its object is *ḥokmâ* and *ḥešbôn* (wisdom and explanation). In v. 27b its object is *ḥešbôn* (an explanation). In v. 29 its object is *ḥišbōnôt* (schemes). Some have argued that *ḥišbōnôt* is the plural of *ḥešbôn*.[25] However, the MT vocalization is the plural of a different word, which is used elsewhere in the OT only in 2 Chron. 26:15, where it means "war machines."[26] *Ḥišbōnôt* should thus be understood to refer to "human inventions, a planned and technically conceived activity which is often wrong, ineffective, or evil."[27] The phonetic similarities between *ḥišbōnôt* and *ḥešbôn* are deliberate, and this is confirmed by the use of the verb "seek" on all three occasions. *Ḥišbōnôt* is thus a deliberate pun on Qohelet's search for an explanation.[28] Something about Qohelet's search

---

25. Fox, *Qohelet*, 243; Longman, *Ecclesiastes*, 207; Rudman, *Determinism*, 187.
26. Spears, "Theological Hermeneutics," 183.
27. Schoors, *Preacher*, 2:447.
28. Spears, "Theological Hermeneutics," 184. It is possible too that there is an intertextual allusion to Gen. 6:5, which speaks of the Lord observing that humankind's wickedness was great and that every inclination of the "thoughts" (*maḥšĕbōt*) of their hearts was evil continually.

has led him into his own version of human schemes. There is "self-directed irony" here: "Qoheleth is, of course, speaking above all about himself."[29]

Qohelet has found that his own search for wisdom "by wisdom" is merely his own particular version of humanity's scheming, which distorts God's creation of humankind as straight (*yāšār*).[30] "In Eccl 7:23–29, the reader is led on a journey to experience Qohelet's ironization of his own empirical epistemology."[31] Precisely why and how this is the case will become more apparent as Qohelet's journey continues.

Theological Implications

This chapter concludes with a profound reflection by Qohelet on his journey and in particular on his epistemology. Verses 23–29 are an important crux for understanding Qohelet's epistemology and Ecclesiastes as a whole.

Our major focus here will be on Qohelet's epistemology and its ironization in this section. It is worth noting, however, that Qohelet's statement in v. 29—God has made humans straight, but they have sought out many schemes—has implications for our previous discussion on theodicy. Qohelet's recognition here of the role of humans in making the world crooked lends support to the free-will approach to theodicy. Human freedom accounts for the moral evil in the world, so that evil is not incompatible with an omnipotent God who is wholly good. As a whole Qohelet's approach to evil cannot be reduced to this; his whole journey is one of protest and struggle. However, v. 29 implies that theologically a theodicy of protest and the free-will defense are not incompatible.

"Wisdom" is the specific means by which Qohelet conducts his search for meaning (v. 23).[32] Reading Qohelet within the context of the OT wisdom corpus, and especially after Proverbs, one initially tends to read "wisdom" positively as that practical and intellectual wisdom that is rooted in the fear of Yahweh and handed on from generation to generation. This is what the text appears to say in chap. 1 and here. As Fox points out, in biblical Wisdom literature "wisdom" and "knowledge" are almost always ethically positive.[33] Indeed, some commentators, like Seow, assume that the meaning of wisdom in Ecclesiastes is very much the same as it is in Proverbs and Job. Ogden, for example, says of "wisdom" in 1:13, "The tool for this investigation was 'wisdom' . . . by which he means the inherited tradition of the wise men together with its

---

29. Fox and Porten, "Unsought Discoveries," 33–34.
30. Spears, "Theological Hermeneutics," 185.
31. Ibid., 187.
32. For a discussion of the terminology of wisdom, see Fox, *Qohelet*, 80–85.
33. Ibid., 82. Two partial exceptions that Fox mentions are Prov. 3:5 and 21:30.

method of observation and reflection."[34] Even those who do not make quite such a strong equation as Ogden still tend to define wisdom in Ecclesiastes in quite general terms and to assume that the methodology of Qohelet is much the same as that in the other wisdom books.[35]

As one proceeds with Ecclesiastes, however, it becomes apparent that "wisdom" means something very different from its predominantly positive usage in Proverbs. One's nagging doubt becomes a strong sense here in chap. 7 that Qohelet's wisdom is quite different from the wisdom that is built on the fear of Yahweh. Fox has given sustained attention to wisdom as part of Qohelet's epistemology in Ecclesiastes.[36] On the basis of 1:12–18, Fox insists that we need to examine carefully Qohelet's epistemology. The problem of knowledge is central to the book, and although Qohelet's epistemology is unsystematic, it is not chaotic. Qohelet's ideas form a coherent whole and allow for systematic exposition.

Fox examines wisdom in Ecclesiastes and concludes that Qohelet adopted an *empirical* methodology; he seeks to derive knowledge from experience and to validate his ideas experientially.[37] Fox characterizes Qohelet's method as "empirical" by analogy to Western philosophical empiricism, although he recognizes that Qohelet does not offer a philosophical theory: "We can say that he holds a primitive form of the type of empiricism (the 'weak' form) that maintains that all knowledge comes from experience because every proposition is either a direct report on experience or a report whose truth is inferred from experience."[38]

Fox does acknowledge that much that Qohelet says comes from traditional learning and that some of his ideas are formulated a priori (e.g., 3:17; 8:12b) or derive from assumptions that lack experiential grounding (e.g., 7:11–12). Nevertheless, Fox maintains that the "empirical" label is justified, first, by Qohelet's method, which looks to experience as the source and warrant of knowledge; and second, by his concept of knowledge, according to which

34. Ogden, *Qoheleth*, 34.
35. Whybray (*Ecclesiastes* [NCBC], 49) simply notes that "Qoheleth's intention is to test the adequacy of human wisdom at its best." Murphy (*Ecclesiastes*, lxi–lxiv, 13) has an extended note on wisdom in Ecclesiastes but fails to detect the serious difference in method between "wisdom" in 1:13, etc., and most of its occurrences in Proverbs. Indeed, Murphy remarkably suggests that "Qoheleth is often in conflict with wisdom teaching, but his methodology is nonetheless that of the sage. He frequently reminds the reader how he applied himself with 'wisdom'" (ibid., lxiii). See also Gladson ("Retributive Paradoxes in Prov. 10–29," 20) for an example of the assumption that Wisdom literature shares a common empirical epistemology. Those scholars, like Gladson, who use "empirical" to describe the general method of wisdom use it in a nontechnical way to refer to the observational and reflective element in wisdom.
36. Fox, "Qohelet's Epistemology"; idem, *Qohelet*, esp. 79–120.
37. Fox, *Qohelet*, 79–120.
38. Ibid., 85.

knowledge is created by thought and dependent on perception.[39] In chap. 7 Qohelet's emphasis on experience and observation is particularly clear in v. 15.

"Empirical" is not the best word to describe Qohelet's epistemology, because classically it refers to dependence solely on sense perception, whereas reason and experience play a major role in Qohelet's epistemology.[40] Greek empiricism developed in the second century AD in debates about medicine. To signal their opposing views doctors introduced the terms "empiricist" and "rationalist." The former argued that knowledge is a complex sort of experience, whereas the latter argued that genuine knowledge involved experience and—crucially—reason. The debate is thus one about true knowledge, the sort manifest in a competent doctor who has mastered medicine. Doctors came to distinguish themselves from lay healers by asserting that their practice was guided by theoretical knowledge. With time, however, an abundance of theories of medicine arose, and empiricism is a reaction to this situation. The empiricists were not hopeful that a true theory of medicine would emerge and asserted that medical knowledge is "just a matter of experience."[41] What counts is that the remedy be successful in experience no matter how much theory or lack thereof accompanies it. The role of reason was controversial among the empiricists, but some inclined toward a role for practical reasoning, whose truth could be validated by experience. Clearly this debate in Greek philosophy is too late to have influenced Qohelet. Indeed, his epistemology cannot be equated with any particular school of Greek philosophy, but it shares with many of the Greeks the sense of human autonomy and the role of reason and experience *and* observation as the route to true knowledge.

Qohelet's epistemology is thus better referred to as "autonomous." Indeed, Fox notes, "We need not suppose that the author has read the Greek philosophy or even heard about its particulars. He does, however, share the fundamental tenet of Greek philosophy: *the autonomy of individual reason*. This is the belief that the individual can and should proceed toward truth by means of his own powers of perception and reason, and that he can in this way discover truths previously unknown."[42]

---

39. Ibid., 80, 85. Cf. Michel, *Untersuchungen*, 24–28, 35–38. Michel (*Qohelet*, 33) notes that the verb "see" occurs forty-six times and often means "critical observation." He suggests that Qohelet is not registering an empirical datum but is critically evaluating what he has perceived. He argues that Qohelet is not an empiricist who engages in various experiences and notes them down, as Fox suggests, but a thinker, an epistemological skeptic. Murphy (*Ecclesiastes*, xxx) notes that the difference between Michel and Fox "may be only verbal."

40. Crenshaw's ("Qoheleth's Understanding of Intellectual Inquiry," 212–13) critique of "empirical" as too restrictive a description of Qohelet's epistemology is thus apt. In *Reading Ecclesiastes*, 230–37, I too described Qohelet's epistemology as empirical but have since concluded that "autonomous" is by far the better description.

41. Frede, "Empiricist View of Knowledge," 230.

42. Fox, *Time*, 81–82 (italics mine).

For Qohelet, investigation of the world "by wisdom" means that he will use his powers of reason applied to his experience and observations rather than traditional knowledge in his inquiry. Fox points out that Qohelet never invokes prior knowledge or anything he heard to argue for his convictions. Qohelet seeks experience, observes it, evaluates it, and then reports his conclusions. Other scholars have also picked up on this autonomous epistemology of Qohelet, although none has examined it as thoroughly as Fox or discerned the ironic contrast with other wisdom literature. Hengel, for example, says of Qohelet's thought, "Its unprejudiced, detached observation and its strictly rational, logical thought lead to a radical criticism of the doctrine of retribution in traditional wisdom and thus indirectly attack a cornerstone of Jewish piety."[43] On 2:1 Whybray says: "It is because 'Solomon' has determined to seek it [happiness, contentment] independently for himself that he discovers that, like his corresponding attempt to rely on his own wisdom and knowledge (1:13, 17), it proves totally unsatisfactory."[44] N. Lohfink is very clear that "wisdom" in Ecclesiastes should not be translated as *Weisheit* (wisdom) but as *Wissen* (knowledge).[45] "'Knowledge,' and not the usual 'wisdom,' is the more exact translation in Qoheleth for the Hebrew *ḥokmâ*."[46]

The significance of Qohelet's epistemology is strengthened by examining the epistemology of other wisdom literature.[47] Contrary to a widespread assumption, wisdom's epistemology is not autonomous.[48] Many of the sages' teachings undoubtedly derive from the observations of generations of wise men but are always shaped in accordance with prior ethical-religious principles. Whatever the actual source of their teaching, the sages do not, according to Fox, offer their experience as the source of new knowledge, and they rarely invoke experiential arguments. The rare appeal to what is seen is a rhetorical strategy and not a fundamental methodological procedure, as with Qohelet. Fox offers Prov. 24:30–34; 7:6–20; and 6:6–8 as examples. The first two passages contain references to what the teacher "saw," in the one

43. Hengel, *Judaism and Hellenism*, 1:126.

44. Whybray, *Ecclesiastes* (NCBC), 52.

45. N. Lohfink, *Kohelet*, 24–25.

46. N. Lohfink, *Qoheleth*, 46.

47. Very little work has been done in this area. Crenshaw ("Wisdom and Authority") explores the rhetoric of wisdom along the lines of threefold warrant: ethos, pathos, and logos. Fox (*Qohelet*, 90) perceptively notes that rhetoric is an expression of an underlying epistemology. Ethos, pathos, and logos will be present in any rhetoric, but, as Fox points out, the question is how they are realized in specific texts. Fox notes that Crenshaw mentions arguments from consensus as the form of logos characteristic in Wisdom literature and thus suggests that "the seemingly empirical arguments in Wisdom Literature are primarily ways of strengthening ethos by creating consensus." Much work remains to be done in this area. O'Dowd's "Wisdom of Torah" makes an important contribution in this direction. Schellenberg's *Erkenntnis* is also an important investigation of Qohelet and OT epistemology.

48. Fox, *Qohelet*, 90.

case with respect to what happened to a lazy man's field, and in the other he "saw" a woman enticing a youth to fornication. As Fox points out, in Prov. 24:30–34 the observation is followed by a lesson, but the observation calls the truth to mind rather than the truth being discovered or inferred from the observation. "The sage does not say that he saw a field gone wild, looked for the cause, and found that its owner was lazy, nor does he claim to have looked at lazy farmers and observed what happens to their fields. Rather he came across a field gone wild, and this sparked a meditation on its causes."[49]

In Prov. 7 the teacher reports observing the seduction but makes no claim to have observed the consequences; these he knows already! Similarly, when the wise man exhorts the pupil, "Go to the ant . . . consider its ways, and be wise" in Prov. 6:6–8, the ant is being used as an illustration of diligence. The observation of the ant is used to emphasize the wise man's point, but not to prove the point in the first place.

Personal experience, Fox points out, is cited more commonly in theodicy.[50] Compare Ps. 37:25, for example: "I have been young, and now am old, yet I have not seen the righteous forsaken or their children begging for bread." Psalm 73:3 is another example: "For I was envious of the arrogant; I saw the prosperity of the wicked." As Fox points out, however,

> Observation in theodicy testifies to old truths; it does not uncover or argue for new ones. . . . Qohelet's use of experience does have certain parallels in theodicy both in the sufferers' complaints and in the defenders' theodicy. He differs in the greater importance he gives to the "I" and, more significantly, in the reasons for which he appeals to the ego. While the sufferers and defenders try to understand what they observe, they, unlike Qohelet, do not observe *in order* to gain knowledge.[51]

Qohelet, however, makes knowledge dependent on the knower's perceiving it. For (the "Greek") Qohelet there is no body of truth standing outside the individual and demanding assent, no Dame Wisdom who was in existence before humankind and who would exist even if all humans were fools. For Qohelet wisdom must be justified through the individual's experience

---

49. Ibid., 91. Crenshaw ("Qoheleth's Understanding of Intellectual Inquiry," 206) insists, contra Fox, that Prov. 7:6–27 and 24:30–34 *are* examples of an observer, like Qohelet, interposing "his subjective consciousness between experience and audience." Frydrych (*Living under the Sun*, 54–56) argues along the same lines. However, this is to fail to note that observation is never neutral; one always gathers data in the perspective of some "torchlight." Observation is theory laden. This is particularly true of Prov. 7:6–27, in which observation clearly operates within a value-laden framework of adultery and prostitution as wrong and dangerous. Proverbs' approach to the world never claims to be autonomous, whereas Qohelet's does.

50. Fox, *Qohelet*, 91–92.

51. Ibid., 92.

and reason. "Qohelet alone of the sages speaks with 'a voice that justifies itself by reference to the good sense of the individual's reflections on his experiences.'"[52]

Fox is surely right about the strong individualism that underlies Qohelet's autonomous epistemology.[53] Crenshaw argues that inherited tradition and individual appropriation are the two essential ingredients of "ethos" in wisdom's rhetoric. "This bipolarity of ethos provides an important corrective to the oft-mentioned individualism which characterizes wisdom thinking."[54] It is precisely this bipolarity that is missing from Ecclesiastes; epistemologically the balance has shifted to the pole of individual assessment. In contrast to the other sages, for Qohelet anything less than certainty is ignorance. "Qohelet seems to start with the expectation that reason can provide certainty, and when he sees that it does not, he is struck by its frailty. The other sages seem more comfortable with the limitations of knowledge."[55]

Examination of Qohelet's epistemology and comparison of this with that of other wisdom literature exposes the ironic use of "by wisdom" in Ecclesiastes. What one expected to be wisdom rooted in the fear of Yahweh turns out to be a quest for certain knowledge resulting from logical analysis of personal experience and observation. When Qohelet says "by wisdom," the reader instinctively fills it with a positive content, but ironically "wisdom" comes to mean its opposite, namely folly! It is here in chap. 7 that the irony of Qohelet's epistemology comes clearly into view. "By wisdom" he could not find wisdom! Instead what he found was Dame Folly, whose embrace he discovered to be more bitter than death. Qohelet *himself* is the sinner who has been seized by Dame Folly.

This does not mean that the problem of Qohelet's epistemology is here resolved, but its irony comes clearly into view and forces the reader to look closely at Qohelet's so-called wisdom in order to see how it could lead him to folly. For the resolution we have to keep reading. But theologically chap. 7 is important in exposing the end of an autonomous approach to the meaning of life—such an approach confronts us with the enigma of life but offers us no way out of this impasse. It brings us into contact with the brokenness of life (vv. 13 and 29) but cannot move us beyond that hopeless point. Verse 29 intensifies the problem of v. 13, for it is not only the world that is broken but

52. Ibid., 95, quoting J. Williams, *Those Who Ponder Proverbs*, 85.

53. Cf. Fisch, *Poetry with a Purpose*, 158. Fisch notes that Ecclesiastes "gives us a radically individualized statement." This is evident in the autobiographical "I" that dominates Ecclesiastes and is readily seen in 1:12–13 and 2:3–8. Fisch distinguishes the "I" of Qohelet from that of the Psalms. The latter may be subjective, but it is never autobiographical in Qohelet's sense. As Fisch points out, Qohelet could have said with Montaigne, "It is my portrait I draw. . . . I am myself the subject of my book."

54. Crenshaw, "Wisdom and Authority," 19.

55. Fox, *Qohelet*, 106.

humans too, so that neutral detached observation—the essence of autonomy—is simply not possible.

Theologically, it is important to note that Qohelet's epistemology is one of general autonomy, not just empiricism. From the Enlightenment four major epistemologies emerged: rationalism (Descartes), empiricism (Hume), idealism (Kant), and as a reaction to these, romanticism. What is not always clearly noted is that *all* of these are a manifestation of human autonomy, which is at the heart of modernity. James Sire makes the important point that a Christian worldview begins with ontology (what is, i.e., God) rather than with epistemology (i.e., how we know about the world). In the seventeenth century, however, an important shift took place to starting with epistemology (implying human autonomy) and then trying to work out what we can know with certainty about the world and God. "In the biblical worldview, in short, everything is first and foremost determined by the nature and character of God. It cannot be said too strongly: *Ontology precedes epistemology.* Though it may not appear to be so at first, to turn this around and presuppose that epistemology determines ontology is devastating to the Christian worldview."[56]

Human autonomy is so ingrained in modern culture, even though it has been challenged but not abandoned under the guise of postmodernism, that it is difficult for us today to see the radicality of the ironization of an autonomous epistemology here in 7:23–29.[57] Much modern theology has been an attempt to make peace with autonomy by conceding the epistemological starting points and seeking to hold on to whatever fragments of theology remain in the light of the various modern or postmodern epistemologies.[58] What is true of modern theology is even more true of biblical studies: it has consistently sought to keep theology apart from its domain in the quest for autonomous scientific analysis.[59] Ecclesiastes 7:23–29 demonstrates that starting with an autonomous epistemology is not wisdom but folly and will lead one not to truth but right into the arms of Dame Folly.

Why is this the case? Verse 29 gives us an important clue: God made humans straight but they have devised many schemes. It is not the world that is crooked but humans, and one of humanity's great schemes, in terms of the biblical metanarrative, is the quest for autonomy as opposed to dependence on the living God. The tree of the knowledge of good and evil, the temptation by the serpent, and the building of the Tower of Babel are all symbolic of this temptation to autonomy. Barth deals with this topic under the title

56. Sire, *Naming the Elephant*, 55–56.

57. Gadamer (*Truth and Method*, 272) asserts, "Enlightenment critique is primarily directed against the religious tradition of Christianity—i.e., the Bible. . . . This is the real radicality of the modern Enlightenment compared to all other movements of enlightenment: it must assert itself against the Bible and dogmatic interpretations of it."

58. The strategy of correlation is a good example of this.

59. See Bartholomew, *Reading Ecclesiastes*, chap. 3.

"The Pride of Man."[60] The pride of humankind consists in our denial of our creatureliness and our attempt to play God by asserting our autonomy. "And so it comes to pass that self-centred man rotating about himself robs God of that which is only His, taking that which belongs only to God. Why? To deck himself out with it, to be as God is, to be God. The mad exchange takes place. It does so, as we have seen, without any prospect that he will really succeed in being God."[61]

In terms strongly reminiscent of Qohelet, Barth notes that the concealment of one's true identity under the guise of autonomy is powerful.[62] Might God not have created humans to be self-sufficient and in control of themselves? In the autonomous exercise of human freedom there is no need to deny God; is this not just humankind coming to full maturity? Barth compares this concealment to the speech of the serpent in Gen. 3, which "like all bad theology—of which this speech is the original—is itself only an interpretation of human existence which does not explicitly express but only implies a call to disobedience."[63] Qohelet's concealment is embodied in his repeatedly naming his autonomous epistemology "wisdom"; however, in 7:23–29 it is exposed as folly and sinful.

It is folly because it seeks truth about the world apart from God, and it is sinful in its inherent idolatry: "Human existence is a loan and is to be held in trust. From its structure as the existence of a rational creature it is clear that it can only be understood as a loan. God alone is truly rational, knowing what He wills and willing what He knows. Creaturely reason as it characterizes man's structure cannot as such try to be self-sufficient."[64] Autonomy always assumes some neutral capacity within humankind by means of which truth can be arrived at apart from God. As Barth notes, however, "As I see it, it is impossible to maintain at one and the same time the concept of man constituted by the Word of God and the idea of a neutral capacity in man. If man has his being in the Word of God, he can do only that which corresponds to the Word of God. The actuality in which he has his being is from the very first orientated in this direction."[65]

What looks like a value-free standpoint turns out to be heavily laden with baggage. Popper evokes this critique in his images of the bucket and the searchlight.[66] An autonomous approach to knowledge, such as that of Qohelet, thinks of our mind as resembling a bucket; we simply accumulate perceptions and knowledge in it. The searchlight theory, by comparison, recognizes that we

60. Barth, CD 4.1:413–78.
61. Ibid., 421–22.
62. Ibid., 420–21.
63. Ibid., 420.
64. CD 3.4:328.
65. CD 3.2:131.
66. Popper, "Bucket and the Searchlight," in Objective Knowledge, 341–61.

always search within a framework, a horizon of expectations. Observations can, under certain circumstances, act like a bomb and destroy the framework, but theory always precedes observation. This is very helpful because it alerts us that it is a particular torchlight, a particular framework, that Qohelet is bringing to his data, in the context of which he keeps coming to the *hebel* conclusion. From a Christian perspective the postulate of neutrality assumed by autonomy is impossible—in our quest for knowledge there will always be some form of faith informing our quest, and the way forward is to reject the many attempts at autonomous knowledge and to engage in *faith seeking understanding*.

Newbigin notes that Christ is the clue to the whole of creation.[67] This strikes the right note of confidence and humility in a Christian epistemology: confidence, because Christ *is* the clue, and humility, because Christ is the *clue* and we do not have all the answers. But this clue needs to be pursued with rigor in all areas of life. Of course, Qohelet has not yet arrived at such a point.

67. L. Newbigin, *The Light Has Come: An Exposition of the Fourth Gospel* (Grand Rapids: Eerdmans, 1982), 3. Newbigin writes, "Jesus is the clue for understanding all that is."

O.
The Enigma
of Political Rule
(8:1–9)

Translation

¹Who is like the wise person and who knows the interpretation¹ of a matter?² The wisdom of a person lightens one's face, and the hardness of one's countenance is changed.³

²I say,⁴ "Keep the command of a king, as in the manner⁵ of an oath to God."

1. *Pēšer* occurs only here in Biblical Hebrew, and so it is difficult to be sure about its translation. In Biblical Aramaic, the noun refers to the interpretation of dreams or solution of riddles (cf. Dan. 2:45; 4:6 [3]; 5:15).

2. *Dābār* means "a word, a thing, a matter." The root *dbr* occurs five times in vv. 1–5.

3. *Yĕšunne'* is the Pual imperfect third masculine singular of *šn'*, meaning "is changed" (GKC §75rr; cf. Lam. 4:1). However, several commentators read the verb actively rather than passively (see Longman, *Ecclesiastes*, 208; Crenshaw, *Ecclesiastes*, 148). Seow (*Ecclesiastes*, 278) emends the text to *yĕšanne'nnû*, thus reading "one changes it." There is little at stake in the meaning of the verse.

4. The Hebrew has no verb after "I." Scholars omit it or emend the text; I have assumed that "say" has fallen out or is implied. See *IBHS* 680n28.

5. Taking the idiom *'al-dibrat* modally (as in the manner) rather than causally (because of the oath to God; RJW §290). Cf. Ps. 110:4.

³Do not be terrified in his presence,[6] leave! Do not persist in an evil matter,[7] for he will do whatever he pleases.

⁴For the word of a king is supreme,[8] and who will say to him, "What are you doing?"

⁵The one who keeps a command[9] will experience no harmful thing. A wise heart knows a time and judgment:

⁶For[10] everything there is a time and a judgment; but[11] the evil of humanity[12] rests heavily upon them.

⁷For no one knows what will happen, for who can tell one when it will happen?

⁸No one has power over the wind[13] to restrain the wind, and no one has power over the day of death. There is no discharge[14] from battle. Evil will not deliver its lord.

⁹All this I have seen, and I gave my heart to every deed that is done under the sun, at a time when[15] one person lords it over another to the other's detriment.

6. Rudman ("Qohelet's Use of *lpny*," 148) proposes that this phrase be translated "Do not be disobedient." He argues that Qohelet is playing on two idioms: that of the royal court and that of serving God. While such an interpretation fits the context, the evidence is speculative. Furthermore, the idiom *nibhal mippānāyw* (be terrified in his presence) is attested in Gen. 45:3 and Job 23:15.

7. Waldman ("*Dābār Raʿ* of Eccl 8:3," 407–8) argues in the light of Akkadian material that *dābār rāʿ* (an evil matter) here means "rebellion." However, the phrase could cover a variety of activities.

8. *Šilṭôn* (supreme) occurs only here and in 8:8 in the OT. *Šilṭôn* is a noun, and syntactically the phrase is similar to that in Ps. 19:9 [10], which states lit. "the judgments of the LORD are truth."

9. The Hebrew has no pronominal suffix attached to "command." Some translators insert one ("his command" or "a royal command") because they believe the command to refer to that of the king. See the interpretation.

10. The particle *kî* occurs four times in vv. 6–7. The meaning of each occurrence is debated (Schoors, *Preacher*, 1:106–7). Seow (*Ecclesiastes*, 281) takes all four as "that," indicating the object of "knows" in v. 5. I have translated them all causally as "for" apart from the second *kî* in v. 6, which is more appropriately translated adversatively as "but." See the interpretation.

11. Adversative use of *kî* (RJW §447).

12. There is a debate over whether *rāʿat hāʾādām* is a subjective or objective genitive. Those who favor the view that *ʾādām* is the object of "evil" take *rāʿat* to mean "trouble" or "misfortune," hence Longman's (*Ecclesiastes*, 210) "people's troubles." However, the idiom "evil of humanity" occurs in Gen. 6:5 along with the adjective *rabbâ*. Qohelet often refers to Genesis, and thus I translate this phrase as the subjective genitive.

13. *Rûaḥ* may refer to "wind" or to "the life breath, the spirit." In context it probably refers to both, picking up the theme of "striving after wind" as well as our lack of control over death.

14. In the OT *mišlaḥat* occurs only here and in Ps. 78:49, where it refers to a detachment of angels sent to carry out God's command. Seow (*Ecclesiastes*, 282) notes that there was legal provision for exemption from war in the OT; in the light of Ps. 78:49 he translates *mišlaḥat* as "substitution" and takes it to refer to the practice, common in the Persian period, of sending substitutes to war on one's behalf. Either way, the point is that one cannot get out of war once in it.

15. *ʿĒt ʾăšer* is the accusative of time. See GKC §118i.

Interpretation

The opening question of v. 1 starts a new section. Although some think v. 1 concludes the previous section,[16] the theme of knowing introduced in v. 1 is picked up again in vv. 5 and 7, and the section is coherent as a whole.

> ¹Who is like the wise person and who knows the interpretation of a matter? The wisdom of a person lightens one's face, and the hardness of one's countenance is changed.

8:1. Verse 1 articulates the traditional wisdom perspective, according to which the wise person is unique in knowing the interpretation of a word, a thing, or a matter. The openness of the expression indicates the range of expertise embodied in the wise person. In context, knowing how to act in a particular situation is the most relevant aspect of the expertise of a wise person. Proverbs 26:4–5 is a great example of this, juxtaposing two opposite responses to the fool. Verse 4 tells one not to answer fools according to their folly, whereas v. 5 instructs one to answer fools according to their folly. This juxtaposition is highly instructive in that it alerts us to the hermeneutical dimension of wisdom. Wisdom involves knowing what is fitting in a particular situation, and this will vary. This aspect of interpreting a matter is especially relevant in this context because Qohelet will go on to discuss how to conduct oneself in the presence of the king.

In the OT it is God who "causes his face to shine" on his people (Num. 6:25; Pss. 31:16 [17]; 67:1 [2]; 80:3, 7, 19 [4, 8, 20]; 119:135). This idiom refers to God's being gracious to his people and granting them shalom. Wisdom in Proverbs is a gift of God, and v. 1b asserts that it makes those who possess it gracious and beneficent like God. Hardness of countenance thus symbolizes the opposite of graciousness, namely, harshness and meanness. Wisdom transforms this into a face open to God and one's neighbor.

Wisdom teachers instruct their disciples about how to live successfully, and one aspect of the wise life is knowing how to behave in the presence of one's superiors. This is a theme that crops up regularly in Proverbs.[17] For example, Prov. 25:15 teaches, "With patience a ruler may be persuaded, and a soft tongue can shatter bone." In this section Qohelet explores the value of traditional wisdom by relating it to being in the presence of the king. Verse 1, like Proverbs, asserts the value of wisdom. To "lighten the face" is an idiom for bringing favor and graciousness—in Prov. 16:15 the light of the king's face is paralleled with his favor. But does traditional wisdom really work when it comes to dealing with the king?

---

16. Lauha (*Kohelet*, 144) even thinks that the verse is a gloss. Longman (*Ecclesiastes*, 208) sees it as a sarcastic comment bridging the two sections.

17. See Prov. 19:12; 20:2; 22:11, 29; 23:1–3.

> ²I say, "Keep the command of a king, as in the manner of an oath to
> God."
> ³Do not be terrified in his presence, leave! Do not persist in an evil
> matter, for he will do whatever he pleases.
> ⁴For the word of a king is supreme, and who will say to him, "What are
> you doing?"

8:2–4. In v. 2 Qohelet advises that one keep the command of the king as
if it were an oath to God, and we know from 5:1–7 that this is therefore to
be taken with full seriousness. Obedience to the king is to be absolute. The
idiom *nibhal mippānāyw* (be terrified in his presence) in v. 3 is attested in
Gen. 45:3 and Job 23:15. In the former verse Joseph's brothers are *dismayed*
in his presence; in the latter Job is *terrified* of God. The Niphal of *bhl*, which
we have here, means "be disturbed, dismayed, terrified." Why would one be
terrified and dismayed in the presence of the king?

The answer lies in the danger of persisting in an "evil matter." The phrase
is ambiguous and could mean a whole variety of things. In context an "evil
matter" probably refers to "a bad idea," a suggestion that the king dislikes.[18]
Once the king's power is regarded as absolute, as v. 2 implies, then any difference of opinion with him ironically becomes an "evil matter." From observation
Qohelet knows (v. 4) that the king's word is absolute, and as far as he can see,
the king is accountable to no one; there is no one to interrogate him about
what he is doing. At any sign of such opposition from the king, therefore,
one should desist and get out of the king's presence fast. Qohelet envisages
the power of the king as absolute: he will do whatever he pleases and no one
will call him to task (vv. 3–4).

Lacking here, of course, is Proverbs' and the OT's sense of the king being
subject to God.[19] Indeed, according to Prov. 8:15–16 it is only by wisdom that
kings reign: "That is, by using Wisdom's gifts of insight, justice, and statecraft
according to cosmic standards, as determined by Yahweh at creation."[20] Proverbs is well aware that abuse of power is an abomination to God (cf. 16:22).
Furthermore, in 29:14 the longevity of a king's reign/throne is proportional
to how he treats the poor. Implied here and present implicitly in the other
passages in Proverbs is that the king will indeed be held accountable by God.
Proverbs also emphasizes that a wise leader will listen to advice. Solomon
asked for a "listening heart" to govern God's people (1 Kings 3:9). Proverbs
28, which contrasts "many rulers" with "an intelligent ruler" (v. 2), is clear in
this context that if one will not listen to *the law*, then even one's prayers are

---

18. So Longman, *Ecclesiastes*, 212.
19. See Prov. 16:12–15; 20:28; 21:1; 29:14; 31:1–9.
20. Van Leeuwen, "Proverbs," 92.

an abomination (v. 9). Proverbs 29:14 warns that if a ruler listens to falsehood, then all his officials will be wicked.

Being wise in the presence of a king should therefore entail respect but also the freedom to give sound advice. But Qohelet observes the power of the king to be absolute, and logically, in such a situation, the "wise" thing to do is never to oppose the king. From this perspective, traditional wisdom just does not work, because any opposition to the king will have bad personal consequences—and anyway, the king will do what he wants.

> ⁵The one who keeps a command will experience no harmful thing. A wise heart knows a time and judgment:
> ⁶For everything there is a time and a judgment; but the evil of humanity rests heavily upon them.
> ⁷For no one knows what will happen, for who can tell one when it will happen?
> ⁸No one has power over the wind to restrain the wind, and no one has power over the day of death. There is no discharge from battle. Evil will not deliver its lord.

8:5–8. Verses 5 and 6a resort to traditional wisdom. Verse 5 is understood by many to refer to the king's command, but the Hebrew has no pronominal suffix on "command," and this is deliberate. Qohelet is referring not to the command of the absolute ruler he has been describing but to obedience to God and king when they are in harmony. He has in mind traditional wisdom such as is expressed in Prov. 24:21–22, in which readers are exhorted to fear the LORD and the king and not to disobey either lest ruin come upon them. In such a context in which king and God are in harmony, then indeed one who keeps a command will experience no harmful thing. Verse 5b harks back to the poem on time in chap. 3. It is not immediately clear how v. 5b relates to v. 5a, but I suggest that "a wise heart" could refer to that of both the one issuing the command, perhaps the king, and the one obeying it. In such a situation there would indeed be nothing to fear from obeying a command. Verse 6a explicitly evokes 3:1.

So far, so good, but this traditional approach is immediately subverted by Qohelet: the evil of humanity rests heavily upon them (v. 6b). "The evil of humanity" may deliberately evoke Gen. 6:5, where the same phrase occurs. Verse 6b is also reminiscent of Eccles. 7:29. In Gen. 6:5 and in Eccles. 7:29 human responsibility for evil in the world is to the fore. Here, however, it becomes the basis for Qohelet's despair over the enigma of life. As often before, he invokes the problem of history (8:7) and the problem of meaning and death (v. 8). The question of v. 7 contrasts with the question in v. 1. No one, not even the wise person, knows what is to come or when something will happen, and no one has power over death. "Wind" could also be translated as "spirit," and possibly Qohelet has both in mind here. "Wind" evokes his refrain that everything is enigmatic, a striving after wind. But no one can control the wind. So it is with the "end" of the human spirit at death: control over death is outside human power.

Contrary to Deut. 20:5–8, which allows a discharge from the army, there is no discharge from battle. "Battle" may be literal, perhaps referring to being sent off by a wealthy landowner to fight a war in his place. Seow notes that this was common practice in the Persian period.[21] "Battle" may also be a metaphor for the struggle of life and against death—one cannot escape. Seow suggests that the imagery here may evoke the battle between Mot (death) and Baal, the god of life in Canaanite mythology.[22]

The final sentence of v. 8 is intriguing: evil will not deliver its owner or lord. This surely refers back to the "evil of humanity" in v. 6, but what does it mean? Krüger suggests that Qohelet means that even the kind of opportunistic behavior proposed in vv. 2–3 will not in the long run save a person.[23] But perhaps we can also see here a reference back to 7:26, in which Qohelet ironically finds himself in the hands of Dame Folly and as "the sinner." Verse 6b suggests that Qohelet will argue in a direction similar to 7:23–29, but he does the reverse. In v. 8b, however, he seems to return to the insights of 7:23–29. One would expect that the owner or lord would control evil, but ironically the owner of evil cannot free himself, and evil will certainly not rescue its owner. This is a powerful image of what Luther calls "the bondage of the will," in which humans are so caught up in evil that they cannot liberate themselves.

> [9]All this I have seen, and I gave my heart to every deed that is done under the sun, at a time when one person lords it over another to the other's detriment.

8:9. "All this I have seen" (v. 9) reminds us that Qohelet's discussion of the absolute power of the king rests on what he has observed.[24] With "and I gave my heart . . ." it also evokes the totality and personal nature of his journey of exploration. He notes that at the very time he is engaged in his journey, government is corrupt: one person lords it over another to another's detriment. This is precisely the problem that results from the unaccountable, absolute rule Qohelet refers to in vv. 2–4.

The wise person *knows* the interpretation of a matter (v. 1), and a wise heart *knows* a time and judgment. But in the context of absolute power the only "wise" thing to do seems to be to acquiesce to it, even though it leads

21. Seow, *Ecclesiastes*, 282–83.
22. Ibid., 283.
23. Krüger, *Qoheleth*, 157.
24. De Jong ("A Book on Labour," 111) describes v. 9 as a "blurred borderline" that connects with the preceding verses but could also introduce v. 10. Beentjes ("Who Is Like the Wise?"), however, argues that v. 9 concludes the preceding pericope.

to oppression of others (v. 9). Furthermore, no one *knows* what will happen or when it will happen.[25]

Theological Implications

Wisdom teaches one how to behave in the king's presence by learning what is fitting in different situations, but Qohelet in 8:1–9 reflects on the value of such wisdom in the context of the absolute power of a king. He envisages the king's word as supreme, and no one holds him accountable. This opens wide the gate for tyranny and all the problems that accompany it, so that one person lords it over another to the latter's detriment (v. 9).

Tyranny is indeed a serious political problem. O'Donovan notes, "Authority belongs to those who, embodying the identity of the community, enact right on its behalf. . . . For the idea to become actual, a third component must be present, power."[26] But it is precisely this power that can be abused: absolute power corrupts absolutely. O'Donovan explains that every conflict over political authority plays itself out before two horizons: the first is where injustice is systematically ignored by those in power; the second is where those in power have no "right of tradition." It is the former problem that Qohelet has in mind, as v. 9b in particular makes clear.

The medieval tradition deals with the problem of such abuse of power under the heading of "tyrannicide." "The tyrant controlled the polity not for the common good but for his own private good; which is to say, the public sphere of action and interaction was effectively shut down, and government was abandoned in the pursuit of private interest."[27] Alongside this, O'Donovan notes the problem of tribalism in which a public order exists, but it is one of communal solidarity and not enacted judgment.

How to respond to tyranny has long been pondered in the Christian tradition. The Reformers agreed that natural and divine law necessarily limit the state's power to command obedience. They disagreed on whether "only some historically particular constitutional arrangements provided for the possibility of removing a supreme magistrate (thus Calvin and Grotius) or whether such a structure was implicitly present in all states (Beza and Althusius)."[28] O'Donovan is himself cautious on the just-revolution approach, noting that political reform is the way to proceed.

As O'Donovan himself recognizes, however, the twentieth century witnessed regimes that did manifest tyrannical rule—for example, apartheid

25. Contra Barolín ("Eclesiastés 8:1–8"), who sees vv. 1–8 as providing hope because justice will triumph over the arrogance of the monarch.
26. O'Donovan, *Ways of Judgment*, 140.
27. Ibid., 146.
28. Ibid., 146n21.

South Africa, Rwanda, Bosnia, and Somalia. In many of these situations tyranny and tribalism coalesced into a terrible evil for those living under it. It is the practical reality of living wisely in such a situation that Qohelet wrestles with. A wise heart may know a time and a judgment, but how does one begin to cope with tyranny?

As the Christian tradition notes, tyranny needs to be resisted, although Christians continue to disagree about the parameters of such resistance. But for Qohelet, as so often for the individual in such a situation, the practical realities are very challenging. There may be a time for judgment, but God, it seems, will not intervene, so what does one do? It is not surprising, therefore, that the next section in this chapter deals with the problem of delayed judgment and injustice.

One answer is, of course, the political alternative to autocracy—namely, democracy. A healthy democracy goes a long way toward muting abuse of power, but it would be foolish to think that contemporary democracies are exempt from the abuse of power. Globalization, for example, with its undermining of the nation-state, has raised acutely the challenge of international law to ensure that unjust, asymmetrical international relations are not increasingly embedded so that the gap between rich and poor continues to widen. In the name of spreading liberty, U.S. President George W. Bush and British Prime Minister Tony Blair led their countries into an unprovoked invasion of Iraq, which resulted in the deaths of thousands of civilians and brought the country to the brink of civil war.

The NT helps with its much fuller revelation of the *eschaton*, when justice will roll down like the waters, and with its doctrine of resurrection. There will be a time of judgment when rulers will give an account of their deeds and receive just compensation. Nevertheless, being wise in an oppressive context such as that described by Qohelet in 8:2–4 can be very costly if one refuses to acquiesce to abusive power and resists it. Inevitably it results in suffering. Suffering, while remaining mysterious, is also illumined by the centrality of the cross to the Jesus event. Suffering, in the sense of taking up one's cross, is now enunciated as an integral part of discipleship, and the NT again and again recognizes that we will suffer (cf. James and 1 Peter, for example) and that God is at work in our suffering. "Everything is a gift, suffering the holiest of all; and the healing of all hurts is found in the Body of One who was broken, the only *pharmakon athanasias*."[29]

In the OT, Joseph and Daniel and his friends stand out as exemplary figures among those who suffered at the hands of absolute rulers. In Isaiah, the Suffering Servant was "taken away by a perversion of justice" (Isa. 53:8); yet out of his anguish, he will see light, and he will find satisfaction through his knowledge (Isa. 53:11). We also have the psalms of lament and the book of

---

29. Andersen, *Job*, 9–10.

Lamentations. In the NT we not only have much teaching about discipleship and suffering, but right at its heart is the cross of Christ. It was in calamity and not serenity that the church was born. P. T. Forsyth came to see this amid the horror of World War I, the first great blow to the evolutionary optimism of the nineteenth century. In his *Lectures for War-Time on a Christian Theodicy*, he writes: "Our faith did not arise from the order of the world; the world's convulsions, therefore, need not destroy it. Rather it rose from the sharpest crisis, the greatest war, the deadliest death, and the deepest grave the world ever knew—in Christ's Cross."[30] But such a perspective requires returning again and again to a foundational trust in God as creator and redeemer, and Qohelet does not begin from here. Thus his epistemology leaves him thoroughly vulnerable to the enigma of what he observes and experiences.

30. Forsyth, *Justification of God*, 57.

P.
The Problem of Delayed Judgment
(8:10–17)

Translation

10Then[1] I observed the wicked buried. They used to go in and out of the holy place,[2] but they were forgotten[3] in the city in which they acted in this way.[4] This too is enigmatic.

1. *Ûbĕkēn* is composed of the conjunction *wĕ*, the preposition *bĕ*, and the particle *kēn*. It is an example of a complex preposition functioning as an adverb (*IBHS* §11.3.2). Seow (*Ecclesiastes*, 284) maintains that the presence of this word means that v. 10 cannot initiate a new section. In my view, however, it does, although the connection between the sections is close.

2. This phrase has generated much discussion about how to understand *wābā'û* (lit. "and they came") following "buried." Serrano ("I Saw," 168–70) emends *qĕburîm* to a form of the verb *qrb* (to approach) and translates this verse, "and then I saw the wicked approach, they entered and went out of the holy place, and they were praised in the city because they acted thus. Indeed this is vanity." Longman (*Ecclesiastes*, 216) takes *wābā'û* to qualify "buried" and translates, "the wicked buried and departed." Seow (*Ecclesiastes*, 284), with others, follows the LXX in reading "brought to burial." Commentators assume that the MT makes no sense as it stands. The Hebrew reads lit. "Thus I observed the wicked buried, and they came, and from the place of the holy one they went." However, the MT is a problem only if we fail to discern the change in temporal reference in the latter part of the verse. "And they came . . ." is what they *used to do*, as the NASB and NRSV recognize in their translations.

3. Longman (*Ecclesiastes*, 218–19) emends the text from the Hithpael of *škḥ* (to forget) to the Hithpael of *šbḥ* (to praise).

4. Seow (*Ecclesiastes*, 285) translates *kēn-'āśû* as "those who acted justly." However, by far the most common meaning of *kēn* is "thus, so," hence "in this way."

11Because[5] the sentence[6] for an evil deed is not speedily executed,[7] therefore the human heart is fully set to do evil.[8]

12For[9] a sinner does evil a hundred times[10] and lengthens one's life. Still[11] I know that it will be well with those who fear God because they fear him.

13And it will not be well for the wicked person, and one's days will not be long like a shadow, because one does not fear God.

14There is an enigma that is done on the earth: there are righteous people who are treated[12] according to the conduct of the wicked, and there are wicked people who are treated according to the conduct of the righteous. I say this too is enigmatic.

15But[13] I recommend joy, for there is nothing better for a person under the sun than to eat and to drink and to rejoice, for this will accompany one in one's labor in the days of one's life that God has given one under the sun.

16When I turned my heart to know wisdom and to observe the task that is done on earth (for one does not see sleep day or night),[14]

5. Taking *'ăšer* as causal (RJW §468).

6. *Pitgām* is one of two Persian loanwords in Ecclesiastes. It is a Persian loanword in Hebrew and Aramaic, being attested in Aramaic documents from Elephantine (Porten and Yardeni, eds., *Textbook*, II, 8.8.2–3) as well as from North Saqqara (Segal, *Aramaic Texts*, no. 1.2–3). It occurs in Esther 1:20 and several times in the Aramaic sections of Daniel and Ezra. It generally means "word" or "matter" but is used here in the specific sense of a word of judgment or sentence.

7. Following the masoretic punctuation, one would translate, "because the sentence is not carried out, an evil deed is quick." But see Seow (*Ecclesiastes*, 286) for why this is unlikely. There is also some discussion about *na'ăśâ* (executed) because some believe that the negative particle *'ên* occurs only before the participle, whereas here it occurs before the Niphal perfect. However, Ginsburg (*Coheleth*, 201) long ago showed that *'ên* may be used with finite verbs (cf. Jer. 38:5; Job 33:15). See Isaksson, *Studies*, 73–74, although he leaves the problem unresolved.

8. Literally "therefore the heart of human beings is full in them to do evil."

9. Taking *'ăšer* as causal (RJW §468). Many translations take it as concessive (even though), but it cannot have this meaning here. See Longman, *Ecclesiastes*, 217n43.

10. In the Hebrew, the word *mě'at* (hundred) is in the construct state. I take *mě'at* to be an ellipsis for "a hundred times." Alternatively, *mě'at* is an archaic absolute (Gordis, *Koheleth*, 297). Seow (*Ecclesiastes*, 287) emends the text to read "the wrong of hundreds."

11. I take *kî gam* as concessive, though there is some discussion about how to interpret it. See, for example, Schoors, *Preacher*, 1:134–36. Murphy (*Ecclesiastes*, 85) and Schoors prefer a concessive understanding of *kî gam* as "although," but Murphy does not try to smooth over the resulting contradiction in the way that Schoors, following Gordis (*Koheleth*, 297), does. Schoors (*Preacher*, 1:135) asserts that reading *kî gam* "as concessive fully fits the context, since, as clearly formulated by Gordis, *ywd'* introduces a restatement of a conventional idea, which Qoh[eleth] does not accept." Ogden understands *kî gam* adversatively as "however."

12. Literally "whom [one] treats them." For this idiom, cf. Esther 9:26.

13. Adversative use of *waw*.

14. Seow (*Ecclesiastes*, 289) argues that this parenthetical clause has been inadvertently transposed from v. 17. See the interpretation.

[17]I observed every work of God. Indeed,[15] no one can comprehend[16] the work that is done under the sun, on account of which[17] one labors to seek, but one does not find. Even if the wise person says he knows, he is unable to find.

Interpretation

"Then I observed" introduces a new section in Ecclesiastes, albeit one that is closely connected to the previous section. Whereas the previous section focused on the (ir)relevance of traditional wisdom to corrupt government, this section picks up the theme of vv. 6–7: there is a time for judgment, but we do not know if or when it will happen. In this section Qohelet develops the theme of delayed judgment on the basis of what he has observed. Traditional wisdom may teach that there is a time and a place for judgment and justice (v. 6), but what if our observation contradicts this and we see justice endlessly delayed? This is the problem Qohelet moves on to in this section, which deals with the problem of the wicked not being speedily punished.

[10]Then I observed the wicked buried. They used to go in and out of the holy place, but they were forgotten in the city in which they acted in this way. This too is enigmatic.

8:10. Longman maintains that v. 10 "vies for the most difficult verse in the book,"[18] mainly because the MT as it stands appears to make no sense. The problem centers on the wicked being forgotten—commentators assume this would be good news for the righteous, and yet Qohelet finds this enigmatic. Thus two approaches are taken to resolve this problem. First, Ginsburg, Delitzsch, Murphy, and Seow retain the verb "forgotten" but translate the phrase along the lines of "those who have acted justly were discarded."[19] However, this involves supplying the adverb "justly," which is not in the text. The second approach, adopted inter alia by Longman,[20] is to emend "forgotten" to "praised." The attractions of both approaches are obvious, but the more difficult MT version should stand.

15. Asseverative use of *kî* (RJW §449).
16. Literally "find."
17. *Bĕšel 'ăšer* is an unusual form in Biblical Hebrew. This idiom is similar to *bĕšel še* found in 4QMMT B 12, C 32 (Qimron and Strugnell, "Unpublished," 405), and a Bar Kokhba letter (DJD II, 165–66).
18. Longman, *Ecclesiastes*, 218.
19. Seow, *Ecclesiastes*, 276. See Ginsburg, *Coheleth*, 398–99; Delitzsch, *Ecclesiastes*, 346; Murphy, *Ecclesiastes*, 79.
20. Longman, *Ecclesiastes*, 218–19.

Qohelet is commenting in v. 10 on the observable lack of temporal judgment of the wicked. He notes as he observes their funerals that they used to inhabit the holy place (i.e., the temple) frequently. This, however, did not affect their wickedness, so that they were hypocrites going through the form of religion but denying its spirit. They are precisely the sort of people Qohelet warns against in 5:1–7 [4:17–5:6]. They lived without any sense that God is in heaven and they mere creatures on earth (cf. 5:2). They should therefore be ripe for judgment, but as far as Qohelet can see, there will never be a time for such judgment. Judgment never came while they were alive, and now they are forgotten, so that they will not even be remembered for what they were really like. One way in which there can be a time for judgment is when a future generation recognizes the evil of a former generation and acknowledges and confesses this evil. But as far as Qohelet can see, not even this limited time of judgment will happen. This he finds enigmatic.

> [11]Because the sentence for an evil deed is not speedily executed,
> therefore the human heart is fully set to do evil.

8:11. The problem with delayed judgment is that it encourages evil: the human heart is fully set to do evil. As with v. 6 it is possible that Qohelet has Gen. 6:5 in mind here. The human capacity for evil is extreme, but Qohelet here relates it to delayed judgment, whereas in Genesis judgment comes because God's patience is finally worn out. In the light of v. 10 it is probably human judgment that Qohelet has primarily in mind, but there is no reason why he should not refer to both human and divine judgment, especially since in Proverbs divine judgment works inter alia through human agents (cf. Prov. 8:15–16). The point is that delayed judgment encourages evil to flourish.

> [12]For a sinner does evil a hundred times and lengthens one's life. Still
> I know that it will be well with those who fear God because they
> fear him.
> [13]And it will not be well for the wicked person, and one's days will not
> be long like a shadow, because one does not fear God.

8:12–13. In vv. 12–13 we hear the confessional voice of Qohelet in relation to the time for judgment, and here he specifically has God's judgment in mind. In v. 12 Qohelet confesses what he "knows" about God's justice despite the prolonging of sinners' lives. Even though a sinner sins continually and lives a long life, Qohelet knows that it will be well with the one who fears God.[21] The confession continues in v. 13 but with an important shift. In contrast to the one who fears God, it will not be well with the wicked and their days

---

21. Murphy ("Qohelet's 'Quarrel' with the Fathers," 241) rightly notes that the fear of God in vv. 12–13 carries the same meaning as in traditional wisdom, i.e., Proverbs.

will not be long, because they do not fear God. As we have observed before, when Qohelet juxtaposes his confessional view with his enigmatic view, he does not resolve the contradictions but leaves them intact. So here, the clear contradiction is left intact: in v. 12a the sinners do prolong their lives, whereas in v. 13b they will not prolong their days! The confessional statement of vv. 12–13 thus affirms the character-consequence structure of Proverbs, but the juxtaposition of contradictory views is not resolved. Thus a gap is opened up in the text between what Qohelet observed and what he knows. The gap represents the immense struggle within Qohelet: how does one resolve the contradiction between what one observes and what one "knows"?

> **14**There is an enigma that is done on the earth: there are righteous people who are treated according to the conduct of the wicked, and there are wicked people who are treated according to the conduct of the righteous. I say this too is enigmatic.

8:14. Verse 14 is a further description of an enigmatic situation of injustice that Qohelet has observed. Justice is turned upside down. The righteous are treated as if wicked and the wicked as if righteous. This too Qohelet cannot comprehend—it is enigmatic, a terrible mystery. Qohelet's strong feelings about this are indicated by the double use of "enigma(tic)," at the beginning and end of this verse.

> **15**But I recommend joy, for there is nothing better for a person under the sun than to eat and to drink and to rejoice, for this will accompany one in one's labor in the days of one's life that God has given one under the sun.

8:15. In v. 15 we hear once again the confessional voice of Qohelet that resonates with the previous *carpe diem* passages. He recommends joy, for there is nothing better than eating, drinking, and rejoicing, for this will accompany one in one's labor under the sun. Whybray notes that Qohelet speaks with gathering confidence in each progressive *carpe diem* passage. The distinguishing mark of this *carpe diem* passage is its being prefaced by "I recommend."[22] The verb "recommend" (*šibbaḥ*) can also mean "laud" or "praise," so that we have here a strong recommendation from Qohelet. The element of joy accompanying one in one's labor and the eating-drinking motif are already found in 2:24 and 5:18 [17].[23] The "better-than" saying is also characteristic of the *carpe diem* passages. Once again it should be noted that this recommendation of joy is juxtaposed in contradictory fashion with v. 14. How, one might ask, can Qohelet recommend joy when the righteous are being treated

---

22. Whybray, "Qoheleth, Preacher of Joy," 87–89.
23. See comments on those sections.

as if wicked and the wicked as righteous? A gap is opened in the reading, and it is not resolved. Again it evokes the tension Qohelet experiences between what he observes and what he "knows."

> [16]When I turned my heart to know wisdom and to observe the task that is done on earth (for one does not see sleep day or night), [17]I observed every work of God. Indeed, no one can comprehend the work that is done under the sun, on account of which one labors to seek, but one does not find. Even if the wise person says he knows, he is unable to find.

8:16–17. In vv. 16–17 Qohelet reflects on his task and the inaccessibility of wisdom. We are familiar with the introductory formula in v. 16 from 2:25 and 7:25. Qohelet's whole person is engaged in the task of knowing wisdom. The parenthetical phrase "for one does not see sleep day or night" has occasioned much discussion. The relevance of "sleep" is not clear, and the idiom "to see sleep" is foreign to the OT.[24] Seow transposes this phrase to v. 17.[25] With Fox, however, it seems best to take the phrase as Qohelet referring to himself.[26] Deprivation of sleep could be related to religious fervor,[27] but with reference to Qohelet it implies intensity *and* disturbance. The unusual idiom of "seeing sleep" makes sense in the context of his quest, based as it is on observation. His autonomous epistemology results in his not *seeing* sleep! What he sees is so disturbing that it prevents him from finding rest. He is fully engaged in the quest, but it is constantly bringing him irresolvable enigmas, and one can imagine the impact of such a state on one's sleep. Qohelet himself shares in the experience he describes in 2:23: even at night his mind does not rest.

Verse 17 begins with a reminder of the comprehensive nature of Qohelet's quest—he observed every work of God. N. Lohfink perceptively notes, "This verse is very important in understanding the whole book, because it makes the action of God equivalent to the activity 'that is carried on under the sun.' . . . What is especially meant is all human activity. This then is at the same time always divine activity. Yet precisely in this dimension it is impenetrable for humans, above all when we ask about the 'all' of divine activity."[28] This statement is thus ironic because what Qohelet can observe is equated with "every work of God." As will become apparent later in Qohelet's journey, there are works of God such as creation and redemption to which an autonomous epistemology can never do justice, but they are crucial to resolving the

---

24. Murphy (*Ecclesiastes*, 81) notes that it can, however, be matched by Terence and Cicero.
25. Seow, *Ecclesiastes*, 289.
26. Fox, *Qohelet*, 255, who goes so far as to emend the text to "my eyes" (253–54).
27. Seow (*Ecclesiastes*, 289) notes that deprivation of sleep is a motif associated with religious fervor in the ancient Near East.
28. N. Lohfink, *Qoheleth*, 110–11.

enigmas Qohelet keeps encountering. There is hubris in his epistemology that leads him to think that he has observed every work of God. The problem is, as Qohelet goes on in v. 17 to explain, that no matter how comprehensively his epistemology is applied it fails to yield the desired results. No one can comprehend the meaning of work and life. The wise person may say he does, but according to Qohelet this is simply untrue—he does not!

Theological Implications

In this section Qohelet's exploration of delayed judgment and its enigma is juxtaposed with his affirmation of judgment and justice. Clearly gaps are left in the argument as a result of the juxtapositions. The lack of observable justice and the longevity of sinners results in people favoring evil, since such a lifestyle—contra Proverbs—appears to bring about long life and security. Qohelet is aware of this, and yet he "knows" that it will be well with those who fear God, but sinners will be punished and will not experience longevity. The gap resulting from the deliberate juxtaposition of these contradictory views is left unfilled, and in v. 14 Qohelet proceeds to another example of injustice. What makes this section particularly interesting is that the juxtaposition appears to be done consciously in v. 12 and v. 13, with v. 12a drawing the reader's attention to the contradiction and thereby making the reader aware that the author is aware of the contradiction.

Similarly, the "better-than" saying in v. 15 is in juxtaposition first to v. 14 and to the earlier example and enigmatic comment. The question that the juxtaposition raises is precisely how one could enjoy life while evil and oppression flourish and the righteous are treated as though they are wicked. How could Qohelet commend joy amid all the enigma he observes? The gap created by this juxtaposition is deliberately left open. Second, the "better-than" saying is juxtaposed with vv. 16 and 17 that follow. Rather than joy and rest, we find a Qohelet with insomnia (v. 16) who simply cannot resolve the enigma of life. One seeks, as he does, but one never finds—contrary to what he confesses he knows in vv. 12–13 and recommends in v. 15. Even if the wise person asserts that he has knowledge, it is not possible—he too cannot find wisdom!

Theologically, v. 17a is most important for the interpretation of Ecclesiastes. Qohelet's autonomous epistemology, the bucket with which he gathers his data, leads him to believe that he has observed "every work of God." In terms of his epistemology, this is true, but this verse alerts us to the hubris and limits of his epistemology—hubris, because it is arrogant to imagine that the works of God are confined to what Qohelet can observe, and limits, because Qohelet's sort of epistemology can never take into account God's works of creation and redemption. Verse 17a is thus yet another place in Ecclesiastes in which Qohelet's epistemology is ironized.

In this section Qohelet wrestles with the problem of delayed judgment. He observes the funerals of the wicked. Hypocritically, they used to participate in the cultus, going in and out of God's house, the temple. But now they are forgotten, and it appears that they will never be brought to justice. He observes the righteous treated as wicked and the wicked rewarded as though righteous, and he agonizes over this problem of delayed justice.

The problem of tyranny and delayed judgment remains an agonizing one in our time. In the context of the metanarrative of Scripture, judgment will not be delayed indefinitely. The return of Christ will be *the* time for judgment. As Berkouwer writes, "No longer will evil be called good and good evil; no longer will darkness be turned into light and light into darkness; no longer will bitter be made sweet and sweet bitter (Isa. 5:20). The conflict between good and evil will come to an end, as will all arguments about motives, intentions, and the nature of good. . . . Error will be exposed: real error, turning away from the Lord."[29] In a way that bears directly on Ecclesiastes, Spykman notes, "The crooked will at last be made straight, the unrequited wrongs made right— the unresolved crimes against humanity, the defamation of God's name, the wanton slaughter of the unborn, indifference to the crying needs of the poor and oppressed."[30]

Nevertheless, in the time between the coming of Christ and the consummation of the kingdom, delayed judgment remains an agonizing problem. The genocide in Rwanda is a powerful example. In the spring and early summer of 1994, out of a population of about 7.5 million, at least 800,000 people were killed in one hundred days. That amounts to 333 murders per hour, or more than 5 people killed every minute. "The dead of Rwanda accumulated at nearly three times the rate of Jewish dead during the Holocaust. It was the most efficient mass killing since the atomic bombings of Hiroshima and Nagasaki."[31] The West stood by while this genocide took place, and adequate justice in the aftermath has been impossible to achieve, so that victims and killers find themselves living side by side and sometimes even in the same house![32] The problem is not just the Hutus who participated in the massacres but the failure of the West to act. "The desertion of Rwanda by the UN force was Hutu Power's greatest diplomatic victory to date, and it can be credited almost single-handedly to the United States."[33]

It is very difficult to imagine the experience of those victims who died, or those who survived the genocide in Rwanda. Stories such as those told in Gourevitch's *We Wish to Inform You* help to give us some sense of the sheer

29. Berkouwer, *Return of Christ*, 160.
30. Spykman, *Reformational Theology*, 556–57.
31. Gourevitch, *We Wish to Inform You*, 3.
32. Ibid., 308.
33. Ibid., 150. Gourevitch's book is most revealing in terms of the abject failure of the West to prevent the genocide in Rwanda.

hell of genocide and the delayed judgment that follows. Gourevitch says of the stories told to him by survivors, "Quite often, I felt that these stories were offered to me the way that shipwrecked people, neither drowned nor saved, send messages in bottles: in the hope that, even if the legends they carry can do the teller no good, they may at some other time be of use to somebody, somewhere else."[34] Qohelet would remind us that again and again both victims and perpetrators are simply forgotten.

There is no easy solution to this sort of problem, hence the enduring relevance of Ecclesiastes. *By faith* the Christian believes that the day of judgment will come and that justice will finally be done, as Qohelet confesses in vv. 12 and 13. This remains a confession of faith and one that the data of life challenge again and again as judgment is delayed and the worst forms of evil flourish. Like us, Qohelet confesses that God's judgment will set matters right, but there is still the question of how to live the present, and that remains unresolved for Qohelet.

34. Ibid., 182.

Q.
The Fate of Death
and the Gift of Life
(9:1–12)

Translation

1For[1] I gave my heart[2] to all this, to explain[3] all this, that[4] the righteous and the wise and their deeds[5] are in the hand of God. However, whether[6] it is love or hate that awaits them,[7] no one knows.

1. Translating *kî* as causal. Longman (*Ecclesiastes*, 224) and Seow (*Ecclesiastes*, 297) take *kî* as an asseverative, translating "indeed." Debate centers on whether v. 1 implies a connection with what precedes or starts a new section. I opt for the latter, but typical of Qohelet's organic logic, v. 1 connects back into chap. 8 and indeed into the whole of Qohelet's journey.

2. MT has *'el-libbî*, whereas the more common construction would be with the direct object marker *'et*. Longman (*Ecclesiastes*, 224n2) leans toward emending the text to *'et*, but the same idiom occurs in 7:2 and a similar usage in 2 Sam. 13:33; 19:20.

3. This verb (*lābûr*) is difficult. The MT vocalization suggests the root *bwr*, "to examine, make clear, explain" (BDB 101), and if this is correct, then this is the only place it occurs in the OT. The root is, however, attested in Arabic and Akkadian. See Seow, *Ecclesiastes*, 297.

4. Nominalizing use of *'ăšer* (RJW §464).

5. Schoors (*Preacher*, 1:60–61) points out that *wa'ăbādêhem* is an Aramaism in its morphology.

6. It is not easy to know how to translate the phrase *gam-'āhăbâ gam-śin'â*, lit. "both love and also hate." Seow (*Ecclesiastes*, 298) takes it to refer to "their deeds," noting that in v. 6 the same words refer to human activities and not to divine and that in v. 6 *gam . . . gam* does not refer to uncertain alternatives. However, the context in v. 6 is clearly that of human activities, whereas the context in v. 1 is that of being in God's hand. Contextually, it is better to see love and hate here as attributes of God and to translate *gam . . . gam* as "whether . . . or."

7. *Lipnêhem* (lit. "before them") can be understood either temporally (in advance) or spatially (before their eyes). It has occasioned some difficulty in determining what is meant. The LXX reads the preceding word *hakkōl* as *hābel*, so that the end of v. 1 reads "all before them

2Everything is the same for every person.[8] There is the same fate for the righteous person and the wicked, for the good,[9] and for the clean and for the unclean, for the one who sacrifices and for the one who does not sacrifice. As it is for the good person, so it is for the sinner. The one who swears an oath is like the one who shuns[10] an oath.

3This is an evil in all that is done under the sun, for there is one fate for all, and furthermore the heart of humans is full of evil, and madness is in their hearts while they live, and after it[11]—to the dead!

4For[12] whoever is united[13] with all the living, there is hope,[14] for a living dog[15] is better than a dead lion.

---

is enigmatic." Taking love and hate to refer to God, I think *lipnêhem* must be read temporally to refer to what awaits humans.

8. As a result of the challenges of reading *hakkōl lipnêhem* in the preceding line, some emend *hakkōl* at the start of v. 2 to read *hābel*, thus yielding with the preceding two words "all before them is enigmatic." However, this is not necessary. The Hebrew reads lit. "everything is as for all," meaning that "everything is the same for everyone."

9. *Laṭṭôb* is regarded by many as problematic because it is not paired with another word as are the words around it. Fox (*Qohelet*, 257) and Seow (*Ecclesiastes*, 299) discern haplography at this point in the MT, and they follow the LXX in adding "and the bad." Longman (*Ecclesiastes*, 225) and Ogden (*Qoheleth*, 146) see *laṭṭôb* as a later addition to the text. Gordis (*Koheleth*, 300) suggests that the absence of "and the evil" may rest on rhythmic grounds. There is nothing at stake theologically in this issue, and I have chosen to retain the MT reading at this point.

10. Following the NRSV. *Yārē'* (shun) is lit. "fear." Seow (*Ecclesiastes*, 299) translates "the one who reveres the oath" in opposition to "the one who swears (falsely)." However, nothing in the Hebrew indicates a false swearing, and thus one's translation depends on how one understands *yārē'*.

11. *'Aḥārāyw* is lit. "after it." The third masculine singular suffix has perplexed commentators because it comes after a series of plural suffixes. The LXX and Syr have plural suffixes. Seow (*Ecclesiastes*, 300) maintains, mainly because of the singular suffix, that the last three words in this verse were wrongly transposed from the following verse. Thus he moves these three words to the end of v. 4 and translates them there as "and unto the dead is finality" (ibid., 296). However, I take the singular "it" to refer to the madness of human life viewed as a whole.

12. Taking *kî* in its causal sense. See the interpretation.

13. Translation of the verb *yibbāḥēr* is difficult. It is the Pual imperfect third masculine singular of *bḥr*, which means "choose, select." Seow (*Ecclesiastes*, 300) retains the Ketib and translates the opening of this verse as "Who is the one who chooses?" However, this does not make much sense in context, and it is probably better to follow some twenty Hebrew MSS, LXX, Symm, and Syr by reading the Qere, *yēḥubbar*, which is the Pual imperfect third masculine singular of *ḥbr*, meaning "be allied with, be joined to." This would assume a textual error because of metathesis.

14. Seow (*Ecclesiastes*, 300) insists that *biṭṭāḥôn* means not "hope" but "confidence" or "certitude." It is true that in 2 Kings 18:19 and Isa. 36:4 the word means "confidence" but not necessarily "certitude," as Seow translates it here. Furthermore, in 2 Kings and Isaiah the context is that of military threat, which is quite different from this verse. In this context, it seems appropriate to translate *biṭṭāḥôn* as "hope."

15. The *lamed* before *keleb* (dog) has occasioned much debate. It could function as a preposition, yielding the translation "it is better for a live dog than . . ." (Longman, *Ecclesiastes*,

⁵For the living know they will die, but the dead know nothing. There is no longer any reward[16] for them, for their memory is forgotten. ⁶Their love, their hate, their jealousy—already it has perished. Never again will they have any share in all that is done under the sun. ⁷Go, eat your bread with joy and drink your wine with a merry heart, for God has already approved your works. ⁸Let your clothes be sparkling[17] at all times, and do not let oil be lacking on your head. ⁹Enjoy life[18] with the woman whom you love all the days of your enigmatic life, that is, all the enigmatic days[19] he has given to you under the sun, for that is your portion in life and in your labor at which you labor under the sun. ¹⁰Whatever your hand finds to do, do with your strength,[20] for there is no work or thought or knowledge or wisdom in Sheol, to which you are going. ¹¹I turned and I observed[21] under the sun that the race is not to the swift,[22] and the battle is not to the mighty, nor is bread for the wise, nor riches to the intelligent, nor favor to the knowledgeable, for time and chance[23] befall all. ¹²Indeed, no one knows one's time. Like fish entangled in an evil[24] net and like birds caught in a snare, so[25] people are ensnared in an evil time, when it suddenly comes upon them.

225; Fox, *Qohelet*, 258), or it could mark dog as a *casus pendens* (GKC §143e), or it could be emphatic, as I take it to be. See Huehnergard, "Asseverative," 591; and *IBHS* §11.2.10i.

16. Seow (*Ecclesiastes*, 301) suggests that *śākār* may here have its economic meaning of "wages," and hence he translates it as "recompense." However, in context "reward" is the better translation. Longman (*Ecclesiastes*, 226) notes that *śākār* may have been chosen because of its assonance with *zēker* (memory).

17. According to Brenner (*Colour Terms*, 90–91), *lābān* refers to brightness rather than hue. *Lābān* is generally translated as "white."

18. Literally "see life." Cf. 2:1 and 3:13 for similar expressions.

19. Some Hebrew MSS and Syr omit this repetitive phrase. Seow (*Ecclesiastes*, 302) suggests that it should be omitted as an instance of dittography. However, repetition has literary significance, not least in Ecclesiastes, and the text makes sense as it stands.

20. The masoretic accents indicate that *bĕkōḥăkā* (with your strength) should be read with the infinitive *la'ăśôt*, yielding "Whatever your hand finds to do with strength, do!" However, we should probably follow several Hebrew MSS, Syr, and Vg in taking *bĕkōḥăkā* with the imperative *'ăśēh* (do), as translated above.

21. This idiom also occurs in 4:1. The only difference is that the "observe" is here an infinitive absolute, whereas in 4:1 it is a finite verb. There is no significant shift in meaning.

22. *Mērôṣ* is not found anywhere else in Classical Hebrew. Seow (*Ecclesiastes*, 307) suggests that it is to be compared with Ethiopic *mĕrwāṣ*, meaning "race, contest."

23. The word *pega'* occurs elsewhere in the OT only in 1 Kings 5:4 [18], where it means "misfortune." The verb *pāga'* means "to meet, to encounter, to reach," so that the noun *pega'* means "incident" or, because of its predominantly negative connotations, something like "accident."

24. The Vg and Tg omit "evil," and Galling (*Prediger*, 114) and Lauha (*Kohelet*, 172) delete it. However, its repetition here and later in this verse is deliberate.

25. Literally "like them."

Interpretation

> ¹For I gave my heart to all this, to explain all this, that the righteous and the wise and their deeds are in the hand of God. However, whether it is love or hate that awaits them, no one knows.

9:1. Verse 1 starts a new section in Ecclesiastes, but as so often with Qohelet it is organically connected into his journey thus far.[26] "All this" refers backward and forward; it is thus anaphoric, so that the opening *kî* should be translated causally as "for" rather than asseveratively as "indeed."[27] "For" indicates the ongoing nature of Qohelet's journey as it winds back and forth in quest of an answer to the value of one's labor under the sun. "Gave my heart" reminds the reader of the intensity and deeply personal nature of Qohelet's quest.

Verses 1–6 are an anguished reflection on the finality of death as the destiny of every person. As so often with Qohelet, he begins with an orthodox statement and then subverts it. He asserts that the righteous and the wise and their deeds are in the hand of God. As noted before, there is no dichotomy in Qohelet's thinking between the righteous and the wise, contrary to the common view among scholars that wisdom's notion of righteous and sinner is different from that of the rest of the OT. For Qohelet, as for Proverbs, to be righteous is to be wise, and to be wise is to be righteous.

To be "in the hand of God" is to be subject to God's sovereignty and power. In Prov. 21:1 the king's heart is said to be in the hand of the LORD, who turns it wherever he wishes. In Proverbs and the rest of the OT, to be in God's hand is a wonderful thing for the righteous and wise, the source of trust and assurance. Verse 1a is therefore a confessional statement about God's sovereignty, stressing that all that the righteous and wise do plus the outcome of their actions is in God's good control.

Qohelet, however, immediately subverts any such positive connotations. As far as he can observe, no one knows whether being in God's hand means that love or hate lies ahead. "Hate" is a strong word, referring to God's wrath and judgment and evoking the strength of Qohelet's feeling at this point. In Isa. 1:14 the same root is used when the LORD says to the Israelites that his

---

26. Scholars do not agree how to divide up chap. 9. Murphy (*Ecclesiastes*, 88) takes 9:1–12 as a section, which he titles "Reflections." Whybray (*Ecclesiastes* [NCBC], 139) has vv. 1–10 as a section, which he is "certain" ends with v. 10. Ogden's analysis is preferable because it takes into account the inclusions and introductory phrases that Murphy (inclusions) and Whybray (introductory phrases) refer to (Ogden, *Qoheleth*, 143–60). According to Ogden, vv. 1–12 are closely linked, with vv. 1–6, 7–10, 11–12, and 13–16 forming subsections. See also Ogden, "Qoheleth IX 1–16." As is apparent from my subdivisions, I prefer to take 9:13–18 as a separate section. Ogden ("Qoheleth IX 1–16," 168) argues that in vv. 13–16 Qohelet affirms wisdom as the highest value, but as is apparent in the next chapter, I read vv. 13–16 more pessimistically.

27. Cf. Longman, *Ecclesiastes*, 224.

soul *hates* their new moon festivals and appointed feasts. "Love" by contrast is the attitude of care and grace of the LORD toward his covenant people (cf. Deut. 4:37). Proverbs 3:33 expresses the traditional understanding of how God's love and hate operate: "The curse of the LORD is on the house of the wicked, but he blesses the abode of the righteous."

As noted in the translation, Seow takes love and hate to refer to "their deeds."[28] However, the context is dominated by God's power and contradictory retribution, so that love and hate clearly refer to God's actions, not those of humans.[29] Because of what follows v. 1, Murphy understands "in the hand of God" as simply a reference to God's power rather than God's benign providence.[30] This is an argument from context that fails to recognize Qohelet's struggle with orthodoxy. His struggle becomes most intense in this chapter: Longman says of 9:1–10 that its message is "among the most clearly pessimistic of the entire book."[31] We must resist the temptation to flatten out the polarities of his struggle, alas, a temptation that commentators on Ecclesiastes find hard to resist. Qohelet knows the traditional view that we are in God's hands, but epistemologically he cannot square what he observes with this view.

Verse 1b is thus a statement stemming from Qohelet's observation of life; as far as he can *see*, one does not know whether the future will be love or hate. This deconstructs v. 1a in the strongest fashion; the righteous may be in God's hands, but it is uncertain whether this means that God's love or hate lies ahead for them. Murphy puts it most clearly, "The customary signs of blessing or curse have been displaced, since there is no comprehension of what God is about."[32]

---

²Everything is the same for every person. There is the same fate for the righteous person and the wicked, for the good, and for the clean and for the unclean, for the one who sacrifices and for the one who does not sacrifice. As it is for the good person, so it is for the sinner. The one who swears an oath is like the one who shuns an oath.

9:2. In contrast to traditional wisdom and the rest of the OT, Qohelet states unequivocally in v. 2 that everything is the same for everyone because all share the same fate, namely death. His emphatic assertion is elaborated with a long list of those people between whom the OT carefully distinguishes. In the covenantal literature of the OT, the righteous and the wicked are carefully

---

28. Similarly, Hertzberg (*Prediger*, 176) and Lauha (*Kohelet*, 166) suggest that human attributes are here referred to; in context it is God.
29. Murphy, *Ecclesiastes*, 90.
30. Ibid.
31. Longman, *Ecclesiastes*, 224.
32. Murphy, *Ecclesiastes*, 90.

distinguished. But for Qohelet, it is the same for both righteous and wicked—both are on the way of death. "For the good" is often taken as problematic because it is not paired with an opposite. However, it serves to underscore Qohelet's point—the good do not escape the fate of death.

"Clean" and "unclean" are terms from the priestly literature of the Torah. Cleanness refers to purity and normality or wholeness. "The insistence on purification of the unclean is a corollary of the idea that Israel, the camp, and especially the tabernacle are holy. Contact between uncleanness and holiness is disastrous. They are utterly distinct in theory and must be kept equally distinct in practice, lest divine judgment fall."[33] For Qohelet, however, death collapses this distinction fundamental to priestly theology. Sacrifice is so important in Leviticus that its first seventeen chapters are devoted to the procedures and occasions for sacrifices. Sacrifice is the means given by the LORD for maintaining and restoring the relationship between God and his people and between members of the covenant community. But for Qohelet it makes no difference whether one sacrifices—death embraces all. It is the same for the good person as it is for the sinner.

In Eccles. 5:1–7 [4:17–5:6] Qohelet, in line with Deuteronomy, urges caution in making vows before God, lest God become angry and destroy the works of one's hands. Here, however, death obliterates that advice—it makes no difference whether one makes a vow or shuns one. In context *yārē'* (shuns) is best understood not as fearing to make a vow but as shunning a vow that has been made. In 5:1–7 this is regarded as catastrophic, but here it makes no difference whatsoever—the one who makes a vow and the one who shuns a vow share the same destiny, namely death. One's ethics (righteous and wicked) and one's worship (clean or unclean, sacrificing or not) make no difference whatsoever—all end up dead.

Qohelet once again manifests knowledge of the Torah. He is familiar with Deuteronomy, as we saw in our discussion of 5:1–7. "Righteous" and "wicked" are common language in the Torah, the Historical books, and the Prophets, in which they have, as here, strong ethical and religious connotations. What is most interesting about v. 2 is that Qohelet is also familiar with the sort of priestly legislation we find in Leviticus. After his reference to the temple in 5:1–7 this should not surprise us, but as historical criticism has developed there has been an unfortunate tendency to see Wisdom as separate from Torah and the Prophets. Here, however, Qohelet is clearly familiar with the central priestly concepts of cleanness and uncleanness, and with sacrifice. This confirms that by Qohelet's time at least there was an organic relationship between Wisdom and Torah.

[3]This is an evil in all that is done under the sun, for there is one fate
for all, and furthermore the heart of humans is full of evil, and

---

33. Wenham, *Leviticus*, 21–22.

> madness is in their hearts while they live, and after it—to the
> dead!

9:3. Verse 3 explains what this common fate of humans is, namely death. For Qohelet the universality of death is "evil," utterly inexplicable and unacceptable. Possibly alluding again to Gen. 6:5, Qohelet despairs not only of the common fate of humankind but of humankind itself; their hearts are full of evil, and madness is in their hearts while they live. His assessment of the human condition is akin here to that of Jeremiah, who out of his own agony discerns that the human heart is desperately wicked and deceitful above all else (Jer. 17:9). The singular suffix attached to "after" should be taken as referring to the entire collective madness of human life viewed as a single whole. In evocative language Qohelet asserts that what follows this madness is death.

> [4]For whoever is united with all the living, there is hope, for a living dog
> is better than a dead lion.
> [5]For the living know they will die, but the dead know nothing. There is
> no longer any reward for them, for their memory is forgotten.
> [6]Their love, their hate, their jealousy—already it has perished. Never
> again will they have any share in all that is done under the sun.

9:4–6. In vv. 4–6, Qohelet explores the possibility that there is some advantage to being alive rather than dead. This is a topic he has explored before in 6:1–6, in which he asserts that it is better to be stillborn than to live amid the enigmas of life. Verse 4 consists of two proverbs that superficially appear to affirm life over death. If one is part of the living, one has hope, and a living dog is better than a dead lion. However, there is a stinger in the tail of these proverbs. In stark contrast to contemporary Western culture, dogs were among the most despised animals in the ancient Near East,[34] whereas lions were among the most admired creatures. "The irony is especially bitter because dogs may have been associated with death and the underworld."[35] Life may be thought to have some advantages over death, but that is like thinking that it is better to be a living dog than a dead lion!

The irony is sustained in v. 5. The "advantage" of living is that you know you will die! But lest this be thought an actual advantage, Qohelet elaborates on his view of death.

The dead know nothing; they cease to be conscious beings.

They receive no reward if they have lived well.

They are not remembered.

---

34. Podechard (*L'Ecclésiaste*, 412) notes that "the dog, an impure animal, is in the Orient an object of contempt (I Sam. xvii,43; II Sam. iii,8; ix,8; xvi,9; Math. xv,26; Apoc. xxii,15)."
35. Seow, *Ecclesiastes*, 301.

All the tumultuous emotions driving their lives—love, hate, jealousy—are
gone forever.
Never again will they share in life.

For Qohelet, death is so awful that it completely overshadows any value to
life.

> [7]Go, eat your bread with joy and drink your wine with a merry heart,
> for God has already approved your works.
> [8]Let your clothes be sparkling at all times, and do not let oil be lacking
> on your head.
> [9]Enjoy life with the woman whom you love all the days of your enig-
> matic life, that is, all the enigmatic days he has given to you under
> the sun, for that is your portion in life and in your labor at which
> you labor under the sun.
> [10]Whatever your hand finds to do, do with your strength, for there is no
> work or thought or knowledge or wisdom in Sheol, to which you are
> going.

9:7–10. After this despairing reflection, the imperatives in vv. 7–10 come
as a shock. Verses 7–10 are the fifth of the *carpe diem* passages in Ecclesiastes.
As with the other *carpe diem* passages, it is crucial to note that this passage
is juxtaposed in a contradictory fashion with vv. 1–6 and vv. 11–18. Contra
many commentators, this is not Qohelet's answer to the enigma of death but
an alternative vision of life.[36] The *carpe diem* section in vv. 7–10 opens in a
particularly strong way. It looks very much like the other juxtaposed *carpe diem*
sayings that we have looked at. The lack of introductory formulae, however,
combined with the several imperatives, enhances the juxtaposed nature of
this advice. As noted previously, the *carpe diem* passages become stronger as
Qohelet's journey proceeds. Ogden points this out here: "The most striking
literary feature of this section is the sudden appearance of a series of imperatives bearing on enjoyment. . . . What is new, however, in this section is the
move from advice to imperative; it gives the enjoyment theme in this case a
more authoritative presentation."[37] There is no "better-than" element, perhaps
because of the sharper, imperative nature of the exhortation. God's approval
of eating and drinking is strongly stated in v. 7b,[38] and as Ogden notes, "Qoheleth does not mean that God will happily sanction *anything* we determine

---

36. Longman (*Ecclesiastes*, 229) is typical of many when he says that "in the light of death,
Qohelet urges his reader/hearer to seek pleasure, specifically to eat and drink."
37. Ogden, *Qoheleth*, 151.
38. Cf. Whybray, "Qoheleth, Preacher of Joy." Murphy is more cautious but acknowledges
that v. 7b refers to God's largesse. All agree on the festive symbolism in vv. 8–9. On eating and
drinking, see my comments on the earlier *carpe diem* passages (2:24–26; 3:10–15, 16–22; 5:18–20
[17–19]; 8:10–15).

to do. From the fuller context, it is clear that Qoheleth locates enjoyment within the divine will; God wills that we enjoy his basic provisions, for he is the one who provides them (cf. 2.24 etc.)."[39] A new element in this *carpe diem* passage is the specific mention of wine. Wine formed part of Qohelet's failed experiment in 2:3, but here it alerts us to the festive nature of the eating and drinking and is approved by God.

The reference to clothing and oil are also new. Brenner examines the biblical evidence on sparkling (white) clothing and concludes that they symbolize "purity, festiveness, or elevated social status."[40] Hengstenberg argues that white is "the colour of serene splendour symbolically shadowing forth glory."[41] Referring to the transfiguration of Christ and the symbolism of white in Revelation, he asserts that white here expresses the *"confident hope of the future glory of the people of God. . . .* The true members of the people of God ought always to be in a festive, joyous mood, inasmuch as they rise by faith above the gloomy present to the glorious future awaiting them."[42] Delitzsch notes that white is in contrast to the black robes of mourning; the garments "are an expression of festal joy, of a happy mood; black and white are, according to the ancients, colour symbols, the colours respectively of sorrow and joy, to which light and darkness correspond."[43] Longman criticizes pietistic commentators for going "with purity" and maintains that white is here a symbol of joy.[44] Festivity is clearly the image evoked in v. 8, but one should not forget that in the *carpe diem* passages this is rooted in a vision of the world as God's creation, so that Hengstenberg is not far off in seeing purity *and* hope here as well. In the hot climate of Palestine, oil protected against dryness and is clearly associated in the OT with joy and gladness. In Ps. 23:5 the LORD anoints one with oil so that one's cup overflows. In Isa. 61:3 the oil of gladness is contrasted with mourning. Thus v. 8b is another exhortation to joy.

The reference to the "woman whom you love" is also a new element in this *carpe diem* passage. Some argue that *'iššâ* (woman) without the article may refer to any woman rather than to one's wife.[45] When the context demands it, however, *'iššâ* without the article may well refer to one's wife (cf. Gen. 30:4, 9; 1 Sam. 25:43; Deut. 22:22). Once we realize that the *carpe diem* vision is rooted in a theology of creation, then the case for this woman being one's

39. Ogden, *Qoheleth*, 152. For a contrary view, see Longman, *Ecclesiastes*, 229.

40. Brenner, *Colour Terms*, 152.

41. Hengstenberg, *Ecclesiastes*, 214.

42. Ibid., 215.

43. Delitzsch, *Ecclesiastes*, 363.

44. Longman, *Ecclesiastes*, 230.

45. Whybray, *Ecclesiastes* (NCBC), 144. He asserts, "Qoheleth nowhere else refers to marriage, and there is no way of telling whether he is here referring specifically to married life." But see Pahk, "Syntactical and Contextual Consideration of *'šh*," for the case that Qohelet is referring to one's wife.

wife is compelling. Thus v. 9a is a positive affirmation of marriage that is to be fully enjoyed in all its dimensions.

As in the other *carpe diem* passages, work is affirmed in v. 10a—one should apply oneself to it diligently. Verse 10 is a reminder once again of how all-embracing the *carpe diem* vision of Qohelet is, because as Whybray points out, "Qoheleth is . . . recommending . . . all useful and intellectual activity."[46] Significantly though, accompanying the stronger hortatory element and intruding on this *carpe diem* passage is a stronger deconstructive element than in any of the others. In v. 9 the life that the reader is exhorted to enjoy is in the context of "all the days of your enigmatic life," and v. 10b undermines v. 10a by confronting it with the empty reality of Sheol. P. Johnston's analysis of Sheol in the OT is illuminating in this context. He argues that it is not simply the OT word for the underworld that is the destiny of all, as here. In the OT it is generally reserved for those under God's judgment and seldom refers to all humanity, and when it does it is only in contexts like this that stress life's absurdity and human sinfulness.[47] Johnston says of 9:9–10: "That all without distinction go to Sheol is part of Qohelet's reflection on the absurdity of observable life. But it is not the book's final word."[48]

This could be taken to support the view that the *carpe diem* passages are Qohelet's advice as to how to respond to the enigma of life, but this is to ignore the boiling point to which Qohelet's struggle has brought him. More than any other of the juxtaposed sections we have looked at, this one witnesses to the enormous tension in the attempt to pursue the logical implications of Qohelet's epistemology while also trying to acknowledge the insights of Israelite life and religion. The two threaten, as it were, to pull each other apart. As the advice to seize the day becomes imperative, so the enigma of life pulls in the opposite direction, and we see here the imminent explosion of Qohelet's attempt to hold on to both. Once again the exhortation to enjoyment should therefore not just be seen as the answer to the problem of the universality of death. The contradiction remains unresolved: how is one to appropriate joy if one is living like a dog?

> [11]I turned and I observed under the sun that the race is not to the swift, and the battle is not to the mighty, nor is bread for the wise, nor riches to the intelligent, nor favor to the knowledgeable, for time and chance befall all.
> [12]Indeed, no one knows one's time. Like fish entangled in an evil net and like birds caught in a snare, so people are ensnared in an evil time, when it suddenly comes upon them.

46. Whybray, *Ecclesiastes* (NCBC), 145.
47. P. Johnston, *Shades of Sheol*, 83.
48. Ibid.

9:11–12. Many commentators regard vv. 11–12 as a separate section, and as so often with Qohelet it is hard to know where one section ends and another begins. "I turned and observed" does indicate a shift in focus, but the theme of evil befalling one is so closely related to v. 1 that I have included vv. 11–12 in this section. In v. 1 Qohelet asserts that one does not know whether love or hate awaits. In these verses, he explores the more disturbing possibility of how hate—he assumes these evils come from God—can ambush one unexpectedly. That his reflections are based on what he *observed* is important; it alerts us once again to the autonomous epistemology guiding his reflections.

In v. 11, using five examples, Qohelet observes that the character-consequence structure of Proverbs is simply not the case. In any race we would expect the fastest to win, but, says Qohelet, the race is not to the swift. If Qohelet had knowledge of Greek culture it is possible that he had a Hellenistic athletic event in mind. N. Lohfink goes so far as to say, "The whole series could summarize the biographical ideal of a young Greek: success in sport as a youth, then a military career, eventually setting up a family, accumulation of wealth, public influence in the polis."[49] Whatever the background and whether or not an actual athletic event is in mind, Qohelet's point is that the outcome is not what we expect. His second example is that of war; we would expect the mighty to triumph, but this is not the case. In Prov. 20:13 and 28:19 living wisely means that one will have plenty of bread. Not so, says Qohelet. Forms of the words "intelligent" (*byn*) and "knowledgeable" (*yd'*) occur in Prov. 1:1–6 to indicate the great advantage of wisdom.[50] Moreover, Prov. 1–9 clearly teaches that wisdom, knowledge, and intelligence do lead to wealth (cf. Prov. 3:2, 10) and favor. But on the basis of what he has observed, Qohelet denies this because time and chance befall everyone, just as does death.

By "time and chance" Qohelet has disaster in mind, the equivalent of "hate" in v. 1. The references to time resonate back to chap. 3, and here the point is that one never knows when evil is going to befall one. Qohelet uses two images to evoke the horror of this experience. The first is that of fish suddenly finding themselves caught in an "evil net." Some suggest that "evil" is reproduced here by mistake, since it occurs later in this verse. But the repetition is deliberate and not only alerts us that this is an image depicting the *human* condition but also reinforces how strongly Qohelet feels about this. Without having any prospect of what lies ahead, a fish may suddenly find itself entangled in a net. So too an unsuspecting bird may find itself caught in a snare. *Paḥ* (snare) most likely refers to a self-springing bird trap.[51] Qohelet does not say so, but it is probably not by chance that for both fish and bird this chance experience leads to death. For Qohelet the unexpectedness of such occurrences mirrors

49. N. Lohfink, *Qoheleth*, 122.
50. See Fox, *Proverbs 1–9*, 28–38.
51. Seow, *Ecclesiastes*, 308.

what he observes among humans: evil suddenly befalls people when they least expect it. He does not comment on the sort of evil he has in mind, but we have a good idea of the range of possibilities from his earlier discussions: poverty, oppression, injustice, corruption, loneliness, and so on. The language in v. 12 is reminiscent of 7:26,[52] but here it is not the sinner who is seized; as he notes in v. 2, "Everything is the same for everyone."

Theological Implications

In this section we witness the deep tension between Qohelet's outworking of his epistemology and his believing affirmation of life. Proverbs teaches the character-consequence structure, but at the opening and conclusion of this section Qohelet finds it thoroughly undermined. In 9:1–6 Qohelet's pessimism hits rock bottom. In terms almost blasphemous he asserts that one simply cannot know whether God's love or hate awaits one. In vv. 1–6 it is the common destiny of *death* that Qohelet finds enigmatic; it is the fate of all, both righteous and wicked, and thus what can possibly be the value of wisdom and righteousness? Neither righteousness, nor cultic cleanliness, nor appropriate sacrifice, nor avoidance of sin appear to make any difference; the end is the same, namely death. Verse 11 similarly subverts the character-consequence structure of Proverbs: swiftness, strength, wisdom, wealth, knowledge—all these make no difference because time and chance befall all.

In stark contrast stand vv. 7–10a, in which Qohelet affirms life: eating, drinking, attention to one's appearance as a sign of life (v. 8), enjoying married life (v. 9), and working hard (v. 10). This is the voice of the orthodox Qohelet, and it affirms the gift of the ordinary in line with the rest of the OT. Rather than seeing time as a curse that creates the context in which we can be ensnared by evil (v. 12) and inevitably drags us toward death amid our love, hate, and jealousy (v. 6), time is here presupposed as the context for life, for life lived to the full. In *Seven Essays on Metaphysics*, Jacques Maritain tells of one day finding himself—a renowned seventy-seven-year-old philosopher—skipping across a hilltop in Toulouse and shouting, "I'm alive, I'm alive!" "Having experienced sudden and utterly surprising rapture at the gift of life, the joy of being invested with existence, the privilege of being rather than not being, Maritain sank to his knees whispering words of praise and thanksgiving."[53] Qohelet knows from faith and life of this experience, and he expresses it with particular force in this *carpe diem* passage.

52. The word for "net" (*māṣôdâ*) is the same word for "snare" in 7:26.
53. Manning, *Ruthless Trust*, 26.

Such an approach to life implies a practice of "receiving the day."[54] As Bass notes, "At the heart of this practice is praise of the One who created the earth and separated the light from darkness. This One is still active in earth and all creatures, including ourselves. Every day, this One offers gifts—life, light, and hours in which to work and eat and love and rest—and invites humankind to join in the ongoing work of caring for creation and all who dwell therein."[55]

Receiving the day is rooted in a view of our world as creation, and Bass suggests the following practices for receiving the day:

1. *Honoring the body, day by day.* Humans are embodied creatures, and rhythms of eating, drinking, and washing are an important part of human identity. People who lose their homes report that the loss of this rhythm is one of the hardest aspects of such loss.[56] Kathleen Norris notes,

> Our culture's ideal self, especially the accomplished, professional self, rises above necessity, the humble, everyday, ordinary tasks that are best left to unskilled labor. The comfortable lies we tell ourselves regarding these "little things"—that they don't matter, and that daily and personal and household chores are of no significance to us spiritually—are exposed as falsehoods when we consider that reluctance to care for the body is one of the first symptoms of extreme melancholia. Shampooing the hair, washing the body, brushing the teeth, drinking enough water, taking a daily vitamin, going for a walk, as simple as they seem, are acts of self-respect. They enhance one's ability to take pleasure in oneself and in the world.[57]

Intriguingly, in this chapter Qohelet specifically refers to such care of the body in v. 8. Crenshaw notes, "The value of white clothes in a hot climate was widely known, and the frequent application of oils to combat the deleterious effect of dry heat on skin was widely practiced by those who could afford it. According to Esther 8:15, Mordecai wore a combination of bright clothes and white garments on a festive occasion."[58] Bread and wine represent the everyday needs of life as well as occasions of celebration,[59] and Qohelet encourages us to enter into these daily activities and rhythms with joy. His reference to enjoying life with the woman you love affirms marriage—the companionship as well as the bodily, sexual dimension.

For Qohelet, like Mordecai, care of the body manifests itself in the aesthetics of one's clothes—he exhorts the reader to "let your clothes be sparkling."

54. See Bass's book with this title: *Receiving the Day: Christian Practices for Opening the Gift of Time.*
55. Ibid., 18.
56. Ibid., 32.
57. Norris, *Quotidian Mysteries*, 40.
58. Crenshaw, *Ecclesiastes*, 162.
59. See Vitz, *Continual Feast*, for a great cookbook that follows the church calendar, enabling one truly to eat and drink and enjoy one's work.

This is not to imply that Christians should constantly be at the height of contemporary fashion; rather, that our receiving of the day should show itself in the fabrics and clothes we wear. Something of the way in which simplicity can manifest itself in great beauty is wonderfully evoked by Sue Bender in her book about a year with the Amish. What initially attracted her to them were their quilts. She was drawn back again and again to a shop in which they were for sale:

> I stared at the quilts. They seemed so silent: a "silence like thunder." . . . Colors of such depth and warmth were combined in ways I had never seen before. At first the colors looked somber, but then—looking closely at a large field of brown—I discovered that it was really made up of small patches of many different shades and textures of color. Greys and shiny dark and dull light brown, dancing side by side, made the flat surface come alive. Lush greens lay beside vivid reds. An electric blue appeared as if from nowhere on the border.[60]

2. *The offering of attention.* Qohelet encourages us to enter into life attentively. The opposite of attention is distraction, and in today's busyness attentiveness suffers. Annie Dillard has made it her task as a writer to attend to the creation. Peterson describes Dillard as an exegete of the creation, just as Calvin is an exegete of Scripture. The doctrine of creation calls us to attention because "Matter is real. Flesh is good. Without a firm rooting in creation, religion is always drifting off into some kind of pious sentimentalism or sophisticated intellectualism. . . . The physical is holy."[61] Dillard spent a year attending to a creek and its surroundings and published her experiences in *Pilgrim at Tinker's Creek*. Her explorations are rigorous and, in turns, puzzling and mysterious. But she "ends up on her feet applauding."[62]

> Emerson saw it. "I dreamed that I floated at will in the great Ether, and I saw this world floating also not far off, but diminished to the size of an apple. Then an angel took it in his hand and brought it to me and said, 'This must thou eat.' And I ate the world." All of it. All of it intricate, speckled, gnawed, fringed, and free. Israel's priests offered the wave breast and the heave shoulder together, freely, in full knowledge, for thanksgiving. They waved, they heaved, and neither gesture was whole without the other, and both meant a wide-eyed and keen-eyed thanks. Go your way, eat the fat, and drink the sweet, said the bell. A sixteenth-century alchemist wrote of the philosopher's stone, "One finds it in the open country, in the village and in the town. It is in everything which God created. Maids throw it on the street. Children play with it." The giant water bug ate the world. And like Billy Bray I go my way, and my left foot says, "Glory," and

60. Bender, *Plain and Simple*, 2–3.
61. Peterson, *Contemplative Pastor*, 68.
62. Ibid., 69.

my right foot says, "Amen": in and out of Shadow Creek, upstream and down, exultant, in a daze, dancing, to the twin silver trumpets of praise.[63]

3. *Attending to God*. Bass's third practice involves making times for God regularly each day: "The Christian practice of receiving the day begins with setting aside a part of each day for attention to God. This piece of time leans deliberately into the wind, grounding us to resist the forces that hurry us on to distraction. . . . Putting down an anchor or two amidst the swells of each day is essential if we are to avoid bobbing on its surface or being washed away by its demands."[64] This is a topic that Qohelet addresses in particular in chap. 5, where he exhorts us to approach God to *listen*. However, even here the sparkling (white) clothes and the embrace of joy imply a concern with purity and life *coram deo*, before the face of God.

4. *Saying no to say yes*. Receiving the day, especially in our frenetic consumer culture, involves choosing what not to do as well as what to do. Qohelet's exhortation to embrace the ordinary is much harder nowadays than it was in his day, with TV, the Internet, and all the things that constitute what Casey calls our dromocratic, namely speed-driven, culture.[65] Recovering the ordinary will mean dispensing with the clutter that fills our lives.

5. *Unmastering the day*. Bass's final step involves a recognition that there is much about our days that we cannot control, and we need to relinquish control at these points. "Saint Francis is reported to have said, 'In baptism we have died the only death that matters.' It is, finally, in this kind of confidence, this kind of trust, that we are free to receive this day as a gift—and also to receive it as a day that bears gifts, including the gift we become when we lose ourselves in faithful living."[66]

Christians are not exempt from the evil day befalling them. In Eph. 6:13 Paul exhorts his readers to take up the armor of God so that they might withstand on the "evil day" and having done all to be still standing. The Nestle-Aland Greek NT indicates no allusion to v. 12 of this chapter, but one wonders if Paul might not have had it in mind. Certainly Paul understands that the evil day by its very nature comes unexpectedly, and that one may find oneself suddenly ensnared in it, but he insists that one has the resources in Christ to come through it still standing, rather than beaten to a pulp.

It is Qohelet's very understanding of just how good life can be that creates the awful tension within him, and in this, the last *carpe diem* passage before the final one in chap. 11, we witness his inability to keep the perspective of enigma and joy apart and in tension. In v. 9 and v. 10b we see signs of the enigmatic

63. A. Dillard, *Annie Dillard Reader*, 424.
64. Bass, *Receiving the Day*, 36–37.
65. Casey, *Getting Back into Place*, xiv. See also P. Virilio, *Speed and Politics*, trans. M. Pollizotti (New York: Semiotext[e], 1986).
66. Ibid., 43.

conclusion tugging away at his affirmation of life. This chapter therefore focuses unequivocally Qohelet's problem: How does one bridge the gap between the despairing enigma of life and the sheer goodness of life? In this chapter, it is particularly the mystery of death that perplexes Qohelet. He appears to regard Sheol as the termination of life, and this casts a question mark over all that precedes death. As Qohelet continues his journey, we must wait to see if and how he resolves this tension that is threatening to implode.

In the light of the fuller revelation in Christ, much of this problem is resolved. Death, we now know, has no sting for the believer but is the stepping stone into God's presence. We await the resurrection of the dead. Nevertheless, this side of the consummation of the kingdom, death and suffering retain their shadow, as does the evil day, so that Qohelet's dilemma remains pastorally relevant.

R.
The Example of a City
(9:13–18)

Translation

¹³This also I observed in relation to wisdom[1] under the sun, and it
made a great impression on me:
¹⁴There was a small city and a few people in it. And a great king came
against it, and he surrounded it and built huge nets[2] against it.
¹⁵But there was[3] a wise commoner[4] in it, and he delivered[5] the city by
his wisdom. But no one paid attention to[6] that commoner.

1. The Hebrew reads lit. "Also I observed wisdom." *Ḥokmâ* (wisdom) is the accusative of limitation (Joüon-Muraoka §126g), so it should be translated "as to, concerning, in relation to wisdom."

2. *Mĕṣôdîm* is the same word translated "snare" in 7:26 and "net" in 9:12. Seow (*Ecclesiastes*, 309) prefers to read *mĕṣûrîm* (siegeworks) with two Hebrew MSS, LXX, Symm, Syr, and Vg. He notes that *mĕṣôdîm* is often thought to be associated with *mĕṣûdâ* or *mĕṣād*. However, these words are always associated with defense and not, as here, offense. What this fails to take into account is the possible play on words between v. 12 and v. 14. "Nets" may here be an image for siegeworks as well as a reminder that this was an evil time for this city.

3. *Māṣā' bāh* (lit. "one found in it") has caused some discussion. Vg, Syr, and Tg all translate the verb as passive, i.e., "there was found in it." However, *māṣā'* is Qal perfect, and we cannot assume the Niphal stem was read. The comparable idiom is found in Gen. 2:20: *lō'-māṣā' 'ēzer* ("one did not find a helper," which translates into English comparably as "there was no helper").

4. Although many translate *miskēn* as "poor," Seow (*Ecclesiastes*, 310) points out that *miskēn* is generally contrasted with the elite of society and is thus the equivalent of the small-holder, the commoner.

5. Seow (*Ecclesiastes*, 310) translates "might have delivered." The perfect may indicate a hypothetical situation, but in context this is to be rejected. Qohelet is describing what he "observed."

6. *Zākar* (lit. "remember") is often found in parallel to expressions like "did not lay these things to heart" (Isa. 47:7) and "come to mind" (Isa. 65:17) in the OT. Such a nuance of "paying attention to" fits well in this context. Cf. Seow, *Ecclesiastes*, 310.

¹⁶And I said, "Wisdom is better than might," but the wisdom of the commoner was despised, and his words were not listened to.
¹⁷The calm[7] words of the wise are better listened to than the shouting of a ruler among fools.[8]
¹⁸Wisdom is better than weapons of war, but one sinner destroys a whole lot of[9] good.

Interpretation

"This also I observed" indicates a new section in Ecclesiastes, although there are connections with what precedes. "In relation to wisdom" means "as an example of wisdom." As becomes apparent in this section, "wisdom" is again used ironically here, because what Qohelet observes subverts traditional wisdom. The anecdote revolves around the proverb in v. 16, "Wisdom is better than might." This proverb reflects the theology of Proverbs particularly as articulated in Prov. 24:3–7: "Wise warriors are mightier than strong ones, and those who have knowledge than those who have strength; for by wise guidance you can wage your war, and in abundance of counselors there is victory" (vv. 5–6 NRSV). However, what Qohelet observed contradicts this perspective.

¹³This also I observed in relation to wisdom under the sun, and it made a great impression on me:
¹⁴There was a small city and a few people in it. And a great king came against it, and he surrounded it and built huge nets against it.
¹⁵But there was a wise commoner in it, and he delivered the city by his wisdom. But no one paid attention to that commoner.
¹⁶And I said, "Wisdom is better than might," but the wisdom of the commoner was despised, and his words were not listened to.

9:13–16. Qohelet observed a small city with few citizens. But a king used his power to lay siege to this city. Qohelet's use of "nets" as an evocative metaphor for the siegeworks refers back to v. 12. This was indeed a case of evil suddenly befalling the city. Verse 15a would appear to confirm that wisdom is better than might. The wisdom of a commoner enabled the city to be rescued from

7. The Hebrew reads lit. "The words of the wise in stillness are listened to." It is unclear whether the words of the wise are spoken "in stillness" or whether they are heard "in stillness." In terms of the parallelism in this verse, the contrast is between the calm words of the wise and the shouts of a ruler, and thus I opt for reading "in stillness" as a reference to "the words."

8. This phrase may be deliberately ambiguous; it could mean "a ruler of fools" or "a ruler among fools."

9. Literally "much," but Longman's (*Ecclesiastes*, 236) translation, "a whole lot of," is more evocative.

the overwhelming power launched against it.[10] However, three things subvert that view: the commoner was not attended to, presumably after the delivery of the city (v. 15); his wisdom was despised; and his words were ignored (v. 16).

This tragic anecdote is comparable to that in 4:13–16, which also deals with wisdom and leadership. As the poor though wise youth became king but was later opposed by the populace in 4:13–16, so here a commoner delivers the city against all odds but is then ignored and, even worse, despised. So although wisdom might appear to be better than might, what value is it if wisdom is ignored and rejected as soon as the crisis is over?

> [17]The calm words of the wise are better listened to than the shouting
> of a ruler among fools.
> [18]Wisdom is better than weapons of war, but one sinner destroys a
> whole lot of good.

9:17–18. Verses 17–18 extend this line of reasoning.[11] Verse 17 is another proverb: the calm words of the wise are better than the shouting of a ruler among fools. Once again this resonates with Proverbs: "One who is calm in spirit has understanding" (17:27b). With wisdom goes a calmness in teaching, and this is infinitely better than the raging of a ruler among fools. Furthermore, according to Proverbs, the wise ruler is open to instruction, unlike this raging fool. The ruler among (or of) fools probably evokes the ruler of the city in v. 14. Verse 18a is a "better-than" proverb: wisdom is better than the instruments of war. This is synonymous with the earlier proverb: wisdom is better than might. The anecdote just described would appear to confirm this. The powerful king came with his instruments of war, his "nets," against the city, but the wisdom of the commoner triumphed over that power. As often with Qohelet, however, there is a stinger in the tail: one sinner destroys a whole lot of good. The sinner is the ruler of fools who ruled over the city delivered by wisdom. His failure to attend to the wisdom that rescued his city subverts for Qohelet the value of wisdom. No wonder Qohelet notes in v. 13 that this occurrence made a great impression on him. Wisdom would appear to be better than might, but from observation he knows that reality is not so straightforward; the value of wisdom can be destroyed by one sinner. What then, he might ask, is the value of "wisdom"?

10. It may be that this anecdote recalls the story of the rebellion of Sheba in 2 Sam. 20. Sheba sets himself against David, and David's forces pursue Sheba to the city of Abel of Beth-maacah, where they besiege the city. A wise woman speaks to Joab and delivers the city by her wisdom, but we are not told how the woman was viewed after the deliverance.

11. Ogden ("Qohelet IX 17–X 20," 31) argues that 9:17–18 is not closely linked with what precedes and that it moves the discussion in a new direction that is continued in chap. 10. As is apparent from my interpretation, however, I see 9:17–18 as closely linked with 9:13–16. This is not to deny the links between this section and what follows; as is often the case with Qohelet, it is difficult to determine section breaks with precision.

Theological Implications

This concluding section of chap. 9 is fraught with irony. Qohelet tells a story of what he observed as an example of "wisdom," but it turns out to be an example of why "wisdom" has no value. Strongly to the fore in this section is the shortcoming of Qohelet's autonomous epistemology—it cannot deal with what Gladson calls retributive paradox, which occurs in all strands of OT literature, not least in Proverbs.[12] Retributive paradox is the recognition that reality does not always fit with the act-consequence structure, so that experience often creates a paradox. Qohelet's anecdote is an excellent example of this. The city's dealing with the commoner is a paradox. In the context of Qohelet's epistemology, however, such a paradox is not just a paradox but fatally subverts the wisdom enterprise. This is in danger of reading the character-consequence structure mechanically—any exception and the whole house collapses.

Taken as a whole, however, Proverbs by no means presents a mechanical character-consequence understanding of retribution. This has been clearly demonstrated in an excellent article on wealth and poverty in Proverbs by Van Leeuwen.[13] He points out that there are large groups of sayings in Proverbs that assert a simple cause and effect relationship whereby righteousness leads to wealth and wickedness to poverty. These are examples of the "character-consequence nexus." However, they do not concern concrete, individual acts and their consequences: "It is the long-term character and direction of a person or group (as 'righteous' or 'wicked') which determines life consequences and 'destiny.'"[14] It is a failure to recognize this long-term character that leads scholars to the mechanical view of retribution in Ecclesiastes.

> These proverbs, when taken by themselves, are the basis for the view of some scholars that the tidy dogmatism of Proverbs does not correspond to reality and is doomed to collapse under the weight of reality, as happened in Job and Qoheleth. Since the foregoing sayings are not always exemplified in human experience, their falsification presumably led to a crisis of faith in Yahweh's maintenance of a just world order.[15]

However, proverbs are by their very nature partial utterances, and this type of mechanical approach does not do justice to the many sayings in Proverbs that manifest a more complex understanding of the way God works in creation. Particularly noteworthy in this respect are the "better-than" sayings in Proverbs (cf. 15:16–17; 16:16, 19; etc.). The overall picture is far more complex, as Van

---

12. Gladson, "Retributive Paradoxes in Prov. 10–29."
13. Van Leeuwen, "Wealth and Poverty," 25–36.
14. Ibid., 27; cf. Fox, *Qohelet*, 132–33.
15. Van Leeuwen, "Wealth and Poverty," 28–29.

Leeuwen notes: *"In general*, the sages clearly believed that wise and righteous behavior did make life better and richer, though virtue did not *guarantee* those consequences. . . . General patterns may be discerned, but many particular events may be unjust, irrational, and ultimately inscrutable."[16]

Van Leeuwen also notes that there *is* a future-oriented retribution perspective in Proverbs. Proverbs lacks a doctrine of resurrection and yet insists on the triumph of God's justice. Van Leeuwen regards this as a hallmark of Yahwistic faith. "The sages' stance is to maintain faith in God's justice, even when they personally cannot see it or touch it, even when the recorded past does not verify it. Here religion provides no escape from the pain or absurdities of existence. The book of Job was inevitable, not because Proverbs was too simplistic, but because life's inequities, as reflected in Proverbs, drive faith to argue with the Deity."[17]

Clearly Qohelet's autonomous methodology demands an empirical certainty that traditional wisdom was well aware that it could not provide. Consequently, rather than Qohelet representing a crisis in wisdom, he should be seen as focusing on the retributive paradox that Proverbs is aware of and subsumes under its more general, long-term, character-consequence understanding. Because Qohelet's epistemology is based on observation and reason alone, however, he moves in the direction of deconstructing the tradition by focusing on the individual exceptions.

Theologically, therefore, this section is important in foregrounding the limits of Qohelet's autonomous epistemology for real life in a good but fallen world—it has no resources for coping with the retributive paradoxes regularly encountered in life. Qohelet's bucket with which he collects his data is full of holes, and it will need to be broken open to take account of larger realities if any resolution to his search is to emerge.

Once again this should not detract from his perceptive analysis of the mystery and pain of retributive paradoxes, of which our contemporary world is full. When the wise are despised and their contribution ignored it is painful and fraught with mystery and enigma—indeed, often incomprehensible. "Even when wisdom is available society tends to disdain it, thereby assuring its own destruction!"[18] However, it is increasingly clear that Qohelet's epistemology does not have the resources for living such paradoxes.

16. Ibid., 32–33. The fuller quote appears in my introduction under "Reading Ecclesiastes within the Context of Proverbs and Job and Its Connection to the Torah."

17. Ibid., 34.

18. Levine, "Humor in Qohelet," 77.

S.
Wisdom, Folly, and Rulers
(10:1-20)

Translation

[1]Dead flies[1] make the perfumer's oil stink and ferment;[2] a little folly is more precious[3] than wisdom and[4] honor.
[2]The heart of a wise person inclines[5] to the right, but the heart of a fool to one's left.

1. The nature of the genitive in *zĕbûbê māwet* (flies of death) has occasioned much debate. The expression could refer to flies of death, meaning poisonous flies (LXX; Tg; Delitzsch, *Ecclesiastes*, 371; C. H. Wright, *Koheleth*, 417) or doomed flies (cf. 2 Sam. 12:5). However, neither of these translations makes sense here, and the genitive should be taken as merely indicating flies that have died in the ointment. Seow (*Ecclesiastes*, 311) insists that *zĕbûbê māwet* cannot have this meaning but should be translated as "a fly that dies." The significance for translation is minimal.

2. *Yabbîaʿ* (ferment) is problematic on two accounts. First, there is no "and" in the Hebrew between "stink" and "ferment." Thus most versions add a conjunction between the two verbs. An asyndeton is assumed: "makes the perfumer's oil stink (and) ferment." Second, *yabbîaʿ* is generally related to the root *nbʿ* (to bubble and, secondarily, to ferment). However, the existence of the verb *nbʿ* in Hebrew is questionable (Seow, *Ecclesiastes*, 312). Fox (*Qohelet*, 265) argues that "to bubble" makes no sense here, and he and Seow (*Ecclesiastes*, 306) argue from the LXX and Syr that the original text may have had *gābîaʿ* (vessel). Thus Seow translates, "A fly that dies causes <a bowl of> perfumer's oil to turn rancid." Contra Fox, "to bubble" and hence ferment would fit well in this context. Either way the meaning of the sentence is clear.

3. *Yāqār* is typically translated "rare" or "precious." Some scholars (e.g., Longman, *Ecclesiastes*, 238; Seow, *Ecclesiastes*, 306) argue that the meaning "heavy" or "weighty" (known in Aramaic) is more suitable in context. However, "precious" fits well in the context, playing as it does on the value of the perfumer's oil.

4. Another case of asyndeton, the conjunction has been added to make the English more readable.

5. There is no verb in this verse. Direction is implied.

³Even when the fool[6] walks along the road his heart is deficient, and he says to everyone he is a fool.

⁴If the ruler's temper[7] rises against you, do not leave your place. For composure will sate[8] great sins.

⁵There is an evil I observed under the sun, indeed,[9] an error that originates from the ruler.

⁶Folly[10] is placed in many[11] exalted places while the rich sit in lowly places.

⁷I observed slaves on horses but nobles walking on foot[12] like slaves.

⁸Whoever digs a pit[13] will[14] fall into it, and whoever breaks through a wall will be bitten by a snake.

⁹Whoever quarries stones may be injured by them, and whoever splits logs may be endangered[15] by them.

¹⁰If the ax is blunt[16] and one does not sharpen its edge,[17] then he must exert more strength, but the benefit of wisdom is to succeed.

6. The Ketib *kĕšehassākāl* seems unusual because it retains the definite article after the temporal *kĕ* and the relative pronoun *še*. However, whether one reads the Ketib or the Qere (no definite article: *kĕšessākāl*) makes no difference in meaning, and Crenshaw (*Ecclesiastes*, 170) asserts that the difference is euphonic.

7. *Rûaḥ* can mean "temper," and this meaning fits well here. Cf. Prov. 16:32.

8. *BHS* suggests an emendation of this verb to a form of *nwʾ* (to prevent). But this is unnecessary and detracts from the repetition of the root *nwḥ* ("leave" and "sate") as well as the wordplay with *rûaḥ*.

9. The *kaph* prefixed to the noun "error" is asseverative rather than comparative as in the NRSV.

10. *Hassekel* is a *hapax legomenon*. The MT vocalizes it as the abstract (folly) rather than the concrete "fool."

11. *Rabbîm* lacks the article, and thus some take it with the next clause and translate "the mighty and the rich." However, with most I take it as modifying "exalted places." The absence of the definite article may be a feature of Late Hebrew (Seow, *Ecclesiastes*, 315).

12. Literally "on the ground."

13. *Gûmāṣ* is a *hapax legomenon*. It is probably an Aramaic loanword (Wagner, *Aramäismen*, 52).

14. According to Longman (*Ecclesiastes*, 243) and most other commentators, the use of the imperfect form of the verb twice in this verse indicates potentiality (GKC §107r). Delitzsch (*Ecclesiastes*, 378) notes, "The futures are not the expression of that which will necessarily take place, for, thus rendered, these four statements would be contrary to experience; they are the expression of a possibility." However, the motif of digging a pit and falling into it is a common one in Proverbs and Psalms, and in my opinion "will" is the most appropriate translation in v. 8, though "may" fits better in v. 9. See the interpretation.

15. This is the only use of the Niphal of *skn* in the OT, but its use is well attested in Postbiblical Hebrew and Aramaic (Jastrow, *Dictionary*, 991).

16. The verb *qēhâ* occurs in Jer. 31:29–30 and Ezek. 18:2, where it means "to numb"; it occurs only here in the Piel and means "to be blunt." It is transitive but should be understood impersonally, or taken to be the adjective *qēheh* (dull, blunt), "a form widely attested in Postbiblical Hebrew for iron implements" (Seow, *Ecclesiastes*, 317).

17. Taking *pānîm* (face) to refer to the edge of the ax (cf. Ezek. 21:16 [21]). However, the edge is normally referred to with the word *peh* (mouth). The dominant alternative, proposed

[11]If the snake bites before being charmed,[18] there is no benefit in having a charmer.[19]

[12]Words from the mouth of the wise person bring grace, but the lips of the fool swallow[20] him.

[13]The beginning of the words of his mouth is folly, but the end of (the words of)[21] his mouth is evil madness.

[14]But the fool talks on and on. No one knows what is to happen,[22] and who can tell anyone what will come after him?

[15]The labor of fools wearies them,[23] for[24] he does not know how to get to the city.

[16]Woe[25] to you, O land,[26] whose king is a lad[27] and whose leaders feast in the morning.

[17]Blessed are you, O land, whose king is of nobility and whose leaders eat at the proper time—for strength and not in order to get drunk.[28]

[18]Through sloth[29] the roof sags, and due to inactivity[30] the house leaks.[31]

---

at least since Jerome, is to treat *pānîm* adverbially as *lĕpānîm* (beforehand). See, for example, Seow, *Ecclesiastes*, 317.

18. The Hebrew can be read in two ways: the masoretic punctuation assumes that the snake bites before it is charmed. However, it is also possible to read *bĕlô'-lāḥaš* (without charm) as referring to the snake as one for which no charm is effective (see Seow, *Ecclesiastes*, 318). I have followed the masoretic punctuation, but see the interpretation.

19. Literally "the master of the tongue."

20. The subject "lips" is plural, whereas the verb is singular. Perhaps "lips" are equated with "mouth." See Whitley, *Koheleth*, 86; GKC §145n. On the meaning of the verb "swallow," see Guillaume, "Note on *bl'*."

21. The words in parentheses are not in the Hebrew but are understood by ellipsis.

22. Some Hebrew MSS, LXX, Symm, Peshitta, Syro-Hexapla, and Vg read "what has happened," apparently considering the future reference redundant in light of the following phrase.

23. The syntax is difficult at this point. First, the verb is feminine, whereas "labor" is masculine. Second, "fools" is plural, but the object suffix attached to the verb is singular. Some emend the verb to the masculine form, but there is biblical precedent for a lack of gender concord (Whitley, *Koheleth*, 87). "Labor" could, however, be treated as a feminine noun (BDB 765). Regarding the difference in number, it is best to take the object suffix as distributive; see Ginsburg, *Coheleth*, 440; Whybray, *Ecclesiastes* (NCBC), 156; Seow, *Ecclesiastes*, 320.

24. The *'ăšer* is causal here.

25. On *'îy*, a shortened form of the word "woe," see 4:10.

26. The LXX and Syr have "city" for "land" here.

27. *Nā'ar* may mean "servant" or "youth, lad."

28. *Šĕtî* is a *hapax legomenon*, but it is a variant of *šĕtîyâ*, found in Esther 1:8, and is common in Postbiblical Hebrew.

29. *'Ăṣaltayim* is a *hapax legomenon*, apparently a dual form of the adjective used as a substantive (see GKC §88b). Some propose emending the text. Others argue that we have here a duality of intentionality, implying intense laziness. Others (e.g., Seow, *Ecclesiastes*, 331; and Longman, *Ecclesiastes*, 251, whom I follow here) argue that the duality anticipates the dual hands in the second colon. See note 30.

30. Literally "sinking of hands."

31. *Yidlōp* is generally taken to mean "drip" and hence "leak." Because *ydlp* in Ugaritic occurs in the same semantic context as *ymk* (collapsed), some suggest that *yidlōp* here may

¹⁹One makes[32] bread for laughter, and wine gladdens the living, but
money answers[33] everything!
²⁰Furthermore, do not curse the king even in your thoughts;[34]
do not curse the rich even in your bedroom,
for a bird of the heavens may[35] carry your voice,
or some winged creature[36] may tell of the matter.

Interpretation

A theme that connects back into chap. 9 and extends through this chapter
is that of the king and government.[37] Verses 4–5 and 16–20 all deal with the
king in one way or another. This chapter lacks any *carpe diem* emphasis and is
typical of much of what we have seen in the previous chapter; Qohelet begins
with traditional wisdom akin to that in Proverbs but then gives it an ironic twist
that subverts the traditional approach. In the process he articulates a different
doctrine of two ways according to which money answers everything.

¹Dead flies make the perfumer's oil stink and ferment; a little folly is
more precious than wisdom and honor.

10:1. The proverb of v. 1 connects back to 9:18b, but also anticipates the
havoc wrought by folly later in this section. In 9:18b Qohelet states that one
sinner destroys much good. Here Qohelet illustrates this by noting that small
though flies may be, they can ruin precious ointment by making what is designed to smell beautiful stink and ferment. In the Hebrew there is no "and"

have a similar meaning. See Moran, "Note on Ps. 119:28," 10; and Greenfield, "Lexicographical Notes I," 208–9.

32. "Makes" is a participle without a subject. See GKC §116t.

33. *Ya'ăneh* may be Qal or Hiphil. LXX and Vg assume Qal, meaning "to answer, respond."
Syriac takes the verb to mean "afflict." The Hiphil means "to preoccupy," which Seow (*Ecclesiastes*, 332–33) supports. But in context, "answers" is by far the best translation. See the
interpretation.

34. *Maddā'* (thought) usually means "knowledge" and is generally taken by extension to
mean "thought." "Knowledge" in the OT may have sexual connotations, and Seow (*Ecclesiastes*,
333) thinks this may be the case here. Hence he translates it as "intimacy." Verse 20 is in parallel
verse form, and "intimacy" would appropriately parallel "bedroom." See Longman (*Ecclesiastes*,
252–53) for five alternative readings aimed at securing parallelism that overlaps in meaning.
However, this is to mistake how parallelism works, and all the ancient versions translate within
the semantic range of "knowledge" and "thought," and "bedroom" in the second line need not
have sexual connotations but merely suggests privacy.

35. See note 14.

36. Literally "lord [or master] of wings." The reference could be to a bird or an insect.

37. See Ogden ("Qoheleth IX 17–X 20") for an overview of the different views of the parameters of this section. Ogden argues that 9:17 moves the discussion in a new direction and that
9:17–10:20 contains a set of variations dealing with the vulnerability of wisdom.

between "stink" and "ferment"; an asyndeton is assumed. Perhaps the point is that by causing fermentation in the oil the flies result in the perfume giving off an awful odor rather than its intended perfume. "Dead flies" could also mean "poisonous flies," which opens the possibility that the fermented perfume may even become toxic. The point is that it takes just one rotten apple to ruin a barrel. Qohelet's proverb is in line with traditional wisdom. One is reminded of proverbs like that in Prov. 26:9: "Like a thorn that goes up into the hand of a drunkard is a proverb in the mouth of a fool." Small though a thorn may be, it can cause serious damage when mishandled.

However, Qohelet immediately subverts the traditional wisdom expressed in his proverb. Thus just a little folly is more "precious" than wisdom. Some scholars prefer to translate *yāqār* (precious) as "weighty." However, "precious" is the more common meaning, and it fits with Qohelet's irony—from the perspective of the owner of the perfume, a few dead flies *are* more valuable than wisdom in that they destroy one's precious ointment. Whereas one might have expected Qohelet to use his proverb to warn against even a little folly, he focuses on the vulnerability of wisdom: wisdom is exceedingly vulnerable to folly, and for Qohelet this makes its value questionable.

> ²The heart of a wise person inclines to the right, but the heart of a fool to one's left.
> ³Even when the fool walks along the road his heart is deficient, and he says to everyone he is a fool.

10:2–3. Verses 2 and 3 revert to articulating the perspective of traditional wisdom. Verse 2 depicts a theme that is fundamental to wisdom, that of the two ways. Here Qohelet notes that the heart of the fool inclines in a different direction from that of the wise person. The main point is that their *heart* directions are antithetical, "heart" being the wisdom expression for the core of a person. "Left" and "right" may also have ethical connotations, with "right" signifying what is good and "left" indicating what is bad (cf. Gen. 48:12–20; Matt. 25:31–46). In Jon. 4:11 the citizens of Nineveh are said to be incapable of distinguishing their left hand from their right; that is, they were unable to discern right from wrong.

The direction of the heart inevitably manifests itself in a person's lifestyle, and in v. 3 Qohelet points out that the folly of the fool is indeed manifest in his lifestyle. "Walks along the road" may be both literal and metaphorical. Psalm 1:1 notes the blessedness of the person who does not walk in the path of sinners, clearly using walking as a metaphor for the lifestyle of the person. The point is that the fool cannot hide the inclination of his heart. It is interesting to note here too that Qohelet describes folly as a deficiency of the heart; in other words folly amounts to something lacking in the human heart. From Proverbs we may assume this to be the fear of the LORD, and v. 3 intriguingly implies that the human heart is not whole without this fear. The description of the fool saying to everyone he is a fool may mean that by his behavior and/or speech he shows himself to be a fool; alternatively it could refer to his calling everyone else a fool. Perhaps the ambiguity is intentional—one of the ways in which the fool manifests his folly is by regarding everyone except himself as a fool.

> ⁴If the ruler's temper rises against you, do not leave your place. For composure will sate great sins.

10:4. Verse 4 is typical of the advice of traditional wisdom. Proverbs 16:14 says, "The rage of a king is a messenger of death, and whoever is wise will appease it." Here in v. 4 there is a wordplay between "temper" (*rûaḥ*), "leave" (*tannaḥ*), and "sate" (*yannîaḥ*). Contrary to 8:2–3, which envisages the king's power as absolute and encourages one to flee his presence, Qohelet here, in line with traditional wisdom, envisages that the wisdom of composure will cause the ruler's anger to abate. The "ruler" probably refers to someone of lesser authority than the king, but the same advice applies. This advice, which is very similar to traditional wisdom, is subverted, however, in what follows, as Qohelet reflects on his observation of political rule.

> ⁵There is an evil I observed under the sun, indeed, an error that origi-
> nates from the ruler.
> ⁶Folly is placed in many exalted places while the rich sit in lowly
> places.
> ⁷I observed slaves on horses but nobles walking on foot like slaves.

10:5–7. Once again it is *observation* that deconstructs traditional wisdom for Qohelet: "There is an evil I observed" (v. 5). The source of the "error" is none other than the ruler. In vv. 5–7 he relates his observation: as a result of an "error" by a ruler, fools are elevated to high positions and the rich are demoted. In the Priestly literature *šĕgāgâ* (error) is used for a sin of inadvertence (cf. Lev. 5:18). Its opposite in that context is a sin of intention. If we can assume that meaning here, then "inadvertently" (perhaps Qohelet is deliberately ironic) a ruler allows the world to be turned upside down. This is imaginatively evoked in vv. 6 and 7: folly—here personified (v. 6)—is placed in exalted positions while the rich, the elite, sit in lowly places. Slaves ride on horses while princes walk on foot like slaves. Horses were costly and were used mainly for military purposes or to carry nobles and kings, but here slaves ride on them.

Commenting on Prov. 30:21–23, Van Leeuwen notes that "it is an instance of the world upside down, a pattern of inversion or chaos that is found throughout the world from ancient times to the present."³⁸ Qohelet envisages a similar

---

38. Van Leeuwen, "Proverbs," 254. See also idem, "Proverbs 30:21–23."

chaotic situation in vv. 6 and 7. In context, the point is that if folly is reigning, then the wisdom of v. 4 will not work. Here Qohelet's pair of opposites is no longer wise person and fool as in v. 2 but folly versus the rich and slaves versus princes. Wealth is a major concern of Qohelet, and here it subtly creeps in as a synonym for wisdom. Verse 19 confirms this false identification. Seow asserts, "Wealth is really not the issue, but the presumed status of these people. The rich are expected to be in the ruling class."[39] But this is to miss an important twist in Qohelet's thinking, as we will see below. It may well be that the wealthy are expected to rule, but in Proverbs it is by wisdom and not by wealth that rulers rule (cf. Prov. 8:16).

> [8]Whoever digs a pit will fall into it, and whoever breaks through a wall will be bitten by a snake.
> [9]Whoever quarries stones may be injured by them, and whoever splits logs may be endangered by them.

10:8–9. Verses 8 and 9 focus on the problem Qohelet discerns with the character-consequence structure in traditional wisdom, a continuation of what he has been discussing. Most scholars take the imperfects of the verbs in vv. 8 and 9 to be perfects of potentiality and translate them all as "may" rather than "will." If we translate the verbs as "may," then Qohelet's only concern in these verses is the accidental happenings of life. However, the image of v. 8a occurs elsewhere in Proverbs and Psalms as "the parade example of the act-consequence view of retribution advocated by K. Koch: the evil-doer will/should fall by the very evil that is perpetrated; wrongdoing is essentially corruptive for the wrong-doer, because it comes back upon him."[40] Proverbs 26:27 states, "Whoever digs a pit will fall into it, and a stone will come back on the one who starts it rolling" (NRSV). A similar motif is found in Pss. 7:15–16 [16–17]; 9:15–16 [16–17]; 35:7–8; 57:6 [7]. The commonality of this motif inclines me toward the view that in v. 8 Qohelet is using a common image to express the character-consequence structure of traditional wisdom. As in the other places where this motif is used, digging a pit is a metaphor for evildoing aimed at other humans. Similarly, breaking through a wall should be taken in parallel as a further example of evildoing, in this case breaking and entering in order to steal. A strong reading of the character-consequence structure in Proverbs would expect evildoers to get their just deserts; thus the one who digs a pit *will* fall into it, and the one who breaks and enters *will* be bitten by a snake (the mortar used for building walls in Israel would be ready homes for snakes when it chipped away and left crevices).

Of course, Qohelet knows that this does not always happen, and in v. 9 he moves on to accidental happenings in which the act-consequence structure

39. Seow, *Ecclesiastes*, 315.
40. Murphy, *Ecclesiastes*, 101–2.

Nobody falls on purpose

appears to have no bearing at all. In v. 9 it is therefore appropriate to translate the imperfects as "may." Qohelet gives two examples of accidental happenings; one may be injured while quarrying stones, and one may be injured in a variety of ways while splitting logs (cf. Deut. 19:5). Qohelet does not comment further on these examples, but we know him well enough by now to know what he is thinking. His epistemology is such that it just takes one unpredictable, uncontrollable accident to shatter traditional wisdom. Any such accident means that life is unpredictable, an enigma.

> [10]If the ax is blunt and one does not sharpen its edge, then he must exert more strength, but the benefit of wisdom is to succeed.
> [11]If the snake bites before being charmed, there is no benefit in having a charmer.

10:10–11. Verse 10 extends the image of the person splitting logs: if one's ax is blunt, it is wise to sharpen it immediately, otherwise one has to exert much more strength to split logs. Thus wisdom brings success. However, this traditional wisdom is subverted by v. 9 and what follows. If one can endanger oneself by splitting logs, it may be better to have a blunt ax than to have a sharp one. This subversion is given a further ironic twist by evoking an image that emphasizes the limits of wisdom in v. 11: What use is a snake charmer if the snake bites before it is charmed or if it bites the owner of the charmer?[41] "Formulated with 'biting' irony, v. 11 demonstrates that even the practical knowledge and skills of the expert do not totally eliminate dangers or guarantee success."[42]

> [12]Words from the mouth of the wise person bring grace, but the lips of the fool swallow him.
> [13]The beginning of the words of his mouth is folly, but the end of (the words of) his mouth is evil madness.
> [14]But the fool talks on and on. No one knows what is to happen, and who can tell anyone what will come after him?
> [15]The labor of fools wearies them, for he does not know how to get to the city.

10:12–15. As with vv. 1–3, 8, and 18, vv. 12–15 express the traditional view of wisdom, but with an ironic twist. Verses 12–15 reflect on the speech of fools in line with the traditional wisdom of Proverbs,[43] thereby affirming the act-consequence structure. Speech is a major theme in Proverbs. The speech of the wise brings grace (v. 12a). This pithy saying is ambiguous in that it could

41. Verse 11 can be read in either way. On snake charming in the ancient Near East, see Astour, "Two Ugaritic Serpent Charms."
42. Krüger, *Qoheleth*, 186.
43. See Bartholomew, *Reading Proverbs with Integrity*, 13–14.

mean either that the result of the speech of the wise is grace or that the wise achieve grace by their speech (cf. Prov. 14:3). Possibly it means both: through their speech the wise mediate grace to others, and in the process that grace rebounds upon them. In terms of the parallelism with v. 12b the emphasis is more likely on winning grace. In contrast to the wise, the speech of a fool brings destruction: the fool is swallowed up by his lips.

Verse 13 elaborates on this by explaining that folly never stands still; it develops and deteriorates. The speech of the fool begins with folly but ends in wicked madness—it has devastating consequences. Nevertheless, the fool just keeps talking (v. 14a). Verse 14b, however, gives this affirmation of traditional wisdom an ironic twist: no one knows what is to come, thus we cannot even be sure that the consequences of folly will eventuate. Once again the character-consequence structure of Proverbs, which flows from the antithesis of two ways, is brought into question. Verse 15, however, further evokes the problem with folly: the fool's labor is wearisome because the fool does not even know the way to the city, where, presumably, he works, and thus he exerts far more energy than is necessary in his labor. As Seow notes, "This verse may provide some clue as to the extent of urbanization in Palestine during Qohelet's time. In an urbanized society, the city is the center of commercial and social intercourse. The way to the city is, therefore, common knowledge; everyone except the most stupid and incompetent knows the way to town."[44]

> ¹⁶Woe to you, O land, whose king is a lad and whose leaders feast in
>   the morning.
> ¹⁷Blessed are you, O land, whose king is of nobility and whose leaders
>   eat at the proper time—for strength and not in order to get drunk.
> ¹⁸Through sloth the roof sags, and due to inactivity the house leaks.
> ¹⁹One makes bread for laughter, and wine gladdens the living, but
>   money answers everything!
> ²⁰Furthermore, do not curse the king even in your thoughts;
>   do not curse the rich even in your bedroom,
> for a bird of the heavens may carry your voice,
>   or some winged creature may tell of the matter.

10:16–20. Verses 16–20 reflect on the advantage of good leadership, a theme common in traditional wisdom. It is terrible for a land to be ruled by an immature king and to have leaders who feast in the morning when they should be governing. *Nāʿar* (lad) can mean "youth" or "servant." The contrast with a king of nobility in v. 17 has suggested to many that "servant" is the right translation here. However, in 1 Kings 3:7 Solomon marvels that he has been made king, even though only a *nāʿar*, who does not know how to go out or to come in. Hence I retain the translation "lad." Either way the point is

---

44. Seow, *Ecclesiastes*, 320.

that it is disastrous to have a king who is immature and has no idea how to govern. The result is that the leaders feast in the morning rather than attending to the business of governance. The "Woe" at the start of v. 16 indicates just how disastrous such government can be for a nation. Isaiah 5:11–13 and 21:5 critique this sort of behavior, and it is also the type of behavior Prov. 31:4–9 condemns. By contrast, the land is blessed whose king is a noble and thus well initiated into governance and whose leaders eat at the right time and in order to gain strength to govern rather than to get drunk. This has the ring of traditional wisdom about it, but the insistence that the king should be a noble, one of the wealthy elite, may hark back to Qohelet's false antithesis of folly and riches in v. 6. This is likely in light of 4:13, where Qohelet affirms that a poor but wise youth (*yeled*) is better than an old, rich king.

Verse 18 is a proverb in accord with traditional wisdom: sloth and inactivity have bad consequences. Many proverbs address this issue (cf. Prov. 6:6–11; 10:26; 13:4; 15:19; 19:24; 20:4; 21:25; 22:13; 24:30–34; 26:13–16; etc.). The two lines in v. 18 express the same thought. In ancient Israel roofs were covered with lime, which cracked with time and thereby allowed rain to drip into the house. Maintenance was thus essential. Neglect of such maintenance would lead to the roof sagging and leaking; the wise person would be proactive in the maintenance of his house.

However, vv. 19 and 20 twist in another direction: bread and wine evoke feasting and remind us initially of the *carpe diem* passages, but the concluding phrase, "but money answers everything," gives the game away. As noted in the translation, Seow proposes that we translate *ya'ăneh* as "preoccupy," hence "And money preoccupies everyone."[45] However, the versions support "answer," and it makes the best sense in the context. As we saw in v. 6, Qohelet attempts in this chapter to position riches as the antithesis of folly, and here we see something of the result. It is money that enables one to feast, and if that is what life is about, then forget the importance of activity and hard work as expressed in the language of traditional wisdom in v. 18, and make money so that you can feast. Ironically, the leaders feasting early in the morning may not be so foolish after all, so that v. 19 subverts vv. 16–17.

Furthermore, if money answers everything, then at all costs one must remain in favor with the elite, and this is the subject addressed in v. 20. The king should not be cursed even in one's "thoughts." Some scholars wonder how an unspoken word could be overheard,[46] and this is one among other reasons why various emendations have been proposed for "thoughts" (see the translation note). Gordis supports "thoughts" and comments, "What is in a man's mind may emerge in sleep . . . or may otherwise be blurted out in an unguarded moment, as experience taught long before Freud's *Psychopathology*

45. Ibid., 328.
46. For example, Whybray, *Ecclesiastes* (NCBC), 158.

of Everyday Life supplied a theoretical explanation."[47] The hyperbole here is deliberate: because money answers everything, one must stay in favor with the king at all costs. In the OT, it is God who knows the inner workings of a person, but here there is an idolatry of wealth and position, so that even within one's thoughts one must not think evil of the king. Similarly with the bedroom; it stands for a place of privacy where one can usually just be oneself without worrying about what others think. But so important to happiness is one's relationship with the king that even here one must not say anything evil about him. As we might say, "walls have ears." The paranoia involved is evoked by the hyperbolic images of v. 20b. A bird or an insect might carry to the king what one thought or said.

Theological Implications

Throughout this chapter Qohelet states the character-consequence structure of traditional wisdom and then problematizes it. The problems of government emerge at the outset and conclusion of this section, and in the process the theme of wealth is foregrounded. His observations about rulers bring traditional wisdom into question. Verse 6 notes that he has observed fools ruling while *the rich* are placed in subjection to them. In vv. 16–20 he asserts the value of mature, wise kings whose leaders govern rather than engage in drunken revelry, but then subverts this through his point that *money* answers everything.

The theme of government and oppression is not a new one in Ecclesiastes, and the reader should consult the other chapters where I have discussed these topics in detail. Suffice it here to note that this chapter is illuminating in terms of *the two ways* of Wisdom literature. The biblical doctrine of two ways is presented most clearly in the OT in Pss. 1–2,[48] the introduction to the Psalter. In Ps. 1 the blessedness of the person whose delight is in the law of the LORD is contrasted with the destiny of the wicked (plural). Verse 6 notes that the way of the wicked will perish, but the LORD watches over the way of the righteous—hence two ways. In Ps. 2 the scene shifts from the individual Israelite to heaven and the nations. Yahweh is on the throne and he laughs at his competitors. P. Miller notes, "If we have moved from a way the individual should walk to the rule of nations and empires, it is still the way of the Lord and the Lord's rule."[49] The image of the two ways is thus comprehensive, applying as much to nations and institutions as to individuals. In terms of Qohelet and his observations of the abuse of power, Miller's comments on

---

47. Gordis, *Koheleth*, 329.
48. In Jesus's teaching, it is most clear in his conclusion to the Sermon on the Mount (see Matt. 7:24–27).
49. P. Miller, *Interpreting the Psalms*, 91.

Ps. 2 are apposite: "In a strange way it is one of the most assuring sounds of the whole Psalter as it relativizes even the largest of human claims for ultimate control over the affairs of peoples and nations. The fiercest terror is made the object of laughter and derision and thus is rendered impotent to frighten those who hear the laughter of God in the background."[50]

This doctrine of two ways is also central to Proverbs, with its two ways, women, and houses. Van Leeuwen has analyzed the root metaphors of Prov. 1–9 and argues persuasively that

> underlying the bipolar metaphorical system of positive and negative youths, invitations/calls, "ways," "women," and "houses" in Proverbs 1–9, is a yet more fundamental reality which these images together portray. These chapters depict the world as the arena of human existence. This world possesses two fundamental characteristics. First is its structure of boundaries or limits. Second is the bipolar human *eros* for the beauty of Wisdom, who prescribes life within limits, or for the seeming beauty of Folly, who offers bogus delights in defiance of created limits.[51]

Van Leeuwen argues that the worldview that Proverbs exhibits is a "carved" one in that "cultural and personal exhortation is grounded in the reality of the created world with its inbuilt normativity."[52] Justice and righteousness are built into the world.

Qohelet's epistemology, as we have seen time and again, problematizes the doctrine of the two ways. In this chapter he asserts it clearly in vv. 2, 8, 12–15, and 16–18 but subverts it in the rest of the chapter as a result of his observation of folly ruling, accidental happenings, and the view that wealth answers everything. His epistemology leads him to regard any exception to the general character-consequence principle as subverting it, although as noted in discussing the theological implications of 9:13–18, the book of Proverbs is well aware of such exceptions or paradoxes. What is intriguing in this chapter is that abandonment of the biblical doctrine of the two ways always generates another two ways.

In this chapter Qohelet's subversion of v. 2, a clear, pithy statement of the doctrine of the two ways, clears the way for a *very different* two ways to appear. Thus in v. 6 the contrast is not between folly and wisdom but between folly and *the rich*. In v. 7 slaves are compared to nobles, the elite. In v. 19 this emphasis on riches in comparison with folly is capped with his statement that "money answers everything." The result is certainly a doctrine of two ways but one very different from that of Proverbs. Now we have folly versus riches,

50. Ibid., 90.
51. Van Leeuwen, "Liminality," 116. See also the theological implications section for 9:13–18.
52. Ibid., 118.

and the latter becomes associated with the king and his elite so that whatever happens one must not even think an evil thought about the king (v. 20).

Theologically, the point is that two ways are unavoidable, but sinners try to reconstrue them to their advantage. In God's world humans inevitably adopt some doctrine of two ways. I will start with some academic examples of this and then follow them with some more down-to-earth examples.

The academic examples come from *philosophy and literary theory*. It is instructive to compare the writings of the postmodern philosopher Jacques Derrida, who has a strong doctrine of two ways, but again one at variance with the biblical picture. At the end of "Structure, Sign and Play," Derrida distinguishes between two interpretations of interpretation.[53] The first, in the tradition of the metaphysics of presence, deciphers the text in search of its true meaning. The second, in good Nietzschean fashion, sets the text in play. Derrida's straightforward reading of Gen. 22 in *The Gift of Death* is a good example of the first interpretation of interpretation. There is nothing unusual about this reading—authorial intention could be said to be firmly in place as a guardrail guiding Derrida's reading of the text.[54] It is Derrida's contemporary application of the reading that is most unusual and disturbing—the extraordinary call of God to Abraham: "Take your son, your only son, Isaac, whom you love . . . and offer him," is secularized into a paradigm for the daily call of our neighbors upon ourselves.

Derrida's performative reading of the Tower of Babel narrative (Gen. 11:1–9) is a good example of his second interpretation of interpretation, of setting a text in play.[55] Suffice it here to note that Derrida uses a French translation whereby the text is read as God invoking God's name "Babel" over the city. This marginally possible—but completely unacceptable—reading is telling in terms of Derrida's philosophy of language.

In his discussion of deconstruction, George Steiner boldly asserts that deconstruction confronts us with a stark choice of two ways:

> It is Derrida's strength to have seen so plainly that the issue is neither linguistic-aesthetic nor philosophical in any traditional, debatable sense—where such tradition and debate incorporate, perpetuate the very ghosts which are to be exorcized. The issue is, quite simply, that of the meaning of meaning as it is re-insured by the postulate of the existence of God. "In the beginning was the Word." There was no such beginning, says deconstruction; only the play of sounds and markers amid the mutations of time.[56]

53. Derrida, "Structure, Sign and Play," 292–93.
54. I allude here to Derrida's statement about authorial intention in *Of Grammatology*, 158.
55. See Bartholomew, "Babel and Derrida."
56. Steiner, *Real Presences*, 120.

There are a variety of types of deconstruction, helpfully distinguishable as "soft" and "boa" deconstructors.[57] J. H. Miller and Harold Bloom are examples of the former and Derrida the embodiment of the latter. Intriguingly, all of these deconstructors have in common a doctrine of "the two ways" when it comes to reading texts.[58] Bloom asserts that the "praxis of poetry" requires one of two views of language: a magical theory that credits language with plenitude of meaning or a nihilistic view that discerns a lack of meaning and randomness in language. He goes on to say:

> All I ask is that the theory of language be extreme and uncompromising enough. Theory of poetry, as I pursue it, is reconcilable with either extreme view of poetic language, though not with any views in between. Either the new poet fights to win freedom from dearth, or from plenitude, but if the antagonist be moderate, then the agon will not take place, and no fresh sublimity will be won. Only the agon is of the essence.[59]

Similarly, Miller describes the two extremes in theory of language as a reciprocal relationship in which nihilism is present always as a latent ghost encrypted in the logocentric system. The two ways are not antithetical, nor may they be synthesized: "Each defines and is hospitable to the other, host to it as parasite."[60]

Derrida's view of interpretation is also constructed around two ways, and this manifests itself in a variety of ways. I have already noted the two interpretations of interpretation, deciphering a text and setting it in play. This is paralleled in his discussion of Jabès and the book in his typology of the rabbi and the poet.[61] Derrida's distinction between the rabbi and the poet symbolizes the two types of interpretation.[62] "The 'rabbinical' interpretation of interpretation is the one which seeks a final truth, which sees interpretation as an unfortunately necessary road back to an original truth. The 'poetical' interpretation of interpretation does not seek truth or origin, but affirms the play of interpretation."[63] Derrida explains:

> Between the fragments of the broken Tables the poem grows and the right to speech takes root. Once more begins the adventure of the text as weed, as outlaw far from *"the fatherland of the Jews,"* which is a *"sacred text surrounded by*

57. I am conflating two typologies here. See Himmelfarb, *On Looking*, 9.
58. See Jeffrey, *People of the Book*, 1ff.
59. Bloom, "Breaking of Form," 4–5.
60. J. Miller, "Critic as Host," 228.
61. Derrida, *Writing and Difference*, 64–78.
62. See ibid., 76: "Everything that is exterior in relation to the book, everything that is negative as concerns the book, is produced *within the book*. . . . One emerges from the book only within the book, because, for Jabès, the book is not in the world, but the world is in the book."
63. Ibid., 311n3.

commentaries" (p. 109). The necessity of commentary, like poetic necessity, is the very form of exiled speech. In the beginning is hermeneutics. But the *shared* necessity of exegesis, the interpretive imperative, is interpreted differently by the rabbi and the poet. The difference between the horizon of the original text and exegetic writing makes the difference between the rabbi and the poet irreducible. Forever unable to reunite with each other, yet so close to each other, how could they ever regain the *realm*? The original opening of interpretation essentially signifies that there will always be rabbis and poets. And two interpretations of interpretation. . . . The book of man is a book of question.[64]

Within this doctrine of the two ways, theology and Christian reflection get damned as irretrievably "logocentric." David Jeffrey suggests that the roots of this perspective lie in gnosticism:

> But deconstruction is itself arguably one of the most evidently gnostic varieties of poststructuralist theory. Like its second-century predecessor as much as the antinomian structuralism of Barthes on which it more nearly draws, deconstruction *ad finem* strives to separate its form of knowledge from any reference to external nature, experience, or historical process. The transcendent principle in both ancient gnosticism and modern deconstruction is an absence, not a presence.[65]

Jeffrey is not alone in discerning gnostic parentage for deconstruction. Milbank, Eco, F. Watson, and Keefer make similar comparisons.[66] Of these, the fullest case is that by Keefer.[67] Keefer argues that deconstruction, like second-century gnosticism, is antinomian, antihistorical, and antiworldly. Epistemologically, knowledge is cut off from "positive externality." The hidden God of gnosticism is an absence, but this God who is inaccessible is also constitutive of everything. With its concern for salvation, gnosticism might appear different from Derrida's philosophy, which manifests no nostalgia for presence. But Keefer argues that any genuine piety is lacking in gnostic texts. Keefer suggests that the sources for Derrida's gnosticism might be Nietzsche and Heidegger; Hans Jonas noticed the similarity of Heidegger's thought to

---

64. Ibid., 67.
65. Jeffrey, *People of the Book*, 356. See ibid., 355–56.
66. Milbank, *Word*, 60–63, 79; Eco, *Interpretation*, 1–43; F. Watson, *Text and Truth*, 77, 80, 82; Keefer, "Deconstruction and the Gnostics." Milbank (*Word*, 61) notes that Derrida is anti-Platonic in his taking the signifying trace to be an absolutely original moment but remains Platonic in seeing this imaging as a lapse. "The further dimension to his scepticism might be described as a kind of Valentinian gnosis, in that it identifies creation with fall and makes both inevitable, though resignation to aesthetic jouissance is the nearest he gets to a motif of redemptive 'return.'"
67. Keefer, "Deconstruction and the Gnostics," 83–87.

gnosticism. A more specific source may be Lautréamont's *Chants de Maldoror*, which Derrida engages positively in *Dissemination*.[68]

For theological assessment of deconstruction this comparison of deconstruction with gnosticism is very important. Jeffrey rightly asserts that the two ways of deconstruction are an unacceptable framework from a Christian perspective:

> Accordingly, for the Christian, theory of poetry cannot responsibly be formulated from either polar view about the nature and properties of language, since such an absolute dichotomization misrepresents reality, either idolizing language (logocentrism) or repudiating it as useful means to understanding (nihilism).
>
> Still more disturbing is the way any such misprision as Bloom's masks the nature of the actual *agon* in which men and women struggle to communicate and commune, to know and to be known, to love and seek truth. Neither Dante nor Eliot, for example, could say with Bloom that whichever theory of language one chooses is immaterial for theorizing about poetry so long as it is "extreme enough and uncompromising"; for the Christian theorist the choice does not lie between sense and nonsense, a surplus of meaning and no certain meaning at all. Rather, it lies more profoundly *between life and death* (Deut. 30:19), *truth and denial of truth* (Rom. 1:25). In the imperfect area of human signification, where we see "as in a mirror enigmatically," the asymptotic character of fallen language is a source of endless frustration as well as momentary joy.[69]

This may seem a long way from Qohelet, but the transmuting of the biblical two ways into a significantly different two ways is instructive. Underlying the doctrine of the two ways is the biblical doctrine of *the antithesis*. "In biblical teaching the antithesis points to a spiritual conflict which cuts across all of life. World history demonstrates this running encounter between two opposing forces—the 'kingdom of light' and the 'kingdom of darkness.'"[70] It was the genius of the twentieth-century Dutch philosopher Herman Dooyeweerd to see that the antithesis and the consequent doctrine of two ways runs not just through daily life but through scholarship as well, so that the objectivity aspired to by post-Enlightenment thinkers is a myth.[71]

What Qohelet demonstrates in this chapter is that denial of the biblical two ways does not eradicate them but transmutes them into an idolatrous two ways, which Proverbs would itself call folly. Through his problematization of the

---

68. Derrida, *Dissemination*, 36ff. Keefer ("Deconstruction and the Gnostics," 86) describes *Chants de Maldoror* as an "explicitly Gnostic text, in the line . . . of Carpocrates, the most violently antinomian of the second-century Gnostics."

69. Jeffrey, *People of the Book*, 8 (italics mine).

70. Spykman, *Reformational Theology*, 67. See also Wolters, *Creation Regained*, chap. 3.

71. For an introduction to Dooyeweerd's thought on this subject, see Kalsbeek, *Contours*, chap. 2. See also Clouser, *Myth of Religious Neutrality*; and Buckley, *At the Origins of Modern Atheism*.

two ways of traditional wisdom, Qohelet ends up with a very contemporary two ways, that of folly versus wealth. For many in our culture *wealth* is the supreme objective, and poverty, its polar opposite, is utter folly. In the film *A Good Year* the lead character, having deviously made millions on the stock exchange in one day, says to his colleagues, "Winning is not everything," and they reply en masse—almost liturgically—"it's the only thing!"

Addictions invariably manifest a transmutation of the biblical two ways. Sex addiction is common nowadays, and in its perspective, life is about sex, so that life without sex is folly. Substance abuse—both alcohol and drug— is pervasive in Western culture today, and as G. Collins notes, once it takes hold, "life is built around getting enough of the drug; all else is of secondary importance."[72] To have the drug is life; not to have it is death and folly.

The idolatry involved in this transmutation of the biblical two ways is evident in v. 20. Whereas in the OT *God* looks on the heart, here one must keep one's thoughts pure of any evil thought about the king, lest one lose favor with those in power who are the source of riches. Riches have become everything and nothing must stand in their way. From Qohelet's earlier reflections (cf. 2:1–11) we know that he too would recognize that to absolutize wealth and power is no answer to the question of life and its meaning. Steiner gets us closer to the resolution of Qohelet's problem. As he perceptively discerns, Derrida's skewed two ways confront us with the real two ways, either God as Creator or nihilism.

---

72. G. Collins, *Christian Counseling*, 384.

T.
Living with the Uncertainties
of God's Providence
(11:1–6)

Translation

> ¹Release[1] your bread upon the surface of the waters,[2] for[3] after many days you may[4] find it.
> ²Give a portion to seven and even to eight, for[5] you do not know what evil will happen on the earth.
> ³If the clouds are full, they will pour out rain[6] on the earth; and whether a tree falls south or north, the place where the tree falls, there it is.[7]

1. *Šalaḥ* is in the Piel stem and means "to send" or "to release" but not "to throw" or "to cast," as it is often translated.

2. "Upon the surface of the waters" should not be confused with *hišlîk 'el-hammayim* ("to throw into the waters"; cf. Exod. 15:25).

3. Causal use of *kî* (RJW §444).

4. The imperfect may have a modal aspect (may find) rather than indicate the future tense.

5. The *kî* could be causal, concessive (even though), emphatic (indeed), or a weakened asseverative. Seow (*Ecclesiastes*, 336) argues for the concessive usage, but in context I take it to be causal.

6. The masoretic punctuation suggests that "rain" is the object of "be full of." One would then have to take the second verb as intransitive: "they empty (themselves out) on the earth." However, it is easier to assume a disjunctive accent on "clouds" and to take "rain" as the object of "empty." See Seow, *Ecclesiastes*, 336.

7. The form of the verb *yĕhû'* has perplexed commentators. Fredericks (*Qoheleth's Language*, 222–23) lists four options: (1) It should be read as the personal pronoun *hû'*. (2) It is the jussive form of *hwh* with additional *aleph*. (3) It is the imperfect of the Aramaic word *hwh*, "to be." (4) It has its origin in the Arabic root *hwh*. Seow (*Ecclesiastes*, 336) argues that *yĕhû'* is to be

⁴The one who watches the wind will not sow, and the one who observes the clouds will not reap.

⁵Just as you do not know the way of the spirit [in] the limbs in the mother's womb,⁸ so you do not know the work of God, who does all things.

⁶In the morning sow your seed, and do not let your hand rest in the evening,⁹ for¹⁰ you do not know which will succeed, whether this or that, or whether both will do equally well.

Interpretation

The key to this section is found in v. 6b—one simply does not know what God is going to do in the future.¹¹ In this respect, this section picks up again on the theme of 10:14 and looks back to the many other places where this issue has surfaced. One cannot be sure of the character-consequence structure, because one cannot be sure of what God is going to do. So how then should one live?

¹Release your bread upon the surface of the waters, for after many days you may find it.

²Give a portion to seven and even to eight, for you do not know what evil will happen on the earth.

11:1–2. The translation of v. 1 is straightforward, but what does it mean?¹² A popular interpretation, going back to Jerome and Tg, understands it to refer to acts of almsgiving or charity. Goethe's lines in his *West-östlicher Diwan*

---

analyzed as the Qal imperfect of *hwh*, with a confusion of the III-weak and III-*aleph* roots, which he says is a common phenomenon in Late Hebrew. As Fredericks (*Qoheleth's Language*, 223) notes, "All renderings, regardless of the view of the word's actual meaning, end in the redundant but emphatic sense of 'where the tree falls, there it is.'"

8. Seow (*Ecclesiastes*, 328) translates this line: "Just as you do not know how the life-breath gets [into] the fetus in the belly of the pregnant woman." Debate centers on whether *rûaḥ* refers to "wind" or to "spirit, life breath" and on the function of the preposition *kĕ* in *ka'ăṣāmîm*. *Kĕ* cannot be a conjunction (GKC §155g), although many translate this line as if two comparisons are expressed. It is probably better to follow many Hebrew MSS and the Tg and read *ba'ăṣāmîm* (in the limbs). *'Eṣem* (bone) can mean "body frame" or "body," especially in the plural. From comparative use in an ancient Near Eastern text, Seow (*Ecclesiastes*, 337) proposes "fetus" as a possible translation.

9. As Fox (*Qohelet*, 277) argues, *babbōqer . . . lā'ereb* does not mean "in the morning . . . until the evening" but "regularly."

10. Causal use of *kî* (RJW §444).

11. On 11:1–6 as a distinct section, see Ogden, "Qoheleth XI 1–6."

12. See Murphy (*Ecclesiastes*, 106) and Fox (*Time*, 311–12) for the various possibilities. Homan ("Beer Production") offers the unusual suggestion that Qohelet is recommending beer production and consumption in difficult times.

witness to the enduring popularity of this reading: "Why do you want to find out where charity flows! Throw your bread into the water—who knows who will enjoy it?"[13] In support of this view modern scholars cite parallels such as that in the Instructions of 'Onchsheshonqy 19.10: "Do a good deed and throw it in the water; when it dries you will find it."[14] Hengstenberg argues that by means of maritime trade imagery "the author admonishes us to secure by benevolence, and by putting completely away that covetous narrow-heartedness, which, in times of distress, so easily creeps into our heart."[15] Seow similarly asserts, "The verse is not about foreign investments, but liberality."[16]

A second line of interpretation, advocated by Delitzsch, Gordis, and many others, is that Qohelet here does refer to maritime trade. Finding support in verses like Isa. 18:2, about a land "that sends [*haššōlēaḥ*] ambassadors by the sea in vessels of papyrus on the waters [*'al-pěnê-mayim*]," this approach argues that releasing one's bread on the waters is a metaphor for trade. Verse 2 would then refer to diversifying trade; literally it would mean dividing one's cargo among several boats, which metaphorically would equate to enterprises.[17] Such trade is risky, but it may yield a good reward—after many days, one may find it. Against this view, Seow argues that if foreign investment were in mind, one would expect to find not just "it" but more than "it" (that is, a profit).[18]

A third line of interpretation regards releasing bread into the water as a metaphor for a senseless act.[19] The bread dissolves, but such an act may have unexpected consequences, because we are ignorant of the future.

Which interpretation one opts for will also depend on how one reads v. 2 and vice versa. Verse 2 is closely related to v. 1 by its syntactical structure (starting with an imperative and concluding with a motive clause with an initial *kî* [for]). If one reads v. 1 as exhorting one to acts of charity, then v. 2 would encourage one to generously share possessions in many different ways. "To seven and even to eight" marks this as a numerical saying so that in mind are not exact numbers but generosity (cf. Prov. 6:16; 30:15–33; Amos 1; 2; etc.). If v. 1 is read as encouraging risky commerce, then v. 2 would refer to diversifying one's business interests to maximize the possibility of success. If with Murphy one reads v. 1 as referring to senseless acts, then one would find in v. 2 an antithesis to v. 1. "If previously the paradox of a possible success was held out (v 1), now one is warned not to bank on taking precautions against mishap."[20]

13. Quoted by Murphy, *Ecclesiastes*, 106.
14. Lichtheim, *Ancient Egyptian Literature*, 3:174.
15. Hengstenberg, *Ecclesiastes*, 235.
16. Seow, *Ecclesiastes*, 335. Krüger (*Qoheleth*, 191–93) holds the same view.
17. Longman (*Ecclesiastes*, 256) holds this view.
18. Seow, *Ecclesiastes*, 335.
19. Galling, *Prediger*; Hertzberg, *Prediger*; Murphy, *Ecclesiastes*, 106, 107.
20. Murphy, *Ecclesiastes*, 107.

Murphy argues that the third interpretation is "vintage Qoheleth"—one cannot even rely on uncertainty![21] It is hard to be sure of the correct interpretation, but in the context of chap. 10, with its emphasis on wealth and riches, the second line of interpretation seems to be the right one. The lengthy period of time anticipated in v. 1b "exactly accords with the idea of commerce carried on with foreign countries, which expects to attain its object only after a long period of waiting."[22] Releasing bread on the water is "a figure taken from the corn trade of a seaport . . . an illustration of the thought: seek thy support in the way of bold, confident adventure."[23] The bread in mind would not be a thick loaf, which would immediately sink, but the flat type of bread common in the ancient Near East. "Find it" does not therefore detract from this reading, contra Seow. It is part of the metaphor. Just as later in a day one might stumble across a loaf of bread one released onto the water earlier, so too adventurous commerce might yield its return with time.

Verse 2 does not tell us to whom to give portions of our "bread," but in context it would refer to investing widely. The motivation for this is the uncertainty of the future: one never knows what evil will take place on earth. Verses 1 and 2 thus resonate with chap. 10. If "money answers everything," then one must do all one can to secure one's future financially. Just as one must never annoy the king, so too one must do all one can to secure one's investments.

> [3]If the clouds are full, they will pour out rain on the earth; and whether a tree falls south or north, the place where the tree falls, there it is.
> [4]The one who watches the wind will not sow, and the one who observes the clouds will not reap.
> [5]Just as you do not know the way of the spirit [in] the limbs in the mother's womb, so you do not know the work of God, who does all things.
> [6]In the morning sow your seed, and do not let your hand rest in the evening, for you do not know which will succeed, whether this or that, or whether both will do equally well.

11:3–6. Verse 3 uses the images of clouds full with moisture and a falling tree to evoke the inevitability of bad things happening and their randomness. If clouds are full it is inevitable that rain will come. If a tree falls, whether it falls north or south (a merism signifying "everywhere"[24] or "anywhere") there it is, and we have no control over it ending up where it does. Humans simply cannot control the future. Verse 5 moves on from the inevitability and

21. Ibid.
22. Delitzsch, *Ecclesiastes*, 392.
23. Ibid.
24. Fox, *Time*, 314.

randomness of events to the limits of human knowledge. Humans are ignorant about so much: we do not know how a child is formed in its mother's womb, and in v. 5b Qohelet extends this ignorance comparably to the works of God, that is, his providential ruling of life—we do not understand it (v. 5). Thus Qohelet's advice in v. 6 is to work hard, but, as he ironically notes, one has no idea what if anything will succeed. Once again, in typical Qohelet fashion, the rug is pulled out from under one's feet. Money may answer everything, but there is no guarantee of it.

Theological Implications

Wealth is a theme that has cropped up repeatedly in Qohelet's journey, and as we saw in chap. 10, once he subverts the two ways of wisdom he is pushed into another two ways, that of riches versus folly. This section exposes the folly of that approach. One can diversify (v. 2), trade abroad (v. 1), work hard (v. 6), but still one has no control over what the future might bring. Wealth simply will not do as the answer to everything (10:19).

Theologically, what is exposed here is the idolatry of wealth. It is not that wealth *per se* is a problem, but it becomes one when it replaces God. Jesus addresses this clearly in Matt. 6:19–21 (cf. Luke 12:33–34), where he exhorts his hearers not to store up treasures on earth, where they are vulnerable to moth and rust, but in heaven, where they are invulnerable. As he says, "Where your treasure is, there your heart will be also." France rightly notes that treasures in heaven are "'stored up' by obedience to God *in all areas of life*."[25]

The idolatry of wealth is a major problem in Western culture today as the gap in the West and internationally between rich and poor increases. With Jesus, Qohelet reminds us that wealth by itself is never secure ground on which to stand. God, and God alone, must be at the center of our lives.

---

25. France, *Matthew*, 138 (italics mine).

U.
Rejoicing and Remembering
(11:7–12:7)

Translation

11:7Truly,[1] light is sweet,
and it is good for the eyes to observe the sun.
8If[2] a person lives many years,
let him rejoice in all of them.[3]
But one should remember
the days of darkness, for they will be many.
All that comes is enigmatic.
9Rejoice, young man,
in[4] your youth,
and let your heart cheer you
in the days of your youth.[5]

1. Emphatic use of *waw* (RJW §438).
2. The meaning of *kî 'im* is debated. Elsewhere in Ecclesiastes it has an exceptive force ("even though": 3:12; 5:11 [10]; 8:15), but here, with Longman (*Ecclesiastes*, 258) and Seow (*Ecclesiastes*, 348), I take *kî* as a (weakened) asseverative and leave it untranslated.
3. There is a further example of a lack of agreement in gender here: the suffix on "all of them" is masculine, whereas the antecedent "years" is feminine.
4. Temporal use of *bě* (RJW §241).
5. *Běḥûrôtekā* is found only here and in 12:1 in the OT. This feminine plural form probably indicates an abstract (Whitley, *Koheleth*, 93).

Follow[6] the ways of your heart
and the vision[7] of your eyes,
and know that for all these things
God will bring you into judgment.
[10]Banish vexation from your heart
and put away evil from your body,
for youth and the dawn of life[8] are an enigma.
[12:1]And remember your Creator[9] in the days of your youth,
before[10] the evil days come
and the years approach when you will say,
"There is no delight in them for me";
[2]before the sun and the light and the moon and the stars grow dark,
and the clouds return
after[11] the rain;
[3]on the day in which[12] the keepers of the house tremble,
and strong men[13] stoop,
and the women grinders[14] cease[15] because they are few,
and those looking through the windows grow dark;
[4]and the doors of the street are shut
as the sound of the mill becomes low,

6. Literally "walk."

7. Ketib has the plural form *mar'ê*, but Qere (with numerous Hebrew MSS, LXX, Syr, and Vg) has the singular *mar'ēh*.

8. *Šaḥārût* occurs only here in Biblical Hebrew. The root means "to be black" and is connected with *šaḥar* (dawn). Hence I follow NRSV and Seow (*Ecclesiastes*, 350–51) in translating "the dawn of life."

9. Strangely, MT has the plural *bôrĕ'eykā*. However, the plural makes no sense in this context and has been explained in several ways: as the plural of majesty (Delitzsch, *Ecclesiastes*, 402); as the result of the frequent confusion in Late Hebrew of III-*aleph* and III-weak roots (Seow, *Ecclesiastes*, 351); as emphatic rather than indicating plurality (according to Schoors, *Preacher*, 1:24, the plural form has been introduced as a *pluralis intensitatis* under the influence of *Elohim* and related forms); or one can follow the ancient versions in reading the singular *bôrĕ'ekā*. Some scholars also find the appearance of "Creator" here jarring and propose alternatives such as "your health" (Ehrlich); "your well" as a metaphor for one's wife (Graetz); and "your pit" (Galling) as a synonym for one's grave (see Seow, *Ecclesiastes*, 351). However, these are unsatisfactory; assuming the consonantal text to be correct, "Creator" must be the meaning.

10. Literally "until when not"; hence "before."

11. Seow (*Ecclesiastes*, 353–54) asserts that "after" makes no sense here and suggests that *'aḥar* be translated "with" as in Ruth 1:15. See the interpretation.

12. This clause connects vv. 3–5 to v. 2.

13. The precise meaning of this phrase in which *ḥayil* (wealth, power, prestige) qualifies "men" is uncertain. It could mean "landowners" (Longman, *Ecclesiastes*, 264), "valiant men" (Seow, *Ecclesiastes*, 355), or "strong men," as I translate it.

14. The Hebrew could mean "(women) grinders" or refer to the molar teeth.

15. *Bāṭēl* is a *hapax legomenon* in the OT but is well attested in Postbiblical Hebrew. It can mean to stop altogether or to suspend one's activity.

and the sound of the birds rises,[16]
and all the daughters of song are humbled.
[5]Furthermore,[17] they fear heights[18]
and terrors[19] in the road.
The almond tree blossoms,[20]
the grasshopper drags itself along,[21]
and the caperberry breaks.
For the human goes to his eternal home,
and mourners walk about in the street,
[6]before the silver cord[22] is snapped,[23]
and the golden bowl is broken,
and the jar is shattered by the well,
and the wheel[24] is crushed at the well,
[7]and the dust returns[25]
to the earth as it was,
and the spirit returns
to God, who gave it.

16. The translation of this line is disputed. There is no subject for the verb, so one either translates "one rises" or "the sound of the birds rises." For an argument for the former based on an Assyrian parallel, see Haupt, "Assyr. *lâm iççûri çabâri*." However, this view, adopted by many, is based on the presupposition that we are dealing with an allegory of old age. To take "the sound of the birds" as the subject, as I do, means taking the *lamed* before "sound" as the asseverative *lamed* or the *lamed* that occasionally occurs before the subject in Late Biblical Hebrew. See Seow, *Ecclesiastes*, 358.

17. *Gam* has an associative function here, linking vv. 4 and 5. See Schoors, *Preacher*, 1:129.

18. Seow (*Ecclesiastes*, 360) translates "even from on high they see," vocalizing the verb as *yir'û* instead of MT *yirā'û*, "they are afraid." See Schoors (*Preacher*, 1:28) for the four different readings of *yr'w*. He notes, "The meaning required by the context is that of . . . 'to be afraid.'"

19. The word is a *hapax legomenon*, but its meaning is derived from *ḥtt*, "to be filled with terror."

20. The ancient translations and most modern commentators take the root of *wĕyānē'ṣ* (blossoms) as *nṣṣ* (to blossom). But some argue that the root is *n'ṣ* (to despise). Thus, for example, Seow (*Ecclesiastes*, 361) reads *wĕyānē'ṣ* as the Hiphil of *n'ṣ* and translates "becomes revolting." With Schoors (*Preacher*, 1:41–42) I take the *aleph* in *wĕyānē'ṣ* as a simple scribal error and read "blossoms."

21. The root *sbl* (to carry, to be laden) occurs in the Qal and Piel but nowhere else in the Hithpael. Much depends on what one takes the "grasshopper" to be. Seow (*Ecclesiastes*, 362) translates "the locust" and takes this to refer to a type of tree that "droops." An Arabic cognate, *sabala*, can mean "drag" or "droop." I take the reference to the grasshopper to be literal and read the Hithpael of the verb as reflexive, hence "drags itself along."

22. *Ḥebel* (cord) can refer to anything long and twining.

23. Reading the Qere with forty-four MSS, rather than the Ketib, which means "removed."

24. The meaning of this noun here is contested. Many take it to refer to a wheellike pulley at a well, but others, such as Dahood ("Canaanite-Phoenician Influence," 213–14) and Seow (*Ecclesiastes*, 367), take it to mean "vessel, jar."

25. For the use of the jussive where we would expect an imperfect, see GKC §109k.

Interpretation

This is the final section of Qohelet's instruction before the narrator makes his concluding comments in 12:8–14,[26] and it is widely recognized as a poem.[27] This section remains deeply in touch with the brokenness of life (11:8c; 12:1–8) but indicates the way out of Qohelet's agonizing tension between affirming joy and running up continually against the enigma of life—the enigma that has plagued Qohelet throughout his journey of exploration.

> [7]Truly, light is sweet,
> and it is good for the eyes to observe the sun.

11:7. The proverb in v. 7 starts the final stage in Qohelet's journey as presented in Ecclesiastes. The initial *waw* ("and," translated "truly") here indicates a shift in focus, but it is the content of the proverb that definitively signals a major change. Through large sections of Ecclesiastes "under the sun" has had decidedly negative consequences, but like the unexpected arrival of spring we find this proverb. Light is sweet: "sweet" is a metaphor of taste and evokes the tasting, the full experiencing, of life as truly good. One is reminded of the psalmist's "Taste and see that the LORD is good" (Ps. 34:8 [9]) and the exhortation to "awaken the dawn" (Ps. 108:2 [3]). "To see the sun" is to be alive as a creature, as one who lives "under the sun." This proverb declares being alive as good, delightful. It thereby hints at the possibility of resolution to Qohelet's struggle. The contrast between light and darkness is common in the Bible, and it is basic to the images throughout 11:7–12:7. We have already come across it in 2:13–14. There death subverted the comparison with wisdom as light. Here, however, there is a sense of resolution—it is delightful to see the sun. Observation has been at the heart of Qohelet's epistemology, but the latter has led him again and again into despair about life. Here, perhaps using

26. This section is generally regarded as a distinct unit. However, there is some debate about its beginning. Some, such as Hertzberg (*Prediger*, 203–4) and Michel (*Qohelet*, 165–66), make 11:7–8 the conclusion of the preceding section. Seow (*Ecclesiastes*, 368) argues that "in the morning" of 11:6 recalls "in the morning" of 10:16 and thus concludes the section 10:16–11:6. Whybray (*Ecclesiastes* [NCBC], 161) isolates 11:7–8 as a separate section, but in terms of theme and vocabulary (rejoice and remember, light and darkness) they are tied closely to the verses that follow. Ogden ("Qoheleth XI 7–XII 8") thinks that this section concludes with 12:8, but since 12:8 reintroduces the voice of the narrator, this is unlikely. In my opinion, 11:7 strikes a very different note from what precedes and fittingly opens Qohelet's final speech. Indeed, Ravasi (*Qohelet*, 332) describes 11:7–8 as "the overture" to Qohelet's grand finale.

27. Longman (*Ecclesiastes*, 258–59, 264–66) does not think that this is a poem, but others (Witzenrath, *Süß ist das Licht*, 5–7; Busto Saiz, "Estructura"; Backhaus, *Zeit und Zufall*, 303–17; Ogden, "Qoheleth XI 7–XII 8"; N. Lohfink, "Freu Dich, Jüngling") have argued that the passage is a carefully constructed unit. Its parallelism, structural symmetry, and use of metaphor (esp. in 12:1–7) indicate its poetic nature.

a quote from Euripides,[28] Qohelet affirms a way of living that enables one to *observe* the sun with joy, to welcome the dawn, as it were. One is reminded of the title of Wilfrid Sheed's book, *In Love with Daylight*, written after long experiences of a struggle with various diseases. As Krüger notes, "This verse formulates an unrestricted affirmation of life."[29]

> [8]If a person lives many years,
> let him rejoice in all of them.
> But one should remember
> the days of darkness, for they will be many.
> All that comes is enigmatic.

11:8. After all that Qohelet has led us through, how is he able to move toward *this* conclusion? The key is found in the two verbs that dominate the poem, *rejoice* and *remember*. Verse 8 introduces them. "Rejoice" is the imperative that governs 11:9–10, and "remember" is the imperative that governs 12:1–7. This is not to suggest that Qohelet here loses touch with the paradoxes of life, but he contextualizes them in the framework of rejoicing and remembrance, and thus moves progressively in this section toward a resolution of his contradictory juxtaposition of joy and enigma.

Up until this section the *carpe diem* passages have always followed enigmatic sections.[30] This shift to having the *carpe diem* section preface and structure the enigmatic section about death is significant, as is the introduction of "remember," which has not yet occurred in a *carpe diem* passage. Previously the two ways of seeing life have been juxtaposed without resolution. This allowing of the *carpe diem* element to shape the whole suggests the possibility of integration and resolution. The bridge element then between the *hebel* and *carpe diem* poles would be rejoicing and particularly *remembering*.

Verse 8 urges one to rejoice in all one's days, however many they are. Joy is thus affirmed no matter what one's age. At the same time one should remember that there will be many days of darkness, because we do not know the future. Here one senses Qohelet moving toward an affirmation of joy over despair but still struggling with how to relate the two. The exhortations and imperatives in vv. 8–10 connect back into the previous *carpe diem* passage in 9:7–10, but the exhortation to "remember" is new. Here it is the days of darkness that must be remembered, for they will be many. All that has gone before fills the

28. Murphy, *Ecclesiastes*, 116. See Euripides, *Iphigenia in Aulis*, 1.1218: "sweet it is to see the light."

29. Krüger, *Qoheleth*, 195.

30. This depends on how one divides up the book. In some cases the *carpe diem* passages may be sandwiched in between enigmatic sections. The point is that, on my understanding, a *carpe diem* section never opens a new section except here in 11:7–12:7.

content of "days of darkness." The phrase includes death but so much more as well: evil days, oppression, aloneness, abusive rule, and so on.

> [9]Rejoice, young man,
> in your youth,
> and let your heart cheer you
> in the days of your youth.
> Follow the ways of your heart
> and the vision of your eyes,
> and know that for all these things
> God will bring you into judgment.

11:9. Verse 9 turns its attention to the young man, the typical recipient of instruction from a wisdom teacher. As with Proverbs (cf. Prov. 1:1–6), however, the instruction should not be restricted to the youth, as this would contradict the exhortation in 11:8 that relates to the whole of one's life. The point is rather to get the foundations for living in place as early as possible. Qohelet affirms joy as he does in the *carpe diem* passages. "Let your heart cheer you" and "follow the ways of your heart" are intriguing exhortations in the light of Qohelet's journey. Longman understands these exhortations to mean that Qohelet's advice is "to pursue whatever they want to do, not to wait or it will be too late. He specifically mentions the *heart* and *eyes* because these are the 'organs of desire.'"[31] However, the exhortation to joy never has this meaning in the *carpe diem* passages, nor does it here. In the context of Qohelet's journey it is also important to note that he repeatedly tells us "I turned/gave my heart" to his explorations. These expressions evoke a picture of his "I" controlling his heart, whereas in v. 9 it is the heart that does the leading. He was under the impression that his journey was from the heart, but these verses raise a question about that. If living according to the ways of one's heart means affirming the *carpe diem* vision, then it is possible that Qohelet was not exploring from the heart as he thought, but very much from the head, which had become dislocated from his deepest heartfelt intuitions as reflected in the *carpe diem* passages. Here we get a true vision of what it means to live "from the heart."

In v. 9c, in contrast to v. 8c, Qohelet includes a reference to something in the future that is certain—the judgment of God. There is development in his thinking here: contrary to v. 8c not everything that comes is enigmatic— there will be a time for judgment, and the young person needs to note that how he rejoices and lives out his life will finally be held to account by God. Longman argues that v. 9aβ is in stark contrast to v. 9c: "After this positive advice, however, he imparts a somber reminder of the coming judgment.

---

31. Longman, *Ecclesiastes*, 261. The early debates about the canonicity of Ecclesiastes centered on the apparent contradiction between 11:9 and Num. 15:39.

Specifically, he will judge them for their youthful enjoyment!"[32] However, as Seow notes,

> For him [Qohelet], the enjoyment of life is both the lot of humanity . . . and a gift of God. . . . Human beings are supposed to enjoy life to the full because that is their divinely assigned portion, and God calls one into account for failure to enjoy. Or, as a passage in the Talmud has it: "Everyone must give an account before God of all good things one saw in life *and did not enjoy.*" . . . For Qohelet, enjoyment is not only permitted, it is commanded; it is not only an opportunity, it is a divine imperative.[33]

> ¹⁰Banish vexation from your heart
> and put away evil from your body,
> for youth and the dawn of life are an enigma.

11:10. Verse 10 confirms this interpretation with its exhortation to the young person to banish vexation from his heart and evil from his body because youth and the origins of life are enigmatic. "Vexation" has cropped up several times in Ecclesiastes (1:18; 2:23; 5:17 [16]; 7:3). This verse resonates with all the previous references to "vexation." In 1:18, for example, much "wisdom" brings vexation and sorrow. But here wisdom involves banishing vexation. Lest we read the exhortations in v. 9 as a license for hedonism, evil is also to be banished from one's body. Following the ways of one's heart will involve refusing to use one's body for evil activities; rather, an embrace of joy and pursuit of life are central to righteousness. The motivation for this is that youth and the dawn of life are an "enigma." Here we see Qohelet still confronted with the mystery of life, but his response is shifting—anger and evil are to be avoided in the light of the mystery of life. "Enigma," such a central term in Ecclesiastes, has here the more positive nuance of mystery and points to the limitations of creaturely knowledge (cf. v. 5) in a more positive way than so often in Ecclesiastes.

12:1–7. "And" at the start of v. 1 links this section back to the preceding one, while also indicating a shift in focus. Whereas "rejoice" has governed 11:7–10, "remember" governs 12:1–7. Here "remember" means much more than intellectual acknowledgment of God as Creator.[34] It refers to allowing the notion of God as Creator to shape one's view of life and one's handling of life's enigmas now. And, if Qohelet has Gen. 1 in mind, then it is that kind of understanding of God as Creator by which Qohelet calls on his readers to

32. Longman, *Ecclesiastes*, 260.
33. Seow, *Ecclesiastes*, 371.
34. In terms of reception history, Kierkegaard's (*Edifying Discourses*, 3:81–94) discussion of the imperative "remember" is noteworthy.

allow their minds and lives to be shaped.[35] So shocking is this imperative that many scholars think Qohelet simply cannot be referring to God as Creator. But the theology of God as Creator is fundamental to traditional wisdom, and it is implicit in the *carpe diem* passages throughout Ecclesiastes.

Remembrance, as Wolterstorff recognizes, involves consciously allowing the great acts of God, remembered in the tradition, to shape one's perspective in the present.[36] The days of darkness will be many (11:8), but the way to joy in the midst of this darkness (12:2–7) is to remember God as *Creator*. In 11:8 the tension between joy and enigma is still present; the command to rejoice is paralleled by the command to remember the days of darkness. This tension is resolved by changing the object of remembrance in 12:1 and putting the days of darkness in the context of such remembrance, as the threefold use of "before" that structures 12:1–7 makes clear. Just as the description of death in this section is metaphorical, so too should "youth" not be taken too narrowly to refer only to the young. The idea is rather that life needs to be built on a foundation of such remembrance.

There has been much discussion about vv. 1–7 and how to interpret them. There are three main ways to read 12:1–7: allegorically, literally, and symbolically. An allegorizing interpretation of this section takes Qohelet to be describing a house or village, but the objects and activities represent old age.[37] Such a reading goes back to the Tg, Talmud, and Ibn Ezra. Delitzsch proposed an allegorical interpretation in which, for example, in v. 2 sun = spirit, light = thinking, moon = soul, stars = the five senses, and clouds = illness.[38] The diversity of interpretations among those who read this section allegorically raises questions about its legitimacy.[39] Opponents of an allegorical reading recognize the metaphorical nature of this section but suggest that death and not just old age is primarily in focus. C. Taylor and Anat see vv. 2–5 as describing the situation at a funeral and consequently, like vv. 6 and 7, relate not just to old age but to death.[40] This approach represents the literal reading

---

35. On *zākar* (remember) in the OT, see H. Eising, "*zākhar*," *TDOT* 4:64–82; and on the philosophy of remembrance, see Wolterstorff, "Remembrance of Things (Not) Past." *Zākar* is not a common word in Ecclesiastes, and while it can be used simply in terms of remembrance as in 9:15, it clearly has a richer nuance in 11:7–12:7, as the objects of *zākar* here indicate. Note, for example, 11:8b. The remembrance of the days of darkness is far more than mere intellectual acknowledgment, as 12:2–7 makes poignantly clear.

36. Wolterstorff, "Remembrance of Things (Not) Past," 131.

37. Crenshaw ("Youth and Old Age") argues that Qohelet's negative description of old age runs counter to the common association of old age with wisdom in the ancient Near East and Israel.

38. Delitzsch, *Ecclesiastes*, 401–27. See Fox (*Time*, 344–45) for a list of many of the decodings proposed in allegorical readings of this passage.

39. A point made strongly by Sawyer ("Ruined House in Ecclesiastes 12") in relation to vv. 2–5.

40. C. Taylor, "Dirge of Coheleth"; idem, *Dirge of Coheleth*; Anat, "Lament."

of the text. A symbolic reading sees something larger depicted through the literal portrayal of death. Fox argues that at a symbolic level Qohelet portrays something of eschatological proportions.[41] He proposes an interpretation that assumes that the text has different levels of meaning. At the literal level there is the funeral and its related sadness. At the second level are the symbols that suggest a disaster of cosmic magnitude. At the third level some images suggest the pains of old age, but they are not allegorical, though there is some indication of an allegory of death.[42] To decide these issues, we must turn to the verses themselves.

> ¹And remember your Creator in the days of your youth,
> before the evil days come
> and the years approach when you will say,
> "There is no delight in them for me";

Verse 1 exhorts young persons to remember their Creator before the evil days come in which it is hard to rejoice. At a literal level, there is clearly a contrast here between youth and old age—the longer one lives, the more possibilities there are for experiencing the enigmas of life. And "the evil days" and the approaching years in which one finds no delight probably refer to the approach of death, the great enigma for Qohelet. However, especially in the context of 11:8, youth should be read not just literally but as a metaphor for getting the foundation of one's life right before the enigmas of life strike. Ellul refers to this situation as one that is still fluid: "For this reason we must remember the Creator in our youth, and in the youth of each thing: situations, societies, associations, cultures, political relations, and churches!"[43] The exhortation to remember one's Creator is "addressed to everyone, including a body of people or an institution."[44] Qohelet would be under no illusions that youth are spared the enigmas of life. As he says in 9:12, "No one knows one's time."

> ²before the sun and the light and the moon and the stars grow dark,
> and the clouds return
> after the rain;

Verse 2 introduces the second of the three "before" clauses. The distinction between "sun" and "light" is found in Gen. 1, where the light is created before the sun. The reference to the clouds returning *after* the rain perplexes commentators, and thus some propose that the preposition 'aḥar be translated as

41. Fox, *Time*, 338–43.
42. Ibid., 344–49.
43. Ellul, *Reason for Being*, 283.
44. Ibid., 287.

"with."[45] However, the common meaning of *'aḥar* is "after," and Longman is right to note that "from a psychological viewpoint, the idea that the clouds are coming after the rain evokes even more pathos."[46] This verse has been read as an image of old age. Thus Longman comments: "In sum, the passage presents images evoking dread and sorrow in the light of encroaching old age and impending death."[47] However, there are similarities here to the language of cosmological catastrophe related to the coming day of the LORD in the prophets that exceed the reference to old age.[48] Especially in the Prophets the darkening of the luminaries are metaphors used to evoke the day of the LORD (cf. Isa. 5:30; 13:10; Jer. 25:10–11; Ezek. 32:7–8; Amos 8:9; Joel 2:2, 10, 31 [3:4]; 3:15 [4:15]; Job 3:6; Matt. 24:29; Mark 13:24–25). The coming of the clouds is also an eschatological motif; in Ezek. 32:7, for example, the sun is covered with a cloud. That the "light" and the "sun" grow dark hints at the undoing of creation itself, bearing in mind the allusion here to Gen. 1. In Eccles. 1:5 part of the endless cycle of nature is that the sun sets, only to rise again. Here, however, it is darkened. Thus Qohelet clearly has something much larger in mind than old age or death.

> [3]on the day in which the keepers of the house tremble,
> and strong men stoop,
> and the women grinders cease because they are few,
> and those looking through the windows grow dark;

Verses 3–6 have multiple possible references. Verses 3 and 4 could describe the hopelessness of life in a formerly vibrant city.[49] Verse 5c clearly refers to the context of a funeral in which the human goes to one's eternal home and mourners walk about the streets, even while the almond tree blossoms and the caperberry bursts open.[50] But as with v. 2 there is an eschatological dimension present that exceeds these literal referents.

In v. 3 the "keepers of the house" are servants of the house but with authority for the care of the house (cf. 2 Sam. 16:21; 20:3). "Tremble" is a strong word with associations of terror (cf. Hab. 2:7). The phrase "strong men" is used

45. So, e.g., Seow, *Ecclesiastes*, 353.
46. Longman, *Ecclesiastes*, 269.
47. Ibid. Fredericks ("Life's Storms") revives a meteorological reading of 12:2–6, according to which imminent death is compared to the approach of a terrible storm. Witzenrath (*Süß ist das Licht*, 49) and Ogden ("Qoheleth XI 7–XII 8," 34) read this second "before" section as an allegory of death. Ogden (ibid., 34–35) reads vv. 6–7 as referring to death, not old age. Sawyer ("Ruined House in Ecclesiastes 12") reads this section as the parable of a ruined house with two discernible levels of interpretation.
48. Seow ("Qohelet's Eschatological Poem," 234) notes that the author "recasts the vision of the end through a radical revision that is reminiscent of prophetic eschatology."
49. Loretz, *Qohelet*, 191–92.
50. Krüger's (*Qoheleth*, 190) interpretation of "breaks."

in the OT of those who are trustworthy or brave or strong; it is often used of soldiers.[51] Seow suggests that "stoop" has here the connotation of "cower" or even "convulse."[52] The language of v. 2a is thus very strong and implies a major catastrophe. The remainder of the verse confirms this—"the woman grinders," those who work in the mill, cease their labor. Work at the mill providing flour for bread would have been an essential service in Israel, and the cessation of such labor is indicative of the catastrophe Qohelet has in mind. The reason given for the cessation of labor is that the women are few, and Fox surmises that the women are few because the others have gone to the funeral.[53] However, this does not do justice to the catastrophic context—perhaps we are to envision many of the women as having suddenly died, or perhaps, which I regard as more likely, the literal details are less important than the evocation of catastrophe. The motif of women "looking through the windows" is a literary idiom evoking dashed hopes.[54] Their eyes grow dim through grief and despair at what is happening. Verse 3 thus presents a picture of major catastrophe. "The scene is reminiscent of passages about imminent destruction brought about by the deity, the mere threat of which causes even the brave and powerful to tremble in terror (Exod 15:14–15; Isa 13:6–8; Amos 2:13–15)."[55]

> [4]and the doors of the street are shut
> as the sound of the mill becomes low,
> and the sound of the birds rises,
> and all the daughters of song are humbled.

Verse 4a continues the theme of societal breakdown. "The doors of the street" refers to the gates that open onto the central business area of the city, where the markets and law courts would operate. But now, even as the mill ceases its work, causing starvation to threaten, so too does the life of the city close down. The result is that in the eerie silence that ensues the only thing to be heard is "the sound of the birds," a sound that is normally obscured by the busy life of the city. This sound may also be more ominous: "The author is probably thinking not of birds singing in joy, as is commonly assumed, but either of birds hooting ominously or of birds of prey making a commotion when they sense death or when they move into a depopulated place. Like the fading sound of the mill, the rising sound of the birds is a sign of death."[56] Thus in Ezek. 39:4 Ezekiel prophesies against Gog that he will be given to

51. Seow, *Ecclesiastes*, 355.
52. Ibid.
53. Fox, *Qohelet*, 302–3.
54. Abramsky, "Woman." That the women are looking through the windows probably implies that a house with a second floor is in mind. See de Geus, *Towns in Ancient Israel*, 82.
55. Seow, *Ecclesiastes*, 377.
56. Ibid., 358.

birds of prey of every kind. The imagery is that of birds gathering around a dying animal, waiting until the animal is weak enough so that they can begin to devour the carcass. "The daughters of song" are probably mourners who chant their laments.[57] They occur in parallel with "birds of song," so that "humbled" should be taken to mean silenced[58]—such is the terror of the times. As the sound of the birds of prey rises, so the sound of lament decreases.

> [5]Furthermore, they fear heights
> and terrors in the road.
> The almond tree blossoms,
> the grasshopper drags itself along,
> and the caperberry breaks.
> For the human goes to his eternal home,
> and mourners walk about in the street,

Verse 5a evokes the social nightmare of the time envisaged. It is a time of terrible fear and anxiety. "Heights" are the places from which attacks can come, not least from the birds of prey, and "terrors in the road" evokes the dangers of traveling. The blossoming of the almond tree could either be an ironic sign of nature continuing amid the catastrophe[59] or a deliberate allusion to Jer. 1:9–12, in which the almond tree is a sign of coming judgment. With the strong allusions to prophetic eschatology present in this section, the latter option is not as unlikely as it may seem. That the blossoming of the almond tree is not a hopeful sign is confirmed by what follows. Nature itself is in travail: the grasshopper drags itself along, having lost its capacity for fast movement, and the caperberry breaks. The breaking of the caperberry is often taken to refer to its use as an aphrodisiac, the point being that it is no longer effective in old age. But the eschatological language in this section inclines one away from seeing here a reference to the impotency of old age; rather, the caperberry breaks in the sense of coming to nothing, falling apart. The grasshopper and the caperberry evoke the end of nature itself.

Verse 5c focuses on the human in the midst of this catastrophe. "The human" refers not to a single individual but to humanity as a whole. The human goes to his "eternal home." The latter expression certainly signifies the grave, but we have to wait until v. 7 to see more precisely how Qohelet perceives this "home." That death is in mind is confirmed by the imagery of mourners in the street. One might ask how there can be mourners when humanity as a whole goes

57. Fox, *Time*, 326. Seow (*Ecclesiastes*, 359–60) suggests that they may be birds of some sort, so that "humbled" refers to them swooping down to attack.

58. Contra Fox (*Time*, 326), who takes "humbled" to refer to the posture of bowing low as a sign of mourning.

59. So Longman, *Ecclesiastes*, 272: "Perhaps this signifies the indifference of the surrounding world to the decline and eventual death of the individual."

to its eternal home, but that is to ignore the poetic character of this section. The point is that death has come comprehensively to the creation.

> [6]before the silver cord is snapped,
> and the golden bowl is broken,
> and the jar is shattered by the well,
> and the wheel is crushed at the well,

Verse 6 introduces the third "before" sequence in 12:1–7. "The silver cord" is often taken to be a metaphor for life, and thus its being broken as a sign of death. However, the word for "cord" can refer to anything long and twisted,[60] and in connection with the golden bowl being broken, it probably refers to the lampstand holding the golden bowl. Thus the imagery here is probably that of the silver cord holding the bowl being snapped so that the bowl falls and is broken. In the OT the "lamp" is particularly associated with the cultus (Exod. 24:33–40; 37:17–24; etc.). In the tabernacle, however, the lamp is made entirely of pure gold, whereas here we have one of silver with a gold bowl. The lamp was a common household artifact, but one made of silver and gold would be very special, though still not of the same status as that in the tabernacle. The imagery here is clearly related to humankind going to its eternal home, and perhaps the image of the breaking of the "lesser lamp" signifies the demise of that creature made in the image of God that is more dignified than anything else in the creation but still creaturely and subject to death. That this human demise is part of a societal demise is indicated by the remainder of v. 6. The jar for drawing water lies shattered at the well, and the wheel used for drawing water lies crushed. This interpretation is preferable to seeing the shattered jar and wheel as images of human death. Throughout this passage the cosmic dimensions have been to the fore, and these everyday images of a jar and a wheel signify the demise of ordinary, daily life "under the sun."

> [7]and the dust returns
> to the earth as it was,
> and the spirit returns
> to God, who gave it.

Verse 7 clearly refers to the death of the human, articulated in terms reminiscent of God's formation of the human from dust and breath in Gen. 2:7. Intriguingly, death is *not* here seen as the end, contra Krüger and many others, who think that for Qohelet death really is the end.[61] The spirit returns to God, who gave it (cf. Eccles. 3:21). Murphy, with many others, argues, "This is a picture of dissolution, not of immortality, as if there were a *reditus animae*

---

60. Seow, *Ecclesiastes*, 364.
61. Krüger, *Qoheleth*, 203.

ad Deum, 'the return of the soul to God.' There is no question of the soul here, but of the life-breath, a totally different category of thought."[62] Similarly, Longman asserts that for Qohelet "death is the end"—what is portrayed is "a prelife situation."[63] However, one wonders. If Qohelet is here presenting death as the end, then what has become of the reference to God's judgment in 11:9, which implies that one will be brought into judgment for how one has lived? One wonders what view of the "soul" Murphy is working with when he sharply distinguishes "soul" from "life-breath." In Gen. 2:7 God breathes into the man formed from the dust, and the man becomes a "soul." Biblical anthropology is far more holistic than Platonic body/soul anthropologies recognize. Qohelet certainly has no developed view of the afterlife, but 12:1–7 is framed by references to the Creator: in 12:1 one must remember one's Creator and in 12:7 the spirit returns to "God, who gave it." Thus, although he overstates the case in terms of OT eschatology, Hengstenberg is moving in the right direction when he comments at this point:

> That the spirit of man does not perish with the body is here . . . most decidedly taught. . . . The return of the soul to God can only be such an one as that of which the apostle speaks in 2 Corinthians v.10. . . . No other meaning than this, "that the soul must one day return to God as its judge," is fitted to prepare the way for the admonition, "remember thy Creator," which is the main feature of this entire section.[64]

Ellul similarly notes that "breath" in Gen. 2 has become "spirit" here, and thus "what returns to God is a spirit fitted out with the person's whole known or hidden history. . . . That is, the person enters into the fulness of life, with everything that his life has been. The breath brings with it the entire history of that particular, unique person who has lived his life in God's presence."[65] Further, if Qohelet had wanted to indicate death as the end, then he could have stated clearly, as in 9:10, that it is *Sheol* to which one is going. One goes *down* to Sheol, and, as P. Johnston has shown, Sheol has decidedly negative connotations in the OT.[66] In 3:21 Qohelet states that one does not know whether the

62. Murphy, *Ecclesiastes*, 120.
63. Longman, *Ecclesiastes*, 273.
64. Hengstenberg, *Ecclesiastes*, 253–54. Contra Schoors ("Koheleth," 303), who concludes, "For Koheleth death seems to indicate complete extinction in which the fate of man is indistinguishable from that of the animal. In sum, in Koheleth's view, death renders the aporia of human life complete." Similarly Crenshaw ("Youth and Old Age," 9) asserts, "The idea is that the creator breathed life into human beings and takes back that life-breath at the moment of death. This understanding of mortality has no positive feature, for the pessimistic refrain dashes all such hope."
65. Ellul, *Reason for Being*, 290–91.
66. On Sheol as the place to which one descends, see P. Johnston, *Shades of Sheol*, 73. On the negative connotations of Sheol in the OT, see Johnston's conclusions (ibid., 83).

human spirit goes upward, but here the implied metaphor is indeed upward; the spirit returns to God, who gave it.[67]

What then are we to make of this passage as a whole? It is methodologically unhelpful to work as Fox does with three different layers of interpretation: the literal, the symbolic, and the allegorical. Presupposed in such a methodology is a philosophy of language that in the long-standing tradition of Aristotle espouses the double-language theory, which posits a sharp distinction between literal and metaphorical language. In recent decades this theory has been vigorously challenged, a challenge summed up in Mary Hesse's evocative assertion, "all language is metaphorical!"[68] In my opinion, 12:1 refers to the individual and his approaching death, but vv. 2–6 connect individual death with the eschatological vision of the day of the Lord, as enunciated in the prophets. Krüger thinks that Qohelet has reduced the cosmic visions of the prophets to the death of the individual,[69] and here they are clearly connected. But it is far more likely that Qohelet works in the opposite direction—from the death of the individual to the end of history[70]—thereby invoking the prophetic vision of God's cosmic judgment. That is why it is so important to "remember your *Creator*" in your youth. Like Genesis and the rest of the OT, Qohelet does not work with the notion of the isolated individual subject here, but conceives of humankind as an integral part of God's creation.

Most hopeful is the return of the spirit to God. As Hengstenberg notes, to see death in this section as the end makes nonsense of Qohelet's insistence that finally judgment comes before God. For this judgment to be a reality, there must be life beyond death, and although Qohelet lived prior to the revelation of the NT, he envisions, albeit without elaboration, that life which is a gift of God returning to God, its eternal home (12:5).

Theological Implications

This final section in Qohelet's journey is very important for an understanding of his journey as a whole. "Rejoice" is the exhortation that governs 11:8–10, and "remember" governs 12:1–7. The darkness and enigma of life remain strongly present in both sections, but the proverb of 11:7 is highly significant, as is the fact that for the first time in the *carpe diem* passages the

---

67. Bream ("Life without Resurrection," 56) calls 12:7 "a remarkably open-ended description, and, in the light of Qoheleth's respect for facts and his refusal to speculate, we may accept it as expressing Qoheleth's realistic agnosticism about what happens at, and after, death. He stuck with the evidence. The Lord gives the spirit, and the Lord takes it away."
68. Hesse, "Cognitive Claims," 3; see also idem, *Models and Analogies in Science*, 150–56.
69. Krüger, *Qoheleth*, 204.
70. Beal ("C[ha]osmopolis") argues along similar lines but with a postmodern twist, which I reject.

enigma of life is set in the context of joy (and remembrance) rather than the other way around.

Like a beacon alerting us to a major shift in Qohelet's perspective and struggle, 11:7 unashamedly affirms life and raises the question of what could have shifted Qohelet from his tense struggle between the *hebel* of life and the affirmation of joy—what is it that has brought such resolution? How has the contradictory juxtaposition of these two opposing approaches to life yielded a positive affirmation of life? The answer is provided in 11:8–10 and 12:1–7.

There is in 11:8–10 a developing affirmation of joy. In v. 8 joy is affirmed, but one must still "remember" the days of darkness, for all that comes is enigmatic. But in vv. 9 and 10, the call to joy is unrestrained, and it is identified as the deepest expression of one's heart. All that comes is no longer enigmatic, for it is judgment that lies ahead—there will be a time for judgment, when the extent to which one has embraced life as God's gift will be accounted for. By the time we reach v. 10, "enigma" has the more positive nuance of mystery and has become the motivation for getting rid of vexation and pursuing righteousness (put away evil).

In 12:1–7 there is a further development in Qohelet's thought, because the object of "remember" is now no longer the days of darkness as in v. 8 but "your Creator." This is a vital step in the resolution of Qohelet's struggle. The theology of remembrance of God as Creator undermines Qohelet's autonomous epistemology, because it is tantamount to making the fear of God (here = "remember your Creator") foundational to Qohelet's search for wisdom rather than the sort of epistemology he had adopted.[71] Indeed, although the reality of death is stronger than ever in this section, the observational language is absent. Remembrance thus presents the *possibility* of the resolution of the tension in Qohelet's juxtapositions of enigma and joy. As Ellul says:

> Remember your Creator. Only here does Qohelet call him by this name, and he does so by design! . . . You may consider yourself autonomous, but you are incapable of knowing what should be done, incapable of knowing what wisdom is. You are a creature. . . . Our problems do not stem from our failure to stay in our garden, like Candide. All the evils, and I choose my words carefully, *all the evils of the world* stem from our taking ourselves to be the Creator.[72]

71. As we have seen, Qohelet does refer to the fear of God, particularly in 5:7 [6]. My point here is that "remember your Creator" is similar in meaning to "the fear of the LORD" in a text such as Prov. 1:1–7. On the latter text, see Whybray (*Proverbs*, 36), who argues that the acquisition of true knowledge begins with the fear of the Lord. In the context of Ecclesiastes, 12:1 is making the same point.

72. Ellul, *Reason for Being*, 280–81. Ellul could well be accused of reading into the text at this point, but if one assumes that Qohelet had Gen. 1–3 in mind, then remembrance of one's Creator may well stress the contrast with wanting to become "like God" by "knowing good and evil." The presence of wisdom motifs in Gen. 1–3 has long been recognized (cf. Blocher, *In the*

I have deliberately used *possibility* above. The description of death and the enigmatic saying in v. 8 balance the goodness of seeing the light (11:7) and remembering the Creator with a weighty reminder of the fragility of life. Something of the juxtaposition remains, and the reader is compelled to look to the concluding verses as to whether the potentiality of remembrance really does provide the key to resolving the juxtaposition.

My analysis of these passages would thus confirm Whybray's view that (1) these *carpe diem* passages "are arranged in such a way to state their theme with steadily increasing emphasis and solemnity"; and (2) "these seven texts are clearly more than mere marginal comments or asides. They punctuate the whole book, forming a kind of *Leitmotiv*; they increase steadily in emphasis as the book proceeds; and the last, the most elaborate of them all, directly addressed to the reader, introduces and dominates the concluding section of the book in which Qoheleth presents his final thoughts on how life should be lived and why. It would be arbitrary to deny that they play a significant part in the exposition of Qoheleth's thought."[73]

Contra Whybray, however, I have suggested that the juxtaposition of the *carpe diem* passages with the enigmatic passages creates gaps that have to be filled. "Remembrance of God as Creator" potentially fills these gaps. For all their penetrating insight, Whybray and Ogden fail to recognize the gaps that the juxtaposition creates. Indeed, scholars who view Qohelet's message as more pessimistic tend to recognize the gaps more easily. The critical question, though, is how one fills the gaps. Whybray and Ogden tend to fill in the gaps positively by seeing the *carpe diem* passages as answers. However, as we have seen again and again in our examination of these passages, they would be most inadequate answers.

Castellino is much closer to the truth when he insists that "one can not deny the presence of a series of 'antitheses' that makes it difficult to assess the true meaning of the book. Due to these 'antitheses,' exegetes are divided when called upon to judge what fundamental note Qohelet really strikes. . . . There is no denying that both sides could substantiate their judgment through an array of apposite quotations."[74] Failure to recognize the juxtapositions/antitheses results in scholars endlessly trying to fill in the (unrecognized) gap created by them. The gap is always then filled in by making one of the poles dominant. Thus Qohelet either becomes mainly skeptical or mainly positive. Recognition of the juxtapositions grants the insight that he is skeptical *and* positive! His autonomous epistemology takes him toward skepticism, but his Jewish background and faith provide him with an undeniably shalomic perspective on life.

Beginning), and Eve's reliance on what she saw rather than on what God as Creator said may well be part of the background here.

73. Whybray, "Qoheleth, Preacher of Joy," 87–88.

74. Castellino, "Qohelet and His Wisdom," 15–16.

Ecclesiastes itself gives us clues as to how the gap between autonomous skepticism and the *carpe diem* perspective is to be filled. The theology of remembrance in 12:1 is important in this respect, but the epilogue is definitive in indicating finally how the narrator intends us to fill in the gaps, and I suggest that 12:13–14 confirms my reading of 12:1 as the bridge that positively resolves the tension/gap between the *carpe diem* element and the enigma statements.

It is easy to overlook the richness evoked in the phrase "remember your Creator," and so it is worth pausing to reflect on its theological and philosophical implications. The word "remember" occurs frequently in Deuteronomy, and a passage that is similar to 12:1 is Deut. 8:18 (NRSV), "But remember the LORD your God, for it is he who gives you power to get wealth, so that he may confirm his covenant that he swore to your ancestors, as he is doing today."[75] In the context of this verse the alternative is the danger of forgetting God (Deut. 8:11–20). Forgetting God involves for Deuteronomy an assertion of human autonomy: "Do not say to yourself, 'My power and the might of my own hand have gotten me this wealth'" (Deut. 8:7). Instead the Israelites are to remember the LORD and allow this remembrance to shape the way they live in the land.

Remembrance in Eccles. 12:1 is thus far more than mere mental assent. It represents the radical difference between a worldview in which humankind is central and autonomous and one in which God is central.[76] In his evenhanded critique of modernity, Charles Taylor notes that "acknowledging the transcendent means being called to a change of identity. . . . Christian faith can be seen in the same terms: as calling for a radical decentering of the self, in relation with God."[77] And in a way that is wonderfully reminiscent of Qohelet, Taylor goes on to note, "Renouncing . . . not only takes you away but also brings you back to flourishing. In Christian terms, if renunciation decenters you in relation with God, God's will is that humans flourish, and so you are taken back to an affirmation of this flourishing, which is biblically called agape."[78] Qohelet's autonomous epistemology puts himself and his consciousness at the center of his quest for knowledge, and in Deuteronomy's language this is a case of "forgetting."

75. Other significant passages in the OT are Judg. 8:34; Neh. 4:14; Pss. 78:35; 137:6; Isa. 17:10; 57:11; Jer. 51:50; Jon. 2:7.

76. Haden ("Qoheleth and the Problem of Alienation," 66) notes in this respect the difference between Qohelet and modern existentialists: "For the existentialist, meaning escapes man because there is no reference point outside of humanity to give life meaning; for Qoheleth, meaning may be elusive and cause the feeling of *hebel*, but nevertheless, meaning exists because God exists." He agrees with Kendall ("Alienation and the Struggle for Existence"): "Man must reaffirm creaturehood, for it is the negations of his limitations as a creature which leads him towards deeper alienation and struggle in life."

77. Charles Taylor, "Catholic Modernity?" 21.

78. Ibid., 22.

Philosophically, Casey gets at the sort of remembering, by contrast with forgetting, that Qohelet has in mind:

> In short, I am calling for a return to memory as more than mere mental "flotsam"—as more than a mere engrammatic inscription of the left-overs, the rags and tatters, of our lives. Remembering, rather, is soul-making, is its very basis. As such, remembering needs itself to be remembered—just as the soul itself needs to be remembered in this soulless time of ours. . . . In fact the right rich remembering is an equiprimordial entrance to the soul's depths. . . . Memory is . . . in many ways the taproot of the rhizomatic structure of the soul itself. . . .
> Soul-making, we can conclude, is ineluctably a remembering, while remembering is itself a main means of reversion to soul. For we see into the depths of the psyche by the re-verting, re-connecting, re-versioning, and re-visioning which remembering in depth alone makes possible. [79]

By "re-verting" Casey has in mind the human capacity to look back, and in Qohelet's case looking back to the primordial origin[80] of all things. But this is lifeless unless such looking back involves a "re-connecting" with that to which one returns. "Re-version" thus becomes a communion and conjunction.[81] Such "re-connection" implies a "re-versioning" (i.e., giving a different version), but of what? Nothing less than of the present, and thus of Qohelet's quest. "Re-versioning . . . cannot be reduced simply to giving another version. . . . It is much more a matter of shifting levels: retelling the tale . . . but at . . . another level of meaning, another stratum of significance."[82] Finally, remembering involves "re-visioning," and Casey discerns three aspects to this:

1. _Re-viewing_: This involves letting our remembered life pass before us.
2. _Re-visualizing_: This is an active approach in which we clarify what has come forth from "re-viewing."
3. _Re-envisioning_: This is the most encompassing mode because it has to do with "visions envisioning the soul itself."[83] Once our lives are re-viewed and re-visualized, we can take account more fully of what has been done, and in Qoheleth's case, said. "Remembering has here truly come into its own. . . . Active remembering allows us to take our lives onwards into new depths. It does so precisely by revivifying old depths."[84] "In remembering we return home to the heartland of the already known, the already-having-happened."[85]

79. Casey, _Spirit and Soul_, 179–80.
80. On this possibility, see ibid., 168.
81. Ibid., 168.
82. Ibid., 172.
83. Heidegger, quoted by Casey in ibid., 175.
84. Ibid., 176.
85. Ibid., 157.

Remembering one's Creator, thus, in all its richness, subverts Qohelet's autonomous epistemology and provides a new starting point for wrestling with the very real issues his journey explored, albeit a starting point with which he was already familiar. His journey is very much like that of Sue Bender, who, in the context of an overly busy life, went to spend a year with the Amish and concludes: "I went searching in a foreign land and found my way home."[86] Remembering one's Creator does not detract from the paradoxes of life but reorients one toward them in a fresh way. Heidegger notes, "Out of memory, and within memory, the soul . . . pours forth its wealth of images—of visions encompassing the soul itself."[87] Qohelet's epistemology yielded the image of enigma in particular, whereas the image of creation evokes and pours forth different images, one's that are developed in passages like Prov. 8 and God's speeches in Job. Enigma remains, but it is enveloped in meaning.

But of course this does not eradicate the difficulties and mysteries of life, and although "remember your Creator" embraces the whole of 12:1–7, the content of this section utterly refuses to ignore the paradoxes of life. This section starts with the exhortation to "remember your Creator" and ends with the human spirit returning to God, who gave it. Thus it is enclosed in creation, but sandwiched in between is Qohelet's strongest reflection on death, both personal and cosmic. In v. 1 the effect of the approaching death of an individual is in view, but in vv. 2–6 the vision becomes one of eschatological judgment in language akin to that of the prophets' description of the day of the LORD. In this way Qohelet connects individual death to the destiny of the creation as a whole, including humanity. "Remembering your Creator" is for Qohelet the key to preparing for personal and cosmic judgment. More than this he is unable to say, but he has found a way to live the mysteries of life without all the answers to his questions. He has no detailed eschatology of hope and of cosmic restoration as is found elsewhere in the OT and fully revealed in the NT, but he has found firm ground in the fear of the LORD, in remembering his Creator rather than trying to play the role of God. It will take Jesus's conquering of death in his resurrection and ascension to resolve the mystery of death that Qohelet pursues so relentlessly.

86. Bender, *Plain and Simple*, xii.
87. Heidegger, "What Is Called Thinking?" quoted in Casey, *Spirit and Soul*, 157.

III.
Frame Narrative: Epilogue
(12:8–14)

Translation

[8]"Utterly enigmatic," says Qohelet, "Everything is enigmatic."
[9]Additionally,[1] because Qohelet was wise, he constantly[2] taught knowledge to the people, and he pondered[3] and sought out[4] and arranged[5] many proverbs.

1. The disjunctive accent on *wĕyōtēr* suggests that it is syntactically distinct from the rest of v. 9. This militates against translating *yōtēr še* as "besides which." *Yōtēr* is thus a noun meaning "an addition" or a substantive used as an adverb, meaning "additionally." *Še* should therefore be read not as a relative pronoun but causally (RJW §474).

2. See Schoors (*Preacher*, 1:116) for this translation of *'ôd*.

3. *Wĕ'izzēn* is usually taken as a *hapax legomenon*, a Piel from *'zn* II, "to weigh." There is an Arabic cognate and noun "scales" from which the word is thought to derive. However, as Longman (*Ecclesiastes*, 275) and Seow (*Ecclesiastes*, 384) point out, the verb more likely derives from *'izzēn*, "to hear, listen." The difficulty is that in all other occurrences in the OT, *'izzēn* is in the Hiphil stem, not the Piel as here. Seow, however, notes that there is semantic overlap between the Hiphil and the Piel, and many Hebrew verbs occur in both stems with no discernible difference in meaning. It should also be noted that all three verbs in this colon are in the Piel stem. *Wĕ'izzēn* should thus be taken to mean "he listened attentively" or, as here, "pondered."

4. This verb also occurs in Prov. 25:2. It has the connotations of searching out, analyzing carefully, deliberating over.

5. Fishbane (*Biblical Interpretation*, 32) suggests that it is likely that *tiqqēn* has here the technical meaning "to edit" or "to arrange." See Seow (*Ecclesiastes*, 385) for the range of possible meanings.

[10]Qohelet sought to find delightful words and he wrote[6] truth plainly.[7]
[11]The words of the wise are like goads,[8] and like nails firmly embedded are the collected sayings[9] that are given by one shepherd.[10]
[12]And besides them,[11] my son, be warned: of the writing of many
books there is no end, and much study[12] is wearisome to the flesh.
[13]The end of the matter, all has been heard. Fear God and keep his
commandments, for this is the whole duty of humankind.[13]
[14]For God will bring every deed into judgment, including every secret
thing, whether good or evil.

Interpretation

[8]"Utterly enigmatic," says Qohelet, "Everything is enigmatic."

12:8. *Restatement of the theme.*[14] Verse 8 takes us back to 1:2 and forms
the *inclusio* of the book, and in the process brings the voice of the narrator—
"says Qohelet"—in once again. As in chap. 1 this alerts us to the theme of

6. See the interpretation for a discussion of the translation of this verb.
7. *Yōšer* is here an adverb rather than a noun. See Schoors, *Preacher*, 1:45–46.
8. On the unusual form of this word see Seow, *Ecclesiastes*, 386–87.
9. *Baʿălê ʾăsuppôt* is a challenging phrase to translate. It occurs only here in the OT, although it is attested in later Jewish literature. In the Talmud it refers to members of the Sanhedrin (*b. Sanhedrin* 12a). Krüger (*Qoheleth*, 207) points out that the phrase could be read personally as "masters of the assemblies" or impersonally as "element of the class 'gathered sayings.'" Long-man (*Ecclesiastes*, 276) translates the phrase as "the masters of collections," Seow (*Ecclesiastes*, 387) as "the mentors of assemblies." Longman notes that the parallelism of this phrase with "the words of the wise" does not require a synonym, but "collected sayings" seems to fit better in the entire verse, and particularly in relation to them being given by one shepherd.
10. There is much debate about whether this expression should be translated "one shepherd" or as "a shepherd." See the interpretation.
11. Fox (*Qohelet*, 326–27; idem, *Time*, 356–57) argues that a disjunctive accent should be placed on *wĕyōtēr* as in v. 9 as a basis for his reading of this verse as a warning against the wise. But the idiom *yōtēr min* is well attested in Postbiblical Hebrew, so the warning is simply not to go beyond the teachings of the wise. See the interpretation.
12. *Lahag* is a *hapax legomenon*. Generally it is taken as a noun from the root *lhg*, not otherwise attested in Hebrew. The meaning derives from an extension of the Arabic cognate meaning "to be devoted" and thus by extension "study." Krüger (*Qoheleth*, 207) proposes to emend the text to *lĕhāgô* from the Qal of *hgh*, and thus it means "read half out loud, consider while mumbling" and by extension "study." Seow (*Ecclesiastes*, 389–90) also relates the verb to the root *hgh* but assumes a haplography of *h* at the end of the verb and translates it "talking."
13. The expression is elliptical. The Hebrew reads lit. "this is all humanity." Seow (*Ecclesiastes*, 390) translates, "for every mortal is to be so."
14. There is much at stake in how we translate and interpret the epilogue. For this reason, I have included more discussion of the technical details in the interpretation section rather than placing them in the footnotes to the translation.

Qohelet's investigation. Situated here it might be taken to imply that this was Qohelet's final conclusion. Thus Longman argues that "in this way the frame narrator indicates that he understands this typically Qohelethine expression to be a proper summary of his message. That message is: there is no ultimate meaning in this world. Once all is said and done, Qoheleth's conclusion is that *everything is meaningless*."[15] However, not only does this assume an unhelpful meaning of *hebel* but it misunderstands the variety of roles that frames in narrative can play.

Caws concludes her analysis of *Reading Frames in Modern Fiction*:

> Each of the preceding essays, dealing with a different aspect of the problems of and the attitudes toward framing, can be seen, nevertheless, to turn around the same group of techniques for putting the selected picture into relief: delays and pauses to surround, with temporal and spatial borders, the central focused part, architectural surrounds to further mark them, repetitions and drastic contrasts to call attention either to the borders or to the dramatic quality of the scene pictured in them, an included picture to develop by nonverbal means the significance of the moral or psychological issues implied in the motifs thrown in relief or an included observer to eye the picture from within it, making an inner frame of vision useful (at times by its very deformation) for the reading from the outer border.[16]

This is helpful in alerting us to the immense variety of roles framing can play. Qohelet's discourse is framed not only by 1:2 and 12:8 but (probably) also by 1:3–11 and 12:9–14. Our concern here, however, is with the function of 12:8 in relation to 1:2. Certainly this inclusion is significant with its emphatic assertion of the enigmatic nature of everything. But *how* is it significant?

Christianson helpfully asserts that 12:8

> is a kind of framing, a formal mark of structure with an emphatic rhetorical function. The inclusion serves to mark off a specific section of text. In this case it surrounds precisely Qoheleth's narration and nothing else. Thinking in different terms, one might compare the inclusion to two identical doors at either end of the same room—serving as the only entrance and exit respectively—or perhaps the ornate covers of a book, which serve to create a unique sign, a feature of separateness. . . . The inclusion is the most obvious structural marker and thematic sign in Ecclesiastes.[17]

Salyer invokes the same image of a doorway, although for him we enter and leave through the same doorway.[18] Strangely, for Salyer 12:8 signals to the

---

15. Longman, *Ecclesiastes*, 276. Many others agree, e.g., Fox, *Time*, 332.
16. Caws, *Reading Frames in Modern Fiction*, 262.
17. Christianson, *Time to Tell*, 98.
18. Salyer, *Vain Rhetoric*, 372.

reader that "not only is an external post of observation about to be tendered, but that Qohelet is no more. The tone of the passage resembles an obituary."[19] The image of a border post is helpful, as is Salyer's notion of 12:8 as the signature of the implied author,[20] but I have no idea where the idea of an obituary comes from, bearing in mind the discussion of Qohelet that follows in 12:9–14.

Christianson's image of book covers is helpful, for it alerts us that 1:2 and 12:8 suggest what Ecclesiastes is about, without necessarily committing one to a view on the topic under discussion.[21] It is helpful to think of 1:2 and 12:8 as the title of the book, as indicating the journey of exploration on which Qohelet takes the reader, but without assuming that this is his conclusion. Indeed, so much in the book itself counters this conclusion that such an assumption is naïve and does no justice to the complexity of the book. Lest we be in any doubt, the epilogue, which is also written by the frame narrator—presumably the same author as that of 12:8—will ensure that Qohelet is not misread in this way. Verse 8 is indeed akin to the signature of the implied author, and his view of Qohelet's journey will become crystal clear in 12:9–14.

12:9–14. *Epilogue.* The words of Qohelet, as we noted in chap. 1, are inserted into a frame by a narrator. Central to the overall interpretation of Ecclesiastes, therefore, is to discern how the voice of the narrator relates to the voice(s) of Qohelet. Historical critics generally see the epilogue as starkly at odds with Qohelet and thus as a later addition providing an orthodox correction to his unorthodox teachings (see "The History of Interpretation" in the introduction). Once we read Ecclesiastes as a text in its totality, however, the relationship between the narrator/epilogist and Qohelet becomes more interesting and important for grasping Ecclesiastes as a whole.

No one has done more than Michael Fox to stimulate fresh examination of Ecclesiastes as a literary whole. However, the relationship of the epilogue to the main body of the text has become particularly important in the light of Fox's reading of the epilogue, according to which the narrator distances himself from Qohelet. Longman has followed Fox in this respect and says of 12:11–14, "he becomes more openly critical, warning his son of the dangers inherent in a writing like the one they just looked at together."[22]

19. Ibid.

20. Ibid.

21. Ogden ("Qoheleth IX 17–X 20," 30) notes, "The further apart the inclusions are, the less useful they become as criteria for establishing the limits of a unit. This is well illustrated by the book of Qoheleth as a whole, for it opens and closes with the theme of vanity (i 2 and xii 8), and although the theme is reiterated throughout, it provides little guide to the relationships between the details embraced within those limits."

22. Longman, *Ecclesiastes*, 284. See also Christianson, *Time to Tell*. For a detailed critique of Fox's view of the epilogue, see Bartholomew, *Reading Ecclesiastes*, 159–71.

> [9]Additionally, because Qohelet was wise, he constantly taught knowledge to the people, and he pondered and sought out and arranged many proverbs.

Here the narrator describes Qohelet positively as *wise*. In the light of the extremes to which the "Greek" voice of Qohelet has gone, this affirmation comes as a surprise and is reminiscent of God's startling affirmation of Job in Job 42:7, in which the LORD expresses his anger against Job's friends because they "have not spoken of me what is right, as has my servant Job." This description of Qohelet as "wise" resonates with the ironic use of "wise" in Qohelet's journey and also indicates from the narrator's perspective that Qohelet does indeed resolve his struggle and arrive at a position that fits with that of traditional wisdom.

Verse 9 also gives us insight into the activities of Qohelet. Like a good pedagogue he constantly taught knowledge to the people. Like Lady Wisdom (cf. Prov. 1–9) Qohelet's voice was continually heard, instructing "the people." Joüon has argued that "Qohelet" was not just a teacher of the elite but an orator of the people.[23] The sophistication of Qohelet's journey makes it hard to imagine that Ecclesiastes was aimed at the people of God as a whole; this work of Qohelet was more likely aimed at those more intellectual Israelites struggling in the postexilic situation with the meaning of life and the influence of Greek philosophy. But that is not the point here; the point is that his focus in his work was to help the people of God acquire knowledge and wisdom.[24]

Verse 9b uses three verbs to describe Qohelet's activity. "Pondered" most likely also has the nuance of "listened," the point being that like any wise person Qohelet listened carefully to others and reflected on what he heard.[25] He searched for wisdom, making use of all resources available to him. That he arranged or edited many proverbs indicates that Qohelet's work was more than that of merely collecting together material—he was deeply involved in interpreting what he gathered. Seow notes, "His editorial task was, thus, not a mechanical one, but hermeneutical, as it were."[26] Thus we have an attractive portrait of Qohelet as a hard-working and creative wise man with a heart for the people of God as a whole.

> [10]Qohelet sought to find delightful words and he wrote truth plainly.

---

23. Joüon, "Sur le nom."

24. On the basis of this emphasis on Qohelet "teaching the people," Gordis (*Koheleth*, 351–52) and N. Lohfink (*Qoheleth*, 142) argue that in this respect Qohelet was more than a sage, that he was quite exceptional. But this rests on a wrong understanding of the wise person. From Prov. 1–9 it is clear that wisdom is directed at the people of God as a whole.

25. Cf. my comments on listening in 5:1–7 [4:17–5:6].

26. Seow, *Ecclesiastes*, 385.

According to v. 10 he was a master of both form (delightful words) and content (he wrote truth plainly). Fox, however, emphasizes that Qohelet *"sought to find* fine words and to write."[27] For Fox this expression is "subtly noncommittal,"[28] the implication being that Qohelet sought to find and to write fine and honest words of truth, but perhaps did not.

Essential to this interpretation is the pointing of "he wrote" as an infinitive absolute, translated "to write," which Fox understands as the direct object of "he sought." The infinitive absolute is not attested by MS evidence but is proposed by the editors of *BHS* as a possible form of the verb. My translation, by comparison, "and he wrote truth plainly," would clearly undermine Fox's interpretation.

In support of this noncommittal reading of v. 10, Fox points out that "to seek" and "to find" are two of Qohelet's theme words, which here remind us that seeking does not necessarily mean finding. Fox alerts us to 8:17 in this respect, arguing that this verse teaches that God made humans unable to comprehend the world, and he implies that this teaching underlies "he sought" and "to find" in the epilogue. Just as the human cannot understand the world no matter how much one searches, so Qohelet was unable to write truth.

With respect to "and he wrote" there are a number of possibilities. First, the passive form *wĕkātûb* could be retained as it is in the LXX and in N. Lohfink's translation of this verse as "and these true sayings are here painstakingly recorded."[29] The difficulty with the passive is that the form is singular, whereas "words" is plural, although that in itself is not conclusive, since the "true words" may be here viewed as a single totality. Second, one could revocalize the text to make the verb an infinitive absolute and thus read it as a continuation of what Qohelet sought. Third, five Hebrew MSS and certain versions (Aquila, Symm, Peshitta, and Vg) understand the verb actively as *wĕkātab*. Such a reading would count strongly against Fox's position, especially if "truth" is understood as "in the profound sense of capturing reality."[30] Regardless of whether the passive form is retained or revocalized as an infinite absolute,[31] both can be understood in opposition to Fox's position.

Context alone will determine a decision in this area, but the tentativeness of Fox's translation at this point makes his translation less likely. A more positive reading of v. 10 can embrace either translation, but Fox's depends on translating this verse as "He sought . . . to write." Remarkably, although without discussion, even Fox in his 1989 paraphrase of Ecclesiastes translates

27. Fox, "Frame-Narrative and Composition," 96 (italics mine).
28. Ibid., 101.
29. N. Lohfink, *Qoheleth*, 142.
30. Murphy, *Ecclesiastes*, 125.
31. Cf. Seow, *Ecclesiastes*, 385.

v. 10b as "and he wrote words that were completely true and honest."[32] Of course, if this is the correct translation, it subverts Fox's position.

Fox finds further support for reading v. 10 as subtly noncommittal in its use of the theme words "seek" and "find." "To find" is certainly one of Ecclesiastes' key words; it occurs seventeen times, and its wide semantic range is exploited by the author in the rhetorical form of antanaclasis, especially in those passages in which it is repeated.[33] Fox is right in seeing a link between the use of these words here and in the main body of Ecclesiastes, especially 7:25–29 and 8:16–17, but his understanding of the link is inadequate. In 7:25–29 and 8:16–17, these two verbs are linked with the limitations of Qohelet's project, but the words themselves do not suggest "not finding." The negative element is stressed by negating "seek" and "find," and the search to find is not always unsuccessful in these passages.[34] Also, where "to find" is used without repetition (as in 9:10, 15; 11:1), it has indeed the meaning of finding.

The use of "seek" and "find" in 12:10 resonates with the previous use of this vocabulary in Ecclesiastes by reminding us that they are connected with Qohelet's encounter with the limitations of human knowledge, but this by no means makes v. 10 subtly noncommittal. Whenever Qohelet has wanted the reader to know that his search leads to "not finding," he has clearly said so, and in the absence of such negating, the context alone could suggest—and would need to do so very clearly—that this is how these words are to be read in v. 10. The context, however, points clearly in the reverse direction, and this on two accounts. First, Fox suggests that the narrator is subtly noncommittal in v. 10 because he wants to create some distance between Qohelet's radical views and his own. In other words, it is the "truth" of Qohelet's presentation that the narrator wants to distance himself from to some extent.[35] But v. 10 is about more than the truth of Qohelet's sayings; it is also about their aesthetic form, as "delightful" indicates. As Crenshaw comments, "Qoheleth devoted time and energy both to the aesthetic of his composition and to the reliability of what he said."[36] Like Crenshaw, Fox translates *ḥēpeṣ* (delightful) as "pleasing," but he never claims that the narrator is distancing himself subtly from the truth and the aesthetic form of Qohelet's sayings. But v. 9 is clear that

32. Fox, *Qohelet*, 348. Similarly in his 2004 commentary, Fox (*Ecclesiastes*, 83) translates v. 10, "Koheleth sought to discover useful sayings and recorded genuinely truthful sayings."

33. On the semantic range of "to find," see Ceresko ("Function of *Antanaclasis*"), who argues that the wisdom poets in particular exploited the ambiguity inherent in "to find" as a form of antanaclasis. The semantic range of "to find" extends to such activities as arrive, reach, overtake, seize, grasp, understand, find, and acquire.

34. See, e.g., 7:27–29 for the ironic play on "finding" and "not finding."

35. Fox understands "truth plainly" as a superlative, which he translates "the most honest words of truth." It is this strong statement of truth that Fox maintains the narrator wants to distance himself from.

36. Crenshaw, *Ecclesiastes*, 191.

Qohelet, like other wisdom teachers, was a master of form. However, if the narrator is subtly noncommittal he would have to be suspicious of both.

Second, to read v. 10 as Fox does is to set it against v. 9a, where Qohelet is described as "wise." Contextually it makes far more sense to read v. 10 as Qohelet achieving what he set out to do, thereby demonstrating his wisdom. That a contradiction exists between the positive affirmation of v. 9a and Fox's reading of v. 10 is confirmed by Fox's discerning a very negative comment about wisdom in general in v. 11 and Qohelet in particular in v. 12. Thus v. 10 does not distance the narrator from Qohelet but aligns the narrator with him. Qohelet succeeded in his search, and ultimately he *did* find. The aesthetic form and the content of his teaching are affirmed. Thus Qohelet's amazing and agonizing journey and his description of it are considered by the narrator as well within the wisdom tradition.

> **11**The words of the wise are like goads, and like nails firmly embedded are the collected sayings that are given by one shepherd.

Verse 11 expands on what Qohelet and other wisdom teachers have in common, namely that their words are like goads and nails and originate from one source, one shepherd—God. Such words prod us into wise action and, like nails firmly embedded, provide us with a place that holds us. It is possible that "goads" and "nails firmly embedded" could be synonyms, the nails being embedded in goads.[37] As Murphy notes, however, "The precise meaning of the metaphor of nails (pegs) is not clear. They can be conceived as giving strength and firmness, and perhaps providing a foundation for life's activities, a basis for a responsible life style."[38]

According to Fox, however, the words of the wise are like goads and nails not because they goad into right action and provide a stable point of anchorage but because they prick and hurt; they are painful and dangerous and one needs to be cautious of them. Fox maintains that v. 11 is unclear and perhaps deliberately ambiguous. However, he argues that if there is parallelism in this verse, we would not expect the comparison to refer to completely different things like encouraging better behavior and being permanent. Fox suggests that the nails, like the goads, are dangerous.

Fox is on weak ground here for two reasons. First, what is being described is not just the words of Qohelet but the "the words of the wise,"[39] and it seems extraordinary that the narrator would create distance between himself and Qohelet by describing the whole corpus of the words of the wise as dangerous, especially in the light of his positive statement in v. 9 about Qohelet being one

37. So Seow, *Ecclesiastes*, 386–87.
38. Murphy, *Ecclesiastes*, 125.
39. This expression recalls the titles in Prov. 22:17; 24:23; 30:1; and 31:1. Galling (*Prediger*, 123–24) suggests that v. 11a is a quotation.

of the wise. A more plausible strategy would be to distinguish Qohelet from other wisdom literature, a strategy that most biblical scholars follow today.

Second, Fox's argument about parallelism in v. 12 as being better accounted for by having both similes referring to the danger and pain of the "words of the wise" is unconvincing. The traditional interpretation also has both similes referring to one thing, namely, the value of the words of the wise, with the two similes developing slightly different aspects of that value: prodding in the right direction, on the one hand, and providing stability, on the other. Indeed, the traditional understanding fits better with the dynamic nature of biblical parallelism, in which there is invariably movement from one line to the next. As Alter puts it, "Literature thrives on parallelism. . . . But it is equally important to recognize that literary expression abhors complete parallelism, just as language resists true synonymity, usage always introducing small wedges of difference between closely akin terms."[40] If in this verse we have in the parallelism the characteristic heightening or intensification that Alter proposes,[41] then the heightening is probably to be located in the "firmly embedded" qualifying "nails." Thus the direction in which the sayings of the wise goad is a direction that is firm, solid, and trustworthy, and the narrator regards Qohelet as squarely in this category.

Fox and Longman translate v. 11b as "that are given by a shepherd" rather than ". . . one shepherd." According to Fox, the shepherd is not God, because in the OT, God is called "shepherd" in his capacity as keeper and savior, and these attributes are not relevant here. Moreover, "shepherd" is never used by itself to refer to God. In Israelite, Egyptian, and Babylonian didactic wisdom literature, God is never called "shepherd." Indeed, he is hardly ever given any metaphorical qualities in wisdom literature. The words of the wise are also never considered as given by God. Furthermore, *'eḥād* (one), which qualifies "shepherd," cannot be read as indicating that there is only one (i.e., a divine) shepherd, since the weight of the verse would then rest there and not on the similes of v. 11a, and the verse would be a theological declaration totally divorced from its context. Thus Fox argues that the reference is simply to a shepherd, any shepherd, and "one" functions simply as an indefinite article, as in 1 Sam. 24:15; 26:20; 1 Kings 19:4–5; and Ezek. 17:7. "In all these cases numerical qualification is not the point, i.e., there is no need to show unity as opposed to plurality. The modifier could be removed with little effect on the sense of the sentence."[42]

Fox's reading is certainly possible, but for a number of reasons it is not as strong as it might appear. First, Fox insists that "one" functions simply as an indefinite article, and he refers the reader to a number of verses where it

40. Alter, *Art of Biblical Poetry*, 10; cf. ibid., chap. 1.
41. Ibid., 19.
42. Fox, "Frame-Narrative and Composition," 103.

apparently functions this way. Remarkably, not one of these verses strongly supports Fox's view. We cannot examine each of the relevant verses in detail here, but careful examination of them bears out the following points. In Ezek. 17:7 "one" is best translated as "another" and is not redundant. In 1 Sam. 24:15 "one" is emphatic and should be translated "a single (flea)." The expression is deliberately repeated in 26:20. In 1 Kings 19:4 the NRSV correctly translates "one" as "solitary" and the expression is repeated in v. 5, although the NRSV does not repeat it. Thus in not one of Fox's examples does *'eḥād* function simply as an indefinite article.

Does this mean then that "one" never functions as the indefinite article? No, but it does alert us to the danger of too quickly assuming that we are dealing with the indefinite article when we encounter *'eḥād*. It is noted by GKC, to which Fox refers, that in only a few passages is a noun made expressly indeterminate by the addition of *'eḥād* in the sense of the indefinite article, and BDB lists the indefinite article as one of eight possible meanings of *'eḥād*.[43] It is therefore possible that *'eḥād* is the indefinite article in v. 11b, but one ought to be cautious about coming to that conclusion, and it seems unlikely that the word is redundant in the compact epilogue of 12:9–14. The idea of "one shepherd" would make sense as indicating the unified source of the diverse words of the wise if it is understood as referring to God as the ultimate source of such wisdom.

Second, Fox is wrong in asserting that God cannot be referred to metaphorically as "one shepherd" because the ideas of him as keeper and savior are irrelevant here. On the contrary, God as the unified source of the diverse words of the wise would explain their value. Furthermore, "goads" were used by shepherds to move animals along the right route, and thus shepherd imagery is already strongly present in this verse,[44] which can be seen to progress naturally to God the shepherd as the one source of wisdom.[45] Thus v. 11 not

---

43. GKC §125b; BDB 25.

44. Fox (*Qohelet*, 348) strengthens the argument that shepherd imagery dominates v. 11 by paraphrasing v. 11b, "and the words of proverb-collectors may smart like the nails a shepherd uses to prod his sheep." It should be noted that this paraphrase makes the reference to the nails more positive than in his translation in "Frame-Narrative and Composition," 96.

45. In my work on Ecclesiastes, I have been struck by its similarities to Deuteronomy. For example,

> Eating and drinking is a dominant motif in Ecclesiastes and Deuteronomy.
> Eccles. 5:1–7 [4:17–5:6] is akin to the Name theology of Deuteronomy.
> Eccles. 5:4–5 [3–4] restates the law of Deut. 23:22–24.
> The exhortation to "beware of anything more than these" in Eccles. 12:12 and that "nothing can be taken away from God's work" in 3:14 is similar to Deuteronomy's exhortation not to add or take anything away from the law.
> The exhortation in Eccles. 12:13 to keep the commandments is a characteristic Deuteronomistic phrase (Weinfeld, *Deuteronomy and the Deuteronomic School*, 336).
> The remembrance motif is common to both Ecclesiastes and Deuteronomy.

only positions Qohelet's teaching among the wise but also traces the origin of such wisdom to one shepherd, namely God.

> [12]And besides them, my son, be warned: of the writing of many books there is no end, and much study is wearisome to the flesh.

Verse 12 therefore warns the reader of the danger of finding wisdom outside the wisdom traditions referred to in v. 11. Contra Fox and Longman, *wĕyōtēr mēhēmmâ* should be translated not as "Furthermore, of these," but as "And besides them." "Be warned" is often used in the OT to refer to giving instruction.[46] The context alone can determine whether this instruction is a warning. The context here indicates that the reader is being warned against going beyond the teaching of the wise; this warning is formulaic, affirming the sufficiency of the texts referred to.[47]

In v. 12 the reasons given for not wandering outside the wisdom tradition are that there is no end to the production of books and much study wearies the flesh. Contra Fox, Qohelet is not warning against the wisdom tradition,[48] but what then is he warning against? Crenshaw asserts that the author is warning "against an open attitude toward the canon."[49] Seow sees v. 12 as akin to the "canonical formula" in Deut. 4:2; 12:32 [13:1]; and Rev. 22:18–19. This formula does not rule out other books from being consulted but establishes the "complete reliability of the respective text for its purpose."[50] Either way this is a remarkable affirmation of Qohelet's journey by the narrator. In a context in which Israelites were being tempted by Greek philosophy, v. 12 would be relevant as a warning against their "folly."

> [13]The end of the matter, all has been heard. Fear God and keep his commandments, for this is the whole duty of humankind.
> [14]For God will bring every deed into judgment, including every secret thing, whether good or evil.

If the author of Ecclesiastes is keenly aware of Deuteronomy or its theology, then it is possible that "one" in Eccles. 12:11 may be related to "one" in Deut. 6:4. Mayes (*Deuteronomy*, 177) also notes that some of the exhortations following Deut. 6:4 have wisdom parallels.

46. Cf. BDB 2094. The form of the verb in 12:12 is Niphal imperative masculine singular. The Niphal infinitive construct form occurs in 4:13, appropriately translated "take advice" by the NRSV. Cf. also Ps. 19:11 [12]. BDB does suggest that in Eccles. 12:12 this verb means only "warn" as in Ezekiel, but that must be argued from the context.

47. Seow, *Ecclesiastes*, 388.

48. Fox, "Frame-Narrative and Composition," 102, 103.

49. Crenshaw, *Ecclesiastes*, 191.

50. Seow, *Ecclesiastes*, 394.

In vv. 13–14 the narrator sums up Qohelet's journey.[51] "All has been heard"—this evokes the wide-ranging, comprehensive nature of Qohelet's quest. "The end of the matter" refers to the ultimate conclusion to the quest we have witnessed. "Fear God and keep his commandments." "Fear" here refers to a holy reverence before God and aligns Qohelet with Proverbs, which makes the fear of God the beginning of wisdom. Thus, as T. S. Eliot notes, the end of the journey is to find oneself at the beginning again, only this time one understands it more fully.

Wisdom is also here related closely to OT torah—"and keep his commandments." Many scholars see a later hand at work here because of the positive reference to law. Fox, for example, finds a strong opposition between wisdom and law in the epilogue.[52] For many commentators, the language about fearing God and keeping his commandments is so alien to Qohelet that vv. 12–14 must be read as a critique of Qohelet.[53] The relationship between these two types of OT material continues to be a matter of discussion among OT theologians.[54] However, this "strong opposition" view is guilty of reading a modern antithesis back into Ecclesiastes. Even so even-handed a scholar as

51. It is common among scholars to discern in vv. 13–14 the voice of a second epilogist, but in the light of the awareness of law in the main body of the book, this seems unnecessary. Sheppard ("Epilogue to Qoheleth," 184–85) notes the similarities in vocabulary between the epilogue and the main body of Ecclesiastes. However, he reads vv. 13–14 as a thematizing of Ecclesiastes that connects with parts of the book but is in tension with the other major thematizing of the book in 1:2 and 12:8. Only in Sirach, in Sheppard's view, do we find the same ideology as in vv. 13–14. For Sheppard (ibid., 189) the epilogue "provides a rare glimpse into a comprehensive, canon-conscious formulation of what the purpose of biblical wisdom is." G. Wilson ("Words of the Wise") rejects a close parallel between 12:9–14 and Sirach. In terms of canonical formation, he proposes that we envisage the development as follows: (a) Proverbs is compiled out of existing collections. (b) The Deuteronomic movement provided a new context in which to interpret wisdom. (c) Apart from the epilogue, Ecclesiastes manifests the critical tendencies of later wisdom. (d) Canonical editors added initial superscriptions to both Proverbs and Ecclesiastes as well as 12:9–14 that picked up themes in Prov. 1:1–8 and made explicit the connection between fearing Yahweh/God and keeping his commandments, which is implicit in Prov. 1–9. The result canonically is that "this movement so binds these two works together that now each must be read in the larger context of the other and in light of the hermeneutical principle laid down in prologue and epilogue" (ibid., 190). Attractive as Sheppard's and Wilson's canonical readings are, they nevertheless depend on a late relating of law and wisdom. See the discussion of this issue in the introduction, "Reading Ecclesiastes within the Context of Proverbs and Job and Its Connection to the Torah."

52. Fox, "Frame-Narrative and Composition," 102, 103.

53. Cf., e.g., Lauha, *Kohelet*, 221–23. The content of vv. 12–14 is decisive for Lauha's understanding of vv. 12–14 as an independent second afterword.

54. See Reventlow, *Problems of Old Testament Theology*, 168–86. As Reventlow says (ibid., 181), "It is at this point, i.e. over the question of the relationship between the various areas of OT thought, that the discussion will have to be continued: in other words, between the conception of order which is characteristic of wisdom (and not just wisdom) and the areas governed by the tradition of salvation history." See Goldingay (*Theological Diversity*, 200–239) for a discussion of the relationship between wisdom and salvation history.

Murphy asserts that the conjunction of the fear of God and obedience to the commandments in v. 13 is not found elsewhere in Ecclesiastes: "The epilogue is obviously putting forth an ideal which has been developed elsewhere and which is not a concern in Ecclesiastes."[55] As we have seen, however, there are clear indications in Ecclesiastes that Qohelet is aware of cultic and other law, and thus the conjunction of law and the fear of God here is not at all surprising. Indeed, the epilogue resonates strongly with 5:1–7 [4:17–5:6].

Verses 13–14 conclude the epilogue and the book. Verse 13b is in the second person and sums up the message of Qohelet in the OT terms of fearing God and keeping his commandments and describes this as "the whole duty of humankind." Thus the first motivation given for revering God is positively that in this way we fulfill our humanity. As Irenaeus noted: "The glory of God is the human being fully alive."[56] Second, in v. 14 we have a negative motivation: the judgment of God, which connects back into 12:1–7.

Theological Implications

For the theological implications of 12:8 see the comments on 1:2. The narrator's affirmation of Qohelet as wise is akin to God's statement in Job 42:7, "My anger is kindled against you and your two friends, for you have not spoken of me what is right, as my servant Job has." God thus affirms the agonizing struggle that Job has gone through before coming to a position of trust and rest in God and finally being able to say that whereas previously he had heard of God, now his eyes see God (42:5). Similarly, the epilogue in Ecclesiastes affirms the journey Qohelet has gone through before coming to that place of remembering his Creator.

Pastorally this is significant, for Ecclesiastes, like Job, holds out hope for those struggling amid the mysteries of what God is up to in their lives and thus in his world. Such agonizing struggles are affirmed and shown to be integral to the Christian life. Job and Ecclesiastes also give us clues as to how to live these struggles. In Ecclesiastes' case the struggle is more intellectual than that of Job. The major clue it yields is that on such a journey of exploration into the meaning of life, one's starting point and thus one's epistemology is crucial.

Van Leeuwen comments on Prov. 1:1–7:

> In Proverbs, faith is not opposed to reason but constitutes its possibility, its connection to reality. Proverbs 1:7 contradicts an assumption basic to most current worldviews—namely, that knowledge of the real world is independent of the "fear" or "knowledge" of God. This modern assumption is expressed, even in works of biblical scholarship, by a variety of separations of "sacred" and

---

55. Murphy, *Ecclesiastes*, 126.
56. Irenaeus, *Against Heresies* 4.20.7 (cf. ANF, 1:490).

"secular" realms: public vs. private, facts vs. values, science vs. religion, reason vs. faith, "objective" vs. (merely) subjective. But the critique of modernity in 1:7 is not just a matter of ideas or perspectives. The very patterns, structures, and institutions of our public and private lives have been largely shaped by reason, science, and technique in the service of modern idols such as wealth, power, pleasure, nation, and unbridled individual "freedom."[57]

It is no accident that the modern idols Van Leeuwen mentions all receive focused attention in Ecclesiastes: wealth, power, nation, and freedom. Ecclesiastes illuminates for us what happens if one tries to understand these entities apart from remembering our Creator or what Proverbs calls the fear of the LORD. You simply cannot make sense of life and continually end up on the slippery slope toward enigma and despair.

In Qohelet's day, Greek philosophy was in the air, and amid the failure of Israel, it was a strong temptation to use such philosophical insights apart from the fear of the LORD to makes sense of life. Ecclesiastes exposes such a quest for what it is, a temptation, which must be resisted by finding one's way back to the starting point and, as T. S. Eliot would remind us, understanding it more fully. That was no easy journey in Qohelet's day and it is no easy journey today. As Barth notes, however, "It is impossible to maintain at one and the same time the concept of man constituted by the Word of God and the idea of a neutral capacity in man. If man has his being in the Word of God, he can do only that which corresponds to the Word of God. The actuality in which he has his being is from the very first oriented in this direction."[58] The legacy of modernity persists in postmodernity to make anything rather than the LORD our starting point. Among postmoderns it is even preferable to admit no starting point—although ironically this itself *is* a starting point—rather than to return to the fear of the LORD and remembrance of one's Creator.

In 12:13 and 14 the epilogist concludes Ecclesiastes by summing up the argument: fear God and keep his commandments. The connection here made between wisdom and law is seen by most commentators as a late addition to the book. As discussed in the introduction (see "Reading Ecclesiastes within the Context of Proverbs and Job and Its Connection to the Torah"), however, this rests on a false antithesis between wisdom and law. Qohelet, as we have seen, is well aware of OT law and alludes to it at several points, and he is familiar with the cultus of the temple where one should go to listen, that is, to be instructed in the law. The imperative to fear God is precisely where Proverbs starts, and the exhortation to keep God's commandments is at the heart of the covenantal faith of Israel. For the epilogist, this is the "whole of humankind," a poignant theological insight. It is only in relationship with

57. Van Leeuwen, "Proverbs," 34.
58. Barth, CD 3.2:131.

God as God and in submission to his will that we find ourselves to be truly alive and on the road to full humanity. As Barth notes, "Basically and comprehensively, therefore, to be a man is to be with God."[59] This indeed is true wisdom, and via a circuitous but necessary route, it is the destination at which Ecclesiastes arrives.

59. Ibid., 135.

Postscript

Postmodernism, Psychology, Spiritual Formation, and Preaching

Emerging from working intensively with Ecclesiastes, one is left with an overpowering sense that it does indeed "make the hands unclean." It is God's word to us and speaks powerfully in our twenty-first-century context. It seemed appropriate therefore to add a postscript giving some indication of how it does this and how it might be appropriated by the church today.

Postmodernism

Personally, I prefer to think of postmodernity as late modernity because it represents the unraveling of modernity rather than a clear move beyond modernity.[1] Postmodernism has problematized modernity and many of its foundational assumptions, but it has not abandoned its roots in human autonomy. David Harvey's diagnosis of the condition of postmodernity is acute;[2] modernity abandoned tradition and religion and embraced reason and human autonomy as the route to truth about the world. Postmodernism has problematized the possibility of reason ever getting us to the truth about the world but is content to live with and indeed to celebrate that impossibility, in what I consider a sort of cheerful nihilism. Thus Derrida, one of postmodernity's great proponents, problematizes what he calls the "metaphysics of presence" but asserts simultaneously that we have no other place to stand. The result is

1. See Goheen and Bartholomew, *Living at the Crossroads*, 107–26.
2. D. Harvey, *The Condition of Postmodernity: An Enquiry into the Origins of Cultural Change* (Oxford: Blackwell, 1989).

that one is left hovering between a deconstructed modernity and a world of historicism in which all is at play—not an easy place in which to live!

Several years ago I was asked to give a lecture on a dialogue between Derrida and Qohelet, a fascinating proposition. Qohelet's Greek epistemology is very modern in its dependence on reason, experience, and observation and in its questioning of religion and tradition. Like Derrida, Qohelet problematizes and deconstructs an epistemology based on human autonomy.[3] Quite unlike Derrida, however, Qohelet ultimately finds resolution and thus an alternative place to stand in remembering his Creator and fearing God.

For all their talk about religion (and I for one am grateful for the way in which postmoderns have brought religion back into academic discussions), Derrida and other postmoderns such as Vattimo never escape their liberal Enlightenment presuppositions. As Gadamer commented on Derrida's and Vattimo's presentations on religion at a meeting in Capri, "Both agree that no matter to what extent we recognize the urgency of religion, there can be no return to the doctrines of the Church."[4] At most they are able to recover a post-Heideggerian, post-Nietzschean form of religion that bears no resemblance to the living religions of our day, let alone orthodox Christianity. This is intriguing, bearing in mind the much ignored explosion of Christianity and Islam in our time.[5]

Qohelet juxtaposes his Greek voice with his Israelite experience of life, and greatly to his credit he refuses to minimize the contradictions between them. Resolution comes through finding his way back via an excruciating journey to that traditional starting point of the Creator, and thereby decentering himself to the appropriate position of creature. Thus Qohelet does indeed point the way back to the "doctrines of the Church," rather than leaving us stranded in no-man's-land.

Qohelet thus helps us to affirm postmodernism's deconstruction of much of modernity while pointing a way toward an old but renewed way that offers real hope in a perplexing world. Missionally, Ecclesiastes is thus exemplary of contextualization,[6] of witnessing to the gospel in our particular time and place. George Steiner notes that Derrida confronts us with a stark choice: either "In the beginning was the Word" or nihilism.[7] Qohelet confronts head-on the

3. Derrida's vocabulary is notoriously difficult to define, but insofar as deconstruction involves the identification of aporia—logical contradictions—in a discourse, then the parallel with Qohelet's critique of traditional wisdom is apt.

4. Gadamer, "Dialogues in Capri," 207.

5. See Jenkins, *Next Christendom*.

6. Whybray ("Qoheleth as a Theologian," 239) aptly describes Qohelet as an apologist. He rejects views of Qohelet as a pessimist, skeptic, cynic, or nihilist and insists that "on the contrary he was a Jewish theologian-teacher whose purpose was, out of a genuine religious faith, to show a young but adult male audience how to maintain their faith in circumstances that militated powerfully against it" (ibid., 245).

7. Steiner, *Real Presences*, 120.

impulse toward nihilism but finds a way through to affirm, "In the beginning." And it is this "grammar of creation"[8] that alone provides a bulwark against the historicism that is so rampant in postmodernism. Amid a crumbling modernity Ecclesiastes exposes the pain of struggling with the questions raised by postmodernism but resists the tendency to collapse creation into fall, as does Derrida, and the move to reduce God to our neighbor, "the other," as does Derrida in his reading of Kierkegaard's *Fear and Trembling*.[9]

Ecclesiastes never lets go of the mysteries of life (cf. 12:1–7) but leads us to that great starting point of the fear of the LORD ("remember your Creator") as *the* place to stand amid the mysteries and enigmas of life, and from which we can embrace life with joy and feasting. It thereby enables us to see the Christian perspective on life as a genuine alternative to modernity and its unraveling in postmodernism.

Psychology

Ecclesiastes cries out for a psychological reading.[10] Zimmermann attempted this but in a speculative manner. There are, however, resources in Kierkegaard and especially the psychiatrist Carl Jung for an insightful analysis of Qohelet's psychological development.

The pervasive use of the first person "I" is the great characteristic of Qohelet's journey. Psychologically this is significant, focusing as it does on the ego and its relation to the self. This is territory that Jung explored in significant detail. For Jung the self is the center of the total person, conscious and unconscious, whereas the ego is the center of conscious personality. The ego is the center of subjective identity, while the self is the locale of objective identity. The self is identified by Jung with the *imago Dei*; it is the creative center where God and humankind meet.

Consequently, the relationship between the ego and the self is vitally important psychologically. Many psychological problems are illuminated in terms of the ego-self relationship. The dominant model among contemporary Jungian analysts is that the first half of life involves the development of the ego, which progressively distinguishes itself from the self. The second half of life involves the ego finding its way toward a healthy, integrated relationship to the self. In terms of this journey of *individuation*, Jung distinguishes between the inflated ego, the alienated ego, and the encounter with the self leading to a healthy relationship between the ego and the self.

8. *Grammars of Creation* was the title of Steiner's 1990 Gifford Lectures.

9. See Derrida, *Gift of Death*, 53–81.

10. A nineteenth-century attempt is that by Root, "Ecclesiastes Considered Psychologically." I am indebted to my colleague in psychology, Brenda Stephenson, for help with this section. We plan to write together a more detailed psychological analysis of Ecclesiastes.

Inflation refers to the identification of the ego with the self. "It is a state in which something small (the ego) has arrogated to itself the qualities of something larger (the Self) and hence is blown up beyond the limits of its proper size."[11] However, this state, which Jungians regard as the initial state of the person, cannot perdure, because the experience of life frustrates the expectations of the inflated ego and results in an estrangement between the ego and the self. "This estrangement is symbolized by such images as a fall, an exile, an unhealing wound, a perpetual torture."[12] This experience of alienation is a necessary stage en route to awareness of and a healthy relationship to the self.

According to Jung, "The self, in its efforts at self-realization, reaches out beyond the ego-personality on all sides; because of its all-encompassing nature it is brighter and darker than the ego, and accordingly confronts it with problems which it would like to avoid. . . . For this reason *the experience of the self is always a defeat for the ego.*"[13] Kierkegaard expresses a similar sentiment:

> So much is said about wasted lives—but only that man's life is wasted who lived on, so deceived by the joys of life or by its sorrows that he never became eternally and decisively conscious of himself as spirit . . . or (what is the same thing) never became aware and in the deepest sense received an impression of the fact that there is a God, and that he, he himself, . . . exists before this God, which gain of infinity is never attained except through despair.[14]

Kierkegaard's depiction of the emergence of the self is important, for it makes explicit the religious dimension that is implicit in Jung's psychology.[15] The inflation of the ego is from this perspective symptomatic of idolatry, with the "I" as the center of one's existence. The journey toward health involves a decentering of the ego, the "I," as *part of* the self and as *constituted by* the self, but not *as* the self. For Kierkegaard as for Jung, the process of moving from an inflated ego through an alienated ego to a healthy ego-self relationship is wrought by pain and struggle, for it is a journey that the ego instinctively resists.[16]

11. Edinger, *Ego and Archetype*, 7.
12. Ibid., 37.
13. Jung, *Mysterium Coniunctionis*, par. 778.
14. Kierkegaard, *Sickness unto Death*, 26–27.
15. The philosophical and theological literature relating to the self is vast. Examples are Weaver, *Self-Love and Christian Ethics*; Weil, *Gravity and Grace*, 23–27, 35–37, 53–54; Ramsey, *Religious Language*, 42–43. On the theology of "I" and of being as encounter, see Barth, *CD* 3.2:244–85.
16. Bakan (*Disease, Pain, and Sacrifice*, 72) argues that "pain is the demand on the conscious ego to work to bring the decentralized part back into the unity of the organism. Pain is the imperative to the ego to assume the responsibility of telic centralization, the ego itself having emerged as a result of telic decentralization."

"Understood psychologically, the central aim of all religious practices is to keep the individual (ego) related to the deity (Self)."[17] This might sound idolatrous until we realize that the self is by definition dependent on that which is outside itself, namely nature, other humans, and above all God. This incidentally is why narrative is such a powerful way to depict epistemology, because it instinctively works against ego inflation by rendering the individual in relation to all the different dimensions of one's life.

Maturity or inner transformation is thus nothing less than an encounter with the self. In his *Answer to Job*, Jung treats the story of Job as a comprehensive account of the encounter with the self.[18] When Job loses everything to which he attached value, he is plunged into despair and a state of alienation. If the self, from a Jungian perspective, is to be recognized as the supreme value, then all lesser attachments, those most closely connected with the inflation of the ego, must be loosened. "Job's life meaning was evidently connected to family, property and health. When deprived of these he fell into despair and entered the dark night of the soul."[19] Job remains convinced of his innocence, thereby demonstrating that he is unconscious of his "shadow." Through his encounters with God, Job is brought to the realization that the ego is ignorant of the self in its totality. "Job's questions have been answered, not rationally but by living experience. What he has been seeking, the meaning of his suffering, has been found. It is nothing less than the conscious realization of the autonomous archetypal psyche; and this realization could come to birth only through an ordeal."[20]

With Job we know what events catalyzed his crisis of meaning, but with Qohelet we do not. This is instructive in itself, because the experience of confrontation with the unconscious takes a variety of forms. Qohelet's sort of struggle is commonly associated with the midlife crisis or "creative illness" that occurs when one moves into the second half of life.[21] Chapter 2 is a fine description of what Jung refers to as the two stages of life. The first involves establishing oneself in the world through accumulation of wealth and status, while the second arises from the crisis of wealth and status losing meaning. Ecclesiastes 5:3 and 7 [2, 6] hint at the source of Qohelet's conflict, namely, that dreams come through much work and that with many dreams come enigmas. Jung would of course pounce on this, with his insistence that the unconscious manifests itself through dreams. For Jung dreams are the "royal road" to knowledge of the self.[22] Disturbing dreams are often a sign

17. Edinger, *Ego and Archetype*, 63–64.
18. The reader should note that despite its insights, *Answer to Job* is a most unusual book, not least theologically.
19. Jung, *Answer to Job*, 81.
20. Ibid., 91.
21. A fine work on midlife transformation is Kidd, *When the Heart Waits*.
22. See Jung, *Dreams*.

of the self, the unconscious, demanding to be heard above the inflated ego. Qohelet's association of dreams with overwork is intriguing in this respect, for it appears to indicate from his own experience that working very hard to achieve wealth and status, an approach characteristic of the first stage of life, results in the unconscious clamoring to be heard via disturbing dreams. As Welch puts it, Jung warns "that there is more to our meaning than the ego would have us believe."[23]

Although we can only speculate about what triggered Qohelet's profound struggle with the meaning of life, this warning from Jung hits the nail on the head with respect to Qohelet's journey. His Greek epistemology confines him to what his ego knows, and his painful journey is one toward a growing awareness of the self of which the ego is only a part. As I suggested in the introduction, the apparent failure of the Israelite experiment in the postexilic era along with a social context of oppression and exploitation may have come home to Qohelet in a deeply personal way, but exactly how, we simply do not know. What we do know is that Qohelet found himself confronted in an unavoidable way with the utter enigma of life.

From a Jungian perspective, Qohelet had two choices: he could repress the experience because of its pain and capacity to wound him deeply, or he could enter the experience, surrender to it, not knowing precisely where it would take him.[24] This is not so much a philosophy of despair as it is an acceptance that says, "I can no longer live my life as I have before. I have to enter this terrifying realm of uncertainty and see where it leads, because all the things that brought me meaning are now in question." Qohelet chooses the latter option, but it is not the easy one; rather, it is a journey of deep suffering that pervades every part of his being.

For Jung, the greatest sin is to live unconsciously, and Qohelet is exemplary in his refusal of that option, although he does not know what the root of the problem is that he is facing. For Jung, to live consciously is to embrace the journey of alienation and pain through which the ego becomes properly aligned with the self. Ironically, Qohelet continually refers to his autonomous observation of life as "turning his heart" toward the different areas of life he explores. I say "ironically" because his epistemology is very much an egocentric one, one of the head rather than the heart. From a Jungian perspective, Qohelet's struggle exposes the misalignment between his ego and his self, but by surrendering to the excruciating journey he embarks on, he opens the way toward realignment of the ego with the self.

23. Welch, *Spiritual Pilgrims*, 81.

24. See Jung (*Memories*, chap. 6, "Confrontation with the Unconscious") for Jung's painful transformation of this sort. Qohelet's surrender to the journey is comparable to Jung's experience of confronting the unconscious and entering into his own breakdown, madness, and unconscious.

Qohelet's constant bumping up against everything being *hebel* is thus a painful confrontation with the limitation of his ego because of its inflation, and of its need to be repositioned in relation to his self. Qohelet's strong emotions and the extremity of the positions he articulates are a sign of the inner turmoil as well as of the fact that a lot of inner, transforming work is going on. But the transformation is not quick, and that is why narrative is helpful in expressing this sort of journey. As Welch notes, for Jung there is a complexity involved in the hearing and telling of one's story.[25] This is certainly true of Qohelet, as I hope this commentary has demonstrated. The *carpe diem* passages grow stronger as the book progresses but so too does the despair and darkness, until the two threaten to tear each other to pieces. In 5:3 and 7 [2, 6] there is some indication of insight into the source of the enigmas Qohelet is struggling with: disturbing dreams resulting from overwork. The points of insight emerge slowly; in 7:23–29 the growing sense that "wisdom" is not what it seems reaches a high point when Qohelet finds that his egocentric "wisdom" has led him right into the arms of Dame Folly, who is more bitter than death.

But the real indication of a turning point comes in the proverb of 11:7: "Truly, the light is sweet and it is good for the eyes to see the sun." This proverb has always struck me as somehow the turning point in Qohelet's journey, and once again Jung is helpful in illuminating Qohelet's journey. For Jung, when the ego begins to approach the center of the self and thus moves toward realignment, the experience can be very powerful. The contrary pole of the self "represents new life and would allow more of the self to come to *light*."[26] This, it seems, is what has happened to Qohelet in 11:7. At an experiential level something has shifted in Qohelet, a sign of the ego reaching toward a healthy alignment with the self. However, this emergence into realignment takes time, so that Qohelet's journey is not yet over at this point. "Jung speaks of two steps in the process of coming to terms with the unconscious. The first step requires hearing the unconscious; the second step involves consciousness relating to this content from the unconscious."[27] Ecclesiastes 11:7 seems akin to step one: Qohelet becomes aware of the self at an intuitive level, and this generates hope and life. What follows after 11:7 to 12:7 is Qohelet gradually unpacking the content of the unconscious.

With its "remember your Creator" 12:1 is highly significant from a Jungian perspective, for it represents a profound realization that the ego is not God but is limited in a creaturely way so that it is dependent on much more than its capacities for observation and experience and reason to find resolution to life's enigmas. "Remember your Creator" represents a decentering of the

25. Welch, *Spiritual Pilgrims*, 81.
26. Ibid., 151 (italics mine).
27. Ibid., 154.

ego and thus a realignment with the self, which is the place where the human communes with God. The mysteries of life do not disappear; 12:1–7 contains Qohelet's strongest evocation of death in all its dimensions, but they are now contained within a remembering of one's Creator and the spirit returning to God, who gave it.

Qohelet has found a resolution to his quest, but it is deeply existential and not just academic. Little wonder the narrator warns that much study wearies the flesh. Qohelet's head "wisdom" has been revealed as folly, but through that painful process of interrogating his previous certainties relentlessly, he has arrived at the beginning, now to understand it more fully and as a more integrated person.

The contemporary psychological significance of Ecclesiastes should not be underestimated. Narcissism is so much a psychological characteristic of our age that Christopher Lasch has referred to our time under the book title *The Culture of Narcissism*. The myth of Narcissus tells the story of a youth who rejected all potential lovers. In reprisal, Nemesis arranged for Narcissus to fall in love with his image reflected in a pool, only to end up dying in despair at being unable to possess the object of his love. Edinger notes that this myth is often misunderstood. Falling in love with one's reflected image means that one does not yet possess oneself; the ego is out of kilter with the self. "Narcissism in its original mythological implications is thus not a needless excess of self-love but rather just the opposite, a frustrated state of yearning for a self-possession which does not yet exist. The solution of the problem of Narcissus is the fulfillment of self-love rather than its renunciation. . . . Fulfilled self-love is a prerequisite to the genuine love of any object, and to the flow of psychic energy in general."[28]

Narcissism is symptomatic of a serious misalignment of the ego with the self, and in our age of modernity and late modernity with its massive overprivileging of the ego, it is not surprising that Western culture is deeply in trouble in this area. Gergen diagnoses our condition in his book *The Saturated Self*: "Critical to my argument is the proposal that social saturation brings with it a general loss in our assumption of true and knowable selves."[29] This brings us right onto the terrain of Ecclesiastes and indicates its value and relevance to the journey of the recovery of the self, a journey indispensable at this time.

Spiritual Formation

Just as modernity has repressed the self, so too has much contemporary Christianity, with its overintellectualization of the faith or its reduction of the

---

28. Edinger, *Ego and Archetype*, 161.
29. Gergen, *Saturated Self*, 16.

faith to emotions or social transformation. All these have their place, but they need to emerge out of an integrated self. Theologically what is at stake is what it means to be human and what salvation is all about. The late art historian Hans Rookmaaker once perceptively posed the question, "Why does Christ save us?" His answer: "In order to make us fully human!"[30] Salvation is about the restoration of our full humanity.

What the Christian tradition of spirituality has long recognized is that what is theologically called *sanctification* is a process of restoration to full humanity characterized by pain and struggle en route to union with God. The mystical tradition has paid detailed attention to the journey toward union with God, as evidenced in writers such as St. John of the Cross, Teresa of Avila, and Thomas Merton. Kierkegaard similarly recognizes that Christianity is about becoming a self through recovery of an existential relationship with God, and that this invariably involves suffering.[31] Simone Weil evokes the pain involved in this transformative journey:

> He whose soul remains ever turned toward God though the nail pierces it finds himself nailed to the very center of the universe. It is the true center; it is not in the middle; it is beyond space and time; it is God. In a dimension that does not belong to space, that is not time, that is indeed quite a different dimension, this nail has pierced through all creation, through the thickness of the screen separating the soul from God.[32]

Weil's description reminds us of the radicality of salvation; God is concerned to transform us at our deepest level of being, and he often does that through the painful journey of loosening our attachments on what makes our life meaningful so that we can find true meaning in him.

30. H. R. Rookmaaker and M. Hengelaar-Rookmaaker, *Our Calling and God's Hand in History* (Carlisle, UK: Piquant, 2003). Here is the full quote from page 171: "Christ died in order that we might be living human beings. He did not die just simply to forgive sins but to achieve much more, to make us new men and women (Romans 6 and Colossians 2). Christ died in order to make normal human life possible, to make freedom and love possible, to make life meaningful. Yes, there is life before death because Christ came. . . . Christ never died in order to make us Christians. . . . Christ died in order that we could be human."

31. The title Westphal gives his commentary on Kierkegaard's *Concluding Unscientific Postscript* is *Becoming a Self.* Bukdahl (*Kierkegaard*, 3) asserts, "The whole of Kierkegaard's writings can be seen as one sustained attempt to isolate and define reality as the internal self-definition of the personality. If this self-definition is successfully carried out, he believed, a person is 'real,' and is in charge of the inner life of the soul as well as of his or her domestic, civic, and private affairs. In ethical terms, internal self-definition of the personality comes when an individual goes beyond what has been thought, in order to exist in that thought. . . . In religious terms, the internal self-definition of the personality can also be defined as the point at which a person encounters the concrete demands of God. Seen from this point of view, it is an interpretation of the peculiar powerlessness and vulnerability of an individual in the world."

32. Weil, *Waiting for God*, 135.

Saint John of the Cross's instructions for seeking union with God express the depth of conversion required for a recovery of our humanity:

> To reach satisfaction in all
> desire its possession in nothing.
> To come to possess all
> desire the possession of nothing.
> To arrive at being all
> desire to be nothing.
> To come to the knowledge of all
> desire the knowledge of nothing.
> To come to the pleasure you have not
> you must go by the way you enjoy not.
> To come to the knowledge you have not
> you must go by a way in which you know not.
> To come to the possession you have not
> you must go by a way in which you possess not.
> To come to be what you are not
> you must go by a way in which you are not.[33]

It is true that the mystical tradition has itself on occasion neglected the self through a Platonic focus on the soul.[34] But at its best this is not the case. Thus Welch begins his book on Teresa of Avila and Jung by noting, "This book is an attempt to help the reader live a fully human yet spiritual life. Its premise is that God calls us into life and into the fullness of our personhood. Centering our life on God does not rob us of our personality, but guarantees it."[35]

It will be obvious from my Jungian reading of Ecclesiastes and from my comments on the theological implications of 12:1–7 that Ecclesiastes is a model of *soul formation*. This becomes apparent as one brings together Jung's insights into the development of the self with the Christian tradition of soul formation. For example, in *Spiritual Pilgrims* Welch has done fine work in bringing the insights of Jung and Teresa of Avila together as a model of spiritual formation. Ecclesiastes can be read along the lines of the formation of the soul in the following ways:

1. Conversion is only the starting point of a process of sanctification or of becoming fully human. Qohelet was a believer, a Solomon-like figure who was steeped in the traditions of Israel. But his journey toward full humanity and thus toward God required that he go through the crisis of faith we encounter in Ecclesiastes.

33. St. John of the Cross, *Ascent of Mount Carmel*, book 1, chap. 13, no. 11.
34. See Butler, *Western Mysticism*, for a good introduction.
35. Welch, *Spiritual Pilgrims*, 1.

2. We can surmise that, like many contemporary Christians in the West, Qohelet spent the early half of his life working very hard, accumulating wealth and status. In the process, although a believer, his ego became less and less aligned with his self, until he could no longer live this way. Surrendering to this crisis, he entered what St. John of the Cross would call a dark night of the soul, with no sense of where this excruciating journey would lead him.

3. Qohelet's journey is thus best understood in relation to the alienation of his inflated ego from his self. His autonomous epistemology with its characteristic "I" exemplifies this, as does his confidence in his approach as "wise" and his constantly bumping up against "everything is utterly enigmatic" as he pursues his journey through his autonomous grid. He thinks that through his epistemology he is turning his heart toward reflection, but ironically it is his heart, his self, that needs surgery. Qohelet is being forced to confront his shadow, "that part of us we fail to see or know."[36] Inter alia this is why the recognition of the irony in Ecclesiastes is so important—it alerts us that things are not what they seem and thereby opens Qohelet and the reader to a way through this journey.

4. The struggle and pain of Qohelet's journey must not be underestimated, a temptation to which academic commentators often succumb. The polarity he experiences between the *carpe diem* affirmation of life and his logical analysis of enigma threaten to tear him apart as his journey progresses. This is the battlefront where his inflated ego encounters his self, and the conflict is excruciating. For new life to come, the inflated ego has to die, and this is experienced as life-threatening and exceedingly painful. "The ego needs life-giving contact with the self. But first, the ego needs to be dis-identified from the self in order to eventually have a relationship with that self. . . . In effect, the many centers where the true self was previously located are now giving way to the true center. This progress corresponds to the pilgrimage to the center in [Teresa of Avila's] *The Interior Castle*."[37]

Teresa of Avila uses the image of a castle and the soul's progress toward the center to depict the journey toward union with God. Her fourth, fifth, and sixth dwelling places correspond to what St. John of the Cross calls the dark night of the soul. The tradition of spirituality is agreed that this journey is exceedingly tough and painful. Nor is it straightforward, but weaves its way organically forward. This resonates with Qohelet's journey—he moves back and forth, revisiting issues, recognizing the irony of his quest, and then plunging into it again.

36. R. A. Johnson, *Owning Your Shadow*, 4.
37. Welch, *Spiritual Pilgrims*, 145.

This is one reason why the logic of Ecclesiastes is so hard to discern, because it is not the scientific logic of a carefully constructed whole, but the organic logic of a soul gradually loosening its ego from its false centers.

5. Understanding Ecclesiastes in terms of soul formation also illumines the destination at which Qohelet arrives. The goal of soul formation is union with God, or, as Jung would put it, realignment of the ego with the self. Ecclesiastes 12:1–7 evokes this powerfully in Qohelet's exhortation to his readers to "remember your Creator before. . . ." "Remembrance" is here far more than mere mental assent; rather, it involves a turning upside down of Qohelet's autonomous epistemology and thus his ego. Remembering involves letting go of false centers and alignment through the self with the true center, God.

Clearly this sketch of the way in which Ecclesiastes depicts soul formation requires detailed development, but we cannot do that here. Suffice it to note that as Peterson puts it, Ecclesiastes is truly a "smooth stone" for pastoral work. According to Peterson, the teaching office of the wise in Israel has a close correlation with pastoral work,[38] and Ecclesiastes has much to offer pastors and spiritual directors as they facilitate soul formation.

Communicating Ecclesiastes

Ecclesiastes 12:9 tells us that Qohelet taught knowledge to the people of God; he was an educator. Wisdom, Brueggemann notes, is one model for education in the OT. "Wisdom in Israel needs to be understood as a serious way in which responsible, reasonable knowledge of the world and passionate trust in God are held together. We have here intellectually mature and theologically sensitive literature. This is a believing reason, or we may say, 'faith seeking understanding.'"[39] Ecclesiastes exemplifies the quality and depth of the sort of education wise men like Qohelet offered to their contemporaries. Wisdom is particularly concerned with human experience, the nuts and bolts of daily life with all its struggles and mysteries and joys. As Peterson points out,

Wisdom had its concrete setting in the daily lives of a people who believed in God as Savior and Creator. That is, the wise men worked in a context previously established and defined by priests and prophets. What they did in that context was not so much announce the word of God as train people in the skills

38. Peterson, "Pastoral Work of Nay-Saying," 166.
39. Brueggemann, *Creative Word*, 68.

of living it. In that way they functioned very much as Christian pastors today in their work between Sundays.[40]

In the previous section I have indicated the relevance of Ecclesiastes to spiritual direction or soul formation. But what of more public communication of Ecclesiastes? After all, Qohelet taught *the people* knowledge. In this regard, we should note three points.

First, Ecclesiastes is a fascinating model of teaching: telling a story with a wise man nicknamed Qohelet as the main character; allowing the reader to experience Qohelet's attraction to Greek epistemology; letting the contradictory juxtapositions of the *carpe diem* passages and the enigmatic conclusions stand so that the reader is forced to reflect on how to fill the gap between them; allowing the irony to slowly emerge; and so on. Christians have a lot to learn from this sophisticated and relevant way of presenting the faith in an ecclesiastical world that is dominated by the three-point sermon or the ten-minute homily. Here is a creative, searching, experientially relevant presentation of wisdom, and we do well to ask what this sort of model might look like in the twenty-first century.

One is reminded in this respect of Kierkegaard's multiple strategies for communicating the faith in his context of a Denmark adrift in Christendom.[41] To get Danes to wrestle personally with the meaning of life, Kierkegaard set about producing a corpus of literature under a variety of pseudonyms and genres. Creative readings of Scripture abound in his works,[42] as do evocative images such as those of knights of infinite resignation and knights of faith. Such works impel the reader to wrestle in order to understand Kierkegaard's view *and* to come to their own conclusions.

I suggest that similar strategies are needed today—creative works like Ecclesiastes and *Fear and Trembling* that take the reader on a journey that becomes their own journey toward recovering their soul. The production of such work will require what John Stott has termed "double listening."[43] "The preacher" needs to have one ear attuned to Scripture and the other to the world in order to facilitate encounter between the Word and the world at this time and this place. Such an approach reminds us of the immense greatness of the gospel and of our infinite capacity to reduce it to something small and irrelevant. Works like Ecclesiastes and *Fear and Trembling* emerge only from a vision of life as a whole and with a strong instinct for what is at stake in human life and culture—nothing less than the glory of God and human well-being.[44]

40. Peterson, "Pastoral Work of Nay-Saying," 166.
41. See Kierkegaard, *The Point of View of My Work as an Author.*
42. See, e.g., his opening meditations on Gen. 22 in *Fear and Trembling.*
43. J. R. W. Stott, *The Contemporary Christian: An Urgent Plea for Double Listening* (Downers Grove, IL: InterVarsity, 1992).
44. See C. S. Lewis, "Weight of Glory," for a sense of the value of human life.

In our day, such strategies need not confine themselves to the written word but could also make use of the film and digital media available. Whatever the medium, the point is that Ecclesiastes cries out for and points us in the direction of serious, deep engagement with the gospel and our world.

Second, Ecclesiastes is a masterly example of contextualization, so that in this sense it is a missionary work par excellence. The author of Ecclesiastes knows intimately the temptations of the intellectuals of his day, and he produces a book that shows that at every point. Instead of simply preaching against Greek epistemology, he takes the reader on the agonizing journey of one Qohelet, who has fallen prey to the lure of such an approach to knowledge amid the demise of Israel. Such indirect communication is undoubtedly required today in our Western, post-Christian cultures. Ours is no longer Kierkegaard's challenge of Christendom but rather that of a decaying, secularized West whose intellectual disembowelment is manifest in the postmodern ideologies of the day. It is in this context that we need to find comparable ways to present the faith.

Third, but by no means least, there is certainly a place for the preaching of Ecclesiastes via the sermon. Ecclesiastes is a highly creative piece of literature, and the preacher will need to find creative ways to allow God's people to hear this text.[45] I have preached Ecclesiastes in a one-hour session as well as over a series of four one-and-a-half-hour sessions. The possibilities are endless. It is important to make sure that congregations have a good working knowledge of Proverbs[46] as the canonical background to Ecclesiastes as well as a robust doctrine of creation. My hope is that in this commentary the sections on theological implications in particular provide clues as to the application of Ecclesiastes. But it is vital to enable congregations to hear the narrative as a whole and not just to expound occasional parts of the whole. Few biblical books are as relevant to the cheerful and not-so-cheerful nihilism of our day, and we need to find creative ways in our particular contexts to hear God's address to us through this book.

Intriguingly, the Wisdom books of the OT are proving very popular among the exploding numbers of Christians in "the South." Jenkins points out in his *New Faces of Christianity*, "In different ways, churches in Africa, Asia, and Latin America show their enthusiasm for those books that are generally known as wisdom literature, books that offer practical means for living in the world. The best known of these are . . . Proverbs and Ecclesiastes."[47] Contemporary African and Asian Christians recognize the genre of wisdom as "an old friend."[48]

45. In terms of hermeneutics and homiletics with a focus on 7:23–29, Spears, "Theological Hermeneutics," is an important source.

46. See Bartholomew, *Reading Proverbs with Integrity*. The best overall commentary available on Proverbs is that by Van Leeuwen, "Proverbs."

47. Jenkins, *New Faces of Christianity*, 57.

48. Ibid., 59.

Chinua Achebe notes, "For the African the proverb is the spice by which Africans chew kola." According to Madipoane Masenya, "If the Wisdom appears like a thick forest to those from the West, to Africans, it is more like a plain."[49]

Van Leeuwen has pointed out that an effect of modernity with its concern for universal truths and concepts has been the denigration and loss of proverbial wisdom.[50] As attention to Proverbs, Job, and Ecclesiastes bears out, this is a significant loss. Perhaps our brothers and sisters in the new centers of Christianity can help those of us in the largely post-Christian West recover the delights and extraordinary riches of the OT Wisdom books and, not least, of Ecclesiastes.

49. Quoted in ibid.
50. Van Leeuwen, "In Praise of Proverbs."

Bibliography

Abraham, W. J. *Canon and Criterion in Christian Theology: From the Fathers to Feminism.* Oxford: Clarendon, 1998.

Abramsky, S. "The Woman Leaning out the Window" [Hebrew]. *Beth Mikra* 80.2 (1980): 114–24.

Ackroyd, P. R. "Two Hebrew Notes." *Annual of the Swedish Theological Institute* 5 (1976): 82–86.

Aelred of Rievaulx. *Spiritual Friendship.* Translated by M. E. Laker. Cistercian Fathers 5. Kalamazoo, MI: Cistercian Publications, 1974.

Aland, B., et al., eds. *Novum Testamentum Graece post Eberhard et Erwin Nestle.* 27th ed. Stuttgart: Deutsche Bibelgesellschaft, 1993.

Allenbach, J., et al., eds. *Biblia Patristica: Index des Citations et Allusions Bibliques dans la Littérature Patristique.* 6 vols. plus supplement. Centre D'Analyse et de Documentation Patristiques. Paris: Centre National de la Recherche Scientifique, 1975–95.

Alonso-Schökel, L. *A Manual of Hebrew Poetics.* Subsidia biblica 11. Rome: Pontifical Biblical Institute Press, 1988.

Alter, R. *The Art of Biblical Poetry.* New York: Basic Books, 1985.

Anat, M. A. "The Lament over the Death of Human Beings in the Book of Qoheleth" [Hebrew]. *Beth Mikra* 15 (1970): 375–80.

Andersen, F. I. *Job: An Introduction and Commentary.* Tyndale Old Testament Commentaries. Downers Grove, IL: InterVarsity, 1976.

Anderson, H., and E. Foley. *Mighty Stories, Dangerous Rituals: Weaving Together the Human and the Divine.* San Francisco: Jossey-Bass, 1998.

Anderson, W. H. U. "The Curse of Work in Qoheleth: An Exposé of Gen. 3:17–19 in Ecclesiastes." *Evangelical Quarterly* 70 (1998): 99–113.

———. "Ironic Correlations and Scepticism in the Joy Statements of Qoheleth." *Scandinavian Journal of the Old Testament* 14.1 (2000): 67–100.

Archer, G. L. "The Linguistic Evidence for the Date of 'Ecclesiastes.'" *Journal of the Evangelical Theological Society* 12 (1969): 167–81.

Aristotle. *Nicomachean Ethics.* Translated by T. Irwin. Indianapolis: Hackett, 1985.

Astour, M. C. "Two Ugaritic Serpent Charms." *Journal of Near Eastern Studies* 27.1 (1968): 13–36.

Aune, D. E. "On the Origins of the 'Council of Javneh' Myth." *Journal of Biblical Literature* 110.3 (1991): 491–93.

Backhaus, F. J. *Denn Zeit und Zufall trifft sie alle: Zu Komposition und Gottesbild im Buch Qohelet.* Bonner biblische Beiträge 83. Frankfurt a.M.: Anton Hain, 1993.

Bakan, D. *Disease, Pain, and Sacrifice: Toward a Psychology of Suffering.* Chicago: University of Chicago Press, 1968.

Baldwin, J. G. "Is There Pseudonymity in the Old Testament?" *Themelios* 4.1 (1978): 6–12.

Barclay, W. *The Gospel of Matthew.* Vol. 1. New Daily Study Bible. Louisville: Westminster John Knox, 2001.

Barolín, D. "Eclesiastés 8:1–8: Consejos para leer entre líneas." *Cuadernos de teología* 20 (2001): 7–22.

Barr, J. *Biblical Words for Time.* Studies in Biblical Theology 1/33. London: SCM, 1962.

Barth, K. *Church Dogmatics.* Edited by G. W. Bromiley and T. F. Torrance. Translated by G. W. Bromiley et al. 4 vols. in 14. Repr., Edinburgh: T&T Clark, 2004.

———. *Homiletics.* Translated by G. Bromiley and D. E. Daniels. Louisville: Westminster John Knox, 1991.

Barthélemy, D. *Les devanciers d'Aquila: Première publication intégrale du texte des fragments du Dodécapprophéton trouvés dans le Désert de Juda, précédée d'une étude sur les traductions et recensions grecques de la Bible réalisées au premier siècle de notre ère sous l'influence du rabbinat palestinien.* Leiden: Brill, 1963.

Bartholomew, C. G. "Babel and Derrida: Postmodernism, Language and Biblical Interpretation." *Tyndale Bulletin* 49.2 (1998): 305–28.

———. "The Composition of Deuteronomy: A Critical Analysis of the Approaches of E. W. Nicholson and A. D. H. Mayes." MA thesis, Potchefstroom University, 1992.

———. "Covenant and Creation: Covenant Overload or Covenantal Deconstruction." *Calvin Theological Journal* 30 (1995): 11–33.

———. *Reading Ecclesiastes: Old Testament Exegesis and Hermeneutical Theory.* Analecta biblica 139. Rome: Pontifical Biblical Institute Press, 1998.

———. *Reading Proverbs with Integrity.* Cambridge, UK: Groves Books, 2001.

———. "A Time for War and a Time for Peace: Old Testament Wisdom, Creation and O'Donovan's Theological Ethics." In *A Royal Priesthood? The Use of the Bible Ethically and Politically: A Dialogue with Oliver O'Donovan,* edited by C. G. Bartholomew, J. Chaplin, R. Song, and A. Wolters, 91–112. Scripture and Hermeneutics Series 3. Grand Rapids: Zondervan, 2002.

Bartholomew, C. G., and M. W. Goheen. *The Drama of Scripture: Finding Our Place in the Biblical Story.* Grand Rapids: Baker Academic, 2004.

Bartholomew, C. G., and T. Moritz, eds. *Christ and Consumerism: A Critical Analysis of the Spirit of the Age.* Carlisle, UK: Paternoster, 2000.

Barton, G. A. *A Critical and Exegetical Commentary on the Book of Ecclesiastes.* International Critical Commentary. New York: Charles Scribner's Sons, 1908.

———. "The Text and Interpretation of Ecclesiastes 5:19." *Journal of Biblical Literature* 27.1 (1908): 65–66.

Barton, J. *Reading the Old Testament: Method in Biblical Study.* Rev. ed. Louisville: Westminster John Knox, 1997.

Barucq, A. *Ecclésiaste: Traduction et commentaire Qohéleth.* Verbum salutis 3. Paris: Beauchesne, 1968.

Bass, D. C. *Receiving the Day: Christian Practices for Opening the Gift of Time.* San Francisco: Jossey-Bass, 2001.

Baumgartner, W. "The Wisdom Literature." In *The Old Testament and Modern Study: A Generation of Discovery and Research,* edited by H. H. Rowley, 210–37. London: Clarendon, 1951.

Bavinck, H. *Reformed Dogmatics.* Edited by J. Bolt. Translated by J. Vriend. 4 vols. Grand Rapids: Baker Academic, 2003–8.

Beal, T. K. "C(ha)osmopolis: Qohelet's Last Words." In *God in the Fray: A Tribute to Walter Brueggemann,* edited by T. Linafelt and T. K. Beal, 290–304. Minneapolis: Fortress, 1998.

Becker, J. *Gottesfurcht im Alten Testament.* Analecta biblica 25. Rome: Pontifical Biblical Institute Press, 1965.

Beckwith, R. T. *The Old Testament Canon of the New Testament Church.* London: SPCK, 1985.

Beentjes, P. C. "Recente visies op Qohelet." *Bijdragen: Tidschrift voor Filosophie en Theologie* 41 (1980): 436–44.

———. "'Who Is Like the Wise?': Some Notes on Qohelet 8,1–15." In *Qohelet in the Context of Wisdom,* edited by A. Schoors, 303–15. Bibliotheca ephemeridum theologicarum lovaniensium 136. Leuven: Leuven University Press, 1998.

Bender, S. *Plain and Simple: A Woman's Journey to the Amish.* San Francisco: Harper & Row, 1989.

Berger, B. L. "Qohelet and the Exigencies of the Absurd." *Biblical Interpretation* 9.2 (2001): 141–79.

Berkouwer, G. C. *The Return of Christ.* Grand Rapids: Eerdmans, 1972.

Berry, W. *Another Turn of the Crank: Essays.* Washington, DC: Counterpoint, 2005.

———. *Life Is a Miracle: An Essay against Modern Superstition.* Washington, DC: Counterpoint, 2000.

———. *What Are People For? Essays by Wendell Berry.* New York: North Point, 1990.

Bianchi, F. "The Language of Qohelet: A Bibliographical Survey." *Zeitschrift für die alttestamentliche Wissenschaft* 105.2 (1993): 210–23.

Bickell, G. *Koheleth's Untersuchung über den Wert des Daseins.* Dem siebenten Internationalen orientalisten-congresse zu Wien hochachtungsvoll überreicht. Innsbruck: Wagner, 1884.

Blenkinsopp, J. "Ecclesiastes 3:1–15: Another Interpretation." *Journal for the Study of the Old Testament* 66 (1995): 55–64.

———. *Wisdom and Law in the Old Testament: The Ordering of Life in Israel and Early Judaism.* Oxford: Oxford University Press, 1995.

Blocher, H. *In the Beginning: The Opening Chapters of Genesis.* Translated by D. G. Preston. Downers Grove, IL: InterVarsity, 1984.

Bloom, H. "The Breaking of Form." In H. Bloom et al., *Deconstruction and Criticism,* 1–31. New York: Continuum, 1979.

Boehl, E. *De aramaismis libri Koheleth: Dissertatio historica et philologica qua librum Salomoni vindicare.* Erlangen: Th. Blaesing, 1860.

Bolin, T. M. "Rivalry and Resignation: Girard and Qoheleth on the Divine-Human Relationship." *Biblica* 86.2 (2005): 245–59.

Bonaventura. *Commentary on Ecclesiastes.* Works of St Bonaventure 7. Translated by R. J. Karris and Campion Murray. St. Bonaventure, NY: Franciscan Institute Publications, 2005.

Bonhoeffer, D. *Ethics*. Edited by E. Bethge. Translated by N. H. Smith. Library of Philosophy and Theology. London: SCM, 1995.

Booth, W. C. *The Rhetoric of Fiction*. 2nd ed. Chicago: University of Chicago Press, 1983.

Bosch, D. J. *Believing in the Future: Toward a Missiology of Western Culture*. Valley Forge, PA: Trinity Press International, 1995.

—————. *Transforming Mission: Paradigm Shifts in Theology of Mission*. American Society of Missiology Series 16. New York: Orbis, 2003.

Botha, M. E. *Sosio-Kulturele Metavrae*. Amsterdam: Buijten en Schipperheijn, 1971.

Bozanich, R. "Donne and Ecclesiastes." *Proceedings of the Modern Language Association* 90.2 (1975): 270–76.

Braaten, C. E., and R. W. Jenson. "Preface." In *Either/Or: The Gospel or Neopaganism*, edited by C. E. Braaten and R. W. Jenson, 1–5. Grand Rapids: Eerdmans, 1995.

Braiterman, Z. *(God) After Auschwitz: Tradition and Change in Post-Holocaust Jewish Thought*. Princeton, NJ: Princeton University Press, 1998.

Branick, V. P. "Wisdom, Pessimism, and 'Mirth': Reflections on the Contribution of Biblical Wisdom Literature to Business Ethics." *Journal of Religious Ethics* 34.1 (2006): 69–87.

Braun, R. *Kohelet und die frühhellenistische Popularphilosophie*. Beihefte zur Zeitschrift für die alttestamentliche Wissenschaft 130. Berlin: de Gruyter, 1973.

Bream, H. N. "Life without Resurrection: Two Perspectives from Qoheleth." In *Light unto My Path: Old Testament Studies in Honor of Jacob M. Myers*, edited by H. N. Bream, Ralph D. Heim, and C. A. Moore, 49–65. Gettysburg Theological Studies 4. Philadelphia: Temple University Press, 1974.

Brenner, A. *Colour Terms in the Old Testament*. Journal for the Study of the Old Testament Supplement 21. Sheffield: JSOT Press, 1982.

Brin, G. *The Concept of Time in the Bible and the Dead Sea Scrolls*. Studies on the Texts of the Desert of Judah 39. Leiden: Brill, 2001.

Brown, C. *Philosophy and the Christian Faith: A Historical Sketch from the Middle Ages to the Present Day*. Downers Grove, IL: InterVarsity, 1969.

Brown, F., S. R. Driver, and C. A. Briggs. *A Hebrew and English Lexicon of the Old Testament*. Oxford: Clarendon, 1907.

Brown, W. P. *Ecclesiastes*. Interpretation: A Bible Commentary for Teaching and Preaching. Louisville: Westminster John Knox, 2000.

—————. "'Whatever Your Hand Finds to Do': Qoheleth's Work Ethic." *Interpretation* 55.3 (2001): 271–84.

Broyde, M. J. "Defilement of the Hands, Canonization of the Bible, and the Special Status of Esther, Ecclesiastes, and Song of Songs." *Judaism* 44.1 (1995): 65–79.

Brueggemann, W. *The Creative Word: Canon as Model for Biblical Education*. Philadelphia: Fortress, 1982.

—————. "Response to J. Richard Middleton." *Harvard Theological Review* 87 (1994): 279–89.

—————. "The Social Significance of Solomon as a Patron of Wisdom." In *Sage in Israel and the Ancient Near East*, 117–32. Winona Lake, IN: Eisenbrauns, 1990.

—————. "Trajectories in Old Testament Literature and the Sociology of Ancient Israel." *Journal of Biblical Literature* 98.1 (1979): 161–85.

Bruns, J. E. "Some Reflections on Coheleth and John." *Catholic Biblical Quarterly* 25 (1963): 414–16.

Bryce, G. E. "'Better'-Proverbs: An Historical and Structural Study." In *Society of Biblical Literature Seminar Papers*, edited by L. C. McGaughy, 343–54. Missoula, MT: Society of Biblical Literature, 1972.

Buckley, M. J. *At the Origins of Modern Atheism*. New Haven: Yale University Press, 1987.

Bühlman, A. "The Difficulty of Thinking in Greek and Speaking in Hebrew (Qoheleth 3.18; 4.13–16; 5.8)." *Journal for the Study of the Old Testament* 90 (2000): 101–8.

Bukdahl, J. *Søren Kierkegaard and the Common Man*. Grand Rapids: Eerdmans, 2001.

Bultmann, R. *Der Stil der paulinischen Predigt und die kynisch-stoische Diatribe*. Göttingen: Vandenhoeck & Ruprecht, 1984.

Burkes, S. L. *Death in Qoheleth and Egyptian Biographies of the Late Period*. Society of Biblical Literature Dissertation Series 170. Atlanta: Scholars Press, 1999.

Burkitt, F. C. "Is Ecclesiastes a Translation?" *Journal of Theological Studies* 23 (1922): 22–28.

Burrell, D. B. *Friendship and Ways to Truth*. Notre Dame, IN: University of Notre Dame Press, 2000.

Burtchaell, J. T. *The Dying of the Light: The Disengagement of Colleges and Universities from Their Christian Churches*. Grand Rapids: Eerdmans, 1998.

Busto Saiz, J. R. "Estructura métrica y estrófica del 'poema sobre la juventud y la vejez': Qohelet 11,7–12,7." *Serafad* 43 (1983): 17–25.

Butler, C. *Western Mysticism: The Teaching of Augustine, Gregory and Bernard on Contemplation and the Contemplative Life*. 2nd ed. New York: Harper, 1966.

Carasik, M. "Qohelet's Twists and Turns." *Journal for the Study of the Old Testament* 28 (2003): 192–209.

Carlebach, J. *Das Buch Koheleth*. Frankfurt: Hermon-Verlag, 1936.

Casey, E. S. *Getting Back into Place: Toward a Renewed Understanding of the Place-World*. Bloomington and Indianapolis: Indiana University Press, 1993.

———. *Spirit and Soul: Essays in Philosophical Psychology*. Dallas: Spring Publications, 1991.

Castellino, G. "Qohelet and His Wisdom." *Catholic Biblical Quarterly* 30 (1968): 15–28.

Catechism of the Catholic Church: With Modifications from the Editio typica. New York: First Image, 1995.

Caws, M. A. *Reading Frames in Modern Fiction*. Princeton, NJ: Princeton University Press, 1985.

Ceresko, A. R. "The Function of *Antanaclasis* (*mṣ'* 'To Find' // *mṣ'* 'To Reach, Overtake, Grasp') in Hebrew Poetry, Especially in the Book of Qoheleth." *Catholic Biblical Quarterly* 44.4 (1982): 551–69.

Childs, B. S. *Introduction to the Old Testament as Scripture*. Philadelphia: Fortress, 1979.

Christianson, E. S. *Ecclesiastes through the Centuries*. Blackwell Bible Commentaries. Malden, MA: Blackwell, 2007.

———. "Qoheleth and the Existential Legacy of the Holocaust." *Heythrop Journal* 38 (1997): 35–50.

———. *A Time to Tell: Narrative Strategies in Ecclesiastes*. Journal for the Study of the Old Testament Supplement 280. Sheffield: Sheffield Academic Press, 1998.

Christianson, E., and T. McWilliams. "Voltaire's Précis of Ecclesiastes: A Case Study in the Bible's Afterlife." *Journal for the Study of the Old Testament* 29 (2005): 455–84.

Clemens, D. M. "The Law of Sin and Death: Ecclesiastes and Genesis 1–3." *Themelios* 19.3 (1994): 5–8.

Clements, R. E. *A Century of Old Testament Study.* Cambridge: Lutterworth, 1976.

Clines, D. J. A. *Job 1–20.* Word Biblical Commentary 17. Waco: Word, 1989.

Clouser, R. A. *The Myth of Religious Neutrality: An Essay on the Hidden Role of Religious Belief in Theories.* Rev. ed. Notre Dame, IN: University of Notre Dame Press, 2005.

Cogan, M. "A Technical Term for Exposure." *Journal of Near Eastern Studies* 27.2 (1968): 133–35.

Collins, G. R. *Christian Counseling: A Comprehensive Guide.* Waco: Word, 1980.

Collins, J. J. *Proverbs and Ecclesiastes.* Atlanta: John Knox, 1980.

Cook, G., et al. *Let My People Live: Faith and Struggle in Central America.* Project coordinator G. Spykman. Grand Rapids: Eerdmans, 1988.

Cox, D. "Sedaqa and Mispat: The Concept of Righteousness in Later Wisdom." *Liber annuus* 27 (1977): 33–50.

Crenshaw, J. L. *Ecclesiastes: A Commentary.* Old Testament Library. Philadelphia: Westminster, 1987.

————. "Ecclesiastes, Book of." In *Anchor Bible Dictionary,* edited by D. N. Freedman, 2:271–80. New York: Doubleday, 1992.

————. "Ecclesiastes: Odd Book In." *Bible Review* 6 (1990): 28–33.

————. "The Eternal Gospel (Eccl 3:11)." In *Essays in Old Testament Ethics: J Philip Hyatt, in Memoriam,* edited by J. L. Crenshaw and J. T. Willis, 23–55. New York: Ktav, 1974.

————. "The Expression *mî yôdēaʿ* in the Hebrew Bible." *Vetus Testamentum* 36.3 (1986): 274–88.

————. "In Search of Divine Presence: Some Remarks Preliminary to a Theology of Wisdom." *Review & Expositor* 74 (1977): 353–69.

————. "Method in Determining Wisdom Influence upon Historical Literature." *Journal of Biblical Literature* 88.1 (1969): 129–42.

————. "Popular Questioning of the Justice of God in Ancient Israel." *Zeitschrift für die alttestamentliche Wissenschaft* 82.3 (1970): 380–95.

————. "Prohibitions in Proverbs and Qoheleth." In *Priests, Prophets and Scribes: Essays on the Formation and Heritage of Second Temple Judaism in Honour of Joseph Blenkinsopp,* edited by R. P. Carroll et al., 115–24. Journal for the Study of the Old Testament Supplement 149. Sheffield: JSOT Press, 1992.

————. "Qoheleth's Understanding of Intellectual Inquiry." In *Qohelet in the Context of Wisdom,* edited by A. Schoors, 204–24. Bibliotheca ephemeridum theologicarum lovaniensium 136. Leuven: Leuven University Press, 1998.

————. "Unresolved Issues in Wisdom Literature." In *An Introduction to Wisdom Literature and the Psalms: Festschrift Marvin E. Tate,* edited by H. W. Ballard Jr. and W. D. Tucker Jr., 215–27. Macon, GA: Mercer University Press, 2000.

————. "Wisdom and Authority: Sapiential Rhetoric and Its Warrants." In *Congress Volume: Vienna, 1980,* edited by J. A. Emerton, 10–29. Vetus Testamentum Supplement 32. Leiden: Brill, 1981.

————. "The Wisdom Literature." In *The Hebrew Bible and Its Modern Interpreters,* edited by D. A. Knight and G. M. Tucker, 369–407. Philadelphia: Fortress, 1985.

————. "Youth and Old Age in Qoheleth." *Hebrew Annual Review* 10 (1986): 1–13.

————, ed. *Studies in Ancient Israelite Wisdom.* New York: Ktav, 1976.

Crouch, W. B. "To Question an End, to End a Question: Opening the Closure of the Book of Jonah." *Journal for the Study of the Old Testament* 62 (1994): 101–12.

Crüsemann, F. "Hiob und Kohelet." In *Werden und Wirken des Alten Testaments: Festschrift für Claus Westermann zum 70 Geburtstag*, edited by R. Albertz, 373–93. Göttingen: Vandenhoeck & Ruprecht, 1980.

———. "The Unchangeable World: The 'Crisis of Wisdom' in Koheleth." In *God of the Lowly: Socio-Historical Interpretations of the Bible*, edited by W. Schottroff and W. Stegemann, 57–77. Translated by M. J. O'Connell. Maryknoll, NY: Orbis, 1984.

Cullmann, O. *Christ and Time: The Primitive Christian Conception of Time and History*. Rev. ed. Translated by F. V. Filson. Philadelphia: Westminster, 1957.

Dahood, M. J. "Canaanite-Phoenician Influence in Qoheleth." *Biblica* 33 (1952): 30–52, 191–221.

———. "Language of Qoheleth." *Catholic Biblical Quarterly* 14.3 (1952): 227–32.

———. "The Phoenician Background of Qoheleth." *Biblica* 47.2 (1966): 264–82.

———. "Qoheleth and Northwest Semitic Philology." *Biblica* 43 (1962): 349–56, 358–59.

———. "Qoheleth and Recent Discoveries." *Biblica* 39.3 (1958): 302–18.

Davidson, R. *The Courage to Doubt: Exploring an Old Testament Theme*. London: SCM, 1989.

Davis, E. F. *Wondrous Depth: Preaching the Old Testament*. Louisville: Westminster John Knox, 2005.

Davis, S. T. "Free Will and Evil." In *Encountering Evil: Live Options in Theodicy*, edited by S. T. Davis, 69–83. Atlanta: John Knox, 1981.

———. Introduction to *Encountering Evil: Live Options in Theodicy*, edited by S. T. Davis, 1–6. Atlanta: John Knox, 1981.

Day, J., R. P. Gordon, and H. G. M. Williamson, eds. *Wisdom in Ancient Israel: Essays in Honour of J. A. Emerton*. Cambridge: Cambridge University Press, 1995.

De Geus, C. H. J. *Towns in Ancient Israel and in the Southern Levant*. Palestina Antiqua 10. Leeuven: Peeters, 2003.

Delitzsch, F. *Proverbs, Ecclesiastes, Song of Solomon*. Translated by M. G. Easton. Grand Rapids: Eerdmans, 1975 (1872).

Dell, K. J. "Ecclesiastes as Wisdom: Consulting Early Interpreters." *Vetus Testamentum* 44.3 (1994): 301–29.

Derrida, J. *Dissemination*. Translated by B. Johnson. Chicago: University of Chicago Press, 1981.

———. *The Gift of Death*. Translated by D. Wills. Chicago: University of Chicago Press, 1996.

———. *Of Grammatology, Corrected Edition*. Translated by G. C. Spivak. Baltimore: Johns Hopkins University Press, 1998.

———. "Structure, Sign and Play in the Discourse of the Human Sciences." In *Writing and Difference*, 278–93. Translated by A. Bass. Chicago: University of Chicago Press, 1978.

———. *Writing and Difference*. Translated by A. Bass. Chicago: University of Chicago Press, 1978.

Dillard, A. *The Annie Dillard Reader*. San Francisco: HarperPerennial, 1994.

Dillard, R. B., and T. Longman III. *An Introduction to the Old Testament*. Grand Rapids: Zondervan, 1994.

Dollimore, J. *Death, Desire and Loss in Western Culture*. London: Allen Lane, 1998.

Drewes, B. F. "Reading the Bible in Context: An Indonesian and a Mexican Commentary on Ecclesiastes: Contextual Interpretations." *Exchange* 34.2 (2005): 120–33.

397

Driver, S. R. *An Introduction to the Literature of the Old Testament*. Repr., Gloucester: Peter Smith, 1972.

Du Plessis, S. J. "Aspects of Morphological Peculiarities of the Language of Qoheleth." In *De fructu oris sui: Essays in Honour of Adrianus van Selms*, edited by I. H. Eybers et al., 164–80. Pretoria Oriental Series 9. Leiden: Brill, 1971.

Eaton, M. A. *Ecclesiastes*. Tyndale Old Testament Commentaries. Downers Grove, IL: Inter-Varsity, 1983.

Eco, U. *Interpretation and Overinterpretation*. Edited by S. Collini. Cambridge: Cambridge University Press, 1992.

Edinger, E. F. *Ego and Archetype: Individuation and the Religious Function of the Psyche*. 1972. Repr., Boston: Shambala, 1992.

Ehlich, K. *"Hbl*—Metaphern der Nichtigkeit." In *"Jedes Ding hat seine Zeit . . .": Studien zur israelitischen und altorientalischen Weisheit: Diethelm Michel zum 65 Geburtstag*, edited by A. A. Diesel et al., 49–64. Beihefte zur Zeitschrift für die alttestamentliche Wissenschaft 241. Berlin: de Gruyter, 1996.

Ehrlich, A. *Randglossen zur hebräischen Bibel*. Vol. 7. Leipzig: Hinrich, 1914.

Ellermeier. F. *Qohelet*. Part 1. 2 sections. Herzberg am Harz: Erwin Junger, 1967–70.

Ellul, J. *The Ethics of Freedom*. Translated by G. W. Bromiley. Grand Rapids: Eerdmans, 1976.

———. *The Reason for Being: A Meditation on Ecclesiastes*. Translated by J. M. Hanks. Grand Rapids: Eerdmans, 1990.

Everson, S., ed. *Epistemology*. Companions to Ancient Thought 1. Cambridge: Cambridge University Press, 1990.

Farmer, K. A. *Who Knows What Is Good: A Commentary on the Books of Proverbs and Ecclesiastes*. International Theological Commentary. Grand Rapids: Eerdmans, 1991.

Fisch, H. *Poetry with a Purpose: Biblical Poetics and Interpretation*. Bloomington: Indiana University Press, 1988.

Fischer, S. "Qohelet and 'Heretic' Harpers' Songs." *Journal for the Study of the Old Testament* 98 (2002): 105–21.

Fishbane, M. *Biblical Interpretation in Ancient Israel*. Oxford: Clarendon, 1991.

Ford, D. F. *Self and Salvation: Being Transformed*. Cambridge: Cambridge University Press, 1999.

Forman, C. C. "Koheleth's Use of Genesis." *Journal of Semitic Studies* 5 (1960): 256–63.

Forsyth, P. T. *The Justification of God: Lectures for War-Time on a Christian Theodicy*. New York: Scribner's Sons, 1917.

———. *Positive Preaching and the Modern Mind*. Repr., Carlisle, UK: Paternoster, 1998.

Fox, M. V. "The Book of Qohelet and Its Relation to the Wisdom School" [Hebrew]. PhD diss., Hebrew University of Jerusalem, 1972.

———. *Ecclesiastes*. Jewish Publication Society Torah Commentary. Philadelphia: Jewish Publication Society, 2004.

———. "Frame-Narrative and Composition in the Book of Qohelet." *Hebrew Union College Annual* 48 (1977): 83–106.

———. *Proverbs 1–9: A New Translation with Introduction and Commentary*. Anchor Bible 18A. New York: Doubleday, 2000.

———. "Qohelet 1.4." *Journal for the Study of the Old Testament* 40 (1988): 109.

———. *Qohelet and His Contradictions*. Journal for the Study of the Old Testament Supplement 71. Sheffield: Sheffield Academic Press, 1989.

———. "Qohelet's Epistemology." *Hebrew Union College Annual* 58 (1987): 137–55.

———. "Time in Qohelet's 'Catalogue of Times.'" *Journal of Northwest Semitic Languages* 24.1 (1998): 25–39.

———. *A Time to Tear Down and a Time to Build Up: A Rereading of Ecclesiastes.* Grand Rapids: Eerdmans, 1999.

———. "Wisdom in Qoheleth." In *In Search of Wisdom: Essays in Memory of John G. Gammie*, edited by L. G. Perdue, B. B. Scott, and W. J. Wiseman, 115–31. Louisville: Westminster John Knox, 1993.

Fox, M. V., and B. Porten. "Unsought Discoveries: Qohelet 7:23–8:1a." *Hebrew Studies* 19 (1978): 26–38.

France, R. T. *Matthew: An Introduction and Commentary.* Tyndale New Testament Commentaries. Grand Rapids: Eerdmans, 1985.

Frede, M. "An Empiricist View of Knowledge: Memorism." In *Epistemology*, edited by S. Everson, 225–50. Companions to Ancient Thought 1. New York: Cambridge University Press, 1990.

Fredericks, D. C. "Chiasm and Parallel Structure in Qoheleth 5:9–6:9." *Journal of Biblical Literature* 108.1 (1989): 17–35.

———. *Coping with Transcience: Ecclesiastes on the Brevity of Life.* Biblical Seminar 18. Sheffield: JSOT Press, 1993.

———. "Life's Storms and Structural Unity in Qoheleth 11:1–12:8." *Journal for the Study of the Old Testament* 52 (1991): 95–114.

———. *Qoheleth's Language: Re-evaluating Its Nature and Date.* Ancient Near Eastern Texts and Studies 3. Lewiston, NY: Edwin Mellen, 1988.

Freud, S. *Interpretation of Dreams.* Translated by A. A. Brill. Hertfordshire, UK: Wordsworth, 1997.

Frydrych, T. *Living under the Sun: Examination of Proverbs and Qoheleth.* Vetus Testamentum Supplement 90. Leiden: Brill, 2001.

Gadamer, H.-G. "Dialogues in Capri." In *Religion*, edited by J. Derrida and G. Vattimo, 200–211. Cambridge, UK: Polity Press, 1998.

———. *Truth and Method.* Translated by J. Weisenheimer and D. G. Marshall. 2nd ed. London: Sheed and Ward, 1989.

Gaede, S. D. *Where Gods May Dwell: Understanding the Human Condition.* Grand Rapids: Zondervan, 1985.

Galling, K. "Kohelet-Studien." *Zeitschrift für die alttestamentliche Wissenschaft* 50 (1932): 276–99.

———. *Der Prediger.* In *Die fünf Megilloth*, by M. Haller and K. Galling, 73–125. 2nd ed. Handbuch zum Alten Testament 18. Tübingen: Mohr/Siebeck, 1969.

Gammie, J. G. "Stoicism and Anti-Stoicism in Qoheleth." *Hebrew Annual Review* 9 (1985): 169–87.

Gentry, P. J. "Hexaplaric Materials in Ecclesiastes and the Role of the Syro-Hexapla." *Aramaic Studies* 1.1 (2003): 5–28.

George, M. K. "Death as the Beginning of Life in the Book of Ecclesiastes." In *Strange Fire: Reading the Bible after the Holocaust*, edited by T. Linafelt, 280–93. New York: New York University Press, 2000.

Gergen, K. J. *The Saturated Self: Dilemmas of Identity in Contemporary Life.* New York: Basic Books, 1991.

Gese, H. "The Crisis of Wisdom in Koheleth." In *Theodicy in the Old Testament,* edited by J. L. Crenshaw, 141–53. Issues in Religion and Theology 4. Philadelphia: Fortress, 1983.

Giese, C. P. "The Genre of Ecclesiastes as Viewed by Its Septuagint Translator and the Early Church Fathers." PhD diss., Hebrew Union College, 1999.

Gilkey, L. *Maker of Heaven and Earth: A Study of the Christian Doctrine of Creation*. Garden City, NY: Doubleday, 1959.

———. *Shantung Compound: The Story of Men and Women under Pressure*. New York: Harper & Row, 1966.

Gilson, E. *The Spirit of Mediaeval Philosophy*. Translated by A. H. C. Downes. Notre Dame, IN: University of Notre Dame Press, 1991.

Ginsberg, H. L. *Koheleth*. Tel-Aviv and Jerusalem: M. Newman, 1961.

———. *Studies in Koheleth*. Texts and Studies of the Jewish Theological Seminary of America 17. New York: Jewish Theological Seminary of America, 1950.

Ginsburg, C. D. *Coheleth, Commonly Called the Book of Ecclesiastes*. London: Longman, Green, Longman and Roberts, 1861.

———. *The Song of Songs and Coheleth (Commonly Called the Book of Ecclesiastes)*. Repr., New York: Ktav, 1970.

Gladson, J. A. "Retributive Paradoxes in Prov. 10–29." PhD diss., Vanderbilt University, 1978.

Glymour, C. "The Epistemology of Geometry." In *The Philosophy of Science*, edited by R. Boyd, P. Gasper, and J. D. Trout, 485–501. Cambridge, MA: MIT Press, 1991.

Goheen, M. W., and C. G. Bartholomew. *Living at the Crossroads: An Introduction to Christian Worldview*. Grand Rapids: Baker Academic, 2008.

Goldingay, J. *Theological Diversity and the Authority of the Old Testament*. Grand Rapids: Eerdmans, 1987.

Good, E. M. *Irony in the Old Testament*. Philadelphia: Westminster, 1965.

———. "The Unfilled Sea: Style and Meaning in Ecclesiastes 1:2–11." In *Israelite Wisdom: Theological and Literary Essays in Honor of Samuel Terrien*, edited by J. G. Gammie, 59–73. Missoula, MT: Scholars Press, 1978.

Gordis, R. *Koheleth—the Man and His World*. 3rd ed. New York: Schocken, 1968.

———. "Qoheleth and Qumran—A Study of Style." *Biblica* 41.4 (1960): 395–410.

———. "Quotations as a Literary Usage in Biblical, Oriental, and Rabbinic Literature." *Hebrew Union College Annual* 22 (1949): 157–219.

———. "Quotations in Wisdom Literature." *Jewish Quarterly Review* 30.2 (1939): 123–47.

Goudzwaard, B., and H. M. de Lange. *Beyond Poverty and Affluence: Toward a Canadian Economy of Care*. Translated and edited by M. R. Vander Vennen. 3rd ed. Toronto: University of Toronto Press, 1995.

Gourevitch, P. *We Wish to Inform You That Tomorrow We Will Be Killed with Our Families: Stories from Rwanda*. New York: Picador, 1998.

Graetz, H. *Kohelet oder der Salomonische Prediger: Übersetzt und kritisch erläutert*. Leipzig: C. F. Winter'sche Verlagshandlung, 1871.

Greenberg, M. "*Nsh* in Exodus 20:20 and the Purpose of the Sinaitic Theophany." *Journal of Biblical Literature* 79.3 (1960): 273–76.

Greenfield, J. C. "Lexicographical Notes I." *Hebrew Union College Annual* 29 (1958): 203–38.

Griffin, D. R. "Creation out of Nothing, Creation out of Chaos, and the Problem of Evil." In *Encountering Evil: Live Options in Theodicy*, edited by S. T. Davis, 101–19. Edinburgh: T&T Clark, 1981.

Guillaume, A. "A Note on *bl'*." *Journal of Theological Studies* 13 (1962): 320–22.

Gunton, C. E. *The One, the Three, and the Many: God, Creation, and the Culture of Modernity.* Bampton Lectures 1992. Cambridge: Cambridge University Press, 1993.

Habel, N. C. *The Book of Job: A Commentary.* Old Testament Library. Philadelphia: Westminster, 1985.

Haden, N. K. "Qoheleth and the Problem of Alienation." *Christian Scholar's Review* 17.1 (1987): 52–66.

Haran, M. *The Biblical Collection: Its Consolidation to the End of the Second Temple Times and Changes of Form to the End of the Middle Ages* [Hebrew]. 2 vols. Jerusalem: Mosad Byalik, 1996–2003.

Harris, R. C. "Ecclesiastical Wisdom and *Nickel Mountain.*" *Twentieth Century Literature* 26.4 (1980): 424–31.

Harrison, C. R. "Qoheleth among the Sociologists." *Biblical Interpretation* 5.2 (1997): 160–80.

———. "Qoheleth in Social-Historical Perspective." PhD diss., Duke University, 1991.

Harrison, R. K. "Garden." In *The International Standard Bible Encyclopedia,* edited by G. W. Bromiley, 2:399–400. Grand Rapids: Eerdmans, 1982.

Harsanyi, M. A., and S. P. Harter. "Ecclesiastes Effects." *Scientometrics* 27.1 (1993): 93–96.

Hauerwas, S. *Naming the Silences: God, Medicine, and the Problem of Suffering.* Grand Rapids: Eerdmans, 1990.

Haupt, P. "Assyr. *lâm iççûri çabâri,* 'Before the Birds Cheep.'" *American Journal of Semitic Languages and Literatures* 32.2 (1916): 143–44.

———. *The Book of Ecclesiastes: A New Metrical Translation, with an Introduction and Explanatory Notes.* Baltimore: Johns Hopkins Press, 1905.

Hayman, A. P. "Qohelet, the Rabbis and the Wisdom Text from the Cairo Geniza." In *Understanding Poets and Prophets: Essays in Honour of George Wishart Anderson,* edited by A. G. Auld, 149–65. Journal for the Study of the Old Testament Supplement 152. Sheffield: JSOT Press, 1993.

Heidegger, M. *Being and Time.* Translated by J. Macquarrie and E. Robinson. Oxford: Blackwell, 1962.

Helsel, P. B. "Warren Zevon's *The Wind* and Ecclesiastes: Searching for Meaning at the Threshold of Death." *Journal of Religion and Health* 46.2 (2007): 205–18.

Hengel, M. *Judaism and Hellenism.* Translated by J. Bowden. 2 vols. Philadelphia: Fortress, 1974.

Hengstenberg, E. W. *A Commentary on Ecclesiastes.* 1869. Repr., Evansville, IN: Sovereign Grace, 1960.

———. "Ecclesiastes." In *A Cyclopaedia of Biblical Literature,* edited by J. Kitto, 1:593–97. Edinburgh: Adam and Charles Black, 1845.

Herrera, R. A. *Reasons for Our Rhymes: An Inquiry into the Philosophy of History.* Grand Rapids: Eerdmans, 2001.

Hertzberg, H. W. *Der Prediger.* Kommentar zum Alten Testament 17.4. Gütersloh: Mohn, 1963.

Hesse, M. B. "Cognitive Claims of Metaphor." *Journal of Speculative Philosophy* 2.1 (1988): 1–16.

———. *Models and Analogies in Science.* Notre Dame, IN: University of Notre Dame Press, 1966.

Hick, J. H. "An Irenaean Theodicy." In *Encountering Evil: Live Options in Theodicy,* edited by S. T. Davis, 39–52. Edinburgh: T&T Clark, 1981.

401

Hillesum, E. *An Interrupted Life: The Diaries, 1941–1943 and Letters from Westerbork.* Translated by A. J. Pomerans. New York: Holt, 1996.

Himmelfarb, G. *On Looking into the Abyss: Thoughts on Culture and Society.* New York: Knopf, 1994.

Hirshman, M. "The Greek Fathers and the Aggada on Ecclesiastes: Formats of Exegesis in Late Antiquity." *Hebrew Union College Annual* 59 (1988): 137–65.

———. "The Preacher and His Public in Third-Century Palestine." *Journal of Jewish Studies* 42.1 (1991): 108–14.

———. "Qohelet's Reception and Interpretation in Early Rabbinic Literature." In *Studies in Ancient Midrash,* edited by J. L. Kugel, 87–99. Cambridge, MA: Harvard University Center for Jewish Studies, 2001.

———. "Rabbinic Views of Qohelet." *Jewish Quarterly Review* 91.3–4 (2001): 477–78.

———. *A Rivalry of Genius: Jewish and Christian Biblical Interpretation in Late Antiquity.* Translated by B. Stein. Albany: State University of New York Press, 1996.

Hitzig, F. *Der Prediger Salomo's.* Kurzgefasstes exegetisches Handbuch zum Alten Testament 7. Leipzig: Weidmann, 1847.

Hoffman, Y. *A Blemished Perfection: The Book of Job in Context.* Journal for the Study of the Old Testament Supplement 213. Sheffield: Sheffield Academic Press, 1996.

Holm-Nielsen, S. "The Book of Ecclesiastes and the Interpretation of It in Jewish and Christian Theology." *Annual of the Swedish Theological Institute* 10 (1976): 38–96.

Homan, M. M. "Beer Production by Throwing Bread into Water: A New Interpretation of Qoh. XI 1–2." *Vetus Testamentum* 52.2 (2002): 275–78.

Hubbard, D. A. "The Wisdom Movement and Israel's Covenant Faith." *Tyndale Bulletin* 17 (1966): 3–33.

Huehnergard, J. "Asseverative *la and Hypothetical *lu/law in Semitic." *Journal of the American Oriental Society* 103.3 (1983): 569–93.

Hume, D. *Dialogues concerning Natural Religion.* London: Penguin Classics, 1990.

Hurvitz, A. Review of *Qoheleth's Language: Re-evaluating Its Nature and Date,* by D. C. Fredericks. *Hebrew Studies* 31 (1990): 144–54.

Hyvärinen, K. *Die Übersetzung von Aquila.* Uppsala: Almqvist & Wiksell, 1977.

Ilibagiza, I., and S. Erwin. *Left to Tell: Discovering God amidst the Rwandan Holocaust.* Carlsbad, CA: Hay House, 2007.

Ingraffia, B. D. *Postmodern Theory and Biblical Theology: Vanquishing God's Shadow.* Cambridge: Cambridge University Press, 1995.

Ingram, D. *Ambiguity in Ecclesiastes.* Library of Hebrew Bible/Old Testament Studies 431. New York: T&T Clark, 2006.

Irwin, W. A. "Ecclesiastes 4:13–16." *Journal of Near Eastern Studies* 3 (1944): 255–57.

———. "Ecclesiastes 8:2–9." *Journal of Near Eastern Studies* 4 (1945): 130–31.

Isaksson, B. *Studies in the Language of Qoheleth: With Special Emphasis on the Verbal System.* Acta Universitatis Upsaliensis. Studi Semitica Upsaliensia 10. Stockholm: Almqvist & Wiksell, 1987.

Jacob, M. "Post-Traumatic Stress Disorder: Facing Futility in and after Vietnam." *Currents in Theology and Mission* 10 (1983): 291–98.

Japhet, S., and R. B. Salters, trans. *The Commentary of R. Samuel Ben Meir (Rashbam) on Qoheleth.* Jerusalem: Magnes, 1985.

Jarick, J. "Aquila's Koheleth." *Textus* 15 (1990): 131–39.

————. "The Hebrew Book of Changes: Reflections on *Hakkōl Hebel* and *Lakkōl Zemān* in Ecclesiastes." *Journal for the Study of the Old Testament* 90 (2000): 79–99.

————. "Theodore of Mopsuestia and the Interpretation of Ecclesiastes." In *The Bible in Human Society: Essays in Honour of John Rogerson*, edited by D. J. A. Clines, P. R. Davies, and M. D. Carroll R., 306–16. Journal for the Study of the Old Testament Supplement 300. Sheffield: Sheffield Academic Press, 1995.

————. "Theodore of Mopsuestia and the Text of Ecclesiastes." In *VIII Congress of the International Organization for Septuagint and Cognate Studies: Paris 1992*, edited by L. J. Greenspoon and O. Munnich, 367–85. Society of Biblical Literature Septuagint and Cognate Studies 41. Atlanta: Scholars Press, 1995.

Jaspers, K. *Nietzsche: An Introduction to the Understanding of His Philosophical Activity*. Translated by C. F. Wallraff and F. J. Schmitz. Baltimore: Johns Hopkins University Press, 1997.

Jastrow, M. *A Dictionary of the Targumim, the Talmud Babli and Yerushalmi, and the Midrashic Literature*. New York: Choreb, 1926.

Jeffrey, D. L. *People of the Book: Christian Identity and Literary Culture*. Grand Rapids: Eerdmans, 1996.

Jenkins, P. *The New Faces of Christianity: Believing the Bible in the Global South*. Oxford: Oxford University Press, 2006.

————. *The Next Christendom: The Coming of Global Christianity*. Oxford: Oxford University Press, 2002.

Jerome. "Commentarius in Ecclesiasten." In *Patrologiae Latine*, edited by J.-P. Migne, 23:1063–1173. Paris: Migne, 1863.

John of the Cross, Saint. *Ascent of Mount Carmel*. Translated by E. A. Peers. London: Burns & Oates, 1983.

John Paul II. *Centesimus Annus*. In *John Paul II and World Politics: Twenty Years of a Search for a New Approach*, edited by U. Colombo Sacco, 76–116. Leuven: Peeters, 1999.

————. *Consecrated Life: Post-Synodal Apostolic Exhortation Vita Consecrata . . . on the Consecrated Life and Its Mission in the Church and in the World*. Sherbrooke, ON: Médiaspaul, 1996.

Johnson, R. A. *Owning Your Shadow: Understanding the Dark Side of the Psyche*. San Francisco: HarperSanFrancisco, 1991.

Johnson, R. E. "The Rhetorical Question as a Literary Device in Ecclesiastes." PhD diss., Southern Baptist Theological Seminary, 1986.

Johnston, P. S. *Shades of Sheol: Death and Afterlife in the Old Testament*. Downers Grove, IL: InterVarsity, 2002.

Johnston, R. K. *Useless Beauty: Ecclesiastes through the Lens of Contemporary Film*. Grand Rapids: Baker Academic, 2004.

Jong, S. de. "A Book on Labour: The Structuring Principles and the Main Theme of the Book of Qohelet." *Journal for the Study of the Old Testament* 54 (1992): 107–16.

————. "God in the Book of Qohelet: A Reappraisal of Qohelet's Place in Old Testament Theology." *Vetus Testamentum* 47.2 (1997): 154–67.

Joüon, P. *A Grammar of Biblical Hebrew*. Translated and revised by T. Muraoka. 2 vols. Subsidia biblica 14/1–2. Rome: Pontifical Biblical Institute Press, 1991.

————. "Sur le nom de Qoheleth." *Biblica* 2.1 (1921): 53–54.

Jung, C. G. *Answer to Job*. Translated by R. F. C. Hull. Bollingen Series 20. Princeton, NJ: Princeton University Press, 1991.

————. *Dreams*. Translated by R. F. C. Hull. Bollingen Series 20. Princeton, NJ: Princeton University Press, 1974.

————. *Memories, Dreams, Reflections*. Rev. ed. New York: Vintage, 1965.

————. *Mysterium Coniunctionis: An Inquiry into the Separation and Synthesis of Psychic Opposites in Alchemy*. Translated by R. F. C. Hull. Bollingen Series 20. Collected Works 14. Princeton, NJ: Princeton University Press, 1963.

Kabasele Lumbala, F., and N. Grey. "Ecclesiastes 3:1–8: An African Perspective." In *Return to Babel: Global Perspectives on the Bible*, edited by J. R. Levison and P. Pope-Levison, 81–85. Louisville: Westminster John Knox, 1999.

Kallas, E. "Ecclesiastes: Traditum et Fides Evangelica. The Ecclesiastes Commentaries of Martin Luther, Philip Melanchthon, and Johannes Brenz Considered within the History of Interpretation." PhD diss., Graduate Theological Union, Berkeley, 1979.

Kalsbeek, L. *Contours of a Christian Philosophy: An Introduction to Herman Dooyeweerd's Thought*. Amsterdam: Duiten and Schipperheijn, 1975.

Kamenetzky, A. S. "Die P'šita zu Ḳoheleth." *Zeitschrift für die alttestamentliche Wissenschaft* 24 (1904): 181–239.

————. "Der Rätselname Koheleth." *Zeitschrift für die alttestamentliche Wissenschaft* 34 (1914): 225–28.

Keefer, M. H. "Deconstruction and the Gnostics." *University of Toronto Quarterly* 55.1 (1985): 74–93.

Kendall, G. A. "Alienation and the Struggle for Existence: Biblical and Ideological Views in Contrast." *Thomist* 47 (1983): 66–76.

Kermode, F. *The Sense of an Ending: Studies in the Theory of Fiction with a New Epilogue*. Oxford: Oxford University Press, 1967.

Kidd, S. M. *When the Heart Waits: Spiritual Direction for Life's Sacred Questions*. San Francisco: Harper & Row, 1990.

Kidner, D. *A Time to Mourn and a Time to Dance*. Downers Grove, IL: InterVarsity, 1976.

Kierkegaard, S. *Edifying Discourses*. Translated by D. F. Swenson and L. M. Swenson. 4 vols. Minneapolis: Augsburg, 1943–46.

————. *Fear and Trembling*. Edited by C. S. Evans and S. Walsh. Translated by S. Walsh. Cambridge: Cambridge University Press, 2006.

————. *The Point of View of My Work as an Author*. New York: Harper & Row, 1962.

————. *The Sickness unto Death: A Christian Psychological Exposition of Edification and Awakening*. Penguin Classics. London and New York: Penguin, 1989.

Kittel, G., and G. Friedrich, eds. *Theological Dictionary of the New Testament*. Translated and edited by G. W. Bromiley. 10 vols. Grand Rapids: Eerdmans, 1964–76.

Kline, M. M. "Is Qoheleth Unorthodox? A Review Article." *Kerux* 13 (1998): 16–39.

Konstan, D. *Friendship in the Classical World*. Cambridge: Cambridge University Press, 1997.

Koosed, J. L. *(Per)mutations of Qoheleth: Reading the Body in the Book*. Library of Hebrew Bible/Old Testament Studies 429. New York: T&T Clark, 2006.

Kraus, M. "Christians, Jews, and Pagans in Dialogue: Jerome on Ecclesiastes 12:1–7." *Hebrew Union College Annual* 70–71 (1999–2000): 183–231.

Kreitzer, L. J. *The Old Testament in Fiction and Film: On Reversing the Hermeneutical Flow*. Biblical Seminar 24. Sheffield: Sheffield Academic Press, 1994.

Krell, D. F. "General Introduction: The Question of Being." In *Martin Heidegger: Basic Writings from Being and Time (1927) to The Task of Thinking (1964), Revised and Expanded Edition*, edited by D. F. Krell, 1–35. London: Routledge, 1993.

Kroeber, R., ed. *Der Prediger. Hebräisch und Deutsch*. Schriften und Quellen der Alten Welt 13. Berlin: Akademie, 1963.

Krüger, T. "'Frau Weisheit' in Koh 7:26." *Biblica* 73.3 (1992): 394–403.

———. *Kohelet*. Biblischer Kommentar Altes Testament 19. Neukirchen-Vluyn: Neukirchener Verlag, 2000.

———. *Qoheleth: A Commentary*. Translated by O. C. Dean Jr. Hermeneia. Minneapolis: Fortress, 2004.

Kugel, J. *The Great Poems: A Reader's Companion with New Translations*. New York: Free Press, 1999.

———. "Qohelet and Money." *Catholic Biblical Quarterly* 51 (1989): 32–49.

Kutler, L. "A 'Strong' Case for Hebrew *mar*." *Ugarit-Forschungen* 16 (1984): 111–18.

Lacy, P. de. "Thematic and Structural Affinities: *The Wanderer* and Ecclesiastes." *Neophilologus* 82 (1998): 125–37.

Lamparter, H. *Das Buch der Weisheit: Prediger und Spruche*. Botschaft des Alten Testaments 16. Stuttgart: Calwer Verlag, 1959.

Lampe, G. W. H., ed. *The Cambridge History of the Bible*. Vol. 2: *The West from the Fathers to the Reformation*. New York: Cambridge University Press, 1969.

Landsberger, B. "Zur vierten und siebenten Tafel des Gilgamesh-Epos." *Revue d'Assyriologie et d'Archéologie orientale* 62 (1968): 97–135.

Lane, D. J. "'Lilies That Fester': The Peshitta Text of Qoheleth (Peshitta Institute Communication 15)." *Vetus Testamentum* 29.4 (1979): 481–90.

Lasch, C. *The Culture of Narcissism: American Life in an Age of Diminishing Expectations*. New York: Norton, 1979.

Laue, L. *Das Buch Koheleth und die Interpolationshypothese Siegfrieds: Eine exegetische Studie*. Wittenberg: Wunschmann, 1900.

Lauha, A. *Kohelet*. Biblischer Kommentar Altes Testament Band 19. Neukirchen-Vluyn: Neukirchener Verlag, 1978.

Lee, E. P. *The Vitality of Enjoyment in Qohelet's Theological Rhetoric*. Beihefte zur Zeitschrift für die alttestamentliche Wissenschaft 353. Berlin: de Gruyter, 2005.

Leibniz, G. W. F. *Essais de théodicée sur la bonté de Dieu, la liberté de l'homme et l'origine du mal*. Paris: Garnier-Flammarion, 1969.

Leiman, S. Z. *The Canonization of Hebrew Scripture*. Hamden, CT: Archon Books, 1976.

Leupold, H. C. *Exposition of Ecclesiastes*. Grand Rapids: Baker Academic, 1952.

Levinas, E. *Totality and Infinity: An Essay on Exteriority*. Translated by A. Lingis. Pittsburgh: Duquesne University Press, 1969.

Levine, É. "The Humor in Qohelet." *Zeitschrift für die alttestamentliche Wissenschaft* 109.1 (1997): 71–83.

Levy, L. *Das Buch Qoheleth. Ein Beitrag zur Geschichte des Sadduzäismus*. Leipzig: J. C. Hinrich'sche Buchhandlung, 1912.

Lewis, C. S. "The Weight of Glory." In *The Weight of Glory and Other Addresses*, 1–15. New York: Macmillan, 1949.

Lewis, J. P. "What Do We Mean by Jabneh?" *Journal of Bible and Religion* 32 (April 1964): 125–32.

L'Hour, J. "Yahweh Elohim." *Revue biblique* 81 (1974): 525–56.

Lichtheim, M. *Ancient Egyptian Literature*. 3 vols. Berkeley: University of California Press, 1973–80.

Limburg, J. *Encountering Ecclesiastes: A Book for Our Time.* Grand Rapids: Eerdmans, 2006.

Loader, J. A. *Ecclesiastes.* Translated by J. Vriend. Text and Interpretation. Grand Rapids: Eerdmans, 1986.

———. *Polar Structures in the Book of Qohelet.* Beihefte zur Zeitschrift für die alttestamentliche Wissenschaft 152. Berlin/New York: de Gruyter, 1979.

———. "Qohelet 3:2–8: A Sonnet in the Old Testament." *Zeitschrift für die alttestamentliche Wissenschaft* 81.2 (1969): 240–42.

Loewenclau, I. von. "Kohelet und Sokrates—Versuch eines Vergleiches." *Zeitschrift für die alttestamentliche Wissenschaft* 98.3 (1986): 327–38.

Lohfink, G. *Jesus and Community: The Social Dimensions of Christian Faith.* Translated by J. P. Galvin. London: SPCK, 1985.

Lohfink, N. "Freu dich, Jüngling—doch nicht, weil du jung bist: Zum Formproblem im Schlussgedicht Kohelets (Koh 11,9–12,8)." *Biblical Interpretation* 3 (1995): 158–89.

———. *Kohelet.* Neue Echter Bibel. Würzburg: Echter, 1980.

———. "Kohelet und die Banken: Zur Übersetzung von Kohelet 5:12–16." *Vetus Testamentum* 39.4 (1989): 488–95.

———. *Qoheleth.* Translated by S. E. McEvenue. Continental Commentary. Minneapolis: Fortress, 2003.

———. "Qoheleth 5:17–19—Revelation by Joy." *Catholic Biblical Quarterly* 52 (1990): 625–35.

———. *Studien zu Kohelet.* Stuttgarter biblische Aufsatzbände 26. Stuttgart: Katholisches Bibelwerk, 1998.

———. "War Kohelet ein Frauenfeind: Ein Versuch, die Logik und den Gegenstand von Koh. 7,23–8,1a herauszufinden." In *Sagesse de l'Ancien Testament,* edited by M. Gilbert, 259–87. Bibliotheca ephemeridum theologicarum lovaniensium 51. Gembloux: Duculot, 1979.

Longman, T., III. *The Book of Ecclesiastes.* New International Commentary on the Old Testament. Grand Rapids: Eerdmans, 1998.

———. "Comparative Methods in Old Testament Studies: Ecclesiastes Reconsidered." *Theological Students Fellowship Bulletin* 7.4 (1984): 5–9.

———. *Fictional Akkadian Autobiography: A Generic and Comparative Study.* Winona Lake, IN: Eisenbrauns, 1990.

———. *Proverbs.* Baker Commentary on the Old Testament Wisdom and Psalms. Grand Rapids: Baker Academic, 2006.

Loretz, O. "'Frau' und griechisch-jüdische Philosophie im Buch Qohelet (Qoh 7,23–8,1 und 9,6–10)." *Ugarit-Forschungen* 23 (1992): 245–64.

———. "Poetry and Prose in the Book of Qohelet (1:1–3:22; 7:23–8:1; 9:6–10; 12:8–14)." In *Verse in Ancient Near Eastern Prose,* edited by J. C. de Moor and W. G. E. Watson, 155–89. Alter Orient und Altes Testament 42. Kevelaer: Butzon & Bercker, 1993.

———. *Qohelet und der alte Orient: Untersuchungen zu Stil und theologischer Thematik des Buches Qohelet.* Freiburg: Herder, 1964.

Lundin, R. *The Culture of Interpretation: Christian Faith and the Postmodern World.* Grand Rapids: Eerdmans, 1993.

Luther, M. *An Exposition of Salomons Booke Called Ecclesiastes or the Preacher.* London: John Daye, 1573.

———. "Notes on Ecclesiastes." In *Luther's Works.* Vol. 15, edited and translated by J. Pelikan, 3–193. St. Louis: Concordia, 1972.

————. *Tischreden.* In *D. Martin Luthers Werke: Kritische Gesamtausgabe.* Vol. 1. Weimar: Böhlau, 1883–1993.

Lyons, W. J. "'Outing' Qoheleth: On the Search for Homosexuality in the Wisdom Tradition." *Theology & Sexuality* 12.2 (2006): 181–202.

Lys, D. *L'Ecclésiaste ou que vaut la vie?* Paris: Letouzey et Ané, 1977.

MacDonald, D. B. "Old Testament Notes." *Journal of Biblical Literature* 18.1–2 (1899): 212–15.

MacIntyre, A. *After Virtue: A Study in Moral Theory.* 2nd ed. Notre Dame, IN: University of Notre Dame Press, 1985.

Mackie, J. L. "Evil and Omnipotence." *Mind* 64 (1955): 200–212. Repr. in *Philosophy of Religion,* edited by B. Mitchell, 92–104. London: Oxford University Press, 1971.

Manning, B. *Ruthless Trust: The Ragamuffin's Path to God.* San Francisco: HarperSanFrancisco, 2002.

Marcus, L. *Auto/Biographical Discourses: Theory, Criticism, Practice.* Manchester, UK: Manchester University Press, 1994.

Maussion, M. *Le Mal, le bien et le jugement de Dieu dans le livre de Qohélet.* Orbis biblicus et orientalis 190. Fribourg: Editions Universitaires; Göttingen: Vandenhoeck & Ruprecht, 2003.

Mayes, A. D. H. *Deuteronomy.* New Century Bible Commentary. Grand Rapids: Eerdmans, 1979.

McConville, J. G. *Deuteronomy.* Apollos Old Testament Commentary 5. Downers Grove, IL: InterVarsity, 2002.

————. "The Old Testament and the Enjoyment of Wealth." In *Christ and Consumerism: A Critical Analysis of the Spirit of the Age,* edited by C. G. Bartholomew and T. Moritz, 34–53. Carlisle, UK: Paternoster, 2000.

McKane, W. *Prophets and Wise Men.* Studies in Biblical Theology 1/44. London: SCM, 1965.

McKenna, J. E. "The Concept of *Hebel* in the Book of Ecclesiastes." *Scottish Journal of Theology* 45.1 (1992): 19–28.

McNeile, A. H. *An Introduction to Ecclesiastes, with Notes and Appendices.* Cambridge: Cambridge University Press, 1904.

Mearsheimer, J. J., and S. M. Walt. *The Israeli Lobby and U.S. Foreign Policy.* Toronto: Viking Canada, 2007.

Meilander, G. C. *Friendship: A Study in Theological Ethics.* Notre Dame, IN: University of Notre Dame Press, 1981.

————. *Things That Count: Essays Moral and Theological.* Washington, DC: Isi Books, 2000.

————, ed. *Working: Its Meaning and Its Limits.* Notre Dame, IN: University of Notre Dame Press, 2000.

Melanchthon, P. "Enarratio Brevis . . . Ecclesiasten." In *Corpus Reformatorum,* vol. 14, edited by C. G. Bretschneider, 89–159. Halle: Schwetschke, 1847.

Merton, T. *Conjectures of a Guilty Bystander.* New York: Doubleday, 1968.

Mettinger, T. N. D. *Solomonic State Officials: A Study of the Civil Government Officials of the Israelite Monarchy.* Coniectanea biblica: Old Testament 5. Lund: Gleerup, 1971.

Michel, D. *Qohelet.* Erträge der Forschung 258. Darmstadt: Wissenschaftliche Buchgesellschaft, 1988.

————. *Untersuchungen zur Eigenart des Buches Qohelet.* Beihefte zur Zeitschrift für die alttestamentliche Wissenschaft 183. Berlin: de Gruyter, 1989.

Middlemas, J. "Ecclesiastes Gone 'Sideways.'" *Expository Times* 118.5 (2007): 216–21.

Middleton, J. R. "Is Creation Theology Inherently Conservative? A Dialogue with Walter Brueggemann." *Harvard Theological Review* 87 (1994): 257–77.

Milbank, J. *The Word Made Strange: Theology, Language, Culture.* Oxford: Blackwell, 2002.

Miles, S. *Consumerism—as a Way of Life.* London: Sage, 1998.

Miller, D. B. "Power in Wisdom: The Suffering Servant of Ecclesiastes 4." In *Peace and Justice Shall Embrace: Power and Theopolitics in the Bible: Essays in Honor of Millard Lind,* edited by T. Grimsrud and L. L. Johns, 145–73. Telford, PA: Pandora, 1999.

———. "Qohelet's Symbolic Use of *hbl.*" *Journal of Biblical Literature* 117.3 (1998): 437–54.

———. *Symbol and Rhetoric in Ecclesiastes: The Place of Hebel in Qohelet's Work.* Society of Biblical Literature. Atlanta: Society of Biblical Literature, 2002.

Miller, J. H. "The Critic as Host." In *Deconstruction and Criticism,* edited by H. Bloom et al., 177–216. New York: Continuum, 1979.

Miller, P. D. *Interpreting the Psalms.* Philadelphia: Fortress, 1986.

Moran, W. L. "Note on Ps. 119:28." *Catholic Biblical Quarterly* 15 (1953): 10.

Mühlenberg, E. "Homilie II: Ecclesiastes 1,12–2,3." In *Gregory of Nyssa, Homilies on Ecclesiastes: An English Version with Supporting Studies,* edited by S. G. Hall, 159–70. Proceedings of the Seventh International Colloquium on Gregory of Nyssa (St Andrews, 5–10 September 1990). Berlin: de Gruyter, 1993.

Muilenburg, J. "A Qoheleth Scroll from Qumran." *Bulletin of the American Schools of Oriental Research* 135 (1954): 20–28.

Müller, H.-P. "Plausibilitätsverlust herkömmlicher Religion bei Kohelet und den Vorsokratikern." In *Gemeinde ohne Tempel = Community without Temple: Zur Substituierung und Transformation des Jerusalemer Tempels und seines Kults im Alten Testament, antiken Judentum und frühen Christentum,* edited by B. Ego et al., 99–113. Wissenschaftliche Untersuchungen zum Neuen Testament 118. Tübingen: Mohr, 1999.

Murphy, R. E. *Ecclesiastes.* Word Biblical Commentary 23A. Dallas: Word, 1992.

———. "The Old Testament as Scripture." *Journal for the Study of the Old Testament* 16 (1980): 40–44.

———. "On Translating Ecclesiastes." *Catholic Biblical Quarterly* 53.4 (1991): 571–79.

———. "Proverbs and Theological Exegesis." In *The Hermeneutical Quest: Essays in Honor of James Luther Mays on His Sixty-fifth Birthday,* edited by D. G. Miller, 87–95. Princeton Theological Monograph Series 4. Allison Park, PA: Pickwick, 1986.

———. "Qohelet Interpreted: The Bearing of the Past on the Present." *Vetus Testamentum* 32.3 (1982): 331–37.

———. "Qohelet's 'Quarrel' with the Fathers." In *From Faith to Faith: Essays in Honor of Donald G. Miller on His Seventieth Birthday,* edited by D. Y. Hadidian, 235–45. Pittsburgh: Pickwick, 1979.

———. *Seven Books of Wisdom.* Milwaukee: Bruce, 1960.

———. "Wisdom in the OT." In *Anchor Bible Dictionary,* edited by D. N. Freedman, 6:920–31. New York: Doubleday, 1992.

———. *Wisdom Literature: Job, Proverbs, Ruth, Canticles, Ecclesiastes, Esther.* Forms of the Old Testament Literature 13. Grand Rapids: Eerdmans, 1981.

———. "Wisdom—Theses and Hypotheses." In *Israelite Wisdom: Theological and Literary Essays in Honor of Samuel Terrien,* edited by J. G. Gammie, 35–42. Missoula, MT: Scholars Press, 1978.

Myers, D. G. "Money & Misery." In *The Consuming Passion: Christianity & the Consumer Culture*, edited by R. Clapp, 51–75. Downers Grove, IL: InterVarsity, 1998.

Newsom, C. A. "Job and Ecclesiastes." In *Old Testament Interpretation: Past, Present, and Future: Essays in Honor of Gene M. Tucker*, edited by J. L. Mays, D. L. Petersen, and K. H. Richards, 177–94. Nashville: Abingdon, 1995.

Nordheimer, I. "The Philosophy of Ecclesiastes." *American Biblical Repository* 12.31–32 (1838): 197–219.

Norris, K. *The Quotidian Mysteries: Laundry, Liturgy, and "Women's Work."* New York: Paulist Press, 1998.

Nouwen, H. J. M. *Clowning in Rome: Reflections on Solitude, Celibacy, Prayer and Contemplation.* London: Darton, Longman and Todd, 2001.

———. *The Road to Daybreak: A Spiritual Journey.* New York: Doubleday, 1990.

———. *The Way of the Heart: Connecting with God through Prayer, Wisdom, and Silence.* New York: Ballantine, 1981.

Noyes, G. R. *A New Translation of Job, Ecclesiastes, and the Canticles.* 3rd ed. Boston: American Unitarian Association, 1867.

O'Callaghan, P. D. *The Feast of Friendship.* Wichita: Eighth Day, 2002.

O'Donovan, O. *The Desire of the Nations: Rediscovering the Roots of Political Theology.* Cambridge: Cambridge University Press, 1996.

———. "Political Theology, Tradition and Modernity." In *The Cambridge Companion to Liberation Theology*, edited by C. Rowland, 235–47. Cambridge: Cambridge University Press, 1999.

———. "Response to Peter Scott." In *A Royal Priesthood? The Use of the Bible Ethically and Politically: A Dialogue with Oliver O'Donovan*, edited by C. G. Bartholomew, J. Chaplin, R. Song, and A. Wolters, 374–76. Scripture and Hermeneutics Series 3. Grand Rapids: Zondervan, 2002.

———. *Resurrection and Moral Order: An Outline for Evangelical Ethics.* Grand Rapids: Eerdmans, 1986.

———. *The Ways of Judgment.* Bampton Lectures 2003. Grand Rapids: Eerdmans, 2005.

O'Dowd, R. P. "The Wisdom of Torah: Epistemology in Deuteronomy and the Wisdom Literature." PhD diss., University of Liverpool, 2005.

Ogden, G. S. "The 'Better'-Proverb (Tôb-Spruch), Rhetorical Criticism, and Qoheleth." *Journal of Biblical Literature* 96.4 (1977): 489–505.

———. "Historical Allusion in Qoheleth IV 13–16?" *Vetus Testamentum* 30.3 (1980): 309–15.

———. "The Interpretation of *dwr* in Ecclesiastes 1.4." *Journal for the Study of the Old Testament* 34 (1986): 91–92.

———. "The Mathematics of Wisdom: Qoheleth IV 1–12." *Vetus Testamentum* 34.4 (1984): 446–53.

———. *Qoheleth.* Sheffield: JSOT Press, 1987.

———. "Qoheleth IX 1–16." *Vetus Testamentum* 32.2 (1982): 158–69.

———. "Qoheleth IX 17–X 20: Variations on the Theme of Wisdom's Strength and Vulnerability." *Vetus Testamentum* 30.1 (1980): 27–37.

———. "Qoheleth XI 1–6." *Vetus Testamentum* 33.2 (1983): 222–30.

———. "Qoheleth XI 7–XII 8: Qoheleth's Summons to Enjoyment and Reflection." *Vetus Testamentum* 34.1 (1984): 27–38.

————. "Qoheleth's Use of the 'Nothing Is Better'-Form." *Journal of Biblical Literature* 98.3 (1979): 339–50.

Origen. *The Song of Songs: Commentary and Homilies.* Translated by R. P. Lawson. Ancient Christian Writers 26. Westminster, MD: Newman Press, 1957.

Pahk, J. Y.-S. "A Syntactical and Contextual Consideration of *'šh* in Qoh. IX 9." *Vetus Testamentum* 51.3 (2001): 370–80.

Paulson, G. N. "The Use of Qoheleth in Bonhoeffer's *Ethics.*" *Word & World* 18.3 (1998): 307–13.

Perdue, L. G. *Wisdom and Creation: The Theology of Wisdom Literature.* Nashville: Abingdon, 1994.

————. *Wisdom and Cult: A Critical Analysis of the Views of Cult in the Wisdom Literature of Israel and the Ancient Near East.* Society of Biblical Literature Dissertation Series 30. Missoula, MT: Scholars Press, 1977.

Perry, T. A. *Dialogues with Kohelet: The Book of Ecclesiastes: Translation and Commentary.* University Park: Pennsylvania State University Press, 1993.

Peterson, E. H. *The Contemplative Pastor: Returning to the Art of Spiritual Direction.* Grand Rapids: Eerdmans, 1989.

————. *Eat This Book: A Conversation in the Art of Spiritual Reading.* Grand Rapids: Eerdmans, 2006.

————. "The Pastoral Work of Nay-Saying." In *Five Smooth Stones for Pastoral Work,* 149–90. Grand Rapids: Eerdmans, 1980.

————. *Run with the Horses: The Quest for Life at Its Best.* Downers Grove, IL: InterVarsity, 1983.

————. *Take and Read. Spiritual Reading: An Annotated List.* Grand Rapids: Eerdmans, 1996.

————. *Working the Angles: The Shape of Pastoral Integrity.* Grand Rapids: Eerdmans, 1987.

Pfeiffer, E. "Die Gottesfurcht im Buche Kohelet." In *Gottes Wort und Gottes Land: Hans Wilhelm Hertzberg zum 70 Geburtstag,* edited by H. G. Reventlow, 133–58. Göttingen: Vandenhoeck & Ruprecht, 1965.

Pieper, J. *Happiness and Contemplation.* Chicago: Regnery, 1968.

Pippert, W. G. *Words from the Wise: An Arrangement by Word and Theme of the Entire Book of the Proverbs.* Longwood, FL: Xulon Press, 2003.

Plantinga, A. "The Free Will Defense." In *The Analytic Theist: An Alvin Plantinga Reader,* edited by J. F. Sennett, 22–49. Grand Rapids: Eerdmans, 1998.

Plantinga, C., Jr. *Not the Way It's Supposed to Be: A Breviary of Sin.* Grand Rapids: Eerdmans, 1995.

Ploeg, J. P. M. van der. *Prediker.* Boeken van het Oude Testament 8. Roermond: Romen, 1953.

Plumptre, E. H. *Ecclesiastes, or The Preacher. With Notes and Introduction.* Cambridge Bible for Schools and Colleges. Cambridge: Cambridge University Press, 1881.

Podechard, E. *L'Ecclésiaste.* Paris: Lecoffre, 1912.

Poincaré, H. *Science and Hypothesis.* London: Scott, 1905.

Polk, T. "The Wisdom of Irony: A Study of *Hebel* and Its Relation to Joy and the Fear of God in Ecclesiastes." *Studia Biblica et Theologica* 6.1 (1976): 3–17.

Popper, K. R. *Objective Knowledge: An Evolutionary Approach.* Oxford: Clarendon, 1972.

Porten, B., and A. Yardeni, eds. *Textbook of Aramaic Documents from Egypt.* 3 vols. Jerusalem: Israel Academy of Sciences and Humanities, 1986–93.

Power, A. D. *Ecclesiastes, or the Preacher: A New Translation, with Introduction, Notes, Glossary, and Index*. London: Longmans, 1952.

Preuss, H. D. *Einführung in die alttestamentliche Weisheitsliteratur*. Stuttgart: Kohlhammer, 1987.

Prior, J. M. "'When All the Singing Has Stopped': Ecclesiastes: A Modest Mission in Unpredictable Times." *International Review of Mission* 91.360 (2002): 7–23.

Pritchard, J. B., ed. *Ancient Near Eastern Texts Relating to the Old Testament with Supplement*. 3rd ed. Princeton, NJ: Princeton University Press, 1969.

Qimron, E., and J. Strugnell. "Unpublished Halakhic Letter from Qumran." In *Biblical Archaeology Today: Proceedings of the International Congress on Biblical Archaeology, Jerusalem, April, 1984*, 400–407. Jerusalem: Israel Exploration Society, 1985.

Rad, G. von. *Wisdom in Israel*. Translated by J. D. Martin. Nashville: Abingdon, 1972.

Ramsey, I. T. *Religious Language*. London: SCM, 1957.

Ranston, H. *Ecclesiastes and the Early Greek Wisdom Literature*. London: Epworth, 1925.

Ratschow, C. H. "Anmerkungen zur theologischen Auffassung des Zeitproblems." *Zeitschrift für Theologie und Kirche* 51 (1954): 36–87.

Ravasi, G. *Qohelet*. Torino: Paoline, 1988.

Redford, D. B. "The Literary Motif of the Exposed Child (Cf. Ex. ii 1–10)." *Numen* 14.1 (1967): 209–28.

Reichenbach, H. *The Philosophy of Space and Time*. Translated by M. Reichenbach and J. Freund. New York: Dover, 1958.

Reventlow, H. G. *Problems of Biblical Theology in the Twentieth Century*. London: SCM, 1986.

———. *Problems of Old Testament Theology in the Twentieth Century*. London: SCM, 1985.

———. "Righteousness as Order of the World: Some Remarks Towards a Programme." In *Justice and Righteousness: Biblical Themes and Their Influence*, edited by H. G. Reventlow and Y. Hoffman, 163–72. Journal for the Study of the Old Testament Supplement 137. Sheffield: Sheffield Academic Press, 1992.

Ricoeur, P. "Biblical Time." In *Figuring the Sacred: Religion, Narrative, and Imagination*, edited by M. I. Wallace, 167–80. Translated by D. Pellauer. Minneapolis: Fortress, 1995.

———. *Time and Narrative*. Translated by K. McGlaughlin and D. Pellauer. 3 vols. Chicago: University of Chicago Press, 1984–88.

———. "Toward a Hermeneutic of the Idea of Revelation." In *Essays on Biblical Interpretation*, edited by L. S. Mudge, 73–118. Philadelphia: Fortress, 1979.

Rist, J. M. *Epicurus: An Introduction*. Cambridge: Cambridge University Press, 1977.

———. *Stoic Philosophy*. Cambridge: Cambridge University Press, 1969.

Rofé, A. "'The Angel' in Qoh 5:5 in Light of a Wisdom Dialogue Formula" [Hebrew]. *Eretz Israel* 14 (1978): 105–9.

Rogers, P. "The Parthian Dart: Endings and Epilogues in Fiction." *Essays in Criticism* 42.2 (1992): 85–106.

Romero, O. *A Martyr's Message of Hope: Six Homilies by Archbishop Oscar Romero*. Kansas City, MO: Celebration Books, 1981.

Root, E. T. "Ecclesiastes Considered Psychologically." *The Old and New Testament Student* 9.3 (1889): 138–42.

Rosin, R. *Reformers, the Preacher and Skepticism: Luther, Brenz, Melanchthon and Ecclesiastes.* Veröffentlichungen des Instituts für Europäische Geschichte Mainz 171. Mainz: Philipp von Zabern, 1997.

Roth, J. K. "A Theodicy of Protest." In *Encountering Evil: Live Options in Theodicy*, edited by S. T. Davis, 7–22. Edinburgh: T&T Clark, 1981.

Rudman, D. "A Contextual Reading of Ecclesiastes 4:13–16." *Journal of Biblical Literature* 116.1 (1997): 57–73.

———. *Determinism in the Book of Ecclesiastes.* Journal for the Study of the Old Testament Supplement 316. Sheffield: Sheffield Academic Press, 2001.

———. "A Note on the Dating of Ecclesiastes." *Catholic Biblical Quarterly* 61.1 (1999): 47–52.

———. "Qohelet's Use of *lpny*." *Journal of Northwest Semitic Languages* 23.2 (1997): 143–50.

Salters, R. B. "Notes on the Interpretation of Qoh 6:2." *Zeitschrift für die alttestamentliche Wissenschaft* 91 (1979): 282–89.

———. "The Word for 'God' in the Peshiṭta of Koheleth." *Vetus Testamentum* 21.2 (1971): 251–54.

Salyer, G. D. "Vain Rhetoric: Implied Author/Narrator/Narratee/Implied Reader Relationship in Ecclesiastes' Use of First-Person Discourse." PhD diss., Graduate Theological Union, 1997.

———. *Vain Rhetoric: Private Insight and Public Debate in Ecclesiastes.* Journal for the Study of the Old Testament Supplement 327. Sheffield: Sheffield Academic Press, 2001.

Sawyer, J. F. A. "Ruined House in Ecclesiastes 12: A Reconstruction of the Original Parable." *Journal of Biblical Literature* 94.4 (1975): 519–31.

Schacht, R. *Making Sense of Nietzsche: Reflections Timely and Untimely.* Urbana: University of Illinois Press, 1995.

Schellenberg, A. *Erkenntnis als Problem: Qohelet und die alttestamentliche Diskussion um das menschliche Erkennen.* Orbis biblicus et orientalis 188. Göttingen: Vandenhoeck & Ruprecht, 2002.

Schiffer, S. *Das Buch Kohelet: Nach der Auffassung der Weisen des Talmud und Midrasch und der jüdischen Erklärer des Mittelalters.* Frankfurt a.M.: Kaufmann; Leipzig: Schulze, 1884.

Schmemann, A. *For the Life of the World.* New York: National Student Christian Federation, 1964.

Schmid, H. H. *Gerechtigkeit als Weltordnung.* Tübingen: Mohr, 1968.

———. *Wesen und Geschichte der Weisheit. Eine Untersuchung zur altorientalischen Weisheitsliteratur.* Beihefte zur Zeitschrift für die alttestamentliche Wissenschaft 101. Berlin: Töpelmann, 1966.

Schoors, A. "Koheleth: A Perspective of Life after Death?" *Ephemerides theologicae lovanienses* 61.4 (1985): 295–303.

———. *The Preacher Sought to Find Pleasing Words: A Study of the Language of Qohelet.* Vol. 1: *Grammar.* Orientalia lovaniensia analecta 41. Louvain: Peeters, 1992.

———. *The Preacher Sought to Find Pleasing Words: A Study of the Language of Qohelet.* Vol. 2: *Vocabulary.* Orientalia lovaniensia analecta 143. Louvain: Peeters, 2004.

———. "La structure littéraire de Qohéleth." *Orientalia lovaniensia periodica* 13 (1982): 91–116.

———. "The Use of Vowel Letters in Qoheleth." *Ugarit-Forschungen* 20 (1988): 277–86.

———. "The Verb *hāyâ* in Qoheleth." In *Shall Not the Judge of All the Earth Do What Is Right? Studies on the Nature of God in Tribute to James L. Crenshaw*, edited by D. Penchansky and P. L. Redditt, 229–38. Winona Lake, IN: Eisenbrauns, 2000.

———. "The Verb *r'h* in the Book of Qoheleth." In *"Jedes Ding hat seine Zeit . . .": Studien zur israelitischen und altorientalischen Weisheit: Diethelm Michel zum 65 Geburtstag*, edited by A. A. Diesel et al., 227–41. Beihefte zur Zeitschrift für die alttestamentliche Wissenschaft 241. Berlin: de Gruyter, 1996.

———. "The Word *ṭôb* in the Book of Qoheleth." In *"Und Mose schrieb dieses Lied auf": Studien zum Alten Testament und zum Alten Orient: Festschrift für Oswald Loretz zur Vollendung seines 70 Lebensjahres mit Beiträgen von Freunden, Schülern und Kollegen*, edited by M. Dietrich and I. Kottsieper, 685–700. Alter Orient und Altes Testament 250. Münster: Ugarit-Verlag, 1998.

Schultz, R. L. "A Sense of Timing: A Neglected Aspect of Qoheleth's Wisdom." In *Seeking Out the Wisdom of the Ancients: Essays Offered to Honor Michael V. Fox on the Occasion of His Sixty-fifth Birthday*, edited by R. L. Troxel, K. G. Friebel, and D. R. Magary, 257–67. Winona Lake, IN: Eisenbrauns, 2005.

Schwartz, M. J. "Koheleth and Camus: Two Views of Achievement." *Judaism* 35.1 (1986): 29–34.

Schwarzschild, R. "The Syntax of *'shr* in Biblical Hebrew with Special Reference to Qoheleth." *Hebrew Studies* 31 (1990): 7–39.

Scott, R. B. Y. *Proverbs, Ecclesiastes*. Anchor Bible 18. Garden City, NY: Doubleday, 1965.

Segal, J. B. *Aramaic Texts from North Saqqâra*. London: Egypt Exploration Society, 1983.

Seow, C. L. *Ecclesiastes*. Anchor Bible 18C. New York: Doubleday, 1997.

———. "Qohelet's Autobiography." In *Fortunate the Eyes That See: Essays in Honor of David Noel Freedman in Celebration of His Seventieth Birthday*, edited by A. B. Beck et al., 275–87. Grand Rapids: Eerdmans, 1995.

———. "Qohelet's Eschatological Poem." *Journal of Biblical Literature* 118.2 (1999): 209–34.

Serrano, J. J. "I Saw the Wicked Buried (Ecclesiastes 8:10)." *Catholic Biblical Quarterly* 16.2 (1954): 168–70.

Shaffer, A. "The Mesopotamian Background of Qohelet 4:9–12" [Hebrew]. In *E. L. Sukenik Memorial Volume*, edited by N. Avigad et al., 246–50. Eretz-Israel 8. Jerusalem: Israel Exploration Society, 1967.

———. "New Light on the 'Three-Ply Cord'" [Hebrew]. In *W. F. Albright Volume*, edited by A. Malamat, 159–60. Eretz-Israel 9. Jerusalem: Jerusalem Exploration Society, 1969.

Sharp, C. J. "Ironic Representation, Authorial Voice, and Meaning in Qohelet." *Biblical Interpretation* 12.1 (2004): 37–68.

Sheppard, G. T. "Epilogue to Qoheleth as Theological Commentary." *Catholic Biblical Quarterly* 39.1 (1977): 182–89.

———. *Wisdom as a Hermeneutical Construct: A Study in the Sapientalizing of the Old Testament*. Beihefte zur Zeitschrift für die alttestamentliche Wissenschaft 151. Berlin: de Gruyter, 1980.

Sherwood, Y. "'Not with a Bang but a Whimper': Shrunken Apocalypses of the Twentieth Century and the Book of Qoheleth." In *Apocalyptic in History and Tradition*, edited by C. Rowland and J. M. T. Barton, 94–116. Journal for the Study of the Pseudepigrapha Supplement 43. London: Sheffield Academic Press, 2002.

Siegfried, K. *Prediger und Hoheslied übersetzt und erklärt*. Handbuch zum Alten Testament II, 3/2. Göttingen: Vandenhoeck & Ruprecht, 1898.

Silberman, L. H. "Death in the Hebrew Bible and Apocalyptic Literature." In *Perspectives on Death*, edited by L. O. Mills, 13–32. Nashville: Abingdon, 1969.

Sire, J. *Naming the Elephant: Worldview as a Concept*. Downers Grove, IL: InterVarsity, 2004.

Skillen, J. W. *In Pursuit of Justice: Christian-Democratic Explorations*. Lanham, MD: Rowman & Littlefield, 2004.

———. *With or against the World? America's Role among the Nations*. Lanham, MD: Rowman & Littlefield, 2005.

Smalley, B. *The Study of the Bible in the Middle Ages*. 3rd ed. Oxford: Blackwell, 1983.

Smelik, K. A. D. "A Re-interpretation of Ecclesiastes 2,12b." In *Qohelet in the Context of Wisdom*, edited by A. Schoors, 385–89. Bibliotheca ephemeridum theologicarum lovaniensium 136. Leuven: Leuven University Press, 1998.

Smit, E. J. "The Tell Siran Inscription: Linguistic and Historical Implications." *Journal of Semitics* 1 (1989): 108–17.

Smit, M. C. *Toward a Christian Conception of History*. Edited and translated by H. D. Morton and H. Van Dyke. Christian Studies Today. Lanham, MD: University Press of America, 2002.

Sneed, M. "(Dis)Closure in Qohelet: Qohelet Deconstructed." *Journal for the Study of the Old Testament* 27 (2002): 115–26.

Snell, D. C. *Twice-Told Proverbs and the Composition of the Book of Proverbs*. Winona Lake, IN: Eisenbrauns, 1993.

Song, C.-S. "Ecclesiastes 3:1–8: An Asian Perspective." In *Return to Babel: Global Perspectives on the Bible*, edited by P. Pope-Levison and J. R. Levison, 87–92. Louisville: Westminster John Knox, 1999.

Sontag, F. "Anthropodicy and the Return of God." In *Encountering Evil: Live Options in Theodicy*, edited by S. T. Davis, 137–51. Edinburgh: T&T Clark, 1981.

Soskice, J. M. *The Kindness of God: Metaphor, Gender, and Religious Language*. Oxford: Oxford University Press, 2007.

Southern, R. W. *Saint Anselm: Portrait in a Landscape*. Cambridge: Cambridge University Press, 1990.

Spangenberg, I. J. J. *Die Boek Prediker*. Skrifuitleg vir Bybelstudent en Gemeente. Kaapstad: N. G. Kerk-Uitgewers, 1993.

———. "A Century of Wrestling with Qohelet: The Research History of the Book Illustrated with a Discussion of Qoh 4,17–5,6." In *Qohelet in the Context of Wisdom*, edited by A. Schoors, 61–91. Bibliotheca ephemeridum theologicarum lovaniensium 136. Leuven: Leuven University Press, 1998.

———. "Irony in the Book of Qohelet." *Journal for the Study of the Old Testament* 72 (1996): 57–69.

———. "Quotations in Ecclesiastes: An Appraisal." *Old Testament Essays* 4 (1991): 19–35.

Spears, A. D. "The Theological Hermeneutics of Homiletical Application and Ecclesiastes 7:23–29." DPhil diss., University of Liverpool, 2006.

Spykman, G. J. *Reformational Theology: A New Paradigm for Doing Dogmatics*. Grand Rapids: Eerdmans, 1992.

Staples, W. E. "The 'Vanity' of Ecclesiastes." *Journal of Near Eastern Studies* 2.2 (1943): 95–104.

Stearns, A. K. *Living through Personal Crisis*. New York: Ballantine, 1984.

Steiner, G. *Grammars of Creation*. New Haven: Yale University Press, 2001.

———. *Lessons of the Masters.* Charles Eliot Norton Lectures, 2001–2002. Cambridge, MA: Harvard University Press, 2003.

———. *Real Presences.* London: Faber & Faber, 1989.

Steinmann, J. *Ainsi parlait Qohèlèt.* Lire la Bible 38. Paris: Cerf, 1955.

Sternberg, M. *The Poetics of Biblical Narrative: Ideological Literature and the Drama of Reading.* Bloomington: Indiana University Press, 1985.

Stiglitz, J. E. *Globalization and Its Discontents.* New York: Norton, 2003.

———. *Making Globalization Work.* New York: Norton, 2006.

Strange, M. "The Question of Moderation in Ecclesiastes 7:15–18." DSacTh diss., Catholic University of America, 1969.

Strodach, G. K. *The Philosophy of Epicurus: The Epicurean and Lucretian Texts Newly Translated with a Commentary and a Study of Classical Materialism.* Evanston, IL: Northwestern University Press, 1963.

Strothmann, W., ed. *Das syrische Fragment des Ecclesiastes-Kommentars von Theodor von Mopsuestia: Syrischer Text mit vollständigem Wörterverzeichnis.* Göttinger Orientforschungen, 1. Reihe, Syriaca 29. Wiesbaden: Harrassowitz, 1988.

Stuart, M. *A Commentary on Ecclesiastes.* New York: Putnam, 1851.

Swinburne, R. *Is There a God?* New York: Oxford University Press, 1996.

Tamez, E. "Ecclesiastes 3:1–8: A Latin American Perspective." In *Return to Babel: Global Perspectives on the Bible,* edited by P. Pope-Levison and J. R. Levison, 75–79. Translated by G. Kinsler. Louisville: Westminster John Knox, 1999.

———. "La teología del éxito en un mundo desigual: Relectura de Proverbios." *Revista de Interpretación Bíblica Latino-Americana* 30 (1998): 25–34.

———. *When the Horizons Close: Rereading Ecclesiastes.* Maryknoll, NY: Orbis, 2000.

———. "When the Horizons Close upon Themselves: A Reflection on the Utopian Reason of Qohélet." In *Liberation Theologies, Postmodernity, and the Americas,* edited by D. B. Batstone et al., 53–68. Translated by P. Lange-Churión. New York: Routledge, 1997.

Tarnas, R. *The Passion of the Western Mind: Understanding the Ideas That Have Shaped Our World View.* New York: Ballantine, 1991.

Taylor, C. "The Dirge of Coheleth." *Jewish Quarterly Review* 4.4 (1892): 533–49.

———. *The Dirge of Coheleth in Ecclesiastes XII: Discussed and Literally Interpreted.* Edinburgh: Williams & Norgate, 1874.

Taylor, C. C. W. "Aristotle's Epistemology." In *Epistemology,* edited by S. Everson, 116–42. Cambridge: Cambridge University Press, 1990.

Taylor, Charles. "A Catholic Modernity?" In *A Catholic Modernity? Charles Taylor's Marianist Award Lecture,* edited by J. L. Heft, 13–37. New York: Oxford University Press, 1999.

Thiselton, A. C. *A Concise Encyclopedia of the Philosophy of Religion.* Oxford: Oneworld, 2002.

———. *The First Epistle to the Corinthians: A Commentary on the Greek Text.* New International Greek Testament Commentary. Grand Rapids: Eerdmans, 2000.

———. *New Horizons in Hermeneutics: The Theory and Practice of Transforming Biblical Reading.* Grand Rapids: Zondervan, 1997.

Thompson, H. O., and F. Zayadine. "The Tell Siran Inscription." *Bulletin of the American Schools of Oriental Research* 212.1 (1973): 5–11.

Torrey, C. C. "The Question of the Original Language of Qoheleth." *Jewish Quarterly Review* 39 (1948): 151–60.

Towner, W. S. "Ecclesiastes." In *New Interpreter's Bible,* edited by L. E. Keck, 5:265–360. Nashville: Abingdon, 1997.

Turner, S. P., and D. E. Chubin. "Another Appraisal of Ortega, the Coles, and Science Policy: The Ecclesiastes Hypothesis." *Social Science Information* 15.4–5 (1976): 657–62.

Uehlinger, C. "Qohelet im Horizont mesopotamischer, levantinischer und ägyptischer Weisheitsliteratur der persischen und hellenistischen Zeit." In *Das Buch Kohelet: Studien zur Struktur, Geschicht, Rezeption und Theologie,* edited by L. Schwienhorst-Schönberger, 155–247. Beihefte zur Zeitschrift für die alttestamentliche Wissenschaft. Berlin: de Gruyter, 1997.

Ullendorff, E. "Meaning of *qhlt.*" *Vetus Testamentum* 12.2 (1962): 215.

Ulrich, E. C. "Ezra and Qoheleth Manuscripts from Qumran (4QEzra and 4QQoh[a, b])." In *Priests, Prophets and Scribes: Essays on the Formation and Heritage of Second Temple Judaism in Honour of Joseph Blenkinsopp,* edited by E. Ulrich et al., 139–57. Journal for the Study of the Old Testament Supplement 149. Sheffield: JSOT Press, 1992.

Vanhoozer, K. J., ed. *Dictionary for Theological Interpretation of the Bible.* Grand Rapids: Baker Academic, 2005.

Vanier, J. *Community and Growth.* Rev. ed. New York: Paulist Press, 2003.

———. *Drawn into the Mystery of Jesus through the Gospel of John.* Ottawa, ON: Novalis, 2004.

Van Leeuwen, R. C. "In Praise of Proverbs." In *Pledges of Jubilee: Essays on the Arts and Culture in Honor of Calvin G. Seerveld,* edited by L. Zuidervaart and H. Luttikhuizen, 308–27. Grand Rapids: Eerdmans, 1995.

———. "Liminality and Worldview in Proverbs 1–9." *Semeia* (1990): 111–44.

———. "Proverbs." In *The New Interpreter's Bible,* edited by L. E. Keck, 5:17–264. Nashville: Abingdon, 1997.

———. "Proverbs 30:21–23 and the Biblical World Upside Down." *Journal of Biblical Literature* 105.4 (1986): 599–610.

———. "Wealth and Poverty: System and Contradiction in Proverbs." *Hebrew Studies* 33 (1992): 25–36.

———. "Wisdom Literature." In *Dictionary for Theological Interpretation of the Bible,* edited by K. J. Vanhoozer, 847–50. Grand Rapids: Baker Academic, 2005.

Vegni. *L'Ecclesiaste secondo il testo ebraico.* Florenz, 1871.

Verheij, A. J. C. "Paradise Retried: On Qohelet 2:4–6." *Journal for the Study of the Old Testament* 50 (1991): 113–15.

Vílchez Líndez, J. *Eclesiastés o Qohélet.* Nueva Biblia Española. Estella, Spain: Verbo Divino, 1994.

Vitz, E. B. *A Continual Feast: A Cookbook to Celebrate the Joys of Family and Faith throughout the Christian Year.* San Francisco: Ignatius, 1985.

Vlastos, G. "Socratic Irony." *Classical Quaterly,* n.s., 37.1 (1987): 79–96.

Vriezen, T. C. *An Outline of Old Testament Theology.* 2nd ed. Oxford: Blackwell, 1970.

Waal, C. van der. *Search the Scriptures.* Translated by T. Plantinga. 10 vols. St. Catharines, ON: Paideia, 1978–79.

Waard, J. de. "The Translator and Textual Criticism (with Particular Reference to Eccl 2:25)." *Biblica* 60.4 (1979): 509–29.

Wadell, P. J. *Friendship and the Moral Life.* Notre Dame, IN: University of Notre Dame Press, 1989.

Wagner, M. *Die lexikalischen und grammatikalischen Aramäismen im alttestamentlichen Hebräisch.* Beihefte zur Zeitschrift für die alttestamentliche Wissenschaft 96. Berlin: Töpelmann, 1966.

Waldman, N. M. "The *Dābār Ra'* of Eccl 8:3." *Journal of Biblical Literature* 98.3 (1979): 407–8.

Waltke, B. K. *The Book of Proverbs: Chapters 1–15.* New International Commentary on the Old Testament. Grand Rapids: Eerdmans, 2004.

Waltke, B. K., and M. O'Connor. *Introduction to Biblical Hebrew Syntax.* Winona Lake, IN: Eisenbrauns, 1990.

Ward, G. *Cities of God.* Radical Orthodoxy Series. London: Routledge, 2000.

Ward, W. A. "Egypto-Semitic *mr,* 'Be Bitter, Strong.'" *Ugarit-Forschungen* 12 (1980): 357–60.

Watson, F. *Text and Truth: Redefining Biblical Theology.* Grand Rapids: Eerdmans, 1997.

———. *Text, Church, and World: Biblical Interpretation in Theological Perspective.* Grand Rapids: Eerdmans, 1994.

Watson, W. G. E. *Classical Hebrew Poetry: A Guide to Its Techniques.* New York: T&T Clark, 2005.

———. *Traditional Techniques in Classical Hebrew Verse.* Journal for the Study of the Old Testament Supplement 170. Sheffield: Sheffield Academic Press, 1994.

Weaver, D. F. *Self-Love and Christian Ethics.* New Studies in Christian Ethics. Cambridge: Cambridge University Press, 2002.

Weeks, S. *Early Israelite Wisdom.* Oxford: Clarendon, 1994.

Weil, S. *Gravity and Grace.* Translated by E. Craufurd. London: Routledge & Kegan Paul, 1952.

———. *Waiting for God.* Translated by E. Craufurd. New York: Harper & Row, 1973.

Weinberg, J. P. "Authorship and Author in the Ancient Near East and in the Hebrew Bible." *Hebrew Studies* 44 (2003): 157–69.

Weinfeld, M. *Deuteronomy and the Deuteronomic School.* Oxford: Clarendon, 1972.

Weitzman, M. P. *The Syriac Version of the Old Testament: An Introduction.* Cambridge: Cambridge University Press, 1999.

Welch, J. *Spiritual Pilgrims: Carl Jung and Teresa of Avila.* New York: Paulist Press, 1982.

Wellek, R., and A. Warren. *Theory of Literature.* 3rd ed. San Diego: Harvest Book, 1984.

Wenham, G. J. *The Book of Leviticus.* New International Commentary on the Old Testament. Grand Rapids: Eerdmans, 1979.

———. *Genesis 1–15.* Word Biblical Commentary 1. Waco: Word, 1987.

Wernik, U. "Will the Real Homosexual in the Bible Please Stand Up?" *Theology & Sexuality* 11.3 (2005): 47–64.

Westphal, M. *Becoming a Self: A Reading of Kierkegaard's Concluding Unscientific Postscript.* West Lafayette, IN: Purdue University Press, 1996.

———. *Suspicion and Faith: The Religious Uses of Modern Atheism.* Grand Rapids: Eerdmans, 1993.

White, C. *Christian Friendship in the Fourth Century.* Cambridge: Cambridge University Press, 1992.

White, G. "Luther on Ecclesiastes and the Limits of Human Ability." *Neue Zeitschrift für systematische Theologie und Religionsphilosophie* 29.2 (1987): 180–94.

White, S. J. "A New Story to Live By?" *The Bible in TransMission* (1998): 3–4.

Whitley, C. F. *Koheleth: His Language and Thought*. Beihefte zur Zeitschrift für die alttestamentliche Wissenschaft 148. Berlin: de Gruyter, 1979.

Whybray, R. N. *Ecclesiastes*. New Century Bible Commentary. Grand Rapids: Eerdmans, 1989.

———. *Ecclesiastes*. Old Testament Guides. Sheffield: JSOT Press, 1989.

———. "Ecclesiastes 1:5–7 and the Wonders of Nature." *Journal for the Study of the Old Testament* 41 (1988): 105–12.

———. "The Identification and Use of Quotations in Ecclesiastes." In *Congress Volume: Vienna, 1980*, edited by J. A. Emerton, 455–61. Vetus Testamentum Supplement 32. Leiden: Brill, 1981.

———. *The Intellectual Tradition in the Old Testament*. Beihefte zur Zeitschrift für die alttestamentliche Wissenschaft 135. Berlin: de Gruyter, 1974.

———. *Proverbs*. New Century Bible Commentary. Grand Rapids: Eerdmans, 1994.

———. "Qoheleth as a Theologian." In *Qohelet in the Context of Wisdom*, edited by A. Schoors, 239–65. Bibliotheca ephemeridum theologicarum lovaniensium 136. Leuven: Leuven University Press, 1998.

———. "Qoheleth, Preacher of Joy." *Journal for the Study of the Old Testament* 23 (1982): 87–98.

———. "Qoheleth the Immoralist? (Qoh 7:16–17)." In *Israelite Wisdom: Theological and Literary Essays in Honor of Samuel Terrien*, edited by J. G. Gammie, 191–204. Missoula, MT: Scholars Press, 1978.

———. *Two Jewish Theologies: Job and Ecclesiastes*. Hull: University of Hull Press, 1980.

Wickham, L. R. "Homily IV." In *Gregory of Nyssa, Homilies on Ecclesiastes: An English Version with Supporting Studies, Proceedings of the Seventh International Colloquium on Gregory of Nyssa (St Andrews, 5–10 September 1990)*, edited by S. G. Hall, 177–84. Berlin: de Gruyter, 1993.

Wiesel, E. *Night*. Translated by M. Wiesel. New York: Hill and Wang, 2006.

Wilch, J. R. *Time and Event: An Exegetical Study of the Use of 'ēth in the Old Testament in Comparison to Other Temporary Expressions in Clarification of the Concept of Time*. Leiden: Brill, 1969.

Williams, A. L. *Ecclesiastes: In the Revised Version, with Notes and Introduction*. Cambridge Bible for Schools and Colleges. Cambridge: Cambridge University Press, 1922.

Williams, J. G. *Those Who Ponder Proverbs: Aphoristic Thinking and Biblical Literature*. Sheffield: Almond, 1981.

Williams, R. J. *Hebrew Syntax: An Outline*. 2nd ed. Toronto: University of Toronto Press, 1976.

Wilson, G. H. "'The Words of the Wise': The Intent and Significance of Qohelet 12:9–14." *Journal of Biblical Literature* 103.1 (1984): 175–92.

Windelband, W. *History of Ancient Philosophy*. Translated by H. E. Cushman. New York: Dover, 1956.

Wingren, G. *Luther on Vocation*. Translated by C. C. Rasmussen. Philadelphia: Muhlenberg, 1957.

Witherington, B. *Jesus the Sage: The Pilgrimage of Wisdom*. Edinburgh: T&T Clark, 1994.

Witzenrath, H. H. "*Süß ist das Licht . . .*" *Eine literaturwissenschaftliche Untersuchung zu Koh 11,7–12,7*. Arbeiten zu Text und Sprache im Alten Testament 11. St. Ottilien: EOS, 1979.

Wölfel, E. *Luther und die Skepsis: Eine Studie zur Kohelet-Exegese Luthers*. Forschungen zur Geschichte und Lehre des Protestantismus 10 Reihe 12. Munich: Chr. Kaiser, 1958.

Wolters, A. M. *Creation Regained: Biblical Basics for a Reformational Worldview.* Grand Rapids: Eerdmans, 1985.

———. *The Song of the Valiant Woman: Studies in the Interpretation of Proverbs 31:10–31.* Carlisle, UK: Paternoster, 2001.

Wolterstorff, N. "The Remembrance of Things (Not) Past: Philosophical Reflections on Christian Liturgy." In *Christian Philosophy*, edited by P. Flint, 118–61. Notre Dame, IN: University of Notre Dame Press, 1990.

———. *Until Justice and Peace Embrace: The Kuyper Lectures for 1981 Delivered at the Free University of Amsterdam.* Grand Rapids: Eerdmans, 1983.

Wright, A. G. "'For Everything There Is a Season': The Structure and Meaning of the Fourteen Opposites (Ecclesiastes 3,2–8)." In *De la Torah au Messie: Mélanges Henri Cazelles*, edited by J. Doré et al., 321–28. Paris: Desclée, 1981.

———. "The Poor but Wise Youth and the Old but Foolish King (Qoh 4:13–16)." In *Wisdom, You Are My Sister: Studies in Honor of Roland E. Murphy, O. Carm., on the Occasion of His Eightieth Birthday*, edited by M. L. Barré, 142–54. Catholic Biblical Quarterly Monograph Series 29. Washington, DC: Catholic Biblical Association of America, 1997.

———. "Riddle of the Sphinx: The Structure of the Book of Qoheleth." *Catholic Biblical Quarterly* 30 (1968): 313–34.

Wright, C. H. H. *The Book of Koheleth Considered in Relation to Modern Criticism, and to the Doctrines of Modern Pessimism, with a Critical and Grammatical Commentary, and a Revised Translation.* London: Hodder & Stoughton, 1883.

Wright, C. J. H. *God's People: Family, Land, and Property in the Old Testament.* Grand Rapids: Eerdmans, 1990.

Wright, G. E. *God Who Acts: Biblical Theology as Recital.* Studies in Biblical Theology 1/8. London: SCM, 1952.

Wuthnow, R. "Introduction: A Good Life and a Good Society: The Debate over Materialism." In *Rethinking Materialism: Perspectives on the Spiritual Dimension of Economic Behavior*, edited by R. Wuthnow, 1–21. Grand Rapids: Eerdmans, 1995.

Yoder, J. H. "Trinity versus Theodicy: Hebraic Realism and the Temptation to Judge God." http://theology.nd.edu/people/research/yoder-john/documents/TRINITYVERSUSTHEODICY.pdf

Young, E. J. *Introduction to the Old Testament.* Grand Rapids: Eerdmans, 1949.

Zaharopoulos, D. Z. *Theodore of Mopsuestia: A Study of His Old Testament Exegesis.* New York: Paulist Press, 1989.

Zimmerli, W. *Das Buch des Predigers Salomo.* Das Alte Testament Deutsch 16/1. Göttingen: Vandenhoeck & Ruprecht, 1962.

———. "Concerning the Structure of Old Testament Wisdom." In *Studies in Ancient Israelite Wisdom*, edited by J. L. Crenshaw, 175–99. New York: Ktav, 1976.

———. "The Place and Limit of Wisdom in the Framework of the Old Testament Theology." *Scottish Journal of Theology* 17 (1964): 146–58.

Zimmermann, F. "The Aramaic Provenance of Qohelet." *Jewish Quarterly Review* 36.1 (1945): 17–45.

———. *Biblical Books Translated from the Aramaic.* New York: Ktav, 1975.

———. *The Inner World of Qohelet.* New York: Ktav, 1973.

———. "The Question of Hebrew in Qohelet." *Jewish Quarterly Review* 40.1 (1949): 79–102.

Zuidema, M. "Athletics from a Christian Perspective." In *Christianity and Leisure: Issues in a Pluralistic Society*, edited by P. Heintzman, G. Van Andel, and T. Visker, 164–91. Sioux Center, IA: Dordt College Press, 1994.

Zurro, E. *Procedimientos iterativos en la poesía ugarítica y hebrea*. Biblica et orientalia 43. Rome: Pontifical Biblical Institute Press, 1987.

Subject Index

Author Index

Hengel, M., 84, 84n350, 272, 272n43
Hengelaar-Rookmaaker, M., 383n30
Hengstenberg, E. W., 45, 45n169, 46n177,
    103n13, 131n17, 189, 189n41, 204n23, 207,
    207n39, 208, 208n47, 304, 304n41, 336,
    336n15, 352n64, 353
Herrera, R. A., 171n64, 171n66, 173, 173n79,
    173n82
Hertzberg, H. W., 39n134, 92n395, 133n29,
    138n1, 253n4, 300n28, 336n19, 342n26
Herzfeld, L., 24
Hesse, M. B., 353, 353n68
Hick, J. H., 260, 260n31
Hillesum, E., 230, 230n27
Himmelfarb, G., 330n57
Hirshman, M., 23, 23n38, 23n39, 27n52
Hoffman, Y., 49n182
Holm-Nielsen, S., 22, 22n29
Homan, M. M., 335n12
Hubbard, D. A., 89, 89n376, 90n379, 98n418
Huehnergard, J., 298n15
Hume, D., 258, 259n27
Hurding, R. F., 126n14
Hurvitz, A., 51n192
Hyvärinen, K., 60n247

IBHS [B. K. Waltke and M. O'Connor],
    103n13, 105n20, 128n2, 128n4, 139n3,
    183n5, 184n21, 202n14, 245n14, 263n2,
    278n4, 287n1, 298n15
Ilibagiza, I., 180n12
Ingraffia, B. D., 173, 173n80
Ingram, D., 41n148
Irwin, W. A., 191n52
Isaksson, B., 51, 68, 68n287, 102n10, 175n2,
    183n2, 215n12, 233n8, 234n18, 245n12,
    263n1, 288n7

Jacob, H. E., 99
Jacob, M., 43n158
Jahn, J., 45
Japhet, S., 24n41
Jarick, J., 28n61, 60n247, 105n21
Jaspers, K., 173n81
Jastrow, M., 215n7, 215n8, 318n15
Jeffrey, D. L., 330n58, 331, 331n65, 332, 332n69
Jenkins, P., 376n5, 388, 388n47
Jenson, R. W., 174n84
Jerome, 61n250
John Paul II (pope), 193, 193n58, 242, 242n39
Johnson, R. A., 385n36
Johnson, R. E., 107n37

Johnston, P. S., 141, 141n18, 142, 142n19, 142n22,
    247n17, 247n19, 305, 305n47, 352, 352n66
Johnston, R. K., 43n158
Jong, S. de, 108n46, 109, 109n48, 208n42, 283n24
Joüon, P., 103n14, 139n6, 312n1, 363, 363n23
Jung, C. G., 378, 378n13, 379, 379n19, 379n22,
    380, 380n24

Kabasele Lumbala, F., 41n151
Kallas, E., 21n22, 27n51, 27n53, 28, 28n58,
    29n65, 30, 30n72, 31n78, 31n79, 33, 33n86,
    33n88, 33n90, 41n146
Kalsbeek, L., 332n71
Kamenetzky, A. S., 60n249, 103n13, 104n18
Kass, L. R., 154n20
Keefer, M. H., 331, 331n66, 331n67, 332n68
Kelsey, M., 126n15
Kendall, G. A., 356n76
Kermode, F., 88n367
Kidd, S. M., 379n21
Kidner, D., 46n177
Kierkegaard, S., 345n34, 377, 378, 378n14,
    383n31, 387, 387n41
Kitto, J., 45n169
Kline, M. M., 108n43
Koch, K., 323
Konstan, D., 198n77
Koosed, J. L., 41n149
Kraus, M., 26n50
Kreitzer, L. J., 43n158
Krell, D. F., 113, 113n64, 113n66
Krüger, T., 63n261, 98n416, 105n24, 110n54,
    138n1, 166n40, 167, 167n47, 168, 169n55,
    234n19, 236n26, 283, 283n23, 324n42,
    336n16, 343, 343n29, 348n50, 351, 351n61,
    353, 353n69, 360n9, 360n12
Kugel, J., 57n230, 158n1, 158n3, 170n60, 214n4,
    216n16, 219, 219n32
Kutler, L., 266n16

Lacy, P. de, 43n158
Lamott, A., 212, 212n62
Lamparter, H., 253n4
Lampe, G. W. H., 28n62
Landsberger, B., 190n45
Landsberger, M., 24
Lane, D. J., 60n249
Lange, H. M. de, 196
Lasch, C., 382
Laue, L., 35, 35n97
Lauha, A., 215n15, 224n1, 280n16, 298n24,
    300n28, 370n52

Index of Scripture and Other Ancient Writings